# CONTENTS

# 5 WHERE TO STAY 81

# 6 WHERE TO DINE 106

# 7 WHAT TO SEE & DO IN SHÀNGHǍI 135

# 8 SHÀNGHǍI STROLLS 199

# LIST OF MAPS

## ABOUT THE AUTHOR

Born in Singapore to a Shanghainese mother and a Chaozhou father, **Sharon Owyang** graduated from Harvard University, and divides her time between freelance travel writing and film projects in the U.S. and China. She has contributed to *Frommer's China* and has also written about Shànghǎi, China, Vietnam, and San Diego for Insight Guides, Compact Guides, the *Los Angeles Times,* and several websites. She speaks Mandarin, Cantonese, and enough Shanghainese to be a curiosity to the locals and to lose to them every time at mahjong. More recently, she was the principal writer of the U.S.-China Media Brief produced by the UCLA Asian American Studies Center.

## ACKNOWLEDGMENTS

Many thanks to Tess Johnston for her friendship and generous help with local information, talks, and trips; Wu Zhede and family for the home-cooked dinners, conversations, and invaluable Shanghai tips; and Hsuan and June Owyang, and Chung and Jeannette Owyang for their generosity throughout the years.

—Sharon Owyang

## HOW TO CONTACT US

In researching this book, we discovered many wonderful places—hotels, restaurants, shops, and more. We're sure you'll find others. Please tell us about them, so we can share the information with your fellow travelers in upcoming editions. If you were disappointed with a recommendation, we'd love to know that, too. Please write to:

*Frommer's Shanghai,* 6th Edition
Wiley Publishing, Inc. • 111 River St. • Hoboken, NJ 07030-5774
frommersfeedback@wiley.com

## AN ADDITIONAL NOTE

Please be advised that travel information is subject to change at any time—and this is especially true of prices. We therefore suggest that you write or call ahead for confirmation when making your travel plans. The authors, editors, and publisher cannot be held responsible for the experiences of readers while traveling. Your safety is important to us, however, so we encourage you to stay alert and be aware of your surroundings. Keep a close eye on cameras, purses, and wallets, all favorite targets of thieves and pickpockets.

## FROMMER'S STAR RATINGS, ICONS & ABBREVIATIONS

Every hotel, restaurant, and attraction listing in this guide has been ranked for quality, value, service, amenities, and special features using a **star-rating system.** In country, state, and regional guides, we also rate towns and regions to help you narrow down your choices and budget your time accordingly. Hotels and restaurants are rated on a scale of zero (recommended) to three stars (exceptional). Attractions, shopping, nightlife, towns, and regions are rated according to the following scale: zero stars (recommended), one star (highly recommended), two stars (very highly recommended), and three stars (must-see).

In addition to the star-rating system, we also use **seven feature icons** that point you to the great deals, in-the-know advice, and unique experiences that separate travelers from tourists. Throughout the book, look for:

**special finds**—those places only insiders know about

**fun facts**—details that make travelers more informed and their trips more fun

**kids**—best bets for kids and advice for the whole family

**special moments**—those experiences that memories are made of

**overrated**—places or experiences not worth your time or money

**insider tips**—great ways to save time and money

**great values**—where to get the best deals

The following abbreviations are used for credit cards:

| | | | | | |
|---|---|---|---|---|---|
| AE | American Express | DISC | Discover | V | Visa |
| DC | Diners Club | MC | MasterCard | | |

## TRAVEL RESOURCES AT FROMMERS.COM

Frommer's travel resources don't end with this guide. Frommer's website, **www.frommers. com,** has travel information on more than 4,000 destinations. We update features regularly, giving you access to the most current trip-planning information and the best airfare, lodging, and car-rental bargains. You can also listen to podcasts, connect with other Frommers. com members through our active-reader forums, share your travel photos, read blogs from guidebook editors and fellow travelers, and much more.

# THE BEST OF SHÀNGHǍI

Featured prominently in the world's newspapers and business and travel magazines in 2010, Shànghǎi, as host of the 2010 World Expo, has once again become the latest "It" city of the world. And yet, even before the Expo shone the world spotlight on China's largest city, visitors have been steadily flocking here throughout the first decade of the 21st century. Much like in the first half of the 20th century, many are drawn by curiosity, a sense of possibility, the lure of potential professional and financial success, or perhaps simply a desire to be in the coolest, brashest, and most exciting city in the new century. Today, Shànghǎi is all that and more. While the city lacks the classical Chinese monuments of Běijīng, its colonial legacy gives it a character all its own. This museum of East meets West on Chinese soil is China's capital of commerce, industry, and finance, and the one city that best shows where China is headed in the 21st century.

Following is a list of Shànghǎi's highlights, both the obvious and the more offbeat choices in this unique city. But don't just take our word for it: Come and experience this dynamic, must-see city for yourself.

## THE MOST UNFORGETTABLE SHÀNGHǍI EXPERIENCES

o **Strolling the Bund:** The most widely known street in Asia, with its gorgeous colonial buildings that were the banks, hotels, trading firms, and private clubs of foreign *taipans* (bosses of old Shànghǎi's trading firms) and adventurers past, deserves to be walked over and over again, especially now that it has been given a US$700-million face-lift. See

# China

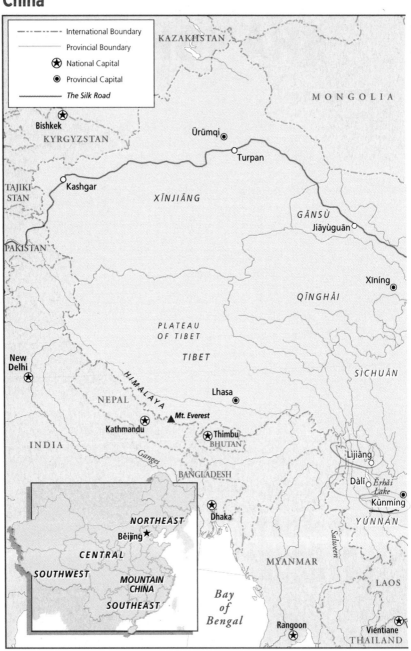

Legend:
- ·—·—· International Boundary
- ········· Provincial Boundary
- ⊛ National Capital
- ◉ Provincial Capital
- —— *The Silk Road*

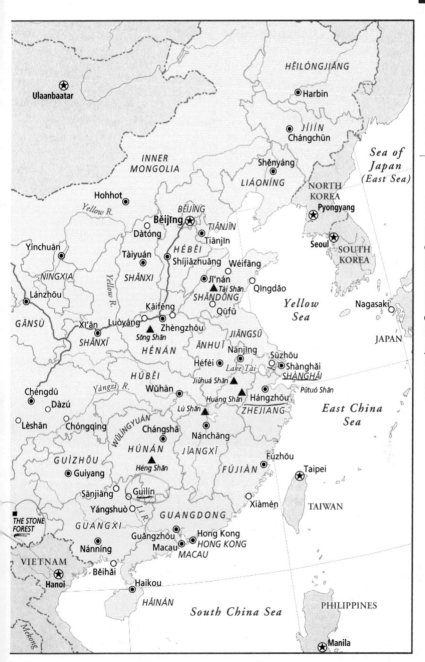

up close the exquisite architectural details of the **Peace Hotel,** the **Customs House,** the **former Hong Kong and Shànghǎi Bank,** and scores of other buildings, some lavishly restored, others closed and awaiting development. Then head across the street to the **Bund Promenade,** which has been widened and gussied up with new trees and park benches. Here you can mingle with the masses while admiring the splendor and grandeur of old Shànghǎi on the one side, and the gleaming promise of new Shànghǎi on the other side of the river. After you've seen it by day, come back again at night for a different perspective. See "Walking Tour 1" on p. 200.

o **Admiring the Collections in the Shànghǎi Museum:** China's finest, most modern, and most memorable museum of historic relics has disappointed almost no visitor since it opened in the heart of People's Square. Make it a top priority, and allow a few hours more than you planned on. See p. 163.

o **Surveying Shànghǎi from Up High:** After crossing the Huángpǔ River from old Shànghǎi to the new Shànghǎi, enjoy the ultimate panorama from either the sphere atop the **Oriental Pearl TV Tower;** the 88th-floor observatory of the **Jīn Mào Tower;** or the 100th-floor all-glass observation deck of the new **Shànghǎi World Financial Center.** All three rank as some of Asia's tallest structures. On a clear day, you can see forever. Alternatively, if you don't want to be glassed in, climb the **Lúpǔ Bridge** in the southern part of the French Concession for a spectacular view of the 2010 World Expo grounds. See p. 188, 187, 190, and 188.

o **Cruising the Huángpǔ River:** A 27km (17-mile) pleasure cruise from the Bund to the mouth of the mighty Yángzǐ River, past endless wharves, factories, and tankers at anchor, gives substance to Shànghǎi's claim as China's largest port and the fact that nearly half of China's trade with the outside world travels these same waters. A shorter 1-hour cruise, and an abbreviated 30-minute cruise from the Pǔdōng side, do not convey the full importance of the river, but they will suffice if you're pressed for time. See p. 165.

o **Shopping 'til You Drop:** To paraphrase a local saying, if you haven't shopped, you haven't been to Shànghǎi. Savvy locals know if you want greater choice and better deals, **Huáihǎi Lù,** with its slew of international boutiques and large department stores, is the place to shop. Branching off and parallel to Huáihǎi Lù, Màomíng Lù, Xìnglè Lù, and Chánglè Lù are also home to a number of delightful small shops. Even if you're the kind of person who only shops once a year, a visit to **Nánjīng Lù,** the "Number One Shopping Street in China" is practically required, if only for a chance to marvel (or shudder) at the sheer numbers of people, people, people everywhere! A pedestrian mall makes strolling and browsing that much easier and that much more crowded. Finally, **Tàikàng Lù,** with its ever-growing block of small shops, artists' studios, and outdoor cafes, makes for a delightful afternoon of shopping. See "Walking Tour 2: Nánjīng Lù" on p. 207, and see chapter 9 for shopping listings.

o **Bargaining for Antiques & Fakes:** Shànghǎi has any number of antiques markets where you can hone your bargaining skills. Two of the top choices are the more touristy **Dōngtái Lù Antique Market** and the slightly more ragtag but colorful **Fúyòu Market** in the old Chinese city (at the western end of Shànghǎi's restored old street, Shànghǎi Lǎo Jiē). Half the fun is in rifling through all the personal collections of memorabilia and antiques that the vendors seem to have scavenged; the other half is in dramatically protesting the high prices quoted, walking away, then being called back by a vendor newly willing to deal. The same process and joys of bargaining apply when trying to purchase knockoff designer goods, but caveat emptor. See p. 228 for warnings about knockoff purchases, and see p. 227 for antiques markets.

o **Rediscovering Shànghăi's Jewish Past:** In the mid–19th century, Sephardic Jews from the Middle East helped make Shànghăi a great city. In the mid–20th century, thousands of Jewish refugees flooded the International Settlement north of the Bund. Today, this history can be encountered at the former **Ohel Moshe Synagogue,** today renamed the **Shànghăi Jewish Refugee Museum,** with an exhibit documenting life in this little-known but important Jewish ghetto. The **Ohel Rachel Synagogue** has also been restored and is open for Shabbat prayers and meals. See p. 170.

o **Soaking in Shànghăi's Night Views:** The night views of the Bund and Pŭdōng are simply not to be missed. Viewing options include dining at one of the Bund restaurants, such as **M on the Bund** or **Laris,** and then crossing the river to **Jade on 36** in Pŭdōng for a nightcap (you can also reverse the order). Better yet, savor the best of both worlds by finishing off the evening at **Vue** bar at Hyatt on the Bund where you can behold the nightlights on both shores of the Huángpŭ River, while soaking in an outdoor Jacuzzi! See chapter 6 for dining options and chapter 10 for bars.

o **Watching the Acrobats:** This has "TOURIST" stamped all over it, but it's nevertheless a totally worthwhile pleasure, especially since Shànghăi's dazzling troupes are rightly considered China's very finest at this ancient craft. See chapter 10.

o **Sampling Shànghăi's Jazz Scene:** The famous **Peace Hotel Jazz Band,** decamped elsewhere for the past 2 years, has at long last returned to its original stomping grounds in the now-restored Peace Hotel. If the band's nightly performances of New Orleans–style jazz, with some members who have been playing here since before the Revolution in 1949, are too tame or nostalgic for you, modern and more improvisational jazz can be heard at a number of true-blue joints: the **Cotton Club, JZ Club,** and the **House of Blues and Jazz.** See p. 249 for jazz bars.

o **Drifting in a Gondola Through a Water Village:** There are any number of picturesque "water villages" near Shànghăi where you can be paddled in a gondola along streams and canals as you pass traditional arched bridges, quaint stone houses, and classical Chinese gardens. Two villages stand out: Tónglĭ and Nánxún. Also, both have additional sights worth seeing and considerably smaller crowds than at tourist traps like Zhōu Zhuāng, but see them soon. See p. 276 and 273.

# THE best SPLURGE HOTELS

o **The Peninsula Shànghăi** (Zhōngshān Dōng Yī Lù 32, Huángpŭ; © 021/2327-2888): The Peninsula Shànghăi marks the return of the Hong Kong and Shànghăi Hotels Limited to Shànghăi after 60 years (the company was originally founded in Shànghăi in 1866)—and what a welcome and glorious return it has been. From its enviable location at the top of the Bund, to its gorgeous Art Deco interiors, from its Rolls-Royce limousines to its standard-setting afternoon tea, from its unmatched in-room amenities to its award-winning fine dining, the Peninsula shows how it's done. Don't miss it! See p. 87.

○ **Park Hyatt Shànghǎi** (Shìjì Dàdào 100, World Financial Center, Pǔdōng; ☏ 021/6888-1234): This exclusive, top-of-the-Hyatt-line hotel is the world's tallest hotel, if height matters to you. It's not the most conveniently located hotel, but the huge rooms (the largest in the city) with high ceilings, elegant decor, comfortable beds, unparalleled views (on a clear day, that is), and thoroughly modern bathrooms with state-of-the-art showers and automated bidets have all garnered high praise. See p. 103.

○ **Fairmont Peace Hotel** (Nánjīng Dōng Lù 20, Huángpǔ; ☏ 021/6321-6888): Shànghǎi's most famous historical hotel was just reopening at press time (after being closed for the last 2 years), and was unavailable for our review, but we are preemptively including it here. We think (and hope), based on a ¥500-million renovation price tag, that the restorations will be faithful and perhaps even surpass our expectations, and that the new joint management by the Fairmont Hotels group and the local Jīnjiāng chain will once again make the Peace Shànghǎi's top destination hotel. See p. 86.

○ **Mansion Hotel** (Xīnlè Lù 82, Xúhuì; ☏ 021/5403-9888): If you want to be transported back in time to Shànghǎi in the 1930s, then the exclusive boutique **Mansion Hotel,** right in the heart of the French Concession, is where you want to lodge. At this refurbished old mansion, you'll get to experience all of today's luxurious amenities in a nostalgic colonial setting. See p. 95.

○ **Amanfayun** (Fǎyún Nòng 22, Xīhújiēdào, Hángzhōu; (☏ 0571/8732-9999): This exclusive luxury resort (disguised as a traditional tea village) is alone worth making a trip to Hángzhōu, especially if you're looking for a quiet and private retreat. Guests stay in traditional (but restored and unmarked) village houses nestled in the hills west of Hángzhōu's famous Xī Hú (West Lake). Rooms have daybeds, sofas, under-floor heating, and free broadband Internet, but no bathtubs or televisions. Yes, the whole of Hángzhōu awaits your exploration, but if you'd just prefer to hike in the surrounding hills, or wake up early and join the monks in prayer at the neighboring Yǒngfú Temple, or simply pamper yourself silly at the Aman spa, it's just as good. See p. 272.

# THE best MODERATELY PRICED HOTELS

○ **Quintet** (Chánglè Lù 808, Jìng Ān; ☏ 021/6249-9088): For those who want to wake up in a typical 1930s Shànghǎi *lòngtáng* (lane) house, and who don't need a lot of hotel facilities, this delightful bed-and-breakfast in the French Concession will deliver the goods. You'll walk on original hardwood floors, but sleep in comfortable, modern beds and have access to Wi-Fi. You'll also smell the aromas and hear the sounds of daily life in the *lòngtáng*. It's nothing fancy, but it's authentic, charming, and reasonably priced. See p. 100.

○ **Captain Hostel** (Fúzhōu Lù 37, Huángpǔ; ☏ 021/6323-5053): Lodged in a 1920s Art Deco building just steps from the Bund, this popular maritime-themed hostel offers clean dorms and simple double "cabins" for around ¥400 after discount, a whopping good bargain for its location. After a hard day's sightseeing, you can sip a cold beer on the rooftop bar (which has fabulous views of Pǔdōng) and be grateful you weren't shanghaied like a sailor of yore. See p. 90.

# THE MOST UNFORGETTABLE DINING EXPERIENCES

o **Tackling Hairy Crab:** The name says it all. The signature dish of Shànghǎi is absolutely scrumptious, but it's seasonal (autumn) and best enjoyed at a big local restaurant. See chapter 6.

o **Rooftop Dining on the Bund:** Whether it's savoring world-class cuisine on the open-air balcony of **M on the Bund,** or enjoying a romantic dinner for two catered by world-renowned chefs in the cupola atop **Three on the Bund,** dining high above Asia's most famous street is a heady experience not to be missed. See p. 111.

o **Eating Xiǎolóng Bāo:** Unless you're a vegetarian, not trying Shànghǎi's favorite (pork) dumpling while you're here is tantamount in some circles to not having visited Shànghǎi at all. The "little steamed breads" spill broth in your mouth when you bite into them. You can find them everywhere, but **Crystal Jade Restaurant** (p. 116) serves up the best in the city. For tips on how to eat it without scalding your tongue, see "Shànghǎi's Favorite Dumpling" on p. 134.

o **Savoring Shànghǎi's Street Food:** This activity could well top all of the others in this category, so fun and delicious is it to snack your way through town on dishes that you'll likely not find at home. You aren't required to try the *chòu dòufu* (stinky tofu), but do have the *shēngjiān bāo* (pork-stuffed fried bread dumplings) and *jīdàn bǐng* (egg pancake). The more locals in the part of town, the more likely you'll find it on any street. Or head to Sìpáilóu Jiē in the old Chinese city or the corner of Chánglè Lù and Xiāngyáng Lù in the French Concession. See p. 118.

o **Dining in a Colonial Mansion:** These days, it's easy to find a restored old mansion for dinner, but two standouts that combine just the right colonial ambience with delicious food are **Fu 1088,** serving excellent Shanghainese cuisine in private dining rooms in a restored mansion, and **el Willy,** dishing out tapas and paella in the loveliest of garden settings. See p. 130 and 120.

# THE best THINGS TO DO FOR FREE

o **People-Watch:** One of our favorite activities. It's free, it's fascinating, and you may learn more about today's China in an hour of people-watching than you would in a day spent on a tour bus. You can do this practically anywhere, at a park or a major intersection, but the best spots may be in People's Square, along Nánjīng Lù Pedestrian Mall, on Huáihǎi Lù, on the Bund Promenade, or at Xīntiāndì, where you are almost certain to see some wild and woolly mix of beleaguered tourists, both Chinese and foreign, along with newly minted business folk, trendy young fashionistas, uniformed school children, strolling seniors, and, of course, whistle-blowing traffic cops. One of the more interesting sights in recent years has been the "matchmaking market" that has sprouted in People's Park (Rénmín Gōngyuán) on weekends as parents show up in droves hoping to find matches for their still-single adult children.

o **Morning Exercises in the Parks and on the Bund:** There's no better way to greet the day than to join the thousands of Shànghǎi residents in their morning tai chi exercises (and occasionally Western ballroom dancing) in Shànghǎi's parks and on the Bund. While the Bund is preferable (the first golden rays hitting the colonial facades are truly something to behold), the newly refurbished Bund promenade seems to have deterred residents from coming out as before. See chapter 7 for details on the Bund and on Shànghǎi parks.

o **Wander the Old Chinese City:** The narrow winding alleys of the old Chinese city may strike some as mysterious and forbidding, but they are neither of these, and are worth exploring even beyond the walking tours in chapter 8. Here is a chance to come upon a wet market, or run into the increasingly rare sight of a night soil worker on his morning rounds (many houses in this part of town still lack indoor plumbing). See it before the bulldozer shows up. See "Walking Tour 3" on p. 214.

o **Stroll the French Concession:** This is the most interesting of the colonial districts left in Shànghǎi, filled with the gorgeous villas, mansions, and apartment houses of the 1920s and 1930s when the French made their mark here. Plenty of Art Deco gems abound, hidden behind years of grime and buried beneath webs of laundry poles, and they await discovery, so keep your head up. See "Walking Tour 4: French Concession" on p. 218.

# SHÀNGHĂI IN DEPTH

While Běijīng may be the capital of China, Shànghăi—the "city above the sea"—is China's economic, financial, and commercial center, its largest city, and the heart of China's future. As China reemerges as a major global power in the 21st century, Shànghăi is the economic engine that is leading the way. As Shànghăi goes, so goes the rest of China. No other super city in the Middle Kingdom, including Hong Kong and Běijīng, or anywhere else in the world, for that matter, is more vibrant or fascinating. Most recently, Shànghăi solidified its credentials as a full-fledged world-class city when it successfully hosted the 2010 World Expo.

None of this should be a surprise when you take a look at Shànghăi's history. Blessed by its location at the mouth of the Yángzĭ River, Shànghăi rose from a fishing village in the 7th century to a major commercial center by the 17th century. In the 19th century, its status as a treaty port enabled all kinds of foreign influences to mix with local Chinese culture, so much so that by the early-20th century, Shànghăi had become known as the Paris of China, and one of the most cosmopolitan and international cities in the world, where foreigners and Chinese alike flocked. But excesses also allowed for the fomenting of revolution, and the city that gave birth to the Communist Party of China in 1921 was also the one most thoroughly shut down after the 1949 Communist victory. With economic reforms in China starting in 1978, however, Shànghăi has once again donned the mantle of progress (at warp speed, no less), and at the beginning of a new millennium, the city has an air of prosperity rediscovered from the heady days of the wealthy foreign concessions.

But make no mistake, today's Shànghăi is no Western-dominated city. Rather, the Shanghainese, influenced by years of foreign exposure, though still unabashedly Chinese at their core, are drawing from the best of both worlds to forge a distinct sensibility, culture, and lifestyle. Not only is Shànghăi a city of finance, but art and architecture, design and fashion are all flourishing here as well—we haven't even touched on the unparalleled shopping and creative dining found in the city.

Not everything is rosy to be sure and growing pains are still everywhere you look, but no city on Earth seems more optimistic about its future than Shànghǎi. Today's Shànghǎi is being hailed, once again, as the New York City or the Paris of China. Perhaps these comparisons are currently necessary to give foreigners a sense of the character and importance of the new Shànghǎi, but the pace and unique nature of Shànghǎi's current evolution suggest that one day in the not-too-distant future, Shànghǎi itself may well be the barometer city to which all others are compared.

# SHÀNGHǍI TODAY

Any discussion of Shànghǎi as China's largest city and its economic, financial, and commercial hub usually starts with a whole lot of numbers. Official figures for 2009 put Shànghǎi's total population at 19 million, of which 14 million were registered permanent residents, and the rest were migrant workers. At the same time, temporary foreign residents numbered more than 100,000 (not counting the more than 300,000 Taiwanese living in Shànghǎi while conducting business), compared with 4,000 in 2000. The United Nations estimates that Shànghǎi's population will stand at 23 million by the year 2015.

Of course, numbers, especially those put out by the Chinese government, seldom tell the full or realistic story, but in the case of Shànghǎi, even when the unverifiable, usually inflated numbers are taken with mountains of salt, they still point to the obviously formidable if unbalanced role Shànghǎi plays in China's economy. While the city has less than 2% of China's population, Shànghǎi accounts for around 5% of China's Gross Domestic Product (GDP), 11% of its financial services, 12% of China's total industrial output, 20% of its manufacturing output, and 25% of the country's trade. Textiles, steel, manufacturing, shipbuilding, and increasingly the retail sector dominate the city's economy, which reports double-digit growth year after year. At the same time, Shànghǎi accounts for around 25% of China's foreign investment, with firms from Volkswagen and Buick to Mary Kay, Amway, Hallmark, and Coca-Cola having invested billions in plants and personnel here. In 2007, more than 500 multinational companies were reported to have their regional corporate headquarters in Shànghǎi. Not since colonial days (1846–1949), when the city was dominated by Western companies, has the port produced such an array of international investments.

Today's business, both domestic and foreign, has made Shànghǎi quite wealthy by Chinese standards, with rising salaries creating an increasingly affluent middle class. The latter comprises mostly white-collar managers, many of whom earn upwards of ¥100,000 a year. China is expected to become the largest luxury market in the world in a few years, led no less by Shànghǎi. As China's longtime center of shopping, Shànghǎi also has plenty of upscale places to dispose of the increased income. Residents are not only forward-looking and business-oriented, but fashionable. Shànghǎi is a city of boutiques, malls, and up-to-date department stores. Year by year, it is catching up with Hong Kong as one of Asia's paradises for shoppers. Everything is writ large here. Shànghǎi is not only home to China's first and largest stock exchange, but it also boasts the world's second-largest department store, China's busiest (and the world's second-busiest) container port, China's tallest building, and the tallest hotel in the world—not to mention more than 13 million mobile phone users. With prosperity, even sales of the venerable bicycle, formerly the chief means of transport in the city, have declined (from one million sales in Shànghǎi in 1990 to less than half that today). Meanwhile, the streets are crowded with more than 600,000 vehicles (including 45,000 taxis) and 280,000 motorcycles.

## Growing Pains

Scratch the surface, however, and a slightly more complex picture emerges. The knock on Shànghǎi has always been that it is a city of appearances, a perception carried over from the early days when what seemed like a European city was in fact built on the backs of millions of Chinese, when its heyday prosperity and wealth masked a much crueler and more dire poverty for millions of Chinese. Today's detractors, often led by Shànghǎi's greatest competitor to the south, Hong Kong, like to claim that for all of Shànghǎi's glamorous exterior, there is no substance behind the flash. Indeed, a closer look beyond appearances shows that many of Shànghǎi's new, handsome buildings remain empty, that your bathroom in the latest brand-new five-star hotel is already showing cracks, and that many more people are, in fact, window-shopping than plunking down cold cash.

The rosy numbers also mask the fact that while Shànghǎi has more than its share of overnight millionaires, ordinary Shanghainese must still be counted as residents of a developing rather than a developed nation. Even taking into account the highly inflated government figures, the city's average annual disposable income for the first three quarters of 2009 was ¥21,871, one of the highest in the country, but still not high enough to keep up with Shànghǎi's massively over-inflated housing prices—the average housing price for new homes in early 2010 was hovering around ¥18,000 to ¥20,000 per square meter, far higher than the nation's average. (In the last few years, housing prices have skyrocketed as a result of the large population influx, wealthy Chinese from around the country purchasing these units as investment properties, speculation, and interestingly enough, the pressure for young men to own a home before they can get married.)

Little wonder, then, that living space is slim (under 140 sq. ft. per person); that many ordinary Shanghainese (lǎobǎixìng), forcibly relocated to the outskirts of town because of megadevelopments and downtown building projects, cannot afford even the smallest of homes; and that many others (including more than two million pensioners) must scrimp by on less than the official minimum wage (Shànghǎi's monthly minimum wage, set at ¥1,120 in mid-2010, is the highest in the country). At the same time, beggars can still be seen congregating at tourist sites, temples, and avenues where visitors are likely to appear. The unemployed, most arriving illegally without residence permits in Shànghǎi, can be sighted sleeping under bridges, awaiting work. To exacerbate matters, inflation, especially of food prices, has been on the rise since 2008, leading to steep increases in the basic cost of living for many. The economic boom has brought other woes as well. Crime is on the rise, prostitution is back in the bars and on the streets (after its complete eradication in the 1950s), and pollution is a major problem.

But Shànghǎi is nothing if not ambitious. This is a city of big dreams. Ever allergic to inactivity and resting on its laurels, Shànghǎi barely had time for the dust to settle from the massive modernization and reconstruction of the 1990s (which *New York Times* writer Ian Buruma hailed as "perhaps the greatest urban transformation since Baron Haussmann rebuilt Paris in the 19th century") before it won the bid in 2002 to host the 2010 World Expo, and embarked on a new phase of building that has once again transformed the city. Indeed, having just completed China's tallest building, the 492m-tall (1,614-ft.) Shànghǎi World Financial Center, in mid-2008, the city has started construction on a new 128-floor, 632m-tall (2,073-ft.) Shànghǎi Tower (nicknamed Shànghǎi Dragon). For the 2010 World Expo, the government is said to have spent between ¥300 billion and ¥400 billion in direct and indirect investment, not just in building the Expo grounds, but also upgrading and expanding the city's two airports and roads, giving its most famous street the Bund a massive face-lift, and adding another seven lines to its subway system in just the last 3 years (another 10 lines are planned for 2020). As a further mark of its ambition and dedication to infrastructure, Shànghǎi is building the world's largest container port, and is creating nine new towns surrounding Shànghǎi, each with a half-million residents.

## Going Green

Additionally, city planners promise that Shànghǎi will soon be not only China's financial and manufacturing capital, but its "green" capital as well. The responsibility for hosting the 2010 World Expo, which had as its theme "Better City, Better Life" has certainly helped fuel Shànghǎi's going green. Already, Shànghǎi has converted Nánjīng Lù to a pedestrian mall, remodeled the Bund and its promenade, revitalized many avenues and villas in the old French Concession, and created 1,800 hectares (4,448 acres) of greenway with trees and lawns (an area equivalent to 4,000 football fields). The government has also done an impressive job rehabilitating the Sūzhōu River, which had been seriously polluted by 80 years of industrial use. Still ongoing is the Huángpǔ River Renovation Project, covering 20km (12 miles) of downtown riverfront on both shores, whereby the harbor will be transformed by green corridors, an elliptical canal, a maritime museum, marinas, riverside parks, and new housing estates.

The Chinese government has also banned the use of ultra-thin plastic bags while requiring shops to charge for thicker plastic carrier bags. In an interesting and ironic twist, hundreds of increasingly environmentally conscious Shanghainese came out in force in early 2008 to protest the extension of the magnetic levitation train line through their neighborhood for fear of radiation and other harmful health effects. These protests led the government to shelve or "reassess" the project (though the latest indications are that the project is back on). Finally, perhaps the most ambitious environmental project yet is the building of an eco-city—the first self-sustaining carbon-neutral city in the world that does no appreciable damage to the environment—that will be home to a half-million people on the wetlands of Dōngtān on Chóngmíng Island at the mouth of the Yángzǐ River. For all the original hoopla surrounding this project, however, it is currently stalled, with work not yet begun on a project originally scheduled to be partially completed by the time of the World Expo.

If you can ignore the inevitable teething pains of any booming city, the present and the future look rosy indeed. The successful hosting of the World Expo has also added to the Shanghainese's optimism. The question of if and when the bubble will burst (consider, in addition to the highly inflated housing prices, that you now generally pay more for a cup of coffee in Shànghǎi than back home, or that while many average Shanghainese may be richer now than they've ever been, rampant speculation and weak regulation of China's financial sectors mean that one's life savings risk being wiped out overnight) does not appear to have deterred Shànghǎi's boosters and all others who would seek a better life from arriving in droves to stake out their share of the spoils. With an unprecedented degree of freedom (at least since the pre-revolutionary days) to express themselves publicly, whether through their fashions or their purchases, just as long as it's not in the arena of politics, Shanghainese seem content, for the moment at least, to go along with their government's experiment of developing a country through economic but not political freedom. Love them or hate them, the Shanghainese—frank, efficient, chauvinistic, and progressive—are using their previous international exposure to create China's most outward-looking, modern, brash, and progressive metropolis.

# LOOKING BACK AT SHÀNGHǍI

## A Small Fishing Village

The first evidence of settlements in the Shànghǎi area actually date to 5000 B.C., though it wasn't until the 5th to 7th centuries A.D. that Shànghǎi appeared on the map as a small fishing village on the banks of the Wúsōng Jiāng (today's Sūzhōu River). It was then a creek known as Hù (for the crab traps in the river), and had its source in nearby Tài Hú (Lake Tài). Eventually Shànghǎi would be known as Hù, and to this day, the name is still in use as a short form to denote the city, for example in the Hùníng Expressway connecting Shànghǎi to Nánjīng. During the Táng Dynasty in A.D. 751, the Shànghǎi region was incorporated into the county of Huátíng, but it was not until 1292 that Shànghǎi, benefiting from its proximity to Hángzhōu, the capital of the Southern Sòng Dynasty (1127–1279), quickly developed from a commercial town (*zhèn*) to a county seat (*xiàn*). By the early 1400s, Míng Dynasty engineers had dredged the Huángpǔ River (also known as *shēn*), making it the main tributary to serve Shànghǎi. In 1553, a city wall was built around what is today's Shànghǎi's Old Town (Nánshì) as defense against Japanese pirates. In 1603, Shànghǎi had its first contact with the Jesuits through local son Xú Guāngqí who was baptized Paul by Jesuit priest Matteo Ricci in Běijīng, and who later deeded some of his land in Shànghǎi (today's Xújiāhuì, meaning Xú family village) to the Catholic Church. By the end of the Míng Dynasty, in 1664, Shànghǎi had become a major cotton and textile center; and its population would soon reach 200,000.

## Foreign Occupation

In 1832, the British-based East India Company explored Shànghǎi and the Yángzǐ River as a potential trading center for tea, silk, and opium, but was rebuffed by proud local officials. Not to be denied, the British eventually forced the Chinese to import British opium (which it produced in British India) by waging the First Opium War between 1839 and 1842 against a weak and corrupt Qīng government that proved no match for the British. The war finally ended with the Treaty of Nánjīng, which opened five Chinese cities, including Shànghǎi, to British consuls, merchants, and their families, and also ceded Hong Kong Island to the British. Soon, the British, French, Americans, Germans, and other foreign powers began to move into Shànghǎi, carving out for themselves sovereign "concessions" where they were not subject to Chinese laws, but to their own as established by their respective governing councils. The British established their concession in 1845, the Americans in 1848 in

Hóngkǒu, north of Sūzhōu Creek, and the French set up their concession in 1849 west of the old Chinese city and south of the British Concession, subjecting themselves to direct French rule through the Conseil d'Administration Municipale. In 1850, the first English-language newspaper in Shànghǎi, the *North China Herald,* was launched.

But peace and calm were elusive. Starting in 1850, a man named Hóng Xiùquán, who believed himself to be Jesus' younger brother, led a group of Tàipíng rebels through southern China in an attempt to overthrow the corrupt Qīng government. Though they bypassed Shànghǎi and established their capital in Nánjīng, an offshoot group, the Small Sword Society, which claimed affiliation with the Tàipíngs, took over Shànghǎi's old Chinese city, driving thousands of Chinese into the foreign concessions. Many Westerners became rich from building housing for the Chinese refugees. The Small Sword Society was eventually defeated by Qīng troops in 1855, though the Tàipíng Rebellion itself didn't end until 1864.

Hardly deterred by these uprisings, the British and the Americans merged their concessions and formed the International Settlement in 1863, subject to rule by the Shànghǎi Municipal Council. In the second half of the 19th century, those seeking fame and wealth were starting to arrive in Shànghǎi in droves to have a go at making their fortune. A number of Sephardic Jew businessmen especially prospered from the opium trade and real estate, and would go on to build some of Shànghǎi's finest buildings of the early 20th century, such as the Children's Palace and the Peace Hotel (1929). By 1871, the term "shanghai," meaning to drug and forcibly kidnap hands for a departing ship, had entered the English language, as during this time, many sailors were literally "shanghaied," waking up at sea on clipper ships bound for China.

> **Impressions**
>
> If God lets Shanghai endure, He owes an apology to Sodom and Gomorrah.
> —A Christian missionary, in concession-era Shànghǎi

While Shànghǎi was starting to prosper, events at the national level were becoming increasingly dire as the Qīng government grew weaker. In 1895, after Japan defeated China in the Sino-Japanese war, the Treaty of Shimonoseki allowed the Japanese to set up factories in Shànghǎi and other ports. Finally in 1911, following the abdication of China's last emperor, Pǔ Yí, the year before, the Republic of China was established under Sun Yat-sen, bringing to an end Chinese imperial rule. The following year, the foreign population in Shànghǎi topped 10,000, a number which only increased as White Russians fleeing the Russian Revolution in 1917 made Shànghǎi's international concessions their temporary home. It is worth noting, however, that even when foreign influx was at its greatest, foreigners never numbered more than 4% of Shànghǎi's total population.

## War & Revolution

As Shànghǎi's wealthy, Chinese and foreigners alike, continued to live the high life and get even richer, corpses started to pile up on the streets, many having perished from cold and hunger, and the seeds of revolution were sown. In 1921, the Chinese Communist Party was founded in Shànghǎi, with Máo Zédōng in attendance. In 1925, in what has come to be regarded as the beginning of the end of Western

## Impressions

*Since the Japanese occupation of the outer city, the International Settlement has been dangerously overcrowded. There is no restriction on sub-letting: the minimum sleeping-space on a floor may cost one dollar sixty cents a month. When the British wished to clear a single street a hundred yards long for defensive purposes they were told that this would mean evicting fourteen thousand people.*
—Christopher Isherwood, on a visit to Shànghăi in 1938

imperial power in China, a student protest on behalf of exploited Shànghăi workers led to students being shot at by the foreign Shànghăi Municipal police. This "May 30th Movement" coalesced anti-foreign sentiment and paved the way for Communist revolutionaries in China.

Also around this time, Shànghăi's triads were making their presence felt as Dù Yuèshēng ("Big-eared Dù") took power from Huáng Jīnróng ("Pockmark Huáng") as head of the powerful Green Gang. On April 12, 1927, Dù's gang assisted Chiang Kai-shek, the new leader of the Kuomintang (Nationalists), in rounding up and executing Communist leaders in Shànghăi at today's Lónghuá Martyrs' Cemetery near Lónghuá Temple, thus forcing the Communists to go underground and initiating a protracted civil war between the two groups. All this time, wealthy Shànghăi continued to prosper and party. During the 1920s and 1930s, this "Paris of the East" reached its zenith as the leading center of trade and finance in Asia, and home to the greatest architecture, finest shops, and most lavish and decadent nightlife. It was this last feature that gave Shànghăi its concurrent reputation as the "Whore of Asia." In 1935, the population was nearly four million, including 60,000 foreigners, of which a little less than half were European Jews who had fled here to escape from Hitler. Shànghăi was then the only place in the world that was willing to accept the "stateless refugees."

But the good times could not and did not last. In 1937 Japan attacked China, taking over the Chinese-administered parts of Shànghăi on August 13. That same year, the Shànghăi Municipal Council tallied 20,000 corpses of homeless people who had died in the streets. The Japanese did not occupy the International Settlement and French Concessions until December 8, 1941. (For the Chinese, World War II has always been known primarily as the Anti-Japanese War.) In 1943, in response to German requests to implement the Final Solution in Shànghăi, the occupying Japanese army forced the stateless Jews into a confined "Designated Area" in Hóngkǒu District. British and American forces also relinquished their extraterritorial powers and concessions to the Chinese that year. World War II finally ended with the Japanese surrender in 1945.

After the war, tensions once again quickly flared between the Communists and Nationalists who had agreed to a temporary truce during the war to fight against a common enemy, the Japanese. After many protracted battles all over the country, Máo Zédōng proclaimed the creation of the People's Republic of China on October 1, 1949, thus ending the civil war (earlier, Communists had "liberated" Shànghăi on May 25 without incident). Chiang Kai-shek, his wife, Soong Mei-ling, and the rest of her

Soong family, except for Soong Ching-ling (the widow of Sun Yat-sen), beat a hasty retreat to Táiwān. Within a year, the remaining colonialists and foreign companies had pulled out of Shànghǎi and the Communist Party began to shut down the city's many industries, including vice industries, and sent the once-thriving city into a slumber for almost 30 years. In 1966, led by the Shànghǎi-based "Gang of Four," which included Máo's wife, Jiāng Qīng, a former Shànghǎi actress, the Cultural Revolution began. Initially a campaign to rid Chinese society of bourgeois elements and to maintain constant class struggle, it descended into social, political, and economic chaos and violence, and ended only in 1976 with the arrest of the Gang of Four.

## Reform & Reawakening

Earlier in 1972, however, China's rapprochement with the outside world had started to take place. After Henry Kissinger undertook several secret missions to Běijīng to reopen relations with the Chinese, Richard Nixon and Premier Zhōu Ēnlái signed the Shànghǎi Communiqué at the Jǐn Jiāng Hotel in 1972, paving the way for normalization of relations between the United States and China, though official ties weren't reestablished until 1979. By then Máo had died (in 1976), and a rehabilitated Dèng Xiǎopíng had initiated "opening and reforms" (gǎigé kāifàng) the year before in 1978. Economic reforms quickly took off, and by 1982, Shànghǎi had opened the Hóngqiáo Development Zone to attract foreign investors.

In 1989, weeks of student protest ended in violence in Běijīng in the Tiān'ānmén massacre. In Shànghǎi, mayor Zhū Róngjī and predecessor Jiāng Zémín maintained calm, which no doubt partially helped Jiāng become China's paramount leader later in 1997 after the death of Dèng Xiǎopíng. Zhū Róngjī became the chief architect of China's economic revolution and China's premier in 1998.

More importantly for Shànghǎi, in 1990 Dèng Xiǎopíng designated Shànghǎi to spearhead China's economic reform, with the Pǔdōng New Area on the east side of the Huángpǔ River slated for development into Shànghǎi's new financial center. Overnight, this former swamp and farmland rapidly transformed into the home of some of China's biggest buildings, including China's first (and largest) stock exchange, the tallest TV tower in Asia, the tallest building in China, and the tallest hotel and the second-largest department store in the world. The building frenzy continued throughout the 1990s and into the 21st century, with new infrastructure seemingly popping up every year, such as the Pǔdōng International Airport, the Nánjīng Lù Pedestrian Mall, the Yán'ān Elevated Expressway, new bridges, tunnels, a high-speed magnetic levitation line, and a public transportation system that, when complete, will overtake London's in size. During this time, Shànghǎi also started to host world events such as the Fortune 500 Global Economic Forum in 1999, the APEC Conference in 2001, and the first Formula One Grand Prix race in China in 2004. As its crowning glory, Shànghǎi won the bid in 2002 to host the World Expo of 2010, thus returning Shànghǎi to what many feel is its rightful place on the world stage.

# SHÀNGHǍI WAYS & MANNERS
## The People

Many of today's Shanghainese had ancestors who came from neighboring areas such as Sūzhōu, Níngbō, Hángzhōu, and even from as far away as Guǎngdōng in the south. The Cantonese who came in with the British as their compradors, and the people from the southern seaport town of Níngbō, who were known as astute bankers, contributed greatly to Shànghǎi's development as a capital of business and trade. It used to be that Shànghǎi was welcoming to anyone who was smart, enterprising, and ambitious, and while that still holds true today, many of today's urban class-conscious Shanghainese tend to regard all non-native Shanghainese with some suspicion and condescension. Migrant peasants from poorer neighboring provinces such as Ānhuī and Jiāngxī who do much of the work deemed too lowly by the Shanghainese, such as construction or trash collection, bear the greatest brunt of disdain.

This chauvinism is not exclusive to the Shanghainese, of course; the term *wàidìrén* is used by Chinese throughout the country to refer to those not of their immediate native soil, and each group naturally tends to think itself superior to all *wàidìrén*. Still, the Shànghǎi brand of chauvinism is particularly strong, and while some of it may be slowly challenged with the increasing influx of educated and ambitious Chinese from other parts of the country, it's still alive and well in the Shanghainese preference for their own dialect whenever possible. Shanghainese is a subcategory of the Wú dialect, one of six major Chinese dialects not including Mandarin, but each of the dialects is so different from the others that some experts consider all to be different languages entirely. Not surprisingly, the Shanghainese consider their dialect the most refined of all.

Perhaps not surprisingly, the Shanghainese's biggest detractors are its main competitors to the north and south, the Běijīngers and the Cantonese respectively. But in general, the Shanghainese have a reputation, valid or not, among many Chinese as being superficial, arrogant, opportunistic, and unpatriotic. This harsh judgment may have more to do with jealousy over economic success than anything else.

Either way, the Shanghainese themselves are too busy to disagree or bother with what they perceive as sour grapes, prefer to think of themselves as cosmopolitan, smart, shrewd, savvy, ambitious, open-minded, progressive, and enterprising, qualities they believe have allowed Shànghǎi to lead the country's economic revolution and move headlong into the 21st century. Generally speaking, the Shanghainese are fashion-setters and conspicuous consumers. That they enjoy a significantly higher standard of living than most other Chinese is, to them, proof that they possess the necessary winning qualities. And indeed, foreign companies doing business in Shànghǎi hail the locals as smart, eager, and hungry to learn. Some Chinese grouse that the Shanghainese are too quick to both please and ape Westerners, but the Shanghainese will just as quickly tell you that their historical exposure to foreigners has made them more open to Western ways, and therefore allowed them to succeed in today's global village. Whether in business (see below) or in social mores, the Shanghainese pride themselves on being pioneers willing to break old rules. Already, Shanghainese men, at least those of the post–Cultural Revolution (1966–76) generation, are considered to be a prime catch for young Chinese women, not necessarily because of their urbaneness or any putative business acumen, but because many younger Shanghainese husbands are known to do all the housework, the cooking, and the grocery shopping for their wives.

Even in China's most cosmopolitan and international city, however, there are still significant differences in customs and modes of behavior between the Shanghainese and foreign visitors. Though Shanghainese today have a remarkable amount of freedom in everything from fashions to critiquing corruption, politics, especially criticism of the government and the Chinese Communist Party, is still a taboo subject for public discussion. If you broach any "embarrassing" topic—including questions about China's handling of political dissidents, the status of Tibet and Táiwān, restrictions on the media, abortion, prison labor, and the Tiān'ānmén Square incident—be prepared for stock answers from most people, especially English-speaking tour guides. Some younger Shanghainese may seem eager to tackle such topics, but Western visitors sometimes find themselves surprised by the sincerely nationalistic responses to such questions. In general, feel free to ask the locals about anything, but remember that visitors can sometimes put their hosts—who may have government jobs—on the hot seat when posing politically sensitive questions. In return, visitors can expect some frank questions, not just from the Shanghainese but from the Chinese in general, about everything from your age and income to your marital status. You may answer such queries as you see fit, vaguely if you wish.

## The Chinese World View

Another discernible difference in world views derives from the profound influence of Confucianism on Chinese society. Even though this uniquely Chinese philosophical tradition (dating to the 5th c. B.C. when its founder, Confucius, 551–479 B.C., formulated a set of social and ethical precepts about the role of an individual in society, and Confucius's students later canonized his teachings, which then became the state philosophy for almost 2,000 years) was completely repudiated during the Cultural Revolution (1966–76) and has never been significantly rehabilitated since, aspects of Confucian philosophy continue to permeate Chinese life and culture to this day. Confucius's laying out of hierarchical relationships (between father and son, husband and wife, older and younger brothers, ruler and subject, and between friends) has led the Chinese to view the individual as part of greater wholes—of the family, foremost; of the workplace; and of the nation. The group has more power than the individual, and it must be consulted before decisions are made.

In practical terms, this translates into a respect for hierarchies. Those of higher rank within any organization, be it a family or a business, hold the power over others and decide what those of lower rank may do. The individual often has far less autonomy and power in Chinese society than in Western societies—even when it comes to apparently insignificant matters. Many Westerners are often shocked to learn that until 2003, Chinese still had to seek permission from their assigned work unit (*dān wèi*) in order to get married. Other Confucian holdovers that generally still endure in modern Shànghǎi are the respect for age, which is synonymous with wisdom and stature; the respect for higher education; and the respect for family matters, which are of more importance than those of work, politics, or world affairs. The importance of *guānxi* or connections in all aspects of Chinese life can arguably be traced back to the Confucian view of the individual as part of a larger nexus of social relationships.

While women are equal to men by law and by Communist dogma, in fact, women are often considered as they once were in traditional Chinese society: second best to men. Male children, who alone continue the family line, are still preferred over females by many couples. Even among foreigners, men are often treated with slightly more respect than women, although modern education and the influx of Western ideas have begun to erode such prejudices at the edges.

Confucianism, which stressed moral and ethical behavior, is mocked in the current exaggerated worship of money and the resultant corruption that now pervades every level of government, party, army, police, state, and private enterprise. Ever since Dèng Xiǎopíng told Chinese peasants that getting rich is glorious (part of his 1982 "opening and reform" *[gǎigé kāifàng]* programs—all but sounding the death knell of Communism), this every-man-for-himself mentality has become the new de facto Chinese ideology. Of course, lip service is paid every now and then, usually on China's National Day (Oct 1), to Communism, or at least to the Communist Party, but all savvy Chinese know to watch out for number one since neither the Party nor anyone else is particularly watching out for them. Periodically, some egregious offender unlucky enough to be caught is given a capital sentence and made an example, but by and large, corruption continues at every level, even as some in the government are doing their best to curb it.

Prices are marked up so high not because one person or party is raking in all the spoils (though sometimes that happens, too), but because everyone along the way is skimming his or her share. These days, even when the *lǎobǎixìng* (ordinary Chinese) complain about corruption and graft, it is usually not out of any true moral or ethical outrage, but from their own failure to get a piece of the pie as well. In April 2008, Chén Liángyǔ, Shànghǎi's former mayor and the Communist Party's top official in the area, was sentenced to 18 years in prison for taking bribes and stealing money from Shànghǎi's pension fund. While President Hú Jǐntāo's government was ostensibly cracking down on corruption, some observers thought that Chén's close association with former Chinese President Jiāng Zémín and his "Shànghǎi faction" were what led to Chén's downfall.

## Doing Business

The vision of one billion consumers for their products has driven countless foreign companies to do business and set up factories in China in the last decade. More than 500 multinational corporations have their regional corporate headquarters in Shànghǎi. However, as almost all foreign companies have discovered, some of whom have pulled out, the consumers have not materialized as envisioned, and government red tape, inertia, corruption, false financial information filed by companies, and "mysterious" Chinese business practices, such as they are, have proven to be significantly more challenging than expected.

Like the rest of Chinese society, Chinese business relies greatly on connections or *guānxi*. Blood ties (however thin, even if it's the fourth uncle of your father's second aunt) and who you know will often get you in the door where a solid business proposal may not. The idea that business deals are often closed not in the boardroom, but indirectly over the umpteenth cup of *máotái* (a potent Chinese spirit) at a Chinese banquet, followed by a night of karaoke singing and more, and that the

# SAVING face

In social or business settings, the Chinese often take great pains to preserve "face," which involves maintaining one's self-respect while deferring important decisions to those of higher rank within a group. "Losing face" means to suffer embarrassment before others. To be criticized roughly by a visitor, for example, or to be asked to do something that is impossible, puts a Chinese person in a difficult position. "Saving face" is achieved by compromising, or sometimes by ignoring a problem altogether. You will seldom be told a direct "no" in response to a difficult or impossible request; instead you may get some more ambivalent answers such as "Maybe" or "I'm not sure" or "We'll see," which is usually tantamount to "No." Many Chinese will go to extremes to avoid settling a dispute or handling a

complaint, because any loss of face in "kowtowing" to another could reflect badly upon their family and China, as well as upon themselves.

What visitors need to do when making requests or issuing complaints in Shànghǎi, then, is to control their tempers, avoid assigning personal blame, seek compromise when possible, and practice patience. A polite approach has a better chance of success than a more aggressive, brutally frank, or simply angry outburst. In a nation renowned for the size and inertia of its bureaucracy, some things are slow to be done, and some things are never done at all. It often helps to ask a person to relay your complaint or demand to a superior, remembering that a response may not be immediate.

outcome is sometimes dependent less on the merits of the deal than on the willingness to play the game, can take foreigners (not to mention their livers, vocal cords, and other body parts) some getting used to. What is at play here, though, is the building of a relationship. Chinese business practices tend to emphasize building a strong relationship before closing a deal, and it is ultimately the quality of the business *relationship* that will determine the success of the venture. Even when a deal is closed, however, there is no guarantee that it will be honored. Any reneging, though, is usually never direct, for that would entail a loss of face (see nearby box); instead, some important element or condition of the deal, which is always out of the control of the Chinese partner, will somehow fall through. As a result, contracts and agreements cannot necessarily be counted on to be worth more than the paper they're printed on. In fact, it is quite common that the Chinese will continue to press for a better deal even after the contract is signed. While the government has tried to establish something resembling an integrated legal system with enforceable pro-business laws, at present the Chinese court system is still enough of a quagmire that many foreign companies often just write off the losses.

As China's commercial center and gateway to the international business community, Shànghǎi's business environment is better regulated and business practices are more codified here than elsewhere in the country, though a number of the same challenges exist. The Shanghainese believe that it is their previous exposure to foreigners that allows them today to be the quickest to adapt to international business practices and ways. But lest the foreigner think the Shanghainese are pushovers in their eagerness to do business, the Shanghainese are some of the shrewdest business and trades people you will likely encounter anywhere. Attitudes towards "getting mine" are just as prevalent (if not more so) here as elsewhere. Many foreign businessmen have discovered, much to their chagrin, that while the Shanghainese may be openly welcoming of foreign expertise and know-how, the hospitality sometimes extends only until they've received all the help they need to make a run of their own enterprises and become competitors to the foreigners who helped them in the first place. Still, the business opportunities are here for the taking, and those who can approach the process with some humility, massive doses of patience (delays are inevitable and you must expect to make several trips to China to solidify your business relationship before even cementing the deal), and as much knowledge as possible about China, the Chinese, and their culture (learning some of the language will also be greatly appreciated) will stand a greater chance of success. See "Etiquette & Customs" in chapter 12, "Fast Facts," for more information.

# SHÀNGHǍI'S ART & ARCHITECTURE
## Eclectic Architecture

For all of Shànghǎi's exalted status as China's economic powerhouse, it has another claim to fame, and that is as a museum of architecture, albeit of the Western variety. Shànghǎi's history as a treaty port has led to it today comprising one of the richest collections of British colonial, Victorian, neoclassical, and Art Deco buildings anywhere in the world. The first three styles were common during the 19th century, and can be seen in many of the buildings in the old British-dominated, business-oriented International Settlement (which ran north of today's Yán'ān Lù into part of Hóngkǒu, and extended west from the Bund), with one of the finest examples being the neoclassical former Hong Kong and Shànghǎi Bank on the Bund. In the 1920s and 1930s, Art Deco took Shànghǎi by storm, and Art Deco apartment buildings sprang up everywhere, especially in the French Concession, whose leafy boulevards and fine villas made it an attractive residential area for many foreigners. Shànghǎi is said to have even more Art Deco buildings than Miami Beach.

At the same time, Shànghǎi has its own unique style of architecture in the *lǐ lòngtáng* (literally "neighbor lane space") lane housing that dominates much of the city. These rows and rows of wood and brick tenements in the settlements' many lanes popped up in the 1850s and 1860s when foreign settlement merchants saw a lucrative opportunity in building housing for the many Chinese who were fleeing the Small Sword Society uprising in the old Chinese city. Everyone conveniently ignored the stipulation in the 1842 Treaty of Nanking that the concessions were for foreigners only. The Chinese stayed on after the rebellions, and the *lǐ lòngtáng* became a fixture. Typically, a row of shops would front a warren of lanes of two-story brick tenement houses, each framed by stone portal doors—called *shíkùmén* (stone gate)—and leading to a small Chinese courtyard. *Shíkùmén* housing evolved over time to incorporate Western decorative devices and motifs as well. There was also a garden-style *lǐ lòng* housing designed more for foreigners, featuring detached or semidetached houses in a variety of styles with accompanying gardens. Apartment *lǐ lòngs* had five- to seven-story apartment buildings sharing a common garden. Since 1949, many *lǐ lòng* houses have been torn down, and more were razed in the 1990s for commercial redevelopment. Many of the remaining *lǐ lòngs* are now designated for preservation.

The frenzy to tear down old buildings was especially acute in the final days of the 20th century, as the Shànghǎi government rushed to modernize and build skyscrapers and malls, but heedless destruction has since stopped. The government realized that conservation, restoration, and redevelopment of old properties has a significant commercial upside, and that modern-day visitors seem to like nothing more than to recapture a flavor of old Shànghǎi in restored projects like Xīntiāndì (p. 116) and some of the converted buildings on the Bund, and that expatriates will pay top dollar to stay in refurbished old houses and apartments. Unfortunately, the quality of preservation of old buildings has been uneven.

Overall, the future of architecture in Shànghǎi looks bright. As China has opened its doors to foreign architects in the building boom of the last 15 years (for example, American architect Ben Wood is responsible for designing both the Xīntiāndì complex as well as the new Wàitānyuán project behind the Bund), Shànghǎi has been the beneficiary of some sublime pieces of modern architecture, such as the Jīn Mào Tower (p. 187), which has since been bested in height by the less interesting but taller Shànghǎi World Financial Center (p. 190). The Shànghǎi Grand Theatre (p. 189), the Shànghǎi Oriental Art Center (p. 248), and Tomorrow Square (Míntiān Guǎngchǎng) housing the JW Marriott Hotel (p. 86) are some other attractive modern buildings. Architecture was also the star at the recent 2010 World Expo which featured many innovative and creative designs in the various country and theme pavilions. A crowd favorite was the cube-shaped "Seed Cathedral" UK Pavilion, looking like a dandelion but made of 60,000 acrylic rods containing seeds from around the world. Unfortunately, the majority of pavilions are to be torn down at the end of the Expo, with only five structures to be retained (p. 184), including the prominent Chinese Pavilion looking like an Oriental crown, and the 1km-long (⅔-mile) Expo Axis.

## But Is It Art?

As recently as a decade ago, Chinese contemporary art was still largely an underground phenomenon, with exhibitions frequently shut down by authorities. Today, the scene has not only gone legitimate, but it has become passionately embraced both locally and internationally. One reason for modern Chinese art's popularity is its comparative affordability: These days, the works of high-profile Chinese artists typically fetch between $20,000 and $500,000 in overseas markets, sums still considerably cheaper than works by artists of similar stature in the West, though a new auction record for Asian contemporary art was set in mid-2008 when Zēng Fànzhì's painting of youths wearing masks and Red Guard scarves was sold for $9.7 million.

Independent, foreigner-owned galleries were some of the first players on the contemporary Chinese art scene, first establishing themselves in Běijīng in the early 1990s. In Shànghǎi, the grandfather of them all was the independent ShanghART Gallery (p. 237) started by Swiss Lorenz Helbling in 1994, and quickly followed by galleries such as Biz Art and Art Scene China. Relocated to much larger premises at 50 Mògānshān Lù, where much of Shànghǎi's nascent art scene has started to coalesce in the last few years, ShanghART represents and shows some of Shànghǎi and China's hottest contemporary artists, such as painter and performance and video artist Xú Zhèn, video installation artist Shī Yǒng, and pop artist Zhōu Tiěhǎi, the last known for his series of paintings anthropomorphizing Joe Camel, and also for his painting of former New York mayor Rudy Giuliani framed by elephant dung. Other famous local artists include photographer Deke Erh (p. 237) and painter Xú Jié, known for her series of China Doll paintings.

Today's Chinese art encompasses everything from pop art and photography to shock art and video installations, but the largely politicized images of the '80s and early '90s have given way to a more sophisticated attempt to capture a subtler contemporary ethos reflecting the tensions of urban Chinese life. When they do occur, political images and statements can sometimes still get an artist into trouble. In general, as is to be expected of a still-young art scene, quality is at best uneven.

What particularly worries some observers of the Shànghǎi art scene is the pressure exerted by the rampant commercial impulse of the city. Whereas foreigners and philanthropic collectors interested in nurturing Chinese talent were the ones collecting Chinese contemporary art in the early days, much of the extraordinary art boom in the last 5 years has been due to an ever-growing Chinese economy and local buyers entering the market. Newly minted millionaires with bagfuls of disposable cash have been engaging—with the help of large auction houses such as Christie's and Sotheby's—in what some observers fear is an irrational exuberance of buying, artificially driving up prices and creating a speculative bubble. Still, Shànghǎi is nothing if not speculative and brash, and if ever there was a city that needed to decorate the walls of its skyscrapers and had the financial wherewithal to do so, Shànghǎi is it. Little wonder, then, that the art scene in Shànghǎi is growing at warp speed and the city is well on its way to becoming if not the nation's art center (that title still belongs to Běijīng), then at least a gateway to some of the country's most interesting and provocative contemporary art.

In addition to 50 Mògānshān Lù, visitors can also view all manner of modern art at the new Rockbund Art Museum (p. 188) just behind the Bund, the Museum of Contemporary Art in People's Park (p. 180), the Zendai Museum of Modern Art at Fāngdiàn Lù 199, Building 28 in Pǔdōng, the Duōlún Modern Museum of Art (p. 178), Tàikàng Lù Art Centre, Creek Art at Guāngfú Lù 428, Shànghǎi Sculpture Space (p. 190), the Shànghǎi Gallery of Art (p. 237), and a plethora of galleries around town. As well, the Shànghǎi Biennale, originally started in 1996 as an all-local affair, is now an international event held every other autumn.

# SHÀNGHǍI IN POPULAR CULTURE: BOOKS, FILM, TV, MUSIC

## Recommended Books

At the top of the list of books on Shànghǎi history is Shànghǎi-born Lynn Pan's nostalgic, romantic, easy-to-read history of the city and its characters, *In Search of Old Shanghai* (Joint Publishing [H.K.] Co., Ltd., 1982). Many accounts of Shànghǎi's history tend to focus on the lurid, the sensational, and the exotic during Shànghǎi's golden age in the first half of the 20th century, including Stella Dong's spicy history of colonial Shànghǎi, *Shanghai: The Rise and Fall of a Decadent City, 1842–1949* (William Morrow, 2000). It suffers, as any general book on Shànghǎi must, from a lack of depth, but it at least summarizes the main events and personalities that came to define the time. Harriet Sergeant's equally entertaining *Shanghai* (Jonathan Cape, 1991) focuses on a shorter period (1920s and 1930s) and uses stories and anecdotes to bring to life Shànghǎi in its heyday.

Considerably more academic but still fascinating, *Beyond the Neon Lights: Everyday Shanghai in the Early Twentieth Century* (University of California Press, 1999) by Hanchao Lu gets past the myth and the hype to examine the daily lives of ordinary Shanghainese in their *shíkùmén* (stone frame) lane housing. Andrew David Field's well-documented *Shanghai Dancing World: Cabaret Culture and Urban Politics, 1919–1954* (The Chinese University Press, 2010) looks at issues of colonialism, sexuality, politics, and Chinese national identity through the prism of Shànghǎi's nightlife during the jazz age. Finally, for a much more comprehensive, long-ranging (but still readable) history, Jeffrey Wasserstrom's meticulously researched *Global Shanghai 1850–2010* (Routledge, 2009) ambitiously takes on the city's history by focusing on seven 25-year installments, and in so doing provides a fascinating and wider perspective on Shànghǎi now and in the future.

As biographies and memoirs go, only the first section of colorful American journalist Emily Hahn's *China to Me* (Blakiston Co., 1946) is set in Shànghǎi, but it offers a vivid and entertaining account of life among the Shànghǎi elite in the 1930s. It includes her encounters with members of the Soong family, who are themselves profiled in great, highly readable detail in Sterling Seagrave's *The Soong Dynasty* (Harper & Row, 1985). *Carl Crow: A Tough Old China Hand* (Hong Kong University Press, 2007) traces the life and times of entrepreneur and businessman Carl Crow in Shànghǎi between the two world wars.

If fiction is your cup of tea, old Shànghǎi comes alive in Vickie Baum's novel *Shanghai '37,* in which different characters' lives collide at the Cathay (Peace) Hotel just before the Sino-Japanese War. No literary masterpiece, it nevertheless succeeds in bringing a tumultuous bygone era to life. *Midnight* (Foreign Language Press, 1957) by Mao Dun, a Chinese novelist who became China's Minister of Culture from 1949 to 1965, is a full epic that vividly brings the violence and corruption of 1930s Shànghǎi to life through the travails of a ruthless industrial capitalist. Shanghainese writer Eileen Chang (Zhāng Àilíng), better known in the West these days for her novella *Lust, Caution,* which spawned the 2007 movie, has a number of well-written novels, but for those with short attention spans, her book of probing short stories, *Love in a Fallen City* (NYRB Classics, 2006), is especially good, and tells of love, longing, and loss in 1940s Shànghǎi.

Far darker visions of Shànghǎi are powerfully evoked in J. G. Ballard's personal novel, *Empire of the Sun* (V. Gollancz, 1984), based on his imprisonment as a child during the Japanese occupation, and in Nien Cheng's *Life and Death in Shanghai* (Grove Press, 1986), a memoir of her imprisonment during the Cultural Revolution. Anchee Min's *Red Azalea* (Pantheon Books, 1994) recounts her extraordinary journey from revolutionary Red Guard to film star in Shànghǎi under the watchful eye of Madame Máo. The more recent Wang Anyi's *The Song of Everlasting Sorrow: A Novel of Shanghai* (Columbia University Press, 2009) is a lyrical, decades-long journey of a 1946 Shanghainese beauty pageant runner-up whose life unfolds against a turbulent backdrop of a changing China.

A welcome antidote to the dark and heavy survival stories is the light and fun series of detective novels by Chinese author Qiū Xiǎolóng, featuring the poetry-writing, murder-investigating Shànghǎi police inspector Chen. Start at the beginning with *Death of a Red Heroine* (Soho Press, 2000). There are five Inspector Chen novels. Those partial to thrillers can also pick up Tom Bradby's *The Master of Rain* (Doubleday, 2002), a murder mystery set in 1920s Shànghǎi involving British lads, Russian prostitutes, and Chinese gangsters.

Finally, for pictorial memoirs on Shànghǎi's colonial architecture, there's no topping Tess Johnston and Deke Erh's *A Last Look: Western Architecture in Old Shanghai Revisited* (2005); *Frenchtown Shanghai: Western Architecture in Shanghai's Old French Concession* (2003); and *Shanghai Art Deco* (2006), all published by Old China Hand Press, and all more widely available in Shànghǎi than in the West. The two have also released a series of books on Western colonial architecture in other parts of China. Architecture fans can also pick up Australian architect Ann Warr's *Shanghai Architecture* (Watermark Press, 2007), a comprehensive guide to the architecture and history of Shànghǎi from the days when it was an old walled city right up to the present. Greg Girard's wonderful photography book *Phantom Shanghai* (Magenta Publishing for the Arts, 2010) gives glimpses of Shànghǎi you'll never see because many of the houses, shops, neighborhoods, and buildings he spent the previous 5 years photographing have all fallen prey to the bulldozer in the name of progress. The estimable Lynn Pan rounds out this section with her latest *Shanghai Style: Art and Design Between the Wars* (Long River Press, 2008), a history of *hǎipài*, that unique brand of Shànghǎi style, aesthetic, and culture that so seamlessly combined the East and West.

## Recommended Films

Old Shànghǎi was the Hollywood of China. Many of its films were produced at the Shànghǎi Film Studios (located in Xújiāhuì on Cáoxī Běi Lù across from the Xújiāhuì Cathedral) during the 1930s and 1940s, often featuring China's top actresses such as Ruǎn Língyù, Zhōu Xuán, and Hú Dié. Another two-bit actress with the stage name Lán Píng was among thousands who never achieved a starring role then, but she had her revenge later, when she met and married the young revolutionary who would become Chairman Máo. Known as Jiāng Qīng after 1949 (and later punished as the leader of the Gang of Four), she helped dictate the nature of Communist cinema, drama, and other arts during the 1950s, 1960s, and 1970s. She was a star on the political stage for decades, but her real dream remained Hollywood.

Today, Shànghǎi is no longer the center of Chinese filmmaking, although the Shànghǎi Film Studio continues to churn out some movie and television projects and the occasional joint-venture film with foreign filmmakers. Films about Shànghǎi, at least those familiar to Western audiences, trade heavily on the nostalgia of the mysterious and romantic 1930s. For Western audiences, the classic is Josef von Sternberg's 1932 film *Shanghai Express*, starring Marlene Dietrich, though none of it was filmed in Shànghǎi, of course. The Shànghǎi underworld of 1930s gangsters and their molls is also stylishly evoked in Zhāng Yìmóu's 1995 film *Shanghai Triad* (*Yáo a yáo yáo dào wàipó qiáo*), starring Gǒng Lì. Steven Spielberg's 1987 film *Empire of the Sun*, based on English author J. G. Ballard's autobiographical novel, takes a look inside the concentration camps of Shànghǎi during the Japanese occupation; some of the most gripping scenes were filmed in the streets of Shànghǎi (using 15,000 local extras) and at the Peace Hotel on the Bund.

Although Hong Kong director Wong Kar-Wai's 2000 award-winning film *In the Mood For Love* (*Huā Yàng Nián Huá*) is set in Hong Kong, it evokes the lives of displaced Shanghainese in the former British colony during the 1960s. Everything in this wonderfully moody movie oozes nostalgia, and the lead actress Maggie Cheung's slim, figure-hugging *qípáo* outfits even sparked a fashion craze in Shànghǎi in 2001. Old-time tailors were forced out of retirement to churn out once again this quintessentially traditional Chinese dress that had fallen so out of fashion until then.

For those who like a little more challenging fare, Taiwanese director Hou Hsiao-hsien's beautiful chamber piece, *Flowers of Shanghai* (*Hǎi Shàng Huā*, 1998), takes place entirely inside four turn-of-the-20th-century opium-filled Shànghǎi brothels, as madams, servants, and courtesans (called *huā* or flowers) despair and connive for the attentions of their patrons. There's nothing lurid or sensational here, only a slow-moving existential meditation that grows increasingly claustrophobic as the evening wears on. Not for those with short attention spans.

More recently, director Ang Lee's trenchant and controversial *Lust, Caution* (*Sè Jiè*, 2007), adapted from Eileen Chang's novella and largely filmed in Shànghǎi, depicts the attempts of a group of young Chinese students to assassinate a Chinese collaborator during the Japanese occupation of Shànghǎi in World War II. The movie's own considerable merits were largely overshadowed by the controversy surrounding it, including the cutting of 7 minutes of explicit footage from the version shown in mainland China, and for the movie's putative sympathetic portrayal of a Japanese collaborator.

The darker side of modern Shànghǎi as seen through the failed dreams and bleak hopes of a lonely Shànghǎi youth is depicted in the stylized low-budget *Sūzhōu River* (*Sūzhōu Hé*, 2000) directed by Ye Lou.

Recent Hollywood films shot with a full or partial Shànghǎi backdrop include *Mission Impossible III* (2006), *The Painted Veil* (2006), *The Great Raid* (2005), *Code 46* (2003), and the not very successful *The White Countess* (2005), the last about a blind American diplomat, his fantasy nightclub, and a family of Russian aristocrats in 1930s Shànghǎi. Most recently, the murder mystery *Shanghai* (2010) directed by Mikael Håfström and starring John Cusack and Gong Li tells the story of an American who returns to 1940s Shànghǎi to investigate the death of a friend. The movie was all set to film in Shànghǎi in 2008, but Chinese authorities denied permission at the last minute, and the production had to relocate to London and Thailand where sets were built to stand in for colonial Shànghǎi.

Finally, a 1998 Austrian documentary by Joan Grossman and Paul Rosdy, *The Port of Last Resort*, tells the story of the Jews who fled Nazi Europe for Shànghǎi from 1937 to 1941.

# EATING & DRINKING IN SHÀNGHǍI

Food plays such an important role in Chinese culture that when people meet, they often greet each other with the words, "Have you eaten?" (*Chī lè ma?*). For the visitor to China, food will (or should) be one of the highlights of your trip. If you're traveling on a group tour, you'll likely be fed fare that is fairly ordinary and generic, and above all inexpensive. Try to sneak out for an independent Chinese meal if possible. Mealtimes are practically sacred, and you'll find, especially if you are on an organized tour, that visits and events are often scheduled around meals, which are usually taken early (11:30am–noon for lunch and 5:30–6pm for dinner). In a city such as Shànghǎi, few businesses or tourist attractions close for the lunch hour, though this is more common in smaller Chinese towns.

Following Daoist principles, Chinese cooking aims for a balance of flavors, textures, and ingredients. Certain foods are thought to have *yáng* (warming) or *yīn* (cooling) properties, and the presence of one should ideally be offset by the presence of its opposite. Seldom is one ingredient used exclusively, and meals should reflect that harmonious blend of meat and vegetables, spicy and bland, and so forth. China has a staggering variety of regional cuisine (see "China's cuisines" on p. 108 in chapter 6) that reflects the different ingredients available in a particular environment, and also emphasizes different cooking methods, and you are encouraged to try as many of these as possible while you are in the country. Chances are that little of it will taste like the food from the neighborhood Chinese restaurant back home; if anything, it'll taste better.

While you can sample most of the diverse Chinese cuisines in Shànghǎi (though admittedly, few ethnic Chinese cuisines make it here entirely intact, as the local preference for sweet invariably finds its way onto most menus), the emphasis here is on Shànghǎi's traditional cuisine, also known locally as *běnbāng cài*. Considered a branch of the Huáiyáng style of cooking, Shànghǎi cooking favors sugar, soy sauce, and oil, and seafood is featured prominently. While it is true, as some critics allege, that traditional Shànghǎi cooking does tend towards the oily and the over-sweet, many typical Shànghǎi dishes are simply delicious and deserve to be tried, as it's likely you won't find much like it back home.

You can find the following typical Shànghǎi dishes in any local restaurant serving *běnbāng cài*: cold appetizers such as *xūnyú* (smoked fish), *kǎofū* (braised gluten), *zuì jī* (drunken chicken marinated in Shàoxīng wine), and *pídàn dòufu* (tofu with "thousand-year-old" eggs); snacks like *xiǎolóng bāo* (steamed pork dumplings with gelatinous broth), *shēngjiān bāo* (pork-stuffed fried bread dumplings), and *jiǔcài hézi* (leek pie); traditional dishes such as *chǎo niángāo* (fried rice cakes), *Shànghǎi cū chǎomiàn* (Shànghǎi fried thick noodles), *shīzǐ tóu* (braised "lion's head" meatballs), *típáng* (braised pig trotters), *méicài kòuròu* (braised pork with preserved vegetables), *yóumèn sǔn* (braised fresh winter shoots), *jiāobái* (wild rice stems), *shuǐjīng xiārén* (crystal prawns), *dàzhá xiè* (hairy crab), *xuěcài máodòu bǎiyè* (bean-curd sheets with soy beans and salted winter greens), and the soup *yānduxiān* (pork-based broth with ham, bamboo shoots, and bean curd skin). Desserts include *bābǎofàn* (eight-treasure glutinous rice) and *dòushā sūbǐng* (red bean paste in flaky pastry).

Regional differences notwithstanding, Chinese food is usually eaten family-style, with a number of dishes to be shared by all. If you find yourself dining solo, you can ask for *xiǎo pán* (small portions), usually about 70% of the full dish and the full cost, though not all restaurants will accommodate this request. Dishes can arrive in random order, though most meals usually begin with cold appetizers (*liáng cài*), then move on to seafood, meat, and vegetable main dishes. Except in Cantonese cuisine when it's taken as one of the first courses, soup is usually served last. Plain rice is typically eaten as an accompaniment in your average proletarian setting, but is seldom voluntarily offered in finer dining, where the emphasis is supposed to be on the subtle flavors of each dish and ingredient, and rice is considered a mere filler. (You can always request rice if it's not automatically offered.) Outside of the more sophisticated restaurants, the food in many places throughout the country can be a bit more greasy than foreigners are used to; if this is a cause for concern, you can specify beforehand *shǎo yóu* ("less oil"), though don't expect this request always to be honored.

In your average Chinese restaurant, dessert, if it exists, usually consists of a few orange wedges and not much else, though Shànghǎi and Cantonese cuisines feature a slightly wider choice of sweets such as red bean pastries (*dòushā sūbǐng*), and sesame seed paste (*zhīma hú*). Tea is usually served free, though if you're asked what kind of tea you want, you'll probably be charged for it. A vintage like *lóngjǐng* tea (from the Hángzhōu) is considerably more expensive than something like your average chrysanthemum (*júhuā chá*) or jasmine tea (*mòlihuā chá*). Napkins and chopsticks should be free, though if you're given a prewrapped package of tissues, you'll likely be charged for opening it, and possibly for the peanuts as well. In general, there is no tipping, though a few restaurants outside the major hotels may add on a service charge, which usually guarantees you won't get much in the way of service.

For a glossary of Chinese dishes, listed in *pīnyīn* with Chinese characters, see chapter 13, "The Chinese Language."

# PLANNING YOUR TRIP TO SHÀNGHǍI

Traveling in China is not as hard as you might think, and in Shànghǎi, it's even easier than that. Of all the cities in China, Shànghǎi is the easiest for an independent traveler to navigate. Tens of thousands of visitors arrive here every year, usually armed with some solid pre-planning, a guidebook, and a sense of adventure. However you choose to visit and whatever your preconceptions about traveling to China, it is important that you read this chapter carefully. It contains all the basics for designing a trip to Shànghǎi and entering China with the right documents in hand.

For additional help in planning your trip and for more on-the-ground resources in Shànghǎi, see "Fast Facts," on p. 281.

## WHEN TO GO

Except for the windy, chilly winter months, Shànghǎi teems with tourists and business travelers, most notably May through October. July and August are unpleasantly hot and humid as a rule; locals often sleep on cots on the sidewalks to escape the pent-up heat of the day in their small apartments. Shànghǎi's busiest tourist periods coincide with its mildest weather in the spring and fall. September and October are really the ideal times to visit, but they're also popular times for meetings and conventions, leading to high hotel occupancy and uncompetitive room rates. To avoid the big crowds and still enjoy decent weather, the best time to visit is in late March or late October/early November. Besides the climate, the other major consideration in the timing of your visit should be the domestic Chinese travel season (see "Holidays" below).

**CLIMATE** Shànghǎi, located on the 31st parallel north, has a climate comparable to that of the southeastern coast of the United States, except that Shànghǎi's summer is hotter. Spring, from mid-March to mid-May, is mild but rainy. Summer, from mid-May to mid-September, is oppressively hot and humid. Winter, from mid-November to mid-March, is damp and chilly, but there is seldom snow and the daytime temperatures are usually above freezing. Autumn, from mid-September to mid-November, is the most comfortable season, being neither too hot nor too rainy, but typhoon-propelled rains can strike in September.

## Shànghǎi's Average Temperatures & Rainfall

|  | JAN | FEB | MAR | APR | MAY | JUNE | JULY | AUG | SEPT | OCT | NOV | DEC |
|---|---|---|---|---|---|---|---|---|---|---|---|---|
| Temp. (°F) | 39.5 | 40.5 | 47.5 | 58.0 | 68.0 | 74.5 | 82.0 | 82.0 | 74.0 | 65.5 | 54.0 | 44.5 |
| Temp. (°C) | 4.2 | 4.7 | 8.6 | 14.4 | 20.0 | 23.6 | 27.8 | 27.8 | 23.3 | 18.3 | 12.2 | 6.9 |
| Days of Rain | 9.0 | 10.2 | 13.1 | 13.5 | 15.0 | 13.1 | 11.4 | 10.0 | 11.6 | 8.4 | 9.1 | 8.6 |

**HOLIDAYS**    National holidays observed in Shànghǎi with days off include **New Year's Day** (Jan 1), **Spring Festival/Chinese New Year** (first day of the lunar calendar: Feb 3, 2011, Jan 23, 2012), **Qingming Festival** (usually Apr 5 on the Gregorian calendar; Apr 4 during leap years), **Labor Day** (May 1), **Dragon Boat Festival** (early June on the lunar calendar), **Mid-Autumn Festival** (Sept on the lunar calendar), and **National Day** (Oct 1).

**Spring Festival,** the Chinese New Year, is the most important holiday. Officially, it is a 3-day national holiday (usually expanded to 7 days, making the weekend after the 7-day holiday normal working days). On the first 3 days, banks, offices, and many workplaces are closed. In reality, the effects of this holiday are felt from 2 weeks before the date until 2 weeks after, as Chinese travel to and from their hometowns, which may be very far from their place of work. The 15th day of the New Year is marked by the Lantern Festival celebrations.

The **National Day** (Oct 1) holidays will also last 7 days. While offices, banks, smaller restaurants, and some sights may be closed for part of each holiday period, you will find in Shànghǎi that hotels that normally cater to business travelers will offer significant discounts during those times.

# Shànghǎi Calendar of Events

Festivals and celebrations are not numerous in Shànghǎi, and many are family affairs, but there are some opportunities to mix with the locals at city parks and other locations at annual public events.

For an exhaustive list of events beyond those listed here, check http://events.frommers.com, where you'll find a searchable, up-to-the-minute roster of what's happening in cities all over the world.

## WINTER

**Lónghuá Temple Bell-Ringing.** On New Year's Eve in the Gregorian calendar (Dec 31), crowds gather at Lónghuá Temple to pray for good fortune as the bell is struck 108 times during a special midnight Buddhist service. Fireworks, dragon and lion dances, folk art shows, and music go on into the wee hours.

**Spring Festival/Chinese New Year (Chūn Jié).** This is the time when Chinese return to their hometowns for family get-togethers, to visit friends, to settle the year's debts, to visit temples to pray for prosperity in the coming year, and to decorate their homes with red paper (signifying health and prosperity). Parks and temples hold outdoor celebrations and put on markets, the best places for tourists to visit. Begins the first day of the lunar calendar: February 3, 2011; January 23, 2012.

**Lantern Festival (Dēng Jié,** sometimes called Yuánxiāo Jié). On the 15th day after Chinese New Year, on the first full moon, people used to parade through town with paper lanterns, while parks and temples displayed more elaborate and fanciful lanterns, all accompanied by fireworks and folk dances. In Shànghǎi in recent years, there's been a minor revival of sorts, especially around the Yù Yuán Old Town Bazaar, but Shanghainese mostly mark the occasion by eating *yuánxiāo* (glutinous rice balls with sweet stuffing). This always falls 15 days after the Spring Festival.

**Guānyīn's Birthday.** Held on the 19th day of the second lunar month, about 50 days after Chinese New Year, in honor of the Goddess of Mercy, Guānyīn, this is a good opportunity to visit one of the Buddhist temples in Shànghǎi and join in the celebrations.

## SPRING

**Shànghǎi International Literary Festival.** Started in 2006 with entirely volunteer help, this festival, which is timed with the Hong Kong Literary Festival to better bring in international authors, is starting to attract a loyal following of bibliophiles. Big names who have held book readings at the Glamour Bar include Booker-prize winners Arundhati Roy and Anne Enright. Local authors are featured as well. Two weekends in early March.

**Lónghuá Temple Fair (Lónghuá Miàohuì).** Beginning on the third day of the third lunar month, this 10-day temple fair, featuring an array of vendors, Buddhist worshippers, and local opera performers, dates from the Míng Dynasty (1368–1644). Typically first or second week of April.

**Tomb Sweeping Festival (Qīng Míng Jié).** This day honors the dead, which in Chinese communities overseas and some rural counties usually entails the sweeping of ancestral graves and the offering of food and wine to the departed. This is now a public holiday. In Shànghǎi this means crowds of tourists from neighboring regions at the main sights. April 4 (Apr 5 in leap year).

**Formula One Grand Prix Racing.** It was hoped that this glamorous event, held in the northwestern suburb of Āntíng, would draw fans from around the world for 3 days of high-speed, high-adrenaline racing featuring the sport's biggest names, but the event has consistently lost money since its Shànghǎi inaugural in 2004. Although a race is scheduled for 2011, F1's future in Shànghǎi remains uncertain after that. April.

**Labor Day.** There's little for the Shànghǎi tourist to do except shopping, shopping, and more shopping. May 1.

**Shànghǎi Spring International Music Festival.** One of many recent festivals instituted by Shànghǎi, this one usually runs for 2 weeks in mid-May and has attracted such performers as the Chicago Symphony Orchestra and the Vienna Choir. It's also when the "Golden Chime" award is given to China's best music DJs.

## SUMMER

**Shànghǎi International Film Festival.** Scores of international films are screened, providing many Chinese with a chance to see films they would ordinarily not be able to. Foreign films are usually dubbed into Chinese. An international jury judges competition films. This is usually preceded by the Shànghǎi TV Festival. May/June.

## AUTUMN

**Mid-Autumn Festival (Zhōngqiū Jié).** Traditionally the time to read poetry under the full moon, this festival, also known as the "Mooncake Festival," and primarily celebrated by the eating of "mooncakes," pastries with extremely rich sweet bean filling, is now an official public holiday. During the Yuán Dynasty (1206–1368), Chinese attempting to revolt against their Mongol rulers sent each other messages hidden inside these cakes. Held on the 15th day of the 8th lunar month (usually Sept).

**Shànghǎi Biennale.** With the art scene thriving in Shànghǎi, this relatively new festival held every 2 years showcases the works, sometimes highly experimental, of local and international artists at the Shànghǎi Art Museum and at various galleries and venues

## Western Holidays in Shànghǎi

**Christmas** has become an increasingly popular holiday in Shànghǎi, celebrated at hotels and restaurants with large dinner parties. As commercial a holiday as it is in the West, **Valentine's Day** has caught on with a vengeance, with hotels and international restaurants offering room and dining packages that would have Cupid working overtime. Western **New Year's** has not caught on to the same extent, although Lónghuá Temple has become *the* place to literally ring in the new year. **St. Patrick's Day** and **Halloween** are celebrated by locals and expatriates at the cafes, bars, and discos.

throughout the city. Usually October to November, even-numbered years.

**Shànghǎi International Arts Festival.** This wide-ranging annual festival features local and international plays, concerts, and music and dance performances at various locations throughout the city. Usually the month of November.

# ENTRY REQUIREMENTS

## Passports

Visitors must have a valid **passport** with a 6-month validity beyond the date of arrival and two consecutive blank pages remaining to allow for visas and stamps that need to appear together.

For information on how to get a passport, see "Passports" in "Fast Facts" on p. 285. The websites listed provide downloadable passport applications as well as the current fees for processing passport applications. For an up-to-date, country-by-country listing of passport requirements around the world, go to the "Foreign Entry Requirement" Web page of the U.S. State Department at **http://travel.state.gov**.

## Visas

All visitors to mainland China (but not the Special Administrative Regions of Hong Kong and Macau) are required to have a **visa.** Tour groups are usually issued a group visa, with the paperwork handled by the travel agency (check with your agent). Individual travelers should apply for visas from your nearest Chinese embassy or consulate. Contact information for all Chinese embassies and consulates can be found at **www.fmprc.gov.cn/eng**. Some consulates require in-person applications while others allow applications by post or courier with extra charges. Visas are typically processed in 3 to 5 business days, though 1-day service is possible if you apply in person and pay extra fees.

The most common type of visa is the single-entry "L" tourist visa, usually good for 30 days, though you can request a longer validity period. Your request may not always be granted, and in some cases, you may be asked to produce supporting documentation (such as a travel agent–issued itinerary or an airline ticket with a return date). If you're going to be leaving and then returning to mainland China (even if you're just making a short trip to Hong Kong), apply for a double-entry visa. There are also multiple-entry 6-month or 1-year visas, which are now increasingly easy to come by. Visas are typically valid for 1 to 3 months after the date of issue.

To apply for a visa, you must complete an **application form,** which you can request by mail or download from the various consular websites. Also required is one **passport photo** per individual traveler (including a child traveling on a parent's passport). Though the visa is valid for the entire country (with a few exceptions that may require special permits), in general, avoid mentioning Tibet or Xīnjiāng on your application.

Following is a list of embassy addresses and visa fees for some countries, along with their respective Web pages that link to the appropriate consular sites and downloadable visa application forms. **Warning:** Visa fees listed are accurate as of press time, but are subject to change at any time.

o **United States:** 2201 Wisconsin Ave., Room 110, Washington, DC 20007 (© **202/338-6688;** fax 202/588-9760; www.china-embassy.org). All visas, whether single or multiple-entry visas are US$130. Applications must be delivered and collected by hand, or sent via a visa agency.

o **Canada:** 515 St. Patrick St., Ottawa, ON K1N 5H3 (© **613/789-3434;** fax 613/789-1911; www.chinaembassycanada.org). Single-entry visas are C$50; double-entry C$75. Applications must be delivered and collected by hand, or sent via a visa agency.

o **United Kingdom:** 31 Portland Place, London W1N 3AG (© **020/7631-1430;** fax 020/7588-2500; www.chinese-embassy.org.uk). Single-entry visas are £30, double-entry £45, with an extra charge of £20 for each package received through the mail.

o **Australia:** 15 Coronation Dr., Yarralumla, ACT 2600 Canberra (© **02/6273-4780;** fax 02/6273-5848; http://au.china-embassy.org/eng). Single-entry visas are A$40; double-entry A$60, with an extra charge of A$50 for each package processed by mail or courier.

o **New Zealand:** 2–6 Glenmore St., Wellington (© **04/472-1382;** fax 04/499-0419; www.chinaembassy.org.nz; www.chinaconsulate.org.nz). Single-entry visas are NZ$140, double-entry NZ$210, with an extra charge of NZ$15 for each package processed by mail or courier.

**GETTING A VISA IN HONG KONG** Nationals of most developed nations require only a valid passport to enter Hong Kong, even though it's a part of China. Chinese visas (single- and double-entry only; multiple-entry visas have to be obtained in your home country) can be easily secured at countless Hong Kong travel agencies, but they are cheapest at the **Visa Office of the PRC,** 26 Harbour Rd., China Resources Building, Lower Block, seventh floor, Wanchai (© **852/3413-2424;** www.fmcoprc.gov.hk; Mon–Fri 9am–noon and 2–5pm), where single-entry visas costs HK$1,020 for U.S. citizens, HK$450 for U.K. citizens, HK$150 for Canadians and Australians. At press time, the office was accepting HK$ cash only. Another outlet to get visas is at the Hong Kong operation of **CTS (China Travel Service),** with a popular branch at 27-33 Nathan Rd., Tsim Sha Tsui (© **852/2315-7188;** fax 852/2315-7292; www.ctshk.com). Or try **Grand Profit International Travel Agency,** 705AA, seventh floor, New East Ocean Centre, 9 Science Museum Rd., Tsim Sha Tsui (© **852/2723-3288**).

**VISA EXTENSIONS**   As a rule, single-entry tourist visas may be extended once for a maximum of 30 days at the local PSB (Public Security Bureau, *gōng'ān jú*) in most cities. In Shànghǎi, head to the Foreign Affairs Section of the PSB (*chūjìng guǎnlǐjú*) which has been relocated to Pǔdōng, at Mínshēng Lù 1500 (✆ **021/2895-1900**, ext. 2; Metro: Shànghǎi Kèjìguǎn/Science and Technology Museum, exit 3). Office hours are Monday through Saturday 9am to 5pm. Extensions usually require 5 business days. Bring your passport and two passport photos.

## Customs

### WHAT YOU CAN BRING INTO CHINA

In general, you can bring in anything for personal use that you will take with you when you leave, including laptops, GPS devices, cameras, video recorders, and other electronic equipment. You're also allowed four bottles of alcoholic beverages and three cartons of cigarettes. Travelers are prohibited from bringing in firearms, drugs, plant material, animals, and food from diseased areas, as well as "printed matter, magnetic media, films, or photographs which are deemed to be detrimental to the political, economic, cultural, and moral interests of China." This last section covers pornography, overtly political and religious material, and anything related to Tibet. In practice, however, small amounts of personal reading material in non-Chinese languages have yet to present a problem. Currency in excess of US$5,000 is supposed to be declared on Customs forms, though most major points of entry seem to have dispensed with the Customs declaration form entirely.

### WHAT YOU CAN TAKE HOME FROM CHINA

Upon departure, antiques purchased in China, defined as any item created between 1795 and 1949, must be accompanied by an official red wax seal before being taken out of the country (see chapter 9, "Shopping," for more details). Any item created before 1795 is prohibited for export. For information on what you're allowed to bring home, contact one of the following agencies:

**U.S. Citizens: U.S. Customs & Border Protection (CBP),** 1300 Pennsylvania Ave. NW, Washington, DC 20229 (✆ **877/287-8667**; www.cbp.gov).

**Canadian Citizens: Canada Border Services Agency,** Ottawa, Ontario, K1A 0L8 (✆ **800/461-9999** in Canada, or 204/983-3500; www.cbsa-asfc.gc.ca).

**U.K. Citizens: HM Customs & Excise,** Crownhill Court, Tailyour Road, Plymouth, PL6 5BZ (✆ **0845/010-9000;** from outside the U.K., 020/8929-0152; www.hmce.gov.uk).

**Australian Citizens: Australian Customs Service,** Customs House, 5 Constitution Ave., Canberra City, ACT 2601 (✆ **1300/363-263;** from outside Australia, 612/6275-6666; www.customs.gov.au).

**New Zealand Citizens: New Zealand Customs,** The Customhouse, 17–21 Whitmore St., Box 2218, Wellington, 6140 (✆ **04/473-6099** or 0800/428-786; www.customs.govt.nz).

## Medical Requirements

If you will be arriving in mainland China from a country with **yellow fever,** you may be asked for proof of vaccination, although border health inspections, when there isn't a health crisis, is cursory at best.

# GETTING THERE & AROUND
## Getting to Shànghǎi
### BY PLANE

Chinese carriers serving international destinations include **Air China** (www. airchina.com), **China Eastern Airlines** (www.flychinaeastern.com), **China Southern Airlines** (www.flychinasouthern.com), and **Hainan Airlines** (www. hnair.com). On direct nonstop flights, flying with one of the above is often cheaper than flying with your country's airline. Chinese airlines frequently "code share" with foreign airlines as well, which means you may end up flying on a Chinese airline jet even if you've purchased a foreign airline ticket, or vice versa. International flights arrive in Shànghǎi at Pǔdōng International Airport (airport code: PVG).

### From North America

Of the North American airlines, **Air Canada** (www.aircanada.ca), **American Airlines** (www.aa.com), **Delta Airlines** (www.delta.com), and **United Airlines** (www. ual.com) all fly to Shànghǎi.

    **Japan Airlines** (www.jal.co.jp) and **All Nippon Airways** (www.ana.co.jp) fly to Shànghǎi via Tokyo. **Korean Air** (www.koreanair.com) and **Asiana Airlines** (us. flyasiana.com) fly via Seoul.

### From the United Kingdom & Europe

Shànghǎi is connected to the U.K. and Europe by **Virgin Atlantic** (www.virgin atlantic.com), **British Airways** (www.britishairways.com), **Air France** (www.air france.com), **Austrian Airlines** (www.austrianair.com), **KLM Royal Dutch Airlines** (www.klm.com), **Lufthansa** (www.lufthansa.com), **Aeroflot** (www.aeroflot.com), **Finnair Airlines** (www.finnair.com), **Scandinavian Airlines** (www.scandinavian. net), and **Turkish Airlines** (www.turkishair.com).

### From Australasia

**Qantas** (www.qantas.com) flies nonstop to Shànghǎi from Sydney, while **Air New Zealand** (www.airnewzealand.com) flies nonstop from Auckland. Alternatively, it may be cheaper to fly one of the other Asian carriers via their home country, such as **Singapore Airlines** (www.singaporeair.com), **Malaysian Airlines** (www.malaysia airlines.com.my), **Garuda Indonesia** (www.garuda-indonesia.com), **Philippine Airlines** (www.philippineairlines.com), or **Thai Airways** (www.thaiairways.com). Other carriers serving Asia Pacific include **Dragonair** (www.dragonair.com), which flies from Hong Kong to Shànghǎi and is partly owned by Cathay Pacific, **Air Macau** (www.airmacau.com.mo), **Royal Brunei Airlines** (www.bruneiair.com), **Royal Nepal Airlines** (www.royalnepal-airlines.com), and **Emirates** (www.emirates.com). Alternatively, those flying from Hong Kong may find it cheaper, though not necessarily more convenient, to take a ferry to either Shēnzhèn or Zhūhǎi in Guǎngdōng Province and connect to Shànghǎi via a Chinese airline such as China Eastern or Hainan Airlines. The Chinese "no-frills" low-cost carrier **China Spring Airlines** (http://chinaspringtour.com) flies from various Chinese cities such as Zhūhǎi, Tiānjīn, Qīngdǎo, and Guìlín, to Shànghǎi.

## Arriving at the Airport

Almost all the international carriers arrive in Shànghǎi at **Pǔdōng International Airport (Pǔdōng Jīchǎng)** (✆ 021/96990; www.shanghaiairport.com), located about 45km (28 miles) east of downtown Shànghǎi. Transportation on the highway to hotels in Pǔdōng and downtown Shànghǎi runs between 50 minutes and 1½ hours depending on traffic. The high-tech airport, designed by French architect Paul Andreu, has two terminals, which have departure halls (international and domestic) on the upper level and arrivals on the lower level, and are connected by three indoor 500m-long (1,640-ft.) corridors and free shuttle buses on the third floor (outside doors 1 and 8 in Terminal 1, and doors 23 and 27 in Terminal 2) running at 10-minute intervals between 6am and midnight. At press time, most of the international airlines were using Terminal 2, as well as Shànghǎi Airlines, Air China, and China Southern for domestic flights. *Note:* To be sure, check with your airline which terminal you will be arriving at and departing from.

Arrival procedures are straightforward at both terminals. Depending on the severity of health issues like SARS, H1N1, or avian flu, visitors may be required to fill out a **health declaration form,** and/or be subjected to a **health check** (involving the reading of your temperature) as you approach immigration. **Immigration forms** are usually distributed in-flight but are also available just before you reach the immigration counters. Depending on your time of arrival, it should take 15 to 30 minutes to clear immigration. Have your passport and completed form(s) ready. Baggage claim is followed by Customs. Foreigners are no longer required to fill in Customs declaration forms and are seldom stopped.

There are ATMs just after immigration, and several other ATMs outside Customs in both terminals. Also here are hotel counters, bank counters for **money exchange,** and a Tourist Information Center (TIC) counter.

In 2010, Shànghǎi also built a brand-new **Terminal 2** at its older airport, **Hóngqiáo International Airport (Hóngqiáo Jīchǎng)** (✆ 021/96990; www.shanghaiairport.com), approximately 19km (12 miles) west of the city center at Shēndá Yī Lù 1 in Mínháng District. Terminal 2 caters largely to flights within China including the Shànghǎi–Běijīng shuttles. At press time, the older Terminal 1 was reserved for the low-cost airline Spring Airlines, and a few Asiana, Korean Air, ANA, and JAL flights connecting to Gimpo Airport in Seoul, and Haneda Airport in Tokyo. Shuttle buses (outside Gate 6 on the Departure Level in Terminal 1, and Gate 1 on the Arrival Level of Terminal 2) connect the two terminals at 15-minute intervals between 6am and 11pm. Arrival procedures at Terminal 2 are fairly routine, and it usually takes about 15 to 20 minutes to retrieve your luggage. There are ATMs and some hotel counters here as well.

## Getting into Town from the Airport

**TAXIS**   The legitimate taxis are lined up in a long queue just outside the arrival halls of both airports (outside Level 1 of Hóngqiáo Airport's Terminal 2). *Never* go with taxi touts who approach you in the arrival halls with "Take taxi?" which is about the extent of their English. At Pǔdōng International Airport, taxis using the highways and the Nánpǔ and Lúpǔ bridges charge ¥170 and up for the 1-hour (or longer) trip to hotels in downtown Shànghǎi, and only slightly less for the nearer hotels in Pǔdōng. From Hóngqiáo Airport, taxis should charge from ¥40 to ¥80, depending on traffic and the location of your hotel, and take from 20 to 40 minutes to transport you. Taxis between the two airports will cost around ¥240 and take 1 to 1½ hours.

Most Shànghǎi taxi drivers are honest, but be sure the meter is on; if not, say, *"Dǎ biǎo!"* If that doesn't work, select another taxi. All legitimate taxi meters are equipped to print out a receipt, which you can ask for by saying, *"Fā piào."* It's a good idea to always get a receipt, which will have the phone number of the taxi company and numerical identification of the driver, should you ever need to recover any lost items. Flag-fall for taxis is ¥12 for the first 3km (2 miles), then ¥2.40 for every subsequent kilometer (⅔ mile). For more tips on taking a taxi, see "Taxi Tips" (p. 42).

**HOTEL SHUTTLES**  A number of Shànghǎi's hotels maintain service counters situated along the walls in the arrival halls in both airports, though these primarily serve only visitors who have made transportation arrangements with the hotel prior to arrival.

**AIRPORT BUSES**  The most economical transfer from Pǔdōng International Airport is via the official **Airport Bus** (✆ **021/6834-6612**). There are 10 Airport Bus Lines connecting the airport and other transportation stops. Airport Bus Line no. 1 goes from Pǔdōng to Hóngqiáo Airport (every 15 min. 7am–11pm; ¥30); Airport Bus Line no. 2 (Jīchǎng Èrxiàn) goes from Pǔdōng (every 15–20 min. 7:20am–11pm; ¥22) to the City Air-Terminal Building (Chéngshì Hángzhàn Lóu) at Nánjīng Xī Lù 1600 (just west of the Shànghǎi Center), with return buses departing for the airport every 15 to 20 minutes from 6am to 9pm; Airport Bus Line no. 5 goes from Pǔdōng to the Shànghǎi Railway Station (Shànghǎi Huǒchē Zhàn); and Airport Bus Line no. 7 connects to the Shànghǎi South Railway Station (Shànghǎi Nán Zhàn). Prices range from ¥16 to ¥30. There are also direct buses to Suzhou and Hangzhou.

From Hóngqiáo Airport, several buses make the run into town. A shuttle, **Mínháng Zhuānxiàn (Airport Special Line),** departs for the Chéngshì Hángzhàn Lóu (City Air-Terminal Building) at Nánjīng Xī Lù 1600 every 20 minutes from 6am to 8pm. Tickets cost ¥4. Airport Bus Line no. 1 (Jīchǎng Yīxiàn) connects Hóngqiáo (buses depart every 20 min. 6am–9pm; ¥30) with Pǔdōng Airport (every 20 min. from 7:20am to last flight).

**SUBWAY**  Metro Line 2 now connects downtown Shànghǎi to Pǔdōng Airport, though the journey will still take a good 45 to 50 minutes. For those with no luggage or light luggage who desire a slightly faster journey, there is Shànghǎi's highly touted magnetic levitation (Maglev) train. However, unless you're staying in the eastern reaches of Pǔdōng, even the Maglev is not that much faster or more convenient than a taxi or airport bus in getting you to your destination. Covering some 30km (19 miles) in 8 minutes, this ultra-high-speed train (¥50 regular ticket, ¥80 same-day round-trip) connects Pǔdōng International Airport to the Lóngyáng Lù metro stop, where you transfer to the subway (Lines 2 and 7). Depending on your hotel's location, you may have to change subways again, and possibly even hail a taxi before you arrive at your hotel's door, all of which makes it inconvenient for travelers with heavy luggage. Maglev trains run every 20 minutes between 6:45am and 9:30pm daily. For information, call ✆ **021/6255-6987.**

In 2010, Metro Line 2 was extended all the way from the new Terminal 2 at Hóngqiáo Airport through downtown Shànghǎi to Pǔdōng Airport. However, you're better off taking the airport shuttle bus than traveling by subway between the two airports (upwards of 90 min.).

# MASS levitation

Shànghǎi's much-hyped mass transit showpiece, the magnetic levitation (**Maglev**) train, started running in late 2003, with trains connecting the 30km (19 miles) between Pǔdōng International Airport and Pǔdōng's Lóngyáng Lù Station in no more than 8 minutes. "While the wheel-track link—which is run on mechanical technology—works like a propeller-driven aircraft, the Maglev line—motored by electrical technology—is like a jet," crowed Xú Kuāngdí, the former Shànghǎi mayor who got the project off the ground during his tenure. Traveling at up to 430kmph (267mph), Maglev (a Sino-German joint venture) has cost Shànghǎi upwards of ¥8.9 billion, making this the most expensive subway spur in the world. Unfortunately, Maglev in its current form is not very practical for travelers with heavy luggage (see above), so the government has largely taken to promoting this more as a tourist attraction, Shànghǎi's latest must-ride (¥50 one-way; ¥80 same-day round-trip). Indeed, on any given day, you'll usually see more sightseeing tourists and students than airport-bound travelers. In 2008, the Chinese government's plans of building a Shànghǎi-Hangzhou Maglev line for the 2010 World Expo that would also connect Pǔdōng International and Hóngqiáo airports met with resistance as Shànghǎi residents came out in force to protest the effects of potential magnetic radiation and noise pollution in their neighborhoods. At press time, the project had been shelved indefinitely.

To get into town from Terminal 2 of Hóngqiáo Airport, take either Metro Line 2 or Metro Line 10 (also stops at Terminal 1).

## BY CAR

Since foreign visitors are not allowed to drive their own vehicles into or within China unless prearranged with a state-recognized travel agency on a specific itinerary (and accompanied by guide and driver), few visitors generally arrive this way.

## BY TRAIN

From Hung Hom Station in Kowloon (Hong Kong), train T100 arrives at the **Shàng-hǎi Railway Station (Shànghǎi Huǒchē Zhàn)** (② 021/6354-3193 or 021/6317-9090) on alternate days at 10am (departing from Hong Kong the day before at 3pm; see www.it3.mtr.com.hk for schedules and fares). Many trains from China's major cities especially to the north and west also arrive here. You must produce your train ticket to attendants at the station exits in order to leave the terminal. The station is located in the northern part of town in Zhábĕi District. You can take the subway (lines 1, 3, 4) into town, or hail a taxi on the lower level of the terminal. There are no currency exchange facilities or ATMs here. Scheduled to open in 2011 is the **Hóngq-iáo Railway Station (Hóngqiáo Huǒchē Zhàn)** west of Hóngqiáo Airport, which will service nearby cities in Jiāngsū Province like Sūzhōu, Wúxī, and Nánjīng. If you arrive here, you can take a taxi or Metro Lines 2 or 7 into town. Many trains from Hángzhōu and some cities in southern China like Xiàmén and Kūnmíng arrive at the **Shànghǎi South Railway Station (Shànghǎi Nán Zhàn)** (② 021/6317-9090) in the southern part of town. The station is accessible via Metro Lines 1 and 3.

## BY BOAT

International arrivals from Kobe and Osaka in Japan are at the **Shànghǎi Port International Cruise Terminal (Guójì Kèyùn Zhōngxīn)** at Dōngdàmíng Lù 500 (*©* **021/6181-8000**), not far north of the Bund. Domestic ships arriving from Dàlián, the Yángzǐ River, and Pǔtuó Shān now arrive at the **Wúsōng Passenger Terminal (Shànghǎi Gǎng Wúsōng Kèyùn Zhōngxīn)** (Sōngbǎo Lù 251; *©* **021/5657-5500**), at the intersection of the Huángpǔ and Yángzǐ rivers. If you arrive here as an independent traveler, you will have to hail a taxi at the passenger terminal to reach your hotel, which is likely another 30 to 45 minutes away.

# Departing Shànghǎi
## BY PLANE

Shànghǎi has air connections with all of China's main cities and many international destinations as well. Almost all international departures and some domestic flights as well leave from Pǔdōng International Airport. *Note:* If you're leaving on a domestic flight, be sure to confirm in advance which airport serves your flight. Arrive at the airport at least 2 hours before departure for international flights, and 1 hour before departure for domestic flights (more if there's any kind of health alert in force, as you'll be required to fill in a health form and have your temperature taken). Note that check-in for international flights officially closes 30 minutes before departure, so budget plenty of time. Visitors no longer need to pay a separate departure tax as this is now included in the cost of the plane ticket. Remember to fill out a departure card, then proceed to emigration with passport, boarding card, and departure card. At Pǔdōng Airport, there are exchange counters just inside the departure hall to convert your remaining *yuán* to your home currency, but you will have to show proof of the initial exchange (either the exchange receipt from the bank or hotel desk, or the ATM withdrawal receipt), and there is now a ¥50 service fee.

For those flying to Běijīng, there are frequent **Shànghǎi-Běijīng shuttle flights** that depart practically hourly from Hóngqiáo Airport (Terminal 2). Fares can start from as low as ¥800 one-way.

Airport-bound passengers not wanting to splurge on a taxi can take the airport bus from the Shànghǎi Airport City Terminal (Shànghǎi Jīchǎng Chéngshì Hángzhàn) at Nánjīng Xī Lù 1600. Buses (¥22) leave for Pǔdōng Airport every 15 minutes between 6am and 7:30pm. Buy your ticket on the bus. Buses for Hóngqiáo Airport (¥4) leave every 20 to 30 minutes between 6am and 8pm.

**Tickets** for domestic flights (and international flights) on Chinese airlines can be purchased at the airport or through travel agencies such as **CITS** (Běijīng Xī Lù 1277, Guólǚ Dàshà; *©* **021/6289-4510** or 021/6289-8899, ext. 263), or the **Shànghǎi Spring International Travel Service,** Dīngxī Lù 1558 (*©* **021/6251-5777**), though there will be a service charge. There are a plethora of other travel agencies all over town offering discounted airline tickets, but you'll usually need to speak some Chinese to get the best deals from them. Whatever you do, shop around. You can also go directly to the airlines and specifically ask for the lowest discounted (*dǎzhé piào*) ticket (they may not automatically give you the lowest rate, so you have to ask). Besides having ticket booths at both airports, Shànghǎi Airlines has an office in town at Jiāngníng Lù 212 (*©* **021/6255-8888;** www.shanghai-air.com), and China Eastern has offices in town at Yán'ān Xī Lù 200 (*©* **021/6247-5953** or

021/6247-2255). Many Chinese also use the website **Ctrip** (www.ctrip.com) to book their e-tickets, which you can do with a credit card or PayPal account. Another popular online Chinese booking service that takes credit cards (surcharge applies) or cash (you pay when the ticket is delivered) is **eLong** (www.elong.net).

## BY TRAIN

Shànghǎi is well connected by train to many major Chinese destinations, including Běijīng (10 hr.), Guǎngzhōu (16 hr.), Hong Kong (18 hr., Train K100), and the nearby towns of Hángzhōu (2 hr.) and Sūzhōu (35 min.). For the Shànghǎi–Tibet train (52 hr. on the Qīnghǎi–Tibet railway), foreigners have to purchase an expensive Tibet tour package in order to travel this way. The website **www.travelchinaguide. com** has Shànghǎi train schedules in English that can be very helpful in planning your trips. At press time, work had commenced on a high-speed rail line between Běijīng and Shànghǎi that would more than halve the travel time to under 5 hours, though details were sketchy about when construction would be complete. For now, five express trains (D302, D306, D308, D314, D322) run every evening between 9:10pm and 9:35pm to Běijīng Station (Běijīng Zhàn), sometimes referred to as Běijīng South (Běijīng Nán Zhàn), arriving between 7:20am and 7:40am (10 hr., ¥730 for soft sleeper; ¥327–¥409 seats). There is also a day-train to Běijīng (D32) with seats only, which leaves Shànghǎi at 10:30am and arrives in Běijīng at 8:50pm. Round-trip Běijīng–Shànghǎi tickets for Z or D trains (return trip within 3–20 days) can be purchased up to 20 days in advance, though the rail authorities can change the purchasing window at any time.

At Shànghǎi's main railway station, **Shànghǎi Huǒchē Zhàn** (inquiries ✆ 021/6317-9090; tickets ✆ 021/9510-5105), which is located north of the Sūzhōu Creek in Zhábèi District and is accessible by taxi or the subway's Metro Lines 1, 3, and 4, there is now a bank of self-service ticket kiosks (in Chinese and English) in the main building, selling tickets for all trains throughout China. In general, train tickets can be purchased 3 to 10 days in advance (up to 20 days in advance for Z or D trains) at the railway station or at any number of satellite ticket offices around town, including one just off the Nánjīng Lù Pedestrian Mall at Guìzhōu Lù 124, and another one at Jīnlíng Dōng Lù 2. Tickets can also be bought through CITS, any travel agency, or through your hotel ticket desk, though fees will of course accrue, ranging from ¥5 at CITS if you purchase it yourself to ¥50 from some hotel ticket desks.

Starting in 2011, high-speed trains bound for cities in Jiāngsū Province like Nánjīng, Wúxī, and Sūzhōu (as well as other destinations yet to be determined at press time) will depart from the **Hóngqiáo Railway Station (Hóngqiáo Huǒchē Zhàn)** in the western part of the city past Hóngqiáo Airport, and accessible via Metro Lines 2 and 10.

Although a few Hángzhōu-bound trains still depart from the Shànghǎi railway station, the majority now leave from the Shànghǎi South Railway Station (Shànghǎi Nán Zhàn) ((✆ 021/6317-9090) in the southern part of town. This station is reachable by Metro Lines 1 or 3.

*Warning:* Larger bags will be X-rayed when you enter the railway station departure hall, so keep any film in your hand luggage.

## BY BOAT

The **Shànghǎi International Ferry Co. Ltd.** (✆ 021/6537-5111; www.shanghai ferry.co.jp) has a weekly sailing to Osaka on Tuesday at 11am, while the **Japan-China International Ferry Co. (Chinajif)** (✆ 021/6325-7642; www.fune.co.jp) operates ships bound for Osaka and Kobe. Ships depart from the **Shànghǎi Port International Cruise Terminal (Guójì Kèyùn Zhōngxīn)** at Dōngdàmíng Lù 500 (✆ 021/6181-8000 or 021/6595-2299), not far north of the Bund. Tickets are available at Dōngdàmíng Lù 908, 15th floor, D-G (✆ 021/6537-5111), or at travel agencies.

Domestic boats bound for Pǔtuó Shān (12 hr.) now depart from the **Wúsōng Passenger Terminal (Shànghǎi Gǎng Wúsōng Kèyùn Zhōngxīn)** (Sōngbǎo Lù 251; ✆ 021/5657-5500), about a 30- to 45-minute taxi ride northeast of the Bund at the mouth of the Yángzǐ River. Tickets can be bought at the terminal or at travel agencies such as CITS.

# Getting Around

Given the size of Shànghǎi and the overcrowded condition of its public buses, taxis and the subway become indispensable for any sightseer. Fortunately, both are relatively inexpensive. Unfortunately, the number of vehicles on the street has multiplied at a much faster rate than roads are being built, so you are likely to be caught in a few traffic jams. Allow for extra time to get to your destination. An adventurous alternative is to travel as many Shànghǎi residents do: by bicycle.

## BY SUBWAY

In the months leading up to the Shànghǎi Expo, the city's subway (*dìtiě*) system (www.shmetro.com), an inexpensive and fast way to cover longer distances, began a massive expansion. At press time, there are 12 lines in various stages of operation, with another 10 lines projected for completion by 2020. Despite the expanded number of lines, the original Metro Lines 1 and 2 are still quite overburdened, especially during morning and evening rush hours and on weekend afternoons. With the recent expansion of the subway system, stops and lines can also get a little confusing. A useful online interactive subway aid can be found at **www.exploreshanghai.com/metro**.

Operating from 5:30am to midnight daily, the subway currently has 12 lines, but for tourists, Lines 1, 2, 4, 7, 9, and 10 are the most useful. **Metro Line 1,** the red line, winds in a roughly north-south direction connecting the Shànghǎi Railway Station in the north, through the French Concession and on down Héngshān Lù to the Shànghǎi South Railway Station and points southwest. In the future, the northern terminus of Metro Line 1 will be Chóngmíng Island. Metro Line 1 connects with **Metro Line 2,** the green line, at People's Square (Rénmín Guǎngchǎng) near Nánjīng Xī Lù. This is the busiest subway station in the city as Metro Line 8 also connects here. Metro Line 2 runs in an east-west direction from Hóngqiáo Railway Station and Hóngqiáo Airport in western Shànghǎi across downtown, under the Huángpǔ River, and through Pǔdōng's most developed areas all the way to Pǔdōng Airport.

**Metro Line 3,** actually more of an aboveground light rail, encircles the western outskirts of the city and also links Shànghǎi's main railway station with the South Station, though it is seldom useful for sightseeing except for its stop near Lǔ Xùn Gōngyuán (Hóngkǒu Stadium Station) and Duōlún Lù cultural street (Bǎoxìn Lù

# taxi TIPS

- Never go with taxi touts or individual drivers who approach you at airports, railway stations, tourist sights, or even outside your hotel. The general rule is never go with a driver who asks you your destination before you even get into the cab.

- In general, always hail a passing cab if possible, as opposed to waiting for taxis that have been waiting for you. Opinions differ on the following point, but if you're staying at an upmarket hotel in Shànghǎi, it is generally safe to go with the taxis called by the doormen, usually from a line of waiting cabs. It sometimes occurs that drivers give kickbacks to the doormen for being allowed to the head of the queue, but in my experience, I have not had, nor have I heard of, problems with hotel-hailed taxis. Some top hotels will give you a piece of paper with the taxi's registration number on it in case of complaints, though there's no guarantee of redress, of course. Some hotels restrict their waiting taxis to those from the Dà Zhòng Taxi Company, which has the best reputation in Shànghǎi for honest and efficient service.

- Always have your destination marked on a map or written down in Chinese, as well as a business card from your hotel with the address in Chinese so you can show it to the taxi driver when you want to get back.

- Check to see that the supervision card, which includes the driver's photo and identification number, is prominently displayed, as required by law. If not, find another cab.

- If the driver's identification number is over 200,000, there's a good chance that the driver is newly arrived in town and may not be familiar with the streets, which is reason enough to find yourself another cab. Caveat emptor: This is not a foolproof way of weeding out inexperienced drivers since a number of new arrivals actually "share" the taxis of more experienced drivers, even if this is against the law.

- Make sure the meter is visible, and that you see the driver reset

Station) north of downtown. **Metro Line 4,** the purple line, forms a ring around the city and connects Pǔdōng to the Shànghǎi Railway Station. **Metro Lines 5** and **6** run in the far southwest reaches of the city and in the eastern part of Pǔdōng respectively, and are not useful for most tourists. **Metro Line 7** connects northwest Shànghǎi with the western French Concession before hitting the Expo stops and Lóngyáng Station in Pǔdōng. **Metro Line 8** runs up Xīzàng Lù all the way from the main Expo stop in Pǔdōng through downtown into Hóngkǒu, while **Metro Line 9** can take visitors all the way from Pǔdōng out to Qībǎo (p. 263) and Shéshān (p. 174) in Sōngjiāng District via stops in the southern part of the French Concession. **Metro Line 10** provides a convenient connection between Hóngqiáo Railway Station and Hóngqiáo Airport in the west and the heart of the French Concession before heading northeast to Hóngkǒu. **Metro Line 11** serves the northwestern suburbs of Shànghǎi. At press time, the post-Expo plans for **Metro Line 13,** which

**PLANNING YOUR TRIP TO SHÀNGHǍI** | Getting There & Around

**3**

it by pushing down the flag, which should happen *after* the taxi has moved off. You should also hear at that time a voice recording in Chinese and English welcoming you to take the taxi. If the driver fails to reset the meter, say, *"Qīng dǎbiǎo,"* and if that fails, find yourself another cab.

o If traveling by yourself, sit up front and take out your map so you can follow (or at least pretend to follow) the taxi's route.

o On the rare occasion that the taxi driver refuses to honor your request after you're en route, make a big show of taking down the driver's identification number and suggesting, by any means available, that you intend to file a complaint. This can sometimes scare the otherwise recalcitrant driver into complying.

o If you're unwittingly riding with a driver who doesn't know the way (and you only realize this after you've been driving in circles or if the driver has had to stop to ask directions), it's best to find yourself another cab.

Unfortunately, even if you have every "right" to not pay the fare, this can sometimes lead to more inconvenience than it's worth (the driver will likely complain loudly or create a scene). At such times, it may be more practical to pay the fare or a portion of it, but, as in the previous example, make a show of taking down the driver's identification number and notifying him/her of your decision to lodge a complaint.

o At the end of the trip, pay the indicated meter fare and no more. Tips are not expected. It's a good idea to carry smaller bills (¥100 notes can sometimes be changed, but don't count on it) to pay your fare.

o Be sure to get a receipt *(fā piào)* with the phone number of the taxi company and the taxi driver's numerical identification, should you need to file a complaint or retrieve lost items. All the legitimate taxis are now equipped with meters that can print receipts.

operates only inside the Expo Park, had not been verified. See the map on the inside back cover for all stops. ***Note:*** There are plans to rename some of these subway lines, though hopefully not during the life of this edition.

Navigating the subway is relatively easy. Subway platform signs in Chinese and English indicate the station name and the name of the next station in each direction, and maps of the complete Metro system are posted in each station and inside the subway cars as well. English announcements of upcoming stops are made on trains. Fares range from ¥3 for the first few stops to ¥10 for the most distant ones. Tickets can be purchased from the ticket vending machines (in both English and Chinese). ***Note:*** Hang onto your electronic ticket, which you have to insert into the exit barrier when you leave.

If you are going to be riding the subway a fair amount, consider purchasing a rechargeable **Shànghǎi Public Transportation Card (Jiāotōng Kǎ),** which costs

¥20, onto which you can add more money, and which can be refunded (but only at certain stations like **Jiāngsū Lǔ**). Instead of inserting your ticket into the slot, simply hold your card over the sensor on the barriers. The card, which can be purchased at Metro stations and convenience stores throughout the city, can also be used to pay for bus, ferry, and taxi rides, with your fare being automatically deducted from the amount remaining on the card.

## BY TAXI

With more than 45,000 taxis in the streets, this is the most common means for visitors to get around Shànghǎi, though as in any urban metropolis, available taxis can be almost impossible to find during rush hour or when it rains. Taxis congregate at leading hotels, but can just as easily—and indeed, should preferably be—hailed from street corners. The large majority of vehicles are fairly clean, air-conditioned, and reasonably comfortable Passat or Santana sedans (both built in the local Shànghǎi factory by Volkswagen). In recent years, overall service has improved noticeably (at least at the top companies), and some cars have recorded messages in English greeting you and reminding you to take all items when you leave.

By and large, most Shànghǎi taxi drivers are honest. If there's a commonly heard complaint, it's less about the dishonesty of taxi drivers than about their inexperience (some drivers may have arrived in town around the same time as you), and their lack of familiarity with local streets. I've sometimes had drivers ask me how to get to my destination, though that is unlikely to happen to you. Instead, you'll just be driven around in circles, the driver unwilling to admit to a foreigner that he or she doesn't know the way. To minimize the chances of this happening to you, stick with the top taxi companies, though it must be said that even then, such an experience may sometimes be simply unavoidable. In general, follow the advice in the box "Taxi Tips," below.

Your best bets for service and comfort are the turquoise blue taxis of **Dà Zhòng Taxi** (✆ **800/6200-1688** or 021/6258-1688), the yellow taxis of **Qiáng Shēng Taxi** (✆ **021/6258-0000**), and the blue taxis of **Jǐn Jiāng Taxi** (✆ **021/6275-8800**). The fare is ¥12 for the first 3km (2 miles) and ¥2.40 for each additional kilometer. After 11pm, flag-fall rises to ¥15 for the first 3km (2 miles). Expect to pay about ¥15 to ¥25 for most excursions in the city and up to ¥60 for longer cross-town jaunts. Carry smaller bills (no larger than ¥50) to pay the fare. If you anticipate a fair amount of taxi travel and don't want to be burdened with cash, you can purchase a taxi/subway card (*Jiāotōng Kǎ*) at ticket counters in subway stations. Cards come in denominations of ¥50 or ¥100, and are easily rechargeable. The fare is automatically deducted from the balance on your card. You can also use this card on the subway. Finally, for taxi service complaints, call ✆ **021/6323-2150;** you may not get your money back, but you might be helping future riders.

## BY CAR

Tourists are forbidden to rent self-drive cars (or motorcycles or scooters) in China because a Chinese driver's license is required (available only to foreigners with an official residency permit). Of course, major hotels are only too happy to rent chauffeured sedans to their foreign guests by the hour, day, or week, at rates that will make you never complain about car rental prices back home again. With a multitude of other transportation options available to tour the city, we do not recommend this method unless time is an issue and cost is not.

## BY BUS

**Public buses** (*gōng gòng qì chē*) charge ¥2, but they are considerably more difficult to use, less comfortable than taxis or the Metro, and for the truly intrepid only. Some buses have conductors, but others only have money slots in the front of the bus with no change given. To figure out which bus number will get you to your destination, ask for help in your hotel. Bus nos. 20 and 37, for example, run between People's Square and the Bund; bus no. 16 connects the Jade Buddha Temple to Old Town; bus no. 65 travels from the Bund to the Shànghǎi Railway Station. Be prepared to stand and be cramped during your expedition, and take care with backpacks and purses, as these are inviting targets for thieves, who frequently seek out foreign visitors on public buses.

## BY BICYCLE

If you've always dreamed of joining in the dance that is millions of Chinese riding their bicycles, Shànghǎi is not the ideal place to fulfill that dream. The huge economic wealth generated in the last decade has resulted, predictably, in an exponential increase in the number of cars on the road and the concomitant decline in popularity of the bicycle (since 1990, sales have dropped from one million to 500,000 bikes per year). Wide avenues and small streets these days are much more likely to be taken up by honking vehicles spewing exhaust, making bicycle-riding appear even more hazardous and intimidating. That said, the bicycle is still the main form of transportation for millions of Shànghǎi's residents. Unfortunately for the visitor, most hotels don't rent bikes (you may get some daft looks if you inquire), and even the Captain Hostel, which used to rent bikes, has since stopped. Those with their hearts set on seeing Shànghǎi on two wheels can rent a basic city bike starting at ¥80 for a day at **China Cycle Tours** (Huáihǎi Zhōng Lù 358, no. 52; ℂ **0/1376-111-5050;** www.chinacycletours.com; daily 9am–6pm) near the Huangpi Road (S) Metro station in the French Concession. Another option is **Bodhi Bikes** (Zhōngshān Běi Lù 2918, Building 2, third floor, Ste. 2308; ℂ **021/5266-9013;** daily 8:30am–5:30pm), near the Cáoyáng Lù Metro station in the northwest part of town. The shop rents bikes at ¥150 a day with a deposit of your passport or ¥2,000. Alternatively, if you plan on doing a significant amount of cycling, consider buying a bicycle (average cost is around ¥400) for a very basic bike without flashy accessories. One of the better places to purchase bicycles is a supermall like Carrefour (see chapter 9).

Whether you rent or buy, be sure the brakes and tires are in good working order. You'll also need a bicycle lock. Helmets are not required in Shànghǎi—few use them—but they are advised for the neophyte China bike rider. In general, stick to a few general principles, namely: Ride at a leisurely pace, stay with the flow, and use the designated bike lanes on the big streets. Should you have a flat or need a repair, there are sidewalk bicycle mechanics every few blocks, and they charge low rates. Always park your bike in marked lots (identifiable by the forest of bikes outside a park, attraction, or major store) watched over by an attendant, and lock your bike or it will be gone by the time you get back. Parking usually costs around ¥.50.

## BY BRIDGE, BOAT & TUNNEL

To shift the thousands of daily visitors between east and west Shànghǎi across the Huángpǔ River, there is now a multitude of routes. Three are by bridge, each handling around 45,000 vehicles a day: the 3.7km-long (2⅓-mile), harp-string-shaped **Nánpǔ Dàqiáo** (built in 1991), and the **Lúpǔ Dàqiáo**, both in the southern part of town; and the 7.7km-long (4¾-mile) **Yángpǔ Dàqiáo** (built in 1993) northeast of the Bund. A fourth route (and the cheapest) is by water, via the **passenger ferry** (*lúndū*) that ordinary workers favor. The ferry terminal is at the southern end of the Bund around Jīnlíng Lù on the west shore (ticket price: ¥2), and at the southern end of Riverside Avenue at Dōngchāng Lù on the east shore. Other routes across the river make use of tunnels, with motor vehicles using the Yán'ān Dōng Lù Tunnel, the Fùxīng Lù Tunnel, the Rénmín Lù tunnel, the Dàlián Lù tunnel, the Xīnjiàn Lù tunnel, and the Dǎpǔ Lù Tunnel, with at least two additional tunnels under construction; Metro Line 2 is filled with German-made subway cars, while Metro Line 4 and Metro Line 8 also make the crossing; and there is also the **Bund Sightseeing Tunnel (Wàitān Guānguāng Suìdào)** equipped with glassy tram cars that glide through a subterranean 3-minute light show with music and narrative (daily 8am–10:30pm [11pm Fri–Sun, 10:30pm May–Oct]; ¥55 round-trip; ¥45 one-way).

## BY FOOT

The best way to see Shànghǎi's sights and experience life at street-level is on foot. Much like downtown New York or Tokyo, Shànghǎi's streets can be almost impossibly crowded at times, but they are always fascinating to stroll. Doing so requires a bit of vigilance, of course, as Shànghǎi pedestrians are distinctly second-class citizens to the motorists who rule the road. Shànghǎi drivers, who drive on the right side of the road, have never been known to give pedestrians the right-of-way; at red lights, vehicles seldom stop when making a right turn, whether pedestrians are in the crosswalk or not. Drivers don't pay much attention to lane markings and will always rush to fill an empty space wherever they can find one, even if it's where you happen to be walking. Besides a sea of humanity, Shànghǎi pedestrians also have to contend with bicycles, scooters, and motorcycles on sidewalks. Happily, there are now surly brown-clad, whistle-blowing traffic assistants at the major roads and intersections to make sure both pedestrians and motorists obey the traffic lights. Jaywalkers who are caught may be fined up to ¥50. In general, whether crossing large avenues or small lanes, look every which way before you cross, take your cues from locals, and you should be just fine.

## City Layout

Shànghǎi, with one of the largest urban populations on Earth (more than 19 million permanent residents), is divided by the Huángpǔ River into Pǔdōng (east of the river) and Pǔxī (west of the river). For the traveler, the majority of Shànghǎi's sights are still concentrated **downtown** in Pǔxī, whose layout bears a distinct Western imprint. After the First Opium War in 1842 opened Shànghǎi to foreign powers, the British, French, Germans, Americans, and others moved in, carving for themselves their own "concessions" where they were subject not to the laws of the Chinese government but to those established by their own governing councils.

Today, the city is divided into districts (*qū*), according to which listings in this book are organized. Today's districts hew fairly close to, but do not follow exactly, the original concession borders. For the traveler, the two most important geographical markers are the **Bund (Wàitān)** and **People's Square (Rénmín Guǎngchǎng)** about a mile to the west. Since the days of the International Settlement, established in 1863 with the melding of the British Concession and the American Concession, the **Bund,** with its signature colonial-era banks and trading houses, has been and still is the symbolic center of the city; from here, **downtown Shànghǎi** opens to the west like a fan. Today's practical and logistical center, however, is **People's Square (Rénmín Guǎngchǎng),** about a mile to the west of the Bund. This is the meeting point of three important subway lines (1, 2, and 8), as well as the location of some major attractions, including the Shànghǎi Museum, Shànghǎi Art Museum, and Shànghǎi Grand Theatre. The Bund and People's Square are linked by several streets, none more famous than **Nánjīng Lù,** historically China's number-one shopping street.

Southwest of the Bund is historic **Nánshì,** Shànghǎi's old Chinese city, which was the first part of Shànghǎi to be settled (and one of the last to be developed, though building is certainly proceeding apace these days). Nánshì used to have a city wall, which followed today's Rénmín Lù and Zhōnghuá Lù circle. As its name suggests, the old Chinese city has retained the greatest number of typically Chinese sights, such as the quintessential Southern-Chinese Garden, Yù Yuán, the famous Húxīntíng Teahouse, several temples, and even part of the old city wall.

A mile or so west of the Bund and the old Chinese city, Shànghǎi's former **French Concession,** established in 1849 and straddling both today's Lúwān and northern Xúhuì districts, is still one of Shànghǎi's trendiest neighborhoods. Chock-full of colonial architecture and attractions, it is home to some of the city's priciest real estate and to its most glamorous shops and restaurants, as seen in the megadevelopment Xīntiāndì.

Farther west still, beyond the Inner Ring Road that wraps around downtown Shànghǎi and the French Concession, is the **Hóngqiáo Development Zone,** where modern commercial and industrial development was concentrated beginning in the 1980s.

While sightseeing is concentrated in downtown Shànghǎi and the French Concession, **north Shànghǎi** has a scattering of interesting sights, including the Jade Buddha Temple, the Lǔ Xùn Museum, and the Ohel Moshe Synagogue; and **south Shànghǎi** has the Lónghuá Pagoda, Xújiāhuì Cathedral, and the Shànghǎi Botanical Garden.

In contrast to the colonial and historical sights of Pǔxī, the district of **Pǔdōng,** lying east of the Huángpǔ River, is all about Shànghǎi's future. Mere farmland before 1990 when then-President Dèng Xiǎopíng designated it as the engine of China's new economic growth, Pǔdōng has sprouted in just a decade to become the city's financial center, and a high-tech and free-trade zone, home to Asia's largest shopping centers, longest bridges, tallest buildings, and the 2010 World Expo site. Modern skyscrapers like the Oriental Pearl TV Tower, the Jīn Mào Building, and the Shànghǎi World Financial Center, which houses the world's highest hotel, the Park Hyatt, and a new slew of swanky international hotels, restaurants, and shopping malls, are attempts to attract the visitor over to the eastern shore of the Huángpǔ. With considerably less choice in the matter, many Shànghǎi residents were also displaced here in the last decade by the destruction of old neighborhoods in Pǔxī. For more information on Shànghǎi's neighborhoods, see "Neighborhoods in Brief" on p. 70.

**MAIN STREETS** In downtown Shànghǎi, the general rule is that east-west streets are named for Chinese cities, while north-south streets are named for provinces and regions. The main east-west street through downtown Shànghǎi is **Nánjīng Lù,** historically China's top shopping street. The portion running west

# Shànghǎi Orientation

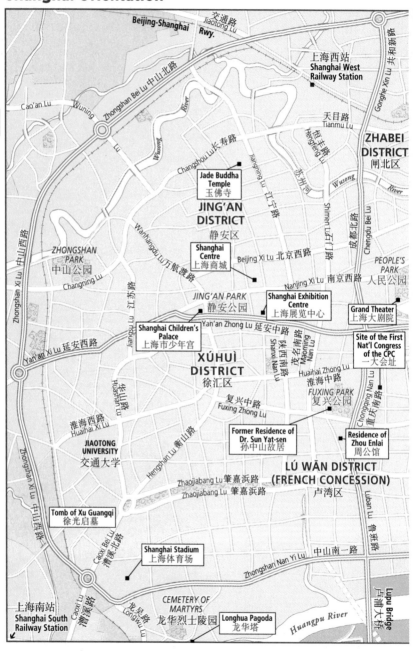

Beijing-Shanghai Rwy.

交通路
Jiaotong Lu

上海西站
Shanghai West
Railway Station

Gonghe Xin Lu 共和新路

Cao'an Lu

Wuning Lu

Zhongshan Bei Lu 中山北路

天目路
Tianmu Lu

桓丰路
Hengfeng Lu

ZHABEI
DISTRICT
闸北区

Changshou Lu 长寿路

River

Jiangning Lu 江宁路

苏州河

Wusong River

Shimen 山门路

成都北路 Chengdu Bei Lu

Jade Buddha
Temple
玉佛寺

JING'AN
DISTRICT
静安区

ZHONGSHAN
PARK
中山公园

Wanhangdu Lu 万航渡路

Shanghai
Centre
上海商城

Beijing Xi Lu 北京西路

PEOPLE'S
PARK
人民公园

Changning Lu

Zhongshan Xi Lu 中山西路

Jiangsu Lu 江苏路

JING'AN PARK
静安公园

Nanjing Xi Lu 南京西路

Shanghai Exhibition
Centre
上海展览中心

Grand Theater
上海大剧院

Shanghai Children's
Palace
上海市少年宫

Yan'an Zhong Lu 延安中路

茂名南路 Maoming Nan Lu

陕西南路 Shanxi Nan Lu

Site of the First
Nat'l Congress
of the CPC
一大会址

Yan'an Xi Lu 延安西路

XÚHUÌ
DISTRICT
徐汇区

Huashan Lu 华山路

Huaihai Zhong Lu
淮海中路

Chongqing Nan Lu 重庆南路

Fuxing Zhong Lu
复兴中路

FUXING PARK
复兴公园

JIAOTONG
UNIVERSITY
交通大学

Huaihai Xi Lu
淮海西路

Former Residence of
Dr. Sun Yat-sen
孙中山故居

Residence of
Zhou Enlai
周公馆

LÚ WĀN DISTRICT
(FRENCH CONCESSION)
卢湾区

Hengshan Lu 衡山路

Zhaojiabang Lu 肇嘉浜路

Zhaojiabang Lu 肇嘉浜路

Luban Lu 鲁班路

Tomb of Xu Guangqi
徐光启墓

Caoxi Bei Lu 漕溪北路

中山南一路 Zhongshan Nan Yi Lu

Zhongshan Xi Lu 中山西路

Shanghai Stadium
上海体育场

Zhongshan Nan Lu 中山南路

Lupu Bridge
卢浦大桥

上海南站
Shanghai South
Railway Station

Caoxi Lu 漕溪路

龙吴路 Longwu Lu

CEMETERY OF
MARTYRS
龙华烈士陵园

Longhua Pagoda
龙华塔

Huangpu River

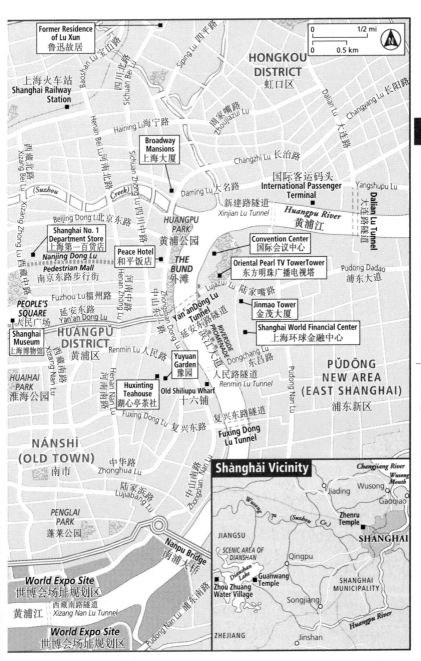

Former Residence
of Lu Xun
鲁迅故居

HONGKOU
DISTRICT
虹口区

上海火车站
Shanghai Railway
Station

Baoshan Lu 宝山路

Sichuan Bei Lu 四川北路

Siping Lu 四平路

Dalian Lu 大连路

Changyang Lu 长阳路

Haining Lu 海宁路

Broadway
Mansions
上海大厦

Changzhi Lu 长治路

Zhoujiazui Lu 周家嘴路

Henan Bei Lu 河南北路

Xizang Bei Lu 西藏北路

(Suzhou

Creek)

Sichuan Zhong Lu 四川中路

Daming Lu 大名路

国际客运码头
International Passenger
Terminal

Yangshupu Lu

Dalian Lu Tunnel
大连路隧道

新建路隧道
Xinjian Lu Tunnel

Huangpu River
黄浦江

HUANGPU
PARK
黄浦公园

Beijing Dong Lu 北京东路

Shanghai No. 1
Department Store
上海第一百货店

Convention Center
国际会议中心

Peace Hotel
和平饭店

Oriental Pearl TV TowerTower
东方明珠广播电视塔

Pudong Dadao
浦东大道

Nanjing Dong Lu
Pedestrian Mall
南京东路步行街

THE
BUND
外滩

Fuzhou Lu 福州路

河南中路
Henan Zhong Lu

Lujiazui Lu 陆家嘴路

Zhongshan Dong Lu 中山东路

Xizang Zhong Lu 西藏中路

PEOPLE'S
SQUARE
人民广场

延安东路
Yan'an Dong Lu

Yan'anDong Lu
Tunnel
延安东路隧道

Jinmao Tower
金茂大厦

Shanghai World Financial Center
上海环球金融中心

Shanghai Museum
上海博物馆

HUANGPU
DISTRICT
黄浦区

Renmin Lu 人民路

RIVERSIDE
PROMENADE
滨江大道

Dongchang Lu 东昌路

PŬDŌNG
NEW AREA
(EAST SHANGHAI)
浦东新区

HUAIHAI
PARK
淮海公园

Xizang Nan Lu 西藏南路

Yuyuan
Garden
豫园

人民路隧道
Renmin Lu Tunnel

Pudong Nan Lu 浦东南路

Henan Nan Lu 河南南路

Huaxinting
Teahouse
湖心亭茶社

Old Shiliupu Wharf
十六铺

NÁNSHÌ
(OLD TOWN)
南市

Fuxing Dong Lu 复兴东路

夏兴东路隧道

Fuxing Dong
Lu Tunnel

Zhonghua Lu
中华路

Lujiabang Lu
陆家浜路

Fuxing Dong
Lu Tunnel

PENGLAI
PARK
蓬莱公园

Zhongshan Nan Lu 中山南路

Nanpu
Bridge
南浦大桥

World Expo Site
世博会场址规划区

黄浦江

西藏南路隧道
Xizang Nan Lu Tunnel

Pudong Nan Lu 浦东南路

World Expo Site
世博会场址规划区

### Shànghǎi Vicinity

Changjiang River
长江

Wusong
Mouth

Jiading

Wusong

Gaoqiao

Zhenru
Temple

JIANGSU

(Suzhou Cr.)

SHANGHAI

SCENIC AREA OF
DIANSHAN

Dianshan Lake

Qingpu

SHANGHAI
MUNICIPALITY

Guanwang
Temple

Zhou Zhuang
Water Village

Songjiang

ZHEJIANG

Jinshan

Huangpu River

from the Bund, through the pedestrian mall, to People's Park (Rénmín Gōngyuǎn), is known officially as **Nánjīng Dōng Lù;** it continues west as **Nánjīng Xī Lù.** Parallel to Nánjīng Lù in the south is **Yán'ān Lù** (originally a creek dividing the International Settlement from the French Concession to the south), which runs west through the downtown corridor all the way to the Hóngqiáo Airport (changing its name in the western segment to Hóngqiáo Lù). Running above Yán'ān Lù is the elevated expressway **Yán'ān Gāojià,** the quickest way to traverse downtown Shàng-hǎi; near the Bund, this leads to the underground tunnel **Yán'ān Dōng Lù Suìdào** that resurfaces on the east side of the river in Pǔdōng. It used to take an hour to drive from the Hóngqiáo District through downtown to Pǔdōng, but the Yán'ān Expressway has cut the travel time to 20 minutes without traffic. To the south, the Fùxīng Lù Tunnel also runs from Pǔxī to the foot of the Nánpǔ Bridge in Pǔdōng.

The major north-south thoroughfares include the **Bund,** on the west shore of the Huángpǔ River (the avenue along the Bund is known as **Zhōngshān Dōng Yī Lù** which becomes **Zhōngshān Nán Lù** as it moves into the South Bund); and **Xīzàng Lù,** which divides Nánjīng Lù into its east and west sectors, and Yán'ān Lù and Huáihǎi Lù into their east and middle *(zhōng)* sectors. Xīzàng Lù also borders People's Square (Rénmín Guǎngchǎng), the site of the Shànghǎi Museum, the Grand Theatre, and the central subway station for both Metro lines.

In the French Concession, the two big avenues are **Huáihǎi Zhōng Lù** (Shàng-hǎi's second-most-famous shopping street) and **Fùxīng Zhōng Lù,** both extensions of the east-west streets that begin downtown at the southern Bund (Zhōngshān Dōng Èr Lù). Crossing them are a number of smaller scenic streets, the liveliest of which are **Ruìjīn Lù** and **Màomíng Lù** near the historic Jǐn Jiāng Hotel. At the western end of the French Concession, the graceful and trendy avenue of **Héngshān Lù** runs south toward the Xújiāhuì shopping area.

Downtown Shànghǎi, the French Concession, large portions of north and south Shànghǎi, as well as the Pǔdōng New Area, are surrounded by the **Inner Ring Road (Nèihuán Gāojià),** an elevated expressway that bears the road name **Zhōngshān** along most of its route. This Inner Ring Road is bisected by the **North-South Elevated Road (Nánběi Gāojià),** which runs above **Chéngdū Běi Lù,** the first major street west of People's Square, a rough dividing line between downtown

## Making Sense of Shànghǎi Street Names

Shànghǎi's main streets, as well as some smaller streets that intersect them, are often mouthfuls to pronounce and difficult to remember at first, but after a few trips through the city, they begin to sort themselves out. One reason that the street names in *pīnyīn* (see appendix) seem so long is that they incorporate the characters for north or south, street or avenue, all running together in the street name.

Zhōngshān East First Road is written in *pīnyīn* as Zhōngshān Dōng Yī Lù. Common items in street names and their English translations are as follows:

| | | | |
|---|---|---|---|
| *Běi* = North | | *Jiē* = Street | |
| *Yī* = First | | *Nán* = South | |
| *Dà Dào* = Avenue | | *Èr* = Second | |
| *Dōng* = East | | *Lù* = Road | |
| *Sān* = Third | | *Xī* = West | |
| *Nòng* = Lane | | *Zhōng* = Central | |

## THE STREETS OF OLD Shànghǎi

Up until the establishment of the People's Republic of China in 1949, many of Shànghǎi's streets bore foreign names, bequeathed to the city by colonial overlords. Here's a partial list of old and new:

**Current street name . . . once known as**

| Current street name | once known as |
| --- | --- |
| Fùxīng Zhōng Lù | Route Lafayette |
| Hénán Lù | Homan Road |
| Héngshān Lù | Avenue Petain |
| Huáihǎi Zhōng Lù | Avenue Joffre |
| Màomíng Běi Lù | Moulmien Road |
| Màomíng Nán Lù | Route Cardinal Mercier |
| Nánjīng Xī Lù | Bubbling Well Road |
| Nánjīng Dōng Lù | Nanking Road |
| Rénmín Lù | Boulevard des Deux Republiques |
| Ruìjīn Èr Lù | Route Pere Robert |
| Ruìjīn Yī Lù | Route des Soeurs |
| Sīnán Lù | Rue Masenet |
| Tiānshān Lù | Lincoln Avenue |
| Xīzàng Nán Lù | Boulevard de Montiguy |
| Yán'ān Dōng Lù | Avenue Edward VII |
| Yán'ān Xī Lù | Great Western Road |
| Yán'ān Zhōng Lù | Avenue Foch West |
| Zhōngshān Dōng Yī Lù | The Bund |

Shànghǎi and the French Concession. A second, even larger ring road is under construction; it will join the airports of east and west Shànghǎi.

## Finding an Address

Nearly all of Shànghǎi's big streets have signs on poles near intersections that give the names in Chinese characters and in *pīnyīn,* which is the alphabetical rendering of those characters (used on maps and throughout this book). Though street numbers are given, few locals pay any attention to them, as navigation is usually by street name, landmarks, and nearby intersections. The only exception is in the case of Shànghǎi's many smaller lanes (*lòngtáng, lòng* for short) branching off the main streets and the smaller intersecting streets. An address sometimes given as Héngshān Lù 9, no. 3, means it's House no. 3 (*sānhào*) situated in Lane no. 9 (*jiǔ nòng*) off Héngshān Lù; Lane no. 9 could well be found between House no. 7 and Lane no. 11; taxi drivers and locals are quite familiar with this system should you need to locate such an address.

The maps in this book cannot fully capture the details of any given area, so it's highly recommended that you buy a map (see "Visitor Information," p. 286) or get one from your hotel concierge. Between the Chinese characters provided in this book's map keys and a second (preferably trilingual) map with English, *pīnyīn,* and characters, you should have no problems comparing the characters with the road signs as you make your way. It's always helpful to have your hotel staff mark your hotel and destination on your map before you set off so that you can show it to taxi drivers or passersby should you get lost. There is, however, no question of truly getting lost even if you wander off the main paths indicated on the maps. Given Shànghǎi's Western influence, it's not difficult these days to find even a marginal English speaker to help you, even if it's just to locate an address on the map and point you in the right direction. Though their daily attitudes may not reflect it, Shànghǎi residents can be quite friendly and helpful to beleaguered foreigners.

# MONEY & COSTS

**THE VALUE OF CHINESE RÉNMÍNBÌ VS. OTHER POPULAR CURRENCIES**

| Yuán (¥) | US$ | Can$ | UK£ | Euro (€) | Aus$ | NZ$ |
|---|---|---|---|---|---|---|
| 1 | 15¢ | 15¢ | 10p | .10€ | 15¢ | NZ20¢ |

Frommer's lists exact prices in the local currency. The currency conversions quoted above were correct at press time. However, rates fluctuate, so before departing, consult a currency exchange website such as **www.oanda.com/convert/classic** to check up-to-the-minute rates.

## Currency

Though it's usually a good idea to change at least some money before you leave home, this scenario doesn't apply as readily to mainland China, as the Chinese *rénmínbì* (RMB), or *yuán* (¥), is not a commonly held currency. Where it's carried, it will most likely be exchanged at a highly unfavorable rate. This shouldn't present too much of a problem for most travelers arriving in Shànghǎi by plane, as airports all have money exchange facilities and ATMs. Those travelers arriving by train from Hong Kong would do well to change a small amount of money in Hong Kong where the *yuán* is readily obtainable.

Currency exchange in China is legal only if conducted at hotels, banks, and stores, at the official rate set by the central government through the Bank of China. This rate is the same at all nationwide outlets, saving travelers the hassle and stress of having to find the best rate. Besides the airport, you can change money at hotel bank desks and at larger branches of the Bank of China. Hotel desks have the convenience of being open long hours 7 days a week, but their services are usually restricted to guests. You'll have to provide your passport for any kind of currency exchange.

Keep all receipts when you change money; you will need them should you wish to reconvert any excess *yuán* into your home currency.

Reject any attempts by private individuals or shops to change money at rates different from the official rate: Not only is this illegal, you may well end up with fake bills. Avoid especially the black-market money-changers who congregate outside branches of the Bank of China that are popular with tourists, such as the one on the Bund.

**YUÁN NOTES & EXCHANGE RATES** Chinese currency is known as both *rénmínbì* (RMB, literally "the people's money") and as *yuán* (¥). However, you'll mostly hear money referred to as *kuài qián,* literally "pieces of money," or *kuài* for short. Bills come in denominations of ¥100, ¥50, ¥20, ¥10, ¥5, ¥2, and ¥1, which also appears as a coin. The next unit down is the *jiǎo* (¥.10), commonly referred to as *máo.* There are notes and coins for ¥.50, ¥.20, and ¥.10. Beyond that is the *fēn* (¥.01), but you'll hardly ever see or have use for it. China being primarily still a cash society, keep a good stock of smaller bills, especially ¥10 notes, for street stalls, convenience stores, and taxis, all of whom will balk if you offer a ¥100 bill first thing in the morning.

After years of being pegged solely to the U.S. dollar, China allowed an appreciation of the *yuán* in 2005, ostensibly pegging it to a basket of currencies (known as a "crawling peg"). However, critics note that since then, the *yuán* has been appreciating steadily against the dollar without much reference to the other currencies (which were never specified), and since the financial crisis of 2008, has once again been all but frozen against the dollar. In mid-2010, the Chinese government again signaled that it would allow the *yuán* to be tracked to a trade-weighted "basket" of currencies, but since none of the details are made explicit, it is difficult to get a clear picture of what is actually happening with the valuation of the *yuán*.

## ATMs

There are many ATMs in China, but only a handful that will accept your foreign-issued card. In Běijīng and Shànghǎi, the situation is improving as more banks have ATMs that are able to accept foreign cards. Check the back of your ATM card to see which network your bank belongs to: **Cirrus** (www.mastercard.com), **PLUS** (www.visa.com), or **AEON** (www.americanexpress.com). Before you leave home, you can contact the proper institutions to locate ATMs currently available in Shànghǎi or ask your bank for a list of ATMs in China and Shànghǎi. Be sure you know your personal identification number (PIN) and daily withdrawal limit before you depart. In general, the ATMs at the major branches of the Bank of China, Hong Kong and Shanghai Bank, Industrial and Commercial Bank of China (ICBC), and China Construction Bank will accept your card, as will a Citibank ATM at the Pǔdōng International Airport (in the arrival hall right after immigration). The above-mentioned bank ATMs usually allow a maximum withdrawal of ¥2,500 per transaction, but it is possible to make another withdrawal the same day. **Note:** Remember that many banks impose a fee every time you use a card at another bank's ATM, and that fee can be higher for international transactions (up to $5 or more) than for domestic ones (where they're rarely more than $3). In addition, the bank from which you withdraw cash may charge its own fee. For international withdrawal fees, ask your bank.

## Credit Cards

Credit cards are another safe way to carry money. They also provide a convenient record of all your expenses, and they generally offer relatively good exchange rates. In China, however, despite the plethora of Visa and MasterCard signs throughout, your international credit card (*guójì xìnyòng kǎ*) is usually accepted only at the top international hotels, and at restaurants and shops catering to foreigners. You can also obtain cash advances (in *yuán*) against your American Express, Visa, MasterCard, and Diners Club card at major branches of the Bank of China (bring your passport). This is an expensive way of getting cash, as there is a minimum withdrawal of ¥1,200 and you'll have to pay a 4% commission plus whatever your card issuer charges you, so use it only as a last resort.

In general, beware of hidden credit-card fees while traveling. Check with your credit or debit card issuer to see what fees, if any, will be charged for overseas transactions. Recent reform legislation in the U.S., for example, has curbed some exploitative lending practices. But many banks have responded by increasing fees in other areas, including fees for customers who use credit and debit cards while out of the country—even if those charges were made in U.S. dollars. Fees can amount to 3% or more of the purchase price. Check with your bank before departing to avoid any surprise charges on your statement.

If you plan to use your credit cards in China, notify your issuer(s) beforehand, as many companies, to prevent fraud, often put a hold on cards that suddenly start registering foreign charges. Loss of credit cards should be reported immediately (see "Lost & Found" in "Fast Facts," p. 284).

| WHAT THINGS COST IN SHÀNGHĂI | YUÁN ¥ |
| --- | --- |
| Taxi from Pǔdōng airport to city center | 190.00 |
| Double room, moderate | 600.00 |
| Double room, inexpensive | 300.00 |
| Airport bus (Pǔdōng) to city center | 22.00 |
| Taxi ride up to 5km (3 miles) | 17.00 |
| Subway ride | 3.00 |
| Local telephone call | 0.50 |
| Dinner for two in top hotel/international restaurants | 1,000.00 |
| Dinner for two in popular local restaurants | 200.00 |
| Steamer of dumplings at a basic local restaurant | 12.00 |
| Bottle of beer at a trendy Shànghǎi bar or hotel | 60.00 |
| Bottle of beer at an ordinary restaurant or store | 24.00 |
| Bottle of beer at the 24-hour neighborhood store | 12.00 |
| Admission to Yù Yuán | 40.00 |
| Theater ticket to Shànghǎi Acrobatics | 200.00 |

## Traveler's Checks

With the proliferation of Shànghǎi ATMs accepting international cards, traveler's checks are becoming a less popular but still acceptable way to bring money into China. However, they are only accepted at major branches of the Bank of China, at foreign exchange desks in hotels, and occasionally at major department stores and shops targeted to foreign tourists. Bigger bank branches will accept checks in any hard currency from any major company, but smaller branches will only accept the currencies of larger economies. The exchange rate for traveler's checks is fractionally better than for cash, though the commission charged on checks (.75%) usually offsets any gains. Most Chinese banks will change U.S. dollars cash into *yuán*, so it's a good idea to have some U.S. dollar notes on hand in case of emergencies. If you carry traveler's checks, be sure to keep a separate record of their serial numbers so you're ensured a refund in case of loss.

You can buy traveler's checks at most banks. They are offered in denominations of $20, $50, $100, $500, and sometimes $1,000. Generally, you'll pay a service charge ranging from 1% to 4%.

The most popular traveler's checks are offered by **American Express** (© **800/807-6233** or 800/221-7282 for card holders—this number accepts collect calls, offers service in several foreign languages, and exempts Amex gold and platinum cardholders from the 1% fee); **Visa** (✆ **800/732-1322**); and **MasterCard** (✆ **800/223-9920**).

# STAYING HEALTHY
## Before You Go

No **vaccinations** are required for entry to China and Shànghǎi, but be sure your inoculations are up-to-date. The standard inoculations are for **polio, diphtheria,** and **tetanus,** while additional inoculations may be against **meningococcal meningitis, cholera, typhoid fever, hepatitis A and B,** and **Japanese B encephalitis.** Some of these vaccinations, such as the one for hepatitis B, may require several shots over a span of several months, so allow enough time before your trip. Mosquito-borne **malaria,** while a cause for concern in more rural parts of China, is not a factor in Shànghǎi. Consult your doctor or a specialist travel clinic about your individual needs.

For the latest information on infectious diseases and health-related travel risks (including the latest update on the ever-changing situation with malaria), contact the **International Association for Medical Assistance to Travelers (IAMAT)** (✆ **716/754-4883** or, in Canada, 416/652-0137; www.iamat.org) for tips on travel and health concerns in China, and for lists of local, English-speaking doctors. The United States **Centers for Disease Control and Prevention** (✆ **800/311-3435;** www.cdc.gov) provides up-to-date information on health hazards by region or country and offers tips on food safety. The website **www.tripprep.com,** sponsored by a consortium of travel medicine practitioners, may also offer helpful advice on traveling abroad. You can find listings of reliable overseas clinics at the **International Society of Travel Medicine** (www.istm.org).

Standard over-the-counter remedies are easily available at drugstores and supermarkets, though you may want to bring your own if you use any regular medications. It's best to stock up on all your prescriptions before you leave, but prescriptions can also usually be filled (at least with a generic equivalent, if not the actual drug) at select Shànghǎi pharmacies if you're in a pinch. (See "Drugstores" in "Fast Facts," p. 282.) Carry the generic name of prescription medicines, in case a local pharmacist is unfamiliar with the brand name. Don't forget an extra pair of contact lenses or prescription glasses, though there are plenty of optometrists in Shànghǎi who can replace your glasses or lenses. Feminine hygiene products such as sanitary napkins are widely available, but tampons are usually sold only in international supermarkets and pharmacies like Watson's.

## Regional Health Concerns

Hygiene standards in Shànghǎi are some of the highest in China, but despite this, the standards of many places are still not up to those in developed nations. Do take precautions here that you may otherwise overlook at home, more so if you plan to travel outside of China's big cities. Still, travelers shouldn't be unduly worried.

**DIETARY RED FLAGS**   The greatest risk to your enjoyment of traveling in China is probably that of stomach upsets caused by low hygienic standards. To minimize this risk, wash your hands frequently, and keep them away from your mouth and eyes; eat freshly cooked hot food, especially if away from the top international hotels; eat only fruit that you peel yourself; and only drink boiled or bottled water bought in supermarkets, larger shops, and convenience stores. *Never drink tap water.* Use bottled water to brush your teeth.

**RESPIRATORY ILLNESSES**  Another common ailment is respiratory illnesses of various kinds, from the common cold (which can be picked up during the long flight over, the overcrowded subways, or the change in temperature and humidity) to upper-respiratory tract infection, often mistaken for a cold, all of which are exacerbated by Shànghǎi's heavy pollution. Standard over-the-counter cold remedies are easily available at drugstores and supermarkets, though you may want to bring your own if you use any regular medications. More serious infections can be treated at any of the clinics that cater to foreigners.

**INFLUENZA**  The SARS crisis hit China in 2003, avian influenza (or "bird flu") struck a chicken farm on the outskirts of Shànghǎi in 2004, and the H1N1 Flu also hit Shànghǎi in 2009, but all three have been brought under control and you should have little to be concerned about. At press time, none of the above was a major concern in Shànghǎi, but check the latest news before you leave (see "Before You Go," above).

**SUN EXPOSURE**  Other ailments to guard against, especially in the summer months, include excessive sun exposure, heatstroke, and dehydration. Shànghǎi's pollution makes most days appear overcast, but the sun still has the power to burn. Shànghǎi's high humidity during the summer can also cause those just coming from drier climes to fatigue quickly. Drink plenty of bottled water.

**SEXUALLY TRANSMITTED DISEASES**  Led by AIDS, sexually transmitted diseases are also on the rise in China. The government denied the existence of AIDS for as long as it could, and while there are now a few public campaigns addressing the issue, there is still a lot of ignorance and silence surrounding AIDS and other sexually transmitted diseases. Condoms, including Western brands, are widely available in Shànghǎi.

## If You Get Sick

If you begin to feel unwell, contact your hotel reception first. The top hotels have in-house doctors or doctors on call who may be able to treat minor ailments and direct you to the best places should further treatment be required.

Shànghǎi has several clinics with the latest equipment and English-speaking, foreign-trained doctors who deliver international-caliber health care. Expect to pay rates comparable to those in the West. In general, avoid Chinese hospitals.

See "Doctors & Dentists" in "Fast Facts" on p. 281 for a list of the top clinics in Shànghǎi that cater to foreigners. Foreign consulates can provide a list of area doctors who speak English. In many cases, you'll be expected to pay the full medical costs upfront. Keep all proof of payment so you can submit your health insurance claim when you return home.

# CRIME & SAFETY

China is one of Asia's safest destinations, and Shànghǎi is one of the safest cities in the world for foreign travelers. Most likely the biggest potential threat you'll encounter will be the **pickpockets** who tend to congregate in crowded places like railway, bus, and subway stations; airports; popular tourist sights; and crowded markets. As always, the standard precautions apply: Leave as many of your valuables as you can in hotel safes; any other valuables should be distributed around your person, and not kept inside your purse or backpack, which can be easily picked. Wear a money belt *inside* your clothes. Always leave one photocopy of your passport and traveler's check receipts at your hotel. Violent crimes and cases of sexual harassment against foreign visitors are quite rare but do occur, so use common sense. Travel with others when possible, rebuff strangers in the streets, and avoid unlighted streets after dark. Beggars can sometimes be seen on Shànghǎi streets.

Visitors should also beware of **scam artists** who will use the pretext of practicing their English to try and befriend you, with the goal of separating you from your money. As far as many Chinese are concerned, there's no such thing as a poor foreigner. These scams can range from "art students" taking you to special shops and pressuring you to buy paintings that are neither authentic, unique, nor worth what's claimed, to the friendly face who'll offer to buy you a meal or a drink at a local haunt, where you'll find yourself with 12 opened bottles of warm beer you didn't order and, if you refuse to pay, several thuggish bouncers standing between you and the door.

**Solicitations** are also commonplace, whether in a bar, karaoke joint, or even your hotel room, where many a China visitor has been telephoned in the wee hours, with a voice on the other end inquiring "Massagee?" (The caller always hangs up when a woman answers.) Not only is there a higher-than-expected incidence of sexually transmitted diseases in China, but there have been reports of men, foolish enough in the first place to accept such invitations, being forced to pay huge sums for services not actually rendered.

If you find yourself a victim of theft, file a police report at the local PSB (Public Security Bureau) known as *gōng ān jú.* Don't expect any redress, necessarily, but at least you'll have the report for insurance claims back home.

In general, there's very little harassment of **solo female travelers,** in and of itself a rare sight among Chinese.

For all travelers, however, if you are planning a night of bar- or club-hopping, do travel in groups and watch your drinks, as stories have surfaced around press time of the appearance of drugs, particular those with sedative properties like Rohypnol (officially known as Flunitrazepam), being slipped into drinks.

Another major hazard that tourists will have to contend with is **traffic.** Even if foreign visitors were allowed to drive (which you are not without a Chinese driver's license), you stand little chance against Chinese motorists who treat lane markings and traffic lights like so much fluffy roadside decoration. Seat-belt rules and speed limits are consistently ignored. There really is only one rule on Chinese roads: Might is right, which kicks pedestrians down to the bottom of the traffic food chain. Still, if you look every which way before you cross, generally go with the flow, and take your cue from locals, there's little cause for concern. Paying greater attention in the streets will also prevent you from falling down open manholes or being hit by debris from Shànghǎi's many construction projects.

## Dealing with Discrimination

In general, there is little overt discrimination in China against non-Chinese, except perhaps for persistent overcharging. But then again, many Chinese have the attitude that *all* foreigners (including ethnic Chinese from Hong Kong, Táiwān, and

Southeast Asia) are moneybags, and will simply overcharge anyone and everyone they can. Ethnic Chinese, on the other hand, can use the "We're all Chinese after all" appeal for better prices, which the *lǎowài* (the somewhat condescending "old foreigner" term applied to non-Chinese) cannot do. Dark-skinned visitors may also have a slightly more difficult time of it than whites, especially outside of the big cities, but beyond the expected gawking and overcharging, those who don't speak Mandarin probably will not notice any difference.

On the other hand, once some sort of communication has been established, non-Chinese tend to receive better treatment from locals than the Chinese dole out to each other. Unfortunately, this situation sometimes even extends to Shànghǎi's top hotels.

# SPECIALIZED TRAVEL RESOURCES

In addition to the destination-specific resources listed below, please visit Frommers. com for other specialized travel resources.

## Travelers with Disabilities

Most disabilities shouldn't stop anyone from traveling. There are more options and resources out there than ever before. China has more citizens with disabilities than any nation on Earth. Despite the fact that some efforts have been made to address their needs (spearheaded for several decades by the son of former Supreme Leader Dèng Xiǎopíng, who is in a wheelchair as a result of persecution during the Cultural Revolution), Chinese with disabilities are still largely hidden from public view, while specialized facilities for them range from sporadic to nonexistent. The situation is fractionally better in Shànghǎi: Sections of some major sidewalks are now equipped with "raised dots" to assist the blind; modern buildings and some major tourist sites have elevators; and a handful of top hotels have wheelchair-accessible rooms, but the bottom line is that Shànghǎi is a city of long stairways (even at most subway stations) and crowded, crumbling sidewalks. Even so, most disabilities haven't stopped travelers from making their way through the Shànghǎi obstacle course and enjoying its many sights.

To minimize the difficulties of navigating a place like China, it's best that you travel with a specialist group (such tours to China are rare, but are slowly starting to catch on). One outlet offering such customized tours to China is **Flying Wheels Travel** (www.flyingwheelstravel.com), which organizes escorted private tours in minivans with lifts. **Access-Able Travel Source** (www.access-able.com) offers extensive access information and advice for traveling around the world with disabilities.

## LGBT Travelers

Shànghǎi is quite tolerant of gay and lesbian travelers, though there are no specialized resources catering to them. This is not all that unusual, given how puritanical Chinese society tends to be in sexual matters, gay or straight. (Walking hand in hand with a same-sex partner won't raise any eyebrows because it is deemed a sign of friendship.) Shànghǎi does have a homosexual community that is becoming increasingly visible, but it is still not officially sanctioned. Because foreigners are perceived as "different" from Chinese in the first place, gay and lesbian travelers should experience no discrimination here. In recent years, a few nightspots have even become identified with a gay, lesbian, and transsexual clientele (see chapter 10). The popular **International Gay & Lesbian Travel Association (IGLTA)** (© 800/448-8550 or 954/776-2626; www.iglta.org) has a few listings for gay-friendly organizations serving inbound visitors to China. **Hermes Tours** (© 877/486-4335; http://hermestours.com) offers small group tours to China.

## Senior Travel

The Chinese generally respect age far more than do their Western counterparts. Increasingly there are more "senior discounts" (for those over 70) offered at tourist attractions. If you book a hotel from an international hotel chain overseas, inquire about but don't expect senior discounts. In Shànghǎi, brace yourself for long stairways at some museums and temples, and impatient crowds everywhere you turn.

**Elderhostel** (© 877/426-8056; www.elderhostel.org) arranges study/travel programs for those age 55 and over (and a spouse or companion of any age) in the U.S. and in more than 80 countries around the world, including China. **ElderTreks** (© 800/741-7956; www.eldertreks.com) also offers expensive small-group tours to China.

## Family Travel

If you have enough trouble getting your kids out of the house in the morning, dragging them thousands of miles away may seem like an insurmountable challenge, especially to a place as seemingly foreign as China. But the difficulties of family travel to China lie less in the "foreignness" of the environment than in the lack of services and entertainment geared towards children.

Hygiene, or rather the lack thereof, presents the other main challenge. Much of China is quite dirty, so young children who have the tendency of putting their hands in their mouths should be closely monitored, while older children should be reminded to wash their hands frequently and to follow the general health tips outlined in the "Staying Healthy" section earlier in this chapter. Challenges notwithstanding, family travel to China can be immensely rewarding, and you shouldn't let the absence of children-friendly resources deter you from venturing here en masse.

The Chinese tend to dote on their children, and you may find your children given the same amount of attention, which usually takes the form of a lot of friendly touching, chatter, and photo sessions with the young ones.

Many hotels in Shànghǎi allow young children (usually under 12) to stay free with their parents, and some hotels provide babysitting service for a fee (though the caretakers are usually just culled from in-house staff).

Unlike most other cities in China, Shànghǎi has plenty of sights to dazzle and distract your children. For Western kids, there are many familiar fast-food and foreign-style eateries, several amusement and theme parks, a natural history museum, a children's palace, the zoo, indoor playgrounds and toy stores in shopping centers, and plenty of parks for rowing, kite-flying, and in-line skating. As a rule, there are special discounts for children at museums and attractions, though discounts are given based on height, not age.

To locate accommodations, restaurants, and attractions that are particularly kid-friendly, refer to the "Kids" icon throughout this guide, and to the "Especially for Kids" section in chapter 7.

Recommended family travel websites include **Family Travel Forum** (www.familytravelforum.com); **Family Travel Network** (www.familytravelnetwork.com); **Traveling Internationally with Your Kids** (www.travelwithyourkids.com); and **Family Travel Files** (www.thefamilytravelfiles.com).

## Women Travelers

Women travelers to China generally have no more difficult a time of it than their male counterparts. You should, however, be prepared for the inevitable questions, whenever casual communication has been established (and especially if you're traveling solo), of whether you are married and have children.

In general, there is very little discrimination against women travelers. If anything, women (who "hold up half the sky" as Máo Zédōng proclaimed) are expected to pull their own weight. Don't expect any help in lugging that heavy bag up and down trains, or for doors to be opened for you.

In response to the greater numbers of women business travelers, several top hotels in Shànghǎi like the St. Regis have started to offer secure "women only" floors, complete with added perks like fine toiletries, women's magazines, and spa services.

Check out the award-winning website **Journeywoman** (www.journeywoman.com), a "real life" women's travel-information network where you can sign up for a free e-mail newsletter and get advice on everything from etiquette and dress to safety.

## Student Travel

Student travelers should not expect special rates or other discounts in Shànghǎi. A few attractions offer discounts to students, but you'll have to produce a Chinese student identity card for that.

### The Ethnic Chinese Foreigner

Ethnic Chinese who are born and raised outside China, but who do not speak any Chinese (and that includes any number of second-generation-on-down Chinese-Americans, Chinese-Britons, Chinese-Australians, and more) usually find themselves in an awkward position when visiting China. Simply by virtue of the fact they look Chinese, they are expected to speak the language, and those who don't are often viewed with a mix of subtle derision and exasperation. At the same time, they are not given the same benefit of the doubt as non-Chinese foreigners (see "Dealing with Discrimination," above). While the reasons for this unfortunate phenomenon are age-old and complex, ethnic Chinese foreigners, like any foreign visitor, can go a long way in endearing themselves to locals by learning some Chinese and displaying some knowledge of Chinese culture and history. Even if you speak with a funny accent, the effort is usually appreciated. Learn the words for "We're all Chinese!" *(Wǒmén dōushì zhōngguórén!)*, and you may well find yourself paying a little more than local but a little less than foreigner prices for that special scarf. Mainland Chinese also tend to look very favorably upon ethnic Chinese foreigners "returning" to the motherland to search for their roots, a process known in Mandarin as *xún gēn*.

## Single Travelers

Single travelers on a group tour to China are often hit with a "single supplement" to the base price. Unfortunately, there is no real way to avoid it unless you agree to room with other single travelers on the trip. If you are traveling by yourself in China, however, you may find that you can sometimes get a smaller "single" room (with one twin or double bed, often called a *dānrén jiān*) for considerably less than the standard double (*biāozhǔn jiān*).

# RESPONSIBLE TOURISM

Responsible tourism is conscientious travel. China doesn't have much by way of organized eco-tourism. Indeed the country as a whole is facing staggering environmental problems as a result of its economic growth, and one can argue that the domestic travel industry contributes to the problem.

For the visitor to Shànghǎi, the main environmental problem you'll likely encounter is pollution. As the standard of living rises for the average Shanghainese, the number of cars on Shànghǎi's streets go up, too.

The local (and central) government are acutely aware of the environmental challenges facing them, and one of the development goals for Shànghǎi is to become China's greenest city (see p. 12 in chapter 2). To that end, the 2010 World Expo, which had as its theme "Better City, Better Life," helped focus a great deal of attention on sustainable urban development. In the years leading up to the Expo, the Shànghǎi government took several measures to walk the talk, including rehabilitating the Sūzhōu River, which had been seriously polluted by 80 years of industrial use; building environmentally friendly and energy-efficient World Expo pavilions; building China's largest waste-to-energy plant; banning the use of ultra-thin plastic bags while requiring shops to charge for thicker plastic carrier bags; and encouraged recycling by introducing separate trash bins for recyclables throughout the city. Shànghǎi also has its first carbon-neutral hotel, **URBN Hotel** (p. 100), and its first carbon-neutral fitness gym, **One Wellness** (p. 100), and some of the new hotels, such as the **PuLi Hotel and Spa** (p. 98) and the **Peninsula** (p. 87), have taken it upon themselves to install energy-saving devices in their rooms.

While it remains to be seen how much of the talk coming out of the World Expo about sustainable living will translate into actual results in the future, visitors can certainly help lessen their environmental impact with basic measures such as recycling, not getting hotel linens washed daily, and walking instead of using motorized transport. Shopping at stores that employ local workers and sell locally produced goods also help to support local economies.

## General Resources for Green Travel

The following websites provide valuable, wide-ranging information on sustainable travel.

o **Responsible Travel** (www.responsibletravel.com) is a great source of sustainable travel ideas; the site is run by a spokesperson for ethical tourism in the travel industry.

o **Sustainable Travel International** (www.sustainabletravelinternational.org) promotes ethical tourism practices, and manages an extensive directory of sustainable properties and tour operators around the world.

- **Carbonfund** (www.carbonfund.org), **TerraPass** (www.terrapass.org), and **Cool Climate** (http://coolclimate.berkeley.edu) provide info on "carbon offsetting," or offsetting the greenhouse gas emitted during flights.

- **Greenhotels** (www.greenhotels.com) recommends green-rated member hotels around the world that fulfill the company's stringent environmental requirements.

- **Environmentally Friendly Hotels** (www.environmentallyfriendlyhotels.com) offers more green accommodations ratings.

- **Volunteer International** (www.volunteerinternational.org) has a list of questions to help you determine the intentions and the nature of a volunteer program. For general info on volunteer travel, visit **www.volunteerabroad.org** and **www.idealist.org**.

# SPECIAL INTEREST & ESCORTED TRIPS

The single biggest decision first-time visitors to China often have to make is whether to travel independently, booking all accommodations and onward transportation on your own as you go; travel on a structured escorted group tour with a group leader, where everything from airfare to hotels, meals, tours, admission costs, and local transportation are included; or travel on an unescorted package tour, which straddles the two by having the basic elements such as airfare, accommodations, and transfers taken care of, but leaving you the freedom to visit sights, shops, and restaurants at your will. Your decision will, of course, depend on your experience and goals. Shàng-hǎi itself can be comfortably explored on your own (especially armed with this guide!); any package tour, escorted or otherwise, is really just a waste of money, unless you are seeking a special theme or expert-guided tour. The rest of China is possible to see on your own, even if you don't speak the language, but it will require a lot of patience, energy, resourcefulness, time, goodwill, and not a little luck.

The unescorted package tour provides convenience, but while it may make economical sense for many destinations in the world because the package ends up being cheaper than buying the individual elements yourself, in China you usually end up paying more for the convenience. The reason is that any foreign tour operators from which you may purchase your package are required to use Chinese state-registered travel agencies to act as local handlers. These local agencies usually quote unconscionably high rates, which become even more exorbitant when your tour operator tacks on the middleman fee. The lack of competition—the Chinese travel agency scene has been dominated since the 1980s by CITS, and to a lesser extent, CTS and CYTS—has only served to keep prices high. In recent years, more private operators have been allowed to compete, but their comparative lack of experience and size still drive most travelers, however grudgingly, to CITS, which is at least established and has some experience with foreigners' whims. Of course, you can book directly with CITS, but there is no guarantee of redress or compensation should something go wrong.

If convenience is paramount and money no object, consider booking with one of the agencies listed in the next section, which can also book unescorted tour packages. You can also check with the China National Tourism Administration (see "Visitor Information" in "Fast Facts" on p. 286) for a list of registered Chinese agencies that can help. In each case, always comparison-shop, as package tours vary widely with regard to choice of airlines, hotels, and other hidden expenses; never go with the first company on the list. Do not under any circumstances book with private Chinese tour agencies or guides online, as many of them are not licensed.

As an alternative for those desiring a more personalized and customized experience, **concierge service providers** creating tailor-made itineraries and private guided tours—a relatively new business in China travel—have also started to appear on the scene. Run by two expatriates in Shànghǎi, **Luxury Concierge China** (Wūlǔmùqí Běi Lù 457, Ste. 403; ✆ **135/0166-2908;** fax 021/6249-2316; www. luxuryconciergechina.com) can custom-design your trip in whole or in part from the minute you land in Shànghǎi. Services provided include itinerary planning, hotel booking, transportation, and private guided tours (art, architecture, culinary, fashion design, history, and shopping).

## Escorted General Interest Tours

Escorted tours are structured group tours, with a group leader. The price usually includes everything from airfare to hotels, meals, tours, admission costs, and local transportation, but not usually domestic or international departures. Most require you to pay upfront. Many, but not all, escorted China tours include Shànghǎi (1–2 nights), but do not cover it in any kind of depth (as with any escorted tour, you'll get little opportunity for serendipitous interactions with locals and you'll likely miss out on some lesser-known gems).

As noted previously, it is possible to travel through China on your own even if you don't speak the language (even more so through an increasingly international city like Shànghǎi), but time, energy, and resourcefulness are required to arrange your own way. For those short on time and who want the security and ease that come from knowing all you have to do is show up, escorted tours have traditionally been and continue to be the preferred way to see China.

Unfortunately, however, China package tours, escorted or otherwise, are usually unbridled attempts at gross profiteering, all at your expense. Foreign tour operators are required to work with, and essentially cede control to, a handful of Chinese travel agencies on the ground (historically the cabal of CITS, CTS, or CYTS), where there is every attempt to pad every pocket (except yours) at every possible level. From the number and location of shopping stops, to the strong suggestions of tipping, to the extra "must-see" sight the guide tries to fob upon you, no attempt to fleece you will be bypassed. Of course, most visitors never realize the full extent to which they are being taken.

While this situation will likely not change without some larger structural changes in the Chinese tourism industry, there are several precautions you can take to ensure you get as much value for your money as possible should you decide to join an escorted tour.

### EVALUATING TOURS

In evaluating tour companies for China, besides the usual considerations of price, itinerary, schedule, size and demographics of the group, physical ability required, types of hotels you're likely to stay at, existence of single supplements if you're traveling alone, and payment and cancellation policies (especially as they pertain to health-related issues like SARS or H1N1), here are some other questions to ask your tour operator:

- **Shopping Stops:** This is how tour guides, drivers, tour operators, and all their kith and kin make money: by ferrying you to as many shopping outlets as possible in between the sights, and then collecting commissions on every item purchased. (Equal opportunity fleecers, they do this to *all* tourists, not just foreigners.) The better foreign tour operators try as much as possible to design their own itineraries, keeping shopping stops to a minimum, but it is difficult to avoid the stops entirely. Ask your tour operator how many of these stops are included, and if they don't know, find another company. This is as sure a sign as any that your company is not a China specialist and is only cobbling together a package without much concern for their clients. If you're stuck at one of these stops, sit them out if possible, as prices are astronomically marked up to begin with, so any discounts promised are no big deal.

- **Additional Costs:** You cannot be too clear on what *exactly* is included in the price of the tour. Watch out especially for additional **tips** that may be asked of you. For what it's worth, there is officially *no* tipping in China. Taxi drivers, your average restaurant waitstaff, and the staff at your typical Chinese hotel do not expect tips and will usually return any change. However, where escorted tours are concerned, there invariably ends up being some form of tipping of guides and drivers. In general, payment for the tour guides and drivers, including reasonable tips, should be included in the initial cost quoted by your tour operator; if your tour operator tells you that tips are not included, you will need to add the anticipated tips onto the initial cost quoted you. As a general rule, despite the nonstop pressure you'll get to tip and tip well, only tip for truly excellent or exceptional service, and then pull together a reasonable (by Chinese standards, not the West's) sum from the group. Some guides claim they would not be making a living wage were it not for tips and shopping commissions, but it's also true that many tour guides make many times more than what an ordinary factory worker makes. Any excessive or misguided tipping merely makes it more difficult on the travelers that follow you.

- **Guides:** The quality of guides in China varies widely, from genuinely knowledgeable and critically thinking guides to those who merely repeat verbatim every bit of propaganda they've had to study to become licensed, to those whose grasp of the English language makes it all sound like Chinese to you. Your chances of encountering the first are considerably greater, though hardly assured, in the big cities where competition has forced the better guides to a level of proficiency and accountability not demanded of guides in smaller towns and areas. Many guides, though, still tend to err on the side of telling foreigners what they want to hear; others don't have much experience beyond their limited purview. Ask your tour company if they will be sending an accompanying guide or tour manager from home to oversee the trip and supplement the local guides. This person, who should be knowledgeable about not only Chinese history and culture, but also the workings of Chinese tourism, is worth paying more for as they can help ensure a smoother trip. Depending on your itinerary and tour operator, you may get a Chinese tour guide who will accompany you throughout China (called a *quánpéi*) as well as local guides in the different cities, or simply local guides at every destination. As noted above, make sure *all* the guides and drivers' fees are included in the tour cost, or factor in the accurate number of guides along the way if you have to prepare for tips.

## TOUR COMPANIES

The following is but a short list of companies offering packages to China that span different interests and budgets. While they are located in North America, the U.K., and Australia, they have representatives around the world, and it's usually possible to fly in on your own and join only the land portion of the tour.

o **Abercrombie and Kent** (U.S.): Classy top-of-the-line luxury-travel company that specializes in tailor-made private tours and escorted small group travel. ℂ **800/323-7308,** fax 630/954-3324, www.abercrombiekent.com (U.S.); ℂ **08450/700610,** fax 08450/700608, www.abercrombiekent.co.uk (U.K.); ℂ **1300/851-800,** www.abercrombiekent.com.au (Australia); ℂ **0800/441-638** (New Zealand).

o **Academic Travel Abroad** (U.S.): Arranges all the tours for the Smithsonian (educational, cultural) and National Geographic Expeditions (adventure, natural history). ℂ **877/EDU-TOUR** (338-8687), fax 202/633-9250, www.smithsonianjourneys.org; ℂ **888/966-8687,** fax 202/342-0317, www.nationalgeographic.org/ngexpeditions.

o **Adventure Center** (U.S.): Touts a plethora of China trips that offer a more adventurous twist on the standard itineraries; activities can include walking, cycling, and even staying at a Hángzhōu farm. ℂ **800/227-8747** (U.S.); **888/456-3522** (Canada); www.adventurecenter.com.

o **China Focus** (U.S.): Its large mainstream tours have received good reviews from travelers on Frommer's message boards; they have been described by an enthusiastic client as "champagne tours at beer prices." Watch out for additional costs to cover extras. ℂ **800/868-8660** or 415/788-8660; fax 415/788-8665; www.chinafocustravel.com.

o **Elderhostel** (U.S.): Popular educational tours for those 55 and older. ℂ **877/426-8056;** www.elderhostel.org.

o **Gecko's Adventures** (Australia): Budget adventures aimed at 20- to 40-year-old travelers who normally journey independently. Uses local accommodations and transport, and has branches worldwide. ℂ **03/9662-2700;** fax 03/9662-2422; www.geckosadventures.com.

o **Helen Wong's Tours** (Australia): Well-regarded, experienced group offering longer stays to savor the "local" experience. ℂ **02/9267-7833;** fax 02/9267-7717; www.helenwongstours.com.

o **Intrepid Travel** (Australia): As its name suggests, adventurous trips with competent guides; good value for money. ℂ **613/9478-2626,** fax 613/9419-4426, www.intrepidtravel.com (Australia); ℂ **877/448-1616** (U.S.).

o **Laurus Travel** (Canada): A small China-only specialist that runs well-received small group tours. ℂ **604/438-7718;** fax 604/438-7715; www.laurustravel.com.

o **Pacific Delight** (U.S.): Popular outfit offering a wide range of mainstream tours, many economical. Also offers special tours for families with children. ℂ **800/221-7179;** www.pacificdelighttours.com.

o **Peregrine Adventures** (Australia): Upmarket counterpart to Gecko's Adventures; emphasizes soft adventure and new angles on standard experiences such as visiting an untouristed part of the Great Wall or checking out Shànghǎi's local food stalls. ℂ **03/9663-8611,** fax 03/9663-8618, www.peregrineadventures.com (Australia); ℂ **800/227-8747** (U.S.).

- **R. Crusoe & Son** (U.S.): Classy outfit offering custom, private, or small tours that include extras such as viewing the terra-cotta warriors in Xi'an up close at eye level. ✆ **888/585-8555;** www.rcrusoe.com.
- **Ritz Tours** (U.S.): The largest China tour operator in the U.S.; offers different China packages with maximum group size at 32; varying ages, popular with families; expect many shopping stops and pressure to tip. ✆ **800/900-2446;** www.ritztours.com.
- **SITA World Tours** (U.S.): Experienced outfit offering different grades of tours to China. Also guarantees its advertised departures so there is no fear of a tour canceling. ✆ **800/421-5643;** www.sitatours.com.

Another option is to visit Shànghǎi on a **themed escorted tour,** such as one on Chinese cooking, shopping, architecture, tai chi, traditional medicine, art, or another topic. Such tours are usually one-time offerings, however, led by experts in the field, so finding them requires research and some luck. Search magazines, newspapers, and the Internet for groups that specialize in your interest.

# STAYING CONNECTED
## Mobile Phones

China's wireless capabilities function on the quasi-universal GSM (Global System for Mobiles) network, which is used by all Europeans, most Australians, many Asians (except in Japan and Korea), and many North Americans as well. In the U.S., T-Mobile, AT&T Wireless, and Cingular use this quasi-universal system; in Canada, Microcell and some Rogers customers are GSM. If you're coming from North America and want to use your GSM phone in China, make sure it's at least a tri-band (900 MHz/1800 MHz/1900 MHz) phone that's been "unlocked" to receive service in China. Also call your wireless operator at home and ask for "international roaming" to be activated on your account. The roaming and international call charges will be predictably exorbitant, so consider buying a prepaid SIM card (known as *quánqiútōng,* about ¥100) in China, which you can install in your GSM phone. SIM cards are available at airports, railway stations, and mobile phone stores. Recharge or top-up cards (*shénzhōuxíng chōngzhí kǎ*) are available at post offices, mobile phone stores, and some news kiosks. If you don't have a GSM phone, you can purchase an older Chinese model in any of Shànghǎi's department stores or phone shops for around ¥300 or more, though depending on the model, don't expect it necessarily to work back in North America.

Alternatively, it's easy to rent a phone in Shànghǎi. There are rental shops in the arrival hall of Pǔdōng Airport; and the city's largest phone company, China Mobile (www.china-mobile-phones.com), can deliver phones to your hotel. Rental costs range from ¥68 to ¥116 a day before airtime (at least ¥7 a minute) and long-distance charges.

Some hotels in Shànghǎi have also started to make available mobile phones for guests staying in executive level rooms, while one hotel, the Peninsula (p. 87), offers free VOIP calling to anywhere in the world for all its guests.

# Internet & E-mail

Travelers in China should find it quite easy to check their e-mail and access the Internet on the road, despite periodic government attempts to block websites, control traffic, and shut down cybercafes. If you find yourself unable to access a popular website or search engine, try returning to it in a day or two; some shutdowns are temporary.

## WITHOUT YOUR OWN COMPUTER

The comparative wealth of the Shanghainese (making personal computers more popular than ever), along with occasional government crackdowns, has reduced the number of **cybercafes,** or *wăngbā* (literally, "net bar") in town. Where they still exist, most of them are smoke-filled dens full of young Chinese playing online video games. Charges range from ¥3 to ¥5 an hour. These days, you will be asked to show your passport at cybercafes before you are allowed to surf the Net. Hotel business centers with broadband Internet access are the old stand-by, but expect to pay significantly higher rates. The most reliable and the cheapest Internet access can be found at the **Shànghăi Library (Shànghăi Túshūguăn),** Huáihăi Zhōng Lù 1557 (© **021/6445-2001**), in a small office on the ground floor underneath the main entrance staircase. It's open from 9am to 8:30pm daily (¥4 per hr.), and is always packed with Chinese students. **Captain Hostel** (Chuánzhăng Qīngnián Jiŭdiàn, Fúzhōu Lù 37; © **021/6323-5053**) charges ¥5 for 15 minutes of broadband access.

## WITH YOUR OWN COMPUTER

These days, many Shànghăi hotels offer **in-room broadband Internet access.** The typical charge is around ¥120 for 24 hours, though an increasing number of hotels are starting to offer it free. If you don't have your own Ethernet cables, hotels can usually provide them, either for free or for a small fee.

**Wi-Fi** (wireless fidelity) has caught on quickly in Shànghăi, with a number of the top business hotels (Westin, Shangri-La, the Peninsula, the PuLi Hotel and Spa, just to name a few) offering wireless "hot spots" in their lobbies, executive lounges, and boardrooms, and also in their rooms. Charges range from free to ¥120 for 24 hours. There are also many cafes and bars around town offering free Wi-Fi.

Mainland China uses the standard U.S.-style RJ11 telephone jack also used as the port for laptops worldwide. Standard electrical voltage across China is 220v, 50Hz, and most laptops can deal with it.

# Newspapers & Magazines

Foreign magazines and newspapers, including *USA Today, International Herald Tribune, South China Morning Post,* and Asian editions of the *Wall Street Journal, Newsweek,* and *Time,* are sold at kiosks in international hotels. For the world according to China's Communist Party, there's the English-language *China Daily,* distributed free at many hotels. The local version, *Shanghai Daily* (www.shanghaidaily.com), a 6-day-a-week newspaper, covers the city with the same propagandistic outlook, but has an occasionally helpful arts and entertainment section appearing on Saturday. Several free, weekly and monthly English-language magazines and newspapers produced

# ONLINE TRAVELER'S toolbox

o **ATM Locators:** Visa ATM Locator (www.visa.com) provides locations of PLUS ATMs worldwide; MasterCard ATM Locator (www.mastercard.com), gives locations of Cirrus ATMs worldwide.

o **China Digital Time** (www.chinadigitaltimes.net) is a U.C. Berkeley–based website that delivers the best collection of China-related news stories from media sources around the world.

o **C-trip** (www.english.ctrip.com) is a Chinese consolidator hotel and airplane booking site that is very popular with many Chinese. English-speaking agents are available to help with bookings.

o **eLong** (www.elong.net) offers excellent prices on both domestic and international flights, which can be booked online or via telephone. Credit cards are accepted (with a 3%–5% surcharge), or pay in cash when the tickets are delivered. English-speaking agents can help with the booking process.

o **Foreign Languages for Travelers** (www.travlang.com) provides a lexicon, with pronunciation guide, of basic useful traveling terms in English, Chinese characters, and *pīnyīn*.

o **Online Chinese Tools** (www.mandarintools.com) has Chinese dictionaries for Mac and Windows users, and also provides conversions between the solar and lunar calendar.

o **The Oriental-List** is a spam- and ad-free moderated mailing list focusing only on travel in China, and is an excellent location to post questions not already covered in this guide. To subscribe, send a blank e-mail to subscribe oriental-list@datasinica.com.

o **Travelchinaguide.com** (www.travelchinaguide.com) is an online tour operator in China. While it offers both package and private tours, the information (especially on train travel and getting around locally) and community sections are the most helpful.

o **Travel Advisories** are available at http://travel.state.gov/travel/cis_pa_tw/tw/tw_1764.html, www.fco.gov.uk/travel, www.voyage.gc.ca, and www.dfat.gov.au.

o **Universal Currency Converter** (www.xe.net/currency) provides the latest exchange rates for any currency against the *yuán*.

o **Weatherbase** (www.weatherbase.com) provides month-by-month temperatures and rainfalls for individual cities in China.

o **The Weather Channel** (www.weather.com) provides current temperatures in Shànghǎi.

o **World Health Organization** (www.who.org) and the **Centers for Disease Control** (www.cdc.gov) both provide information on health concerns that may affect travelers around the world, including in China.

expressly for travelers and expatriates in Shànghǎi such as *that's Shanghai, City Weekend,* and *Shanghai Talk* can be useful for entertainment listings (not always accurate) and restaurant reviews. See "Visitor Information" in "Fast Facts" on p. 286.

## Telephones

The international **country code** for China is **86.** The **city code** for Shànghǎi is **021.**
**To call Shànghǎi:**

1.    Dial the international access code: **011** from the U.S. or Canada; **00** from the U.K., Ireland, or New Zealand; or **0011** from Australia.
2.    Dial the country code **86** for China.
3.    Drop the first zero and dial the city code **21** (for Shànghǎi) and then the number.

**To call within China:** Local calls in Shànghǎi require no city code; just dial the eight-digit Shànghǎi number (or the three-digit emergency numbers for fire, police, and ambulance). Calls from Shànghǎi to other locations in China require that you dial the full domestic city code (which always starts with **0**). Similarly, if you are calling a Shànghǎi number from outside the city but within China, dial the city code (021) and then the number. Public pay phones require either a deposit of a ¥1 coin or an IC card (*àicēi kǎ*) available from post offices, most convenience stores, and street stalls.

**To make international calls:** To make international calls from China, first dial 00 and then the country code (U.S. or Canada 1, U.K. 44, Ireland 353, Australia 61, New Zealand 64). Next you dial the area code and number. For example, if you wanted to call the British Embassy in Washington, D.C., you would dial 00-1-202-588-7800.

You can also use your calling card (AT&T, MCI, or Sprint, for example) to make international (but not domestic) calls from Shànghǎi. The local access number for **AT&T** is ℂ **10-811;** for **MCI** ℂ **10-812;** for **Sprint** ℂ **10-813.** Check with your hotel for the local access numbers for other companies. The directions for placing an international calling-card call vary from company to company, so check with your long-distance carrier before you leave home. To save money, however, use an **IP card** (*àipì kǎ*), available from post offices, most convenience stores, and street stalls, but bargain for less than the face value of the card (in other words, you should bargain to pay around ¥80 for a ¥100 card). Depending on where you call, a ¥50 card can yield you up to an hour's talk time. Instructions in English should be on the back of the card.

**For directory assistance:** Dial 114 if you're looking for a number inside Shànghǎi. If you want numbers for other cities in China, dial zero, the city code, followed by 114. Dial 116 for numbers to all other countries.

**For operator assistance:** If you need operator assistance in making a call, it's best to ask your hotel for help.

**Toll-free numbers:** Numbers beginning with 800 within China are toll-free, but calling a 1-800 number in the U.S. from China is not toll-free. In fact, it costs the same as an overseas call.

3

PLANNING YOUR TRIP TO SHÀNGHǍI

Staying Connected

# SUGGESTED ITINERARIES

See Shànghǎi in a day? Even though many visitors on organized tours do, I don't recommend it. While the city may lack the large-scale palaces and awesome sights of Běijīng, Shànghǎi is one of the most exciting cities in the world right now, and requires at least 2 or 3 days to soak in its unique vibe and energy. Still, if a day or two is all the time you have, I want to help you make the most of it with a ready-made itinerary that allows you to have an unforgettable trip.

**4**

While Shànghǎi's sights are scattered around town, the 1-day highlights are clustered together, sparing visitors the need to fight Shànghǎi traffic. The second day takes in Shànghǎi's lesser-known but no less delightful sights on both land and water. For those staying a third day, I suggest an overnight trip to nearby Hángzhōu (or a day trip to Sūzhōu or one of the water villages in the Yángzǐ River delta).

## Neighborhoods in Brief

The Shànghǎi municipality consists of 14 districts, four counties, and the Pǔdōng New Area, and covers an area of 6,341 sq. km (2,448 sq. miles), with its urban area measuring 2,643 sq. km (1,020 sq. miles). The seven main urban districts, running from east to west, are identified here.

**Pǔdōng** Located across the Huángpǔ River from the Bund, Pǔdōng (literally "east of the Huángpǔ") was formerly backwater farmland before 1990 when it was targeted by then–Chinese President Dèng Xiǎopíng to lead Shànghǎi and the rest of China into a new age of economic growth. Today, it is home to the Lùjiāzuǐ Financial with its many modern economic monuments (Jīn Mào Tower, Shànghǎi World Financial Center), the Shànghǎi stock exchange, Asia's second-largest department store, a riverside promenade, the Pǔdōng International Airport, and the 2010 World Expo grounds.

**Huángpǔ (Downtown Shànghǎi)** The city center of old Shànghǎi lies in a compact sector west of the Huángpǔ River and south of Sūzhōu Creek. It extends west to Chéngdū Běi Lù (the North-South Elevated Hwy.), and encompasses the Bund, People's Square (Rénmín Guǎngchǎng), and the Shànghǎi Museum. The district now also stretches to the south to encompass **Nánshì,** the old Chinese city, with the Old Town Bazaar, Yù Yuán (Yù Garden), Shànghǎi's old city wall, and the Confucian Temple.

**Hóngkǒu (Northeast Shànghǎi)** Immediately north of downtown Shànghǎi, across Sūzhōu Creek, this residential sector along the upper Huángpǔ River was originally the American Concession before it became part of the International Settlement in colonial days. Today, it's a developing neighborhood with a few sights: the Ohel Moshe Synagogue, the Lǔ Xùn Museum, and the Duōlún Lù Commercial Street.

**Lúwān (French Concession)** Beginning at Xīzàng Lù at the eastern end of People's Square and continuing west to Shǎnxī Nán Lù, this historic district was the domain of the French colonial community up until 1949. The French left their mark on the residential architecture, which boasts such tourist sights as Fùxīng Park, the historic Jǐn Jiāng Hotel, the shops along Huáihǎi Zhōng Lù, the Xīntiāndì development, and the former residences of Sun Yat-sen and Zhōu Ēnlái.

**Jìng Ān (Northwest Shànghǎi)** North of the French Concession and part of the former International Settlement, this district has its share of colonial architecture, as well as the modern Shànghǎi Centre. Two of the city's top Buddhist shrines, Jìng Ān Sì and Yùfó Sì (Jade Buddha Temple), are located here, as are a number of Shànghǎi's top hotels and restaurants.

**Xúhuì (Southwest Shànghǎi)** West of the French Concession and south along Héngshān Lù, this area is one of Shànghǎi's top addresses for cafes, bars, and shops. Sights include the Xújiāhuì Cathedral, Lónghuá Pagoda, the Shànghǎi Botanical Garden, and the former residence of Soong Ching-ling.

**Chángníng (Hóngqiáo Development Zone)** Starting at Huáihǎi Xī Lù, directly west of the Xúhuì and Jìng Ān districts, this corridor of new international economic ventures extends far west of downtown, past Gǔběi New Town and the Shànghǎi Zoo, to the Hóngqiáo Airport.

# THE BEST OF SHÀNGHǍI IN 1 DAY

This "greatest hits" itinerary takes in Shànghǎi's top attractions—the best of East and West, past, present, and future—including a world-class museum; China's number-one shopping street; Shànghǎi's most famous colonial landmark, the Bund; one of the world's tallest buildings in Pǔdōng; and a classical Chinese garden and temple complex. All of these landmarks can be traced in a loop around Pǔxī (west of the Huángpǔ River), with a quick detour into Pǔdōng (if you have more than a day, save Pǔdōng for the second day), but it can be strenuous, so do fortify yourself with a hearty breakfast before setting off in the morning. There are plenty of dining options along the way, so feel free to stop at restaurants other than those recommended here, especially if you've been delayed by shopping, sightseeing, or just people-watching. In the evening, I recommend taking in the Shànghǎi Acrobats, and ending with a nightcap or late supper amid the lights on the Bund. **Start:** *Metro to Rénmín Guǎngchǎng (People's Square).*

## 1 Shànghǎi Museum (Shànghǎi Bówùguǎn) ★★★

This modern, state-of-the-art museum, often cited by visitors as Shànghǎi's premier attraction, has as impressive a collection of historical artifacts as you'll see in any museum in China. It's possible to tour all 11 exhibition rooms, but if your time is limited, pick four or five of the most interesting to you. The bronze and stone sculpture galleries on the first floor, the painting gallery on the third, and the jade gallery on the fourth are generally considered the most impressive. The audio phone with narratives of the major exhibits is worth renting. Allow at least an hour, preferably two. See p. 164.

Emerge from the north exit of the museum onto:

## 2 Rénmín Guǎngchǎng (People's Square)

Shànghǎi's central square was once part of colonial Shànghǎi's horse-racing track. To the northwest, the building with the curved crucible roof is the **Shànghǎi Grand Theatre** (p. 189), the city's premier venue for international performances, dances, and concerts. Just behind it, though out of view, is the colonial clock tower marking today's **Shànghǎi Art Museum** (p. 182). Directly to your north is Shànghǎi's **City Hall.**

Head northeast across Rénmín Dàdào to:

## 3 Shànghǎi Urban Planning Museum (Shànghǎi Chéngshì Guīhuà Zhǎnshìguǎn) ★★

Even if you've had your fill of museums, duck into this modern Microlite glass building and head straight for the third floor. Your jaw will drop at the huge scale model of urban Shànghǎi as it will look in 2020. It is usually at this moment that visitors begin to grasp the enormous physical and social engineering experiment that is Shànghǎi, and understand why Shànghǎi really will be the city of the future. See p. 176.

Cross Xīzàng Lù and head north until you reach:

## 4 Nánjīng Lù Pedestrian Mall

This is China's "Number One Shopping Street," which needs to be seen and experienced, especially the sea of humanity that crowds the plaza on any given day. These days, the street is lined as much with modern shopping centers as with the old colonial holdovers, all covered in neon lights, of course. It takes about 20 to 30 minutes to walk to the end without stopping for any major breaks, and considerably more if you like to shop. See "Walking Tour 2: Nánjīng Lù" on p. 207. Otherwise, hop on board the electric **sightseeing trolley** (¥2) that will take you to the end of the pedestrian mall at Hénán Zhōng Lù.

Continue east on Nánjīng Dōng Lù, passing along the way the Peace Hotel, one of Shànghǎi's most gorgeous Art Deco buildings. Soon you'll arrive at:

## 5 The Bund ★★★

The most famous street in Asia during the first half of the 20th century, this embankment was where the foreign powers who entered Shànghǎi after the Opium War of 1842 erected their Western-style banks and trading houses. Today it is a veritable museum of architecture featuring building styles from Art Deco and Gothic to late Renaissance and classic European. It's also home to some of the swankiest shops, restaurants, and bars in Shànghǎi. See "Walking Tour 1: The Bund & Beyond" on p. 200 for a history of the buildings.

# The Best of Shànghǎi in 1–2 Days

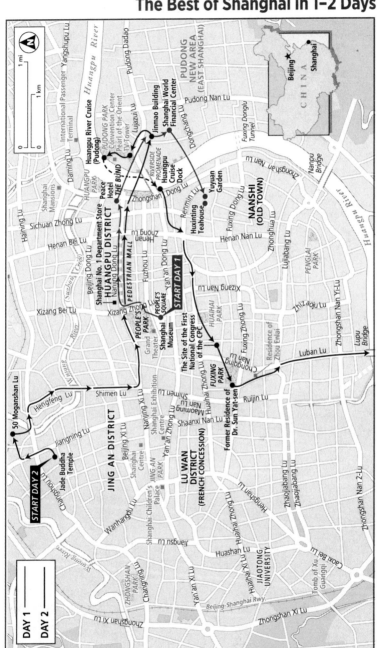

## 6 Dining on the Bund ☕

If the weather is nice, I suggest the ultimate of Shànghǎi dining experiences: rooftop dining on the Bund at either M on the Bund (Guǎngdōng Lù 20; ✆ 021/6350-9988; see p. 111) or New Heights at Three on the Bund (Zhōngshān Dōng Yī Lù 3; ✆ 021/6321-0909; see p. 113). The former was the restaurant that put Shànghǎi on the world dining map, while the latter serves more casual bistro fare. From either rooftop, soak in the views of Pǔdōng across the Huángpǔ River.

After lunch, if you are staying for a second day, walk to the southern end of Zhōngshān Dōng Yī Lù and head west on Yán'ān Dōng Lù. Take a left (south) onto Sìchuān Nán Lù and head all the way down past Rénmín Lù onto Lìshuǐ Lù and eventually Jiǔjiǎochǎng Lù. You are now in Shànghǎi's Old Town (jump ahead to #8).

If you have only 1 day, head back up the Bund to Nánjīng Lù where you have a number of options for crossing the river to Pǔdōng. You can walk west on Nánjīng Lù to the Nanjing Road (E) subway station and take Metro Line 2 for one stop to Lùjiāzuǐ; or you can cross via the Bund Sightseeing Tunnel (entrance at Běijīng Lù), complete with tram cars and tacky flashing lights; or you can just hop a taxi through the Yán'ān Lù Tunnel to Pǔdōng and the:

## 7 Jīn Mào Tower ★★★ or Shànghǎi World Financial Center ★★

The architecturally perfect Jīn Mào Tower with its 88th-floor observatory is one of my favorite buildings to take visitors for a 360-degree view of Shànghǎi, but it was recently eclipsed in height by the neighboring Shànghǎi World Financial Center (SWFC). SWFC's vertiginous 100th-floor all-glass observation deck is stunning, but it's not for the faint-hearted.

Take a taxi back across the river to:

## 8 Old Town

This is the center of the old Chinese city, the first part of Shànghǎi to be settled and where foreigners seldom ventured during the Concession days. These days, the mysterious and foreboding alleys have given way to a sprawling temple bazaar, anchored in the south by **Shànghǎi Old Street (Shànghǎi Lǎo Jiē)**, full of reconstructed Míng and Qīng dynasty shop houses proffering a wide variety of souvenirs, antiques (mostly fake), and delightfully tacky tchotchkes. At the eastern end of the street is the Daoist **Temple of the Town God (Chénghuáng Miào**, p. 169). In the center of the Old Town complex is a main square with the **Bridge of Nine Turnings (Jiǔqū Qiáo)** and the classic mid-lake pavilion **Húxīntíng Teahouse (Húxīntíng Cháshè)**. See p. 187.

To the north of the teahouse is:

## 9 Yù Yuán (Yù Garden) ★

Billed as the most complete Chinese classical garden in urban Shànghǎi, Yù Yuán can be interesting for those who've never seen a Chinese garden up close before, even if you have to fight your way through the tourist throngs. It's full of rock gardens, ponds, bridges, and pavilions all laid out to simulate a microcosm of the universe. Allow at least an hour. See p. 160.

When you exit Yù Yuán, you can wander some more through the cluster of shops or head south to the aforementioned **Shànghǎi Old Street** for souvenir shopping. At the western end of the street at Hénán Lù, you can catch a taxi back to your hotel so you can freshen up for:

## 10 A Night with the Shànghǎi Acrobats

Though this screams "tourist" in every way, few visitors are disappointed with their night spent watching the contortionist, juggling, unicycling, and plate-spinning acts of the justifiably world-famous **Shànghǎi Acrobatic Troupe** at the **Shànghǎi Centre Theatre (Shànghǎi Shāngchéng Jùyuàn).** Performances usually start at 7:30pm and last 90 minutes. *Tip:* Tell your hotel concierge to book tickets while you are out sightseeing, as shows are sometimes sold out at the last minute. See p. 243.

If you fancy a nightcap or even a late dinner, you have a multitude of options. You can head back to the Bund (night views are quite different and worth returning for) for a late supper at **Mr & Mrs Bund** at Bund 18 (p. 112) or go directly to the hottest bar in town, **Bar Rouge** also at Bund 18 (p. 251) or any of the dining establishments at **Three on the Bund** (p. 113). Alternatively, check out any of the bars and restaurants at Shànghǎi's other glamorous see-and-be-seen hot spot, **Xīntiāndì** (p. 116) in the former French Concession. Wherever you end up, sit back, relax, and promise yourself another visit to Shànghǎi in the near future.

# THE BEST OF SHÀNGHǍI IN 2 DAYS

If you've already made your way through "The Best of Shànghǎi in 1 Day," your second full-day tour should be a bit more relaxed, though no less eclectic, and it covers a much wider swath of territory. Start the day early in northwest Pǔxī by beating the crowds to view some exquisite jade Buddhas, then hurtle into Shànghǎi's future by visiting the city's tallest buildings in Pǔdōng (east of the Huángpǔ River). Come back down to earth—or rather, sea level—with a short cruise on the Huángpǔ River. Spend the afternoon strolling the former French Concession, with some of the city's finest colonial architecture and historical houses, or climb the Lǔpǔ Bridge for a view of the former World Expo grounds. Spiff up your final evening with a jazz concert. *Start:* Jade Buddha Temple (Yùfó Sì).

## 1 Jade Buddha Temple (Yùfó Sì)

If possible, arrive first thing in the morning to beat the tour bus crowd. The highlights at this Buddhist temple are two luminous white jade Buddhas brought from Burma in 1881. The larger and more impressive is in the Cángjīng Lóu in the back and the sleeping Buddha is in the Wòfó Sì northwest of the main hall. Throughout, you can observe the workings of a typical Buddhist temple, though this one is geared squarely for tourism.

Those with an interest in the Chinese contemporary art scene can take a detour up north to **Mògānshān Lù 50,** a collection of industrial warehouses converted into artists' studios and galleries. It's a very short taxi ride, or if you prefer to walk, head east on Ānyuǎn Lù for a block to Chānghuá Lù. Turn left (north) for 5 long blocks, and take a right onto Mògān Shān Lù until you arrive at the compound entrance. Otherwise, take a taxi from the Jade Buddha Temple to **Nánjīng Xī Lù Metro Station.** Take Metro Line 2 to reach Lùjiāzuǐ Metro stop in Pǔdōng, Shànghǎi's financial district.

## 2 Jīn Mào Tower ★★★ or Shànghǎi World Financial Center ★★

You can now visit three observation towers in Pǔdōng: the eyesore Oriental Pearl Tower with its globes meant to simulate pearls, the architecturally perfect Jīn Mào Tower, or the tallest building in China, the Shànghǎi World Financial Center (SWFC). I recommend either the Jīn Mào with its 88th-floor observation deck, or SWFC's all-glass 100th-floor observatory. See p. 187 and 190.

After your heady visit, walk toward the river to the riverside promenade **Bīnjiāng Dàdào.**

## 3 Coffee Break ☕

If you have to have your frappuccino or latte with full trimmings, this is the best Starbucks to get your fix (Fù Dù Duàn, Bīnjiāng Dàdào; ℂ 021/5878-1332), for it comes with a stunning view of the Bund across the river. Sit outside on a nice day and be lulled into the flow of river traffic.

From here, if you want to get on with your day without taking an hour or so out for a Huángpǔ River Cruise, head south on Fùchéng Lù for about 20 minutes to the **Passenger Ferry Terminal (Lún Dù Mǎ Tóu)** at Dōngchāng Lù, and take the water taxi (¥2) bound for Jīnlíng Lù on the other side of the Huángpǔ River. This short ferry ride will give you a chance to get on the water, while watching ordinary Shanghainese people get to and from work. From the Jīnlíng Lù ferry terminal, take a taxi ahead to #5.

If you fancy a bit of a short cruise, head north on the Riverside Promenade (Bīnjiāng Dàdào) all the way past the twin-globe **International Convention Center (Guójiā Huìyì Zhōng Xīn)** to the dock **Dōngfāng Míngzhú Yóulǎn Mǎtóu** on Fēnghè Lù where you can purchase tickets to:

## 4 Huángpǔ River Cruise ★

This is actually a shorter version of the regular 1- to 3-hour Huángpǔ River Cruise which typically departs from the Pǔxi side, but in a busy day, this cruise (40 min.) along the city's main shipping artery will give you a quick but wonderful opportunity to see Shànghǎi's working wharves and to take in the changing skyline. Boats depart hourly from 10am to 4pm. See p. 165.

Take a cab to:

## 5 Xīntiāndì ★

This trendy pedestrian mall of restaurants, bars, and boutiques in restored *shíkùmén* (stone frame gate) houses is good for a stroll, if only to see how today's hip young Shanghainese like to spend their free time and hard-earned *yuán*. There's also a small *shíkùmén* museum (p. 116). The capitalistic lifestyle on display here is especially ironic given that the development is anchored in the south by the **Site of the First National Congress of the Communist Party** (p. 185), the birthplace of China's Communist Party. Pop in for a quick look at the room where Máo and company conceived their grand plans.

6 Delicious Dumplings 🍲

Any of the restaurants and bars in Xīntiāndì can provide refreshments, but I recommend Crystal Jade Restaurant (Fěicuì Jiǔjiā) (on the second floor of the south block, Xīngyè Lù 123, Xītiādì, South Block, House 6–7, Unit 2F–12A&B; ℂ 021/6385-8752; see p. 134) for some of Shànghǎi's best *xiǎolóng bāo* dumplings. The *dāndān miàn* (hand-pulled noodles in a spicy peanut sauce) is a must-try as well.

For part of the afternoon, I recommend:

## 7 Strolling the French Concession & Climbing the Lǔpǔ Bridge

The French Concession, the most picturesque of Shànghǎi's neighborhoods, full of colonial mansions, leafy parks, and tree-lined avenues, is best appreciated on foot. See "Walking Tour 4: French Concession" on p. 218. If time is short, I recommend taking a cab from Xīntiāndì to **Fùxīng Gōngyuán,** one of Shànghǎi's loveliest parks and worth a stroll-through for photo opportunities of card-playing seniors and tai chi practitioners. From the park, visit **Sūn Zhōngshān Gùjū,** Sun Yat-sen's former residence, and—time and interest permitting—**Zhōu Gōng Guǎn,** the former residence of Chairman Máo's second in command, Zhōu Ēnlái. Otherwise, you can walk or take a taxi to any of the sights listed on the itinerary that appeal to you, because you likely won't have time to cover the whole route on foot. Or if you prefer something a little more invigorating and panoramic, take a taxi to the **Lǔpǔ Bridge (Lǔpǔ Dàqiáo)** (p. 188) and climb to the viewing platform for a bird's-eye view of the city and the structures left over from the 2010 World Expo (p. 184).

If you are visiting Shànghǎi for more than 2 days, I recommend taking an overnight trip to Hángzhōu for the third day. Unless you're traveling by private car, it's best to take an evening train (p. 265) to Hángzhōu the night before so you can make the most of your day there. If Hángzhōu doesn't appeal to you, or if this is your last night in Shànghǎi, then by all means, jazz it up!

## 8 Live Jazz

There is a multitude of options for evening jazz in the city. The storied **Peace Hotel Jazz Bar Band** has finally returned to its original abode (p. 249), playing all the usual pleasing popular standards in a splendid Art Deco environment. For more funk or experimental jazz, try the **Cotton Club** (p. 248) or **JZ Club** (p. 249).

# THE BEST OF SHÀNGHǍI IN 3 DAYS

Having sampled the highlights of Shànghǎi in just 2 days, make your third and final day a little different by skipping out of town and heading for nearby Hángzhōu, once described by Marco Polo as "the finest, most splendid city in the world." Unless you're traveling by private car, I recommend taking the train down to Hángzhōu the night before for a more relaxed visit the next day (though it is possible to take an early train in the morning as well). I haven't packed too much in this suggested itinerary because Hángzhōu's famed West Lake (Xī Hú) is best appreciated at a leisurely pace. Alternatively, you can also visit Sūzhōu, or any of the water villages of the Yángzǐ River delta, of which Tónglǐ and Nánxún are recommended in chapter 11 (p. 273) on your third day. The itinerary below takes in the highlights of Hángzhōu (p. 264). **Start:** *Líng Yǐn Sì (Temple of the Soul's Retreat)* by taxi, or bus no. K7 or Y1.

## 1 Líng Yīn Sì (Temple of the Soul's Retreat) ★

Hángzhōu's most famous temple complex gets impossibly crowded, so it's wise to start off here first thing in the morning. The highlight here is the Buddhist rock carvings of Fēilái Fēng (Peak That Flew from Afar), dating back more than 600 years. Afterwards, head for the large main temple to see the giant gilded Buddha.

If you are a tea connoisseur, you can follow the main path of Fēilái Fēng past Yǒngfú Temple and onto the grounds of **Amanfayun,** a hotel now occupying what was once Fǎyún Cūn, a village of tea farmers. Here along the Fǎyún Pathway is the **Tea House** where you can sip, purchase, and learn all about tea from the surrounding area. Or you can take a cab to the **Chinese Tea Museum (Zhōngguó Cháyè Bówùguǎn)** or directly to **Lóngjǐng Village** if you are interested in purchasing tea directly from the villagers. You should speak some Mandarin or have someone with you who does. Whatever you do, avoid the tourist trap at the Dragon Well Tea Park (Lóngjǐng Wēnchá). Otherwise, take a cab or bus no. K7 or Y1 from Líng Yǐn Sì to the Shangri-La Hotel. Across the street is Hángzhōu's most famous sight:

## 2 Xī Hú (West Lake) ★★★

Despite modernization at the eastern lakeshore and attempts to enlarge the lake in the west by dredging another causeway, Hángzhōu's most famous lake has managed for the most part to retain its tranquillity and loveliness, much of which can be best appreciated by strolling the lake. For now, take a **lake cruise ★★★** on one of the large passenger ferries, which also stops at **Xiǎo Yíng Zhōu (Island of Small Seas)** in the middle of the lake. On your return, you can wander along **Gūshān Dǎo (Solitary Island),** which is home to a pretty park, the Zhèjiāng Provincial Museum, and Hángzhōu's famous restaurant, Lóu Wài Lóu.

## 3 Lóu Wài Lóu Lunch 🍲

Lóu Wài Lóu (Gūshān Lù 30; ✆ 0571/8796-9023; see p. 273), a Hángzhōu institution, is the spot for lunch, even if it's the spot for all the tour groups in town as well. Try local specialties such as Beggar's Chicken *(jiàohuà jī)*, shrimp with *lóngjǐng* tea leaves *(lóngjǐng xiārén),* and *dōngpō* pork.

## 4 Lakeshore Promenade ★

Walk off lunch along the Bái Causeway (Bái Dī) in the northern part of the lake. Cross **Duàn Qiáo (Broken Bridge),** and take a leisurely stroll to the pedestrian mall of Húbīn Lù edging the northeast part of the lake. Make your way by foot or taxi to the southern end of the lake.

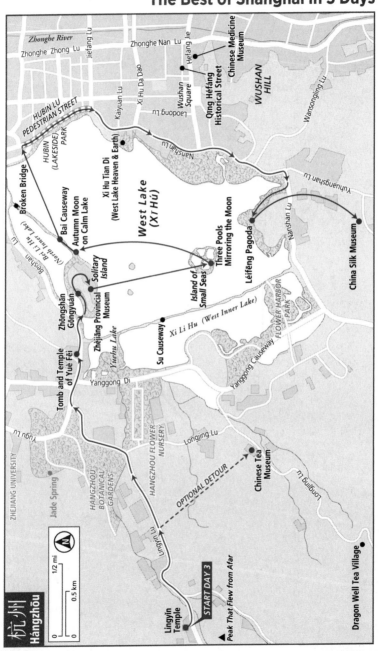

Hángzhōu 杭州

Zhonghe River
Zhonghe Zhong Lu
Zhonghe Nan Lu
Jiefang Lu
Hefang Jie
Chinese Medicine Museum
WUSHAN HILL
Xi Hu Da Dao
Kaiyuan Lu
Wushan Square
Laodong Lu
Qing Héfāng Historical Street
Wansongling Lu
HUBIN LU PEDESTRIAN STREET
Nanshan Lu
Broken Bridge
HUBIN (LAKESIDE) PARK
Xi Hu Tian Di (West Lake Heaven & Earth)
Bai Causeway
Autumn Moon on Calm Lake
West Lake (Xī Hú)
Yuhuangshan Lu
Běishān Lu
Bái Dī (North Inner Lake)
Solitary Island
Three Pools Mirroring the Moon
Léifēng Pagoda
Nanshan Lu
China Silk Museum
Zhōngshān Gōngyuán
Zhejiāng Provincial Museum
Island of Small Seas
FLOWER HARBOR PARK
Tomb and Temple of Yuè Fēi
Yuehu Lake
Su Causeway
Xi Li Hu (West Inner Lake)
Yanggong Causeway
Yanggong Di
Yúqu Lu
HANGZHOU FLOWER NURSERY
Longjing Lu
Chinese Tea Museum
Longjing Lu
ZHEJIANG UNIVERSITY
Jade Spring
HANGZHOU BOTANICAL GARDENS
OPTIONAL DETOUR
Lingyin Lu
START DAY 3
Peak That Flew from Afar
Lingyǐn Temple
Dragon Well Tea Village

1/2 mi
0.5 km

## 5 Léi Fēng Tǎ (Léi Fēng Pagoda) ★

This rebuilt Buddhist pagoda has some of the best panoramic views of the lake, as well as of the hills and tea plantations of Lóngjǐng village to the west, and the modern skyscrapers of downtown Hángzhōu to the east.

Take a short taxi ride to:

## 6 ZhōngguóSīchóu Bówùguǎn (China Silk Museum) ★

This surprisingly comprehensive exhibit of the history and art of silk weaving reminds us that Hángzhōu, too, produced its share of silk.

By now, it's almost time to wind down. Hop a cab to:

## 7 Xī Hú Tiāndì ★

This is Hángzhōu's version of Shànghǎi's Xīntiāndì (p. 268), complete with trendy restaurants and bars where you can take a refresher before heading for the railway station to board your evening train back to Shànghǎi.

# WHERE TO STAY

There are two types of hotels in China: **Sino-foreign joint venture hotels,** which are Chinese-owned properties with foreign management, and wholly **Chinese-owned-and-managed hotels.** The former tend to be four- and five-star hotels (see below for more on the rating system) with familiar brand names, while the latter can range from five-star outfits to unrated hovels. Two of the biggest Chinese hotel management groups are the Jīn Jiāng chain and the Héngshān chain, both of which started with flagship hotels in Shànghǎi, but have now extended their management to hotels around China.

The Chinese government ranks hotels on an almost meaningless star system whereby five-star accreditation is handed out by a central authority, while ranks of four stars and below are determined by local authorities, none of whom are beyond being wined, dined, and having their palms greased (a little or a lot). **Five-star hotels** have the complete facilities and services of any international luxury hotel, but even among its ranks, quality varies more than it should. **Four-star hotels** come close, often lacking only a few technical requirements (such as a swimming pool or other facility). Both levels are popular choices for Western travelers, providing English-speaking staff and clean, comfortable, even luxurious accommodations. Foreign-managed hotels have foreign staff at the top levels, though increasingly the Chinese are filling more of these positions even in joint-venture hotels. For Western travelers, your first choice should be foreign-managed hotels followed by the top Chinese-managed outfits. In general, four- and five-star Chinese-managed hotels do not match their foreign-managed counterparts in service or maintenance of facilities.

**Three-star hotels** are almost always Chinese managed. Few of them have English-speaking staff. In the bigger cities, three-star hotels are adequate for the budget traveler who merely needs a decent place to spend the night. In many parts of China, however, the three-star hotel is the best you'll find.

Due to the comparative lack of cleanliness (rather than safety issues), **two-** and **one-star hotels,** as well as unrated hotels and basic guest houses catering to the rugged backpacking traveler, are generally best avoided, if possible. In some parts of China, these hotels are not even allowed to accept foreign travelers. *Note:* The zero- to three-star rating system I use in the following reviews does not correspond to the Chinese star-rating system. For details on Frommer's star-rating system, see p. viii.

In general, most hotel rooms, no matter how basic, have the following: a telephone whose line you can plug into your laptop computer; air-conditioning, either centrally or individually controlled, which often doubles as a heater; a television that usually receives only local Chinese channels, if that; and some sort of potable water, either in the form of hot water thermoses that are delivered to your room after you check in, or bottled water and an electric kettle. Except for the top hotels, most hotels do not have exclusively nonsmoking rooms. If they tell you they do, but put you in a room that reeks of every previous smoker, they mean the room is a nonsmoking room *for the moment!*

*Note:* It's quite common to receive telephone calls in the middle of the night (even in four- and five-star hotels, alas) inquiring if you would like *ànmó* (literally "massage," but in this case, a not-so-subtle euphemism for sexual services). The caller usually hangs up if a woman answers, or occasionally if a man answers in a non-Chinese language. However, bolder callers have learned enough to say "Massagee?" when they hear a foreign male's voice. If you are not amused, and complaining to the hotel staff doesn't work (much of this calling actually comes from in-house), unplug your phone.

In general, payment for your room is made upfront; many, but not all, of the three-star-and-up hotels catering to foreigners accept foreign credit cards. Asked how long you're staying, always say 1 day (or you'll be asked to pay for however many days you plan on staying). You can then pay as you go. Keep all receipts, from proof of your room payment to any room key deposit you might have to make. The top hotels usually levy a service charge of 10% to 15%, though this may be waived or included in the final negotiated price at smaller hotels. Children under age 12 usually stay free in their parent's room.

With practically every international hotel chain and brand name represented in Shànghǎi, and more on the way (watch out for the Waldorf Astoria, W, and another Four Seasons, and two more Shangri-La's, among others, in the next few years), as well as the establishment of some very nice **boutique hotels** in the last few years, the visitor is spoiled for choice when it comes to high-end accommodations. Even more appealing, and unique to Shànghǎi, these luxury accommodations come in a range of styles, from modern luxury towers to restored Art Deco hotels to elegant colonial mansions. Prices are high, but the fierce competition from the glut of hotels has led to significant discounts during parts of the year. However, these discounts disappear almost entirely during big conventions, meetings, and special citywide events, such as the annual Formula One Grand Prix race in the spring. Midrange accommodations are plentiful in Shànghǎi, but few foreigners choose these mostly three-star hotels when big discounts are available from the top hotels. In the last few years, **bed-and-breakfasts** have started appearing in Shànghǎi, and have become a welcome alternative to the cookie-cutter chain hotels. Shànghǎi's budget hotels, few and far between, charge more than elsewhere in China, with the exception, perhaps, of Hong Kong and Běijīng.

Because Shànghǎi is more of a financial, commercial, and industrial city than a tourism-driven one, hoteliers like to claim that they have no low season. In reality, you can get the biggest discounts between December and February, while rates are highest from May through October.

## Saving on Your Hotel Room

The **rack rate** is the maximum rate that a hotel charges for a room. Shànghǎi frequently hosts international conventions and large special events such as the Formula One Grand Prix, so the top hotels will charge rack rates during these occasions. During all other times, however, almost no one pays more than 90% of this rate. On average, you can usually expect a discount of 20% to 40%, and occasionally even up to 60% to 70% during the low season. To lower the cost of your room:

○ **Do not book ahead.** As a general rule, you can get the best rates in China by simply showing up at a hotel and bargaining, assuming, of course, that there is room. For much of the year, most Chinese hotels are never full and your chances of getting a lower rate are much better on the spot than if you booked months in advance (perhaps paying double what you might in person). In addition, there is no guarantee that the booking you make will be honored, especially at local Chinese hotels. That said, most travelers to China (especially first-timers) who are not familiar with the language tend to find the prospect of negotiating on the spot daunting, not to mention highly inconvenient if you have to drag your luggage around until you find a suitable hotel. Those who want to get the best deal but also be assured of a place to stay can book a hotel for the first night, and then bargain in person once you've reached your destination. To bargain in person, it's helpful to keep in mind the general discounting structure mentioned above, as well as the discounted rates offered by various websites (see below).

○ **Book online.** If you have to or would like to stay at a specific joint-venture hotel during a particularly busy time, the best rates are usually offered on the hotel's website. Some of them also offer Internet-only discounts. Beware that these rates fluctuate constantly according to inventory. Unless there's a major event going on, the further in advance you book, the smaller the discount you'll likely receive. Hotel prices quoted by services like Travelocity and Expedia can occasionally be quite competitive, especially closer to the time, but such rates can usually be matched by the hotels themselves. Several top international hotels such as the Marriott chain also have a "look no further" policy whereby they will match the lowest rates offered on any non-hotel-affiliated websites.

○ **Dial a central booking number.** With the better hotels, you can sometimes get better rates with their toll-free central booking numbers than by calling the hotels directly.

○ **Do not book through Chinese hotel agencies or websites specializing in Chinese hotels.** As a general rule, do not book with any online Chinese travel agencies and hotel-booking sites, as not all of them are licensed and you have no guarantee of getting a room or your money back. Whatever prices these sites quote you, you can usually obtain the same discount if you contact the hotels directly and may even beat that discount as you won't have to pay the agency's markup (usually 10%). That said, there's no harm in consulting hugely popular Chinese travel websites such as Ctrip (www.english.ctrip.com) and eLong (www.elong.com) if only to get a sense of your beginning price for negotiation.

## Look Before You Buy

When bargaining for a room at a hotel, always ask to see the room first to avoid any rude surprises after you've put your money down. This is standard practice at all Chinese hotels, and any receptionist who tells you otherwise is merely being lazy. Most of the top hotels will be more reluctant to show their rooms, but politely insist if it's important enough to you.

# How to Choose the Right Location for You

No district has a complete lock on convenience for the traveler, because the main tourist sites are scattered around the sprawling city, and shuttling by taxi and Metro is cheap and efficient. In general, hotels in Huángpǔ, Lúwān, and Jìng Ān districts have the most to see in their immediate neighborhoods.

For the average visitor on a short stay, the downtown district of **Huángpǔ,** which encompasses the city center, the Bund, and the eastern half of Nánjīng Lù, and which has a number of top hotels like the Westin, JW Marriott, and a slew of hotels along or just off the Nánjīng Lù Pedestrian Mall, offers the convenience of being able to walk to central sites such as the Bund, People's Square, Shànghǎi Museum, and Shànghǎi Grand Theatre. New, tony hotels along the Bund (the Peninsula, the recently reopened Peace Hotel, and the Waldorf Astoria), the South Bund, and the old Chinese city also make this district a top choice, though the downtown area tends to shut down by 10pm.

Those looking for a more exciting nightlife would do well to be based in the **Lúwān District** just southwest of the Bund, or the northeastern part of the Xúhuì District just to the west of Lúwān. This former French Concession area is one of the most pleasant areas to stay, whether as a tourist or resident. There is a good sprinkling of international-caliber hotels here, but even more attractive are the wide, tree-lined streets, hundreds of colonial mansions and Art Deco apartments hidden inside narrow lanes ripe for exploring, excellent restaurants in colonial settings, and colorful nightlife around Xīntiāndì, Tàikàng Lù, and Héngshān Lù. Some of the best shopping in town is also found here along Huáihǎi Lù and Màomíng Lù.

North of Lúwān and west of Huángpǔ District, **Jìng Ān District (Northwest Shànghǎi)** has its share of colonial mansions (more of the British than of the French variety), some fine restaurants, and many top hotels including the Four Seasons, the Portman Ritz-Carlton, and the Hilton.

To the west, the sprawling western district of **Chángníng** and the Hóngqiáo Development Zone is primarily a foreign investment and residential area, most easily accessible by taxi, as there is no subway service out here yet. A handful of top international hotels based here, such as the Regent, Sheraton, and Marriott, cater mostly to business travelers, but there are some excellent restaurants in the district worth checking out.

To the east of city center, just across the Huángpǔ River, the **Pǔdōng New Area** has less to offer sightseers, as it's still primarily a business district. With several of Shànghǎi's best hotels, and subway links to downtown (Metro Lines 2 and 4), however, it can now serve as a base for tourists as well.

The following hotel listings are arranged first by location, then by price. The **Very Expensive** category lists hotels with rack rates over ¥2,380 per night; the **Expensive** category lists hotels with rack rates of ¥1,360 to ¥2,380 per night; the **Moderate** category, rack rates of ¥680 to ¥1,360 per night; and the **Inexpensive** category, rack rates of under ¥680. Each listing also includes the average discount you can expect at that establishment.

*Note:* Maps for accommodations are in chapter 7, with specific map page numbers noted in the listing descriptions following all reviews.

# best HOTEL BETS

- **Best Newcomer:** From its storied location at the top of the Bund to its beyond-luxurious in-room amenities, the **Peninsula Shànghǎi** easily takes top honors and also sets a new standard for Shànghǎi's luxury hotels. The "urban resort" **PuLi Hotel and Spa** is a close runner-up, successfully creating a haven of peace and tranquillity in the midst of a busy urban jungle. See p. 87 and 98.

- **Best Service:** This is an impossibly difficult category with fierce competition, but our vote goes to the **St. Regis Shànghǎi,** which has refined service to a whole new level with its customized "Lifestyle Butler Service": No request seems too frivolous or difficult for the hotel's 24-hour butlers, not even escorting guests on city tours. A close second is the *consistently* friendly and efficient service at the **Pǔdōng Shangri-La.** In Pǔxī, the **PuLi Hotel and Spa**'s staff is wonderfully accommodating and impressively thorough in getting right all the details. See p. 104, 103, and 98.

- **Best Hotel Perks:** The **Peninsula Shànghǎi** lets all guests call home anywhere in the world for free (using a VOIP system)—need I say more? Oh, and there's also the walk-in closets and dressing room with weather panel and nail dryer, the three-in-one printer/fax/copier, the multimedia reader, the free Wi-Fi, the Nespresso machine, and of course, the all-important mood lighting. See p. 87.

- **Best City Views:** Le Royal Méridien, the tallest hotel in Pǔxī, also has the most stunning 360-degree views of the whole city. The **Park Hyatt** in Pǔdōng is taller (it's the tallest hotel in the world), but you need the help of a clear day to fully enjoy the view. See p. 87 and 103.

- **Best View of the Bund:** The nearby Grand Hyatt and Park Hyatt are higher, but the **Pǔdōng Shangri-La** is closer and at just the right elevation for a spectacular view of Shànghǎi's European architecture across the Huángpǔ River. The view is even better at night when this riverfront "colonial scroll" of banks and trading houses is lit up. See p. 103.

- **Best View of the Bund & Pǔdōng:** **Hyatt on the Bund** provides unique views of both the Bund and Pǔdōng's skyscrapers; one of our favorite things to do is to sit and watch the Huángpǔ river traffic from the hotel's VUE bar. See p. 91.

- **Best Whiff of Old Shànghǎi:** The legendary Peace Hotel has the advantage of renown, but since it was not open for review at press time, the French Concession **Mansion Hotel** with its romantic period furnishings best takes us back in time to the '30s and '40s when life was a cabaret, even—or maybe especially—in Shànghǎi. See p. 95.

- **Best Setting: Rùijīn Hotel,** located on the former Morriss Estate in the French Concession, has one of the loveliest colonial settings with four original villas (and several faux additions) amid sprawling manicured lawns that are lovely to stroll. See p. 94.

# HUÁNGPǓ (DOWNTOWN)
## Very Expensive

**Fairmont Peace Hotel (Hépíng Fàndiàn)** 和平饭店   After more than a 2-year renovation, Shànghǎi's best-known historic hotel is back in business. Originally built in 1929, the Peace—known in its heyday as the Cathay Hotel—is where Noël Coward wrote *Private Lives* in 1930, and Steven Spielberg filmed scenes for *Empire of the Sun*. Although the hotel had just reopened and was unavailable for review at press time, expect that many of the original highlights of the hotel, including the masterpiece Art Deco lobby, the magnificent rooftop views, the world-famous Jazz Bar, and the "Nine Nations" deluxe suite (each decorated in the style of a particular country, for example, Chinese, British, American, French, Indian, and others) should all be well preserved, with guest rooms elegantly appointed and fitted with the latest state-of-the-art amenities. The Fairmont Hotels chain now manages the hotel with the local Jiǎnjiāng group, which means that service should be a considerable improvement from before.

Nánjīng Dōng Lù 20 南京东路20号 (on the Bund); see map p. 136. ✆ **021/6321-6888.** Fax 021/6329-0300. www.fairmont.com/peacehotel. 270 units. ¥2,900 standard; ¥3,500 executive level; from ¥7,000 suite. AE, DC, MC, V. Metro: Nanjing Rd. (E). **Amenities:** 3 restaurants, deli, lounge, bar; babysitting; concierge; executive-level rooms; health club w/Jacuzzi and sauna; indoor pool; 24-hr. room service; spa. *In room:* A/C, TV/DVD, movie library, CD player, fridge, hair dryer, minibar, MP3 docking station, Wi-Fi.

**JW Marriott (Wànháo Jiǔdiàn)** 万豪酒店 ★★   Conveniently located a short walk from the main People's Square subway station and attractions such as the Shànghǎi Museum, Grand Theatre, Nánjīng Lù Pedestrian Mall, and Xīntiāndì, this is a handsome five-star hotel lodged primarily on the 38th to 60th floors of Tomorrow Square, a fascinating futuristic tower. Boasting a penthouse library billed as the tallest in the world by *Guinness World Records*, and China's first Mandara Spa, the hotel has luxurious rooms furnished with three telephones, CD radio, laptop safe, thick bathrobes, and brilliant city views. Marble bathrooms have separate showers with power massage jets and antifog mirrors. Service is top-notch.

Nánjīng Xī Lù 399 南京西路３９９号 (at Huángpí Běi Lù, west side of People's Square); see map p. 136. ✆ **800/228-9290** or 021/5359-4969. Fax 021/6375-5988. www.marriott.com. 342 units. ¥2,500 standard; ¥3,150 executive level; from ¥3,900 suite (regular 30% discounts, up to 60% pending occupancy). AE, DC, MC, V. Metro: People's Square. **Amenities:** 3 restaurants, deli, 2 lounges; babysitting; concierge; executive-level rooms; health club w/Jacuzzi and sauna; indoor/outdoor pool; 24-hr. room service; spa. *In room:* A/C, TV, movie library, CD player, fridge, hair dryer, minibar, Wi-Fi (¥120 per day).

**The Langham, Yangtze Boutique, Shànghǎi (Shànghǎi Lángyán Yángzǐ Jīngpǐn Jiǔdiàn)** 上海朗延扬子精品酒店 ★   Located a block south of the Nánjīng Lù pedestrian mall and a block east of People's Square, this striking, 1934 Art Deco hotel has undergone a complete overhaul from a three-star outfit into a handsome, ultraluxurious boutique hotel. The luxe interiors combine the best of colonial Shànghǎi ambience with the most modern amenities, including plush beds, a 42-inch LCD TV in the bedroom, and a 19-inch LCD set in the large marble bathroom. Ask for a room with a balcony, which, though small, provides a delightful perch to take in the hubbub of the city. The staff was very friendly and helpful, and housekeeping very prompt in replacing amenities missing from the room during my stay. The hotel also boasts a fine Cantonese restaurant, **T'ang Court.**

Hànkŏu Lù 740, 汉口路740号, (east of Xīzàng Zhōng Lù, 1 block south of Nánjīng Dōng Lù); see map p. 136. ⓒ **021/6080-0800.** Fax 021/6080-0801. www.langhamhotels.com. 96 units. ¥3,300–¥3,600 standard; ¥4,000 suite (30%–50% discounts). AE, DC, MC, V. Metro: People's Square. **Amenities:** 3 restaurants, lounge, bar; airport transfers; babysitting; concierge; health club and spa; room service. *In room:* A/C, TV/DVD, hair dryer, minibar, MP3 docking station, Wi-Fi (¥5 per min., ¥120 per day).

### Le Royal Méridien Shànghăi (Shànghăi Shìmào Huángjiā Aìmĕi Jiŭdiàn)
上海世茂皇家艾美酒店 ★   Occupying part of the tallest building in Pŭxī at 66 stories, Le Royal Méridien probably has the most perfect location in town at the western end of the Nánjīng Lù Pedestrian Mall, and steps from all the museums and subway stops of People's Square and People's Park. The ultramodern hotel offers luxuriously appointed rooms with floor-to-ceiling windows (with all the de rigueur breathtaking views of Pŭxī and Pŭdōng farther in the distance), 42-inch plasma TV, DVD and CD player, and sofa seating in each room. All guests are also entitled to free admission to the Museum of Contemporary Art (MOCA) in nearby People's Park. Service is friendly and efficient. The hotel also features the excellent French restaurant **Allure.**

Nánjīng Dōng Lù 789 南京东路789号 (east of People's Square, at the western end of Nánjīng Lù Pedestrian St.); see map p. 136. ⓒ **021/3318-9999.** Fax 021/6361-3388. www.lemeridien.com/royalshanghai. 761 units. ¥3,400–¥3,800 standard; ¥4,100 executive level; from ¥4,300 suite (40%–50% discounts). AE, DC, MC, V. Metro: Rénmín Guangchang. **Amenities:** 4 restaurants, lounge, bar, juice bar; babysitting; children's programs; concierge; executive-level rooms; health club w/Jacuzzi and sauna; indoor heated pool; 24-hr. room service; spa. *In room:* A/C, TV/DVD, CD player, hair dryer, Internet (¥5 per min., ¥120 per day), minibar.

### The Peninsula Hotel, Shànghăi (Shànghăi Bàndăo Jiŭdiàn) 上海半岛酒店 ★★★
Newly opened in late 2009, the luxurious Peninsula Hotel sets a new standard for luxury hotels in Shànghăi. Located at the top of Shànghăi's most famous street next to the former British Consulate, the 14-story Peninsula is the only property allowed to be built on the Bund in the last 60 years. Tops at the hotel are the guest rooms, large, elegant, and fully appointed with walk-in closets, a nail dryer, a Nespresso coffee machine, a three-in-one printer, fax, and copier, a 46-inch plasma TV, a multimedia reader, free Wi-Fi, and a VOIP system that allows guests to call home anywhere in the world for free. What is especially impressive is the hotel getting right all the smallest details to ensure maximum guest comfort: Afraid you might wake up in the dark confused as to where you are? Wave your hand and the bedside lighting panel will slowly illuminate. Deluxe rooms with Bund and river views are well worth splurging on. Fully expect the refined and attentive service for which the Peninsula is well known. Those not staying here can still drop in for Peninsula's famous high tea (daily 2–6pm), with a traditional 1930s tea dance held the first Saturday of every month.

Zhōngshān Dōng Yī Lù 32 中山东一路32号, No. 32, The Bund (at Bĕijīng Dōng Lù); see map p. 136. ⓒ **021/2327-2888.** Fax 021/2327-2000. www.peninsula.com. 235 units. ¥3,200–¥4,800 standard; from ¥6,400 suite (30%–40% discounts). AE, DC, MC, V. Metro: Nanjing Rd. (E). **Amenities:** 3 restaurants, lounge, bar; airport transfer; babysitting; children's programs; concierge; health club w/Jacuzzi and sauna; indoor pool; 24-hr. room service; spa. *In room:* A/C, TV/DVD, movie library, CD player, fax, fridge, hair dryer, minibar, MP3 docking station, free Wi-Fi.

**The Westin Shànghǎi (Shànghǎi Wēisītīng Dàfàndiàn)** 上海威斯汀大饭店 ★ ☺

Located a 5-minute walk from the Bund, the award-winning Westin offers large guest rooms headlined by Westin's patented Heavenly Bed, and plushly furnished with a large work desk, fax machine, high-speed Internet access, and deluxe bathroom that includes a separate stall with a "rainforest" shower. The Westin Kids Club is nearly unique in Shànghǎi, consisting of a separate area with adjoining outdoor terrace and paddle pool. Adults, meanwhile, can avail themselves of the sybaritic experience at the hotel's Banyan Tree Spa. Service throughout is impeccable. Besides the Bund, the old Chinese city (Nánshì) can also be reached on foot (20 min.).

Hénán Zhōng Lù 88 河南中路 8 8 号, Wàitān Zhōngxīn (3 blocks west of the Huángpǔ River); see map p. 136. ☏ **888/WESTIN-1** (937-8461) or 021/6335-1888. Fax 021/6335-2888. www.westin.com. 570 units. ¥3,600 standard; ¥4,300 executive level; from ¥3,950 suite (40%–50% discounts). AE, DC, MC, V. Metro: Nanjing Rd. (E). **Amenities:** 3 restaurants, deli, 2 lounges, juice bar; babysitting; children's programs; concierge; executive-level rooms with 24-hr. and IT butler service; state-of-the-art health club w/Jacuzzi and sauna; indoor/outdoor pool; 24-hr. room service; spa. *In room:* A/C, TV/DVD, movie library, fax, fridge, hair dryer, Internet (¥120 per day), minibar.

## Expensive

**Howard Johnson Plaza Hotel (Gǔ Xiàng Dàjiǔdiàn)** 古象大酒店    Not your dowdy, functional Howard Johnson back home, Shànghǎi's version is a modern 27-story tower just south of the new Century Square (Shìjì Guǎngchǎng) on the Nánjīng Lù Pedestrian Mall and with easy access to the Bund. Rated five stars, though lacking the excitement and luxury of the top hotels in this category, the hotel has rooms furnished with redwood furniture, comfortable beds with down bedding, robes, and full amenities. Marble bathrooms are large and clean. Service is friendly enough, if a little tentative.

Jiǔjiāng Lù 595 九江路 5 9 5 号(south of Nánjīng Dōng Lù, west of Húběi Lù); see map p. 136. ☏ **800/820-2525** or 021/3313-4888. Fax 021/3313-4880. www.howardjohnsonplazahotel.cn. 360 units. ¥2,075 standard; ¥2,325 executive level (club room); from ¥2,820 suite (40%–50% discounts). AE, DC, MC, V. Metro: People's Square or Nanjing Rd. (E). **Amenities:** 2 restaurants, lounge, bar; babysitting; concierge; executive-level rooms; health club and spa w/Jacuzzi and sauna; indoor pool; 24-hr. room service. *In room:* A/C, TV, fridge, hair dryer, minibar, Wi-Fi.

**Radisson Hotel Shànghǎi New World (Shànghǎi Xīn Shìjiè Lìshēng Dàjiǔdiàn)** 上海新世界丽笙大酒店    Opened in 2005, Shànghǎi's second Radisson hotel is a five-star outfit, but its service falls a little short of the service at top hotels in this category, such as the Westin and the JW Marriott. What it does have is one of the best hotel locations in town, right next to the Nánjīng Lù Pedestrian Mall and directly across from People's Square. Most of the guest rooms, located in a 47-story City Tower capped by a flying saucer, are furnished in a contemporary style, and are perfectly comfortable and well appointed with all the usual five-star amenities, including free broadband Internet access. The staff tries hard to please.

Nánjīng Xī Lù 88 南京西路 8 8 号 (west of Xīzàng Zhōng Lù); see map p. 136. ☏ **800/333-3333** or 021/6359-9999. Fax 021/6358-9705. www.radisson.com/shanghaicn_newworld. 520 units. ¥2,300 standard; ¥2,700 club room; from ¥3,500 suite (30% discounts). AE, DC, MC, V. Metro: People's Square. **Amenities:** 3 restaurants, lounge, bar; babysitting; concierge; health club w/sauna; indoor pool; 24-hr. room service. *In room:* A/C, TV, fridge, hair dryer, minibar, free Wi-Fi.

**Renaissance Shànghǎi Yùyuán Hotel (Shànghǎi Yùyuán Wànlì Jiǔdiàn)**
上海豫园万丽酒店 ★  Located a 3-minute walk from Yù Garden and its surrounding shops, a 5-minute walk from the Bund, and a quick taxi ride from the French Concession, this is the first top-caliber modern hotel to open in the old Chinese city. The signature Renaissance whimsy is apparent in the funky blue and green color-themed rooms, which are plush and come with all the expected five-star amenities. East-facing rooms have the best views of Yù Garden and Pǔdōng. The staff is helpful and friendly. With the nearby Metro Line 10 and the Rénmín Lù tunnel to Pǔdōng now in operation, this hotel is well situated for tourists.

Hénán Nán Lù 159 河南南路159号 (at Fúyòu Lù, just west of Yù Garden); see map p. 156. ✆ **021/2321-8888.** Fax 021/5350-3658. www.renaissancehotels.com/shasy. 340 units. ¥2,000 standard; ¥2,400–¥2,550 executive level; from ¥3,200 suite (40%–50% discounts). AE, DC, MC, V. Metro: Yu Yuan (Yu Garden). **Amenities:** 2 restaurants, bar; babysitting; concierge; executive-level rooms; 24-hr. health club w/Jacuzzi and sauna; indoor pool; room service; spa. *In room:* A/C, TV, fridge, hair dryer, minibar, Wi-Fi (¥120 per day).

**Sofitel Hyland Hotel (Hǎilún Bīnguǎn)** 海伦宾馆 ★  This handsome, contemporary, Accor-managed four-star tower in the heart of the pedestrian sector of Nánjīng Lù has a superb downtown location. Recently refurbished rooms are comfortable with all the modern amenities associated with this luxury brand. Sofitel Club rooms are slightly larger and include a Western buffet breakfast. There's a European vibe to the hotel. Service is efficient, if a bit brusque at times.

Nánjīng Dōng Lù 505 南京东路 505号 (on Nánjīng Lù Pedestrian Mall); see map p. 136. ✆ **800/221-4542** or 021/6351-5888. Fax 021/6351-4088. www.sofitel.com/asia. 401 units. ¥1,870 standard; ¥2,788 executive level; from ¥2,550 suite (30%–40% discounts). AE, DC, MC, V. Metro: Nanjing Rd. (E). **Amenities:** 2 restaurants, bar; babysitting; concierge; executive-level rooms; health club w/sauna; room service. *In room:* A/C, TV, fridge, hair dryer, minibar, Wi-Fi (¥120 per day).

**The Waterhouse at South Bund (Shuǐshè Jiǔdiàn)** 水舍酒店  If post-industrial chic is your preferred style, consider staying at this newly opened boutique hotel lodged inside a 1930s warehouse near the Shíliùpǔ Wharf. With exposed brick, broken plaster walls, and splotchy concrete stairwells, it's hard not to feel like you're staying in a bomb shelter at times, albeit one that's a member of Design Hotels. But this bunker also has shiny wooden floors, glass windows, and lots of modern furniture and amenities to make up for any dystopian tendencies. No two rooms are alike here (some are noisier than others, some have showers only, so be sure to request a room with a bath if that matters to you), but all rates include breakfast, unlimited local phone calls, and complimentary nonalcoholic beverages from the minibar. The hotel is also home to the restaurant **Table No. 1,** opened and run by several former chefs at London's Maze restaurants. A rooftop cocktail bar has stunning views of the Huángpǔ River and Pǔdōng. The hotel was in its soft opening at press time, but the staff was friendly and helpful.

Máojiāyuán Lù 1-3 毛家园路1–3号 (north of Cool Docks, Zhōngshān Nán Lù 479); see map p. 156. ✆ **021/6080-2988.** Fax 021/6080-2999. www.waterhouseshanghai.com. 19 units. ¥1,600–¥1,900 standard; from ¥2,900 suite (30%–40% discounts). AE, DC, MC, V. No Metro. **Amenities:** Restaurant, lounge, bar; concierge; health club; room service. *In room:* A/C, satellite TV/DVD, CD player, fridge, hair dryer, minibar, MP3 docking station, free Wi-Fi.

**5**

## CHINESE business MOTELS

It may sound a bit dodgy, but for many Chinese business travelers to Shànghǎi, the no-frills business chain motels (such as the Jǐnjiāng Inn, Super Motel, and Green Tree Inn chains) that have sprouted up around town have become a popular lodging option. Usually housed in dull, unremarkable buildings, these motels have basic, but relatively new and clean rooms (some even with very modern decor) with air-conditioning, hot water, television, telephone, and even broadband Internet for the business or professional traveler who would prefer to stay away from the backpacking hostel scene. There is usually a restaurant on the premises that serves *jiā cháng cài* (homestyle Chinese cooking), as well as a business center that can handle airplane and train bookings. Not much English is spoken at these places, so it may be more suitable for foreigners who already have some grasp of Chinese. Still, if you're bemoaning the lack of decent but affordable lodgings in town, here are three of the better-located choices. **Jǐnjiāng Star (Jǐnjiāng Zhīxīng),** located downtown in Huángpǔ District at Fújiàn Nán Lù 33 (℃ 021/6326-0505; www.jj-inn.com), has basic in-suite standard rooms for ¥349; **Green Tree Inn (Gélín Háotài)** at Yán'ān Zhōng Lù 1111, just west of Fùmín Lù (℃ 021/3617-4888; www.998.com), has standard rooms starting at ¥399; while **Super Motel 168 (Mótài Yán'ān Xī Lù Diàn),** located in western Shànghǎi at Yán'ān Xī Lù 1119 (℃ 021/5117-7777; www.motel168.com), across from the Longemont Shànghǎi (p. 101), has standard rooms starting at ¥298.

## Moderate

**Park Hotel (Guójì Fàndiàn)** 国际饭店 One of the swankiest hotels in old Shànghǎi, the historic Park Hotel was the tallest building in Asia when it opened in 1934 at the north end of what was then Shànghǎi's race course (today's People's Square/Rénmín Guǎngchǎng). A pale version of yesteryear's glory, today's hotel nevertheless retains some of its past elegance in a nicely restored Art Deco lobby. For a four-star hotel, rooms are unexciting but functional, and the marble bathrooms are compact but clean. Ask for a room with a view of Nánjīng Lù (south). Service is adequate.

Nánjīng Xī Lù 170 南京西路 1 7 0 号 (north of People's Park, west of Xīzàng Lù); see map p. 136. ℃ 021/6327-5225. Fax 021/6327-6958. www.parkhotel.com.cn or http://park.jinjianghotels.com. 252 units. ¥1,245–¥1,500 standard; ¥1,700 executive level; from ¥2,100 suite (40% discounts). AE, DC, MC, V. Metro: People's Square. **Amenities:** 2 restaurants, bar; babysitting; concierge; executive-level rooms; health club; 24-hr. room service. *In room:* A/C, TV, fridge, hair dryer, Internet, minibar.

## Inexpensive

**Captain Hostel (Chuánzhǎng Qīngnián Jiǔdiàn)** 船长青年酒店 This maritime-themed hostel, lodged in a 1920s Art Deco–style building, is one of the most popular budget options in town. Among its recommendations, a superb location just off the Bund, clean "sailor bunk" dorms, comfortable if no-frills standards with in-suite bathrooms, and a rooftop bar offering views of the Huángpǔ River and Pǔdōng to rival those at the considerably more expensive bars and restaurants on the Bund, but with cold beer at half the price. All the usual hostel facilities, including a small Internet cafe, are also available.

Fúzhōu Lù 37 福州路37号 (just west of the Bund); see map p. 136. ℂ **021/6323-5053.** Fax 021/6321-9331. www.captainhostel.com.cn. 21 units. ¥500–¥600 standard (30% discounts); ¥90 dorm beds. AE, DC, MC, V. Metro: Nanjing Rd. (E). **Amenities:** Restaurant, bar; concierge; Internet. *In room:* A/C, TV (in some).

**East Asia Hotel (Dōngyà Fàndiàn)** 东亚饭店 ✦ If you don't mind the lack of frills and services, staying right in the thick of the Nánjīng Lù Pedestrian Mall doesn't come any cheaper than this. Located in the neoclassical former Shànghǎi Sincere Department Store, this hotel features rooms and furnishings that are a bit drab and subject to the usual wear and tear, but are still adequate for a few nights' stay for those on a budget. Guests are mostly Chinese, but bilingual signage and the staff's tenuous grasp of some English terms make this a manageable option for the foreigner. The deluxe rooms facing Nánjīng Lù are worth spending an extra ¥40.

Nánjīng Dōng Lù 680 南京东路 6 8 0 号 (just west of Zhèjiāng Zhōng Lù); see map p. 136. ℂ **021/6322-3223.** Fax 021/6322-4598. 164 units. ¥400–¥520 standard; from ¥660 suite (30% discounts). AE, DC, MC, V. Metro: People's Square. **Amenities:** Restaurant, bar/lounge; concierge; room service. *In room:* A/C, TV, hair dryer.

# HÓNGKǑU (NORTHEAST SHÀNGHǍI)

## Very Expensive

**Hyatt on the Bund (Shànghǎi Wàitān Màoyuè Dàjiǔdiàn)** 上海外滩茂悦大酒店 ★★The second Grand Hyatt to open in Shànghǎi, this handsome contemporary hotel boasts a northern Bund address, but is actually situated on the western bank of the Huángpǔ River in Hóngkǒu, and is about a 10-minute walk from the Bund. All luxuriously appointed rooms have flatscreen LCD TVs, DVD players, and iPod docking stations. Floor-to-ceiling windows allow breathtaking views of either the Bund or Pǔdōng, while suites give you the best of both worlds. Staff is exceedingly friendly and helpful and the hotel's restaurants consistently provide quality dining. As Hóngkǒu district and the western shore of the Huángpǔ River continue to develop, look for this hotel to be much in demand for its river location. For now, travelers can benefit from highly competitive room rates.

Huángpǔ Lù 199 黄浦路199号 (north of the Bund, on the northeast side of Sūzhōu Creek); see map p. 136. ℂ **021/6393-1234.** Fax 021/6393-1313. www.shanghai.bund.hyatt.com. 631 units. ¥3,000–¥3,200 standard; ¥3,500 executive level; from ¥5,000 suite (up to 50% discount pending occupancy). AE, DC, MC, V. Metro: Nanjing Rd. (E) (about 1 mile away). **Amenities:** 4 restaurants, bar; babysitting; concierge; executive-level rooms; health club w/Jacuzzi and sauna; indoor pool; 24-hr. room service; spa. *In room:* A/C, TV/DVD, CD player, fridge, hair dryer, minibar, MP3 docking station, Wi-Fi (¥120 per day).

## Expensive

**Broadway Mansions Hotel (Shànghǎi Dàshà)** 上海大厦 The Art Deco Broadway Mansions just north of the Bund was originally built in 1934 as an exclusive residential hotel by the British. It was sold to the Japanese in 1937, but later housed the Foreign Correspondents' Club of China after World War II. These days, the exterior could use a touch-up, but the interiors have been transformed into a modern hotel offering spacious rooms with high ceilings, firm beds, overhead bedside reading lights, and all the expected amenities. The rooms facing Sūzhōu Creek are absolutely worth the extra cost, as there are few other places where you can wake up to the creek, the Bund, *and* Pǔdōng outside your window. Service is adequate.

Běi Sūzhōu Lù 20 北苏州路２０号 (north of the Bund across the Sūzhōu River, just west of the Wàibáidù Bridge); see map p. 136. ⓒ **021/6324-6260.** Fax 021/6324-1565. www.broadwaymansions. com/en/index.htm. 253 units. ¥2,200–¥2,500 standard; ¥3,800 suite (up to 50% discounts in low season). AE, DC, MC, V. Metro: Nanjing Rd. (E) (about 1 mile away). **Amenities:** 3 restaurants, bar; concierge; executive-level rooms; health club and spa; 24-hr. room service. *In room:* A/C, TV, fridge, hair dryer, Internet (¥80 per day), minibar.

## Moderate

**Astor House Hotel (Pǔjiāng Fàndiàn)** 浦江饭店　Built in 1860 and reconstructed in late Renaissance style on its present site in 1910, this hotel north of the Bund is China's oldest, and the first place to use telephones and electric lights in the country. More recently, this cheap backpackers' favorite in the last decade has upgraded into a somewhat pricey, three-star outfit with executive-level rooms. Refurbished standard rooms have firm and comfortable beds, and bathrooms are large and clean. Visitors can also choose from four restored "celebrity rooms," once occupied by famous visitors such as U.S. President Ulysses S. Grant in 1879 (no. 410), Scott Joplin in 1931 and 1936 (no. 404), Bertrand Russell in 1920 (no. 310), and Albert Einstein in 1922 (no. 304). Service is adequate at best.

Huángpǔ Lù 15 黄浦路１５号 (northeast side of Sūzhōu Creek, north of the Bund); see map p. 136. ⓒ **021/6324-6388.** Fax 021/6324-3179. www.pujianghotel.com. 116 units. ¥1,280 standard; ¥1,680 celebrity room and executive level (20%–40% discounts). AE, DC, MC, V. Metro: Nanjing Rd. (E) (about 1 mile away). **Amenities:** 2 restaurants, bar; concierge; executive-level rooms; 24-hr. room service. *In room:* A/C, TV, hair dryer, Internet (¥60 per day), minibar (in some).

# LÚWĀN (FRENCH CONCESSION)
## Very Expensive

**88 Xīntiāndì Hotel** 88 新天地酒店 ★　Part of the trendy Xīntiāndì dining and entertainment complex in the heart of the French Concession, this small, luxury boutique hotel in the toniest of surroundings screams urban chic. All rooms here are plush residences, tastefully decorated with a combination of modern amenities, Chinese furnishings, and large, comfortable beds. Other welcome perks include a fax machine, free broadband connection, and kitchen facilities. Lake views are pleasant and worth the extra ¥200, and service is fine, though not particularly memorable.

Huángpí Nán Lù 380 黄陂南路３８０号 (south block of Xīntiāndì); see map p. 140. ⓒ **021/5383-8833.** Fax 021/5383-8877. www.88xintiandi.com. 53 units. ¥3,300–¥3,500 standard; from ¥3,800 suite (30%–40% discounts). AE, DC, MC, V. Metro: Huangpi Rd. (S). **Amenities:** Restaurant; concierge; health club w/Jacuzzi and sauna; indoor swimming pool; room service. *In room:* A/C, TV, fridge, hair dryer, minibar, free Wi-Fi.

**Jīn Jiāng Hotel (Jīn Jiāng Fàndiàn)** 锦江饭店　The Jīn Jiāng Hotel opened its doors in 1929 as the Cathay Mansions, but is best remembered as the location for the signing of the Shànghǎi Communiqué by President Nixon and Zhōu Ēnlái in 1972, reestablishing U.S.–China relations. Today's complex includes: the 1929 North Building (Běilóu or the Cathay Building), remodeled as a five-star hotel; the central Grosvenor House (1931), with its facade an imitation of the Barclay-Vesey Building in New York City, redone as a five-star all-suite deluxe hotel; and the old South Building, most recently renovated in 2005 into another five-star outfit (Cathay Garden). The Grosvenor House contains a presidential suite with Chairman Máo's desk and easy chair (with a concealed compartment on the right side for a pistol). The Art Deco rooms in the North Building were renovated in 2009 and have high ceilings and modern furnishings. Service, still lagging behind the international chains, is adequate though hardly exemplary. Staff still struggles occasionally with English.

Màomíng Nán Lù 59 茂名南路 5 9 号 (1 block north of Huáihǎi Zhōng Lù); see map p. 140. ☎ **021/3218-9988.** Fax 021/6472-5588. http://jj.jinjianghotels.com. 442 units. ¥3,300 standard (North Building); ¥3,300 executive level (South Building); from ¥4,200 suite (30% discounts). AE, DC, MC, V. Metro: Shanxi Rd. (S). **Amenities:** 4 restaurants, lounge; babysitting; concierge; executive-level rooms; health club w/sauna; indoor pool; 24-hr. room service. *In room:* A/C, TV/DVD, fridge, hair dryer, Internet (¥2 per min., ¥90 per day), minibar.

**Okura Garden Hotel Shànghǎi (Huāyuán Fàndiàn)** 花园饭店 ★  Once the top hotel in the French Concession, the five-star Japanese-managed Okura was built in 1990 on the site of the 1920s French Club and Cercle Sportif. The fine Art Deco features of the original structure have been preserved in its east lobby and grand ballroom with its gorgeous elliptical stained-glass ceiling. As well, the sprawling lawns with the gazebo were once the strolling grounds for Máo Zédōng. Recently renovated rooms are of average size, with marble bathrooms that contain automated bidets. The Okura lacks the latest high-tech in-room gadgets of newer hotels, and it rather ungenerously charges guests staying in standard rooms a small fee to use the pool and health club (free for executive-level rooms), but the friendly and highly efficient staff does their best to make your stay as pleasant as possible.

Màomíng Nán Lù 58 茂名南路 5 8 号 (1 block north of Huáihǎi Zhōng Lù); see map p. 140. ☎ **021/6415-1111.** Fax 021/6415-8866. www.gardenhotelshanghai.com. 492 units. ¥2,100–¥2,500 standard; ¥3,400–¥3,800 executive level; from ¥4,500 suite (40% discounts). AE, DC, MC, V. Metro: Shanxi Rd. (S). **Amenities:** 5 restaurants, 3 bars; babysitting; concierge; executive-level rooms; health club w/ Jacuzzi and sauna; indoor pool; 24-hr. room service; 2 lighted outdoor tennis courts. *In room:* A/C, TV, fridge, hair dryer, Internet (¥2 per min., ¥120 per day), minibar.

**Pullman Shànghǎi Skyway Hotel (Shànghǎi Sīgéwēi Pōěrmàn Dàjiǔdiàn)** 上海斯格威铂尔曼大酒店  This eye-catching, 52-story, thoroughly modern hotel dominates the skyline in the southern tip of the French Concession. Guests on upper floors are treated to dramatic city views, with south-facing rooms affording some of the most direct views of the former Expo grounds. Rooms are comfortable and well-appointed, and the hotel's facilities are still relatively new and shiny, but for an Accor-managed hotel, service is a bit brusque and uneven. Being mere steps away from the hip dining and shopping complex Tiānzǐfáng, however, is a treat.

Dàpǔ Lù 15 打浦路15号 (south of Nánchāng Lù); see map p. 140. ☎ **021/3318-9988.** Fax 021/5301-0000. www.pullmanhotels.com. 645 units. ¥3,000–¥3,600 standard; ¥4,000 executive level; from ¥10,800 suite (30% discounts). AE, DC, MC, V. Metro: Dapuqiao. **Amenities:** 4 restaurants, 3 bars; babysitting; concierge; executive-level rooms; health club w/Jacuzzi and sauna; indoor pool; 24-hr. room service. *In room:* A/C, TV, fridge, hair dryer, minibar, Wi-Fi (¥ 100 per day).

# Expensive

**Pudi Boutique Hotel (Pǔdī Jīngpǐn Jiǔdiàn)** 璞邸精品酒店 ★ 🔥  One of the earlier arrivals (2007) on the boutique hotel scene, the Pudi, well situated in the heart of the French Concession, goes all out to spoil its guests silly. Upon arrival in the dark lobby with its colorful fish tanks, you're whisked up to your very large room for a private check-in, after which you have your choice of pillows (goose down, perhaps?) and five different brands of amenities. Each room also has a fax, copier, and scanner, along with its own specially commissioned art, which guests can purchase. The Pudi tries to distinguish itself with funky twists like a plasma TV that swivels between the bedroom and the living area, and a bedside clock that projects the time onto the ceiling, though some guests might find the latter a little disturbing. The hotel tries hard with its butler service and its ratio of two staff for every guest. Some guests have complained of excessive noise, but the hotel's very reasonable prices are a bargain for the luxuries on offer. After being managed by Accor, the hotel has recently gone local.

Yàn dāng Lù 99 雁荡路99号 (south of Nánchāng Lù); see map p. 140. © **021/5158-5888.** Fax 021/5157-0188. www.boutiquehotel.cc. 52 units. ¥1,677 standard; ¥2,277 suite (20%–30% discounts). AE, DC, MC, V. Metro: Huangpi Rd. (S). **Amenities:** Restaurant, rooftop bar, cigar lounge; babysitting; concierge; fitness room; rooftop Jacuzzi; 24-hr. room service. *In room:* A/C, TV/DVD, fridge, hair dryer, Internet (free), minibar.

## Moderate

**City Hotel (Chéngshì Jiǔdiàn) 城市酒店**   Located right in the center of town, the four-star 26-story City Hotel is a professional outfit attracting largely business clientele. The modern guest rooms are fairly plain and simple, and superior rooms run small, but all are otherwise comfortable enough with firm beds and clean bathrooms. Service and amenities have improved considerably in the last few years, with the staff seemingly more comfortable communicating in English. With highly competitive room rates (which can be up to 50% off on online hotel booking sites), this is an attractive midrange option.

Shǎnxī Nán Lù 57 陕西南路 5 7 号 (south of Yán'ān Zhōng Lù); see map p. 140. © **021/6255-1133.** Fax 021/6255-0211. www.cityhotelshanghai.com. 270 units. ¥1,300–¥1,500 standard; ¥1,800 executive level (40% discounts); from ¥2,700 suite. AE, DC, MC, V. Metro: Shanxi Rd. (S) (5 blocks). **Amenities:** 3 restaurants, bar; concierge; executive-level rooms; fitness center w/sauna; indoor pool; 24-hr. room service. *In room:* A/C, TV, fridge, hair dryer, Internet (free), minibar.

**Ruìjīn Hotel (Ruìjīn Bīnguǎn) 瑞金宾馆**   Right in the heart of the French Concession, this 1930s colonial-style hotel is located on the well-manicured grounds of the former Morriss Estate. Owner of the *North China Daily News,* the oldest English-language newspaper in China, Morriss also bred greyhounds, which he would race at the dog track located just behind his compound. Today, a number of faux "old" houses have been added to the four original villas on this grand estate occupying a whole city block. Guest rooms, located in the largest of the original villas, are comfortable enough, with firm beds with fresh soft linens. Ask for a garden-view room. The facilities and the service may not be the finest for what you're paying, but the overall atmosphere of colonial Shànghǎi, at least the refined version of it, is lovely.

Ruìjīn Èr Lù 118 瑞金二路 1 1 8 号 (south of Fùxīng Zhōng Lù); see map p. 140. © **021/6472-5222.** Fax 021/6473-2277. www.ruijinhotelsh.com. 61 units. ¥1,320 standard; from ¥2,400 suite (30% discounts). AE, DC, MC, V. Metro: Shanxi Rd. (S). **Amenities:** Restaurant, bar; concierge; room service. *In room:* A/C, TV, fridge, hair dryer, Internet, minibar.

# XÚHUÌ (SOUTHWEST SHÀNGHĂI)
## Very Expensive

### Regal International East Asia Hotel (Fùháo Huánqiú Dōngyà Jiǔdiàn)
富豪环球东亚酒店   The internationally managed, 22-story Regal Hotel has bright, modern guest rooms that were renovated in 2008, and come with bedside electronic controls, robes, slippers, and all the amenities of a five-star establishment. There's also a dedicated ladies floor with extra amenities. The hotel's Shànghăi International Tennis Center offers some of the city's best sporting facilities, including a center court that seats 1,200 spectators. There's a 12-lane bowling alley and an indoor squash court. The hotel is located along trendy Héngshān Lù in the French Concession, the Metro is a block away, and the shopping district of Xújiāhuì is a 10-minute walk away. Service is efficient enough, but drops off when it gets busy. *Tip:* Request a room number that ends in "9"—these are significantly larger than the rest.

Héngshān Lù 516 衡山路 5 1 6 号 (west of Wúxing Lù); see map p. 140. © **800/222-8888** or 021/ 6415-5588. Fax 021/6445-8899. www.regal-eastasia.com. 330 units. ¥2,600–¥3,000 standard; ¥4,100 executive level; ¥4,900 suite (30%–40% discounts in low season, otherwise 10%–20%). AE, DC, MC, V. Metro: Hengshan Rd. **Amenities:** 3 restaurants, patisserie, bar; babysitting; concierge; executive-level rooms; large health club and spa w/Jacuzzi; large indoor pool; 11 championship tennis courts; 24-hr. room service. *In room:* A/C, TV, fridge, hair dryer, Internet, minibar.

## Expensive

### Héngshān Picardie Hotel (Héngshān Bīnguǎn) 衡山宾馆   Located just
south of the Regal International Hotel, this four-star French modern hotel, formerly the Picardie Apartments built in 1934, offers a comfortable stay at reasonable prices. Recently renovated rooms are spacious and equipped with modern furniture and full amenities. If all the standard rooms are being discounted to the same rate (as they often are), be sure to ask for the higher-end deluxe standards, as these have large bathrooms that come with a separate tub and shower and even a television set. Service has improved greatly from a few years ago. It's a short walk to the subway, shops, and restaurants just up Héngshān Lù, and only a slightly longer walk to the Xújiāhuì area to the south.

Héngshān Lù 534 衡山路 5 3 4 号 (south of Huáihăi Lù at the intersection with Wănpíng Lù); see map p. 140. © **021/6437-7050.** Fax 021/6437-2927. www.hengshanhotel.com. 240 units. ¥2,080–¥2,320 standard; ¥2,960 executive level; ¥4,000 suite (20%–40% discounts). AE, DC, MC, V. Metro: Hengshan Rd. **Amenities:** 4 restaurants, bakery, lounge; babysitting; concierge; executive-level rooms; health club; 24-hr. room service; spa; free Wi-Fi. *In room:* A/C, TV, fridge, hair dryer, Internet (free), minibar.

### Mansion Hotel (Shǒuxí Gōngguǎn Jiǔdiàn) 首席公馆酒店 ★   Located in a
French Concession villa built in 1932 for one of the partners of Shànghăi's most infamous gang boss Du Yue Sheng, this exclusive boutique hotel is as luxurious and old school as they come. The lobby, cluttered with overstuffed armchairs, traditional Chinese furnishings, old gramophones, and colonial-era bric-a-brac, immediately transports guests back to old Shànghăi. Rooms are individually decorated in a combination

of Eastern and Western motifs, but all feature comfy king-size beds, armchairs with ottomans, Bose iPod sound docks, and 42-inch flatscreen TVs, while the marble bathrooms boast separate Jacuzzi tubs and high-pressure full body showers. Rooftop dining with superb views rounds out the whole dandy experience. For all its opulence, service is inconsistent and guest reactions have ranged from ecstatic to underwhelmed.

Xīnlè Lù 82 新乐路82号 (west of Xiāngyáng Běi Lù); see map p. 140. © **021/5403-9888.** Fax 021/5403-7077. www.chinamansionhotel.com. 32 units. ¥2,050 standard; ¥4,000 suite (30%–40% discounts). AE, DC, MC, V. Metro: Shanxi Rd. (S). **Amenities:** 2 restaurants, lounge; babysitting; concierge; 24-hr. room service. *In room:* A/C, TV, CD player, fax, fridge, hair dryer, minibar, MP3 docking station, free Wi-Fi.

**Tàiyuán Villa (Tàiyuán Biéshù)** 太原别墅 ★ 🎁    Run by the same folks at the Ruìjīn Hotel (p. 94), this villa is a more peaceful and possibly nicer option than the Ruìjīn. Also known as the Marshall House for American general George Marshall who stayed here between 1945 and 1949 when he was mediating between Máo Zédōng and Chiang Kai-shek, this magnificent mansion, originally built in 1920, was one of many homes of Jiāng Qīng (also known as Mme. Máo) between 1949 and 1976. Today this storied villa has dark wood paneling, a grand circular stairwell, and  large, comfortable rooms (now carpeted and adorned with classical furniture and comfortable beds). Villa guests can use the pool and business center in the new, modern annex that usually caters only to long-term guests. The grounds are some of the quietest you'll find in central Shànghǎi.

Tàiyuán Lù 160 太原路 1 6 0 号 (south of Yǒngjiā Lù, east of Yuèyáng Lù); see map p. 140. © **021/6471-6688.** Fax 021/6471-2618. www.ruijinhotelsh.com. 13 units. ¥2,000 standard; ¥5,000 master suite (30%–50% discounts). AE, DC, MC, V. Metro: Hengshan Rd. **Amenities:** Restaurant; concierge; fitness center; indoor pool; room service. *In room:* A/C, TV, fridge, hair dryer.

## Moderate

### Courtyard Shànghǎi Xújiāhuì (Shànghǎi Xīzàng Dàshà Wànyí Jiǔdiàn)
上海西藏大厦万怡酒店    Housed in a tall tower capped by a Tibetan-style temple, the Courtyard, newly opened in early 2009, is a thoroughly modern, four-star hotel that offers a comfortable stay at very reasonable prices. Rooms are spacious and furnished with modern furniture, LCD televisions, and all the standard amenities. Though the hotel caters mostly to business travelers, its convenient location next to the Xújiāhuì shopping area and subway station makes it an appealing option for tourists as well.

Hóngqiáo Lù 100 虹桥路 100 号 (west of Cáo Xī Běi Lù); see map p. 140. © **021/6129-2888.** Fax 021/6129-2999. 364 units. ¥1,000 standard; ¥1,550 executive-level; from ¥2,000 suite (30%–40% discounts). AE, DC, MC, V. Metro: Xújiāhuì. **Amenities:** Restaurant, deli; babysitting; concierge; executive-level rooms; health club w/Jacuzzi and sauna; indoor pool; 24-hr. room service. *In room:* A/C, TV, fridge, hair dryer, minibar, Wi-Fi (¥60 per hr., ¥120 per day).

## Inexpensive

### Magnolia Bed & Breakfast    Conveniently located near the lively cafes and restaurants around Dōnghú Lù, this bed-and-breakfast in a quaint three-story French Concession house is a great choice for those looking for a more local stay. The rooms (two per floor) run a little small, but are clean with wooden floors, comfortable beds, high-pressure showers, and original art work by local artists. The Ink and Water suite on the top floor is more spacious, and also has a bathtub and small balcony. You are

near the street so you will see and hear the sights and sounds of daily life. Those who are sensitive to noise may want to pack earplugs. The community room on the ground floor (where breakfast is served) has a Nespresso coffee machine, a computer, and books and information on local sights. Co-owner Miranda Yao and her staff are very friendly and helpful, and do their best to ensure a most pleasant stay.

Yánqìng Lù 36 延庆路36号 (south of Dōnghú Lù).; see map p. 140. ☎ **1381-794-0848.** www.magnolia bnbshanghai.com. 5 units. ¥650–¥1,200 standard. DC, MC, V. Metro: Changshu Rd. **Amenities:** Concierge. *In room:* A/C, TV, fridge, hair dryer, free Wi-Fi.

# JÌNG ĀN (NORTHWEST SHÀNGHǍI)

## Very Expensive

### Four Seasons Hotel Shànghǎi (Shànghǎi Sìjì Jiǔdiàn) 上海四季酒店 ★★★

Well located in the thick of Pǔxī (Nánjīng Lù is a 5-min. walk and the Shànghǎi Museum a 10-min. stroll), the modern 37-story Four Seasons offers top-quality pampering. Each guest room is lavishly furnished with classical furniture, three telephones, thick robes, and DVD/CD players. The patented Four Seasons bed alone is worth the stay. Marble bathrooms have a separate shower and tub. Best of all, this hotel delivers impeccable service, from its 24-hour butler service for each guest to the highly efficient, friendly but discreet, multilingual staff throughout the hotel.

Wēihǎi Lù 500 威海路500号 (at Shímén Yī Lù, btw. Nánjīng Xī Lù and Yán'ān Zhōng Lù); see map p. 144. ☎ 800/819-5053 or 021/6256-8888. Fax 021/6256-5678. www.fourseasons.com. 422 units. ¥3,600–¥4,100 standard; from ¥5,400 suite; ¥500–¥700 extra for executive lounge benefits (up to 40% discount pending occupancy). AE, DC, MC, V. Metro: Nanjing Rd. (W). **Amenities:** 4 restaurants, lounge; free airport transfers; babysitting; children's programs; concierge; executive-level rooms; state-of-the-art health club and spa w/Jacuzzi and sauna; indoor pool; 24-hr. room service. *In room:* A/C, TV/DVD, movie library, CD player, fridge, hair dryer, minibar, MP3 docking station, Wi-Fi (¥120 per day).

### Hilton Hotel (Jìng Ān Xīěrdùn Dàjiǔdiàn) 静安希尔顿大酒店

Shànghǎi's first foreign-owned hotel (1987), the comparatively low-profile 43-story Hilton still rates among the city's top hotels, even as it's been eclipsed in recent years by an increasing number of ever-more-opulent luxury outfits. Renovated guest rooms are spacious and bright with firm beds and classic furniture, flatscreen televisions, bedside controlled lighting, and broadband connection. Besides a slew of fine international restaurants, the hotel also boasts the Spa at the Hilton (with reflexology, seaweed treatments, acupuncture, and more), which has few rivals. Above all, however, it's the hotel's top-notch service and highly competent staff that make it a favorite of Western business travelers. Its prime location—within walking distance of the attractions of Héngshān Lù and the French Concession—doesn't hurt either.

Huáshān Lù 250 华山路２５０号 (1 block south of Yán'ān Zhōng Lù); see map p. 144. ☎ 800/445-8667 or 021/6248-0000. Fax 021/6248-3848. www.hilton.com. 741 units. ¥2,330 standard; ¥2,880 executive level; from ¥4,180 suite (up to 50% discount pending occupancy). AE, DC, MC, V. Metro: Jing'an Temple. **Amenities:** 5 restaurants, lounge, 2 bars; babysitting; children's programs; concierge; executive-level rooms; state-of-the-art health club and spa w/Jacuzzi and sauna; indoor pool; 24-hr. room service; outdoor tennis court. *In room:* A/C, TV, fridge, hair dryer, Internet (¥120 per day), minibar, Wi-Fi (rooms on 26th floor and up, ¥160 per day).

**Portman Ritz-Carlton Hotel (Shànghǎi Bōtèmàn Lìjiā Dàjiǔdiàn)** 上海波特曼丽嘉大酒店 ★★★　Despite some heavy competition, the 50-story Portman, having just undergone a $40-million renovation, is still tenaciously guarding its position as Shànghǎi's top choice hotel for many business travelers and world leaders. Offering all the luxury and service associated with the Ritz-Carlton brand, the Portman exudes every elegance, from the two-story lobby, with its fiber-optic lighting, laminated stacked-glass sculptures, and marble and limestone walls, to rooms that are plush and well fitted with LCD televisions with DVD players, thick duvets, three phones, and all the amenities you could want. Service is as you'd expect—professional and excellent. The adjacent Shànghǎi Centre provides one-stop shopping with airline offices, a medical clinic, a supermarket, automatic teller machines, a performing arts theater, upscale boutiques, and a little-known cafe called Starbucks.

Nánjīng Xī Lù 1376 南京西路１３７６号 (Shànghǎi Centre); see map p. 144. ☏ **800/241-3333** or 021/6279-8888. Fax 021/6279-8800. www.ritzcarlton.com. 610 units. ¥4,200 standard; ¥4,800 executive level; from ¥5,200 suite (up to 50% discount pending occupancy). AE, DC, MC, V. Metro: Jing'an Temple. **Amenities:** 4 restaurants, 2 lounges; babysitting; concierge; executive-level rooms; health club and spa w/Jacuzzi and sauna; indoor pool; 24-hr. room service; indoor tennis court; spa. *In room:* A/C, TV, CD player, fridge, hair dryer, minibar, Wi-Fi (¥120 per day).

**The PuLi Hotel and Spa (Pǔlí Jiǔdiàn)** 璞麗酒店 ★★★　Described as an "urban resort," the PuLi Hotel and Spa is all that and more. Though it's located right in the center of town next to the Yán'ān Lù Elevated Highway, you won't find a more comfortable quiet oasis in the middle of Shànghǎi's concrete jungle. Blessedly set off from the road by a grove of bamboo, the hotel also adjoins the back of Jīng'ān Park. Decor throughout is classy and understated: Sleek modern furniture is complemented by Chinese flourishes like dragon screens, *shíkùmén* brick, and imperial black inkstone surfaces. The luxuriously appointed rooms are also fitted with low heat-emission glass windows and automated sunshades to help conserve energy, even as you avail yourself of the plush chaise longue, swiveling flatscreen TV, and free beverages from the minibar. The hotel serves an excellent breakfast, which you can have in the restaurant, in the Long Bar, in your room, or on-the-go. To top it off, service is first-rate: The staff does a very thorough job following up on guest requests. With the pampering Anantara Spa and the innovative **Jing'an Restaurant** (p. 125) on the premises, you may not want to leave this oasis.

Chángdé Lù 1 常德路1号 (at Yán'ān Lù); see map p. 144. ☏ **021/2216-6973.** Fax 021/3251-8977. www.thepuli.com. 229 units. ¥3,380–¥3,580 standard; from ¥3,980 club level; from ¥7,080 suite (30%–40% discounts). AE, DC, MC, V. Metro: Jing'an Temple. **Amenities:** 2 restaurants, lounge, bar; babysitting; concierge; health club and spa w/Jacuzzi and sauna; indoor pool; 24-hr. room service; spa. *In room:* A/C, TV/DVD, movie library, CD player, fridge, hair dryer, minibar, MP3 docking station, free Wi-Fi.

***Swissotel Grand Shànghǎi (Shànghǎi Hóng'ān Ruìshì Dàjiǔdiàn)*** 上海宏安瑞士大酒店　Not the flashiest hotel in town, this solid Swiss brand nevertheless delivers a perfectly comfortable stay with all the usual luxurious amenities and helpful, friendly service. For those with a sweet tooth, a Swiss gourmet bakery proffers a decadent selection of chocolate treats. Further recommending this hotel is its highly convenient location right atop the Jìng Ān Temple subway station and right next to the City Air Terminal Building, which is the terminus for the Pǔdōng and Hóngqiáo airport shuttles. And for trivia lovers, the six-story apartment building in front of the hotel was once home to the Shànghǎi writer Eileen Chang (Zhāng Àilíng; she lived on the fifth floor), who wrote the original story on which the 2007 movie *Lust, Caution* is based.

Yùyuán Lù 1 愚园路1号 (at Chángdé Lù); see map p. 144. ☎ **021/5355-9898.** Fax 021/6288-9638. www.shanghai.swissotel.com. 467 units. ¥3,240 double; ¥4,140 executive level; from ¥4,940 suite (40%–50% discounts). AE, DC, MC, V. Metro: Jing'an Temple. **Amenities:** 2 restaurants, lounge; babysitting; concierge; executive-level rooms; health club and spa w/Jacuzzi and sauna; indoor pool with children's paddling pool; room service. *In room:* A/C, TV, fridge, hair dryer, minibar, Wi-Fi (¥120 per day, free in executive-level rooms and suites).

## Expensive

**Hotel Equatorial (Guójì Guìdū Dàjiǔdiàn)** 国际贵都大酒店　This four-star hotel, located just north of the Hilton, has resuscitated its reputation from the late 1990s when it was perceived as a somewhat sordid hotel where solicitations were commonplace. International management of the 27-story tower, provided by a Singapore group, now seems determined to maintain a squeaky-clean image and has improved the overall quality of stay quite a bit. Recently renovated guest rooms are bright and airy, with just enough room for a work desk, coffee table, and two chairs. Fitness facilities are extensive. The generally helpful staff speaks fairly good English. With discounts averaging 50%, this is an attractively priced, perfectly comfortable option if the Hilton next door proves too dear.

Yán'ān Xī Lù 65 延安西路 6 5 号 (south of Jing Ān Gōngyuán); see map p. 144. ☎ **021/6248-1688.** Fax 021/6248-1773. www.equatorial.com. 507 units. ¥1,865–¥2,025 standard; ¥2,835 executive level; from ¥3,645 suite (up to 60% discounts pending occupancy). AE, DC, MC, V. Metro: Jing'an Temple. **Amenities:** 5 restaurants, deli, lounge; babysitting; concierge; executive-level rooms; health club w/Jacuzzi and sauna; large indoor pool; 24-hr. room service; lighted outdoor tennis court. *In room:* A/C, TV, fridge, hair dryer, Internet (¥ 120 per day), minibar.

**JIA Shànghǎi** 上海家合酒店　★★　Lodged in a refurbished 1926 neoclassical building on Nánjīng Lù, the chic boutique hotel JIA (Mandarin for "home") wants to be your home away from home. Brought to you by the owner of the Philippe Starck–designed JIA Hong Kong, JIA Shànghǎi has maintained the building's original facade and structure, but has gussied up the interiors with some highly eclectic, modern design. While the interiors and bespoke furniture may not be to everyone's taste, the large, comfortable rooms, with fully equipped kitchenettes, microwaves, board games, and iPod docking stations that pipe your tunes to the room's stereo speakers, should make most people feel quite at home. Additional perks include free breakfasts and free local calls. Though the hotel attracts a trendy set, the vibe here is refreshingly informal.

Nánjīng Xī Lù 931 南京西路931号 (at Tàixìng Lù); see map p. 144. ☎ **021/6217-9000.** Fax 021/6287-9001. www.jiashanghai.com. 55 units. ¥2,000–¥2,600 standard; from ¥4,000 suite (30%–40% discounts). AE, DC, MC, V. Metro: Nanjing Rd. (W). **Amenities:** Restaurant, lounge, bar; babysitting; concierge; 24-hr. room service. *In room:* A/C, TV/DVD, CD player, fridge, hair dryer, minibar, MP3 docking station, free Wi-Fi.

**Shànghǎi Hotel (Shànghǎi Bīnguǎn)** 上海宾馆　This four-star 23-story tower under local management caters mostly to Chinese guests, but the staff can handle non-Chinese guests as well. Guest rooms are fully modernized, with all the usual amenities, a work desk, and room for two chairs and a coffee table. If you want to be near the French Concession with convenient access to the trendy cafes of Héngshān Lù, but the prices at the adjacent Hilton and Equatorial hotels are too steep, the Shànghǎi will work. Though rack rates here are marked high, in reality the hotel gives up to 60% discounts and more to remain competitive.

Wūlǔmùqí Běi Lù 505 乌鲁木齐北路５０５号 (west of the Hilton, south of Yán'ān Zhōng Lù); see map p. 144. ☏ **021/6248-0088.** Fax 021/6248-1056. www.shanghai.jinjianghotels.com. 527 units. ¥1,588–¥1,988 standard; from ¥3,188 suite (up to 60% discounts). AE, DC, MC, V. Metro: Jing'an Temple. **Amenities:** 3 restaurants; concierge; small health club w/Jacuzzi and sauna; 24-hr. room service. *In room:* A/C, TV, fridge, hair dryer, Internet (¥ 90 per day), minibar.

**URBN Hotel (Yǎyuè Jiǔdiàn)** 雅悦酒店    Open in late 2007, this factory warehouse–turned–boutique hotel with a Zen garden–style courtyard prides itself on being the first carbon-neutral hotel in Shànghǎi: The hotel's furnishings and materials are locally sourced or recycled, and the hotel will pay for carbon offsets, which may explain the more expensive rates charged here. Rooms are decorated in a simple, contemporary style, but have all the necessary amenities, including DVD players and iPod docking stations. The living spaces are designed to be multifunctional, so you may find your bed on a platform facing a sunken wraparound lounge area, which can be innovative or impractical, depending on your needs. Not all guests may be willing to accept some of the hotel's design and functional quirks (such as the use of fluorescent lightbulbs) and occasionally spotty service, but this "green" property has its heart in the right place. Guests may also use the nearby boutique One Wellness gym, billed as the first carbon-neutral gym in Shànghǎi. The hotel's **Downstairs** restaurant offers wonderful alfresco dining in the warm summer months.

Jiāozhōu Lù 183 胶州路183号 (south of Xīnzhá Lù); see map p. 144. ☏ **021/5153-4600.** Fax 021/5153-4610. www.urbnhotels.com. 26 units. ¥2,000–¥2,600 standard; ¥5,000 courtyard room; ¥8,000 penthouse (30%–50% discounts). AE, DC, MC, V. Metro: Jing'an Temple. **Amenities:** Restaurant, lounge; free airport transfers; concierge; access to nearby gym; 24-hr. room service. *In room:* A/C, TV/DVD, CD player, fridge, hair dryer, minibar, MP3 docking station, free Wi-Fi.

## Moderate

**Old House Inn (Lǎo Shí Guāng Jiǔdiàn)** 老时光酒店    One of the earliest outfits of its kind on the hotel scene, this boutique hotel in a 1930s French Concession lane house remains one the more reasonably priced. Those nostalgic for old Shànghǎi Chinese style will surely love the rooms, some a little small, but all tastefully and elegantly refurbished with classic Chinese furniture, four-poster beds with wispy mosquito netting, and gorgeous hardwood floors. Bathrooms, however, are thoroughly modern. Breakfast is included. The inn's central location puts you in the heart of the French Concession within minutes. There have, however, been complaints of insufficient heating during the winter months.

Huáshān Lù Lane 351, no. 16 华山路３５１弄１６号 (in a lane just west of Chángshú Lù); see map p. 144. ☏ **021/6248-6118.** Fax 021/6249-6869. www.oldhouse.cn. 12 units. ¥640–¥1,250 standard. AE, DC, MC, V. Metro: Jing'an Temple. **Amenities:** Restaurant, bar. *In room:* A/C, TV, hair dryer, minibar, free Wi-Fi.

**Quintet ★**    Independent travelers seeking a change from the usual hotel chains should definitely seek out this charming bed-and-breakfast inside a 1933 French Concession house that has been in the owner's family for three generations. Restored in 2008, the five rooms vary in size, and some have stairs leading to the ensuite baths. Rooms are intimate and boast a wonderful combination of old (original wood floors) and new (full amenities including DVD players and free Wi-Fi). Breakfast (from the all-day restaurant in the building, the excellent **Closed Door Café**) is included, and can even be served in bed if so desired. The B&B's location on Chánglè Lù smack in the heart of the French Concession is ideal for those who want to explore on their own. Owner Fay and her excellent staff can also help with everything from airport transportation and tour planning to arranging Chinese cooking classes and in-room massages.

Chánglè Lù 808 长乐路808号 (west of Chángshú Lù).; see map p. 144. ⓒ **021/6249-9088.** Fax 021/6249-2198. www.quintet-shanghai.com. 5 units. ¥800–¥1,100 standard. No credit cards. Metro: Changshu Rd. **Amenities:** Restaurant; concierge. *In room:* A/C, TV/DVD, CD player, fridge, hair dryer, minibar, MP3 docking station, free Wi-Fi.

# CHÁNGNÍNG/HÓNGQIÁO DEVELOPMENT ZONE (WEST SHÀNGHĂI)
## Very Expensive

**The Longemont Shànghăi (Shànghăi Lóngzhīmèng Dàjiŭdiàn)** 上海龙之梦大酒店  Bringing a dose of luxury to the western part of Shànghăi, the Longemont (formerly the Regent Shànghăi) boasts some of the largest rooms in town, with wonderful city views and all modern amenities including comfortable beds, 42-inch plasma televisions, bedside control of lights and curtains, iPod docking stations, and free broadband Internet. Bathrooms are modern and equipped with rainforest showers. The hotel also has a plethora of fine dining options, a Guerlain Spa, and Shànghăi's biggest indoor pool. Though there's not much of interest for the tourist within walking distance, the main sights are only a 10- to 15-minute taxi ride away.

Yán'ān Xī Lù 1116 延安西路１１１６号 (just east of Pānyú Lù); see map p. 152. ⓒ **021/6115-9988.** Fax 021/6115-9977. www.thelongemonthotels.com. 425 units. ¥3,700–¥3,900 standard; from ¥4,500 suite (30%–40% discounts). AE, DC, MC, V. No Metro. **Amenities:** 4 restaurants, deli, cigar bar and lounge; babysitting; concierge; health club w/Jacuzzi and sauna; indoor pool; 24-hr. room service; spa. *In room:* A/C, TV/DVD, CD player, fridge, hair dryer, Internet (free), minibar, MP3 docking station.

**Shànghăi Marriott Hotel Hóngqiáo (Shànghăi Wànháo Hóng Qiáo Dàjiŭdiàn)** 上海万豪虹桥大酒店 ★  This grand five-star Marriott is the top hotel address in the Hóngqiáo Airport neighborhood and appeals primarily to conference delegates and travelers whose business takes them to western Shànghăi. (Count Microsoft's Bill Gates as one of its previous guests.) Renovated in 2007, guest rooms are large and gracefully appointed with comfortable beds and DVD players. The zoo is a short walk away, but other attractions require a short taxi ride to town. The hotel is often sold out during weekdays, but offers substantial discounts on weekends.

Hóngqiáo Lù 2270 虹桥路２２７０号 (6.4km/4 miles east of Hóngqiáo Airport); see map p. 152. ⓒ**800/228-9290** or 021/6237-6000. Fax 021/6237-6222. www.marriott.com. 313 units. ¥2,656 standard; ¥3,320 executive level; from ¥4,150 suite (up to 50% discounts). AE, DC, MC, V. **Amenities:** 3 restaurants, deli, lounge, sports bar; babysitting; concierge; executive-level rooms; health club w/Jacuzzi and sauna; indoor pool; 24-hr. room service; outdoor tennis court. *In room:* A/C, TV/DVD, fridge, hair dryer, minibar, Wi-Fi (¥120 per day).

**Sheraton Shànghăi Hóngqiáo Hotel (Hóngqiáo Xīláidēng Shànghăi Tàipíngyáng Dà Fàndiàn)** 虹桥喜来登上海太平洋大饭店 ★  Business travelers love this 27-story, five-star Sheraton, not just for the location (halfway btw. the old Hóngqiáo Airport and downtown), but for the highly efficient service and the lush yet homey atmosphere. Rooms are a tad on the small side, but are lushly decorated with rich carpeting, overstuffed chairs, and a classical rollout desktop right

# airport HOTELS

The closest five-star hotel to the Hóngqiáo Airport is the **Marriott Hotel Hóngqiáo** (p. 101), which is still about 6.4km (4 miles) to the east. The Australian-managed 205-unit **Argyle International Airport Hotel Hóngqiáo (Huá Gǎng Yǎ Gé Jiǔ Diàn,** Kōng Gǎng Yī Lù 458; ☎ **021/ 6268-7788;** fax 021/6268-5671) is the nearest major hotel within a 5-minute ride from the airport. Modern efficient standard rooms start at around ¥ 600.

There are several hotels serving Pǔdōng Airport. The best of the lot, **Ramada Pǔdōng Airport Shànghǎi Hotel** (Shànghǎi Jīchǎng Huáměidá Dàjiǔdiàn, Qīháng Lù 1100; ☎ **021/3849-4949;** fax 021/6885-2889; www.ramada airportpd.com), is a 2- to 3-minute free shuttle ride or a 10-minute walk from

the airport. The hotel has 370 units. Rooms (¥880–¥1,080 standard) are clean and comfortable with the usual amenities, including safes and in-room movies. Both Western and Chinese dining are available. If you want to be really close to the terminal and don't mind basic accommodations, the gigantic **Motel 168** (Mótè 168 Shànghǎi Pǔdōng Jīchǎng Kōnggǎng Bīnguǎn, Yínbīn Dàdào 6001; ☎ **021/3879-9999;** fax 021/6885-2526; www.motel168.com) is located right on top of the Maglev station, just a few minutes' walk from both airport Terminals 1 and 2. The hotel has clean rooms with all the basic amenities, including free Internet, all for price levels starting around ¥398.

under Chinese artwork. Bathrooms are sleek and modern with glass sinks. The hotel can arrange tee times and transportation to the Shànghǎi International Golf and Country Club. Its deli, Bauernstube, is the best.

Zūnyì Nán Lù 5 遵义南路 5 号 (1 block north of Yán'ān Xī Lù); see map p. 152. ☎ **800/325-3535** or 021/6275-8888. Fax 021/6275-5420. www.sheraton.com/shanghai. 587 units. ¥2,550 standard; ¥3,260 executive-level; from ¥2,890 suite (40%–50% discounts). AE, DC, MC, V. **Amenities:** 4 restaurants, deli, lounge, bar; babysitting; concierge; executive-level rooms; health club w/Jacuzzi and sauna; indoor pool; 24-hr. room service; free Wi-Fi in lobby. *In room:* A/C, TV, fridge, hair dryer, Internet (¥120 per day), minibar.

## Expensive

**Crowne Plaza Shànghǎi (Shànghǎi Yínxīng Huángguān Jiǔdiàn)** 上海银星皇冠假日酒店    With the opening of a nearby subway stop, this four-star business hotel, which used to be handy only if you were in town for the Shànghǎi International Film Festival (the hotel is next to Shànghǎi Film City [Shànghǎi Yǐngchéng]), is now a fine midrange choice. A Crowne Plaza Club wing opened in mid-2008, but renovations in the last few years have improved the old facilities. Service remains friendly and attentive, and rooms are large and quite luxurious with firm, comfortable beds and modern amenities. Bathrooms run small throughout.

Pānyú Lù 400 番愚路 4 0 0 号 (north of Huáihǎi Xī Lù, off Xīnhuá Lù); see map p. 152. ☎ **800/465-4329** or 021/6145-8888. Fax 021/6280-3353. www.shanghai.crowneplaza.com. 580 units. ¥2,200 superior; ¥2,600 deluxe; ¥3,500 executive level (up to 45% seasonal discounts). AE, DC, MC, V. Metro: Jiaotong University. **Amenities:** 3 restaurants, deli, bar; babysitting; concierge; executive-level rooms; health club w/sauna; indoor pool; 24-hr. room service. *In room:* A/C, TV, fridge, hair dryer, Internet (¥ 120 per day), minibar.

# PŬDŌNG (EAST OF RIVER)
## Very Expensive

**Grand Hyatt Shànghǎi (Shànghǎi Jīn Mào Jūnyuè Dàjiǔdiàn)** 上海金茂君悦大酒店 ★★ The Grand Hyatt is no longer the world's tallest hotel, having been eclipsed by its sister property the Park Hyatt in the neighboring Shànghǎi World Financial Center, but it's still highly attractive to many travelers. Running from the 54th to the 88th floors of the Jīn Mào Tower, the ultraluxurious Grand Hyatt is more of a novelty hotel than a practical one. True, the views of the Bund and Pǔdōng are astonishing, when you are not fogged in, that is; the guest rooms, which combine Art Deco and traditional Chinese motifs with high-tech designs, are lush and luxurious; and the fine dining options are unparalleled, but the burden of renown has also made the staff a bit standoffish. The hotel's high-flying address means you should allow extra time to get to your destination. Those prone to vertigo would do well to choose another *pied-à-terre*.

Shìjì Dà Dào 88 世纪大道 8 8 号, 54th Floor, Jīn Mào Tower (southeast of the Oriental Pearl TV Tower); see map p. 148. ✆ **800/233-1234** or 021/5049-1234. Fax 021/5049-1111. www.hyatt.com. 555 units. ¥3,500–¥3,800 standard; ¥4,150 executive level; from ¥5,400 suite. AE, DC, MC, V. Metro: Lujiazui. **Amenities:** 6 restaurants, 2 lounges; babysitting; concierge; executive-level rooms; health club w/Jacuzzi and sauna; indoor sky pool; 24-hr. room service; spa. *In room:* A/C, TV, fridge, hair dryer, minibar, Wi-Fi (¥120 per day).

**Park Hyatt Shànghǎi (Shànghǎi Bǎiyuè Jiǔdiàn)** 上海柏悦酒店 ★★ The Park Hyatt Shànghǎi is scaling new heights of luxury. Occupying the 79th to 93rd floors of the 101-story, 492m (1,614-ft.) Shànghǎi World Financial Center, this exclusive Hyatt brand now lays claim to the world's tallest hotel. Designed to be a cool refuge (in temperature and style) from the hustle and bustle of Shànghǎi, the hotel has a direct elevator that whisks guests up to the 87th-floor lobby. Happily, a damper has been installed on the 90th floor, which should greatly reduce if not eliminate entirely the occasional swaying that guests staying at the neighboring and similarly high-flying Grand Hyatt would sometimes feel on a windy day. Guest rooms, reached via dimly lit vaultlike hallways, are the largest in the city (55sq. m/592 sq. ft. and up), and some of the most comfortable with high ceilings, daybeds, DVD players, iPod docking stations, and flatscreen plasma TVs. Bathrooms are in a courtyard style with large rain showers and separate powder rooms, but the toilet lid that lifts automatically is perhaps trying a little too hard. Service is fine if not particularly memorable, but the views are brilliant when you're not socked in by clouds or smog.

Shìjì Dà Dào 100 世纪大道100号, World Financial Center (southeast of the Oriental Pearl TV Tower); see map p. 148. ✆ **021/6888-1234.** Fax 021/6888-3400. www.shanghai.park.hyatt.com. 174 units. ¥5,000–¥5,700 standard; from ¥11,500 suite (40%–50% discounts). AE, DC, MC, V. Metro: Lujiazui or Dongchang Lu. **Amenities:** 2 restaurants, lounge, 3 bars; babysitting; concierge; health club and spa w/Jacuzzi and sauna; indoor pool; 24-hr. room service. *In room:* A/C, TV/DVD, CD player, fridge, hair dryer, minibar, MP3 docking station, free Wi-Fi.

**Pǔdōng Shangri-La Hotel (Pǔdōng Xiānggélǐlā Fàndiàn)** 浦东香格里拉饭店 ★★★ With the addition of a sleek new tower annex boasting a slew of trendy designer restaurants, the Himalayan-themed Chi spa, and a second health club and pool, not only is the Shangri-La currently the biggest and boldest hotel in town, but it has the best location in Pǔdōng, with unbeatable views of the Bund across the river. All guest rooms in the 36-story Grand Tower are spacious and superbly appointed with more amenities than you know what to do with, including DVD players, fax machines, 32-inch LCD TVs, and safes equipped to recharge your laptop computer. Original River Wing rooms have just been renovated with more classical furnishings. Staff is delightfully friendly and the service is of a high international caliber.

Fùchéng Lù 33 富城路33号 (southwest of the Oriental Pearl TV Tower/Dōngfāng Míngzhū, adjacent to Riverside Ave./Bīnjiāng Dà Dào); see map p. 148. ℂ **800/942-5050** or 021/6882-8888. Fax 021/6882-6688. www.shangri-la.com. 950 units. ¥1,850–¥3,000 standard; ¥2,250–¥3,750 executive level; from ¥4,050 suite (40% discounts). AE, DC, MC, V. Metro: Lujiazui. **Amenities:** 6 restaurants, deli, 2 lounges, 2 bars; babysitting; concierge; executive-level rooms; 2 health clubs w/Jacuzzi and sauna; 2 indoor pools; 24-hr. room service; spa; tennis court. *In room:* A/C, TV/DVD (Grand Tower rooms only), CD player (in some), fax (in some), fridge, hair dryer, minibar, free Wi-Fi.

### Ritz-Carlton Pǔdōng (Shànghǎi Pǔdōng Lìsī Kǎěrdūn Jiǔdiàn  Fàndiàn)

上海浦东丽思卡尔顿酒店　The second Ritz-Carlton to open in Shànghǎi was too new to review at press time, but guests can likely expect all the luxury and high-caliber service that is associated with the brand. Lodged in the upper 18 levels of the 58-story South Tower of the Shànghǎi International Finance Center (IFC), the hotel is like an Art Deco jewelry box (beige and gold dominate in the main areas) with Chinese flourishes. Rooms should please even the most exacting visitor: Amenities include 400-thread-count bed linens, a 42-inch LCD TV with Blu-ray disc player, and a Bose Wave Music System with iPod dock, among other indulgences. Expect the views from the hotel to be stellar on a good day: panoramic, but not so high up as to miss all the details. The hotel is well situated in Lùjiāzuǐ with easy access to sights like the Jīn Mào Building, the Shànghǎi World Financial Center, the Riverside Promenade, and the slew of luxury shops at Shànghǎi IFC. The subway station is nearby as well.

Shìjì Dàdào 8 世纪大道8号，Shànghǎi IFC; see map p. 148. ℂ **021/2020-1888.** Fax 021/2020-1889. www.ritzcarlton.com. 285 units. ¥5,300 standard; ¥5,500 executive level; from ¥10,000 suite (40% discounts). AE, DC, MC, V. Metro: Lujiazui. **Amenities:** 4 restaurants, lounge, bar; babysitting; concierge; executive-level rooms; health club w/Jacuzzi and sauna; indoor pool; 24-hr. room service; spa. *In room:* A/C, TV/DVD, CD player, fridge, hair dryer, minibar, MP3 docking station, Wi-Fi (¥120 per day in standard rooms, free in other rooms).

### St. Regis Shànghǎi (Shànghǎi Ruìjí Hóngtǎ Dàjiǔdiàn) 上海瑞吉红塔大酒店★★

The handsome St. Regis might well be *the* luxury hotel at which to stay in town were it not for its less-convenient location in Pudong. Standard rooms are large (48 sq. m/157 sq. ft.), and gorgeously furnished with comfortable sofas, ergonomic Herman Miller "Aeron" chairs, Bose CD radios, and "rainforest" showers in the spacious marble bathrooms. But what sets the St. Regis apart from its competitors is its signature 24-hour butler service, which the hotel initially pioneered and which other hotels have tried to copy. As part of their "Lifestyle Butler Service," St. Regis butlers can press clothing, make dinner reservations, and even act as tour guides about town, escorting guests interested in the Chinese art scene to galleries or the private studios of local Chinese artists. A ladies-only floor features women butlers and a host of special in-room amenities including toiletries by Bulgari. Service is top-notch throughout.

Dōngfāng Lù 889 东方路 8 8 9 号 (south central Pǔdōng); see map p. 148. ℂ **800/325-3589** or 021/5050-4567. Fax 021/6875-6789. www.stregis.com. 328 units. ¥3,390 standard; ¥3,970 executive level; from ¥4,270 suite (up to 60% discounts). AE, DC, MC, V. Metro: Pudian Rd. or Century Ave. **Amenities:** 3

restaurants, lounge; babysitting; concierge; executive-level rooms; health club w/aerobics classes; indoor pool; 24-hr. room service; spa. *In room:* A/C, TV/DVD, movie library, CD player, fax, fridge, hair dryer, minibar, Wi-Fi (¥120 per day).

# Expensive

### Courtyard by Marriott Hotel Pǔdōng (Shànghǎi Qílǔ Wànyí Dàjiǔdiàn)
上海齐鲁万怡大酒店 The Courtyard is a thoroughly modern and busy four-star hotel catering to business travelers. The government of wealthy Shāndōng Province owns the building, sparing no expense in maintaining its handsome facilities. The lobby lounge boasts a striking lattice wood and glass partition. Renovated in 2007, the comfortable rooms are of average size, with modern furniture gussied up with the Courtyard's signature floral motifs. Staff is friendly and tries hard. The subway is just 2 blocks away, so a nonbusiness traveler could stay here comfortably, especially if a bargain room rate can be secured. The hotel runs a free shuttle to Yù Yuán on weekends.

Dōngfāng Lù 838 东方路 8 3 8 号 (at intersection with Wéifáng Lù); see map p. 148. ℂ **021/6886-7886.** Fax 021/6886-7889. www.marriott.com/shacy. 318 units. ¥1,495 standard; ¥1,985 executive level; from ¥2,315 suite (up to 50% discounts). AE, DC, MC, V. Metro: Century Ave. **Amenities:** 2 restaurants, lounge; babysitting; concierge; executive-level rooms; health club w/sauna; 24-hr. room service. *In room:* A/C, TV, fridge, hair dryer, Internet (¥ 80 per day), minibar.

### Four Points by Sheraton (Fúpéng Xīláidēng Yóuyóu Jiǔdiàn) 福朋喜来登
由由酒店 ★ This internationally managed Starwood property is worth consideration for independent travelers, as its proximity to both the Nánpǔ Bridge and Fùxīng Lù Tunnel, as well as the Tángqiáo subway station, puts guests within 10 to 15 minutes of the Bund and downtown. Considerably more luxurious than the more functional Four Points brand in North America, Shànghǎi's Four Points (previously a local hotel) offers comfortable lodgings with a welcome dollop of luxury. Rooms are designed in a pleasing contemporary style and come with comfortable beds and all the usual amenities. Glassed-off bathrooms are bright and modern. Service is quite professional and room rates are highly competitive.

Pǔdōng Nán Lù 2111 浦东南路 2 1 1 1 号 (at Pūjiàn Lù, near the Nánpǔ Bridge); see map p. 148. ℂ **800/810-3088** or 021/5839-9909. Fax 021/5870-7003. www.fourpoints.com/pudong. 326 units. ¥1,780–¥1,980 standard; from ¥3,680 suite (40% discounts). AE, DC, MC, V. Metro: Tángqiáo. **Amenities:** 3 restaurants, lounge, bar; babysitting; concierge; executive-level rooms; health club and spa w/Jacuzzi and sauna; 24-hr. room service. *In room:* A/C, TV, fridge, hair dryer, Internet (¥100 per day), minibar.

### Holiday Inn Pǔdōng (Shànghǎi Pǔdōng Jiàrì Jiǔdiàn) 上海浦东假日酒店
This thoroughly Western, 32-story Holiday Inn offers excellent value, after discounts, among four-star hotels in Pǔdōng. Guest rooms are spacious and bright, with bird's-eye maple furniture, comfortable beds, and all the amenities you'll likely need. The white tile bathrooms are spotless, and service is efficient and professional. Given the hotel's tourist-unfriendly location in the middle of the business district of south central Pǔdōng, little wonder most of its guests are business travelers, but individual tourists occasionally find their way here as well. The Metro 4 subway station is also nearby, allowing access to the rest of Shànghǎi.

Dōngfāng Lù 899 东方路 8 9 9 号 (south-central Pǔdōng); see map p. 148. ℂ **800/465-4329** or 021/5830-6666. Fax 021/5830-5555. www.holiday-inn.com. 352 units. ¥1,500 standard; ¥2,000 executive level; from ¥2,000 suite (up to 50% discounts in low season). AE, DC, MC, V. Metro: Pudian Rd. **Amenities:** 3 restaurants, lounge, bar; babysitting; concierge; executive-level rooms; health club and spa; indoor pool; 24-hr. room service. *In room:* A/C, TV, fridge, hair dryer, Internet (¥80 per day), minibar.

# 6

# WHERE TO DINE

Gastronomes never had it so good in Shànghǎi. With restaurants serving a mind-boggling variety of Chinese cuisine, as well as a wide range of top-notch international fare, Shànghǎi is arguably mainland China's best city for eating. Běijīng boosters will disagree, of course, and it was not always so 15 years ago, but the prosperous 1990s that saw Shànghǎi once again take to the world stage have reawakened the demand for *la bella vita,* as seen in the explosion of dining establishments in the last few years. For Shànghǎi residents, ever-attuned to the latest trends and tastes, eating out and trying new restaurants is now a pastime that rivals shopping.

While some of Shànghǎi's top restaurants can be found in hotels, there are scores of well-run private establishments that rival if not surpass the quality of hotel food, and usually at lower prices. Significantly improved hygiene standards should also allay any concerns you may have about eating out. Shànghǎi provides the unusual opportunity of dining one moment in a traditional teahouse and another in a restored colonial mansion; missing out would be a shame.

Don't expect the Chinese food here to taste the same as that at home; expect it to be light years better. While you can eat your way through China by sampling all the regional Chinese restaurants in Shànghǎi, the emphasis is on Shànghǎi's own renowned cuisine, commonly referred to as *běnbāng cài.* Usually considered a branch of Huáiyáng cuisine (see box below on "China's cuisines"), Shànghǎi cooking has traditionally relied on soy sauce, sugar, and oil. The most celebrated Shànghǎi dish is hairy crab, a freshwater delicacy that reaches its prime every fall. Also popular are any number of "drunken" dishes (crab, chicken) marinated in local Shàoxīng wine, and braised meat dishes such as lion's head meatballs and braised pork knuckle. Shànghǎi dim sum and snacks include a variety of dumplings, headlined by the local favorite *xiǎolóng bāo,* as well as onion pancakes and leek pies, all of which deserve to be tried. For more on Shànghǎi cuisine, see chapter 2, "Shànghǎi in Depth."

Those hankering for a taste of home will also find that Shànghǎi is the most foreign-belly-friendly city in China. From the trendiest Continental cuisine to the most recognizable fast-food chains, there is a staggering range of options guaranteed to take the edge off any homesick cravings. Many Asian and European cuisines are well represented, with Italian, Spanish, French, Japanese, Thai, and Indian cooking of good enough quality to satisfy a discerning overseas palate. World-renowned chefs like Jean-Georges Vongerichten, David Laris, and Paul Pairet have also chosen to launch their China flagship restaurants here. Where Shànghǎi particularly excels is in the bold new tastes that are arising from the mix of East and West.

At the other end of the dining scale, the American fast-food chains of McDonald's and KFC are ubiquitous. So are Starbucks, Häagen-Dazs, and Pizza Hut. Subway is in the mix, along with Hooters, and Cold Stone Creamery. Check the local expatriate magazines for location details.

According to the corporate travel index published by *Business Travel News,* the corporate dining tab in Shànghǎi in 2010 (said to lag behind London's, but to exceed San Francisco's) averages around $302 per person per day, but most travelers can get by well below that amount. While Shànghǎi's top international restaurants tend to charge Western prices, you can have an excellent meal for two at a relatively upscale Chinese restaurant for ¥150 to ¥300. Some of the best local foods can be had for less than that. (Prices quoted for a Chinese meal are for two bowls of rice and between two and four dishes.) The key is to mix it up with a combination of local and international dining. If you want to try Shànghǎi's more famous Western restaurants, consider going at lunchtime, when lunch specials and set menus can cost less than half of what you would spend at dinner. Hotel restaurants frequently levy a 15% service charge, but few private restaurants do. There is no tipping in restaurants, and the waitstaff will usually run after you to return your change.

The Shanghainese love affair with eating has spawned a dizzying number of restaurant openings (and closings) on any given week, a vexing matter not only for restaurant owners, but travel writers as well. What follows is a list of mostly established restaurants (with an emphasis on those outside of the big hotels) that should, barring any unforeseen health-related crisis, still be thriving by the time you read this. Consult the local English-language weeklies for new restaurant listings.

The widest variety of dining options is in the Lúwān (French Concession), Jìng Ān, and Xúhuì districts. This is also where you'll find some of the most ambient restaurants located inside colonial mansions on large, sprawling estates. With some of the city's top international restaurants and unimprovable views, the Bund is also another prime dining spot.

As well, Shànghǎi has a number of **food streets** (*měishí jiē*) lined with Chinese restaurants of every ilk, though not all of them have English menus or English-speaking staff. They are: **Huáng Hé Lù,** northwest of the Park Hotel (Huángpǔ); **Yúnnán Lù,** east of Xīzàng Lù and south of Yán'ān Dōng Lù (Huángpǔ); **Yùyuán Zhī Lù,** northwest of Jìng Ān Temple (Jìng Ān); and **Zhápǔ Lù,** north of Sūzhōu Creek and east of Sìchuān Běi Lù (Hóngkǒu). Locals love **Shòuníng Lù,** south of Huáihǎi Lù between the old Chinese city and the French Concession for the restaurants specializing in spicy crawfish (*xiǎolóngxiā*), and **Sì Pái Lóu Lù** in the old Chinese city south of Fāngbāng Zhōng Lù and west of Zhōnghuá Lù is chock-full of roadside stalls selling all kinds of delicious local foods. **Wújiāng Lù,** just off

Nánjīng Xī Lù by the Nánjīng Xī Lù Metro station (Huángpǔ), has become a lot more gentrified and upscale with the inclusion of more Western restaurants.

*Note:* Maps for dining establishments are in chapter 7, with specific map page numbers noted in the listing descriptions following all reviews. For tips on dining etiquette, see "Etiquette & Customs" in "Fast Facts," p. 282. For more tips and a menu guide to the city's most popular dishes, see chapter 2, "Shànghǎi in Depth."

# best DINING BETS

o **Best International Dining: Laris** at Three on the Bund and **T8** in Xīntiāndì top the list for their consistently creative and tasty global cuisine over the years. See p. 113 and 116.

---

## CHINA'S cuisines

China has a vast number of regional cuisines, which have traditionally been classified according to four main cooking styles. Below is a summary of the four styles and their various sub-branches:

**BĚIJĪNG/NORTHERN** Běijīng or Northern cuisine is typically characterized by strong, robust flavors and hearty ingredients; pork and lamb dominate, the latter also due to the Muslim influence in the northwestern part of the country. Staples are heavy noodles and breads instead of rice. **Uighur** or **Xīnjiāng** cuisine falls under this rubric. *Jiǎozi,* small chunks of meat and vegetables wrapped in dough and boiled, are popular snacks also eaten during the Chinese New Year.

**HUÁIYÁNG/SHÀNGHǍI** Huáiyáng cuisine, encompassing the coastal areas of eastern China, and said to require the most skill, aims to preserve the basic flavor of each ingredient in order to achieve balance and freshness. River fish, farm animals, birds, and vegetables feature prominently, and braising and stewing are more common than stir-frying. Red sauces (from soy sauce, sugar, and oil) are popular. **Shànghǎi-, Hángzhōu-, Sūzhōu-,** and **Yángzhōu**-style cooking are all minor variations on the same theme.

**CANTONESE** Considered the most refined and sophisticated of the cuisines, the emphasis here is on freshness and lightness, with steaming and stir-frying the cooking methods of choice. Seafood dominates, but just about anything edible is fair game—the Cantonese are known for being the most adventurous eaters. Top hotels all have Cantonese restaurants, which are always the first choice for Chinese if they're trying to impress a guest. Cantonese dim sum, featuring little morsels of food like shrimp dumplings, barbecue pork crisps, and egg tarts, is widely popular.

**SÌCHUĀN** Sìchuān cooking, born in the damp interior of southwestern China, relies heavily on chilies, peppers, peppercorns, and garlic; spicy and pungent flavors are the result. Popular dishes include *gōngbǎo jīdīng* (diced chicken with chili and peanuts) and *mápó dòufu* (spicy tofu with minced pork). Sìchuān hot pot (*huǒguō*) is also a favorite. Although popular in Shànghǎi, Sìchuān cooking has seldom made it here intact: The local preference for sweet and salty is readily apparent on many a Sìchuān menu in town. Other southwestern cuisines, such as **Guìzhōu** and **Yúnnán**, which are themselves subdivided into various ethnic minority cuisines, tend to be spicy and sour.

- **Best Shànghǎi Dining:** It's almost unfair to have to pick one or two since the city abounds in restaurants serving delicious local fare. But I like **Fu 1088,** which has the best smoked fish in town, and a colonial mansion setting to boot, for elegant contemporary Shànghǎi cuisine, and the longstanding **Jíshì** for no-frills down-home cooking. See p. 130 and 132.

- **Best Room with a View:** Competitors try, but it's hard to beat Shànghǎi's grand dame of world-class Continental dining, **M on the Bund,** for its glamorous roof-top setting and Bund and riverfront views. See p. 111.

- **Best Teahouse:** The most famous teahouse in China, with its eaves soaring over the pond by Yù Yuán (Yù Garden), is Shànghǎi's own **Húxīntíng,** a welcome haven in the crunch of Old Town shopping and mass tourism. See p. 187.

- **Best Xiǎo Lóng Bāo (Dumpling):** **Crystal Jade Restaurant** in Xīntiāndì claims the crown with the thinnest dumpling wrapper in town, and perfect *xiǎolóng bāo* that are served at just the right temperature. The Taiwanese joint **Dǐng Tài Fēng (Din Tai Fung)** comes in a close second. See p. 116 and 117.

- **Best Cantonese:** The best Cantonese restaurants are still to be found in hotels, and there is none better than **Yi Long Court** at the Peninsula Shànghǎi, where traditional and new Cantonese dishes are prepared with the greatest care and judiciousness by master Hong Kong chefs. See p. 112.

- **Best French: Mr & Mrs Bund,** Paul Pairet's modern French eatery, takes the prize for its creative and delicious cuisine that's all the more fun for being shared, and available till the wee hours of the morning. **Jean Georges** at Three on the Bund proves a worthy challenger with superb and creative entrees and wickedly sinful desserts. See p. 112 and 113.

- **Best Asian (Non-Chinese): Simply Thai,** with several outlets, serves consistently delicious, authentic Thai food in the most charming of environments. Outside of hotel restaurants, the best Japanese cuisine and freshest sushi can be found, if you're lucky enough to get a seat, at **Sushi Oyama. Chor Bazaar** is your best source for tasty Indian fare that is easy on the wallet. See p. 122, 121, and 130.

- **Best Tongue Twister (Due to Spicy Food):** For the spiciest Chinese food, **Dī Shuǐ Dòng** will give you chilies straight up by way of Húnán Province. Your sweat glands will be working overtime. See p. 118.

- **Best Vegetarian:** The French Concession **Zǎo Zǐ Shù** takes its mission seriously (its name is also a pun that exhorts diners to become vegetarians as soon as possible, *zǎo chī sù*). There's no smoking, no MSG, no alcohol, and no dairy, but plenty of organic tea, fruit appetizers, flavorful vegetables, mushrooms, and tofu doubling as meat. See p. 118.

# RESTAURANTS BY CUISINE

## AMERICAN

Blue Frog (Chángníng, $$$, p. 130)
Element Fresh ★ (Jìng Ān, $, p. 129)

KABB ★ (Lúwān, $$$, p. 117)
Malone's (Jìng Ān, $$, p. 128)

KEY TO ABBREVIATIONS:
**$$$$** = Very Expensive   **$$$** = Expensive   **$$** = Moderate   **$** = Inexpensive

## BĚIJĪNG

Xīndàlù China Kitchen ★★ (Hóngkǒu, $$$, p. 116)

## CANTONESE

Crystal Jade Restaurant ★★★ (Lúwān, $$, p. 116)
Dynasty ★ (Chángníng, $$$, p. 131)
Yi Long Court ★★★ (Huángpǔ, $$$$, p. 112)
Zen ★ (Lúwān, $$$, p. 117)

## CONTINENTAL/FUSION

Jing'an Restaurant ★★ (Jìng Ān, $$$$, p. 125)
Laris ★★★ (Huángpǔ, $$$$, p. 113)
Mesa ★ (Jìng Ān, $$, p. 128)
M on the Bund ★★ (Huángpǔ, $$$$, p. 111)
New Heights ★ (Huángpǔ, $$, p. 113)
T8 ★★★ (Lúwān, $$$$, p. 116)

## DIM SUM

Crystal Jade Restaurant ★★★ (Lúwān, $$, p. 116)
Dynasty ★ (Chángníng, $$$, p. 131)
Zen ★ (Lúwān, $$$, p. 117)

## DUMPLINGS

Crystal Jade Restaurant ★★★ (Lúwān, $$, p. 116)
Dīng Tài Fēng ★ (Lúwān, Pǔdōng, $$, p. 133)
Jià Jiā Tāng Bāo (Huángpǔ, $, p. 115)
Nánxiáng Mántou Diàn (Huángpǔ, $, p. 115)

## FRENCH

Franck ★★ (Xúhuì, $$$$, p. 120)
Jade on 36 ★★ (Pǔdōng, $$$$, p. 133)
Jean Georges ★★★ (Huángpǔ, $$$$, p. 113)
Mr & Mrs Bund ★★★ (Huángpǔ, $$$$, p. 112)

## GERMAN

Paulaner Bräuhaus ★ (Xúhuì, Lúwān, $$, p. 123)

## HONG KONG

Xīn Wàng (Huángpǔ, Lúwān, $, p. 119)

Yi Long Court ★★★ (Huángpǔ, $$$$, p. 112)

## HOT POT

Hǎi Dǐ Lāo (Chángníng, $$, p. 131)
Hot Pot King ★ (Xúhuì, $$, p. 122)
Kuo Bee Pen Da (Jìng Ān, $$$, p. 126)

## HÚNÁN

Dī Shuǐ Dòng ★★ (Lúwān, $$, p. 118)
Gǔ Yì ★★ (Jìng Ān, $$, p. 128)

## INDIAN

Chor Bazaar ★ (Chángníng, $$$, p. 130)
Kebabs on the Grille ★ (Huángpǔ, $$$, p. 112)
Vedas (Xúhuì, $$$, p. 122)

## INDONESIAN

Bali Laguna (Jìng Ān, $$$, p. 126)

## INTERNATIONAL

Wagas (Pǔdōng, $$, p. 134)
Xīntiāndì Restaurant Mall (Lúwān, $$$, p. 116)
Y's Table ★ (Pǔdōng, $$$$, p. 133)

## IRISH

O'Malley's (Xúhuì, $$, p. 123)

## ITALIAN

Danieli's ★★ (Pǔdōng, $$$$, p. 132)
Va Bene ★★ (Lúwān, $$$, p. 117)

## JAPANESE

Haiku by Hatsune ★ (Xúhuì, $$$, p. 121)
Shintori Null II ★★ (Jìng Ān, $$$$, p. 126)
Sushi Oyama ★★★ (Xúhuì, $$$$, p. 121)

## NEPALESE

Nepali Kitchen (Jìng Ān, $$$, p. 126)

## SEAFOOD

People on the Water ★ (Jìng Ān, $$$, p. 127)
Wáng Bǎo Hé ★ (Huángpǔ, $$$$, p. 112)
Yi Long Court ★★★ (Huángpǔ, $$$$, p. 112)

## SHÀNGHǍI

Art Salon ★ (Lúwān, $$, p. 117)
Bǎoluó ★ (Jìng Ān, $$, p. 127)

Crystal Jade Restaurant ★★★
(Lúwān, $$, p. 116)
Fu 1088 ★★★ (Chángníng, $$$$, p. 130)
The Grape (Xúhuì, $, p. 123)
Guì Huā Lóu ★★ (Pǔdōng, $$$$, p. 132)
Jíshì ★★ (Xúhuì, $$, p. 122)
Lú Bō Láng (Huángpǔ, $$, p. 115)
Méilóngzhèn ★★ (Jìng Ān, $$, p. 128)
Shànghǎi Old Station Restaurant ★
(Xúhuì, $$$, p. 121)
Shànghǎi Uncle ★ (Huángpǔ,
Pǔdōng, Xúhuì, $$$, p. 114)
Sū Zhè Huì (Jade Garden) ★★
(Pǔdōng, $$, p. 134)
1221 ★★ (Chángníng, $$, p. 132)
Wáng Bǎo Hé ★ (Huángpǔ, $$$$, p. 112)
Whampoa Club ★★ (Huángpǔ,
$$$$, p. 113)
Xīndàlù China Kitchen ★★
(Hóngkoǔ, $$$, p. 116)
Xīn Jí Shì ★★ (Lúwān, $$$, p. 117)
Yè Shànghǎi ★ (Lúwān, $$$, p. 117)

**SÌCHUĀN**
Bā Guó Bù Yī (Chángníng, $$, p. 131)

South Beauty ★ (Jìng Ān, $$$, p. 127)

**SINGAPOREAN**
Rendezvous (Jìng Ān, $$, p. 129)

**SPANISH**
el Willy ★ (Xúhuì, $$$$, p. 120)
Restaurant Martin ★ (Xúhuì,
$$$$, p. 120)

**TAIWANESE**
Dīng Tài Fēng ★ (Lúwān,
Pǔdōng, $$, p. 133)

**THAI**
Simply Thai ★★ (Xúhuì, $$$, p. 122)

**UIGHUR**
Shànghǎi Xīnjiāng Fēngwèi Fàndiàn
(Xúhuì, $$, p. 123)

**VEGETARIAN**
Gōngdélín (Huángpǔ, $$, p. 114)
Zǎo Zī Shù ★ (Lúwān, $$, p.118)

**YÚNNÁN**
Lost Heaven ★★ (Huángpǔ, $$$, p. 114)

# HUÁNGPǓ (DOWNTOWN)

## Very Expensive

**M on the Bund (Mǐshì Xīcāntīng)** 米氏西餐厅 ★★ CONTINENTAL Lodged atop a handsome, seven-story colonial building on the Bund, this is the restaurant that put Shànghǎi dining on the world map in 1999. All Art Deco elegance, M boasts a terrace that affords unsurpassed views of the Bund, the Huángpǔ River, and Pǔdōng's skyscrapers, as well as a "Glamour Room" for nightly dinner and drinks. The menu changes frequently to take advantage of fresh local ingredients, but signature dishes include the slow-baked leg of lamb and the sublime Pavlova dessert. Increased competition from the neighboring Bund restaurants has forced service to improve in recent years after a drop-off. M has consistently been on the must-try list of many visitors, largely due to its previous renown and its glamorous environs, but where the quality, taste, and creativity of the food are concerned, quite a few expats prefer restaurants like Laris and T8.

Zhōngshān Dōng Yī Lù 5 中山东一路 5 号, 7th floor (entrance on side street at Guǎngdōng Lù 20); see map p. 136. ☎ **021/6350-9988.** www.m-restaurantgroup.com. Reservations required. Meal for 2 ¥600–¥1,000. AE, DC, MC, V. Daily 6-10:30pm; Tues-Fri 11:30am-2:30pm; Sat-Sun brunch 11:30am-3pm; Sun tea 3:30-5:30pm. Metro: Nanjing Rd. (E).

**Mr & Mrs Bund** ★★★ FRENCH  French brasserie cuisine never had it so good, creative, or playful. At international chef sensation Paul Pairet's excellent new modern French eatery—lodged on the sixth floor of the lavishly restored Chartered Bank of India, Australia, and China building on the Bund—the atmosphere is festive, and the more than 100 dishes on the menu are meant to be shared, family-style. Signature and more popular dishes are featured in the Rookie menu. Do try the foie gras light crumble, meunière bread (think butter and truffles), jumbo shrimp in citrus jar, steamed "Black Cod in the Bag," "Long Short Rib Teriyaki," and the to-die-for lemon tart. If none of that appeals, you can simply select your fish or viand to be cooked in a style (and sauce) of your own choosing. An Enomatic machine in the center of the restaurant dispenses 32 wines by the glass. Service is first-rate, and though the decor in classic black and red suggests formality, the place is surprisingly unpretentious. Request a table by the window for nighttime views of Pǔdōng.

Zhongshan Dong Yi Lu 18, 中山东一路 1 8 号，  Bund 18; see map p. 136. ✆ **021/6323-9898.** www. mmbund.com. Reservations required. Meal for 2 ¥700–¥1,200. AE, DC, MC, V. Mon–Fri business lunch (set menu) 11:30am–2pm; daily 6:30–10:30pm (4am Tues–Sat). Metro: Nanjing Rd. (E).

**Wáng Bǎo Hé** 王宝和 ★ SHÀNGHǍI/SEAFOOD  With an opening date stretching back to 1744, this restaurant claims to be Shànghǎi's oldest. It also claims to be the best place to feast on Shànghǎi's famous hairy crab, though you're just as likely to lose some hair when you see the final tab (a kilo/2¼ lb. of crab will cost around ¥380). This brightly lit restaurant is often full, and your average diner on any given night will likely be a government official, China's next billionaire, or a Japanese or Southeast Asian crab aficionado with kilos of disposable income. Crab dominates the menu, of course, from dumplings and soup to the whole hairy monster, which is typically steamed and eaten with a dipping sauce of ginger, soy sauce, and black vinegar. True crab aficionados then put the whole crab back together after eating, as if it had never been dismantled, piece by succulent piece. Wash it all down with the restaurant's famous Shàoxīng wine.

Fúzhōu Lù 603 福州路 6 0 3 号 (west of Zhèjiāng Zhōng Lù); see map p. 136. ✆ **021/6322-3673.** Reservations required. Meal for 2 ¥400–¥800. AE, DC, MC, V. Daily 11am–1pm and 5–9pm. Metro: Nanjing Rd. (E).

**Yi Long Court (Yì Lóng Gé)** 逸龙阁 ★★★ CANTONESE/SEAFOOD  Under the guidance of Michelin star chef Tang Chi Keung, fresh from the Peninsula Tokyo, this restaurant in the Peninsula Shànghǎi serves up some of the finest haute Cantonese cuisine in town. Classic Hong Kong–style Cantonese cuisine means the emphasis is on seafood, and you can't go wrong with most of the meticulously prepared seafood dishes. Do try the delicious scallops stuffed with minced shrimp, beef with oyster sauce, the light and flaky barbecued pork puffs, and for dessert, the chilled sesame pudding, all complemented by a wide range of quality teas. The Western-style dining room with Art Deco flourishes provides a handsome setting, and table service is impeccable.

Zhōngshān Dōng Yī Lù 32 中山东一路 3 2 号 (Peninsula Hotel, by Běijīng Dōng Lù); see map p. 136. ✆ **021/2327-6742.** Reservations required. Meal for 2 ¥600–¥1,200. AE, DC, MC, V. Daily 11:30am–2:30pm and 6–10:30pm. Metro: Nanjing Rd. (E).

## Expensive

**Kebabs on the Grille** ★ INDIAN  Spicy North Indian cuisine comes to the Cool Docks in the South Bund, but what sets this freshly scrubbed restaurant apart

# THREE ON THE bund (WÀI TĀN SĀN HÀO) 外滩三号

One of the splashiest and most luxurious developments to hit Shànghǎi, **Three on the Bund** is a "lifestyle destination" that was one of the first outfits to bring some world-class swank to the Bund in the last decade. Built in 1922, this former Union Insurance Company Building now houses an art gallery, exclusive fashion outlets (including a Giorgio Armani store), and a luxurious Evian spa, but it's the fine-dining restaurants, all with stunning vistas of the Bund and Pǔdōng, that draw the crowds. For even more exclusive and intimate dining, the domed **Cupola** atop the building offers private dining for two, service by a private butler, and a menu from any of the following outlets. *Note:* Reservations required at Jean Georges, Laris, Whampoa Club, and the Cupola; reservations recommended at New Heights.

**Three on the Bund** is located at Zhōngshān Dōng Yī Lù 3 (entrance on side street at Guǎngdōng Lù 23); see map p. 136. ✆ **021/6323-3355.** www.threeonthebund.com. Metro: Nanjing Rd. (E).

**Jean Georges** ★★★ (fourth floor; ✆ **021/6321-7733;** daily 11:30am–2:30pm and 6–11pm). From *amuse-bouche* to dessert, it's the finest contemporary and light French fare from world-renowned chef Jean-Georges Vongerichten. You'll be singing the *Marseillaise* after the foie gras brûlée with dried cherries and candied pistachios. There are more than 5,000 bottles of wine to choose from, and a 30-seat wine cellar private dining room, all cloaked in dark blue and deep wine hues. Expect a dinner for two to hover immodestly around ¥2,000.

**Whampoa Club** ★★ (fifth floor; ✆ **021/6321-3737;** daily 11:30am–2:30pm and 5:30–11pm). Classic Shànghǎi dishes learned from a passel of old-time Shànghǎi master chefs are given a creative spin here. Indulge in the tasting menu, which was delicious when I was there, and don't miss the tea-smoked eggs with caviar. A professional tea sommelier can help with selecting from more than 50 teas from all over China.

**Laris** ★★★ (sixth floor; ✆ **021/6321-9922;** daily 11:30am–2:30pm and 6–10:30pm). In a light, breezy setting, larger-than-life Australian chef David Laris creates wonderful "New World" cuisine inspired by his previous culinary stints in Hong Kong, Vietnam, Macau, and London (as executive chef of Mezzo). Seafood gets top billing here (scallops on parsnip mash, and cod filet with mono miso are signature dishes), with a crustacean-stocked seafood bar. A special Chocolate Room (which churns out the Laris signature chocolate) gets raves from guests. Save room for the "Pandan Leaf Panna Cotta."

**New Heights** ★ (seventh floor; ✆ **021/6321-0909;** daily 10am–2am) is the option for casual, more affordable bistro-type fare, with rooftop views of the Bund and Pǔdōng rivaling that of M on the Bund next door. There's also free Wi-Fi here for those with their own laptops. Dinner for two should be in the ¥400 range.

is its kebabs, finished off at individual grill sets at your table. The tandoori chicken is melt-in-your-mouth good, and the various curries spicy and flavorful. The mutton skewers and "Magic Mushrooms" should also be tried. Staff is friendly and helpful. Dinners can add up, but the restaurant has very reasonably priced business lunches for ¥70 and an all-you-can-eat Sunday brunch for ¥140 per person.

Zhōngshān Nán Lù 479, No. 8 中山南路 4 7 9 号 (inside the Cool Docks, south of Fùxīng Dōng Lù); see map p. 156. ℂ **021/6152-6567.** www.kebabsonthegrille.com. Reservations recommended. Meal for 2 ¥200-¥300. AE, DC, MC, V. Daily 11am–10:30pm. Metro: Nánpu Bridge.

**Lost Heaven on the Bund Yunnan Folk Cuisine (Wàitān Huāmǎ Tiāntáng Yúnnán Cāntīng)** 外滩花马天堂云南餐厅 ★★ YÚNNÁN  If you fancy some different flavors from the typical Shanghainese cuisine, get thee to Lost Heaven. Steps from the Bund, this restaurant, popular with expats and locals, serves cuisine from the Tea Horse Trail (primarily that of the Dǎi, Bái, Nàxi, and Miáo minorities of Yúnnán Province in southwest China) with lots of Tibetan, Thai, and Burmese influences. Wooden floors and chairs, dark lighting, modern mood music, and photographs of Yúnnán's minorities and snow-capped mountains create just the right ambience. There's a separate menu (with pictures) of house favorites, as well as good English explanations of the various mushrooms and mountains of Yúnnán. Try the Yúnnán wild vegetable cake, Jicong mushrooms with assorted vegetables salad, Yí tribe stir-fry spicy beef, and spicy cod steamed in banana leaf. The tasty "Simmered Vegetables in Tamarind Juice," a typical West Yúnnán dish, actually comes with pork. Lost Heaven's original, smaller, outlet is in the French Concession.

Yán'ān Dōng Lù 17 延安东路 1 7 号 (east of Sìchuān Nán Lù); see map p. 136. ℂ **021/6330-0967.** www. lostheaven.com.cn. Metro: Nanjing Rd. (E). Xúhuì branch: Gāoyóu Lù 38 (by Fùxīng Xī Lù). ℂ **021/6433-5126.** Reservations recommended. Meal for 2 ¥200-¥300. AE, DC, MC, V. Daily noon–2pm and 5:30–10:30pm. Metro: Shanghai Library.

**Shànghǎi Uncle (Hǎishàng Āshū)** 海上阿叔 ★ SHÀNGHǍI  Bring a big appetite to this cavernous and brash red-themed restaurant in the basement of the Bund Center, where old Shànghǎi favorites are given a delightful modern makeover. Menu favorites include the unbelievably tender pine seed pork rib, Shànghǎi traditional smoked fish, Uncle's crispy pork of flame (cooked five ways while preserving its crispy skin and tender flesh), and the fusion-influenced cheese-baked lobster with homemade noodles. The tin-foil-wrapped, salt-baked live fish is also refreshingly light. Mezzanine booths have the best viewing spots.

Yán'ān Dōng Lù 222 延安东路 2 2 2 号, Wàitān Zhōngxīn (Bund Center), Basement (btw. Hénán Zhōng Lù and Jiāngxī Zhōng Lù); see map p. 136. ℂ **021/6339-1977.** Xúhuì branch: Tiānyáoqiáo Lù 211, 2nd floor (north of Nándān Dōng Lù); ℂ **021/6464-6430.** Metro: Xújiāhuì. Reservations recommended. Meal for 2 ¥200-¥300. AE, DC, MC, V. Daily 11am–11pm. Metro: Nanjing Rd. (E).

## Moderate

**Gōngdélín** 功德林 ♨ VEGETARIAN  Shànghǎi's most well-known vegetarian restaurant has more than half a century of experience and has grown a bit stodgy—not to mention greasy—in its old age. Its renown still counts for something, though, as crowds continue to pack in here for the *sùjī* (vegetarian chicken), *sùyā* (vegetarian duck), and other mock imitations of fowl, pork, seafood, and traditional Chinese dishes, all cleverly made from tofu and soy products.

Nánjīng Xī Lù 445 南京西路 4 4 5 号 (south side of Nánjīng Xī Lù, btw. Rénmín Gōngyuán and Chéngdū Běi Lù); see map p. 136. 📞 **021/6327-0218.** Reservations recommended for dinner and Fri-Sun. Meal for 2 ¥75–¥200. AE, DC, MC, V. Daily 11am–2pm and 5–9pm. Metro: Nanjing Rd. (W).

**Lù Bō Láng** 绿波廊 ⓦ SHÀNGHǍI    Housed in a three-story traditional Chinese pavilion just south of Yù Yuán and Jiǔ Qū Qiáo (Bridge of Nine Turnings), this restaurant has become a de rigueur stop on the average tourist itinerary strictly on the basis of its celebrity guest list (Queen Elizabeth II, Fidel Castro, President Bill Clinton, and others). Specialties such as the seasonal *Yángchéng Hú* crab, shark's fin, and President Clinton's favorite *sānsī méimao sū* (pasty stuffed with pork, bamboo, and mushrooms) sell well, though prices are generally inflated. The automatic 10% service charge is a guarantee that you won't get much in the way of service.

Yùyuán Lù 115 豫园路 1 1 5 号 (south shore of teahouse lake); see map p. 156. 📞 **021/6328-0602.** Reservations recommended. Meal for 2 ¥120–¥250. AE, DC, MC, V. Daily 7am–12:30am. Metro: Yu Garden.

# Inexpensive

**Jiā Jiā Tāng Bāo** 佳家汤包 DUMPLINGS    For many locals, this no-frills eatery just north of People's Square on one of Shànghǎi's "food streets" is one of the most famous and popular joints in town for Shànghǎi's favorite dumpling *xiǎolóng bāo*, with long lines inevitably forming during meal times. The restaurant serves several different kinds of dumplings (made only after you've ordered them) and not much else (though they do have the old-fashioned glass-bottled Coca-Cola). Order and pay at the front counter (there's no English menu, but you can point to the Chinese translations at the back of this book). The most basic is the pork-filled *chúnxiānròu tāngbāo* (with 12 in a steamer) or you can go all out with the pork and crab-roe version *xièfěn xiānròu tāngbāo*. For nonpork eaters, there's also a chicken dumpling *jīdīng xiānròu tāngbāo*. This is definitely a local experience you should try, but get here early as half the menu is usually sold out after lunch.

Huánghé Lù 90 黄河路 9 0 号 (north of Nánjīng Lù); see map p. 136. 📞 **021/6327-6878.** Meal for 2 ¥20–¥50. No credit cards. Daily 6:30am–7pm. Metro: People's Square.

**Nánxiáng Mántou Diàn** 南翔馒头店 DUMPLINGS    This two-story dumpling restaurant just west of the Bridge of Nine Turnings (Jiǔ Qū Qiáo) in Old Town would be the ideal place to take a load off and refortify with some of Shànghǎi's most famous snacks if it weren't always jammed to the rafters with scores of like-minded tourists. What they all come for is the award-winning *Nánxiáng xiǎolóng* (¥12 for a steamer of 16 dumplings), steamed pork dumplings with delicious broth that squirts all over the moment you bite into the wrapper. Impossibly long lines form for the takeout counter on the first floor where glass windows allow you to watch the cooks at work. Three dining rooms on the second floor offer a greater choice of snacks, including spring rolls with crab stuffing and salty cashew nut crisps. There's a picture menu to help in ordering; otherwise, just point or wait for help, which may be a while coming. This place is much more popular with tourists than locals.

Yùyuán Lù 85 豫园路 8 5 号 (west shore of teahouse lake); see map p. 156. 📞 **021/6355-4206.** Meal for 2 ¥24–¥80. No credit cards. Daily 7am–8pm. Metro: Yu Garden.

# HÓNGKŎU DISTRICT (NORTHEAST SHÀNGHǍI)

## Expensive

**Xīndàlù China Kitchen** 新大陆 ★★ BĚIJĪNG/SHÀNGHǍI Xīndàlù is worth the trip to Hóngkǒu as it's easily the best place in town for succulent and tasty Peking duck done just right. Roasted in special wood ovens sent over from Běijīng, the duck here rivals some of the best in the capital itself. The restaurant, whose name means "New China," also features a dumpling and noodle section, along with traditional cuisine from Shànghǎi, Suzhou, and Hangzhou, but done in a modern, sophisticated style devoid of the usual oil and grease. In addition to the duck, try the smoked fish, the braised pork chop, or the delicious "Beggar's Chicken" (which has to be ordered in advance). Food presentation and service are sophisticated and the open kitchen allows you to watch the chefs at work—it's a grand time all around.

Huángpǔ Lù 199 黄浦路 1 9 9 号 (1st floor, Hyatt on the Bund, near Wǔchāng Lù); see map p. 136. ✆ **021/6393-1234,** ext. 6318. Reservations required. Meal for 2 ¥300-¥400. AE, DC, MC, V. Daily 11:30am-2:30pm and 5:30-10:30pm. No Metro.

# LÚWĀN DISTRICT (FRENCH CONCESSION)

## Expensive

**Xīntiāndì Restaurant Mall** 新天地 INTERNATIONAL A Starbucks stands at its entrance, the First National Congress of the Communist Party at its flanks, and in its midst, brilliant restorations of Shànghǎi's colonial Shíkù Mén ("stone gate") architecture. The place is **Xīntiāndì** (literally "New Heaven and Earth"), an upscale cultural mall where the moneyed East meets the moneyed West. Here you'll find the city's hottest dining spots. Located downtown a block south of the Huángpí Nán Lù Metro station, Xīntiāndì is a 2-block pedestrian mall with enough good eating to require weeks to experience it all. The best and the priciest are listed below. (See map p. 140.)

**T8** ★★★ (North Block, House 8; ✆ **021/6355-8999;** www.t8shanghai.com; lunch 11:30am-2:30pm, tea 2:30-5:30pm, dinner 6:30-11:30pm) is the restaurant whose service and chefs easily rival, if not eclipse, those at M on the Bund, only with less attitude. Service and management are superb and unobtrusive, the decor is super chic, and the food is irresistible. Although there have been several chefs in the last decade, T8 has consistently been voted one of the top restaurants in town, and is highly recommended. The seasonal menu emphasizes Western dishes with Asian influences, and the latest recommendations include the pigeon popcorn, the sesame-crusted tuna, and the Wagyu beef. Do not miss the to-die-for chocolate addiction plate.

**Crystal Jade Restaurant** 翡翠酒家 ★★★ 🍴 (South Block/Nánlǐ 6–7, second floor–12A & B; ✆ **021/6385-8752;** www.crystaljade.com; Mon–Fri 11:30am–3pm and 5–10:30pm; Sat–Sun 10:30am–3pm and 5–10:30pm) serves up arguably the best *xiǎolóng bāo* (steamed dumplings with broth) and *lāmiàn* (hand-pulled noodles) south of the Yángzǐ. Must-tries include Shànghǎi steamed pork dumplings (the aforementioned *xiǎolóng bāo*), *lāmiàn* in Sìchuān style (noodles in a spicy peanut broth), roast pork buns, and the *hóngyóu cháoshǒu* (wontons with chili sauce). Reserve in advance or risk a long wait. There are two other branches at Huáihǎi Zhōng Lù 300, Hong Kong New World Building, B10, ✆ **021/6335-4188;** and Nánjīng Xī Lù 1038, #719, ✆ **021/5228-1133.**

**Va Bene (Huá Wàn Yì)** 华万意 ★★ (North Block, House 7; ✆ **021/6311-2211;** Sun–Thurs 11:30am–2:30pm and 6–10:30pm; Fri–Sat 11:30am–3pm and 6–11pm) is an upscale Italian diner (from the owners of Hong Kong's Gaia) with warm Tuscan decor, patio dining, and a wide range of antipasti, pasta, and gourmet pizzas, all made from the freshest ingredients.

**Paulaner Bräuhaus (Bǎoláinà)** 宝莱纳 ★ (North Block, House 19–20; ✆ **021/ 6320-3935;** daily 11am–2am) is the Shànghǎi standby praised for its excellent German food, with authentic brews to match.

**KABB (Kǎibó Xīcāntīng)** 凯博西餐厅 ★ (North Block, House 5, Unit 1; ✆ **021/ 3307-0798;** Mon–Fri 7am–midnight, Sat–Sun 7am–2am) is a spiffy American bar and comfort-food cafe.

**Dǐng Tài Fēng** 鼎泰丰 ★ (South Block, House 6, second floor, Unit 11A; ✆ **021/6385-8378;** daily 11am–2:30pm and 5–11pm), an upscale Taiwanese restaurant, serves *xiǎolóng bāo* dumplings (that come in a very close second to Crystal Jade's dumplings), as well as a whole host of Taiwanese dishes and snacks.

**Xīn Jí Shì** 新吉士 ★★ (Tàicāng Lù 181, No. 2, North Block; ✆ **021/6336-4746;** daily 11am–1:30pm and 5–9:30pm), a very popular but homey Shànghǎi eatery, features delicious local favorites such as braised home-cooked pork (*hóng shāo ròu*) and glutinous rice with red dates.

**Yè Shànghǎi** 夜上海 ★ (South Block, House 6; ✆ **021/6311-2323;** daily 11:30am–2:30pm and 5:30–11pm) is an elegant touch of old Shànghǎi, which Hong Kong visitors claim is better than the original Yè Shànghǎi restaurant back home.

**Zen (Xiānggǎng Cǎidié Xuān)** 香港彩蝶轩 ★ (South Block, House 2; ✆ **021/6385-6395;** daily 11:30am–11:30pm), a modern Cantonese restaurant by way of Hong Kong, serves excellent dim sum for lunch.

## Moderate

**Art Salon (Wū Lǐ Xiāng)** 屋里香 ★ SHÀNGHǍI    It's Matisse meets Shànghǎi when you dine in this cozy, somewhat ramshackle art salon lodged in a French Concession storefront. Paintings and art works by contemporary Chinese artists adorn the colorful walls, while mismatched traditional Chinese chairs and tables cram every available nook and cranny, but no matter, the overall effect is one of idiosyncratic charm. The fairly extensive Chinese-only menu bulges with some excellent homemade local specialties. Happily, the brothers who own the place speak excellent English and can translate or make the appropriate recommendations. You can't go wrong with many of the dishes, but worth mentioning are the *pídàn dòufu* (preserved eggs with tofu), the fresh cucumbers with garlic appetizer, *hóngshāo huángyú* (braised yellow croaker), and their very own Shàoxìng-influenced *méigān cài shāo ròu* (braised pork with preserved mustard greens). Service is best described as deliberate, as the owners seem to place a premium on a leisurely appreciation of both the food and the art. Patrons are, of course, free to purchase anything that catches their eye, from the chopsticks in their hands and the chairs beneath them to the art on the walls.

Nánchāng Lù 164 南昌路 1 6 4 号 (btw. Yándāng Lù and Sīnán Lù); see map p. 140. ℂ **021/5306-5462.** Reservations recommended for dinner. Meal for 2 ¥100–¥200. No credit cards. Daily noon–2pm and 5–10pm. Metro: Shanxi Rd. (S).

**Dī Shuǐ Dòng** 滴水洞 ★★ 🐟 HÚNÁN   Rivaling Sìchuān cuisine in spiciness (though relying more on straight chilies and less on the mind-numbing, tongue-lashing peppercorn), the lesser-known cooking of Húnán Province can be tried at this delightful restaurant atop a flight of rickety wooden stairs inside a small French concession storefront. Highly recommended are *zīrán páigǔ* (cumin ribs), *gān guō jī* (chicken in chili pot), *suān dòujiǎo ròuní* (mashed pork with sour beans), *dòujiāo yútóu* (fish head steamed with red chili), and the spiced bullfrog leg. Or order just about anything in sight and plenty of cold beer to douse the fiery flames in your mouth. Service by the batik-clad waitstaff is no-nonsense, even occasionally impatient, but the food is superb and shouldn't be missed.

Màomíng Nán Lù 56 茂名南路 5 6 号 (north of Chánglè Lù); see map p. 140. ℂ **021/6253-2689.** Meal for 2 ¥80–¥140. No credit cards. Daily 10am–1am. Metro: Shanxi Rd. (S).

**Zǎo Zī Shù** 枣子树 ★ VEGETARIAN   This restaurant's name literally means "jujube tree," but the three characters that greet visitors upon arrival also cleverly play on the pun *zǎo chī sù*, advocating the early adoption of a vegetarian diet. Pleasant and contemporary, the restaurant takes its mission seriously: Fruit is served as an appetizer; organic tea is the norm; alcohol, dairy, and MSG are shunned; and

## SHÀNGHǍI'S street FOOD

For all of Shànghǎi's glamorous world-class restaurants located in restored colonial edifices or the most modern of skyscrapers, some of the city's best (not to mention cheapest) food can be found on its streets. At holes-in-the-wall or flimsy makeshift stalls about town, you can find everything from your average *ròubāo/càibāo* (meat and vegetable buns) and *shāomài* (glutinous rice dumplings) to Shànghǎi's classic snacks like *cōng yóu bīng* (scallion pancakes), *jiǔcài hézi* (leek pie), *xiǎolóng bāo* (pork-filled soup dumplings; see p. 134), and even *chòu dòufu* (stinky tofu), to the Muslim-influenced *yángròu chuàn* (spicy grilled lamb skewers). A perennial favorite is *shēngjiān bāo*, medium-size buns filled with fatty ground pork, shallow-fried on the bottom, then steamed, and sprinkled with sesame seeds and chives. You can eat it plain or dip it in black

*Zhènjiāng* vinegar. But the *pièce de résistance* of Shànghǎi street food has to be *jīdàn bīng* (egg pancake), a kind of local breakfast burrito. Batter is poured onto a hot round griddle to form a thin crepe. A fresh egg is added, along with a dash of bean paste, chili sauce, chives, finely diced pickled mustard greens, and the optional salty cruller (*yóutiáo*). The whole thing is then folded into a square or a roll and presto—a most tasty breakfast you won't find back home.

Though these snacks are available on many a Shànghǎi street corner, those in the know head for **the corner of Chánglè Lù and Xiāngyáng Lù** in the French Concession, where you can find some of the best street breakfasts and snacks in town. **Sìpǎilóu Lù** in the old Chinese city (south of Fāngbāng Lù and west of Zhōnghuá Lù) also features many food stalls selling all kinds of local snacks.

# COFFEE, tea & SOMETHING ELSE

The number of Western-style cafes and coffee bars that have sprouted in Shànghǎi in the last few years can almost make you forget that the Chinese have traditionally been tea drinkers. You can credit (or blame) Starbucks for the java jolt, but if you are in need of a caffeine fix, consider branching out and spreading the wealth a little. The following is a list of unusual local teahouses and cafes that offer much more than your average cup of overpriced joe:

**Old China Hand Reading Room** (Shàoxīng Lù 27, by Shǎnxī Nán Lù, Xúhuì; *©* 021/6473-2526; daily 10am–midnight). The most charming coffeehouse in town, it has Qīng Dynasty furniture, old manual typewriters, and beautiful photographs taken by owner and photographer Deke Erh. Sip your tea, coffee, or fruit juice while browsing through hundreds of old and new books and magazines.

**Old Film Café** (Duōlún Lù 123, near Sìchuān Běi Lù, Hóngkǒu; *©* 021/5696-4763; daily 10am–1am). A bit out of the way up by the Duōlún Lù Culture Street (p. 178), but here is a rare opportunity for film lovers to see some Chinese and Russian films dating back to the 1920s. Order a cup of tea, select a flick, and settle in for some culture with your caffeine.

**Wagas** (Huáihǎi Zhōng Lù 300, Hong Kong New World, B107, Lúwān; *©* 021/6335-3739; daily 9:30am–9pm). Who needs Starbucks when you can have Italian illy brand coffee? Wagas serves it straight up, with lounge chairs, a mellow soundtrack, Wi-Fi, gourmet panini, and a lot of healthy menu items like smoothies. There's another branch at Nánjīng Xī Lù 1168, CITIC Square, LG12A (*©* 021/5292-5228).

smoking is definitively prohibited. The bean curd skin roll is a delicious appetizer, while the sweet-and-sour vegetarian pork and the pot with vegetable and curry are popular can't-go-wrong choices. Avoid the vegetarian steak with pepper sauce, though. Spinach dumplings and soup noodles with vegetables are also hearty alternatives for those less inclined to edible fungi. Waitstaff is friendly and helpful.

Sōngshān Lù 77 嵩山路 7 7 号, 1st floor (inside the Shànghǎi Huánggōng complex, south of Huáihǎi Lù, 1 block east of Huángpí Nán Lù); see map p. 140. *©* **021/6384-8000.** Reservations recommended. Meal for 2 ¥80–¥140. AE, DC, MC, V. Daily 11am–9pm. Metro: Huangpi Rd. (S).

## Inexpensive

**Xīn Wàng** 新旺 HONG KONG   Informal, inexpensive, yet tasty dining at its best, this small chain dishes up a hodgepodge of Chinese comfort foods guaranteed to please all comers. Rice, noodles, and congee form the base of most dishes, after which it's strictly variations on a theme. *Yángzhōu chǎofàn* (fried rice), *xiānxiā yúntūn miàn* (shrimp wonton noodles in soup), *mìzhī chāshāo fàn* (barbecue pork rice)—they're all here, along with casseroles, simple sandwiches, fruit juices, and milk teas. The scene is typically chaotic, the waitstaff is usually harried, but the food is delivered quickly. There is another popular branch at Hànkǒu Lù 309 (*©* 021/6360-5008).

Chánglè Lù 175 长乐路 1 7 5 号 (btw. Màomíng Nán Lù and Ruìjīn Yī Lù); see map p. 140. *©* 021/6415-5056. Meal for 2 ¥40–¥70. No credit cards. Daily 7am–5am. Metro: Shanxi Rd. (S).

# XÚHUÌ DISTRICT (SOUTHWEST SHÀNGHǍI)

## Very Expensive

**el Willy** ★ SPANISH   This contemporary Spanish restaurant is a favorite with expats, and frequently garners a host of awards from the local English-language life-style and dining magazines. This might lead some to expect the restaurant to be the greatest thing since the invention of paella, which it is not, but there are enough tasty dishes here for a perfectly fun and enjoyable evening, especially when you throw in the cozy French Concession mansion (the Diage house) with glass windows, one of the best *el fresco* garden settings in town, and the irrepressible charms of chef Guillermo "Willy" Trullas Moreno. Recommended tapas dishes (with the de rigueur modern twist) include the seared foie gras, scallop ceviche, seared red tuna loin, and lamb skewers with smoked eggplant, while the paellas are trusty standbys. There is a wide selection of wines and sherries, which just might make up for the average service.

Dōnghú Lù 20, 1st floor 东湖路 2 0 号 (north of Huáihǎi Zhōng Lù); see map p. 140.Ⓒ **021/5404-5757.** www.elwilly.com.cn. Reservations required. Meal for 2 ¥400–¥800. AE, DC, MC, V. Mon–Sat 5:30–10:30pm. Metro: Changshu Rd.

**Franck** ★★ FRENCH   Squirreled away in the French Concession in charming Ferguson Lane—a trendy little warren of shops, offices, and restaurants—is this cozy French restaurant serving the most authentic bistro fare in town. The red walls are adorned with French movie posters and maps. The menu, which changes daily, is carted around on a blackboard by the attentive and friendly staff, while owner Franck, originally from Aix-en-Provence, attends to every table. Menu choices are all solid here, judging from the many French-speaking repeat diners. You can't go wrong with the cold cuts or the *terrine de campagne* for starters, and classic *poulet rôti* (using free-range chicken from Mongolia, no less) and *tartare de boeuf* for main courses. When the delectable *confit de canard* makes an appearance, be sure to pounce on it. The extensive wine list has some pleasant French finds that complement the dishes well, and a small *boulangerie* sells meats and cheeses if you want to pack for a picnic the next day.

Wǔkāng Lù 376, Ferguson Lane 武康路 3 7 6 弄 (south of Húnán Lù); see map p. 140.Ⓒ **021/6437-6465.** Reservations recommended. Meal for 2 ¥400–¥600. AE, DC, MC, V. Daily 6–10:30pm. No Metro.

**Restaurant Martin** 小红楼 ★ SPANISH   If you have an unlimited expense account and are just hankering for some haute Spanish cuisine, head over to three-star Michelin chef Martin Berasategui's restaurant in Xújiāhuī Park. To be sure, Berasategui oversees the menu from Spain, while his two protégés Maxime Fanton and Yago Márquez execute his vision in a 1921 red-brick mansion that was once the original EMI recording studio. There are several menu options here, including selections from Berasategui's award-winning San Sebastian restaurant (try the *Jamon Iberico*), but some other appetizers have been a bit hit-or-miss. You can't go wrong just going straight for the suckling pig and the seafood paella. (**Note:** If you want the whole suckling pig, it has to be pre-ordered.) Save room for the caramelized house-made cinnamon brioche with *café con leche* ice cream. Restaurant Martin some-times suffers from the heavy weight of expectations associated with the chef's renown (not to mention the sky-high prices), but the classics are reliable, the presentation impeccable, and the service highly attentive.

Héngshān Lù 811 衡山路 8 1 1 号 (in Xújiāhuì Gōngyuán); see map p. 140. ✆ **021/6431-9811.** Reservations required. Meal for 2 ¥700–¥1,400. AE, DC, MC, V. Daily 11:30am–2:30pm and 6:30–10:30pm (bar is open 9:30pm–1am/2am Fri–Sat). Metro: Hengshan Rd. or Xújiāhuì.

**Sushi Oyama** 大山 ★★★ JAPANESE   Located on the top floor of a lovely French Concession house and above the Spanish restaurant el Willy, Sushi Oyama serves the finest quality sushi in town. It's all omakase (chef's special) all the time, which means you give yourself over to the freshest fish selections of the day (flown in from Japan) by chef/owner Takeo Oyama. Selections (including dessert) are often of the exquisite melt-in-your-mouth variety, the sakes available are perfectly complementary, and service is highly attentive. Of course, it all comes at a price, a set price of ¥800 per person, not including drinks. The other downside to this fine restaurant is that it normally takes a week to secure a reservation as there are only 22 places available on any given night. However, you could try to make a reservation the moment (or even before) you get into town and who knows, you may get lucky. At press time, Chef Oyama was about to open another restaurant, Kappo Yu, at Wúxìng Lù 33 (✆ **021/6466-7855**), that would serve a similar *kaiseki*-style 10-course menu of seasonal dishes for ¥690.

Dōnghú Lù 20, 2nd floor 东湖路 2 0 号 (north of Huáihǎi Zhōng Lù); see map p. 140. ✆ **021/5404-7705.** Reservations required. Meal for 2 ¥1,600 and up. AE, DC, MC, V. Mon–Sat 5:30–10:30pm. Metro: Changshu Rd.

## Expensive

**Haiku by Hatsune** ★ JAPANESE   Sushi and sashimi purists might want to stay away, as it's all about the California-style rolls at this chic, highly popular Japanese haunt. Decor is minimalist, with low-slung banquettes and garden views. Favorites include the Moto-roll-ah, and 119 rolls (your standard spicy tuna roll), while the more adventurous can try the Alex Foie roll (seared foie gras with unagi, tempura, and shrimp). There's also a whole range of standard Japanese dishes like tempura, shabu shabu, and a variety of *izakaya*-style small dishes perfect for sharing. *Itadakimasu!*

Táojiāng Lù 28B 桃江路 28B 号 (btw. Héngshān Lù and Wūlūmùqí Lù); see map p. 140. ✆ **021/6445-0021.** Reservations recommended. Meal for 2 ¥200–¥300. AE, DC, MC, V. Daily 11:30am–2pm and 5:30–10:30pm. Metro: Hengshan Rd. or Changshu Rd.

**Shànghǎi Old Station Restaurant (Shànghǎi Lǎo Zhàn)** 上海老站 ★ SHÀNGHǍI   Located in a 1921 French monastery, this restaurant easily boasts one of the most atmospheric and nostalgic colonial settings in town. A mosaic-tiled corridor, lined with traditional lamps, antique gramophones, old photos, and even a painting of Jesus Christ, leads to a main dining hall where you can find the real novelty of this restaurant: two traditional railway carriages (an 1899 German wagon once serving the Qīng empress dowager Cíxǐ Tàihòu, and a 1919 Russian carriage used by Sòng Qìnglíng or Mme. Sun Yat-sen) running off the side of the building and providing additional seating. The food holds its own well enough, with traditional Shànghǎi dishes such as sautéed fresh shrimps, fried hairy crab (seasonal), special vegetarian duck, powdered crabmeat with tofu, and mushroom and vegetable buns making an impression. Don't expect the royal treatment in this Orient Express, as service is mostly perfunctory.

Cáoxī Běi Lù 201 漕溪北路 2 0 1 号 (opposite the Xújiāhuì Cathedral); see map p. 140. ☏ **021/6427-2233.** Reservations recommended. Meal for 2 ¥150–¥320. No credit cards. Daily 11:30am–2pm and 5:30–10pm. Metro: Xújiāhuì.

**Simply Thai (Tiāntài Cāntīng)** 天泰餐厅 ★★ THAI   This restaurant off trendy Héngshān Lù is a top choice with many Shànghǎi expatriates (Thais included) for unpretentious, authentic, and reasonably priced Thai food. The setting is a cozy, two-story cottage with olive green walls adorned with simple Thai friezes, and the food is comfortingly familiar with a few interesting twists. Especially pleasing are the refreshing pomelo (grapefruit) salad with pineapple appetizer, *tom yam* shrimp soup, *panaeng* pork curry, and seafood with glass noodle salad. The busy waitstaff puts on a friendly face. Patio dining in the warmer months provides a lovely respite from the city bustle. There is another branch at Xīntiāndì (☏ **021/6326-2088**).

Dōngpíng Lù 5 东平路 5 号, Unit C (btw. Héngshān Lù and Yuèyáng Lù); see map p. 140. ☏ **021/6445-9551.** Reservations recommended. Meal for 2 ¥150–¥300. AE, DC, MC, V. Daily 11am–11pm. Metro: Hengshan Rd. or Changshu Rd.

**Vedas** 维达斯饭店 INDIAN   Dine like a maharajah at this elegant Indian restaurant deep in the French Concession. With an open kitchen, wood paneling, and Indian music lilting in the background, Vedas gets high marks for authentic and flavorful dishes from all over the subcontinent. Full tandoori choices await, including the more unusual tandoori broccoli, which is quite popular. Try, too, the Kesari chicken *tikka*, lamb *rogan josh,* and the delightful mushroom *methi* (mushroom with fenugreek). Wash it all down with lots of strong masala tea. Service is attentive and considerate.

Jiànguó Xī Lù 550 建国西路 5 5 0 号 (by Wūlǔmùqí Nán Lù); see map p. 140. ☏ **021/6445-3670.** www.vedascuisine.com. Reservations recommended. Meal for 2 ¥200–¥300. AE, DC, MC, V. Daily 11:30am–2:30pm and 5:30–11:30pm. Metro: Hengshan Rd.

# Moderate

**Hot Pot King (Lái Fú Lóu)** 来福楼 ★ HOT POT   Unlike most hot pot restaurants, which are packed, chaotic, and decor-free, Lái Fú Lóu provides some of the most elegant hot pot dining in town. Decor is sleek, with soft gray chairs and dark brown wooden tables spaced far apart, affording diners some welcome privacy. Your biggest decision will be to pick your soup base: There's a wide variety here from which to choose, including a special chicken soup stock, fish, or pig bone soup. Many folks opt for the *yuānyáng* version, which contains both a potent spicy stock and a more benign, pork-based broth. Besides all the usual meat and vegetable ingredients, the restaurant also specializes in handmade *yúwán* (fish balls) and *dànjiǎo* (egg-wrapped dumplings).

Huáihǎi Zhōng Lù 1416 淮海中路 1 4 1 6 号, 2nd floor (at intersection of Fùxīng Xī Lù); see map p. 140. ☏ **021/6473-6380.** Reservations recommended. Meal for 2 ¥80–¥120. AE, DC, MC, V. Daily 11am–4am. Metro: Changshu Rd.

**Jíshì (Jesse Restaurant)** 吉士 ★★ SHÀNGHǍI   The progenitor of the Xīn Jíshì restaurants around town, this down-home restaurant in a tiny French concession cottage is one of my favorites for unrepentantly old-fashioned and delicious Shanghainese comfort food. The must-try's here include the wine-marinated crab, jujubes stuffed with glutinous rice, soy sauce stewed pork, and when in season, the *hóngshāo jiāo bái* (soy-braised wild rice stems). Service is brusque as the harried waitstaff is often eager to clear your table to accommodate the lines out the door. Don't expect to get in here without a reservation.

Tiānpíng Lù 41 天平路 41 (south of Huáihǎi Lù) ); see map p. 140. (*C*) **021/6282-9260.** Reservations required. Meal for 2 ¥120–¥200. AE, DC, MC, V. 11am–midnight. Metro: Xújiāhuì.

**O'Malley's (Ōu Mǎ Lì Cāntīng)** 欧玛莉餐厅 ☺ IRISH   Best known as one of Shànghǎi's top bars and music spots, O'Malley's also sports a menu of Irish, English, and American favorites that range from bangers and mash to hearty helpings of mashed potatoes and flavorful steaks and burgers. Service is friendly and efficient. The old two-story mansion has been decorated like a down-and-out Irish pub, with plenty of cozy booths and tables on its main floor and balcony. In summertime, the large front lawn has courtyard dining and a children's playground, a handy feature during popular weekend brunches. The beers, of course, are quite good.

Táojiāng Lù 42 桃江路 4 2 号 (1 block west of Héngshān Lù); see map p. 140. (*C*) **021/6437-0667** or 021/6474-4533. Meal for 2 ¥80–¥150. AE, MC, V. Mon–Sat 11am–2am; Sun 10am–1am. Metro: Hengshan Rd. or Changshu Rd.

**Paulaner Bräuhaus (Bǎoláinà)** 宝莱纳 ★ GERMAN   Highly popular with local businessmen and their families, Shànghǎi's biggest beer house is a massive 1930s three-story structure isolated from the road by a large green courtyard that serves as a summer beer garden. The in-house German-style brewery makes its own Münchner ale and lager, which goes down well with heaps of sauerkraut, sausages, cabbage, and bratwurst.

Fēnyáng Lù 150 汾阳路 1 5 0 号 (2 blocks east of Héngshān Lù, near the Dōngpíng Lù intersection); see map p. 140. (*C*) **021/6474-5700.** Meal for 2 ¥80–¥160. AE, DC, MC, V. Mon–Fri 5:30pm–2am; Sat–Sun 11am–4pm and 5:30pm–2am. Metro: Changshu Rd.

**Shànghǎi Xīnjiāng Fēngwèi Fàndiàn** 上海新疆风味饭店 UIGHUR   Got lamb? Credible northwest Chinese cuisine can be found at this Uighur restaurant. Amid fake foliage and a miniature model of Xīnjiāng Province's Tiān Shān (Heavenly Lake), patrons are treated to a fun, raucous, and hearty dining experience complete with whooping and dancing waiters. The Uighurs are Muslim, so lamb dominates the Chinese-only menu. Definitely try the juicy *kǎo quányáng* (roast lamb), though if you plan to dine after 7pm, call ahead and reserve a portion, as this popular dish often runs out early. Other favorites include *kǎo yángròu* (barbecue lamb skewers), *dà pán jī* (chicken with cardamoms, peppers, tomatoes, onions, and potatoes), and *lǎohǔ cài*, a refreshing Xīnjiāng salad of cucumbers, tomatoes, and red onions. Noodles (*miàntiáo*) or baked bread (*bǐng*) make good accompaniments, as does Xīnjiāng black beer (*Xīnjiāng píjiǔ*).

Yíshān Lù 280 宜山路 2 8 0 号 (south of Nándān Lù); see map p. 140. (*C*) **021/6468-9198.** Reservations recommended. Meal for 2 ¥120–¥240. No credit cards. Daily 10am–2am (nightly dancing at 7:30pm). Metro: Xújiāhuì (20 min. away).

## Inexpensive

**The Grape (Pútao Yuán Jiǔjiā)** 葡萄园酒家 ⚓ SHÀNGHǍI   Located in part of a stunning, domed former Russian Orthodox church (though little of it is obvious in today's restaurant), the Grape was one of the first Shànghǎi eateries to attract foreign residents. Today, this friendly, down-to-earth (except for the clusters of plastic grapes that hang overhead) cafe keeps a core group of expats and locals happy with its reasonably priced homemade Shànghǎi cuisine and friendly service. The phoenix-tail shrimps with garlic, steamed clams with eggs, spicy chicken, and braised fresh bamboo shoots are all worth trying.

Xīnlè Lù 55 新乐路 5 5 号 (2 blocks west of Shǎnxī Nán Lù, btw. Huáihǎi and Yán'ān Lù); see map p. 140. ℂ **021/5404-0486.** Meal for 2 ¥70–¥140. No credit cards. Daily 11am–midnight. Metro: Shanxi Rd. (S).

## VENI, VIDI, VECI, vino?

Less than a decade ago, if visitors wanted to sip some fine wine in Shànghǎi, they had to head over to a high-end joint venture hotel restaurant and pay some rather exorbitant prices for a limited selection of foreign varietals. Happily for the wine connoisseur in the last few years, **wine bars** and shops have sprouted in Shànghǎi like grapes on a Napa vine, and many restaurants now pride themselves on stocking a wide variety of international brands. Foreign wineries look at Shànghǎi as a burgeoning market, with the result that many suppliers have entered the Chinese market in recent years. For those interested in sampling more local fare, the Chinese wine industry is still relatively young, but is quickly learning and growing from its joint ventures (successful or not) with foreign partners. Brands like Changyu (China's largest wine company), Dragon Seal, Hua Dong, Great Wall, and Dynasty are the better-known Chinese vintners, but quality still varies wildly, and foreigners often find Chinese wines to be more vapid than what they are used to back home. If you fancy a pre- or post-prandial glass (or bottle), the following wine bars and restaurants will serve you well. Prices are generally higher than what you might pay at home for a similar bottle (due partly to high import duties), but outlets often have wine-tastings and special deals, especially when introducing new wines.

**Enoteca** (Ānfú Lù 53–57, east of Wūlǔmùqí Lù, Xúhuì; ℂ **021/5404-0050;** www.enoteca.com.cn; daily 10am–midnight). Pleasant, welcoming place in the French Concession serving a good selection of affordable old- and new-world wines with delicious tapas and sandwiches. A second branch has opened right next to Xīntiāndì (Tàicāng Lù 58, west of Jìnán Lù, Lúwān; ℂ **021/5306-3400**).

**Just Grapes** (Dàgǔ Lù 462, Jìng Ān; ℂ **021/3311-3205;** www.justgrapes.cn; daily 10:30am–10:30pm). This wine shop labels its large selection of international wines (around 400 at last count) according to the wine's general characteristics and its predominant flavors, instead of by country or region, all to help demystify the wine-buying experience. There is a connecting wine lounge and restaurant that serves only a few wines by the glass.

**Napa Wine Bar and Kitchen** (Jiāngyīn Lù 57, near Huángpí Lù, Huángpǔ; ℂ **021/6318-0057;** www.napawine barandkitchen.com; daily 6pm–midnight). Located in a restored Tudor mansion near People's Square with a 40-seat wine bar, large dining room, and outdoor area, this classy outfit has a wine list with over 700 labels, paired with a tasty menu of wine-inspired dishes. In general, you get decent value for your money and knowledgeable and helpful advice if needed.

## SHÀNGHǍI'S BEST FOR brunch

Calling all gluttons! When it comes to chowing down, Shànghǎi's restaurants know how to put on a buffet. Weekend brunches (mostly held in the big hotels Sun 11am–2:30pm) are not necessarily cheap (and a 15% gratuity is added to your tab), but they are sumptuous events and extremely popular among expatriates and Shànghǎi residents alike. Here's a sampling of the best hotel brunches:

**Yi Café at the Shangri-La** (Fùchéng Lù 33, second floor; ☏ 021/6882-8888) sets the standard high with the most extensive international brunch in town. Surely you can find something to eat from 10 food stations that span the globe's cuisine. Or maybe you'd like to try them all. The cost is ¥298, with champagne costing extra. The **Stage** in the Westin Hotel (Hénán Zhōng Lù 88; ☏ 021/6335-1888) has garnered raves for its kids' corner; parents can now feast

the afternoon away (¥498 with free-flowing champagne) while their children play under supervision. **Le Bistrot All Day Dining Restaurant** in Le Royal Meridien Hotel (Nánjīng Dōng Lù 789; ☏ 021/3318-9999, ext. 7008) is another popular choice with its full international spread of everything from foie gras to sushi to an outdoor barbecue in the summer, with as much Mumm Brut as you want for ¥418. The **Marriott Café** at the JW Marriott (Nánjīng Xī Lù 399; ☏ 021/5359-4969, ext. 6422) outdoes the competition with its 360-degree bubbly brunch: a feast of sushi, oysters, lobsters, and unlimited champagne (¥458) against a backdrop of stunning city views and live jazz.

Outside the hotels, **M on the Bund** (p. 111) has the best views to go with your Bloody Mary and eggs Benedict; and **Mesa** (p. 128) serves the best healthy brunch around.

# JÌNG ĀN DISTRICT (NORTHWEST SHÀNGHǍI)

## Very Expensive

**Jing'an Restaurant** ★★ CONTINENTAL    Overlooking Jing'an Park, this classy restaurant on the second floor of the PuLi Hotel and Spa serves some delightfully tasty, chef-billed "hybrid nonesuch cuisine," which means the menu covers everything from artisan breakfasts to bistro lunches to more experimental, innovative dinner choices. Eschewing trendiness, Kiwi chef Dane Clouston is more about playing with the subtle and sophisticated flavors and textures of seasonal ingredients. Lunch is prix fixe and the only occasion to have the delightful Jing'an Burger, sandwiching a thin slab of foie gras, and sized just right (no Big Mac's here). Dinner recommendations include wonderful appetizers: pastrami of salmon and foie gras with smoked chocolate. The slow-roasted Wagyu beef and the maple-roasted duck breast main courses also fare well. Or you may just want to start with dessert first, with the lemon curd pie, strawberry trifle, and the five-spice *panna cotta* (cooked cream), all worth the extra calories. Service is attentive without being intrusive.

Chángdé Lù 1, 2nd floor, PuLi Hotel and Spa 常德路 1 号 (by Yán'ān Zhōng Lù); see map p. 144. ☏ 021/2216-6988. www.jinganrestaurant.com. Reservations recommended. Meal for 2 ¥600–¥1,000. AE, DC, MC, V. Daily 6:30–10am (11am Sun), noon–2:30pm, and 7–10:30pm. Metro: Jing'an Temple.

**Shintori Null II (Xīndūlǐ Wúèr Diàn)** 新都里无二店 ★★ JAPANESE This nouvelle Japanese restaurant in the western part of the French Concession is the epitome of cool, if you like dining in a cold and dystopian industrial bunker. A bamboo-lined concrete walkway and silent automatic sliding doors lead to the main dining pit, which features a long communal table in the center, and an all-chrome open kitchen in the back. The second floor has some of the best perches for people-watching as well as private dining areas sectioned off by blinds. As expected, the crowd is well-heeled, black-clad, and a bit precious. Sushi and sashimi are fresh and popular, but a fun way to go may be to make a meal from a selection of appetizers, such as cuttlefish in butter sauce, Peking duck rolls, foie gras on radish, and vermicelli noodles served in an ice bowl. Save room for the green tea tiramisu dessert. Service is efficient and friendly, which lends some much-needed warmth to the place.

Jùlù Lù 803 巨鹿路 8 0 3 号 (west of Fùmín Lù); see map p. 144. ⓒ **021/5404-5252.** Reservations required. Meal for 2 ¥400–¥700. AE, DC, MC, V. Mon-Fri 5:30-10:30pm; Sat-Sun 11:30am-2pm and 5-11pm. Metro: Changshu Rd.

# Expensive

**Bali Laguna (Bālí Dǎo)** 巴厘岛 INDONESIAN Bali Laguna is widely acclaimed for its exquisite setting, perched over a lily pond in the heart of Jìng Ān Park. With an exotic Southeast Asian decor, views of the surrounding garden, and discreet sarong-clad waitstaff, there are few more genteel or romantic places to dine in Shànghǎi. The food is fairly authentic, rated above average though falling short of a rave. Tasty choices include *otak-otak* (grilled fish cake), chicken satay, king prawns with vermicelli and lemon grass, and stir-fried mushrooms with herbs and vegetables. Dining is on the second floor; reserve ahead for a window table. The bar on the first floor is open nightly until 1am.

Huáshān Lù 189 华山路 1 8 9 号 (inside southwest entrance to Jìng Ān Park); see map p. 144. ⓒ **021/6248-6970.** Reservations recommended. Meal for 2 ¥150–¥250. AE, DC, MC, V. Daily 11am-2:30pm and 6-10:30pm. Metro: Jing'an Temple.

**Kuo Bee Pen Da (Guō Bǐ Pén Dà)** 锅比盆大 HOT POT Diners come to this Taiwanese hot pot chain not for its decor (unremarkable at best), but for its spicy soup bases and fresh homemade dumplings. A curry soup base is the house specialty, but you can also choose the Thai-style hot and sour soup base, the satay soup base, or the *yuānyang* combination (of curry soup and pork-based broth in a different compartment). There's the usual selection of meats, seafood, and vegetables to cook in the bubbling broth, as well as the restaurant's handmade dumplings. Half of the fun here is in creating your own dipping sauces, and there's a wide range of ingredients to choose from, including mashed fresh garlic, parsley, chili oil, peanut sauce, spicy sesame oil, and XO sauce. This is as fun as cooking your own food gets.

Huáshān Lù 301-1 华山路 3 0 1 - 1 号 (across from the Hilton Hotel); see map p. 144. ⓒ **021/6249-8877.** Reservations recommended. Meal for 2 ¥150–¥300. AE, DC, MC, V. Daily 11am-4am. Metro: Changshu Rd.

**Nepali Kitchen (Níbó'ěr Cāntīng)** 尼泊尔餐厅 NEPALESE Fancy a trip to the Himalayas, if only through your taste buds? A favorite with many Shànghǎi expats, this charming three-story restaurant with colorful walls, pictures of snowy mountain ranges, and cushion seating in the back serves fairly authentic Nepali and Tibetan dishes. The cheese balls appetizer and the stir-fried tenderloin beef Nepali-style are always popular starters. For main courses, the Nepali-style grilled fish, the curries, and barbecues are also quite good. Service falls off a bit when it gets busy, which happens almost every night during prime dining hours; an early start will at least get you a little more attention.

Jùlù Lù 819, No. 4 巨鹿路 8 1 9 号 (west of Fùmín Lù); see map p. 144. ✆ **021/5404-6281.** Meal for 2 ¥200-¥300. AE, MC, V. Mon-Sat 11am-2am; Sun 10am-1am. Metro: Changshu Rd.

**People on the Water (Shuǐshàng Rénjiā)** 水上人家 ★ SEAFOOD   Located in the basement of the Hilton Hotel, this elegant, award-winning restaurant specializes in fresh seafood from Níngbō, in case the restaurant's blue hues, flowing water, glass bridge, and tanks of fresh fish hadn't already alerted you. Though the average diner cannot discern any real differences between Níngbō and Shanghainese cuisine, here you'll find some wonderfully subtle and unusual combinations of flavor and ingredients in the seafood dishes you're not even likely to encounter in even many local restaurants. Popular dishes include the deep-fried crab with sinfully thick roe, steamed snow cabbage with yellow fish, clams on a sizzling plate, and braised river eel. The shrimp with crispy seaweed is unusual, if not to everyone's taste. The staff can be helpful, but service drops off considerably when it gets busy.

Huáshān Lù 250 华山路 2 5 0 号, Lower Lobby (basement of the Hilton Hotel); see map p. 144. ✆ **021/6248-7777,** ext. 1830. Reservations required. Meal for 2 ¥150-¥300. AE, DC, MC, V. Daily 11am-2:30pm and 5:30-10:30pm. Metro: Jing'an Temple.

**South Beauty (Qiào Jiāng Nán)** 俏江南 ★ SÌCHUĀN   There are five South Beauty locations around town, but this one in an old financier's mansion off the old Avenue Edward VII (today's Yán'ān Lù) gets raves for its glamorous ambience. Given a contemporary makeover complete with Chinese motifs, lattice paneling, and wooden floors, the restaurant is huge, with a lounge, bar, cigar room, and different dining areas, including a patio that can be quite romantic at night. The food is not excessively spicy here, perhaps to accommodate local and expatriate tastes, but you can always request them to *jiā là* (pile on the spicy). Start with the Four Seasons Cold Dish Platter where you can select four appetizers from a wide range of choices; graduate to the "Australian Beef Tender in Hot Oil with Stones" (tender and succulent as the name suggests), and the delicious "Lan Style Spare Ribs with Chili and Spices." Save room for the *dan-dan* noodles in spicy peanut sauce. I found the staff to be attentive and efficient, but there have been occasional complaints of poor service.

Yán'ān Zhōng Lù 881 延安中路 8 8 1 号 (just east of Tóngrén Lù); see map p. 144. ✆ **021/6247-5878.** Reservations recommended. Meal for 2 ¥200-¥400. AE, DC, MC, V. Daily 11am-11:30pm. Metro: Nanjing Rd. (W).

# Moderate

**Bǎoluó** 保罗 ★ 🍴 SHÀNGHǍI   One of the few constants in this ever-changing town is the long line that invariably forms outside Bǎoluó every evening. A seemingly tiny diner occupying a mere unit in a row of tightly packed Chinese houses until you step inside, the restaurant actually stretches four houses deep, every square inch buzzing with barely controlled chaos. The story goes that Bǎoluó's owner—a bicycle repairman who lived in this very lane—started the restaurant in his own home, but gradually bought up his neighbors' houses as business boomed. The extensive menu features many local favorites given a slight twist, including *huíguō ròu jiābǐng* (twice-cooked lamb wrapped in pancakes), *sōngshǔ lúyú* (sweet-and-sour fried fish), *xièfěn huì zhēnjūn* (braised mushroom with crabmeat), and the sinfully fatty, but absolutely delicious *hóng shāoròu* (braised pork belly).

Fùmín Lù 271 富民路 2 7 1 号 (north of Chánglè Lù, 1 block east of Chángshú Lù); see map p. 144.
℡ **021/6279-2827.** Reservations recommended. Meal for 2 ¥80–¥150. No credit cards. Daily 11am–
6am. Metro: Changshu Rd.

**Gǔ Yì** 古意 ★★ HÚNÁN   Offering spicy Húnán in an elegant if uninteresting
environment, the cramped and therefore perennially packed Gǔ Yì caters to a better-
dressed crowd that tries to hold off breaking a sweat for as long as possible, to no
avail in the end, of course. Tops here are the fresh seafood dishes dressed in a variety of spices and ingredients direct from Húnán. Adventurous types may want to try
the signature shredded pig's ear in chili oil. If not, there are plenty of other recommended dishes, including roasted shrimp on skewers, smoked pork and preserved
beans, and lamb with cumin spice. Note that most fowl dishes are served with bones
intact. Because tables are packed close together, nonsmokers find there's no escap-
ing any secondhand smoke from a neighboring table. Waitstaff could be friendlier,
but the excellent food makes up for these little inconveniences. Reserve in advance
or risk a very long wait.

Fùmín Lù 87 富民路 8 7 号 (north of Jùlù Lù); see map p. 144. ℡ **021/6249-5628.** Reservations recommended. Meal for 2 ¥160–¥240. No credit cards. Daily 11:30am–2pm and 5:30–10:30pm. Metro:
Changshu Rd.

**Malone's (Mǎlóng Měishì Jiǔlóu)** 马龙美式酒楼 AMERICAN   Originally part
of a chain from Canada (opened in 1994), Malone's is a popular sports bar and
restaurant in the American image, complete with wooden floors, dartboards, a pool
table, a small stage, and a dance floor. The TV monitors over the long bar are tuned
to international sports programs, and a decent dance band plays until closing on
weekends, when it gets very crowded. The 100-entry menu is a comprehensive if
overpriced version of American sports bar fare, with potato skins, Buffalo wings,
fries, sandwiches, grilled steaks, and gigantic hamburgers. Unfortunately, service is
hit or miss: If the waitstaff has any experience, they're careful not to show it.

Tóngrén Lù 255 同仁路 2 5 5 号 (2 blocks northwest of Shànghǎi Centre); see map p. 144. ℡ **021/6247-
2400.** www.malones.com.cn. Meal for 2 ¥80–¥180. AE, DC, MC, V. Daily 11am–2am. Metro: Jing'an
Temple.

**Méilóngzhèn** 梅陇镇 ★★ SHÀNGHǍI   Established in 1938, Méilóngzhèn is a
Shànghǎi institution that still draws the crowds after all these years. Its cuisine has
evolved over time from strictly regional fare to one incorporating the spices, vinegars,
and chilies of Sìchuān cooking. Seafood is featured prominently, and popular favorites include deep-fried eel, lobster in pepper sauce, Mandarin fish with noodles in
chili sauce, Sìchuān duck, and Méilóngzhèn special chicken, served in small
ceramic pots. Renovations have turned the once-stodgy surroundings into a sparkling modern restaurant. Staff alternates between attentive and harried. There is
another branch in the Westgate mall at Nánjīng Xī Lù 1038 (℡ **021/6255-6688**).

Nánjīng Xī Lù 1081 南京西路 1 0 8 1 号, Building 22 (east of Shànghǎi Centre at Jiāngníng Lù); see
map p. 144. ℡ **021/6253-5353.** Reservations recommended. Meal for 2 ¥120–¥240. AE, DC, MC, V.
Daily 11am–2pm and 5–10pm. Metro: Nanjing Rd. (W).

**Mesa (Méisà)** 梅萨 ★ CONTINENTAL   This modern minimalist restaurant
with stark walls, floor-to-ceiling windows, and an open kitchen serves up the comfort
foods of home while making good use of fresh local ingredients. The menu changes
frequently, but established favorites include the beetroot Carpaccio with goat

## Chinese on the Cheap

Fast, tasty, and cheap Chinese food can always be found in the point-and-choose **food courts** that blanket the basements (usually) of the large shopping malls and department stores. A multitude of stalls proffer everything from basic stir-fries to Hong Kong–style dim sum, Southern-style casseroles to Northern-style noodles and dumplings. Simply point and choose from the dishes or models on display. Prices are very reasonable, allowing you to try a variety of dishes. You will have to purchase coupons or a card to pay for your food at each stall. The **Megabite** (Dàshídài) food courts in Hong Kong Plaza (Huáihǎi Zhōng Lù 282, Lúwān) and Raffles City Mall (Xīzàng Zhōng Lù 268, Huángpǔ) are excellent places to sample the goods.

cheese, soy and ginger salmon with green tea soba, T-bone steak, and beef pie. Wines, chosen from an impressive list, are served in specially imported glasses. Save room for the homemade desserts. There is alfresco dining on the second-floor patio during the warmer months. This is as comfortable and as unpretentious as fine dining gets. On weekends, Mesa also serves one of the best home-style brunches in town.

Jùlù Lù 748 巨鹿路 7 4 8 号 (east of Fùmín Lù); see map p. 144. ☎ **021/6289-9108.** Reservations required. Meal for 2 ¥90–¥200. AE, DC, MC, V. Mon-Fri 11:30am-2:30pm and 6-11:30pm; Sat-Sun 9:30am-5pm and 6-11:30pm. Metro: Changshu Rd.

**Rendezvous (Fú Lè Jū)** 福乐局 SINGAPOREAN   The restaurant's decor may not be terribly creative (wall posters of Singapore compete with red and green tinsel hanging from the ceiling), but happily, the food served at this restaurant tucked away on the south side of the Kerry Center is authentic and mouthwatering Singaporean and Malaysian fare, as evidenced by the mostly Singaporean clientele. The menu is extensive, filled with curry, chili *blanchan* (chili mixed with shrimp paste), and *nonya* dishes and snacks found at the best of Singapore's hawker stalls. Worth trying are the *laksa* (rice noodles in a spicy coconut soup), the chili crab (Singapore style), spicy Assam fish head, and *sambal* prawns. Finish up with the *bubur chacha* dessert (yam, sweet potato, and sago in coconut milk) or an *ice kachang* (red or green bean with shaved ice). Service is friendly and efficient.

Nánjīng Xī Lù 1515, No. 107 南京西路 1 5 1 5 号, 1st floor (on the south side of Kerry Center/Jiālì Zhōngxīn, at Tóngrén Lù); see map p. 144. ☎ **021/5298-6126.** Meal for 2 ¥160–¥250. AE, DC, MC, V. Daily 11am-9:30pm. Metro: Jing'an Temple.

## Inexpensive

**Element Fresh (Yuán Sù)** 元素 ★ AMERICAN   Even for a city as international and modern as Shànghǎi, finding a reasonably priced, delicious fresh salad on a consistent basis is not as easy as you might imagine. Thankfully, Element Fresh fills the niche for healthy dining by serving up a range of soups, salads, and sandwiches that are fresh, light, healthy, and an instant cure for any homesickness. This eatery has proved so popular that this original in Shànghǎi Centre has now spawned seven other branches. Also on the menu is a slew of smoothies, fresh fruit and vegetable juices, pastas, and a handful of Asian set meals, as well as some very popular breakfast sets. The place is jam-packed at lunchtime, as is the patio during warmer months. Another centrally located branch is on the fifth floor of the KWah Centre at Huáihǎi Zhōng Lù 1028 by Xiāngyáng Nán Lù (☎ **021/5403-8865**).

Nánjīng Xī Lù 1376 南京西路 1 3 7 6 号, no. 112 (ground floor, Shànghǎi Centre); see map p. 144. ☎ **021/6279-8682**. www.elementfresh.com. Reservations recommended. Meal for 2 ¥35–¥140. AE, DC, MC, V. Daily 7am–11pm (midnight Fri–Sat). Metro: Jing'an Temple.

# CHÁNGNÍNG DISTRICT/ HÓNGQIÁO DEVELOPMENT ZONE (WEST SHÀNGHǍI)

## Very Expensive

**Fu 1088 (Fú 1088)** 福一零八八 ★★★ SHÀNGHǍI   Tucked away behind an iron gate on a busy one-way street, this gem of a restaurant in a three-story mansion offers some of the best Shanghainese cuisine in town, and a much more fulfilling dining experience than its sister restaurant, Fu 1039. Guests here are in for a treat—dining is all in individual private rooms (there are 17 of them, seating 2 to 12 people), each furnished with early-20th-century furniture, cherry wood chairs, and chandeliers. Start with the chilled drunken chicken with rice-wine shaved ice, and the most delicious *xūn yú* (smoked fish) you'll ever taste, especially because it's served warm. For main dishes, dig into the glorious braised pork with soy and rock sugar, the deep-fried prawn with wasabi mayonnaise, and the steamed egg with crabmeat. Two local dishes you're unlikely to find back home that are also worth trying include *huáiyáng dàzhǔ gānsī* (bean curd sheet with garden greens and shrimp in thick soup), and the sautéed water bamboo in soy sauce. Service is very courteous and highly efficient. There is a ¥300 minimum charge per person, but for spot-on Shanghainese cuisine that is neither too sweet nor too oily, Fu 1088 is well worth the splurge.

Zhènníng Lù 375 镇宁路 3 7 5 号 (north of Yùyuán Lù); see map p. 152. ☎ **021/5239-7878**. Reservations required. Meal for 2 ¥600–¥900. AE, DC, MC, V. Daily 11am–2pm and 5:30pm–midnight. Metro: Jiangsu Rd.

## Expensive

**Blue Frog (Lán Wā)** 蓝蛙 ☺AMERICAN   This longstanding popular chain has outlets all over town, but this one in the Gubei area is extremely family-friendly with a large menu of familiar Western comfort foods (from nachos and chicken wings to juicy burgers and steaks) and a separate play area for kids. Portions are generous, the service is efficient, and best of all, the restaurant offers all kinds of specials, including discounted happy hour drinks every day and two-for-one burgers every Monday evening. Other branches are in the French Concession at Màomíng Nán Lù 207, #6 (☎ **021/6445-6634**), and in Pǔdōng at the Super Brand Mall, ground floor, no. 27, Lùjiāzuǐ Lù 168 (☎ **021/5047-3488**).

Hóngméi Lù 3338, #30 Hóngméi Leisure Pedestrian Street 虹梅路 3 3 3 8 弄 3 0 号 (south of Yán'ān Zhōng Lù); see map p. 152. ☎ **021/5422-5119**. www.bluefrog.com.cn. Reservations recommended. Meal for 2 ¥150–¥300. AE, DC, MC, V. Daily 10am–late. Metro: Hóngqiáo Rd.

**Chor Bazaar (Qiáobùlā Yìndù Cāntīng)** 乔布拉印度餐厅 ★ 🍴 INDIAN   Not many tourists make it out here to the northwest part of the city, but if you're in the vicinity, Chor Bazaar (*chor* means "thieves" in Hindi, and Chor Bazaar is a flea market in Mumbai) offers delicious Indian dishes at prices considerably cheaper than those at Indian restaurants downtown. The atmosphere is casual, the service top-notch. Menu items should be mostly familiar, but the quality is pleasantly high throughout. The flavorful chicken *tikka masala* and the chicken lollipops are standouts, as are the spinach lamb curry and the *baingan bharta* (eggplant curry). All of this complemented with freshly baked breads (naan and chapatti) and finished off with some delightfully crispy *jalebis* (deep-fried pretzels in syrup). The large number of Indian families dining here will reassure you of the cuisine's authenticity.

Jiānhé Lù 530 剑河路 5 3 0 号 (near Xiānxiá Xī Lù, next to the Xījiāo Bǎilián Century Mart); see map p. 152. (②) **139-1613-1209.** Reservations recommended. Meal for 2 ¥150-¥300. No credit cards. Daily 11am-11pm. Metro: Beixinjing Rd.

**Dynasty (Mǎn Fú Lóu)** 满福楼 ★ CANTONESE/DIM SUM   Long regarded as one of Shànghǎi's top Cantonese restaurants, Dynasty boasts the same chefs (many from Hong Kong) who routinely cater dinners for visiting heads of state at special banquets and luncheons. For their expertise, you can expect not the usual steaming, braising, or stir-frying, but some very creative methods of cooking, including boiling live fish, cut up in pieces, in a rich chicken broth, or roasting, then quick-frying chicken in boiling oil. The large tables with white tablecloths and the open dining space are thoroughly Cantonese, like the menu, where you can't go wrong with the fresh seafood dishes (prawns and lobster are good bets), the classic crispy roasted chicken, or the dim sum lunch.

Yán'ān Xī Lù 2099 延安西路 2 0 9 9 号 (3rd floor, Renaissance Yangtze Shànghǎi Hotel); see map p. 152. (②) **021/6275-0000,** ext. 2230. Reservations required. Meal for 2 ¥200-¥400. AE, DC, MC, V. Daily 11am-2:30pm and 6-10:30pm. No Metro.

## Moderate

**Bā Guó Bù Yī** 巴国布衣 SÌCHUĀN   Those seeking Sìchuān fare with some pizzazz can find it at this popular, batik-themed eatery where chili alerts in the Chinese-only menu will let you know what you're in for. Start your evening with the *fūqī fèipiàn* appetizer (cold beef and tongue doused in chili oil and peanuts), then graduate to *làzi jīdīng* (chicken nuggets in a sea of red chili peppers), *huíguō ròu* (twice-cooked pork with chili and scallions), and the delicious *shuǐzhǔ yú* (fish slices and vegetables in a flaming spicy broth), closing with *dāndān miàn* (noodles in spicy peanut sauce). In between, be kind to yourself with lots of cold water and beer breaks; you'll need them to put out the three-alarm fire in your mouth. There are "face-changing" (*biàn'niàn*) Sichuan Opera performances nightly at 7:40pm.

Dìng xī Lù 1018 定西路 1 0 1 8 号 (north of Yán'ān Xī Lù); see map p. 152. (②) **021/6270-6668** or 021/5239-7779. Reservations required. Meal for 2 ¥100-¥200. AE, DC, MC, V. 11:30am-2pm and 5-9:30pm. Metro: Zhongshan Park.

**Hǎi Dī Lāo** 海底捞 HOT POT   This clean and sleek branch of the popular chain of Sìchuān hot pot restaurants doesn't see many foreigners, but locals love it for its inexpensive, large selection of tasty hot pot ingredients and the restaurant's warm and friendly service. The do-it-yourself aspects are fun and start with a bar where you can mix your own dipping sauces from a large selection of condiments. Definitely order the *gōngfū miàn* (Kung-Fu noodles), whipped up and hand-pulled for you at your table (don't try this at home); after that, you have your pickings of just about every kind of land and sea ingredient you can imagine (the restaurant's name literally means scooping or dredging the ocean floor). The lamb from Inner Mongolia (*nèiméng yángròu*) and the fatty beef (*féi niú*) are also house specialties. It's an adventurous, fun time, and though the menus are in Chinese only, the staff is helpful and friendly and you can really just point to what other diners are having. Reservations are required if you don't want to wait (though snacks and tea are provided).

Wúzhōng Lù 1100 吴中路１１００号 (near Wànyuán Lù); see map p. 152. ℂ **021/5422-3132.** Reservations recommended. Meal for 2 ¥100–¥200. V. Daily 24 hr. No Metro.

**1221** ★★ SHÀNGHǍI  Located at the end of an alley between the center of town and the Hóngqiáo district, the classy "One-Two-Two-One (Yī Èr Èr Yī)" has been quietly serving consistently fine food at reasonable prices for more than a decade. Offering Shànghǎi cuisine (with a touch of East/West fusion cooking) that's neither too greasy nor too sweet, this chic, tastefully decorated restaurant has a large and endearingly loyal following in the expatriate and business community. Most things on the menu will delight, but some standouts include drunken chicken, Shànghǎi smoked fish, lion-head meatballs, and braised pork with preserved vegetables. Also worth trying are the spicy Sìchuān beef with sesame bread, and the crispy duck. Wash it all down with eight-treasure tea (*bābǎochá*), steeped with streams of hot water skillfully poured from long-sprouted teapots. The efficient, no-nonsense service could be friendlier, but that seems a small quibble in an otherwise excellent dining experience.

Yán'ān Xī Lù 1221 延安西路１２２１号 (btw. Pānyú Lù and Dīngxī Lù); see map p. 152. ℂ **021/6213-6585.** Reservations recommended. Meal for 2 ¥120–¥250. AE, DC, MC, V. Daily 11am–2pm and 5–11pm. No Metro.

# PŬDŌNG NEW AREA

## Very Expensive

**Danieli's (Dānní'àilì)** 丹尼艾丽 ★★ ITALIAN  Italian fine dining at its best, which in this case includes an extensive wine list and the city at your feet, Danieli's is a treat if you're in the area. Tasteful and elegant, this restaurant atop the St. Regis Hotel is laid out with an open kitchen and a handful of window tables, which you should request when you make your reservation. The menu, which changes every few months, features all manner of excellent *pesci* and *carni*, especially the grilled beef tenderloin, and the pastas hold their own as well. Save room for the sinful desserts (the tiramisu and warm chocolate cake are excellent), washed down with some delightfully bracing Italian illy coffee. Healthy business lunch sets are offered during the week, and there's a delectable Sunday brunch. From the service to the food, everything is done just right here.

Dōngfāng Lù 889 东方路８８９号 (29th floor, St. Regis Hotel); see map p. 148. ℂ **021/5050-4567,** ext. 6370. Reservations required. Meal for 2 ¥400–¥700. AE, DC, MC, V. Daily 11:30am–2:30pm and 6–10:30pm. Metro: Pudian Rd. or Century Ave.

**Guì Huā Lóu** 桂花楼 ★★ SHÀNGHǍI  Restaurants serving regional cuisine are a dime a dozen, so it's nice to find one that does things just a little bit differently, and with a little more care. This award-winning restaurant in the Pǔdōng Shangri-La is such an outlet, serving up some excellent, very refined regional cuisine along with Cantonese and Sìchuān dishes, in an equally refined setting. You can't go wrong with most of the restaurant's signature dishes that have their own menu. The fried river shrimp, deep-fried duo of Mandarin fish (with both lemon and sweet and sour flavors), braised bean curd with ham and vegetable, braised pork belly, and "Lion's Head" meatballs with crabmeat roe are all excellent. Osmanthus tea (*guìhuā chá*) serves as a refreshing complement. Table service is stylish and impeccable.

Fùchéng Lù 33 富城路３３号 (1st floor, River Wing, Pǔdōng Shangri-La Hotel); see map p. 148. ✆ **021/6882-8888,** ext. 220. Reservations recommended. Meal for 2 ¥400–¥700. AE, DC, MC, V. Mon–Fri 11:30am–3pm; Sat–Sun 11am–3pm; daily 5:30–10:30pm. Metro: Lujiazui.

**Jade on 36** 翡翠36 ★★ FRENCH   At this restaurant designed by Adam D. Tihany and lodged on the 36th floor of the Pǔdōng Shangri-La Hotel, you can expect fine contemporary French cuisine with exceptional city views. The original chef Paul Pairet whose "avant-garde" cuisine got Jade onto many "Best of" restaurant lists has departed, but current chef Fabrice Giraud is holding his own, with a menu offering more straightforward classic French offerings but with the de rigueur twist. Mix and match from the a la carte offerings (a simple onion soup, anyone? Or red-poached foie gras?), or leave it to the chef's choice with the Jade Aqua or Jade Terra Firma sets. Save room for the delightful cappuccino (really the tiramisu). Prices are predictably high, but service is first-rate. Request a table by the window.

Fùchéng Lù 33 富城路３３号 (36th floor, Pǔdōng Shangri-La Hotel); see map p. 148. ✆ **021/6882-8888,** ext. 280. www.jadeon36.com. Reservations required. Meal for 2 ¥2,000. AE, DC, MC, V. Daily 6pm–midnight. Metro: Lujiazui.

**Y's Table** ★ INTERNATIONAL   If you're with a group of people who can't agree on what to eat, then Y's Table, with its options of 12 different caterers covering Japanese, Chinese, Italian, Korean, and Western sandwiches and desserts, is one place to go, especially if you find yourself in Pǔdōng. Located in the bowels of the Shànghǎi World Financial Center, this high-end food court is also the place to sample, in one sitting, gourmet dishes from several well-regarded outlets around town. Try the *lāmiàn* (hand-pulled noodles) from Crystal Jade Kitchen, or the thin-crust pizzas from Pizza Salvatore Cuomo and Grill or the all-you-can-eat Japanese and Korean barbecue from Yakiniku. This cavernous hall lacks the usual liveliness of your average shopping center food court (prices here are comparatively higher of course), but you can't say there's nothing to eat.

Shìjì Dàdào 100 世纪大道１００号, Basement 2 (inside Shànghǎi World Financial Center); see map p. 148. ✆ **021/6877-6865.** www.ystable.com. Meal for 2 ¥300–¥700. AE, DC, MC, V. Daily 11am–3pm and 5–10pm. Metro: Lujiazui.

## Moderate

**Dīng Tài Fēng (Din Tai Fung)** 鼎泰丰 ★ DUMPLINGS/TAIWANESE   How ecstatic are those who live and work in Pǔdōng that they no longer have to go across the river for *xiǎolóng bāo*, Shànghǎi's famous pork and crab dumplings, now that the Taiwanese chain has opened a branch in the Super Brand Mall. Many a local *xiǎolóng bāo* aficionado claim the dumplings here are the best in town, and I certainly think they are in the running. It's easy to gorge yourself just on dumplings here, but there is a host of noodle and rice dishes that are comfort food for many Chinese and they're also worth trying, such as *niúròu miàn* (beef noodle soup) or the fried rice with pork and egg. In between bites, see if you can identify any of the Chinese celebrities drawn on the walls here.

Lùjiāzuǐ Xī Lù 168 陆家嘴西路１６８号, 3rd floor, Unit 24 (inside Super Brand Mall/Zhèng Dà Guǎngchǎng); see map p. 148. ✆ **021/5047-8882.** Meal for 2 ¥120–¥180. AE, DC, MC, V. Daily 11am–10pm. Metro: Lujiazui.

# SHÀNGHĂI'S FAVORITE dumpling

*Xiǎolóng bāo,* literally "little steamer buns," are popular in many parts of China, but nowhere more so than in the Shànghǎi region. The characteristic that distinguishes this little dumpling from all others is the hot broth inside that will trickle into your mouth, or squirt onto your neighbor's lap, depending on how you handle it. *Xiǎolóng bāo* is made by wrapping ground pork and a gelatinous soup in as thin a dough wrapper as possible. Sometimes, powdered crabmeat is added *(xièfěn xiǎolóng).* After steaming, the gelatin has melted and the pork is bathed in a delicious hot oil, all *inside* the wrapper. **Tip:** Never bite directly into a *xiǎolóng bāo* right out of the steamer, as the scalding broth can cause some serious tongue damage! Expert *xiǎolóng bāo* eaters usually hold the top of the dumpling with their chopsticks, with a spoon underneath. Nibble at the skin on top and let the broth trickle onto the spoon, or wait a few seconds for the broth to cool, then slurp the whole thing into your mouth. If desired, you can add some vinegar and ginger.

To be expected, the question of which place serves the best *xiǎolóng bāo* in town is a contentious one. **Nánxiáng Mántou Diàn** (p. 115) in Old Town may have the imprimatur of tradition, history, and fame, while locals may like the no-frills and inexpensive **Jiā Jiā Tāng Bāo** (p. 115) north of People's Square, but for modern connoisseurs who prefer their dumpling wrapper skins paper-thin and still able to seal in the juices, there's a healthy competition going between the upstart Taiwanese chain **Dīng Tài Fēng** (p. 133) and the Singapore-originated **Crystal Jade Restaurant** (p. 116). For our wrappers, I like Crystal Jade by a skin, though, of course, you can resolve the question for yourself by trying all four outlets!

**Sū Zhè Huì (Jade Garden)** 苏浙汇 ★★ SHÀNGHĂI   This branch of one of the more highly regarded and popular Shànghǎi chain restaurants offers diners its signature local dishes as well as Hong Kong–style dim sum in a classy and refined setting. Unadorned glass panels, marble floors, cream-colored chairs, and muted lighting all take a back seat to the food here. You can't go wrong with much of the menu: tea-smoked duck, wine-preserved green crab, and *mìzhī huǒfǎng* (pork and taro in candied sauce) are all house specialties that live up to their renown; the noodles with scallions and small shrimp are some of the most delicious in town; and *qícài dōngsǔn* (fresh winter shoots with local greens) is something you're unlikely to get back home. Service is highly efficient.

Dōngfāng Lù 877 东方路 8 7 7 号 (just north of the St. Regis hotel); see map p. 148. ☎ **021/5058-6088.** Meal for 2 ¥120–¥200. AE, DC, MC, V. Daily 11am–10:30pm. Metro: Century Ave.

**Wagas** INTERNATIONAL   With many outlets around town, this highly popular cafe is best known for its simple but tasty sandwiches, salads, wraps, burgers, pastas, and smoothies, all served up sans preservatives, additives, or MSG. There is Wi-Fi for those who simply cannot be offline. Another branch in Pǔdōng is at Thumb Plaza, Fangdian Lu 199 (☎ **021/5033-6277**).

Pǔdōng Nán Lù 999, G104 浦东南路 9 9 9 号 (west of Shāngchéng Lù, near Bà Bǎi Bàn); see map p. 148. ☎ **021/5134-1075.** Meal for 2 ¥120–¥200. AE, DC, MC, V. Daily 7am–10pm. Metro: Century Ave.

# WHAT TO SEE & DO IN SHÀNGHǍI

Shànghǎi has precious few sights on the scale of the Forbidden City or the Great Wall, but the treasures it does have—its colonial neighborhoods, historic homes, museums, parks, and shopping avenues, not to mention Asia's most famous street—speak to a unique legacy all its own. This chapter describes Shànghǎi's treasures, with a special focus on the city's four top attractions: the **Bund, Yù Yuán** (and **Old Town**), the **Shànghǎi Museum,** and the **Huángpǔ River Cruise.**

The average tourist usually blows through town in about 2 days, but 3 days is a minimum to do any real sightseeing, as attractions are scattered all over the city. Even then, Shànghǎi is about more than just its buildings. The city, one of the most exciting in the world, demands time to soak in its energy, appreciate its complexity, and sample its many attractions, which may not be apparent on the surface. Bear in mind that sights outside Shànghǎi, such as Sūzhōu, Hángzhōu, or the water villages of Nánxún, and Tónglǐ (all covered in chapter 11) require day trips.

## HOW TO SEE SHÀNGHǍI

The best way to see Shànghǎi is on your own, armed with a good map and this book, and using a combination of taxis, subways, and your own two feet. Most attractions, including museums, mansions, places of worship, parks, and gardens, are open daily, unless otherwise noted. Allow an hour or two to visit each of these sights. Transportation facilities and many of the sights described here are very user-friendly, even for the non-Chinese-speaking, first-time visitor. Because Shànghǎi's traffic is getting worse by the day, if you are traveling long distances between attractions, consider taking the subway, where available, to the Metro stop nearest the attraction, then hopping a taxi the rest of the way.

# Huángpǔ (Downtown) & Hóngkǒu
# (Northeast Shànghǎi)

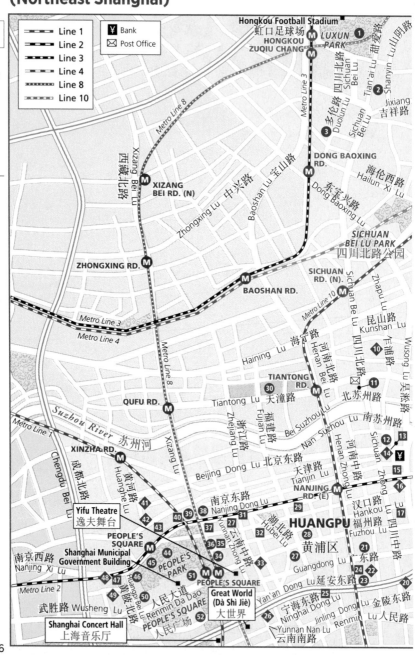

Line 1
Line 2
Line 3
Line 4
Line 8
Line 10

¥ Bank
✉ Post Office

Hongkou Football Stadium
虹口足球场
HONGKOU
ZUQIU CHANG
LUXUN PARK ①

甜爱路 Tian'ai Lu
四川北路 Sichuan Bei Lu
Shanyin Lu 山阴路
多伦路 Duolun Lu
Sichuan Bei Lu
Tian'ai Lu
Jixiang ②
吉祥路 ③

DONG BAOXING RD.
东宝兴路
Dong Baoxing Lu

海伦西路
Hailun Xi Lu

XIZANG BEI RD. (N)
西藏北路 Xizang Bei Lu

Metro Line 8

Zhongxing Lu 中兴路
Baoshan Lu 宝山路

SICHUAN BEI LU PARK
四川北路公园

ZHONGXING RD.
中兴路

SICHUAN RD. (N).
四川北路
Sichuan Bei Lu
Zhapu Lu

BAOSHAN RD.
宝山路

Metro Line 10

昆山路 Kunshan Lu
乍浦路
Wusong Lu 吴淞路

Metro Line 3
Metro Line 4

Haining Lu
海宁路 Haining Lu
河南北路 Henan Bei Lu
四川北路

⑩

QUFU RD.
曲阜路

Metro Line 8
Xizang Lu 西藏路

TIANTONG RD.
天潼路
Tiantong Lu
Bei Suzhou Lu 北苏州路
✉
⑪

⑫ ⑬
⑭ ¥
⑮

Metro Line 1
Suzhou River 苏州河

Chengdu Bei Lu 成都北路

XINZHA RD.
新闸路

黄河路 Huanghe Lu

Tiantong Lu 天潼路
福建路 Fujian Lu
浙江路 Zhejiang Lu
南苏州路 Nan Suzhou Lu
Henan Zhong Lu 河南中路
Sichuan

Beijing Dong Lu 北京东路

天津路
Tianjin Lu

NANJING RD. (E)
南京东路

⑯

汉口路 Hankou Lu
⑰

Yifu Theatre
逸夫舞台

㊶
㊷ ㊸
㊵ ㊴ ㊳ ㊸
Nanjing Dong Lu 南京东路
㊲
㊱
㉙

HUANGPU
黄浦区

湖北路 Hubei Lu
㉜ ㉘
㉗

福州路
Fuzhou Lu 四川中路

PEOPLE'S SQUARE

南京西路 Nanjing Xi Lu
Shanghai Municipal Government Building

Metro Line 2

㊺
㊹
㊻
㊼
㊽ ㊿ ㊾
PEOPLE'S PARK
㊱ ㊲
PEOPLE'S SQUARE
云南中路 Yunnan Zhong Lu
㉝

Guangdong Lu 广东路
㉑
㉒ ㉒
㉓

⑳

㊿ 51
52
人民大道 Renmin Da Dao
PEOPLE'S SQUARE
人民广场

Great World
(Dà Shì Jiè)
大世界

Yan'an Dong Lu 延安东路

宁海东路 Ninghai Dong Lu
㉕
㉖

金陵东路 Jinling Dong Lu 人民路 Renmin Lu

Shanghai Concert Hall
上海音乐厅

武胜路 Wusheng Lu

黄陂北路 Huangpi Bei Lu

Yunnan Nan Lu
云南南路

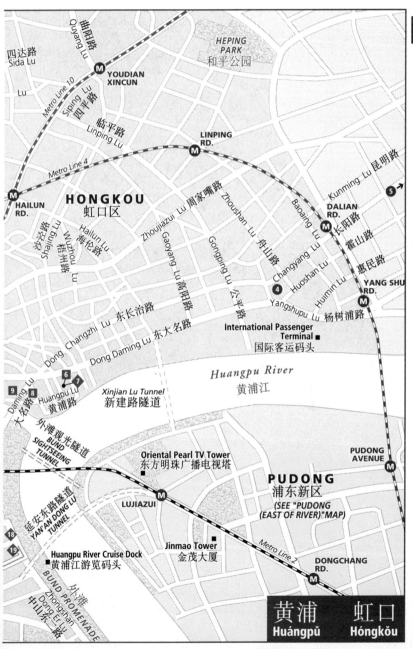

四达路
Sida Lu

曲阳路
Quyang Lu

M YOUDIAN
XINCUN

Lu

Metro Line 10

四平路
Siping Lu

临平路
Linping Lu

Metro Line 4

HEPING
PARK
和平公园

LINPING
RD.
M

昆明路
Kunming Lu

5 ↗

M
HAILUN
RD.

HONGKOU
虹口区

Hailun Lu

沙泾路
Shajing Lu

梧州路
Wuzhou Lu

海伦路
Hailun Lu

周家嘴路
Zhoujiazui Lu

舟山路
Zhoushan Lu

高阳路
Gaoyang Lu

公平路
Gongping Lu

白保路
Baoding Lu

昌阳路
Changyang Lu

DALIAN
RD.
M

长阳路
Changyang Lu

霍山路
Huoshan Lu

惠民路
Huimin Lu

YANG SHU
RD.
M

4

Huoshan Lu

杨树浦路
Yangshupu Lu

东长治路
Dong Changzhi Lu

东大名路
Dong Daming Lu

International Passenger
Terminal ■
国际客运码头

6 7

Huangpu River
黄浦江

Daming Lu
9 8

黄浦路
Huangpu Lu

大名路

Xinjian Lu Tunnel
新建路隧道

外滩观光隧道
BUND
SIGHTSEEING
TUNNEL

延安东路隧道
YAN AN DONG LU
TUNNEL

18

19

Oriental Pearl TV Tower
东方明珠广播电视塔 ■

LUJIAZUI
M

PUDONG
浦东新区

(SEE "PUDONG
(EAST OF RIVER)"MAP)

PUDONG
AVENUE
M

Jinmao Tower
金茂大厦 ■

Metro Line 2

DONGCHANG
RD.
M

Huangpu River Cruise Dock
黄浦江游览码头 ■

中山东二路
Zhongshan
Dong Er Lu

BUND PROMENADE
外滩

黄浦
Huángpǔ

虹口
Hóngkǒu

# Key for Huángpǔ & Hóngkǒu

## ACCOMMODATIONS ■

Astor House Hotel **8**
(Pǔjiāng Fàndiàn)
浦江饭店

Broadway Mansions Hotel **9**
(Shànghǎi Dàshà)
上海大厦

Captain Hostel **17**
(Chuánzhǎng Qīngnián Jiǔdiàn)
船长青年酒店

East Asia Hotel **31**
(Dōngyà Fàndiàn)
东亚饭店

Fairmont Peace Hotel **15**
(Hépíng Fàndiàn)
和平饭店

Howard Johnson Plaza Hotel **32**
(Gǔ Xiàng Dàjiǔdiàn)
古象大酒店

Hyatt On The Bund **6**
(Shànghǎi Wàitān Màoyuè Dàjiǔdiàn)
上海外滩茂悦大酒店

Jínjiāng Star **25**
(Jǐnjiāng Zhīxīng)
锦江之星

JW Marriott **47**
(Wànháo Jiǔdiàn)
万豪酒店

Le Royal Meridien Shànghǎi **37**
(Shànghǎi Shìmào Huángjiā Àiměi Jiǔdiàn)
上海世茂皇家艾美酒店

Park Hotel **43**
(Guójì Fàndiàn)
国际饭店

Radisson Hotel Shànghǎi New World **40**
(Shànghǎi Xīn Shìjiè Lìshēng Dàjiǔdiàn)
上海新世界丽笙大酒店

Sofitel Hyland Hotel **29**
(Hǎilún Bīnguǎn)
海伦宾馆

The Langham, Yangtze Boutique, Shànghǎi **35**
(Shànghǎi Lǎngtíng Yángzǐ Jīngpǐn Jiǔdiàn)
上海朗廷 扬子精品酒店

The Peninsula Hotel, Shànghǎi **13**
(Shànghǎi Bàndǎo Jiǔdiàn)
上海半岛酒店

The Westin Shànghǎi **24**
(Shànghǎi Wēisītīng Dàfàndiàn)
上海威斯汀大饭店

## ATTRACTIONS ●

China Tobacco Museum **5**
(Shànghǎi Yāncǎo Bówùguǎn)
上海烟草博物馆

Duōlún Lù Culture Street **3**
(Duōlún Lù Wénhuà Jiē)
多伦路文化街

Lǔ Xùn Park and Memorial Hall **1**
(Lǔ Xùn Jìniànguǎn)
鲁迅纪念馆

Lǔ Xùn's Former Residence **2**
(Lǔ Xùn Gùjū)
鲁迅故居

Madame Tussauds Museum **39**
(Dùshā Fūrén Làxiàngguǎn)
杜莎夫人蜡像馆

Moore Memorial Church **36**
(Mù'ēn Táng)
沐恩堂

Museum of Contemporary Art/MOCA **45**
(Shànghǎi Dāngdài Yìshù Guǎn)
上海当代艺术馆

Ohel Moshe Synagogue **4**
(Móxī Huìtáng)
摩西会堂

Rénmín Gōngyuán **44**
(People's Park)
人民公园

Rockbund Art Museum **12**
(Shànghǎi Wàitān Měishùguǎn)
上海外滩美术馆

黄浦 **Huángpǔ**　虹口 **Hóngkǒu**

# Lúwān (French Concession) & Xúhuì (Southwest Shànghǎi)

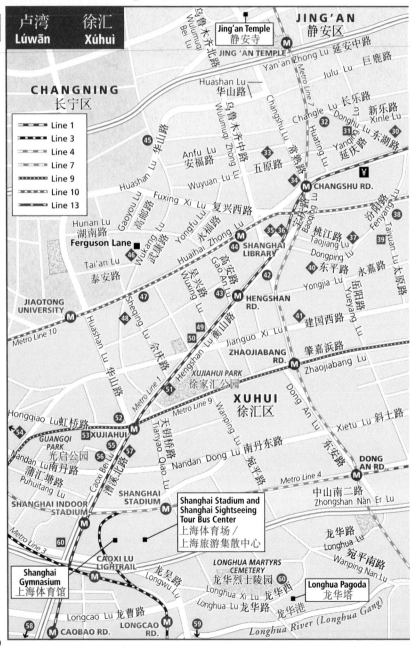

卢湾 **Lúwān**  徐汇 **Xúhuì**

**CHANGNING** 长宁区

Line 1
Line 3
Line 4
Line 7
Line 9
Line 10
Line 13

Jing'an Temple 静安寺
**JING'AN** 静安区
JING 'AN TEMPLE

Yan'an Zhong Lu 延安中路
Julu Lu 巨鹿路
Metro Line 7
Huashan Lu 华山路
Changle Lu 长乐路
Donghu Lu 东湖路
新乐路 Xinle Lu

Wulumuqi Bei Lu 乌鲁木齐北路
Wulumuqi Zhong Lu 乌鲁木齐中路

Anfu Lu 安福路
五原路
Changshu Lu 常熟路
Huaihai Lu
Yanqing Lu 延庆路

Wuyuan Lu 五原路

Huashan Lu 华山路
Gaoyou Lu 高邮路
Fuxing Xi Lu 复兴西路
Yongfu Lu 永福路
Baoqing Lu
桃江路 Taojiang Lu
Dongping Lu 东平路
Fenyang Lu 汾阳路
Taiyuan Lu 太原路

**CHANGSHU RD.**
¥

Hunan Lu 湖南路
**Ferguson Lane**
Wukang Lu 武康路
武康路
Gao'an Lu 高安路
Gao'an Lu
**SHANGHAI LIBRARY**

Tai'an Lu 泰安路

**JIAOTONG UNIVERSITY**
Metro Line 10
Huashan Lu 华山路
Sheqing Lu 余庆路
Wuxing Lu 吴兴路
Gao'an Lu

**HENGSHAN RD.**
Yongjia Lu 永嘉路
东平路 Dongping
永嘉路 Yongjia Lu
Yueyang Lu 岳阳路
Yongjia Lu

Hengshan Lu 衡山路
Jianguo Xi Lu 建国西路
Jianguo Xi Lu
**ZHAOJIABANG RD.**
Zhaojiabang Lu 肇嘉浜路
肇嘉浜路

Metro Line 1
**XUJIAHUI PARK** 徐家汇公园

**XUHUI** 徐汇区

Hongqiao Lu 虹桥路
Metro Line 9
Tianyao Qiao Lu 天钥桥路
Wanping Lu 宛平路
Nandan Dong Lu 南丹东路
Dong An Lu 东安路
Xietu Lu 斜土路

**GUANGQI PARK** 光启公园
Nandan Lu 南丹路
Puhuitang Lu 蒲汇塘路
Caoxi Bei Lu 漕溪北路
**XUJIAHUI**
**DONG AN RD.**

**SHANGHAI INDOOR STADIUM**
**SHANGHAI STADIUM**
Nandan Dong Lu 南丹东路
Wanping Lu 宛平路
Metro Line 4
Zhongshan Nan Er Lu 中山南二路
中山南二路

Metro Line 3
**Shanghai Stadium and Shanghai Sightseeing Tour Bus Center** 上海体育场／上海旅游集散中心

**CAOXI LU LIGHTRAIL**
Longhua Lu 龙华路
Wanping Nan Lu 宛平南路

**Shanghai Gymnasium** 上海体育馆
Longwu Lu 龙吴路
龙坞路
**LONGHUA MARTYRS CEMETERY** 龙华烈士陵园
Longhua Xi Lu 龙华西
Longhua Lu 龙华路
龙华港
**Longhua Pagoda** 龙华塔

Longcao Lu 龙曹路
**LONGCAO RD.**
**CAOBAO RD.**
*Longhua River (Longhua Gang)* 龙华港

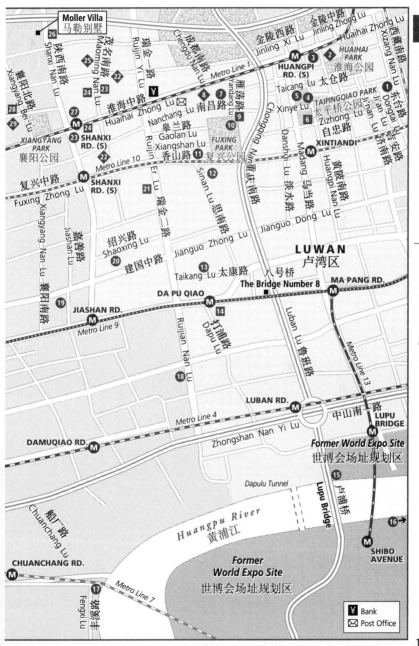

Moller Villa
马勒别墅

金陵西路 金陵中路
Jinling Xi Lu  Jinling Zhong Lu

26 Shanxi Nan Lu
陕西南路

Chengdu Nan Lu
成都南路

Maoming Nan Lu
茂名南路

Ruijin Yi Lu
瑞金一路

Yandang Lu
雁荡路

25

22

Metro Line 1

Huaihai Zhong Lu
淮海中路 南昌路

淮海公园
HUAIHAI
PARK

HUANGPI
RD. (S)
黄陂南路

Huaihai Zhong Lu
Xizang Nan Lu
西藏南路

Huaihai Zhong Lu
淮海中路

Dongtai Lu
东台路

Jinan Lu
济南路

Ji'an Lu
吉安路

3

2

淮海公园

1

Taicang Lu 太仓路

TAIPINGQIAO PARK
太平桥公园

Xinye Lu

5

4

6

Zizhong Lu
自忠路

XINTIANDI
新天地

24

23

27

M

24

SHANXI
RD. (S)
陕西南路

23

22

XIANGYANG
PARK
襄阳公园

Xiangyang Bei Lu
襄阳北路

28

29

Nanchang Lu 南昌路

8

7

9

10

Gaolan Lu
皋兰路

Xiangshan Lu
香山路

11

FUXING
PARK
复兴公园
复兴公园

Fuxing Zhong Lu
复兴中路

M

SHANXI
RD. (S)
陕西南路

Metro Line 10

Sinan Lu 思南路

Chongqing Nan Lu 重庆南路

Danshui Lu 淡水路

Madang Lu 马当路

Huangpi Nan Lu 黄陂南路

12

Xiangyang Nan Lu 襄阳南路

Jiashan Lu 嘉善路

Er Lu Ruijin 瑞金二路

21

Jianguo Zhong Lu 建国中路

Shaoxing Lu
绍兴路

20

Jianguo Zhong Lu
建国中路

Jianguo Dong Lu
建国东路

LUWAN
卢湾区

Taikang Lu 太康路

13

八号桥
The Bridge Number 8

MA PANG RD.

DA PU QIAO
打浦桥

M

14

Ruijin Nan Lu

Dapu Lu 打浦路

Luban Lu 鲁班路

Metro Line 13

19

JIASHAN RD.
嘉善路

M

Metro Line 9

18

LUBAN RD.
鲁班路

M

中山南一路

LUPU
BRIDGE

M

DAMUQIAO RD.

M

Metro Line 4

Zhongshan Nan Yi Lu
中山南一路

Former World Expo Site
世博会场址规划区

Chuanchang Lu
勤厂路

Dapulu Tunnel

Lupu Bridge
卢浦桥

15

16

SHIBO
AVENUE

CHUANCHANG RD.

M

Huangpu River
黄浦江

Former
World Expo Site
世博会场址规划区

M

17

Metro Line 7

Fengxi Lu

Bank ¥

Post Office ✉

141

# Key for Lúwān & Xúhuì

## ACCOMMODATIONS ■

88 Xīntiāndì Hotel **6**
88 新天地酒店

City Hotel **26**
(Chéngshì Jiǔdiàn)
城市酒店

Courtyard Shànghǎi Xújiāhuì **53**
(Shànghǎi Xīzàng Dàshà Wànyí Jiǔdiàn)
上海西藏大厦万怡酒店

Héngshān Picardie Hotel **50**
(Héngshān Bīnguǎn)
衡山宾馆

Jǐn Jiāng Hotel **23**
(Jǐn Jiāng Fàndiàn)
锦江饭店

Magnolia Bed and Breakfast **31**

Mansion Hotel **28**
(Shǒuxí Gōngguǎn Jiǔdiàn)
首席公馆酒店

Okura Garden Hotel **24**
(Huāyuán Fàndiàn)
花园饭店

Pudi Boutique Hotel **9**
(Pǔdǐ Jingpǐn Jiǔdiàn)
璞邸精品酒店

Pullman Shànghǎi Skyway Hotel **14**
(Shànghǎi Sīgéwēi Pōěrmàn Dàjiǔdiàn)
上海斯格威铂尔曼大酒店

Regal International East Asia Hotel **49**
(Fùháo Huánqiú Dōngyà Jiǔdiàn)
富豪环球东亚酒店

Ruìjīn Hotel **21**
(Ruìjīn Bīnguǎn)
瑞金宾馆

Tàiyuán Villa **39**
(Tàiyuán Biéshù)
太原别墅

**卢湾 Lúwān　徐汇 Xúhuì**

## DINING ◆

Art Salon (Wùlǐxiāng) **8**
屋里香

Dì Shuǐ Dòng **25**
滴水洞

El Willy **30**

Enoteca **33**

Franck **46**

Haiku by Hatsune **36**

Hot Pot King (Lái Fú Lóu) **34**
来福楼

Jíshì (Jesse Restaurant) **48**
吉士

O'Malley's (Ōu Mǎ Lì) **35**
欧玛莉餐厅

Paulaner Brauhaus (Bǎoláinà) **37**
宝莱纳

Restaurant Martin **51**

Shànghǎi Old Station Restaurant **57**
(Shànghǎi Lǎo Zhàn)
上海老站

Shànghǎi Xīnjiāng Fēngwèi Fàndiàn **54**
上海新疆风味饭店

Simply Thai (Tiāntài Cāntīng) **40**
天泰餐厅

Sushi Oyama **30**
大山

The Grape (Pútáo Yuán) **29**
葡萄园酒家

Vedas 维达斯饭店 **41**

Xīn Wàng 新旺 **22**

Xīn Tiāndì 新天地 **5**

Zǎo Zǐ Shù 枣子树 **2**

# Jìng Ān (Northwest Shànghǎi) & Zhábĕi

**Line 1**
**Line 2**
**Line 3**
**Line 4**
**Line 7**
**Line 8**
**Line 10**
**Line 11**

Zhongshan Bei Lu 中山北路
ZHENPING RD. 镇坪路
Metro Line 3
Metro Line 4
Suzhou River 苏州河
Xi Suzhou Lu 西苏州路
Moganshan Lu 莫干山路 ❶
PUTUO 普陀区
Changshou Lu 长寿路
Metro Line 7
Jiangning Lu 江宁路
CHANGSHOU RD. 长寿路
Anyuan Lu 安远路 ❷
Haifang Lu 海防路
Changping Lu 昌平路
Shanxi Bei Lu 陕西北路
CHANGPING RD. 昌平路
Kangding Lu 康定路
Jiaozhou Lu 胶州路
Changde Lu 常德路
Xikang Lu 西康路
Xinzha Lu 新闸路
JING'AN 静安区
Changshou Lu 长寿路 ❹⁰
Wuning Nan Lu 武宁南路
Wanhangdu Lu 万航渡路
Beijing Xi Lu 北京西路
Fengxian Lu
❸⁹
Shanghai Airport City Terminal 城市航站楼
Zhenning Lu 镇宁路
Tongren Lu 铜仁路
❶³
❶⁴
❶²
❶⁵
❸⁸
JING AN TEMPLE
Metro Line 11
Jiangsu Lu
Yu Yuan Lu 豫园路
❸⁶ ❸⁷
Huashan Lu
❸⁵
❶⁶
JIANGSU RD. 江苏路
Metro Line 2
Nanjing Xi Lu
❸¹ ❸² ❸³ ❸⁴
❶⁷
❶⁸
富民路 ❶⁹
Fumin Lu
❸⁰
❷³
Julu Lu 巨鹿路
❷⁸
❷⁴
❷²
❷¹
❷⁰
华山路
Huashan Lu
❷⁹
❷⁷
❷⁶
Changle Lu 长乐路
❷⁵
Changshu Lu
Metro Line 1
0    1/4 mi
0    0.25 km
N
静安 闸北
Jìng'an  Zhábĕi
XUHUI 徐汇区
CHANGSHU RD. 常熟路

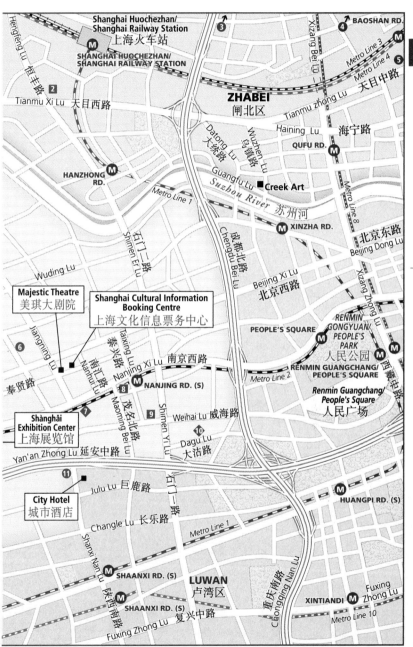

Shanghai Huochezhan/
Shanghai Railway Station
上海火车站
SHANGHAI HUOCHEZHAN/
SHANGHAI RAILWAY STATION

❸

❹ BAOSHAN RD.

❺

Metro Line 3

Metro Line 4

Hengfeng Lu

Tianmu Xi Lu 天目西路

天目中路

ZHABEI
闸北区

Tianmu zhong Lu

Xizang Bei Lu

Haining Lu 海宁路

QUFU RD.

HANZHONG
RD.

Datong Lu 大统路

Wuzhen Lu 乌镇路

Guangfu Lu

■ Creek Art

Metro Line 1

Suzhou River 苏州河

Chengdu Bei Lu

成都北路

XINZHA RD.

北京东路
Beijing Dong Lu

Metro Line 8

Wuding Lu

Shimen Er Lu
石门二路

Beijing Xi Lu

北京西路

Majestic Theatre
美琪大剧院

Shanghai Cultural Information
Booking Centre
上海文化信息票务中心

Taixing Lu 泰兴路

PEOPLE'S SQUARE

Xizang Zhong Lu

RENMIN
GONGYUAN/
PEOPLE'S
PARK
人民公园

Jiangning Lu

Nanhui Lu 南汇路

Nanjing Xi Lu 南京西路

RENMIN GUANGCHANG/
PEOPLE'S SQUARE

Metro Line 2

❻

❽

NANJING RD. (S)

Renmin Guangchang/
People's Square
人民广场

奉贤路

Maoming Bei Lu 茂名北路

Shimen Yi Lu

❾

Weihai Lu 威海路

Shànghǎi
Exhibition Center
上海展览馆

❼

❿
Dagu Lu
大沽路

Yan'an Zhong Lu 延安中路

City Hotel
城市酒店

⓫

Julu Lu 巨鹿路

石门一路

Changle Lu 长乐路

Metro Line 1

HUANGPI RD. (S)

Shanxi Nan Lu

陕西南路

SHAANXI RD. (S)

LUWAN
卢湾区

Chongqing Nan Lu 重庆南路

XINTIANDI

Fuxing
Zhong
Lu

SHAANXI RD. (S)
Fuxing Zhong Lu 复兴中路

Metro Line 10

# Key for Jìng Ān and Zhábĕi

## ACCOMMODATIONS ■

Four Seasons Hotel Shànghǎi **9**
(Shànghǎi Sì Jì Jiǔdiàn)
上海四季酒店

Green Tree Inn **23**
(Gélín Háotài)
格林豪泰

Hilton Hotel **28**
(Jìng'ān Xīěrdùn Dàjiǔdiàn)
静安希尔顿酒店

Hotel Equatorial **30**
(Guójì Guìdū Dàjiǔdiàn)
国际贵都大酒店

JIA Shànghǎi **8**

Old House Inn **26**
(Lǎo Shí Guāng Jiǔdiàn)
老时光酒店

Portman Ritz-Carlton Hotel **13**
(Bōtèmàn Dàjiǔdiàn)
波特曼丽嘉酒店

Quintet **25**

Shànghǎi Hotel **29**
(Shànghǎi Bīnguǎn)
上海宾馆

Swissotel Grand Shànghǎi **39**
(Shànghǎi Hóng'ān Ruìshì Dàjiǔdiàn)
上海宏安瑞士大酒店

The PuLi Hotel and Spa **35**
(Pǔlì Jiǔdiàn)
璞麗酒店

URBN Hotel **39**
(Yǎyuè Jiǔdiàn)
雅悦酒店

## ATTRACTIONS ●

Children's Municipal Palace **31**
(Shì Shàonián Gōng)
市少年宫

Jìng Ān Gōngyuán **33**
(Jìng Ān Park)
静安公园

Jìng Ān Sì **36**
(Jìng Ān Temple)
静安寺

Moller Villa **11**
(Héngshān Mǎlè Biéshù)
衡山马勒别墅

Ohel Rachel Synagogue **6**
(Lāxīěr Yóutài Jiàotáng)
拉西尔犹太教堂

Shànghǎi Circus World **3**
(Shànghǎi Mǎxì Chéng)
上海马戏城

Shànghǎi Glasses Museum **4**
(Shànghǎi Yǎnjìng Bówùguǎn)
上海眼镜博物馆

Shànghǎi Railway Museum **5**
(Shànghǎi Tiělù Bówùguǎn)
上海铁路博物馆

Yùfó Sì **2**
(Jade Buddha Temple)
玉佛寺

**Jing'an & Zhábĕi**
静安 闸北

**SHOPPING** ●
50 Mògānshān Lù **1**
莫干山路５０号

City Mall **37**
(Jiǔbǎi Chéngshì Guǎngchǎng)
久百城市广场

Friendship Store **40**
(Yǒuyì Shāngdiàn)
友谊商店

Shànghǎi Centre **14**
(Shànghǎi Shāngchéng)
上海商城

**DINING** ◆
Bǎoluó **20**
保罗

Bali Laguna **32**
(Bālídǎo)
巴厘岛

Element Fresh **12**
(Yuán Sù)
元素

Gǔ Yì **18**
古意

Jing'an Restaurant **34**

Just Grapes (Táo Zuì) **10**
萄醉

Kuo Bee Pen Da **24**
(Guō Bǐ Pén Dà)
锅比盆大

Malone's **15**
(Mǎlóng)
马龙美式酒楼

Méilóngzhèn **7**
梅陇镇

Mesa (Méisà) **19**
梅萨

Nepali Kitchen (Níbō'ěr Cāntīng) **22**
尼泊尔餐厅

People on the Water **27**
(Shuǐshàng Rénjiā)
水上人家

Rendezvous (Fú Lè Jú) **16**
福乐局

Shintori Null II **21**
(Xīndūlǐ Wúèr Diàn)
新都里无二店

South Beauty **17**
(Qiào Jiāng Nán)
俏江南

# Pǔdōng (East of River)

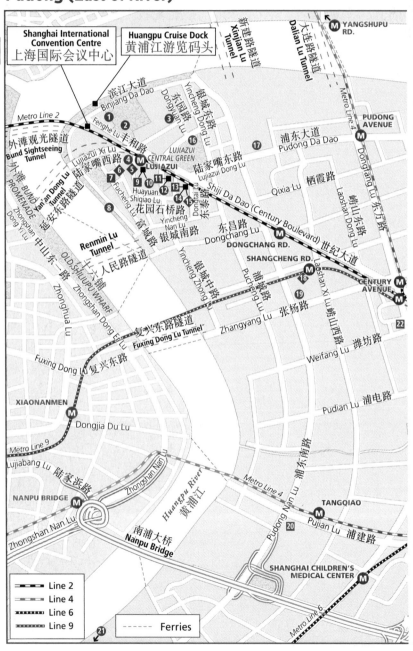

Shanghai International
Convention Centre
上海国际会议中心

Huangpu Cruise Dock
黄浦江游览码头

新建路隧道
Xinjian Lu
Tunnel

大连路隧道
Dalian Lu Tunnel

M YANGSHUPU
RD.

滨江大道
Binjiang Da Dao

银城东路
Yincheng
Dong Lu

东园路
Dongyuan Lu

浦东大道
Pudong Da Dao

PUDONG
AVENUE

Metro Line 2

M PUDONG
AVENUE

Fenghe Lu 丰和路

❶

❸

Metro Line 4

东方路
Dongfang Lu

外滩观光隧道
Bund Sightseeing
Tunnel

LUJIAZUI
CENTRAL GREEN

❶❻

❶❼

浦东大道
Pudong Da Dao

崂山东路
Laoshan Dong Lu

陆家嘴西路
Lujiazui Xi Lu

M
LUJIAZUI

陆家嘴东路
Lujiazui Dong Lu

栖霞路
Qixia Lu

栖霞路
Qixia Lu

延安东路隧道
Yan'an Dong Lu
Tunnel

BUND
PROMENADE

❼

❻ ❺ ❹

❾ ❿ ❶❶

富城路
Fucheng Lu

❶❷ ❶❸

石桥路
Shiqiao Lu

东泰路

❶❹ ❶❺

世纪大道
Shiji Da Dao (Century Boulevard)

中山东一路
Dongshan

Dong Yi Lu

花园石桥路
Huayuan
Shiqiao Lu

富城路
Fucheng Lu

Yincheng
Nan Lu

银城南路

东昌路
Dongchang Lu

DONGCHANG RD.

SHANGCHENG RD.

崂山西路
Laoshan Xi Lu

M

M CENTURY
AVENUE

❽

M M

人民路隧道
Renmin Lu
Tunnel

银城中路
Yincheng Zhong Lu

浦城路
Pucheng Lu

❶❽

22

中山东二路
Zhongshan Dong Er Lu

❶❾

张杨路
Zhangyang Lu

潍坊路
Weifang Lu

OLD SHILIUPU WHARF
十六铺

Zhongshan Dong Er Lu

复兴东路隧道
Fuxing Dong Lu Tunnel

Zhangyang Lu 张杨路

潍坊路
Weifang Lu

中华路
Zhonghua Lu

中山东二路
Zhongshan Dong Er Lu

Fuxing Dong Lu 复兴东路

浦电路
Pudian Lu 浦电路

XIAONANMEN

M

Dongjia Du Lu

Metro Line 9

陆家浜路
Lujiabang Lu 陆家浜路

Metro Line 4

浦东南路
Pudong Nan Lu

NANPU BRIDGE

M

中山南路
Zhongshan Nan Lu

Zhongshan Nan

Huangpu River 黄浦江

TANGQIAO

❷❶

M

浦建路
Pujian Lu 浦建路

南浦大桥
Nanpu Bridge

SHANGHAI CHILDREN'S
MEDICAL CENTER

M

| | Line 2 |
| --- | --- |
| | Line 4 |
| | Line 6 |
| | Line 9 |

Ferries

Metro Line 6

❷❶

Huangpu River 黄浦江

杨浦大桥
Yangpu Bridge

Pudong Da Dao 浦东大道

Luoshan Lu 罗山路

Rushan Lu

BEIYANGJING RD. Ⓜ

Taolin Lu

MINSHENG RD. Ⓜ 张杨路

Fushan Lu

Shangcheng Lu

Zhangyang Lu

Minsheng Lu

Ⓜ YUANSHEN
STADIUM

Fangdian Lu

福山路

Shiji Da Dao (Century Boulevard) 世纪大道

Yanggao Zhong Lu 杨高中路

**Oriental Art Center**
东方艺术中心

Metro Line 9 (under construction)

㉓ ㉕
㉔ Xiangcheng Lu
㉖ 向城路

Dingxiang Lu 丁香路

木蓟路 Changliu Lu

芳甸路

㉛
㉚
迎春路

Ⓜ PUDIAN RD.

Jindai Lu 锦绣路

Henuan Lu

Yinchun Lu

Jinxiu Lu 锦绣路

Ⓜ PUDIAN
RD.

SHANGHAI KEJI GUAN/ Ⓜ
SCIENCE & TECHNOLOGY MUSEUM ㉗

PSB
公安局

㉘

Metro Line 2

㉙

CENTURY PARK
(SHIGI GONGYUAN)
世纪公园

TOMSON
GOLF COURSE →
汤臣高尔夫球场

Metro Line 4

Metro Line 6

Yanggao Nan Lu 杨高南路

Huamu Lu 花木路

Jinxiu Lu 锦绣路

Ⓜ Ⓜ LANCUN
RD.

SHIJI GONGYUAN/
CENTURY PARK

Ⓜ

**Shànghǎi New International Exposition Center**
(Shànghǎi Xīn Guójì Bólǎn Zhōngxīn)
上海新国际博览中心

Pujian Lu 浦建路

0                1/4 mi
0        0.25 km

Ⓝ

LONGYANG RD. Ⓜ

㉜ ㉝

Longyang Lu 龙阳路

㉞

MAGLEV LINE TO
PUDONG INT'L. AIRPORT

# Key for Pǔdōng

**ACCOMMODATIONS** ■

Courtyard by Marriott Hotel Pǔdōng **22**
(Shànghǎi Qílǔ Wànyí Dàjiǔdiàn)
上海齐鲁万怡大酒店

Four Points By Sheraton **20**
Fúpéng Xīláidēng Yóuyóu Jiǔdiàn)
福朋喜来登由由酒店

Grand Hyatt Shanghai **11**
(Jīn Mào Jūn Yuè Dàjiǔdiàn)
上海金茂君悦大酒店

Holiday Inn Pǔdōng **26**
(Pǔdōng Jiàrì Jiǔdiàn)
上海浦东假日酒店

Motel 168 **33**
(Shànghǎi Dàzhòng Merrilyn Air Terminal Hotel,
Mótài 168 Shànghǎ Pǔdng Jīchǎng
Kōnggǎng Bīnguǎn)
上海莫泰浦东机场空港宾馆
上海大众美林阁空港宾馆 两个宾馆

Park Hyatt Shànghǎi **13**
(Shànghǎi Bǎiyuè Jiǔdiàn)
上海柏悦酒店

Pǔdōng Shangri-La Hotel **7**
(Pǔdōng Xiānggélǐlā Fàndiàn)
浦东香格里拉大饭店

Ramada Pǔdōng Airport Shànghǎi **34**
(Shànghǎi Jīchǎng Huáměidá Dàjiǔdiàn)
上海机场华美达大酒店

Ritz-Carlton Pǔdōng **9**
(Shànghǎi Pǔdōng Lìsī Kǎěrdūn
Jiǔdiàn Fàndiàn)
上海浦东丽思卡尔顿酒店

St. Regis Shànghǎi **24**
(Shànghǎi Ruìjí Hóngtǎ Dàjiǔdiàn)
上海瑞吉红塔大酒店

**ATTRACTIONS** ●

Bīnjiāng Dà Dào (Riverside Promenade) **8**
滨江大道

China Pavilion / Expo Axis (Zhōngguó Guǎn
中国馆

Himalayas Art Museum **30**
(Shànghǎi Xīmǎlāyǎ Měishùguǎn)
上海喜玛拉雅美术馆

Jīn Mào Tower (Jīn Mào Dàshà) **12**
金茂大厦

Lùjiāzuǐ Lǜdì **16**
(Lùjiāzuǐ Central Green)
陆家嘴绿地

Oriental Pearl TV Tower **2**
(Dōngfāng Míngzhū Guǎngbō Diànshì Tǎ)
东方明珠广播电视塔

Shànghǎi Bank Museum **17**
(Shànghǎi Shì Yínháng Bówùguǎn)
上海市银行博物馆

Shànghǎi Municipal History Museum **2**
(Shànghǎi Shì Lìshǐ Bówùguǎn)
上海市历史博物馆

Shànghǎi Natural Wild Insect Kingdom **1**
(Shànghǎi Dàzìrán Yěshēng Kūnchóngguǎn)
上海大自然野生昆虫馆

Shànghǎi Ocean Aquarium **3**
(Shànghǎi Hǎiyáng Shuǐzúguǎn)
上海海洋水族馆

Shànghǎi Science and Technology Museum
(Shànghǎi Kējìguǎn)
上海科技馆

Shànghǎi Wild Animal Park **32**
(Shànghǎi Yěshēng Dònwùyuán)
上海野生动物园

Shànghǎi World Financial Center **14**
(Shànghǎi Huánqiú Jīnróng Zhōngxīn
上海环球金融中心

Shìjì Gōngyuán (Century Park) **29**
世纪公园

浦东
**Pǔdōng**

**SHOPPING** ●
A.P. Plaza **27**
(Yàdà Shènghuì Lǚyóu Gòuwù Guăngchăng)
亚大盛会旅游购物广场

IFC Mall **10**
(Guójīn Zhōngxīn Shāngcháng)
国金中心商场

Nextage Department Store **19**
(Shànghăi Dìyī Bābăibàn Xīnshìjì Shāngshà)
第一八佰伴新世纪商厦

Super Brand Mall **4**
(Zhèngdà Guăngchăng)
正大广场

**DINING** ◆
Danieli's **25**
(Dānníàilì)
丹尼艾丽

Din Tai Fung **5**
(Dǐng Tài Fēng)
鼎泰丰

Guì Huā Lóu **6**
桂花楼

Jade on 36 **6**

Sū Zhè Huì **23**
(Jade Garden)
苏浙汇

Wagas **18 & 31**

Y's Table **15**

# Chángníng/Hóngqiáo Development Zone (West Shànghǎi)

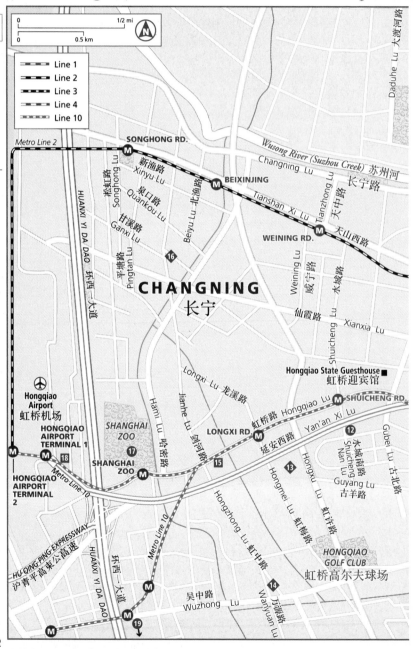

JINSHAJIANG RD. Ⓜ

长宁
**Chángníng**

虹桥开发区
**Hóngqiáo Development Zone**

❶
*CHANGFENG PARK*
长风公园

Metro Line 3

Metro Line 4

Jiangsu Lu 江苏路

Zhenning Lu 镇宁路

*ZHONGSHAN PARK*
中山公园

愚园路 ❷

*ZHONGSHAN PARK*

ZHONGSHAN PARK
Ⓜ

Yuyuan Lu

Ⓜ JIANGSU RD.

古北路 Gubei Lu

Yihua Lu 宜化路

Anhua Lu 安化路

定西路 Dingxi Lu

Wuyi Lu 武夷路

Yan'an Xi Lu 延安西路

Metro Line 2

Ⓜ LOUSHANGUAN RD.

*TIANSHAN PARK*

Tianshan Lu 天山路 天山公园

YAN'AN RD. (N)
Ⓜ

❻ ❺ ❹

华山路 Huashan Lu

兴国路 Xingguo Lu

遵义路 Zunyi Lu

Panyu Lu 番禺路

Xingfu Lu 幸福路

❸

*HUASHAN PARK*
华山公园

Fahuazhen Lu 法华镇路

❿ ❾

Xinhua Lu 新华路

Zhongshan Xi Lu (Inner Ring Expressway)

ZHONGSHAN XI LU (INNER RING EXPRESSWAY)

⓫

*HONGQIAO PARK*
虹桥公园

**Shanghai Film Art Centre** ■
上海影城

❼

Hongqiao Lu 虹桥路

淮海西路

Ⓜ YILI RD.

Huaihai Xi Lu

**JIAOTONG UNIVERSITY**

Metro Line 10

*SONG QINGLING MAUSOLEUM/ INTERNATIONAL CEMETERY*
宋庆龄陵园/ 万国公墓

Ⓜ SONGYUAN RD.

Songyuan Lu 宋园路

❽

Ⓜ HONGQIAO RD.

**XUHUI**
徐汇

Wuzhong Lu 吴中路

中山西路 Zhongshan Xi Lu

Metro Line 3

Nandan Lu 南丹路

Metro Line 4

**YISHAN RD.**
Ⓜ

**SHANGHAI INDOOR STADIUM**
Ⓜ

Yishan Lu 宜山路

# Key for Chángníng/Hóngqiáo Development Zone

**ACCOMMODATIONS ■**

Argyle International Airport Hotel
  Hóngqiáo **18**
(Huá Gǎng Yǎ Gé Jiǔdiàn)
上海华港雅阁酒店

Crowne Plaza Shànghǎi
(Shànghǎi Yínxīng Huángguān Jiǔdiàn) **7**
上海银星皇冠假日酒店

Shànghǎi Marriott Hotel Hóngqiáo **15**
(Shànghǎi Wànháo Hóngqiáo Dàjiǔdiàn)
上海万豪虹桥大酒店

Sheraton Shànghǎi Hóngqiáo Hotel **10**
(Hóngqiáo Xǐláidēng Shànghǎi
  Tàipíngyáng Dà Fàndiàn)
虹桥喜来登上海太平洋大饭店

Super Motel 168 **4**
(Mótài 168 Yán'ān Xī Lù Diàn)
莫泰１６８延安西路店

The Longemont Shànghǎi **3**
(Shànghǎi Lóngzhīmèng Dàjiǔdiàn)
上海龙之梦大酒店

**DINING ◆**

1221 **5**

Bā Guó Bù Yī **6**
巴国布衣

Blue Frog **13**
(Lán Wā)
蓝蛙

Chor Bazaar **16**

Dynasty **11**
(Mǎn Fú Lóu)
满福楼

Fu 1088 **2**
(Fú 1088)
福一零八八

Hǎi Dǐ Lāo **14**
海底捞

**ATTRACTIONS ●**

Dino Beach **19**
(Rèdài Fēngbào Shuǐshàng Lèyuán)
热带风暴水上乐园

Shànghǎi Chángfēng Ocean World **1**
(Shànghǎi Chángfēng Hǎiyáng Shìjiè)
上海长风海洋世界

Shànghǎi Sculpture Space **8**
(Shànghǎi Chéngshì Diāosù Yìshù
  Zhōngxīn)
上海城市雕塑艺术中心

Shànghǎi Zoo **17**
(Shànghǎi Dòngwù Yuán)
上海动物园

**SHOPPING ●**

Carrefour **12**
(Jiālèfú)
家乐福

Hongqiao Friendship Shopping Centre **9**
(Hóngqiáo Yǒuyì Shāngchéng)
虹桥友谊商城

长宁
**Chángníng**

虹桥开发区
**Hóngqiáo Development Zone**

# Key for Nánshì (Old Town) & Southeast Shànghǎi

**ACCOMMODATIONS** ■
Renaissance Shànghǎi Yùyuán Hotel **10**
(Shànghǎi Yùyuán Wànlì Jiǔdiàn)
上海豫园万丽酒店

The Waterhouse at South Bund **15**
(Shuǐshè Jiǔdiàn)
水舍酒店 **1**

**DINING** ◆
Kebabs on the Grille **17**

Lǜbōláng **5**
绿波廊

Nánxiáng Mántóu Diàn **4**
南翔馒头店

Sì Pái Lóu Lù Food Street **7**
四牌楼路小吃街

**SHOPPING** ●
Cool Docks **16**
(Lǎo Mǎ Tóu)
老码头

Fúyòu Market/Cáng Bǎo Lóu **9**
福佑市场 / 藏宝楼

South Bund Fabric Market **19**
(Nán Wàitān Qīng Fǎng Miànliào
Shìchǎng )
南外滩轻纺面料市场

**ATTRACTIONS** ●
Báiyún Guàn **11**
白云观

Chénghuáng Miào **6**
(Temple of the Town God)
城隍庙

Chénxiāng Gé **1**
沉香阁

Dǒngjiādù Tiānzhuǎtáng **18**
(Dǒngjiādù Catholic Church)
董家渡天主堂

Húxīntíng Teahouse **3**
(Húxīntíng Cháshè)
湖心亭茶社

Museum of Folk Art **20**
(Mínjiān Shōucángpǐn Chénlièguǎn)
民间收藏品陈列馆

Shànghǎi Old City Wall
and Dàjìng Gé Pavilion **12**
(Shànghǎi Gǔ Chéng
Qiáng Dàjìng Gé)
上海古城墙大镜阁

Shànghǎi Lǎo Jiē **8**
(Shànghǎi Old Street)
上海老街

Wén Miào **13**
(Confucius Temple)
文庙

Xiǎo Táoyuán Qīngzhēn Sì **14**
(Small Peach Garden Mosque)
小桃园清真寺

Yù Yuán **2**
(Yù Garden)
豫园

南市
Nánshì

# Nánshì (Old Town) & Southeast Shànghǎi

RENMIN GONGYUANI
PEOPLE'S PARK
人民公园

RENMIN
GONGYUAN/
PEOPLE'S PARK

RENMIN GUANGCHANG/
PEOPLE'S SQUARE

Fujian Nan Lu 福建南路

Renmin Guangchang/
People's Square
人民广场

Yan'an Dong Lu 延安东路

Zhejiang Nan Lu 浙江南路

Jinling Dong Lu 金陵东路

Renmin Lu 人民路

Yunnan Lu Food Street
云南路美食街

Line 1
Line 4
Line 8
Line 9
Line 10

Fuyou Lu 福佑路

YU GARDEN

DASHIJIE

Huaihai Dong Lu 淮海东路

HUANGPI
RD. (S)

Metro Line 1

Hua Hai Dong Lu 淮海东路

Dajing Lu 大境路

Fangbang Zhong Lu 方浜中路

Metro Line 8

Chongqing Nan Lu 重庆南路

Huangpi Nan Lu

Dongtai Lu 东台路

Fuxing Dong Lu 复兴东路

复兴中路

Fuxing Zhong Lu

Metro Line 10

LAOXIMEN

XINTIANDI

黄陂南路

Xizang Nan Lu 西藏南路

Zhonghua Lu 中华路

Wenmiao Lu
文庙路

LUWAN
卢湾区

MADANG RD.

Xujiahui Lu 徐家汇路

Metro Line 9

LUJIABANG RD.

Xietu Dong Lu

斜土东路

- - - - Ferries

(i) Tourist Information

0 ——— 1/4 mi
0 ——— 0.25 km

N

XIZANG RD. (S)

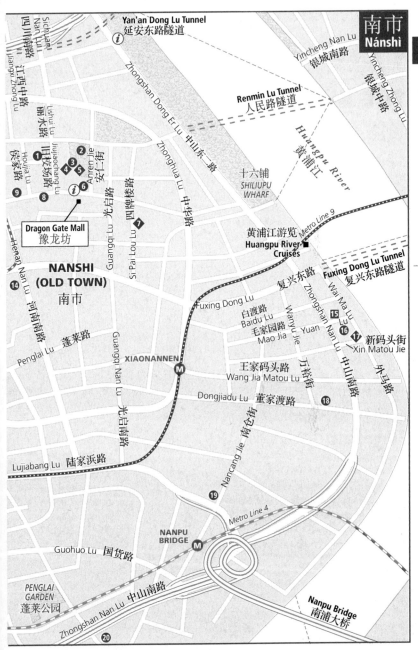

南市
Nánshi

Yan'an Dong Lu Tunnel
延安东路隧道

Renmin Lu Tunnel
人民路隧道

Yincheng Nan Lu
银城南路

Yincheng Zhong Lu
银城中路

Zhongshan Dong Er Lu 中山东一路

Zhonghua Lu 中华路

Sichuan Nan Lu
四川南路

Jiangxi Zhong Lu

Lishui Lu 丽水路

Houjia Lu 侯家路

Jiujiaochang Lu 旧校场路

Anren Jie 安仁街

十六铺
SHILIUPU
WHARF

Huangpu River 黄浦江

Metro Line 9

Guangqi Lu 光启路

Si Pai Lou Lu 四牌楼路

Dragon Gate Mall
豫龙坊

黄浦江游览
Huangpu River
Cruises

NANSHI
(OLD TOWN)
南市

Fuxing Dong Lu Tunnel
复兴东路隧道

Henan Nan Lu 河南南路

Penglai Lu 蓬莱路

Guangqi Nan Lu 光启南路

Fuxing Dong Lu

复兴东路

Baidu Lu 白渡路
Mao Jia 毛家园路
Mao Jia

Zhongshan Nan Lu 中山南路

Wanyu Jie
Yuan

Wai Ma Lu 外马路

新码头街
Xin Matou Jie

XIAONANNEN

Wang Jia Matou Lu
王家码头路

Wanyu Jie 万裕街

Dongjiadu Lu 董家渡路

Lujiabang Lu 陆家浜路

Nancang Jie 南仓街

Metro Line 4

NANPU
BRIDGE

Guohuo Lu 国货路

PENGLAI
GARDEN
蓬莱公园

Zhongshan Nan Lu 中山南路

Nanpu Bridge
南浦大桥

Of course, if you are severely pressed for time and only have a day, an **organized tour** in the company of an English-speaking guide can be a hassle-free if superficial way to cover the major sights. Your hotel travel desk or a travel agency (see "Organized Tours," later in this chapter) can arrange this.

The last and least advised option is to hire a car for the day through your hotel, an expensive option that will easily cost you upwards of ¥800 a day for a car and driver. It's cheaper if you hire a taxi for the day yourself on the streets.

# THE BUND (WÀI TĀN) 外滩

The Bund (which means the "Embankment") refers to Shànghǎi's famous waterfront running along the west shore of the Huángpǔ River, forming the eastern boundary of old downtown Shànghǎi. Once a muddy towpath for boats along the river, the Bund was where the foreign powers that entered Shànghǎi after the Opium War of 1842 erected their distinct Western-style banks and trading houses. From here, Shànghǎi grew into Asia's leading city in the 1920s and 1930s, a cosmopolitan and thriving commercial and financial center. Many of the awesome colonial structures you see today date from that prosperous time and have become an indelible part of Shànghǎi's cityscape. After 1949, the street came to symbolize Western dominance over China and was shuttered.

For the past 3 years, in preparation for the 2010 World Expo, the government spent around ¥5 billion on renovating the Bund, and today it has regained much of its previous glory. A four-lane avenue (cut down from 11) now fronts the old buildings, vehicular traffic having been diverted to an underground tunnel. The Bund buildings all received face-lifts and some even got new tenants. On the east side of the road, a significantly widened, 2.6km-long (1.6-mile) raised promenade, with new trees, vending machines, and 2,000 benches, affords visitors pleasant strolls along the river and marvelous views of both the Bund and Pǔdōng across the river. Pǔdōng's new skyscrapers and modern towers—constituting Shànghǎi's "21st-Century Bund"—may dominate today's skyline, but the city's core identity and history are strictly rooted in this unique strip on the western shore. For years, the Bund was the first sight of Shànghǎi for those arriving by boat; it should be your first stop as well.

## Essentials

Stretching for 1.6km (1 mile) along the western edge of the Huángpǔ River, the original Bund runs from Sūzhōu Creek in the north to Jīnlíng Lù in the south. On the west side of the main avenue (Zhōngshān Dōng Yī Lù) that runs along the Bund are the colonial edifices of yore, while the eastern side is taken by the **Bund Promenade,** a newly widened and lengthened, raised embankment that acts as a dike against the Huángpǔ River, because downtown itself, situated on a soggy delta, is slowly sinking below the river level. The strip south of Jīnlíng Lù used to be the Shíliùpǔ Wharf area; today, it's increasingly referred to as the South Bund (Nán Wàitān). The Bund is pleasant to stroll at any hour, but is often crowded with tourists and vendors selling snacks and souvenirs. Early mornings used to see tai chi practitioners and ballroom dancers out in force, but they have been scarcer since the renovations. Early to midmorning on weekdays is best for avoiding the crowds and for photography. If possible, try to return here at night when the Bund buildings are all aglow.

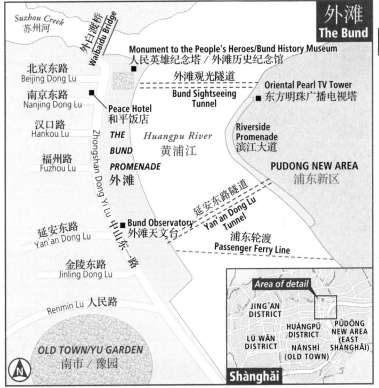

## Exploring the Bund

The highlights of the Bund are undoubtedly the colonial-era buildings lining the west side of Zhōngshān Dōng Yī Lù, standouts of which include the **former British Consulate, Customs House, former Hong Kong and Shànghǎi Bank, former Shànghǎi Club** (now the Waldorf Astoria Hotel), and the **Peace Hotel.** For more details on these buildings, many of which have been skillfully restored, and a more complete walking guide to this gallery of European architecture, see chapter 8, "Shànghǎi Strolls."

Besides its landmark colonial architecture, however, the Bund has a few other small attractions. On its north end, the rehabilitated Sūzhōu Creek enters the Huángpǔ River beneath the 18m-wide (59-ft.) iron **Wàibáidù Bridge,** built in 1906 to replace the original wooden toll bridge constructed in 1856 by an English businessman. The bridge was most recently restored in 2009. On the river shore stands a granite obelisk, **Monument to the People's Heroes,** erected in 1993, and dedicated to Chinese patriots (as defined by the Communist Party) beginning in the 1840s. The **Bund History Museum** (9am–4:15pm; free admission), which contains a few artifacts and some interesting photographs of the Bund, stands at its base; however, at press time, the museum was closed for renovation. Just south of the monument used to be the park **Huángpǔ Gōngyuán,** originally the British Public Gardens built in 1868. In the early days, only Chinese servants accompanying their foreign masters were allowed to enter the park. Dogs were also prohibited, leading in later years to the apocryphal NO CHINESE OR DOGS ALLOWED sign being attributed to the park. The park was eventually opened to Chinese in 1926, but today, has simply become part of the Bund promenade with the recent renovations. South of here, across from the Peace Hotel, is the entrance to the pedestrian **Bund Sightseeing Tunnel (Wàitān Guàngguāng Suìdào)** (daily 8am–10:30pm, 11pm Fri–Sun; admission ¥55 round-trip, ¥45 one-way) located under the Huángpǔ. Complete with tram cars and a light show, the tunnel connects downtown Shànghǎi to the Pǔdōng New Area and the Oriental Pearl TV Tower. Also here is a **statue of Chén Yì,** Shànghǎi's first mayor after 1949 and a dead ringer for Máo Zédōng, at least in bronze.

Farther south down the Bund Promenade are scores of vendors, a few restaurants, and excellent overlooks facing the river. At the intersection with Yán'ān Dōng Lù, you'll also notice a picturesque **Signal Tower,** a slender, round brick tower that served as a control tower for river traffic during colonial days. First built in 1884, the tower was rebuilt in 1907, and also relayed weather reports. In 1993 during the widening of Zhōngshān Lù, it was moved 20m (66 ft.) to its current site. About a 20-minute walk farther down the promenade are the docks for the Huángpǔ River cruises (p. 165).

# YÙ YUÁN (YÙ GARDEN) 豫园

Yù Yuán is a pleasant enough, well-contained classical Chinese garden, if not quite the loveliest of its kind, as local boosters would have you believe. Bearing the burden of being the most complete classical garden in urban Shànghǎi and therefore a must-see for every tourist, this overexposed garden overflows daily with hordes of visitors, and is no longer the pastoral haven it once was. Built between 1559 and 1577 by local official Pān Yǔnduān as the private estate for his father, Yù Yuán (meaning "Garden of Peace and Comfort") is a maze of Míng Dynasty pavilions, elaborate rockeries, arched bridges, and goldfish ponds, all encircled by an undulating dragon wall. Occupying just 2 hectares (5 acres), it nevertheless appears quite expansive, with room for 30 pavilions.

## Essentials

Yù Yuán is located at the heart of Old Town (Nánshì), a few blocks southwest of the Bund in downtown Shànghǎi (Metro: Yu Garden [Line 10]). The main entrance and ticket window (② **021/6355-5032** or 021/6326-0830; www.yugarden.com.cn) are on the north shore of the Húxīn Tíng pond. It is open from 8:30am to 5:30pm (last ticket 5pm), and admission is ¥40. The least crowded time to visit is early morning. Allow 2 hours for a leisurely tour of this site.

WHAT TO SEE & DO IN SHÀNGHǍI | Yù Yuán (Yù Garden)

> ### Impressions
>
> *Seen from the river, towering above their couchant guardian warships, the semi-skyscrapers of the Bund present, impressively, the facade of a great city.*
> —Christopher Isherwood, 1938

# Yù Yuán (Yù Garden)

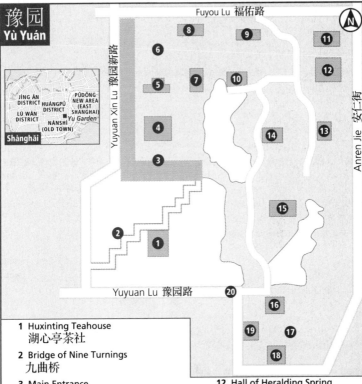

1 Huxinting Teahouse
湖心亭茶社

2 Bridge of Nine Turnings
九曲桥

3 Main Entrance
进口

4 Three Ears of Corn Hall
三穗堂

5 Hall for Viewing the Grand Rockery
仰山堂

6 The Grand Rockery
大假山

7 Pavilion for Viewing Frolicking Fish
鱼乐榭

8 Hall of Gathering Grace
萃秀堂

9 Pavilion of Ten Thousand Flowers
万花楼

10 Nine Lion Study
九狮轩

11 Treasury Hall
藏宝楼

12 Hall of Heralding Spring
点春堂

13 Hall of Harmony
和煦堂

14 Tower for Beholding the View
会景楼

15 Hall of Jade Magnificence
玉华堂

16 Hall of Serenity
静观厅

17 Inner Garden
内园

18 Acting and Singing Stage
古戏台

19 Tower for Watching Waves
观涛楼

20 Exit
出口

# Exploring Yù Yuán

The layout of Yù Yuán, which contains several gardens-within-gardens, can make strolling here a bit confusing, but if you stick to a general clockwise path from the main entrance, you should get around most of the estate and arrive eventually at the Inner Garden (Nèi Yuán) and final exit. The major sites from the northern entrance clockwise to the east and south are as follows:

**SĀNSUÌ TÁNG (THREE EARS OF CORN HALL)**   This is the first and largest of the garden's grand pavilions, although it was built in 1760 after Yù Yuán had been sold to a group of merchants. The highlight here is the fine window and woodbeam carvings of rice, millet, wheat, fruit, and other emblems of a plentiful harvest. The building was used as a meeting place for local officials and for proclaiming imperial announcements.

**YÁNGSHĀN TÁNG (HALL FOR VIEWING THE GRAND ROCKERY)**
Immediately north of the Three Ears of Corn Hall, this graceful two-story tower with upturned eaves serves as the entrance to the marvelous rock garden behind. Its upper story, known as Juǎnyǔ Lóu (Chamber for Gathering Rain), provides a fine view of the Grand Rockery.

**DÀ JIǍ SHĀN (THE GRAND ROCKERY)**   A pond separates the viewing hall from the Grand Rockery, which consists of 2,000 tons of rare yellow stones fused together with rice glue and designed by a famous garden artist of the Míng, Zhāng Nányáng. The twisted mountainlike sculpture, intended to evoke peaks, ravines, caves, and ridges, stands 14m (46 ft.) high and was the highest point in the city during the garden's construction. East of the pond is **Jiàn Rù Jiǎ Jìng (the Corridor for Approaching the Best Scenery);** notice the beautiful vase-shaped door frames. Off the corridor to the east, you'll find the small **Yúlè Xiè (Pavilion for Viewing Frolicking Fish)** with schools of happy carp and goldfish swimming in a stream that appears much longer than it actually is (less than 50m/164 ft.). Northeast of the rockery is the **Cuì Xiù Táng (Hall of Gathering Grace);** to the east is **Wànhuā Lóu (Pavilion of Ten Thousand Flowers),** where a 4-century-old gingko tree stakes out the front courtyard.

**DIǍN CHŪN TÁNG (HALL OF HERALDING SPRING)**   If you continue east from the Grand Rockery and the Pavilion of Ten Thousand Flowers, you will come to two halls in the northeast section of Yù Yuán: the northern **Cángbǎo Lóu (Treasury Hall),** and the most famous historical building in the garden, **Diǎn Chūn Táng (Hall of Heralding Spring).** It was here in 1853 that the secret Small Sword Society (Xiǎodāo Huì) plotted to join the peasant-led Tàipíng Rebellion based in Nánjīng, which aimed to overthrow the Qīng Dynasty. The uprising was a bloody one in Shànghǎi, forcing countless Chinese to flee into the British Concession. Rebels ruled the Chinese city for a year before being put down by a combination of Chinese and Western soldiers. Today, there is a small collection of uprising artifacts in this hall, including weapons and coins minted by the rebels.

**HÉXÚ TÁNG (HALL OF HARMONY)**   South of the rebels' old headquarters, past the **Kuài Lóu (Tower of Joy)** perched atop a pile of rocks, is the glass-enclosed **Hall of Harmony,** worth stepping inside to examine its display of old Qīng Dynasty furniture, fashioned by hand from banyan tree roots.

Just to the west of this hall is a wonderful **dragon wall** with a lifelike clay carving of a dragon's head perched at the end and gray tiles along the top evoking the dragon's body. Such walls are used throughout to divide the garden into different sections. A detour west of this wall leads to a bamboo grove and eventually to the airy **Jiǔshī Xuān (Nine Lion Study).**

**YÙ HUÁ TÁNG (HALL OF JADE MAGNIFICENCE)**    This hall opens into a southern courtyard with the most celebrated stone sculpture in the garden, **Yù Líng Lóng (Exquisite Jade Rock).** This honeycomb slab was reportedly originally procured by the Huìzōng emperor of the Northern Sòng (reigned A.D. 1100–26) from the waters of Tài Hú (Lake Tài) where many of the bizarre rocks and rockeries found in classical Chinese gardens were submerged to be naturally carved by the currents. Such rocks represent mountain peaks in classical Chinese garden design, and this rock satisfies the three elements of appearance (that it be rough, craggy, and pitted). Water poured into the top of this boulder will spurt out through its numerous holes; incense lighted at its base will swirl outward from its openings. Destined for the emperor, the rock was reportedly shipwrecked in the Huángpǔ River, and was later retrieved by Pān Yǔnduān and placed here across from his study.

**NÈI YUÁN (INNER GARDEN)**    South of Exquisite Jade Rock is the entrance to the Inner Garden, which was constructed in 1709 and made a part of Yù Yuán only in 1956. This is often the quietest section of the garden, particularly in the morning. Its **Hall of Serenity (Jìngguān Táng)** at the north entrance and **Tower for Watching Waves (Guāntāo Lóu)** are magnificent, as is the ornately carved **Acting and Singing Stage (Gǔ Xìtái)** to the south. Local artists and calligraphers sometimes use these and other pavilions to display (and sell) their works. The exit from Yù Yuán is located next to the Inner Garden entrance (west); it puts you on Yùyuán Lù, which leads back to the Old Town pond and the Húxīngtíng Teahouse.

# SHÀNGHǍI MUSEUM (SHÀNGHǍI BÓWÙGUǍN)
# 上海博物馆

Frequently cited as the best museum in China, the Shànghǎi Museum has 11 state-of-the-art galleries and three special exhibition halls arranged on four floors, all encircling a spacious cylindrical atrium. The exhibits are tastefully displayed and well lit, and explanatory signs are in English as well as Chinese. For size, the museum's 120,000 historic artifacts cannot match the world-renowned Chinese collections in Běijīng, Taipei, and Xī'ān, but are more than enough to fill the galleries on any given day with outstanding treasures. Many foreign visitors to the museum often rank it as Shànghǎi's very best site.

## Essentials

Located downtown on the south side of People's Square (Rénmín Guǎngchǎng) at Rénmín Dà Dào 201 (© **021/6372-3500;** www.shanghaimuseum.net), the museum has its main entrance on the north side of the building, facing the three monumental structures that now occupy the north half of the square (Grand Theatre to the west, City Hall in the middle, Shànghǎi Urban Planning Exhibition Center to the east).

Metro Lines 1, 2, and 8 have their main stations on the northeast corner of People's Square. The Shànghǎi Museum is open daily from 9am to 5pm (no tickets distributed after 4pm). Admission is free, though there is a limit of 5,000 visitors a day, so if you visit on the weekend, be sure to arrive early. Audio phones providing narratives of the major exhibits in English, French, Japanese, Spanish, German, and Italian are available for rent (¥40 plus a deposit of ¥400 or your passport) at the counter to your left as you enter the lobby.

## Exploring the Shànghǎi Museum (Shànghǎi Bówùguǎn)

Unlike many museums in China, the Shànghǎi Museum is arranged by theme rather than by dynasty. Though visitors all have their individual favorites, the Bronze Gallery and the Stone Sculpture Gallery on the first floor and the Painting Gallery on the third floor are generally considered the most impressive. Elevators, escalators, and stairways serve each floor. A large gift shop on the ground floor sells museum reproductions, books, postcards, and gifts; and smaller shops are located on the other floors.

Begin your tour on the first floor at the **Ancient Chinese Bronze Gallery,** which boasts a marvelous collection of more than 400 bronzes from the 18th to the 3rd centuries B.C. typically reserved for use only by nobles and royalty. Standouts include two wine vessels with animal mask designs, one in the shape of an ox (*zūn*) and the other a traditional pot (*hé*) used by the king of Wú, both dating from the Late Spring and Autumn Period (770–476 B.C.). There's also a typical food vessel on three legs (*dǐng*) from the Western Zhōu Dynasty (1100–771 B.C.), the shape of which is said to be the inspiration for the museum building, which certainly resembles an ancient *dǐng* from afar. The **Ancient Chinese Sculpture Gallery** has sculptures spanning the Warring States period to the Míng Dynasty (475 B.C.–A.D. 1644), including a kneeling clay figure playing a bamboo flute from the Eastern Hàn (A.D. 25–200) and a Buddhist image of Sakyamuni in stone from the Northern Qí (A.D. 550–577).

On the second floor, the **Ceramics Gallery** contains many tricolor figurines from the magnificent Táng Dynasty (A.D. 618–907) and delicately painted and fired pots from the Míng Dynasty (A.D. 1368–1644) kilns at Jǐngdé Zhèn; the gallery is definitely worth a tour if you love your china.

On the third floor, the **Painting Gallery** contains many ancient, original works on silk scrolls, including landscapes from the Míng Dynasty and Buddhist scrolls from the Táng and Sòng (A.D. 960–1279) dynasties. Typical is the ink brush scroll by Emperor Zhào Jí (A.D. 1083–1135) of the Sòng Dynasty titled for its subjects, *Willow, Crows, Reed, and Wild Geese.* The **Calligraphy Gallery** shows the various styles of artistic "handwriting" developed in China over many centuries, with specimens as old as the Táng Dynasty. Altogether, the museum owns some 15,000 of these fine scrolls. The **Seal Gallery** has intricate carved chops in stone used by emperors and their courts to notarize official documents. On this floor, displays show the basic elements of calligraphy, explaining the relationship between Chinese painting and calligraphy, and demonstrating how the artists' tools were used.

The fourth floor has a splendid **Jade Gallery,** with intricately carved jade wine vessels, jewelry, and ornaments, some from as early as the Liángzhǔ Culture (31st–22nd c. B.C.). The **Coin Gallery** displays coins that predate the First Emperor's

南京东路步行街

Nanjing Xi Lu 南京西路

Nanjing Dong Lu PEDESTRIAN MALL

PEOPLE'S
PARK
人民公园

**M** PEOPLE'S
SQUARE

**M** PEOPLE'S
SQUARE

Mu'en Church
沐恩堂

**Museum of
Contemporary Art
(MOCA)**
上海当代艺术馆

**Shanghai Urban Planning
Exhibition Hall**
上海城市规划展示馆

**Shanghai Art
Museum**
上海美术馆

**City Hall**
市人大市政府

Fuzhou Lu 福州路

Huangpi Bei Lu 黄陂北路

**Shanghai Grand
Theater**
上海大剧院

Renmin Da Dao 人民大道

Xizang Zhong Lu 西藏中路

PEOPLE'S SQUARE
人民广场

Entrance

**Great World**
大世界

**Shanghai Museum**
上海博物馆

Wusheng Lu 武胜路

延安东路
Yan'an Dong Lu

**M** DASHIJIE

= = Line 1
= = Line 2
= = Line 4

JING'AN
DISTRICT

Shànghǎi
Museum

PǓDŌNG
NEW AREA
(EAST
SHANGHAI)

LÚ WĀN
DISTRICT

HUÁNGPǓ
DISTRICT

NÁNSHÌ
(OLD TOWN)

**Shànghǎi**

上海博物馆及其周边
**Shànghǎi Museum & Environs**

reign (221–207 B.C.), as well as gold coins from Persia discovered on the Silk Road. The **Míng and Qīng Furniture Gallery** has elaborately carved screens inlaid with jade from the Qīng Dynasty (A.D. 1644–1911), a six-poster canopy bed, and a wonderful, folding wooden armchair from the Míng Dynasty (A.D. 1368–1644). The **Minority Nationalities' Art Gallery** displays some lovely costumes, jewelry, dioramas, and ceremonial creations from the more remote, non-Hàn Chinese reaches of the Chinese empire, most of them dating from the early 20th century.

# HUÁNGPǓ RIVER CRUISE
黄浦江游览

The Huángpǔ River (Huángpǔ Jiāng) is the city's shipping artery both to the East China Sea and to the mouth of the Yángzǐ River, which the Huángpǔ joins 29km (18 miles) north of downtown Shànghǎi. It has also become a demarcating line between two Shànghǎis, east and west, past and future. On its western shore, the colonial landmarks of the Bund serve as a reminder of Shànghǎi's 19th-century struggle to reclaim a waterfront from the bogs of this river (which originates in nearby Diānshān Hú or Lake Diānshān); on the eastern shore, the steel-and-glass skyscrapers of the Pǔdōng New Area point to a burgeoning financial empire of the future.

The Huángpǔ's wharves are the most fascinating in China. The port handles the cargo coming out of the interior from Nánjīng, Wǔhàn, and other Yángzǐ River ports, including Chóngqìng, 2,415km (1,500 miles) deep into Sìchuān Province. From Shànghǎi, which produces plenty of industrial and commercial products in its own right, as much as a third of China's trade with the rest of the world is conducted each year. A boat ride on the Huángpǔ is highly recommended: Not only does it provide unrivaled postcard views of Shànghǎi past and future, but it will also afford you a closer look at this dynamic waterway that makes Shànghǎi flow.

## Essentials

There are several ways to tour the Huángpǔ River. If you have time, a 3-hour (60km/37-mile) voyage along the Huángpǔ to the mouth of the Yángzǐ River and back allows for the most leisurely and complete appreciation of the river. There are also shorter river cruises (1 hr.) that ply the main waterfront area between the two suspension bridges, Nánpǔ Qiáo in the south, and Yángpǔ Qiáo in the north, and an even shorter (30-min.) cruise from Pǔdōng (see "Quick Cruise from Pǔdōng," below).

Many boat companies offer cruises; one of the main ones is the **Shànghǎi Huángpǔ River Cruise Company (Shànghǎi Pǔjiāng Yóulǎn Yǒuxiàn Gōngsī)** (✆ **021/6318-8888** or 021/6374-0091; www.pjrivercruise.com). They typically have a daily, full 3-hour afternoon cruise (2–5pm) to Wúsōng Kǒu and back. Cost is ¥150. As well, there are hour-long cruises (¥100) every day departing at 30-minute to 1-hour intervals between 9:30am and 4:30pm from the Bund to the Yángpǔ Bridge. This company also offers a nightly cruise (45–60 min.; ¥100) every half-hour between 7pm and 8:30pm. Cruise schedules vary depending on the season, and on Saturday and Sunday, additional cruises are sometimes added, so check ahead. During the World Expo, authorities commandeered for Expo use a number of boats from different boat companies, resulting in a disruption to regular sailing schedules. Although regular sailings should be restored by the time you read this, check ahead for the latest accurate sailing times. Boats all depart from the Shíliùpǔ Wharf (Shíliùpǔ Lǚyóu Jíshàn Zhōngxīn) at Wài Mǎ Lù 19, 1 block east of Zhōngshān Nán Lù 171, and just north of Fùxīng Dōng Lù. Tickets can be purchased through your hotel desk or at the Shíliùpǔ Wharf ticket office at Wài Mǎ Lù 80.

## Cruising the Huángpǔ

Between the stately colonial edifices along the Bund, the glittering skyscrapers on the eastern shore of Pǔdōng, and the unceasing river traffic, there is plenty to keep your eyes from ever resting. From the dock, the boat will usually head south first, past the **Cool Docks** (a dining, shopping, and entertainment complex) on the South Bund to the 3.7km-long (2⅓-mile), harp string–shaped **Nánpǔ Dàqiáo (Nánpǔ Cable Bridge)** built in 1991. As the boat turns around and heads back up north, you'll see everywhere signs of the Huángpǔ River Restoration Project, whereby 20km (12 miles) of downtown waterfront on both shores (especially on the Pǔxī) are being turned into marinas, riverside parks, and housing and shopping complexes.

# Huángpǔ River Cruise

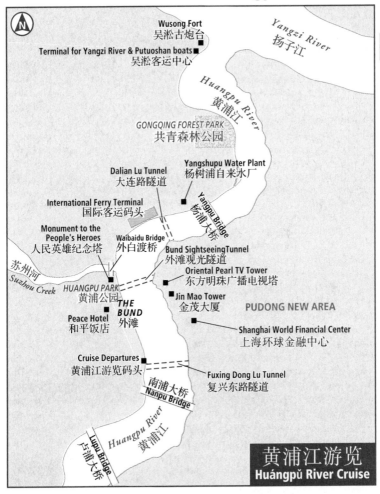

Map labels:

Wusong Fort 吴淞古炮台

Terminal for Yangzi River & Putuoshan boats 吴淞客运中心

Yangzi River 扬子江

Huangpu River 黄浦江

GONGQING FOREST PARK 共青森林公园

Yangshupu Water Plant 杨树浦自来水厂

Dalian Lu Tunnel 大连路隧道

International Ferry Terminal 国际客运码头

Yangpu Bridge 杨浦大桥

Monument to the People's Heroes 人民英雄纪念塔

Waibaidu Bridge 外白渡桥

Bund SightseeingTunnel 外滩观光隧道

Oriental Pearl TV Tower 东方明珠广播电视塔

Suzhou Creek 苏州河

HUANGPU PARK 黄浦公园

Jin Mao Tower 金茂大厦

PUDONG NEW AREA

THE BUND 外滩

Peace Hotel 和平饭店

Shanghai World Financial Center 上海环球金融中心

Cruise Departures 黄浦江游览码头

Fuxing Dong Lu Tunnel 复兴东路隧道

Nanpu Bridge 南浦大桥

Lupu Bridge 卢浦大桥

Huangpu River 黄浦江

黄浦江游览 Huángpǔ River Cruise

Even on overcast days (the norm in Shànghǎi), the single greatest pieces of eye candy as you head north are still the granite offices, banks, consulates, and hotels of the Bund. Sadly for purists these days, however, the **Peace Hotel** with its stunning green pyramid roof and the **Customs House** with its big clock tower no longer have your undivided attention, but have to compete with the towering, 21st-century space-age skyscrapers that have sprouted in the background. Up close, though, the grandeur of the Bund, especially now with the restored Bund Promenade, is still undeniable.

As the ship heads north, on the Pǔdōng shore is the architectural perfection of the **Jīn Mào Tower,** now flanked in the back by the even taller **World Financial Center.** Also on the Pǔdōng shore is the can't-miss Oriental Pearl Tower, the Shàng-hǎi International Convention Center with its twin glass globes, and a slew of hotels, offices, and malls of the Lùjiāzuǐ Financial Area.

Back on the western shore, north of the obelisk that is the Monument to the People's Heroes is **Sūzhōu Creek (Sūzhōu Hé),** formerly called the Wúsōng River. Originating in Tài Hú (Lake Tài), the 120km-long (75-mile) river was once much busier than the Huángpǔ, but silt in the lower reaches eventually diminished water traffic. The creek is spanned by **Wàibáidù Bridge,** which once linked the American Concession in the north (today's Hóngkǒu District) and the British Concession south of the creek. At 18m (59 ft.) wide, with two 51m-long (167-ft.) spans, this bridge has seen all forms of traffic, from rickshaws to trams to motorcars. Elderly Shanghainese still recall the days of the Japanese occupation when they had to bow to Japanese sentries guarding the bridge and seek special permission to cross.

North of the Sūzhōu Creek hugging the west shore are the old "go-downs" or warehouses of the many foreign trading firms. This area, known as Hóngkǒu District, and the district to the east, Yángpǔ District, have been marked for rapid development after Pǔdōng, though new modern towers (all no more than 3 years old) have already started to stake out the skyline. Less than a mile farther on is the **International Passenger Terminal,** where international cruise ships tie up. The Huángpǔ River jogs east at this point on its way to the Shànghǎi shipyards, where cranes and derricks load and unload the daily logjam of freighters from the world's other shipping giants (United States, Japan, Russia, Norway). Eventually, all of this waterfront will be developed into a series of marinas and a combination of industrial and recreational areas, including a section that will be Shànghǎi's answer to "Fisherman's Wharf."

Before the Huángpǔ slowly begins to curve northward again, you'll pass the English castle–style **Yángshùpǔ Water Plant** originally built by the British in 1882. The **Yángpǔ Cable Bridge,** like the **Nánpǔ Cable Bridge** to the south, is one of the largest such structures in the world. With quite a long span, some 602m (1,975 ft.), the Yángpǔ Bridge is considered the world's first "slant-stretched" bridge. Its total length is about 7.6km (4¾ miles), and 50,000 vehicles pass over its six lanes daily.

What impresses river passengers even more than the long industrial shoreline is the traffic slinking up and down the waterway, from the flotilla of river barges to the large rusting hulls of cargo ships. The Huángpǔ is, on the average, just 183m (600 ft.) wide, but more than 2,000 oceangoing ships compete with the 20,000 barges, fishing junks, and rowboats that ply the Huángpǔ every year. As the river curves north, you'll pass the small island, **Fùxīng Dǎo,** which is to be developed into an ecological and recreational theme park.

The Huángpǔ eventually empties into the mighty Yángzǐ River at **Wúsōng Kǒu,** where the water during high tide turns three distinct colors, marking the confluence of the Yángzǐ (yellow), the Huángpǔ (gray), and the South China Sea (green). Before this, there's an ancient **Wúsōng Fort,** from which the Chinese fought the British in 1842. The passenger terminal (**Wúsōng Passenger Terminal;** ☎ 021/5657-5500) for Yángzǐ River cruises is also here. This marks the end of Shànghǎi's little river and the beginning of China's largest one. As your tour boat pivots slowly back into the narrowing passageway of the Huángpǔ, you can look forward to a return trip that should be more relaxed.

## QUICK cruise FROM PǓDŌNG

A brief (40-min.), but dramatic cruise along the Huángpǔ can also be picked up on the Pǔdōng side of the river. The cityscapes on both sides will give you a sweeping perspective of Shànghǎi old and new.

Tickets for the Pǔdōng cruise can be purchased at the Oriental Pearl TV Tower ticket booth or at a kiosk near the dock (Dōngfāng Míngzhú Yóulǎn Mǎtóu; ✆ 021/5879-1888) on Fēnghé Lù. To reach the dock, walk along the north-west side of the TV Tower grounds on Fēnghé Lù, past the Insect Museum and the twin-globed Convention Center, straight on to the right-hand side of the sail-shaped pavilion on the river shore. Departures take place nearly every hour at 10am, 11am, noon, 2pm, 3pm, and 4pm (more may be added during peak times); tickets are ¥50 to ¥70. Night cruises depart from May to October at 7 and 8pm.

# TEMPLES, CHURCHES, MOSQUES & SYNAGOGUES

Not known for its temples, Shànghǎi's most popular Buddhist shrine with visitors is the Jade Buddha Temple (Yùfó Sì). The Lónghuá Temple is also on the route of some tourists; its pagoda is the most interesting one in Shànghǎi. Shànghǎi also has several active Christian churches and an Islamic mosque where foreign visitors may worship or visit. But what really sets religious Shànghǎi apart, at least in China, is its Jewish legacy, most powerfully evoked by the reopening of the Ohel Moshe Synagogue as a museum and study center, and the Ohel Rachel Synagogue for Shabbat services.

## Temples

**Báiyún Guàn** 白云观　Originally built in 1863 in a different location, and moved here in 2004, this temple is one of only two Daoist temples in China to possess the precious Míng Dynasty Daoist Scripture (*dàozàng*)—the other is the much larger Báiyún Guàn in Běijīng. The two-story temple is housed in a courtyard building with red walls, lattice windows and doors, and a beautiful ornamented roof. Incense-bearing supplicants pray before a dizzying array of gilded Daoist deities, each entrusted with a specific cause. If your timing is right, you may be able to catch a Daoist service, which is highly ritualized, often resembling pageants complete with music, chanting, and processions of monks in colorful robes.

Dàjìng Lù 239 大境路２３９号, Huángpǔ (east of Rénmín Lù, next to Dàjìng Gé); see map p. 156. ✆ 021/6328-7236. Admission ¥5. 8am–4:30pm. Metro: Dàshìjiè or Yu Garden.

**Chénghuáng Miào (Temple of the Town God)** 城隍庙　Every Chinese city once had its Temple of the Town God, the central shrine for Daoist worship. Shàng-hǎi's version dates from 1403 when local official Qín Yùbó, who had been posthu-mously designated as Shànghǎi's patron town god by the Míng Dynasty Hóngwǔ emperor (A.D. 1328–98), was finally honored with his own temple, though it didn't take on its present name until 1929. During the Cultural Revolution (1966–76), the temple, which had grown to become more of a marketplace, was destroyed. In the

# jewish SHÀNGHĂI

As China's most international city, Shànghǎi experienced several waves of Jewish immigration, each leaving its mark. The first to arrive, in the late 1840s, were the Sephardic Jews. Businessmen who made their fortunes in opium and property, they built large estates and as many as seven synagogues, and were responsible for some of Shànghǎi's finest architecture. The Sassoons, who emigrated from Baghdad in the mid-19th century, were the first Jewish family to make a fortune in Shànghǎi, and both the Peace Hotel on the Bund and the villa estate next to the zoo (now the Cypress Hotel) were their creations. Silas Hardoon was a later Jewish real estate baron whose great estate was razed to make way for the Sino-Soviet Shànghǎi Exhibition Center on Yán'ān Xī Lù (south of the Portman Hotel). Meanwhile, the legacy of the Kadoories, another wealthy Jewish family from Baghdad, is the stunning

"Marble House" on Yán'ān Xī Lù, today the city's most popular and impressive Children's Palace.

The second wave of Jewish immigrants comprised Russian Jews fleeing the Bolsheviks at the beginning of the 20th century. They were followed in the 1930s by a third wave of European Jews who were fleeing Hitler, and who landed here only because Shànghǎi was the only city in the world at that time willing to accept these "stateless refugees." Just before World War II, the numbers of Jews in Shànghǎi topped 30,000. In February 1943, to appease the Germans who wanted the Japanese to implement the Final Solution in Shànghǎi, the occupying force of the Japanese army forced the "stateless Jews" into a "Designated Area" in Hóngkǒu District (north of the Bund), marked by today's Zhōujiāzuǐ Lù in the north, Huìmín Lù in the south, Tōngběi Lù in the east, and Gōngpíng Lù in the west. Tens of thousands of Jews

early 1990s, the temple and surrounding bazaar area, which encircled part of Yù Yuán, were extensively restored to become one large complex devoted to the god of commerce. The temple's main courtyard is usually jammed with worshippers praying before the statues of Huò Guāng (a local military hero) in the front hall, and the town god in the back. The smell of incense is overpowered only by the smell of money wafting from the nearby shops.

Fāngbāng Zhōng Lù 249 方浜中路 2 4 9 号, Huángpǔ (Old Town Bazaar, north side of Fāngbāng Zhōng Lù near Ānrén Lù); see map p. 156. (℘) **021/6386-5700.** www.shchm.org. Admission ¥10. 8:30am–4:30pm. Metro: Yu Garden.

**Chénxiāng Gé** 沉香阁  Pān Yǔnduān, the official who built Yù Yuán, had this Buddhist temple built to honor his mother in 1600. During the Cultural Revolution (1966–76) it was all but destroyed and abandoned. In 1989, restoration began, culminating in its reopening as a Buddhist nunnery and small Old Town tourist attraction in 1994. The centerpiece is an altar with a golden statue of the Buddha. The Buddha's vault is adorned with images of 384 disciples, created since 1990 by a single master craftsman. Guānyīn (the Goddess of Mercy) is highly venerated here.

Chénxiānggé Lù 29 沉香阁路 2 9 号, Huángpǔ (1 block west off Jiùjiāochǎng Lù, the western boundary of the Old Town Bazaar); see map p. 156. (℘) **021/6328-7884.** Admission ¥5. 7am–4pm. Metro: Yu Garden.

lived cheek by jowl in this "ghetto," where the local synagogue became the center of their material and spiritual lives until the end of the war.

Travelers interested in the Jews in Shànghǎi can still visit that center, the **Ohel Moshe Synagogue (Móxī Huìtáng),** Chángyáng Lù 62, Hóngkǒu (✆ **021/ 6512-6669;** daily 9am–5pm [last ticket sold 4:30pm]). Built in 1927 by the Ashkenazi Jewish community of Shànghǎi, it no longer serves as a synagogue, but as the **Shànghǎi Jewish Refugee Museum (Yóutài Nánmín Zài Shànghǎi Jìniànguǎn)** devoted to the history of the Jews in Shànghǎi. Following renovations, the museum now has an annex in the back that features an exhibition of Jewish life in Shànghǎi from 1933 to 1945. Tickets cost ¥50 (¥10 for students).

The best way to visit this synagogue, Huǒshān Park (Huǒshān Gōngyuán), where there is a memorial to Jewish refugees, the Marble Hall, and the *lòngtáng*

(lane) row houses of Hóngkǒu that formed Shànghǎi's "Little Vienna," is on the wonderful **"Tour of Jewish Shànghǎi"** ★ conducted by appointment with Dvir Bar-Gal (✆ **0130/0214-6702;** www.shanghai-jews.com).

The tour will also pass by **Ohel Rachel Synagogue (Lāxī'ěr Yóutài Jiàotáng)** at Shǎnxī Běi Lù 500, behind the Portman Ritz-Carlton Hotel. It was built in 1920 by Jacob Sassoon in memory of his wife, Rachel, and is today considered one of the world's most endangered monuments. For many years home to the Shànghǎi Education Commission, it reopened in May 2010 as a living synagogue for Shabbat prayers and meals.

Travelers interested in learning more about the Jewish community in Shànghǎi, attending Shabbat dinners, or participating in religious services should contact the **Shànghǎi Jewish Center,** Hóngqiáo Lù 1720, Shang-Mira Garden Villa no. 2 (✆ **021/6278-0225;** fax 021/6278-0223; www.chinajewish.org).

**Jìng Ān Sì (Jìng Ān Temple)** 静安寺   Always lively and crowded, this garishly decorated temple has the longest history of any shrine in Shànghǎi (about 17 centuries, though the shopping annex is considerably more recent, as is the 63m/207-ft.-tall gold pagoda at the back, completed in 2010). The temple's chief antiquities are a Míng Dynasty copper bell (the Hóngwǔ Bell) that weighs in at 3,175 kilograms (3.5 tons) and stone Buddhas from the Northern and Southern States period (A.D. 420–589). Although its name means "Temple of Tranquillity," it is hardly the place for quiet meditation these days, nor was it in the past. Before 1949, this was Shànghǎi's richest Buddhist monastery, presided over by the Abbott of Bubbling Well Road (Nánjīng Xī Lù, as it was known in colonial times because of a well that was located in front of the temple), an imposing figure who kept seven mistresses and a White Russian bodyguard. Today's Southern-style main halls all have renovations using Burmese teakwood (*yóumù*).

Nánjīng Xī Lù 1686 南京西路 1 6 8 6 号, Jìng Ān (corner of Huáshān Lù); see map p. 144. ✆ **021/ 6256-6366.** Admission ¥30. 7:30am–5pm. Metro: Jing'an Temple.

**Lónghuá Sì (Lónghuá Temple)** 龙华寺 ★★   Shànghǎi's largest and most active temple is one of its most fascinating, featuring the city's premier pagoda, the delicate Lónghuá Tǎ. Local lore has it that the pagoda was originally built around

A.D. 247 by Sūn Quán, the king of the Wú Kingdom during the Three Kingdoms period, but today's seven-story, eight-sided, wood-and-brick pagoda, like the temple, dates to the Sòng Dynasty (A.D. 960–1279). For a long time the tallest structure in Shànghǎi, today it can only be admired from a distance. The extensive temple grounds are often crowded with incense-bearing supplicants. There are four main halls (only a century old), the most impressive being the third, Dàxióng Bǎo Diàn (Grand Hall) where a gilded statue of Sakyamuni sits under a beautifully carved dome, flanked on each side by 18 *arhats* (disciples). Behind, Guānyīn, the Goddess of Mercy, presides over a fascinating tableau representing the process of reincarnation: A boat in the bottom right corner indicates birth, while death awaits at the bottom left corner. Behind the third and fourth halls is a basic, but popular vegetarian restaurant (11am–2pm). Lónghuá is also famous for its midnight bell-ringing every New Year's Eve (Dec 31–Jan 1). The Bell Tower's 3,000-kilogram (3.3-ton) bronze bell, cast in 1894, is struck 108 times to dispel all the worries said to be afflicting mankind. For a small fee, you, too, can strike the bell, but three times only.

Lónghuá Lù 2853 龙华路 2 8 5 3 号, Xúhuì; see map p. 140. ✆ **021/6456-6085.** Admission ¥10. 7am–5pm. Metro: Lóngcáo Rd.

**Wén Miào (Confucius Temple)** 文庙   Built in 1855 on the site of an earlier temple, and restored in 1999 to celebrate the 2,550th birthday of Confucius, this temple honoring China's great sage offers quiet refuge from the crowded streets of the old Chinese city. As at all Chinese Confucian temples, there's a *língxīn mén* (gate) leading to the main hall, Dàchéng Diàn. Inside are statues of Confucius flanked by his two disciples, Mèngzǐ (Mencius) and Yánhuī, and his two favorite musical instruments, a drum and set of bells. To the northeast, the Zūnjīng Gé, formerly the library, now houses a display of unusually shaped rocks. Back near the entrance, Kuíxīng Gé is a three-story 20m-high (66-ft.) pagoda dedicated to the god of liberal arts, and the only original structure left on these tranquil grounds. A lively book market is held here on Sunday mornings.

Wénmiào Lù 215 文庙路 2 1 5 号, Huángpǔ (north side of Wénmiào Lù, 1 block east of Zhōnghuá Lù); see map p. 140. ✆ **021/6377-1815.** Admission ¥10. 9am–4:30pm. Metro: Laoximen.

**Yùfó Sì (Jade Buddha Temple)** 玉佛寺 ★ ♨   Though an active Buddhist monastery today, the real emphasis at Shànghǎi's most popular temple is squarely on tourism. What the busloads come for are the temple's two gorgeous white jade Buddhas, each carved from an individual slab of Burmese jade and brought to Shànghǎi in 1881 by the monk Huígēng, who was on his way back from Burma to his hometown on nearby Pǔtuó Shān (Pǔtuó Island). Northeast of the main Dàxióng Bǎo Diàn (Treasure Hall of the Great Hero), the Cángjīng Lóu houses the first of the two treasures: a lustrous, beatific, seated Buddha weighing 205 kilograms (452 lb.), measuring 1.9m (6¼ ft.), and adorned with jewels and stones. The other Buddha is found northwest of the main hall in the Wòfó Sì, where a less impressive, but still beautiful 1m-long (3¼-ft.) sleeping Buddha reclines, his peaceful expression signaling his impending entry into nirvana. Opposite it is a larger, coarser replica donated by the Singapore Buddhist Friendship Association in 1988.

Ānyuǎn Lù 170 安远路 1 7 0 号, Pǔtuó (northwest Shànghǎi, west of Jiāngníng Lù, 6 long blocks north of Běijīng Xī Lù); see map p. 144. ✆ **021/6266-3668.** Admission ¥20. 8am–4:30pm. Metro: Changshou Rd.

# Mosques & Churches

In addition to the two cathedrals listed below, other major Catholic churches include **Bóduōlù Táng (St. Peter's Church),** Chóngqìng Nán Lù 270, Lúwān (📞 021/6467-0198), originally built in 1933 but rebuilt in 1995, and which now holds services in English on Saturday at 5pm and Sunday at 10:30am; **Shèng Ruòsè Táng (St. Joseph's Church),** built in 1860 at Sìchuān Nán Lù 36, Huángpǔ (📞 021/6328-0293 or 021/6336-5537); and **Jūnwáng Tiānzhǔ Táng (Christ the King Catholic Church),** also called the Good Shepherd Church, Jùlù Lù 361, Jìng Ān (📞 021/6217-4608).

Other active Protestant places of worship that open their doors to foreign worshippers include **Huái'ēn Táng (Shànghǎi Grace Church),** opened in 1910 at Shǎnxī Běi Lù 375, Jìng Ān (📞 021/6253-9394); **Jǐnglíng Táng (Youag John Allen Memorial Church),** built in 1923 at Kūnshān Lù 135, east from Sìchuān Běi Lù, Hóngkǒu (📞 021/6324-3021 or 021/5539-1720), the place where Chiang Kai-shek wed Soong Mei-ling; and **Zhūshèng Táng (All Saints Church),** Fùxīng Zhōng Lù 425 at Dànshuǐ Lù (📞 021/6385-0906), a lively church in the French Concession that recently began holding services again.

For the locations of additional cathedrals, churches, mosques, and places of worship and the times of services, inquire at your hotel.

### Dǒngjiādù Tiānzhǔtáng (Dǒngjiādù Catholic Church) 董家渡天主堂

Located in the southern part of the old Chinese city, this was the first large cathedral in Shànghǎi, built in 1853 in the early Spanish baroque style. It's a fine-looking building with arched roofs, thick pillars, and lotus-designed bas-reliefs inside. Chinese couplets are inscribed on both inside and outside walls, and four of the church bells are said to be original.

Dǒngjiādù Lù 185 董家渡1 8 5 号, Huángpǔ (west of Zhōngshān Nán Lù); see map p. 156. 📞 **021/6378-7214.** Services Mon–Sat 7am; Sun 6am, 8am. No Metro.

### Guójì Lǐbài Táng (Héngshān Community Church) 国际礼拜堂 Established

in 1925 and also called the International Church, this is the best known of Shànghǎi's Protestant churches among foreign residents and visitors, and is the largest in use. The ivy-covered English-style building and grounds are beautiful, fully in keeping with this upscale, colonial-style shopping district on the fringes of the French Concession. Special services for foreign passport holders are currently held here on Sundays at 2 and 4pm.

Héngshān Lù 53 衡山路5 3 号, Xújiāhuì (west of Wūlǔmùqí Nán Lù); see map p. 140. 📞 **021/6437-6576.** Services Sun 7:30 and 10am, English-language service 2 and 4pm. Metro: Hengshan Rd.

### Moore Memorial Church (Mù'ēn Táng) 沐恩堂 This church was established

by American missionaries in 1887 and expanded in 1931 to seat more than 1,000 worshippers. It has built up a local membership that numbers in the thousands since reopening in 1979 after its closure during the Cultural Revolution (1966–76). Originally the Methodist church of Shànghǎi, the nondenominational church has a Chinese woman serving as its pastor. Two bishops were consecrated here in 1988, the first in China in 3 decades; the same year, American evangelist Billy Graham preached here.

Xīzàng Zhōng Lù 316 西藏中路3 1 6 号, Huángpǔ Qū (east side of Rénmín Guǎngchǎng); see map p. 136. 📞 **021/6322-5069.** Services Sun 7:30 and 9am, 2 and 7pm. Metro: People's Square.

Temples, Churches, Mosques & Synagogues

# SHÉ SHĀN cathedral

For those who can't get enough of Shànghăi's European-style churches, one of the best is located in Sōngjiāng County, a 40-minute trip from Shànghăi. Situated on the western peak of Shé Shān (Shé Mountain), Shé Shān Cathedral (Shé Shān Táng) was originally built by the Jesuits in 1866 as the Holy Mother Cathedral, and rebuilt between 1925 and 1935 as the Basilica of Notre Dame. Laid out in the shape of a cross, this majestic brick structure has a 38m-tall (125-ft.) bell tower on top of which stands a replacement bronze Madonna and Child statue (the original was destroyed in the Cultural Revolution). Catholic pilgrims from neighboring areas flock here on Sundays, holy days, and especially during the month of May (in 1874, Pope Pius IX declared a full amnesty to any Catholic who made the pilgrimage to the Marian Shrine at Shé Shān during May), many of them making the trek up the hill via the south gate. Along the way are a number of shrines and grottoes. The church (© 021/5765-1521; 8am–4pm) holds Mass Monday through Saturday at 7am (6:30am in summer) and Sunday at 8am.

Behind the church is an astronomical **observatory** (© 021/5765-3423; 7:30am–5pm), founded in 1900 by the French Catholic Mission. The eastern half of Shé Shān consists mostly of a Forest Park, various recreational theme parks, and a tourist resort with the luxurious **Le Méridien Shé Shān** hotel (Línyīn Xīn Lù 1288; © 021/5779-9999). To reach Shé Shān, take Metro Line 9 to the Shéshān or the Dòngjīng stop (about 40 min. from downtown Shànghăi); from there you can take a taxi to the mountain (about ¥15). Public bus nos. 90 and 91 (from outside the subway station) ply the same route, but take longer.

**Xiǎo Táoyuán Qīngzhēnsì (Small Peach Garden Mosque)** 小桃园清真寺 Shànghăi's largest and most active mosque dates from 1917, though the current reconstruction is from 1925. Its main prayer hall can hold several hundred worshippers (restricted to Muslim males only). There is a separate worship hall for women. The courtyard contains a minaret (for calls to prayer). Shànghăi's other mosque that welcomes foreign visitors is the Sōngjiāng Mosque (Sōngjiāng Qīngzhēnsì), located in the southwest suburb of Sōngjiāng (© 021/5782-3684). Shànghăi's oldest mosque (1870) is at Fúyòu Lù 378.

Xiǎo Táoyuán Jiē 52 小桃园街 5 2 号, Huángpǔ Qū (southwest of Chénghuáng Miào at Fùxīng Dōng Lù and Hénán Nán Lù); see map p. 156. © 021/6377-5442. Sunrise–sunset. No Metro.

**Xújiāhuì Tiānzhǔtáng (St. Ignatius Cathedral)** 徐家汇天主堂 ★ Once known as St. Ignatius, this is Shànghăi's great cathedral, opened by the Jesuits who had a church here as early as 1608 (today's structure dates to 1910). The Jesuits were invited here by a local, high-ranking Míng Dynasty official, landowner, and scientist, Xú Guāngqí (the district's name, Xújiāhuì, means "Xú Family Village"), who was himself converted to Catholicism by the Jesuits' most famous missionary to China, Matteo Ricci (1553–1610). Xú is buried in a public park named after him on Nándān Xī Lù, southwest of the cathedral. As a missionary center, the cathedral grounds once included a library, an orphanage, a college, a publishing house, and its own weather station. Today, only the church, part of the school, and the reopened library (p. 189) remain. This largest of Shànghǎi's cathedrals, with space for more than 2,500 inside, sports a gargoyled roof and twin red-brick spires which were destroyed in the Cultural Revolution (1966–76) and rebuilt in 1980. Its vast interior of altars, stone columns, Gothic ceilings, stained-glass windows, and paintings of the Last Supper and Stations of the Cross is yet another chapter in Shànghǎi's living history of European architecture, though there is currently a multiyear project underway to replace the traditional, Western-style stained glass with glasswork imbued with Chinese motifs and characteristics (for example, using a phoenix, the traditional Chinese symbol for rebirth, to signify the Resurrection).

Pǔxī Lù 158 浦西路１５８号, Xúhuì (west side of Cáoxī Běi Lù); see map p. 140. ℂ **021/6438-2595.** Services Mon–Sat 6:15 and 7am, with additional Mass Sat 6pm, Sun 6, 7:30, and 10am; open to visitors Sat–Sun 1–4pm. Metro: Xújiāhuì.

# PARKS & GARDENS

Shànghǎi's parks are splendid places for a stroll, combining scenic vistas with people-watching. They are particularly lively at dawn, when locals gather for their morning exercises ranging from *tàijí quán* (tai chi) to ballroom dancing. Due to the scarcity of play space for children, nearly all parks have a children's section, however small or dilapidated.

In addition to those listed below, Shànghǎi has many smaller parks that offer some reprieve from the urban jungle. One of the newest is in the Xújiāhuì District, **Xújiāhuì Gōngyuán,** built in 1999 on the former grounds of the Great Chinese Rubber Works Factory and the EMI Recording Studio (today's Restaurant Martin), with entrances at Zhàojiābāng Lù and in the west at the intersection of Héngshāng Lù and Yúqìn Lù. The park has a man-made lake with a sky bridge running across the park, and offers a pleasant respite for Xújiāhuì shoppers. The nearest subway stop is Xújiāhuì. **Zhōngshān Gōngyuán,** Chángníng Lù 780, Chángníng District (Metro: Zhongshan Park), built in 1914 as Jessfield Park, once contained the campus of St. John's University, Shànghǎi's first international college; today, it is known for its extensive rose and peony gardens, and a large children's play area.

**Bīnjiāng Dà Dào (Riverside Promenade)** 滨江大道 ★ Pǔdōng's answer to the Bund, this strip of green along the east bank of the Huángpǔ River offers a fine view of the Bund at a distance. After dark, when the Bund's buildings are lit up and beacon lights sweep the river lanes, the view is one of the best in Shànghǎi. The Riverside Promenade also affords marvelous views of Pǔdōng's skyscrapers, and the Shànghǎi International Conference Center and its twin globes. Extending from Dōngchāng Lù and the river ferry terminal in the south to Táidōng Lù in the north, the 2.5km-long (1½-mile) promenade consists of manicured lawns, flower beds, and a broad walkway dotted with kiosks. Starbucks and Häagen-Dazs have staked out the best spots in the middle section around the Shangri-La hotel, so you can now have your view and your latte and ice cream, too.

East shoreline, Huángpǔ River 黄浦江东岸, Pǔdōng (entrances on either side of Lùjiāzuǐ Lù); see map p. 148. Free admission. 6:30am–11pm (midnight in summer). Metro: Lujiazui.

**Fùxīng Gōngyuán (Fùxīng Park)** 复兴公园 ★ ☺ Formerly a private estate in the French Concession, Fùxīng Park was purchased by foreign residents and opened to the French public on July 14, 1909. It was popularly known as French Park, styled after your typical Parisian city park with wide, tree-lined walks and flower beds. Today, this is one of the city's most popular parks, home to a number of restaurants and nightclubs, as well as to pleasant fountains, a children's playground with a carousel and bumper cars, a rose garden to the east, 120 species of trees, and, near the north entrance, a statue of Karl Marx and Friedrich Engels in front of which Chinese couples often practice ballroom dancing.

Gāolán Lù 2 皋兰路 2 号, Lúwān (west entrance Gāolán Lù, north entrance Yándāng Lù, southeast entrance Chóngqìng Nán Lù off Fùxīng Zhōng Lù); see map p. 140. ⓒ **021/6372-6083.** Free admission. 6am–6pm. Metro: Huangpi Rd. (S).

**Jìng Ān Gōngyuán (Jìng Ān Park)** 静安公园  This pleasant little park was completely remodeled in 1999 when the new Jìng Ān Metro station was created. Its north side consists of a sunken cement courtyard, flanked by a few shops, cafes, and the Metro entrance; the south side, dominated by a pond that is an artful re-creation of a classic Southern Chinese garden, is a pretty spot to stroll, people-watch, or enjoy an evening drink at the bar in the adjacent Indonesian restaurant (Bali Laguna). Mornings are a perfect time to watch (or join) tai chi classes, while Sunday morning (8:30–11am) brings out the polyglots (mostly Chinese who want to practice their English) to the multilanguage corner (*wài yǔ jiǎo*) at the eastern end of the park.

Huáshān Lù 189 华山路 1 8 9 号, Jìng Ān (south of Jìng Ān Temple); see map p. 144. ⓒ **021/6248-3238.** Free admission. Dawn to very late. Metro: Jing'an Temple.

**Lùjiāzuǐ Lǜdì (Lùjiāzuǐ Central Green)** 陆家嘴绿地  Located just north of the Jīn Mào Tower, this sprawling, 10-hectare (25-acre) park with an expansive lawn has a large lake in the shape of Pǔdōng; radiating from it are paths that outline a magnolia, the city flower of Shànghǎi. Clusters of willows, maples, and gingko trees provide plenty of shade. It's the kind of place that inspires impromptu picnics, kite flying, a lazy afternoon nap, and even hot-air ballooning in the warmer months. The park is so high-tech that it even has a series of in-ground audio speakers that occasionally pipe out New Age mood music.

Lùjiāzuǐ Lù 160 陆家嘴路 1 6 0 号, Pǔdōng (east of the Oriental Pearl TV Tower; north of the Jīn Mào Tower); see map p. 148. ⓒ **021/5887-5487.** Free admission. 24 hr. Metro: Lujiazui.

**Rénmín Gōngyuán/Rénmín Guǎngchǎng (People's Park/People's Square)** 人民公园／人民广场  Shànghǎi's "Central Park" and central square are built on the site of colonial Shànghǎi's horse-racing track (dating to as early as 1863), once a favorite amusement for the British community and upper-class Chinese. Today, the original 12 hectares (30 acres) of the racecourse have been parceled out into a quiet, pleasant park in the north (complete with a small lake, rock garden, the Museum of Contemporary Art [p. 180], the Moroccan drinking and dining establishment Barbarossa [p. 251], amusement rides, and clusters of old folks playing mah-jongg and chess, who on the weekends put up listings for their single children and grandchildren who are too busy to date or find mates), and Rénmín Guǎngchǎng (People's Square) to the south. Opened in 1951 and renovated in 1994, with an intermediary spell as a public reckoning ground during the early days of the Cultural Revolution (1966–76), the square is now Shànghǎi's cultural and traffic center, with an underground shopping arcade, the central subway station, the Shànghǎi Museum, the Grand Theatre, the 20-story Municipal Hall, and the Shànghǎi Urban Planning Exhibition Hall. Besides being a magnet for locals who come here to feed the pigeons, fly their kites, and gossip on the benches, the square, surrounded as it is by some of Shànghǎi's tallest and most modern buildings, is also a wonderful place to take in exactly how much Shànghǎi has grown up.

Nánjīng Xī Lù 231 南京西路 2 3 1 号, Huángpǔ Qū (at Huángpí Lù); see map p. 136. ☏ **021/6372-0626.** Free admission. 6am–late. Metro: People's Square.

### Shànghǎi Zhíwùyuán (Shànghǎi Botanical Gardens) 上海植物园 ★ ☺

Somewhat inconveniently located in the southwest part of town, the city's premier and largest garden provides a pleasant reprieve from the urban hustle, but is not worth a special trip unless you really like your plants. The extensive grounds, covering 81 hectares (200 acres), are divided into different sections featuring peonies, roses, bamboo, azaleas, maples, osmanthus, magnolias, and orchids (considered the best in China). There are also a garden of medicinal plants and a greenhouse dedicated to tropical plants, but the hallmark section is the Pénjǐng Yuán (Bonsai Garden), which requires a separate admission (¥7), with hundreds of bonsai displayed in a large complex of corridors, courtyards, pools, and rockeries. There are restaurants, exhibition halls, vendors' stalls, and several children's playgrounds dotted throughout the park. The park is extremely crowded on weekends.

Lóngwú Lù 1111 龙吴路 1 1 1 1 号, Xúhuì; see map p. 140. ☏ **021/5436-3369.** www.shbg.org. Admission ¥15 garden only; ¥40 includes conservatory and Bonsai Garden. 7am–5pm. Metro: Shílóng Rd.

### Shìjì Gōngyuán (Century Park) 世纪公园 ★ ☺

Built to herald the new millennium, this sprawling 140-hectare (346-acre) park lies at the southern terminus of Century Boulevard (Shìjì Dà Dào), which runs from the Oriental Pearl TV Tower. Designed by a British firm, the park is divided into seven scenic areas, including a minigolf course, a beach area complete with man-made cobblestone beach, a bird-protection area, and an international garden area. The center of the park contains a lake where fishing poles and paddleboats can be rented. There's plenty here to distract the kids, but it's an even better place to watch local families enjoy themselves.

Jǐnxiù Lù 1001 锦绣路 1 0 0 1 号, Pǔdōng (south entrance at Huāmù Lù, next to Metro station); see map p. 148. ☏ **021/3876-0588.** Admission ¥10. 7am–6pm (to 5pm Nov 16–Mar 15). Metro: Century Park.

### Xúhuì Bīnjiāng Gōnggòng Kāifàng Kōngjiān (Xúhuì Riverside Public Open Space) 徐汇滨江公共开放空间 ★

As part of the Huángpǔ River Restoration project, about 40 hectares (100 acres) of riverfront land west of the Lǔpǔ Bridge all the way down to the old Lónghuá Airport are being rehabilitated to become a vast open space made up of parks, gardens, and a pretty riverside promenade running around 6.5km (4 miles). Still incomplete at press time, this "corniche" is currently best accessed in its central segment around Lónghéng Lù. Here, you'll find a Maritime Tower, which was once the water tower for the airplane factory that used to service the old Lónghuá Airport. At the foot of the tower, the Lónghuá Bridge extends across the tributary Lónghuá Gǎng. As you walk farther north along the riverbank, you'll see two large cranes, remnants from the days when this reclaimed area was the Jiāngnán Shipyard. In the future, there will be more gardens and recreation areas built, as well as water taxis plying the Huángpǔ River (across the river is the former World Expo zone, post-Expo development plans of which are still uncertain). Off the beaten tourist track, this riverside promenade currently provides some lovely strolls, refreshing breezes, and pretty river views.

West shoreline, Huángpǔ River 黄浦江西岸, Xúhuì (at press time, best entrances from either Lónghéng Lù or Dōng'ān Lù); see map p. 140. Free admission. 24 hr. Metro: Chuanchang Rd.

# MUSEUMS & MANSIONS

In its quest to become the cosmopolitan and culturally savvy city worthy of hosting the World Expo in 2010, Shànghǎi set a mildly ambitious goal of establishing 100 museums. To meet this quota, everything from navy ships to Chinese medicines has been encased in glass and given its own building. To spare the time-limited traveler, the more worthwhile sights have been given their own listings and more detailed descriptions below, while some of the more specialty museums are listed in a separate box (p. 179). Many of Shànghǎi's museums and historic residences are housed in the European mansions and estates of colonial Shànghǎi where the setting is often the chief attraction. While lighting and display are seldom state of the art and English signage can be spotty or nonexistent, simply touring these fine storehouses is fascinating enough.

## Duōlún Lù Culture Street (Duōlún Lù Wénhuà Jiē) 多伦路文化街 ★　A

20-minute walk south from Lǔ Xùn Gōngyuán (Lǔ Xùn Park and Memorial Hall) is Duōlún Lù, Shànghǎi's culture street, an attraction opened in 1998, angling off Sìchuān Běi Lù in the historic Hóngkǒu District. This district north of the Bund was the original American Concession, but merged with the British Concession to form the International Settlement in colonial Shànghǎi. By the time the writer Lǔ Xùn (p. 179) moved into the neighborhood in the 1930s, the area had become a Japanese enclave. Other famous progressive artists and writers (Máo Dùn, Guō Mòruò, Dīng Líng), many of whom were part of the League of Leftist Writers, lived here as well during that time, making this area around Duōlún Lù (formerly Darroch Rd.) known as a cultural and literary center.

　　The stately brick homes and shops on this .8km (½-mile) stretch of the street have been preserved and refurbished, and cars are now banned, making it a fine pedestrian mall of bookshops, teahouses, antiques shops, and historic homes. As you enter from Sìchuān Běi Lù, the **Duōlún Museum of Modern Art** (no. 27; ✆ **021/6587-2530;** www.duolunmoma.org; Tues–Sun 10am–6pm; admission ¥10) on your left showcases the works of international modern artists. A few doors down at no. 59, Hóng Dé Táng (Great Virtue Christian Church) is a church built in 1928 with upturned Chinese eaves. The street curves to the right, passing the stately bell tower Xī Shí Zhōng Lóu (no. 119); the wonderful Old Film Café (no. 123), where you can sip coffee while watching old Chinese movies from the 1920s and 1930s; and antiques and curio shops selling everything from art to Máo memorabilia. At Lane 201, no. 2 is the League of Leftist Writers Museum (9:30am–4pm; admission ¥5). The last architectural treasure on the curving lane is the Kǒng Residence, a splendid 1924 creation sadly not open for public viewing. The street is not really worth a special trip out here, but if you're interested in Shànghǎi's colonial architecture, or if your travels take you to Hóngkǒu, then Duōlún Lù is a must.

Duōlún Lù at Shǎnxī Běi Lù 多伦路, Hóngkǒu (3 blocks north of Dōng Bǎoxìng Lù Light Rail Station); see map p. 136. Free admission. Sunrise–late. Metro: Dongbaoxing Rd.

## Himalayas Art Museum (Shànghǎi Xīmǎlāyǎ Měishùguǎn) 上海喜玛拉雅美

术馆　Located by Century Park in Pǔdōng, the recently renamed Himalayas Art Museum (formerly the Zendai Museum of Modern Art) may be off the beaten path for your average visitor, but should attract contemporary art aficionados. On the small side, this active museum nevertheless packs it full of original and more

# unusual MUSEUMS

Shànghǎi has an inordinately large number of unusual museums, usually of interest only to specialists or aficionados. To wit: China's only eyeglasses museum can be found at the **Shànghǎi Glasses Museum** (Shànghǎi Yǎnjìng Bówùguǎn, Bǎochǎng Lù 533, Zhábèi District, ☏ **021/5697-7528;** admission ¥10; Tues–Wed and Fri–Sat 9–11am and 1:30–4pm; Chinese signage only); while an interesting collection of musical instruments seldom seen in the West can be viewed at the **Museum of Oriental Musical Instruments** (Shànghǎi Dōngfāng Yuèqì Bówùguǎn, Gāo'ān Lù 18, near Héngshān Lù, Xúhuì District; ☏ **021/5465-1834;** free admission; Mon–Fri 9–11am and 1:30–4pm). It's a smoker's paradise in China (where an estimated 350 million people smoke) and also here at the **China Tobacco Museum** (Shànghǎi Yāncǎo Bówùguǎn, Chángyáng Lù 728, near Tōngbèi Lù, Yángpǔ District; ☏ **021/6166-5907;** www.tobaccomuseum.com.cn; free admission; Tues, Thurs, and Sat 9am–4pm), the world's largest museum of its kind with seven exhibition halls. The **Shànghǎi Auto Museum** (Shànghǎi Qìchē Bówùguǎn, Bóyuán Lù 7565, Āntíng Town; ☏ **021/6955-0055;** www.shautomuseum.gov.cn; admission ¥60; Tues–Sun 9:30am–4:30pm [last ticket 4pm]), by the Formula One racetrack out in the suburb of Āntíng, traces the history of the automobile both in China and around the world; train spotters might want to check out the **Shànghǎi Railway Museum** (Shànghǎi Tiělù Bówùguǎn, Tiānmù Dōng Lù 200, Zhábèi District; ☏ **021/5122-1987;** www.museum.shrail.com; admission ¥10; Tues–Sat 9–11am and 2–4pm).

experimental works of Chinese artists in a range of mediums, including photography, sculpture, and video installations. There are also guided tours of the museum (in Chinese), lectures, concerts, and film programs.

Fāngdiàn Lù 199, No. 28 芳甸路199弄28号, Pǔdōng (at Thumb Plaza by Yíngchūn Lù); see map p. 148. ☏ **021/5033-9801.** Free admission. 10am–9pm. Metro: Shanghai Science and Technology Museum.

**Lǔ Xùn Park and Memorial Hall/Former Residence of Lǔ Xùn (Lǔ Xùn Gōngyuán/Lǔ Xùn Gùjū)** 鲁迅公园／鲁迅故居 What was originally Hóngkǒu Park (1905), once a foreigners' park opened to the Chinese only in 1928, has been renamed for China's best-known 20th-century writer, Lǔ Xùn (1881–1936), who lived in this neighborhood from 1927 until his death. Known as the "father of modern Chinese literature" because of his role in developing the modern style of Chinese prose as well as in helping simplify the Chinese script, Lǔ Xùn was a prolific writer who translated science-fiction novels into Chinese just as easily as he penned scathing critiques of Confucianism and the alternately submissive and arrogant Chinese character. Extolled as a political revolutionary (Máo Zédōng penned an inscription on Lǔ Xùn's tomb, which lies at the north end of the park), Lǔ Xùn was himself deliberately never a member of the Communist Party. One can only imagine what his scathing pen would have had to say about China's current headlong rush into capitalism.

At the eastern end of the park is a memorial hall devoted to his life, the Lǔ Xùn Jìniànguǎn. The main exhibit room on the second floor displays his many books and old photographs, as well as his hat, goatskin gown, and death mask. Signs are in English. A bookstore here sells English-language copies of some of his most famous works, such as *The Story of Ah Q*. A 10-minute walk east of the park, **Lŭ Xùn's Former Residence** is a three-story brick house where he lived from 1933 to his death, and is still largely decorated as it was then. Exhibits here include an original writing brush as well as a clock marking his exact time of death on October 19, 1936: 5:25am.

Dōng Jiāngwān Lù 146 东江湾路 1 4 6 号, Hóngkǒu; see map p. 136. Park: free admission; includes Lŭ Xùn's tomb; 6am–6pm. Lŭ Xùn Memorial Hall (inside park on east side; ✆ **021/6540-2288**): free admission; 9am–4pm. The Former Residence of Lŭ Xùn, Shānyīn Lù 9 Lane 132 山阴路9 弄 1 3 2 号, Hóngkǒu (from park, take a left out the main entrance, follow Tián'ài Lù south until it curves left onto Shānyīn Lù): admission ¥8; 9am–4pm. Metro: Hongkou Football Stadium.

## Madame Tussauds Museum (Dùshā Fūrén Làxiàngguǎn) 杜莎夫人蜡像馆

This museum is the sixth Madame Tussauds in the world and the first in mainland China. Located on the 10th floor of the New World Shopping Center on the north side of People's Square, the museum features more than 70 wax figures, including a mix of Chinese and foreign icons like Princess Diana, Bill Gates, Jackie Chan, Bill Clinton, Barack Obama, Chinese Olympian Liu Xiang, and late Hong Kong singer and actor Leslie Cheung, all placed in seven themed areas, including music, film, sports, history, and heroes. Billed as the most interactive Madame Tussauds yet, the museum lets visitors have their photos taken shooting hoops with Yáo Míng, playing soccer with David Beckham, or simply gazing into the eyes of Audrey Hepburn—the celebrity of choice to be photographed with, according to surveys conducted in major Chinese cities.

Nánjīng Xī Lù 68, 10th floor 南京西路 6 8 号 1 0 楼, Huángpǔ (in the New World Department Store); see map p. 136. ✆ **021/6358-7878.** www.madame-tussauds.com.cn. Admission ¥135. 10am–9pm. Metro: People's Square.

## Moller Villa (Héngshān Mǎlè Biéshù) 衡山马勒别墅

Garish, hideous, and mesmerizing at the same time, it's hard to take your eyes off this gigantic gingerbread mansion (at Yán'ān Zhōng Lù in the northwest corner of the French Concession). An eclectic mix of architectural styles from faux Gothic to Tudor, this mansion of brown-tiled steeples, gables, and spires was built by Swedish shipping magnate Eric Moller in 1936, so the apocryphal story goes, for his daughter, who envisioned the house in a dream, a version since debunked by the daughter herself. Whatever the genesis, the flamboyant house, with its marble pillars, chandeliers, dark wood paneling, and beautiful stained-glass windows epitomized the excesses of colonial Shàng-hǎi. Previously closed to the public in its incarnation as the headquarters of the Shànghǎi Communist Youth League, the mansion has been restored and is now an overpriced boutique hotel. Unfortunately, the restoration included the addition of several ugly imitation buildings in the back. Whatever was said about the original mansion, it was at least that: original.

Shǎnxī Nán Lù 30 陕西南路 3 0 号, Jing Ān (intersection with Yán'ān Zhōng Lù); see map p. 144. ✆ **021/6247-8881.** 24 hr. Metro: Shaanxi Rd. (S).

## Museum of Contemporary Art/MOCA (Shànghǎi Dāngdài Yìshù Guǎn) 上海当代艺术馆

Opened in 2005, this beautiful, three-story glass structure houses Shànghǎi's first contemporary art museum, and has become a good pacesetter in

China's contemporary art scene today. While not in the same league as better-known MOCAs around the world, the museum's two floors of exhibition space connected by a curving ramp are enough to showcase plenty of goofy, interesting, ridiculous, sublime, "this-is-art?" paintings, photographs, and installations by Chinese and international artists. For those immune to the charms of modern art, the building itself is quite interesting and can be appreciated gratis from the outside or at the door if you simply tell them you're going to the Art Lab restaurant on the third floor, where you can sip cocktails on the rooftop terrace.

Nánjīng Xī Lù 231 南京西路 2 3 1 号, Gate 7, People's Park, Huángpǔ (inside People's Park/Rénmín Gōngyuán); see map p. 136. *✆* **021/6327-9900.** www.mocashanghai.org. Admission ¥20. 10am–9:30pm. Metro: People's Square.

## Museum of Folk Art (Mínjiān Shōucángpǐn Chénlièguǎn) 民间收藏品陈列馆

Another step closer to reaching Shànghǎi's planned 100 museums, this one showcases collections of just about any folk arts and crafts you can think of, which can be quite interesting if you like your Chinese tchotchkes. Rotating exhibits have included tiny shoes for bound feet and 1930s cigarette labels. If this doesn't grab you, come see the significantly more interesting building housing the exhibits. This was the original Sānshān Guild Hall (Sānshān Huìguǎn), the only one remaining of several guildhalls that used to dot the neighborhood. Funded by merchants from Fújiàn Province, it was built in 1909, in a traditional style with upturned eaves, carved beams, and colorfully painted rafters. The stage, in particular, stands out for its elaborate carvings.

Zhōngshān Nán Yī Lù 1551 中山南一路 1 5 5 1 号, Huángpǔ (at Nán Chēzhàn Lù, 2 blocks east of Xīzàng Nán Lù); see map p. 156. *✆* **021/6313-5582.** Free admission. 9am–4pm. Metro: Xizang Rd. (S).

## Propaganda Poster Art Center (Xuānchuánhuà Yìshù Zhōngxīn) 宣传画艺术中心

If you have just the wall space for some revolutionary art, this place has just the right "left" poster for you. Tucked away in the basement of a French Concession apartment building is the personal collection of a private individual, Mr. Yáng Pèimíng. It comprises more than 5,000 Communist propaganda posters from 1949 to 1979. The presentation is a bit haphazard, but the posters themselves are quite interesting. Chairman Máo figures prominently, of course, as do eager, ruddy-cheeked young workers and fervent Red Guards. Vintage posters are for sale as well (from around ¥700 and up), but not necessarily the most interesting ones. The center is worth a peek if you're in the area.

Huáshān Lù 868 华山路 8 6 8 号, Building B, Basement, Chángníng (west of Wúkàng Lù); see map p. 140. *✆* **021/6211-1845.** Admission ¥20. 10am–5pm. No Metro.

## Rockbund Art Museum (Shànghǎi Wàitān Měishùguǎn) 上海外滩美术馆

Housed in the former Royal Asiatic Society building (1932) designed by George Wilson of Palmer and Turner (Shànghǎi's darling architectural firm in the 1920s and 1930s), this contemporary art museum is currently the anchor of the Wàitānyuán development project, and aims to be a big player in promoting contemporary visual art in Shànghǎi. Combining Art Deco with Chinese flourishes (balconies and octagonal *bagua* designs, for example), the main building (worth a peek even if you aren't into the art) has a lecture hall on the first floor, a library on the second, and exhibit halls on the third and fourth floors, as well as in an adjoining building, and space outdoors for larger installations. Audio guide rental costs ¥5 with deposit.

Hǔqiū Lù 20 虎丘路20号, Huángpǔ (east of Sìchuān Lù, north of Běijīng Dōng Lù); see map p. 136. ℂ 021/3310-9985. www.rockbundartmuseum.org. Admission ¥15. Tues–Sun 10am–6pm (last tickets sold 5:30pm). Metro: Nanjing Rd. (E).

### Shànghǎi Art Museum (Shànghǎi Měishùguǎn) 上海美术馆 ★

Relocated in 2000 to the historic clock tower building on the northwest end of People's Square, the museum is more to be seen for its 1930s monumental interior architecture than for its art. The artwork in the 12 exhibit halls is certainly noteworthy, ranging from modern traditional oils to recent pop canvases, but it's overwhelmed by the fastidiously restored, wood and marble interiors of this 1933 five-story, neoclassical landmark. People's Square, today's Rénmín Guǎngchǎng, was a racecourse in colonial times, and today's clock tower, erected in 1933, marks the location of the original grandstand of 1863. After 1949, the building was used as the Shànghǎi Museum and the Shànghǎi Library. Today, in addition to the artwork, there is a classy American restaurant, Kathleen's 5, on the fifth floor.

Nánjīng Xī Lù 325 南京西路 3 2 5 号, Huángpǔ (northwest edge of People's Park at Huángpí Lù); see map p. 136. ℂ 021/6327-2829. www.sh-artmuseum.org.cn. Admission ¥20. 9am–5pm (last tickets sold 4pm). Metro: People's Square.

### Shànghǎi Bank Museum (Shànghǎi Shì Yínháng Bówùguǎn) 上海市银行博物馆

Another notch in the Shànghǎi museum belt, this one would seem to be a natural for this finance-oriented city. Unfortunately, the museum is only open to individual tourists on Wednesday afternoons from 1 to 4pm; the rest of the time, it caters only to tour groups with prior arrangements. Chronicling the history of Chinese banking from the Míng Dynasty (1368–1644) to the present are more than 2,000 relics, including photographs of old-fashioned private banks, an account recording machine from the 1920s, and even a "6-billion-yuán" paper note (which could only buy 70 grains of rice during the period just before the 1949 revolution). If this interests you, call the museum to see if you can't somehow sweet-talk your way in. Enough public requests may make them change their entrance policy.

Pǔdōng Dà Dào 9, 7th floor 浦东大道 9 号 7 楼, Pǔdōng (inside the Industrial and Commercial Bank building, at intersection with Pǔdōng Nán Lù); see map p. 148. ℂ 021/5878-8743. Admission ¥5. Mon–Fri 9–11:30am and 1–4pm, by appointment only; open to individual visitors Wed 1–4pm. Metro: Lujiazui.

### Shànghǎi Municipal History Museum (Shànghǎi Shì Lìshǐ Chénlièguǎn) 上海市历史陈列馆 ★★

This excellent museum in the basement of the Oriental Pearl TV Tower in Pǔdōng tells the history of Shànghǎi with an emphasis on the colonial period between 1860 and 1949. Fascinating exhibits include dioramas of the Huángpǔ River, the Bund, Nánjīng Lù, and foreign concessions, evoking the colorful street life and lost trades of the 19th and early 20th centuries; dozens of models of Shànghǎi's classic avenues and famous buildings; and a vehicle collection with trolley cars (the city line opened in 1908), 1920s sedans, and a U.S. jeep (popular after World War II), among others. Other intriguing bits include a gorgeously ornate wedding palanquin, boulders marking the concessions' boundaries, and visiting chits used in brothels. The museum takes about an hour to tour. Tickets are purchased at the Oriental Pearl TV Tower gate. Audio headsets (¥30) can enhance your visit, but are not crucial, as displays are well annotated in English and Chinese.

Lùjiāzuǐ Lù 2 陆家嘴路 2 号, Oriental Pearl TV Tower basement, Pǔdōng; see map p. 148. ℂ 021/5879-3003. Admission ¥35. 9am–9pm. Metro: Lujiazui.

### Shànghǎi Museum of Arts and Crafts (Shànghǎi Gōngyì Měishù Bówùguǎn)

上海工艺美术博物馆 ★　This gorgeous, three-story late French Renaissance mansion was built in 1905 for the French Concession's Chamber of Industry director. The expansive lawns, sweeping marble staircases, stained-glass windows, dark wooden paneling, and ceiling beams of the mansion obviously appealed to many others as well, as it became the residence of Chén Yì, Shànghǎi's first mayor after 1949. For aficionados of Cultural Revolution (1966–76) history, it also served for a time as the residence of Lín Lìguǒ's (Lín Biāo's son's) mother-in-law, who tore down the glasshouse that used to be in the eastern section of the residence. After 1960, this became the Shànghǎi Arts and Crafts Research Center. Its many rooms were converted into studios where visitors could watch artisans work at traditional handicrafts. Today, some of the artists' studios remain, but it has been largely rearranged as a formal museum of the crafts produced in Shànghǎi over the past 100 years. On display are fine carvings in jade, wood, ivory, and bamboo, as well as gorgeously stitched costumes and tapestries, intricately painted vases and snuff bottles, and a variety of folk crafts from paper lanterns to dough figurines. A salesroom is attached, of course. Expect high prices, but also high quality.

Fēnyáng Lù 79 汾阳路 7 9 号, Xúhuì (at intersection with Tàiyuán Lù); see map p. 140. ℂ 021/6431-1431. Admission ¥8. 9am–4:30pm. Metro: Changshu Rd.

### Shànghǎi Natural History Museum (Shànghǎi Zìrán Bówùguǎn)

上海自然博物馆 ☺　Unlike most of Shànghǎi's museums, which are glossy and modern, this museum, like its contents, has seemingly been frozen in time (specifically 1956, when the museum was first located here), which perversely makes it a rather delightful visit. There is the usual collection of animals, mummies, and fossils, including in the central atrium a complete specimen of a 140-million-year-old dinosaur skeleton from Sìchuān Province. The top floor houses a gallery of stuffed creatures, which have been known to scare some of the young ones (and a few adults, too). Much more interesting for adults is the building itself, a beautiful classical structure that used to be the Cotton Exchange in colonial days. The mosaic floors and stained-glass windows in the lobby only hint at the grand building that once was.

Yán'ān Dōng Lù 260 延安东路 2 6 0 号, Huángpǔ (at Hénán Nán Lù); see map p. 136. ℂ 021/6321-3548. Admission ¥5. Tues–Sun 9am–5pm (last ticket sold 3:30pm). Metro: Nanjing Rd. (E).

### Shànghǎi Postal Museum (Shànghǎi Yóuzhèng Bówùguǎn)

上海邮政博物馆 Located on the north shore of Sūzhōu Creek, this museum is worth a quick visit not just for its philatelic exhibits, but equally for the handsome building in which it's housed: a 1924 structure with a Beaux Arts facade. There's a baroque-style bell tower, and the roof provides pretty views of the rehabilitated Sūzhōu River and of Pǔdōng. Exhibits trace the history of the postal service in China, and show off everything from rare stamps to mailboxes throughout the ages. There are also amusing reprimands from the Postal Commissioner to his staff in 1911 for smoking and slacking on the job.

Běi Sūzhōu Lù 250 北苏州路 2 5 0 号, Hóngkǒu (at Sìchuān Běi Lù); see map p. 136. ℂ 021/6362-9898. Free admission. Wed–Thurs and Sat–Sun 9am–4pm. Metro: Tiantong Rd.

### Shànghǎi Public Security Museum (Shànghǎi Gōng'ān Bówùguǎn)

上海公安博物馆　Big Brother is watching. This modern museum surveys the history of Shànghǎi's "homeland security," with a focus on its police department, originally

# AFTER expo

Shànghăi's turn on the world stage in the form of the 2010 World Expo (May 1–Oct 31, 2010) has come and gone. At the outset of the Expo, 70 million visitors (95% Chinese citizens) and 200 countries and international organizations were expected to participate, and while final attendance figures were not available at press time, the Expo can largely be considered a success vis-à-vis legitimizing Shànghăi as a bona fide international city. The Expo's theme, "Better City, Better Life," with its focus on science, technology, business, and sustainable urban development, not only signaled China's continuing rise as a world power concerned about future development, but also provided the Chinese government with an opportunity to remind Chinese citizens of the progress they had made ("better life") under the Party's leadership in the last 20 years.

For the Expo, the government is said to have spent ¥300 billion to ¥400 billion in direct and indirect investment: building pavilions and walkways for the fair (covering 5.28 sq. km/2 sq. miles of land on both sides of the Huángpŭ River in the south of the city), and significantly upgrading public infrastructure. The success of the Expo in rousing patriotic fever, and what effects this greater national pride will have, remain to be seen. For the Shanghainese, at least, the result of suffering through years of upheaval and construction has been a much-improved city infrastructure that now includes two new airport terminals, 12 subway lines, and a host of tunnels that make traffic and commuting much more manageable. As well, revitalized districts such as the Bund (north and south) have made the city more attractive.

established in 1854. There are few signs in English, but some very interesting artifacts. The second floor has miscellaneous relics, from uniforms and pistol cases to tiny spy cameras and stuffed homing pigeons, but the going gets good on the third floor with grizzly photos and actual weapons (saws, axes, sawed-off shotguns) from Shànghăi's more famous cases. Look for a human skull impaled with a scissor blade, and the stuffed police dog (b. 1946, d. 1957). There are also items deemed threats to public security: gambling devices, opium pipes, pirated videos, drug paraphernalia, and even books on the banned *Fălúngōng* spiritual movement. The fourth floor has displays on firefighting and Shànghăi's crime busters, while the fifth floor is, oddly, given to temporary art exhibits.

Ruìjīn Nán Lù 518 瑞金南路 5 1 8 号, Lúwān (south of Xiétŭ Lù); see map p. 140. ℂ **021/6472-0256.** Admission ¥8. Mon–Sat 9am–4:30pm. Metro: Damuqiao Rd. or Luban Rd.

### Shànghăi Urban Planning Museum (Shànghăi Chéngshì Guīhuà Zhănshìguăn)
上海城市规划展示馆 ★★ Filmmakers and science-fiction writers have imagined it, but if you want to see what a city of the future is really going to look like, take yourself over to this museum on the eastern end of People's Square. Housed in a striking, modern, five-story building made of Microlite glass, this is one of the world's largest showcases of urban development and is much more interesting than its dry name suggests. The highlight is on the third floor: an awesome, vast, scale

Those who didn't make it to the Expo missed a fascinating collection of eye-catching architecture. At press time, the majority of pavilions were expected to be torn down after the Expo, with the exception of five landmarks (all environmentally friendly buildings clustered together on the Pǔdōng side around Shàngnán Lù [Metro: Yaóhuá Lù]) which will be turned into **permanent exhibitions.** Most prominent among them is the towering 69m-high (226-ft.) bright-red **China Pavilion** (called the Oriental Crown) with six floors expanding out and up. It is estimated to have cost upwards of ¥1.4 billion to build, can hold up to 50,000 visitors a day, and was the scene of up to 3-hour waits during the Expo. The roof is built with 56 wooden brackets, representing the 56 ethnic groups in China, and also harvests rainwater. The building is due to be turned into a national history museum after the Expo. North of the China Pavilion is the spaceshiplike **Expo Performance Center.** West of these two structures is the **Expo Axis,** a 1km-long (⅔-mile) walkway along Shàngnán Lù, with two levels underground and two aboveground; it is designated for commercial outlets after the Expo. The two remaining permanent structures lying west of the Axis are the **Expo Center** (an impressive glass structure that's largely a conference center) and the **Theme Pavilion** (designated as an exhibition center, and highly energy-efficient with rooftop solar panels). Post-Expo access to these sites had not been determined when this book went to press, so please check with your hotel concierge for the latest information.

model of urban Shànghǎi as it will look in 2020, a master plan full of endless skyscrapers punctuated occasionally by patches of green. The clear plastic models indicate structures yet to be built, and there are many of them. Beleaguered Shànghǎi residents wondering if their current cramped downtown houses will survive the bulldozer (chances are not good) need only look here for the answer. The fourth floor also has displays on proposed forms of future transportation, including magnetic levitation (maglev), subway, and light-rail trains that are going to change even the face of the Bund. The museum is well worth an hour of your time.

Rénmín Dà Dào 100 人民大道１００号, Huángpǔ (northeast of the Shànghǎi Museum; entrance on east side); see map p. 136. ☏ **021/6372-2077.** Admission ¥30. Tues–Thurs 9am–5pm (last ticket sold 4pm); Fri–Sun 9am–6pm (last ticket 5pm). Metro: People's Square.

**Site of the First National Congress of the Communist Party (Zhōnggòng Yīdà Huìzhǐ)** 中共一大会址  This historic building of brick and marble—a quintessential example of the traditional Shànghǎi style of *shíkùmén* (stone-framed) houses built in the 1920s and 1930s—contains the room where, on July 23, 1921, Máo Zédōng and 12 other Chinese revolutionaries founded the Chinese Communist Party. Also present were two Russian advisors. The delegates had to conclude their meeting on Nánhú Lake in Zhèjiāng Province when police broke up the party. The original teacups and ashtrays remain on the organizing table. As the anchor of the urban renewal project that spawned the open-air mall Xīntiāndì, this museum has been expanded to include several new galleries. There is the expected hagiographic treatment given the history of the Communist Party, but also more interesting displays of a Qīng Dynasty bronze cannon, swords and daggers used by rebels during the Tàipíng and Small Swords rebellions in 19th-century Shànghǎi, and a boundary stone used to demarcate the entrance to the British Concession, dated May 8, 1899.

Xīngyè Lù 76 兴业路 7 6 号, Lúwān (south end of Xīntiāndi); see map p. 140. ℂ **021/5383-2171.** Free admission. 9am–5pm (last entry at 4pm). Metro: Huangpi Rd. (S).

### Soong Ching-ling's Former Residence (Sòng Qìnglíng Gùjū) 宋庆龄故居

Soong Ching-ling (1893–1981) is revered throughout China as a loyalist to the Communist cause. Born in Shànghǎi to a wealthy family, she married the founder of the Chinese Republic, Dr. Sun Yat-sen, in 1915. Unlike the rest of her family members (the most famous being her youngest sister Soong Mei-ling, who married Chiang Kai-shek) who all fled China after 1949, Soong Ching-ling stayed and was given many important political and cultural posts in the Communist government. This 1920s villa, built by a Greek sea captain in the French Concession, served as her residence from 1948 to 1963. Little is changed at this two-story house with white walls and green shutters, with many of the rooms much as Soong left them. The first floor houses the living and dining areas; her upstairs office, bedroom, and the bedroom of her devoted maid, Lǐ Yàn'é, are now open to the public. There are two black sedans in the garage, one presented to her by Stalin in 1952. An annex just inside the gate displays relics from her life, including her Wesleyan College diploma, phonograph records, family photos, and letters from the likes of Indian Prime Minister Jawaharlal Nehru and American correspondent Edgar Snow. Soong Ching-ling died in Běijīng in 1981, but is buried with her parents and her maid in the Wànguó Cemetery in western Shànghǎi.

Huáihǎi Zhōng Lù 1843 淮海中路 1 8 4 3 号, Xújiāhuì (east of Tiānpíng Lù); see map p. 140. ℂ **021/ 6437-6268.** Admission ¥20. 9am–4:30pm. Metro: Jiaotong University.

### Sun Yat-sen's Former Residence (Sūn Zhōngshān Gùjū Jìniànguǎn) 孙中山故居纪念馆 ★

Sun Yat-sen (1866–1925), beloved founder of the Chinese Republic (1911), lived here with his wife, Soong Ching-ling, from June 1918 to November 1924, when the address would have been 29 Rue de Moliere. Here, Sun's wife later met with such literary stars as Lǔ Xùn and George Bernard Shaw (at the same dinner party), as well as political leaders including Vietnam's Ho Chi Minh (in 1933). Led by an English-speaking guide, visitors enter through the kitchen on the way to the dining room. Sun's study is upstairs, complete with ink stone, brushes, maps drawn by Sun, and a "library" of 2,700 volumes (look closer and you'll see they're merely photocopies of book spines). The bedroom and the drawing room contain more original furnishings, including an original "Zhōngshān" suit, similar to the later Máo suit. The backyard has a charming garden.

Xiāngshān Lù 7 香山路 7 号, Lúwān (west of Fùxīng Park at Sīnán Lù); see map p. 140. ℂ **021/6437-2954** or 021/6385-0217. Admission ¥20. 9am–4pm. Metro: Shaanxi Rd. (S).

### Zhōu Ēnlái's Former Residence (Zhōu Gōng Guǎn) 周公馆

China's most revered leader during the Máo years, Premier Zhōu Ēnlái (1898–1976), used to stay at this ivy-covered house when he visited Shànghǎi in 1946. His old black Buick is still parked in the garage. The backyard has a small courtyard garden, where there is a statue of Zhōu. The house was used more as an office than residence, and it served before the revolution as the Communist Party's Shànghǎi office. Zhōu kept a spartan room on the first floor (his threadbare blankets are neatly folded on the bed); newspapers were produced on the second floor; and a dorm was maintained in the attic. Signs are in Chinese only.

Sīnán Lù 73 思南路 7 3 号, Lúwān (2 blocks south of Fùxīng Zhōng Lù); see map p. 140. ℘ **021/6473-0420.** Free admission. 9am–4pm. Metro: Shaanxi Rd. (S).

# SPECIAL ATTRACTIONS

Many of Shànghǎi's top attractions aren't easily categorized. The city's many Children's Palaces, the historic Great World amusement center, and the world's tallest hotel are three examples of the many unusual sights you can view in Shànghǎi.

**Children's Municipal Palace (Shì Shàonián Gōng)** 市少年宫 ★ ☺   Initiated by China's honorary president, Soong Ching-ling, Children's Palaces provide after-school programs for high-achieving children, with advanced instruction in music, art, science, sports, and computers. Of the two dozen children's palaces in the city, this is the largest, the nicest, and the most visited. Besides meeting children and peeking in on their classes, you'll be able to admire the gorgeous colonial setting. Built between 1918 and 1931 by a Jewish family from Baghdad, the Kadoories, this sprawling mansion was known in colonial Shànghǎi as the Marble Hall for its grand hallways and gigantic marble ballroom with ornate fireplaces and glittering chandeliers, all reasonably well preserved despite years of children's activities. To tour this Children's Palace, it's best to call ahead for an appointment or make arrangements through CITS or your hotel concierge.

Yán'ān Xī Lù 64 延安西路 6 4 号, Jìng Ān (near Huáshān Lù); see map p. 144. ℘ **021/6248-1850.** Free admission. Mon–Fri 4:30–6pm; Sat–Sun 9am–4pm. Metro: Jing'an Temple.

**Húxīntíng Teahouse (Húxīntíng Cháshè)** 湖心亭茶社 ★   Shànghǎi's quintessential teahouse has floated atop the lake at the heart of Old Town, in front of Yù Yuán, since 1784. It was built by area cotton-cloth merchants as a brokerage hall. Tea drinking was forbidden inside until the late 1800s, when it became what it is today. Believed to be the original model for Blue Willow tableware, the five-sided, two-story pavilion with red walls and uplifted black-tiled eaves has served everyone from visiting heads of state to local laborers. This is the place in Shànghǎi to idle over a cup of tea, seated in front of the open windows. Húxīntíng (meaning "midlake pavilion") is reached via the traditional Bridge of Nine Turnings, so designed to deflect evil spirits who are said to travel only in straight lines.

Yùyuán Lù 257 豫园路 2 5 7 号, Huángpǔ (at pond in the center of the Old Town Bazaar); see map p. 156. ℘ **021/6373-6950.** Free admission. 8:30am–9pm. Metro: Yu Garden.

**Jīn Mào Tower (Jīn Mào Dàshà)** 金茂大厦 ★★★   Built in 1998 as a Sino-American joint venture, this 421m-high (1,381-ft.) second-tallest building in China (to its neighbor the Shànghǎi World Financial Center) is simply sublime. Blending traditional Chinese and modern Western tower designs, the building, which boasts 88 floors (eight being an auspicious Chinese number), consists of 13 distinct tapering segments, with high-tech steel bands binding the glass like an exoskeleton. Offices occupy the first 50 floors, the Grand Hyatt hotel the 51st to the 88th floors, while a public observation deck on the 88th floor ("the Skywalk") offers views to rival those of the nearby Oriental Pearl TV Tower (its admission charge is also lower).

High-speed elevators (9m/30 ft. per sec.) whisk visitors from Level B1 to the top in less than 45 seconds. The view from there is almost too high, but exquisite on a clear day. You can also look down at the 152m-high (499-ft.) atrium of the Grand Hyatt. Access the building through entrance no. 4.

Shìjì Dà Dào 2 世纪大道 2 号, Pŭdōng (3 blocks southeast of Oriental Pearl TV Tower); see map p. 148. ⓒ 021/5047-5101. Admission ¥88. 8:30am–10:30pm (last ticket sold 10pm). Metro: Lujiazui.

### Lŭpŭ Bridge (Lŭpŭ Dàqiáo) 卢浦大桥 ★★

Looking for something a little more heady and panoramic than wandering museums and shops? Go climb a bridge! The Lŭpŭ Bridge, located in the southern part of the French Concession and spanning the Huángpŭ River, is the longest steel arch bridge in the world, spanning 550 meters (1,804 ft). An elevator from Lŭbān Lù underneath the bridge transports visitors to the main deck, from where you then climb the easy 367 steps up the arch of the bridge to the viewing platform at the top, which is about the size of a basketball court (just imagine the commercials Michael Jordan could film bouncing basketballs from here). The prime bird's-eye view from the top—of river traffic, the former 2010 World Expo grounds (centered around the striking red China Pavilion to the southeast), and futuristic buildings stretching into the distance—is simply spectacular. And though the viewing platform is not officially open at night, some intrepid locals have been known to make the after-dark climb and lived to tell about the even more stunning night views. The bridge was temporarily closed to visitors during the World Expo, but should be reopened by the time you read this.

Lŭbān Lù 909 鲁班路909号, Lúwān (south of Lónghuá Dōng Lù); see map p. 140. ⓒ **800/620-0888** or 021/6305-8355. www.lupubridge.com/lp/about_en.php. Admission ¥38. 8:30am–4pm. Metro: Luban Rd.

### Oriental Pearl TV Tower (Dōngfāng Míngzhū Guăngbō Diànshì Tă) 东方明珠广播电视塔

The earliest symbol of the new China, this hideous gray tower with three tapering levels of pink spheres (meant to resemble pearls) still holds a special place in many a local heart and is still one of the first stops in town for Chinese visitors. Built in 1994 at a height of 468m (1,535 ft.), it is hailed as the tallest TV tower in Asia and the third-tallest in the world. Visit for the stunning panoramas of Shànghăi (when the clouds and smog decide to cooperate) and the stellar Shànghăi Municipal History Museum (p. 182) located in the basement. Various combination tickets are available for the tower and museum, but for most folks, the observation deck in the middle sphere (263m/863 ft. elevation), reached by high-speed elevators staffed by statistics-reciting attendants, is just the right height to take in Shànghăi old and new, east and west. Those partial to vertiginous views can ascend to the "space capsule" in the top sphere (350m/1,148 ft. elevation).

Lùjiāzuĭ Lù 2 陆家嘴路2号, Pŭdōng; see map p. 148. ⓒ **021/5879-1888.** Admission ¥100–¥150, depending on sections visited. 8am–9:30pm. Metro: Lujiazui (Exit 1).

### Peace Hotel (Hépíng Fàndiàn) 和平饭店 ★★★

Having reopened after a 2-year renovation, this Art Deco palace is the ultimate symbol of romantic colonial Shànghăi. Built in 1929 by Victor Sassoon, a British descendant of Baghdad Jews who'd made their fortune in opium and real estate, the building was originally part office/residential complex known as the Sassoon House, and part hotel, the Cathay Hotel, one of the world's finest international hotels in the 1930s. Sassoon himself had his bachelor's quarters on the top floor where he threw lavish parties for the city's top denizens, and where you can again if you rent out the new Sassoon Presidential Suite. Or simply stroll through the wings of the finely restored lobby, and if possible (the hotel was not open for review at press time), head to the roof for a superb view of the Bund, Nánjīng Lù, the hotel's famous green pyramid roof, and Pǔdōng across the Huángpǔ River. Famous guests in the past have ranged from Charlie Chaplin and Noël Coward to Douglas Fairbanks and Mary Pickford.

Nánjīng Dōng Lù 20 南京东路２０号, Huángpǔ (on the Bund); see map p. 136. ℂ **021/6321-6888.** Free admission. 24 hr. Metro: Nanjing Rd. (E).

**Shànghǎi Grand Theatre (Shànghǎi Dà Jùyuàn)** 上海大剧院 ★  A truly grand, eight-story, space-age complex of glass and more glass, Shànghǎi's Grand Theatre, boasting three theaters (the largest seating 1,800), is the city's premier venue for international performances, plays, and concerts. There used to be guided tours allowing visitors to view the main auditorium (second floor), the VIP Room (third floor), and the Ballet Studio (fifth floor), but unfortunately, visiting hours for individuals have been restricted to Monday between 9 and 11am. Otherwise, your only chance to check out the theater is to attend an evening performance. Tour groups can visit at any time with prior arrangements.

Rénmín Dà Dào 300 人民大道３０号, Huángpǔ (across from the Shànghǎi Museum); see map p. 136. ℂ **021/6386-8686.** www.shgtheatre.com. Admission (for tours) ¥40. Tours Mon 9–11am. Metro: People's Square.

**Shànghǎi Library (Shànghǎi Túshūguǎn)** 上海图书馆  Opened in 1996, this city library is a state-of-the-art facility with many modern reading rooms, including one devoted to foreign periodicals (fourth floor; Mon–Fri 8:30am–5pm). The collection includes almost two million rare scrolls, manuscripts, and books that can be viewed upon request, though you'll have to apply for a temporary library card. Downstairs, west of the main entrance, is a low-priced Internet cafe.

Huáihǎi Zhōng Lù 1557 淮海中路１５５７号, Xúhuì (btw. Wūlǔmùqí Zhōng Lù and Húnán Lù, near American Consulate); see map p. 140. ℂ **021/6445-5555.** Free admission (but temporary library card at ¥10 required to read publications). 8:30am–8:30pm. Metro: Hengshan Rd.

**Shànghǎi Library Bibliotheca Zi-Ka-Wei (Shànghǎi Túshūguǎn Xújiāhuì Cángshū Lóu)** 上海图书馆徐家汇藏书楼 ★  The Jesuits established in 1847 as part of their mission in Xújiāhuì a library (Bibliotheca Zi-Ka-Wei), which is now partially reopened to the public. The first of the two buildings that constitute the present library has a second-floor public reading room presided over by two boxwood friezes, one of St. Ignatius of Loyola on his deathbed, and the other of St. Francis. But the real treasure is in the adjacent two-story Bibliotheca built in 1897, with a first floor designed in a Chinese style with separate alcoves for the keeping of local records, and the second floor given over to the collection of Western books. Here, stacked neatly on wall-to-wall, floor-to-ceiling shelves are some 560,000 musty, fragile volumes in about 20 languages including Latin, English, French, German, Chinese, and Russian, and covering everything from literature and philosophy to politics, history, and religion. The oldest book, a Latin tome by John Duns Scotus, dates to 1515. Remarkably, the library, which had become a part of the Shànghǎi City Library in 1956, did not lose a single volume during the Cultural Revolution (1966–76), as librarians defended the collection zealously from Red Guards. The Bibliotheca is only open for touring on Saturday afternoons, but the reading room is open to the public during regular business hours. Special-interest groups can call ahead to arrange a private tour.

Cáoxī Běi Lù 80 漕溪北路８０号, Xúhuì (just north of Xújiāhuì Cathedral); see map p. 140. ✆ **021/6487-4095.** Free 15-min. library tours Sat 2–4pm. Reading room: Mon–Sat 9:30am–7pm. Metro: Xújiāhuì.

### Shànghǎi Old City Wall and Dàjìng Gé Pavilion (Shànghǎi Gǔ Chéngqiáng Dàjìng Gé) 上海古城墙大境阁

In 1553 during the Míng Dynasty, Shànghǎi built a city wall to defend itself against Japanese pirates. Following the course of today's Rénmín Lù and Zhōnghuá Lù, the wall measured 8.1m (27 ft.) high and 4.8km (3 miles) around, and had 10 gates. All that remains today is 50m (164 ft.) of wall at this intersection of Dàjìng Lù and Rénmín Lù (the rest was pulled down in 1912). The visible section of the remaining wall dates to the Qīng Dynasty, as is evident by brick markings bearing the names of Qīng emperors Xiánfēng (1851–61) and Tóngzhì (1862–74). The newly rebuilt Dàjìng Gé Pavilion atop the wall was one of the 30 towers along the structure. There's a small exhibit here on life in the old Chinese city.

Dàjìng Lù 269 大境路２６９号, Huángpǔ (just east of intersection with Rénmín Lù); see map p. 156. ✆ **021/6326-6171.** Admission ¥5. 9am–4pm. Metro: Dàshìjiè.

### Shànghǎi Sculpture Space (Shànghǎi Chéngshì Diāosù Yìshù Zhōngxīn) 上海城市雕塑艺术中心

In the vein of the recent Shànghǎi trend of converting abandoned industrial buildings into art centers, the space formerly occupied by the No. 10 Steel Plant of Shànghǎi (covering a total area of 50,000 sq. m/538,195 sq. ft.) on the edges of the French Concession has now been partially converted into a sprawling urban sculpture art center complete with galleries, artists' studios, restaurants, offices, and outdoor exhibition space. The original red-brick warehouses have been wonderfully preserved and are just as interesting architecturally as what they now house, from sculptures and installations to artwork by Chinese and international artists. If you like your art in 3D, this place, still being developed, is worth a visit.

Huáihǎi Xī Lù 570-588 淮海西路570－588号, Chángníng (east of Kǎixuán Lù); see map p. 152. ✆ **021/6280-7844.** www.sss570.com. Free admission to the grounds. Entrance fees for special exhibitions vary. Tues–Sun 10am–4pm. Metro: Hóngqiáo Rd.

### Shànghǎi World Financial Center (Shànghǎi Huánqiú Jīnróng Zhōngxīn 上海环球金融中心 ★★

Opened in the middle of 2008, this tapering, 101-story, 492m-high (1,614-ft.) glass tower, resembling a giant, old-fashioned bottle opener, is the tallest building in China, and the tallest in the world, vis-à-vis the height to which visitors can ascend—which, in this case, is the stunning, all-glass 100th-floor observatory at a height of 474m (1,555 ft.). (The building, designed by American architect William Pedersen and developed by Minoru Mori and the Mori Group, which built the Roppongi Hills complex in Tokyo, is technically the third tallest in the world.) The rarefied air and views from up top are unparalleled, but can be stomach-churning for those prone to vertigo. The 94th-floor exhibition space, and the 97th-floor skybridge are nothing special, but the tony Park Hyatt Hotel on the 79th to 93rd floors is certainly good for a meal or drink after your visit, as are the restaurants in the basement.

Shìjì Dàdào 100 世纪大道100号, Pǔdōng; see map p. 148. ✆ **021/5878-0101.** www.swfc-observatory. com. 94th floor only ¥100; 94th–97th floors ¥110; 94th–100th floors ¥150. Daily 8am–11pm (10pm last entry). Metro: Lujiazui.

**Xīntiāndì (New Heaven and Earth)** 新天地 ★★★ Shànghǎi's trendiest lifestyle destination, this 2-block complex of high-end restaurants (some of Shànghǎi's best), bars, shops, and entertainment facilities, mostly lodged in refurbished traditional Shanghainese *shíkùmén* (stone-frame) housing, is the first phase of the Tàipíng Qiáo Project, an urban renewal project covering 52 hectares (128 acres) that resulted in the relocation of 3,500 families. Busloads of domestic Chinese tourists traipse through in the evenings, Western visitors feel like they've never left home, and hip young Shanghainese flood here to enjoy the good life they feel they're due. Besides the many shopping and dining establishments (separately reviewed), there is a *shíkùmén* museum (at Xīnyeè Lù and Mǎdāng Lù) showcasing the interiors of a typical lane house.

Bounded by Tàicāng Lù, Huángpí Nán Lù, Zìzhōng Lù, and Mǎdāng Lù, Lúwān; see map p. 140. ℂ **021/3307-0337.** Shíkùmén museum admission ¥20. Museum 10am-10pm. Hours for restaurants and shops vary. Metro: Huangpi Rd. (S).

# ESPECIALLY FOR KIDS

Compared to other Chinese cities, Shànghǎi has a relatively large number of attractions for children. Listed elsewhere in this chapter, the Oriental Pearl TV Tower, the Jīn Mào Tower, and the Shànghǎi Museum of Arts and Crafts may amuse the kids, but the following should appeal particularly to younger foreign travelers (and often to their parents, too) while in Shànghǎi.

**Dino Beach (Rèdài Fēngbào Shuǐshàng Lèyuán)** 热带风暴水上乐园 ★
The best water park in Shànghǎi boasts Asia's largest wave pool (.8 hectares/2 acres). As well, there are eight water slides, the longest measuring almost 150m (500 ft.), three swimming pools for kids, a mile-long river with rapids, and organized beach volleyball and water polo games. Factor in a slew of fast-food outlets, and you come up with the closest thing to an American-style water park in China.

Xīn Zhèn Lù 78 新镇路 7 8 号, Míngháng (Qībǎo Zhèn, south of Shànghǎi-Hángzhōu Hwy.); see map p. 152. ℂ **021/6478-3333.** www.dinobeach.com.cn. Admission ¥100-¥200; children under 1.5m (59 in.) half-price; free for toddlers under .8m (31 in.). Open summer only: 10am-11pm. Metro: Qībǎo.

**Jīn Jiāng Amusement Park (Jīn Jiāng Lèyuán)** 锦江乐园 Shànghǎi's most complete modern amusement park, the Jīn Jiāng has a loop-the-loop roller coaster, merry-go-rounds, and bumper cars, as well as a haunted house. There's also a special playground for preschoolers. The "Gorge Drifting Waterland" is a watersports area open only during summer.

Hóngméi Lù 201 虹梅路 2 0 1 号, Xúhuì (at Hùmíng Lù); see map p. 140. ℂ **021/5420-4956.** Admission ¥80; includes 6 rides. 8:45am-5pm. Metro: Jinjiang Park.

**Shànghǎi Chángfēng Ocean World (Shànghǎi Chángfēng Hǎiyáng Shìjiè)** 上海长风海洋世界 ★ Also known as Aquaria 21, this excellent underwater-world aquarium features a "touch pool" so that kids can mingle with the sea life (crabs, starfish, urchins). The main tank is stocked with seahorses, tuna, turtles, rays, and patrolling sharks fed by keepers in diving suits. There's also an arena of penguins from Peru and Chile. In fact, you can journey through a series of aquatic habitats, from the Amazon River to Antarctica. Scuba gear is provided for those who want diving lessons.

Dà Dū Hé Lù 451 大渡河路 4 5 1 号, Chángníng (Gate 4, Chángfēng Gōngyuán, west of Inner Ring Rd.); see map p. 152. ☎ **021/6223-8888.** www.oceanworld.com.cn. Admission ¥130 adults, ¥90 children 1–1.4m (39–55 in.), free for children under 1m (39 in.). 8:30am–5pm. Metro: Jinshajiang Rd.

## Shànghǎi Circus World (Shànghǎi Mǎxì Chéng) 上海马戏城 ★

This glittering modern arena for acrobatic and circus performances, opened in the northern suburbs in 1999, has a 1,638-seat circus theater with a revolving stage, computer-controlled lighting, and state-of-the-art acoustics. The complex also includes a gigantic animal house with rooms for elephants, tigers, lions, chimps, horses, and pandas. The celebrated Shànghǎi Acrobatic Troupe occasionally stages its 20-act performances here (p. 143). During other times, this venue plays host to a variety of large-scale magic and acrobatic shows, as well as the annual Shànghǎi International Magic Festival and Competition, held in early November. Check with your hotel for the current performers, schedules, and tickets.

Gònghé Xīn Lù 2266 共和新路 2 2 6 6 号, Zháběi (north of railway station, near Zháběi Gōngyuán); see map p. 144. ☎ **021/5665-6622,** ext. 2027. Tickets ¥80–¥600 depending on show. Metro: Shanghai Circus World.

## Shànghǎi Natural Wild Insect Kingdom (Shànghǎi Dàzìrán Yěshēng Kūnchóng Guǎn) 上海大自然野生昆虫馆

The birds and the bees, the beetles and the butterflies, all your usual creepy crawlies are on display in this museum housing several galleries, including a tropical rainforest and a reptile cave. Some of the insect models can be pretty tacky to adult eyes, but kids like the interactive exhibits where they can feed critters and catch fish.

Fēnghé Lù 1 丰和路 1 号, Pǔdōng (west of Oriental Pearl TV Tower, north of International Convention Center); see map p. 148. ☎ **021/5840-6950.** Admission ¥50 adults, ¥30 children 18 and under. Mon–Thurs 9am–5pm; Fri–Sun 9am–5:30pm. Metro: Lujiazui.

## Shànghǎi Ocean Aquarium (Shànghǎi Hǎiyáng Shuǐzú Guǎn) 上海海洋水族馆 ★

Shànghǎi's biggest and best aquarium, and Asia's largest, opened in 2002 in Pǔdōng, next to the Oriental Pearl TV Tower. Its state-of-the-art facilities boast 28 exhibit areas for more than 10,000 sea creatures from all continents: sharks, jellyfish, turtles, lionfish, sea otters, Yángzǐ sturgeon, and more. The centerpiece is the massive, sparkling, glass-surround observation tunnel. Adventurous visitors can make special arrangements to dive in the shark tank, though it could well cost you an arm and a leg.

Yínchéng Běi Lù 158 银城北路 1 5 8 号, Pǔdōng (east of Oriental Pearl TV Tower); see map p. 148. ☎ **021/5877-9988.** www.sh-aquarium.com. Admission ¥135 adults, ¥90 children under 1.4m (55 in.), free for children under .8m (31 in.). 9am–6pm (last ticket sold 5:30pm); July–Aug 9am–9pm (last ticket 8:30pm). Metro: Lujiazui.

## Shànghǎi Science and Technology Museum (Shànghǎi Kējì Guǎn) 上海科技馆 ★★

This hands-on interactive science museum, opened in 2001, has received raves from expatriate families with children. There are five main interactive exhibits, which can be visited in any order. The "Earth Exploration" exhibit is a journey to the center of the Earth, complete with fossils. "Children's Technoland" has a walk-in heart and brain, as well as a simulated construction zone with soft foam bricks. The vast "Light of Wisdom" area has more than 100 interactive stations that bring scientific principles to life. "Cradle of Designers" gives you the chance to design your own cards or create your own video. "Spectrum of Life" is a simulated tropical rainforest with robotic beetles and a bat cave. There are also two IMAX 3D cinemas and an iWerks theater here. Weekends are crowded; the best time to visit is on weekdays in the late afternoon, when the school excursions are over.

Shìjì Dà Dào 2000 世纪大道２０００号, Pǔdōng (north side Shìjì Gōngyuán); see map p. 148. © **021/ 6862-2000.** www.sstm.org.cn. Admission ¥60 adults, ¥45 students (with ID), ¥20 children under 1.2m (4 ft.). Tues–Sun 9am–5:15pm (last ticket sold 4:40pm). Metro: Shanghai Science and Technology Museum.

### Shànghǎi Wild Animal Park (Shànghǎi Yěshēng Dòngwùyuán) 上海野生动物园
Shànghǎi's only drive-through safari, home to some 5,000 animals (200 species), is located all the way out by the Pǔdōng International Airport. At least the South China tigers, lions, cheetahs, zebras, giraffes, camels, bears, elephants, hippos, and flamingos have more legroom here than in the Shànghǎi Zoo. Buses transport visitors through the grounds, and there's also a walk-through area with birds, monkeys, seals, and sea lions.

Nánfāng Gōnglù 南方公路, Nánhuì (east Pǔdōng); see map p. 148. © 021/6118-0000. Admission ¥120, half-price children under 1.2m (4 ft.). 8am–5pm. No Metro.

### Shànghǎi Zoo (Shànghǎi Dòngwùyuán) 上海动物园
One of China's best, this zoo still has a long way to go to equal the better preserves in the West. It was a private estate of the Sassoon family, then a city golf course, before its conversion to a zoo in 1954. There are plenty of open spaces for children to play, but the spaces for animals are quite confined and depressing. Expect the usual performing seals and elephants. The panda center, a 20-minute stroll northwest from the entrance, has small indoor and outdoor areas. There are about 6,000 specimens (600 species) here, as well as a children's zoo and recreation center with playground equipment and a Ferris wheel.

Hóngqiáo Lù 2831 虹桥路２８３１号, Chángníng (1 mile east of Hóngqiáo Airport); see map p. 152. © **021/6268-7775,** ext. 8000. Admission ¥40, free for children under 1.2m (4 ft.). Nov–Feb 7am– 4:30pm; Mar and Oct 7am–5pm; Apr–Sept 6:30am–5pm. Metro: Shanghai Zoo.

# ORGANIZED TOURS

Most Shànghǎi hotels have tour desks that can arrange a variety of day tours for guests. These tour desks are often extensions of **China International Travel Service (CITS),** now rebranded locally as **Jǐn Jiāng Tours.** CITS has its head offices near the Shànghǎi Centre at Běijīng Xī Lù 1277, Guólǚ Dàshà (© **021/6289-4510** or 021/6289-8899, ext. 263; www.citsusa.com). There's another branch at the Bund at Jīnlíng Dōng Lù 2 (© **021/6323-8770**) where you can purchase airline and train tickets.

Jǐnjiāng Tours operates many of the English-language group tours in Shànghǎi, even those booked in hotels. If you have little time, **group tours** are convenient, efficiently organized, and considerably less expensive than private tours. The **Jǐn Jiāng Tours Center,** which has its head office near the Jǐn Jiāng and Okura Garden hotels at Chánglè Lù 191 (© **021/5466-7936** or 021/6466-2828, ext. 0), offers several City Explorer group tours, including a half-day Shànghǎi tour and a 1-day tour of Shànghǎi by bus, with English-speaking guide and lunch, for ¥400; sites include Yù Yuán, the Bund, Jade Buddha Temple, Xīntiāndì, People's Square, the Shànghǎi Museum, and a quick drive-by of Pǔdōng. Another option is **Gray Line**

Shànghǎi, located at Běijīng Xī Lù 1399, A/5F (© 021/6289-5221; www.grayline. com), part of the international chain, which offers half-day (around ¥306) and full-day tours (around ¥496) of Shànghǎi.

Group tours aren't for everyone, as they are extremely rushed. At major sites, group tour participants are shown only a fraction of what's there. A good guide can outline the history and culture of a place, but there is usually no more than an hour to see a major site. Most of the commentary is delivered during the bus ride.

As an alternative, **Big Bus Tours** (Hànkǒu Lù 515, Huì Jīn Tower, Room 1205, Huángpǔ; © 021/6351-5988; www.bigbustours.com) has recently inaugurated two tour routes covering all the major landmarks in Pǔxī and Pǔdōng on its open-top double-decker buses. Your ticket (¥300) allows you to hop on/off at your leisure at any of the designated stops within a 24-hour period, and also includes audio commentary on the buses, free tickets to the Jade Buddha Temple, the Bund Sightseeing Tunnel, and a free River Cruise. Tickets can be purchased through your hotel, from the company's website, or on the bus (one of the main stops is at the northeast corner of People's Square opposite Madame Tussauds by Metro Exit 7).

Of course, travel agencies can arrange in-depth private tours, customized to fit your itinerary or interest (such as education, art, food, or the martial arts). These tours include an English-speaking guide, driver, and private car for the day. The Jīn Jiāng Optional Tours Center offers a full-day private tour of the city, including door-to-door service, air-conditioned car, English-speaking guide, and lunch, at a cost of around ¥1,500 for one person, ¥1,000 per person for two people, and ¥900 per person for three to four people. Travel agencies and hotel tour desks can also act as ticketing agents for nighttime entertainment, too (such as acrobatics, operas, circuses, and Huángpǔ River cruises).

In addition to Jīn Jiāng, another proven private travel agency providing group day tours, private tours, tickets, and hotel bookings to international clients is the **China Spring International Travel Service,** Dīngxī Lù 1558 (© 021/6251-5777; fax 021/6252-3734; www.chinaspringtour.com), which also maintains a 24-hour Tourist Information Line (© 021/6252-0000).

As an alternative, concierge service providers like **Luxury Concierge China** (Wūlǔmùqí Běi Lù 457, Ste. 403; © 1350-166-2908; fax 021/6249-2316; www. luxuryconciergechina.com) can customize itineraries and provide private guided tours for those with special interests such as art, architecture, or shopping. Other recent successful tours have included a sidecar drive of the French Concession, and a fashion designer tour where guests were able to meet with Shànghǎi's up-and-coming designers.

Some other more specialized tour operators include: **Bodhi Bikes** (Zhōngshān Běi Lù 2918, Building 2, third floor, Ste. 2308; © 021/5266-9013; www.bodhi. com.cn), which offers bicycle tours of Shànghǎi by night, as well as day trips to Chóngmíng Island and other nearby mountains; **China Cycle Tours** (© 0/1376-111-5050; www.chinacycletours.com) has daily half-day and 1-day tours of Shàng-hǎi by bicycle, as well as a Chinese massage bike tour (includes a 1-hour massage in your meanderings), and a nightly city tour. **Shanghai Sideways** (© 0/1381-761-6975; www.shanghaisideways.com) arranges motorbike and sidecar tours of the city on a vintage 750cc Changjiang motorcycle, with a 4-hour tour costing ¥1,100 for the first passenger, and ¥750 for the second. There are also 1- and 2-hour tours.

# STAYING ACTIVE

Most visitors to Shànghǎi do not come intending to pursue outdoor recreation or sports, but there is a wide range of such activities. Hotels routinely provide exercise machines, weights, aerobic and workout areas, swimming pools, locker rooms, and, less often, tennis and squash courts, all at little or no charge to their guests. It is possible to use some hotels' fitness facilities even if you are not a guest (although the fees can be steep). Joggers in Shànghǎi will find the early morning streets and public parks conducive to running. Shànghǎi has its own annual international marathon, the Toray Cup (run in mid-Nov).

Golf and bowling are two of the most popular recreational sports in Shànghǎi, pursued by well-to-do locals, foreign residents, and overseas visitors, but you can also enjoy kite-flying, traditional *tàijí quán,* and even go-cart racing if time and energy allow.

Spectator sports include Formula One racing, professional basketball, interleague soccer, and international badminton.

## Activities from A to Z

**BOWLING (BǍOLÍNG QIÚ)**    Bowling experienced a boom in China during the 1990s, when more than 15,000 alleys were built, many of them in Shànghǎi. There are good alleys in the **Regal International East Asia** hotel. The **Orden Bowling Center** at Héngshān Lù 10 (*©* 021/6474-6666) is open 24 hours. Rates run from ¥8 to ¥30 per line at Shànghǎi bowling halls, depending on the quality of the facility and the time of day (the later, the more expensive); shoe rentals toe the line at ¥3 to ¥10.

**GO-KARTING (KǍDĪNG CHĒ)**    The best track for a Formula One drive in miniature is the indoor arena at **Disc Kart** (Díshìkǎ Sàichēguǎn, Zǎoyáng Lù 609 [near Metro Line 3, Jinshajiang Rd. Station]; *©* **021/6285-7778;** www.karting china.com), where the timing system is high-tech, the carts have new Honda engines, and the driving goes on into the wee hours (2pm–2am). An outdoor alternative is the **Qūyáng Racing Cart Club,** Zhōngshān Běi Yī Lù 880 (*©* **021/6531-6800;** Mon–Thurs 10am–5:30pm; Fri–Sun 9am–6pm).

**GOLF (GĀO'ĚRFŪ QIÚ)**    Greens fees at Shànghǎi's dozen or more golf courses run from ¥400 to ¥830 on weekdays, ¥830 to ¥1,660 on Saturday and Sunday. Caddies cost ¥90 to ¥200 and club rental costs ¥250 to ¥450. All courses require advance reservations; summer weekends are particularly crowded. One of Shànghǎi's best is the **Sheshan International Golf Club** (Shéshān Gāo'ěrfū Qún), Línyīn Xīn Lù 288, Shéshān National Tourism Resort, Sōngjiāng District (*©* **021/5779-8008;** www. sheshangolf.com), about 30 minutes outside the city. Vijay Singh and Tiger Woods have both played here in the HSBC Champions Tournament on the Nelson and Haworth course featuring natural forest and man-made lakes.

Other top courses include the world-class, Robert Trent Jones, Jr.–designed **Shànghǎi International Golf and Country Club** (Shànghǎi Guójì Gāo'ěrfū Xiāngcūn Jùlèbù), Xīnyáng Cūn, Zhūjiājiǎo (*©* **021/5972-8111;** Wed–Mon 9am–5pm), an hour's drive west of Shànghǎi in Qīngpǔ District; the **Shànghǎi Riviera Golf Resort** (Shànghǎi Dōngfāng Bālí Gāo'ěrfū Jùlèbù), Yángzǐ Lù 277, Nánxiáng Town, Jiādìng District (*©* **021/5912-6888;** Tues–Fri 9am–10pm; Sat–Sun 8am–10pm), a Bobby J. Martin–designed 18-hole par-61 course with a driving range and

# SHÀNGHǍI spas

In most people's minds, Shànghǎi may not be readily associated with the spa experience, but those addicted to their mud wraps, body polishes, and lomi lomi massages can now get some world-class pampering at a number of classy, brand-name spas in town. In fact, it has become de rigueur for every top hotel worth its salt (rub) to have a brand-name spa.

One of the most sybaritic of the lot is **Chi,** the Himalayan-themed spa at the Shangri-La Hotel Tower (Fùchéng Lù 33; ℂ **021/6882-8888,** ext. 460), delivering top-of-the-world treatments at predictably sky-high prices. The world-famous **Banyan Tree Spa,** located on the third floor of the Westin Hotel (Nánjīng Dōng Lù 88; ℂ **021/6335-1888;** www.banyan treespa.com), is beautifully designed using the theme of the Chinese five elements (wood, water, fire, earth, and metal). A host of beauty, hair-care, and massage treatments are available at steep international spa prices. Also from Thailand, the **Anantara Spa** at the PuLi Hotel and Spa (Chángdé Lù 1; ℂ **021/2216-6899;** www.spa.anantara.com/shanghai) specializes in tea treatments, while the **Spa at the Hilton** (Huáshān Lù 250; ℂ **021/6248-0000,** ext. 2600) continues to dole out some of the city's consistently best massages, especially

its signature *shēntǐ* massage, which combines Swedish with Chinese massage. The worldwide **Chuan Spa** at the Langham, Yangtze Boutique (Hànkǒu Lù 740; ℂ **021/6080-0722;** www.chuan spa.com), offers treatments guided by the principles of traditional Chinese medicine to restore harmony and balance.

Many expats and discerning locals head for **Dragonfly Therapeutic Retreat** (Xīnlè Lù 206; ℂ **021/5403-9982;** www.dragonfly.net.cn), which has an exotic Asian ambience with all the standard treatments at just the right prices (often less than half the rates at hotel spas), though its recent rapid expansion has resulted in somewhat uneven service at different branches. The small but excellent **Shui Urban Spa** (Wūkāng Lù 376, Ferguson Lane, fifth floor; ℂ **021/6126-7800;** www.shuiurbanspa.com.cn) features a variety of pampering treatments by very strong and skilled English-speaking massage therapists. For the truly intrepid, **Fùníng Point Pressure Massage Center of Blind People** (Fùxīng Lù 597; ℂ **021/6437-8378**) offers invigorating Chinese massages for around ¥45 an hour. Little to no English is spoken here, however.

year-round night golfing; the **Tomson Golf Club** (Tāngchén Gāo'ěrfū Jùlèbù), Lóngdōng Dà Dào 1, also in Pǔdōng, with reservations available through the Inter-Continental Hotel Pǔdōng (ℂ **021/5833-8888;** Mon 1–10pm, Tues–Sun 8am–10pm); and Shànghǎi's only 54-hole course, the **Shànghǎi Bīnhǎi Golf Club** (Bīnhǎi Gāo'ěrfū Jùlèbù), Bīnhǎi, Nánhuì, located near the Pǔdōng Airport (ℂ **021/5805-8888** or 021/3800-1888; www.binhaigolf.com; call for hours).

**HEALTH & FITNESS CLUBS** Some hotels offer day rates to outsiders. The **Spa at the Hilton** (ℂ **021/6248-0000,** ext. 2600; 6am–11pm), for example, charges ¥480 per day for use of its gym, pool, tennis and squash courts, sauna,

## Formula One Fever

Formula One racing officially roared into China with the Shànghǎi Grand Prix in September 2004. Located in the northwestern suburb of Āntíng in Jiādìng County, about 40 minutes from People's Square, the Shànghǎi International Circuit (Shànghǎi Guójì Sàichēchǎng), which will host F1 races at least through 2011, features a stunning track in the contours of a Chinese character, and a 10-story glass-and-steel grandstand. Tickets range from ¥180 for practice sessions to ¥3,980 for top seats overlooking the finish line on the last day. For more information, call (©) **021/9682-6999** or 021/6330-5555, or visit www.icsh.sh.cn. To get to the track, you can now take Metro Line 11 out to the Shànghǎi Circuit stop.

Jacuzzi, locker rooms, and exercise room. The most complete range of fitness facilities in town is offered by the **Shànghǎi International Tennis Centre Club,** attached to the Regal International East Asia Hotel, Héngshān Lù 516, third floor, Xúhuì (© **021/6415-5588,** ext. 82), with its 25m (82-ft.) indoor lap pool, aerobics studio, exercise machines, simulated golf range, 12-lane bowling alley, and 10 of China's best indoor and outdoor tennis and squash courts (daily 6am–11pm). Among private fitness clubs, one of the best offering day passes is the **Clark Hatch Fitness Center** at the Radisson Plaza Xing Guo Hotel, Xìngguó Lù 78 (© **021/6212-9998,** ext. 3300), which has a vast array of state-of-the-art equipment (daily 6am–11pm) and single-entry passes for ¥200. The boutique fitness club **One Wellness** at Yánpíng Lù 98 (near Xīnzhá Lù; © **021/6267-1550;** www.onewellness.com.cn) claims to be the first carbon-neutral gym in China and features a gourmet health-food cafe and free Internet stations and Wi-Fi. Daily hours are 6am to 11pm, and a day pass costs ¥300.

**KITE-FLYING (FÀNG FĒNGZHENG)** Chinese have been flying their invention of kites for more than 2,000 years. The best places to buy and to fly local Shànghǎi kites are in the public parks and in People's Square in front of the Shànghǎi Museum.

**TAI CHI (TÀIJÍ QUÁN)** These venerable and graceful "shadow-boxing" exercises, which tens of thousands of Shanghainese practice every morning before work, and Wǔ Shù, the martial arts forms developed in China, can be learned at the **Shànghǎi Wǔshù Center (Wǔshù Yuàn),** Nánjīng Xī Lù 595, Huángpǔ (© **021 6253-3120**), or at the **Lóngwǔ International Kung Fu Center,** Màomíng Nán Lù 1 (© **021/6287-1528;** www.longwukungfu.com).

**YOGA (YÚJIĀ)** You can now practice your sun salutations at a number of places, including **Karma Yoga** in Pǔdōng (Pǔchéng Lù 172, third floor; © **021/3887-0669;** www.karmayoga.com.cn), one of the largest studios in the city with everything from hatha to hot yoga, and **Y+ Yoga Centre** (Fùxīng Lù, Lane 299, no. 2; © **021/6433-4330;** www.yplus.com.cn), offering ashtanga, bikram, and prenatal yoga, as well as Pilates.

## Spectator Sports

Check local listings or your hotel desk for current sports in town. The **Chinese National Basketball League (CNBL)** has been building a strong following across China since its inception in 1994. Each team is allowed to hire two foreign players (usually Americans). The powerful Shànghǎi Sharks (home team of 2.26m/7 ft. 5 in. Yáo Míng, now playing for the Houston Rockets in the NBA) play most of their home basketball games from November through April in Lúwān Stadium, Zhàojiābāng Lù 128 (© **021/6427-8673** or 021/6467-5358). Tickets are ¥30 to ¥200. **Shànghǎi Stadium,** Tiānyáoqiáo Lù 666, Xúhuì (© **021/6426-6666** or 021/6426-6888, ext. 8268), is the usual venue for big sporting events (soccer, track, and field). **Shànghǎi Zhábeǐ Stadium,** Gònghé Xīn Lù 475, Chángníng (© **021/5690-8609**), is a popular venue for rugby tournaments.

# SHÀNGHǍI STROLLS

Despite its immense and dense population, Shànghǎi is one of China's great cities for walking. Much of the street-level fascination comes from the European architecture left over from colonial days (1842–1949), when Shànghǎi was sliced up by the Western powers into foreign concessions. Shànghǎi's present cityscape is an amalgam of Art Deco mansions from that colonial period, *lòngtáng* (walled brick town house rows) with distinctive *shíkùmén* (stone frame gates) from the local Chinese tradition, and malls and towers of glass and steel from international modernism.

Walking Shànghǎi is not without its obstacles. Sidewalks are often crowded not only with other pedestrians, but with bicycle parking lots, construction sites, vendors and their carts, card players, laundry strung between doors and trees, cars brazenly parked on walkways, and motorcycles and bicycles zooming along as if the sidewalks were extensions of the streets. You'll also have to contend with the pollution and dust, occasional raw odors, and jarring sounds, so much so that a half-day's walk can sometimes leave you exhausted. But it is really only in walking that you'll get a chance to discover aspects of Shànghǎi you would otherwise miss from a speeding taxi or a tour bus: that faded colonial mansion hidden under years of grime, or that vegetable market teeming with local housewives—scenes that are themselves rapidly disappearing from today's Shànghǎi.

Walking just about anywhere in Shànghǎi requires vigilance. The basic rule of survival is that cars have the right of way even when they shouldn't. *Cars always have the right of way, even when pedestrians have a green light, so look both ways and always be prepared to yield.* At least at major roads and intersections, brown-clad, whistle-blowing traffic assistants now help direct pedestrian traffic. On smaller streets, simply follow the lead of locals. Above all, slow down and savor a walk through China's biggest, most densely packed city, where past and future, East and West, meet at every corner. The best way to see Shànghǎi, despite its hazards, is on foot.

**THE BUND & BEYOND**

| START: | **Wàibǎidù Bridge, Sūzhōu Creek (Metro: Nanjing Rd. [E]).** |
|---|---|
| FINISH: | **Yán'ān Dōng Lù, south Bund.** |
| TIME: | **2 hours.** |
| BEST TIMES: | **Weekday mornings or late afternoons; nighttime for the lights, not the sights.** |
| WORST TIMES: | **Weekends bring out the crowds on the Bund Promenade. Evenings are pretty, with the lights on the Bund buildings and the river, but the architecture cannot be viewed well after dark.** |

**8**

The Bund & Beyond

SHÀNGHǍI STROLLS

Defining the eastern boundary of downtown Shànghǎi, the Bund (Wài Tān) refers to both sides of the wide avenue (Zhōngshān Dōng Yī Lù) that runs north and south along the western shore of the Huángpǔ River. After a 2-year, ¥5-billion expansion project in preparation for the World Expo of 2010, the Bund reopened to great fanfare with a wider and longer **Bund Promenade** on the east side of the street, affording terrific pedestrian-only walks along the river shore with unparalleled views of Pǔdōng across the river. Our stroll concentrates on the colonial-era European-style architecture on the west side of the street, all of which received face-lifts in the most recent renovations.

The colonial era began in Shànghǎi after the Treaty of Nánjīng ended the First Opium War in 1842. The British and other Western nations moved in, establishing foreign enclaves (concessions) and opening up the city to trade. Consisting of mud flats and streams that were drained, the Bund (which means embankment) became the chief shipping, trading, and financial district of the colonialists. Shànghǎi's foreign population grew from 10,000 in 1910 to 60,000 by 1940, and it was during this period that the great buildings that still line the Bund were built. Many of the more notable buildings were designed by the architectural firm Palmer and Turner, including the Customs House, the former Hong Kong and Shànghǎi Bank, the Bank of China, and the Peace Hotel.

War with Japan signaled the end to the Bund's colonial heyday, the first bomb dropping on the Peace Hotel on August 14, 1937. In January 1943, the Japanese occupation of Shànghǎi put an end to the city's foreign concessions. Shortly after the Communist triumph of 1949, the last of the foreign trading houses abandoned the Bund. In the decades since, many of the buildings, occupied sporadically by local banks, organizations, and businesses, fell into disrepair, but since the late 1990s, there has been a concerted effort to restore the Bund's architectural grandeur, to refurbish the colonial interiors, and to open them to a curious public. With the renovations of the last 3 years establishing luxury hotels, and high-end shops and restaurants as new tenants on the street, the Bund has once again become the city's focal point, all of which makes for a fascinating walking tour. In addition, the route will also take in part of the area behind the Bund known as Wàitānyuán ("head-stream of the Bund"), which the Shànghǎi government is developing into a highly ambitious complex of shops and restaurants in historical buildings connected by courtyards and gardens, pedestrian-only streets, and aerial walkways.

# Walking Tour 1: The Bund

1 Wàibáidù Qiáo (Wàibáidù Bridge)
外白渡桥

2 Bund Sightseeing Avenue
(Wàitān Guānjǐng Dàdào)
外滩观景大道

3 Former British Consulate
英国领事馆旧址

4 Yuánmíngyuán Lù
圆明园路

5 Rockbund Art Museum
上海外滩美术馆

6 Jardine Matheson Building (now the
Shànghǎi Foreign Trade Building)
上海外贸大楼

7 Bank of China (Zhōngguó Yínháng)
中国银行

8 Peace Hotel (Hépíng Fàndiàn)
和平饭店

9 Swatch Art Peace Hotel
(formerly Palace Hotel, no. 19)
和平饭店南楼

10 Bund 18 (formerly Chartered Bank of
India, Australia and China)
外滩18号

11 Russo-Chinese Bank Building (now the
China Foreign Exchange Trade System
Building)
(Zhōngguó Wàihuì Jiāoyì Zhōngxīn)
中国外汇交易中心

12 Shànghǎi Customs House
(Shànghǎi Hǎiguān)
上海海关

13 Hongkong and Shànghǎi Bank (now the
Shànghǎi Pǔdōng Development Bank)
(Shànghǎi Pǔdōng Fāzhǎn Yínháng)
上海浦东发展银行

14 Intersection of Fúzhōu Lù and Jiāngxī Lù

15 Hospital of the Shànghǎi Navigation
Company (now the Bangkok Bank and
the Thai Consulate) (Màngǔ Yínháng)
曼谷银行

Monument to the People's Heroes/
Bund History Museum
人民英雄纪念塔 / 外滩历史纪念馆

16 Three on the Bund
(formerly the Union Insurance
Company Building)
(Wàitān Sān Hào)
外滩三号

17 Shànghǎi Club (Yīngguó Zǒng Huì)
英国总会

Begin at the northern end of the Bund (Zhōngshān Dōng Yī Lù) on the southern
shore of Sūzhōu Creek at:

## 1 Wàibǎidù Bridge

This steel span bridge was built in 1907 to replace the wooden Garden Bridge
that once connected the American Settlement north of the Sūzhōu Creek to
the British Concession. On the north side of the bridge, you can see a number
of colonial holdovers: to the left (west), the former **Broadway Mansions** (now
Shànghǎi Mansions), an Art Deco apartment building constructed in 1934,
which later housed the Foreign Correspondents Club after World War II; and

to the right on the north side of the street, the marvelous old **Astor House Hotel,** built in 1860 and reconstructed in 1906. The hotel was the first to use telephones and electric lights in China. Albert Einstein stayed here in 1921 and 1923 (and you can, too, in his former room, in today's Pǔjiāng Hotel). South of the Pǔjiāng is the former and again current **Russian Consulate,** built in 1917, which served as a seamen's hotel in intervening years.

From the southeastern end of the bridge, looking south, you will find yourself at the beginning of the refurbished:

## 2 Wàitān Guānjīng Dàdào (Bund Sightseeing Avenue)

The patches of greenery that you see here used to be part of the famous (or infamous) **Huángpǔ Gōngyuán (Huángpǔ Park).** Today, very little remains of the notorious park, originally built by the British in 1868, which in colonial days was reputed to have a sign posted forbidding entrance by dogs and Chinese. Actually, they were just 2 out of 10 park prohibitions, but the underlying attitude toward the Chinese was clear. Today's sightseeing avenue is dominated at the northern end by an obelisk, the **Monument to the People's Heroes.** This is a great spot to take in views of Pǔdōng across the river, as well as of the Bund buildings you'll soon be seeing up close.

Cross to the west side of the Bund at Nán Sūzhōu Lù. Straight ahead is the:

## 3 Former British Consulate (Nos. 33–53)

This large, sprawling compound with the two stately gray and tan granite buildings was the former British Consulate, first established here in 1852 after the British victory in the Opium War of 1842, and rebuilt in 1873. From this perch at the top of the Bund, the British oversaw the growth and development of Shànghǎi into an economic powerhouse in the first half of the 20th century. There were other consulate buildings here, but none remain. Today's compound, also enclosing the early English Gothic-style former **Union Church** (originally built in 1886, and given a complete face-lift in 2010) and neighboring hall, are currently managed by the Peninsula Hotel just to the south, itself newly built and opened in 2010. At press time, the former British Consulate buildings were being used to receive official guests for the World Expo, with future plans for it yet uncertain.

Follow the curve of Nán Sūzhōu Lù north, noting across the street on the south shore of Sūzhōu Creek the only remaining building of the Shànghǎi Rowing Club, built in 1904. Take a left (south) at:

## 4 Yuánmíngyuán Lù

Behind the Bund, this street is part of what is known as Wàitānyuán (including the parallel Hǔqiū Lù to the west, which was known as Museum Road in the 1930s), an area that was home to many cultural and religious institutions in the 1930s. It has been slated by the Shànghǎi government for long-term redevelopment, while preserving a number of heritage buildings. (When complete, Wàitānyuán will be bordered by Nán Sūzhōu Lù in the north, Sìchuān Lù in the west, the Bund on the east, and Diānchí Lù in the south.) The initial phase included making this a pedestrian-only street at the center of Wàitānyuán

Plaza, and restoring the buildings along the western side. Starting at the top at no. 209, the former **China Baptist Publication Society Building** is a superb red and brown brick structure by Ladislav Hudec, completed in 1930. Running south, in a row of gorgeous buildings (pick your favorite) are the 1927 **Lyceum Building,** the 1923 **Associated Mission Building,** the 1927 **Somekh Mansion,** the 1933 **YWCA** (the YWCA's primary mission was to educate, not proselytize, and was the only foreign organization allowed to continue operating after 1949), the 1904 **Yuanming Yuan Apartments,** and the stately 1908 **Ampire Building.** To the east is the Peninsula Hotel with its gallery of luxury shops.

Turn right (west) at Běijīng Dōng Lù, passing the 1897 Andrews and George Building, and the 1929 National Industrial Bank of China, and take a right (north) onto Hǔqiū Lù where you'll find:

## 5 Rockbund Art Museum

The museum (p. 181) is housed in the Palmer and Turner–designed former Royal Asiatic Society (RAS) building (completed 1932), an Art Deco structure with Chinese motifs like the balcony and octagonal *bagua* designs in front. When the building was home to the RAS, it once housed a collection of around 15,000 volumes, which miraculously survived World War II and the Cultural Revolution, and can be consulted at the Shànghǎi Library Bibliotheca Zi-Ka-Wei (p. 189). Take a peek inside even if you're not interested in the art.

Head back south to Běijīng Dōng Lù and take a left (going east), past the Peninsula Hotel all the way back to the Bund. The two buildings north of Běijīng Dōng Lù are the former **Banque de L'Indo-Chine** (no. 29), a French classic structure built in 1911, and the **Glen Line Building** (no. 28), built in 1922, both now occupied by the Everbright Bank. The Glen Line Building was the American Consulate for a brief spell after World War II. South of Běijīng Dōng Lù on the Bund, you'll find:

## 6 Jardine Matheson Building (No. 27, now the Shànghǎi Foreign Trade Building)

Completed in 1922, this was one of the first and most powerful foreign trading companies to take root in Shànghǎi. Its founders, Scotsmen William Jardine and James Matheson, had been some of the earliest profiteers from the opium trade. Next door is the former **Yangtze Insurance Building** (no. 26, now the Agricultural Bank of China), built in 1916. The building at no. 24 Zhōngshān Dōng Yī Lù is now the **Industrial & Commercial Bank of China** (formerly the Yokohama Specie Bank), possessed of a nicely restored lobby and worth a quick peek to whet your appetite for the splendors that lie ahead.

The last building on this block is the:

## 7 Bank of China (No. 23)

Built in 1937 by the Chiang Kai-shek Nationalist government, this Art Deco building with a Chinese roof has always been and still is the **Bank of China.** During its construction, there was a competition between the bank director H. H. Kung (Chiang Kai-shek's brother-in-law) and Victor Sassoon, the owner of the Peace Hotel next door, for the claim to the tallest building on the Bund.

Sassoon won, barely, with the addition of a small tower on top of the Peace Hotel. Take a look inside the bank for its grand interior.

Next door, on the corner of Nánjīng Lù, is a Bund landmark, the:

## 8 Peace Hotel (No. 20)

Built in 1929 as both the private residence of the Sassoon family and as a grand hotel, the **Cathay,** this is a living museum of Art Deco, capped by its famous pyramid roof. Noël Coward wrote his play *Private Lives* at the Peace Hotel in 1930, W. Somerset Maugham was a guest, and Steven Spielberg later filmed part of *Empire of the Sun* (based on J. G. Ballard's memoir of growing up as an expatriate during the Japanese occupation) here. Step in for a spot of tea, if you need a break or simply check out the restored Art Deco lobby of the hotel which reopened in July 2010 after a 2-year restoration.

Immediately across Nánjīng Lù is the:

## 9 Swatch Art Peace Hotel (formerly Palace Hotel, No. 19)

Built between 1904 and 1909 by the Sassoons, this white-and-red-brick hotel started as the Palace Hotel, was later the South Building of the Peace Hotel, but has most recently been restored by the Swiss Swatch Group into a swanky hotel cum artists' studios, with exhibition space dedicated to contemporary art. Even if the various Swatch-brand watches (including one marked "Opium Commission" in reference to the hotel hosting the first meeting of the International Opium Commission in 1909) in the ground floor boutiques don't tempt you, take a gander at the grand interiors of the building, which have been lovingly restored.

## 10 Take a Break ☕

Stop for a coffee or a refresher either on the roof terrace of the Swatch Art Peace Hotel or head for the Sibilla Boutique Café on the ground floor of Bund 18, the next building to the south. The cafe serves Italian coffee, panini, and a range of desserts amid the glittering chandeliers and marble.

## 11 Bund 18 (formerly Chartered Bank of India, Australia, and China, No. 18)

Built in 1923, this striking building with the two Ionic stone columns was completely redeveloped into a high-end commercial and restaurant complex in 2004. Occupants include the popular French eatery Mr & Mrs Bund, a raft of high-end boutiques, and the hippest bar in town on the roof.

Next door to the south, the former **North China Daily News Building** (no. 17, now the AIA Building), completed in 1921 in a late-Renaissance style, was originally home to the oldest English-language newspaper in China, the *North China Daily News,* where American writer Emily Hahn once worked. It now houses the American International Assurance Company (AIA). At the end of the block, the former **Bank of Taiwan Building** (no. 16, now the China Merchants Bank), with its simple classical lines, was built in 1924 and was actually a Japanese bank (Taiwan was occupied by Japan in 1895), despite its name.

In the next block of the Bund, across Jiǔjiāng Lù, is the:

## 12 Russo-Chinese Bank Building (No. 15, now the China Foreign Exchange Trade System Building)

Built in 1901, this was the first tile-face construction in Shànghǎi, a wide and squat edifice. Next door is the modernistic former **Bank of Communications Building** (no. 14, now the Bank of Shànghǎi/Shànghǎi Federation of Trade Unions), built in 1940, its large entrance framed in copper sheets.

Cross Hànkǒu Lù to a venerable landmark, the:

## 13 Shànghǎi Customs House (No. 13)

Built in 1927, the classical-style Customs House is fronted by four massive granite Roman columns and topped by a rising bell tower (known as "Big Ching"). The repainted lobby has beautiful mosaics of Chinese junks, but the rest of the building consists mostly of crowded offices that are not open to the public.

Next door is the even more spectacular:

## 14 Hong Kong and Shànghǎi Bank (No. 12, now the Shànghǎi Pǔdōng Development Bank)

This gorgeous classic European building with grand columns and archways, and capped by a huge dome, was built in 1923 (G. L. Wilson of Palmer and Turner was the chief architect). Inside the massive revolving doors, the restored dome and lobby are the most magnificent on the Bund. The foyer, supported by marble columns, is decorated with eight gold-trimmed mosaic panels, each a salute to one of the world's financial capitals at that time (Bangkok, Hong Kong, Tokyo, New York, London, Paris, Calcutta, and of course Shànghǎi). The bank's lobby is also stunning, restored in alabaster and polished wood. The English hailed it as the most spectacular building ever erected between the Suez Canal and the Bering Strait. Between 1955 and 1995, this building served as Shànghǎi's city hall.

Head back out to the Bund and take a detour right (west) onto Fúzhōu Lù past a Tudor-style house (no. 44, Fúzhōu Lù), formerly the Caldbeck, MacGregor & Company wine importers. Head to the:

## 15 Intersection of Fúzhōu Lù & Jiāngxī Lù

This intersection has four somewhat dilapidated but still grand colonial buildings. Notice the two identical Art Deco structures on the northeast (today's Metropole Hotel) and southeast (formerly the Hamilton House, an apartment complex that has a newly renovated restaurant on the ground floor) corners, both built by Palmer and Turner. The building at the northwest corner lodged the Shànghǎi Municipal Council, the governing body of the International Settlement. Just a bit farther west at Fúzhōu Lù 209 is the former American Club, a classic red-brick American Georgian–style building with marble columns. Today, it's the Shànghǎi People's Court. In the old days, Fúzhōu Lù was both the red-light district and the location of Shànghǎi's publishing houses and bookstores, with many of the latter still located at the western end of the street.

Head back up (east) Fúzhōu Lù to the Bund and turn right. The building at no. 9 is currently the China Merchant Holdings Company with its ground floor now developed into yet another luxury boutique; next to it stands the former:

## 16 Hospital of the Shànghǎi Navigation Company (No. 7, now the Bangkok Bank)

This handsome late French Renaissance building is one of the oldest buildings on the Bund, built in 1906. It was the site of China's first telephone switchboard. Next door is the former **Commercial Bank of China** (no. 6), an English Gothic structure. It was built in 1906, but what you see today, though still intriguing, is a stripped-down version of the original, which had many more pillars, cornices, and chimneys. In the continuation of the trend to develop the Bund buildings, no. 6 is now home to several swanky dining and shopping establishments. Next door on the north corner of Guǎngdōng Lù is the former headquarters of the **Nishin Navigation Company** (no. 5, now the Huáxià Bank Building). Another modernistic, Western-style building, it was constructed in 1925 by its Japanese owners. Today, it's home to a slew of restaurants, but is best known for its seventh-floor inhabitants, the restaurant and bar M on the Bund.

On the south side of Gūngdōng Lù is:

## 17 Three on the Bund (formerly the Union Insurance Company Building, No. 3)

One of the toniest addresses in town, this newly restored Renaissance-style building from 1922 is the first of the traditional Bund buildings to be developed into a high-end retail and restaurant complex. Besides hosting world-renowned chefs like Jean-Georges Vongerichten and David Laris, the building is home to the Evian Spa, luxury shops including Giorgio Armani's flagship store, and an art gallery showing the works of contemporary Chinese artists. Entrance is on Guǎngdōng Lù.

Next door to the south is one of the most famous buildings on the Bund, the former:

## 18 Shànghǎi Club (No. 2)

Built in 1910, this was once the city's most extravagant private club, an English Renaissance structure with elaborate white columns and baroque attic windows. It housed the famous black-and-white granite **Long Bar,** at more than 30m (98 ft.), reputedly the longest bar in the world; this was the watering hole for the "old boys' club" that ruled colonial Shànghǎi. For much of the late–20th century, this was the Dōng Fēng Hotel. Today, it has been transformed into part of the tony **Waldorf Astoria Hotel.** The last building on the block, at the corner of Yán'ān Dōng Lù, is the former **Asiatic Petroleum Building,** also known as the **McBain Building** (no. 1, now the China Pacific Insurance Company). Built in 1916, it's a substantial structure employing the ubiquitous baroque pillars, Roman stone archway, and Greek columns.

You can conclude your walk at this point, or cross Zhōngshān Dōng Lù, take a quick look inside the tiny Bund Repository inside the Signal Tower, and head north on the new Bund promenade for more views of the Bund skyline and Pǔdōng. Or you can take a much-deserved break in one of the cafes or restaurants on the west side of the street.

## 19 Winding Down 🍷

Head to the north side of Guǎngdōng Lù for the elevator to M on the Bund (seventh floor). M offers a splendid lounge, world-class Mediterranean cuisine, and a spacious balcony overlooking the Bund and the Huángpǔ River. Alternatively, Three on the Bund (south side of Guǎngdōng Lù opposite M) features top-notch French cuisine at Jean Georges (fourth floor), inventive Shanghainese dining at the Whampoa Club (sixth floor), creative "new world" cuisine at Laris (sixth floor), and inexpensive cafe food at New Heights (seventh-floor terrace). All are open for lunch and dinner.

## WALKING TOUR 2  NÁNJĪNG LÙ

| | |
|---|---|
| START: | **Shànghǎi Centre (Metro: Jing'an Temple).** |
| FINISH: | **Peace Hotel, the Bund (Metro: Nanjing Rd. [E]).** |
| TIME: | **2 to 3 hours (for the western half, from Shànghǎi Centre to People's Square/Xīzàng Lù); another 2 to 3 hours to tour the eastern half of Nánjīng Lù (from Xīzàng Zhōng Lù to the Bund). Those who want to see it all should allot a full day (7km/4½ miles).** |
| BEST TIMES: | **Any weekday starting by 9:30am or at 2:30pm (if you're only going to walk a portion), to avoid midday crowds.** |
| WORST TIMES: | **Weekends are impossibly crowded. Most stores aren't open before 10am, but they stay open late, often until 10pm.** |

Nánjīng Lù is the most famous shopping street in China, long celebrated for its large department stores, silk shops, and fashionable clothing stores. In colonial Shànghǎi, this was the main thoroughfare running through the International Settlement, built originally as a pathway to successive horse-race tracks. Today, this famous stretch is known as **Nánjīng Dōng Lù (Nánjīng Road East)**, while the western portion, **Nánjīng Xī Lù,** is the current name for the former Bubbling Well Road, so named because of a now-displaced well located at the western end of the street (today's intersection with Huáshān Lù). **People's Park (Rénmín Gōngyuán)** is the half-way point, dividing the eastern and western sections. Today's Nánjīng Lù still has remnants of its past retail glories, but the department stores have been modernized and Western-style boutiques are rapidly cornering the fashion trade. There are still plenty of colonial period structures sandwiched in along the avenue (hotels, offices, department stores). If you're short on time or want to save your legs, begin your stroll at People's Park (at Xīzàng Zhōng Lù) and head east for the river along the **Nánjīng Lù Pedestrian Mall.** You can walk either the east or west half of Nánjīng Lù in a little more than an hour, if you don't stop—but you should.

---

To begin, take a taxi or walk straight east from the Jing'an Temple Metro station down Nánjīng Xī Lù to:

## 1 Shànghǎi Centre (Shànghǎi Shāngchéng; No. 1376)

This premier all-in-one complex is home to the 42-floor Portman Ritz-Carlton Hotel, expensive residential apartments (mostly for foreign business families), a medical clinic, a supermarket, ATMs, and upscale boutiques and restaurants. Starbucks is here, but if you need a more substantial breakfast, a light salad lunch, or a fresh fruit smoothie, pay a quick visit to the diner Element Fresh (Unit 112).

If you have plenty of time, cross the street south to the:

## 2 Shànghǎi Exhibition Centre (Shànghǎi Zhánlǎn Zhōngxīn)

Built in 1955 with help from the Soviet Union (then a staunch Communist ally), this somber, grandiose monument to socialist realism is yet another chapter in Shànghǎi's history of foreign architecture. Eye-catching on the outside, it has a decaying air on the inside, where there are regular exhibits that are not very interesting. Before 1955, this was the site of the 11-hectare (26-acre) Hardoon Gardens, a colonial-era fantasy estate built by millionaire Silas Hardoon.

Continue east along the north side of Nánjīng Xī Lù across Xīkāng Lù and take a quick peek into:

## 3 Plaza 66 (Hénglóng Guǎngchǎng, No. 1266)

This is as upscale and as Western a shopping mall as you'll find in Shànghǎi, arguably with the city's largest collection of luxury brand shops under one roof. Hermès, Dior, Versace, Cartier, Louis Vuitton—they're all here. Don't let the lack of foot traffic fool you—customers, when they do show up, drop off *yuán* notes by the suitcase-full. One shop reportedly had to shutter for a few hours just to count the bills.

Head east 1 block and turn left (north) onto Shǎnxī Běi Lù for 1½ blocks, crossing Běijīng Xī Lù. Halfway up the block on the east side of the street is the former:

## 4 Ohel Rachel Synagogue (Yóutài Jiàotáng, Shǎnxī Běi Lù, No. 500)

Built in 1920 by Jacob Sassoon (uncle to Victor Sassoon who built the Peace Hotel) in memory of his wife Rachel, this Greek Revival–style vine-trellised synagogue served the wealthy Sephardic Jewish community until 1952. It was renovated and sanctified for the visit of Hillary Clinton in 1998, and reopened in May 2010 as a living synagogue for the Jewish community to use for Shabbat and holiday services. It also has been on the list of the 100 most endangered sites of the World Monuments Watch.

Head back down (south) Shǎnxī Běi Lù and cross to the south side of Nánjīng Lù. If you're interested in ceramics, take a peek inside:

## 5 Shànghǎi Jīngdé Zhèn Porcelain Artware (No. 1185)

This corner emporium carries a full array of classic Chinese pottery and porcelain, much of it from factories and artisans in Jīngdé Zhèn, one of China's most celebrated pottery centers (located up the Yángzǐ River from Shànghǎi).

Continue east on the south side of Nánjīng Xī Lù until you come to Màomíng Běi Lù and the giant **Uniqlo Store** (the biggest in the world and their flagship store in Shànghǎi) at the corner. This also marks the start of the pedestrian food street:

# Walking Tour 2: Nánjīng Lù

1 Shànghǎi Centre (Shànghǎi Shāngchéng)
上海商城

2 Shànghǎi Exhibition Centre
(Shànghǎi Zhǎnlǎn Zhōngxīn)
上海展览中心

3 Plaza 66 (Hénglóng Guǎngchǎng)
恒隆广场

4 Ohel Rachel Synagogue (Yóutài Jiàotáng)
犹太教堂

5 Shànghǎi Jǐngdé Zhèn Porcelain Artware
(Jǐngdé Zhèn Yìshù Cíqì)
景德镇艺术瓷器

6 Wújiāng Lù Leisure Street
吴江路休闲街

7 Wáng Jiā Shā Dumpling Restaurant
王家沙饺子馆

8 Former International Recreation Club

9 Tóng Yì Lǐ Lòng
同益里弄

10 Tomorrow Square (Míngtiān Guǎngchǎng)
明天广场

11 Shànghǎi Art Museum
(Shànghǎi Měishù Guǎn)
上海美术馆

12 People's Park (Rénmín Gōngyuán)
人民公园

13 Park Hotel (Guójì Fàndiàn)
国际饭店

14 Pacific Hotel (Jīnmén Dàjiǔdiàn)
金门大酒店

15 Moore Memorial Church (Mù'ēn Táng)
沐恩堂

16 Nánjīng Lù Pedestrian Mall
(Nánjīng Lù Bùxíng Jiē)
南京路步行街

17 The No. 1 Department Store
(Shànghǎi Dìyī Bǎihuò Shāngdiàn)
上海第一百货商店

18 Shànghǎi No. 1 Provisions Store
(Shànghǎi Dìyī Shípǐn Shāngdiàn)
上海第一食品商店

19 Shànghǎi Fashion Company
(Shànghǎi Shízhuāng Gōngsī)
上海时装公司

20 Huálián Commercial Building
华联商厦

21 Century Square (Shìjì Guǎngchǎng)
世纪广场

THE BUND PROMENADE
外滩

Zhongshan Dong Yi Lu 中山东一路

Peace Hotel
和平饭店

Henan Zhong Lu 河南中路

NANJING RD. (E) M

Shanxi Nan Lu 山西南路

Fujian Zhong Lu 福建中路

Hubei Lu
湖北路

Bar Tazza D'Oro

Zhejiang Zhong Lu 浙江中路

PEOPLE'S SQUARE

Xizang Zhong Lu 西藏中路

Barbarossa

Huanghe Lu 黄河路

Kathleen's 5

Huangpi Bei Lu 黄陂北路

Chengdu Bei Lu 成都北路

JW Marriott
Lobby Lounge

Wujiang Lu
吴江路

Qinghai Lu 青海路

NANJING RD. (W) M

Shimen Lu 石门路

Maoming Lu 茂名路

Xinzha Lu 新闸路

Beijing Xi Lu 北京西路

Shanxi Bei Lu 陕西北路

Yan'an Zhong Lu 延安中路

"Take a Break"

Jing'an Station
静安站

## 6 Wújiāng Lù Leisure Street

One of five food streets in Shànghăi, this recently renovated pedestrian lane is lined with shops, restaurants, coffee shops, bars, and food stalls, and is a great spot for people-watching. If you need a refresher at this point, **Cristal Restaurant** at 269 Wújiāng Lù, fourth floor (✆ **021/6136-1388**), is good for everything from a stiff cappuccino to a delicious pasta.

Otherwise, continue east along Wújiāng Lù passing JIA Hotel (in a refurbished 1920s building) and cross Tàixìng Lù. Take a left at Shímén Yī Lù back to Nánjīng Lù. Just to the left on the south side of the street is:

## 7 Wáng Jiā Shā Dumpling Restaurant (No. 805)

One of Shànghăi's oldest and most popular diners for cheap local eats has been renovated. You can watch women wrapping *xiăolóng bāo* dumplings through the glass windows. Or join the crowds in ordering up your own steamer of dumplings.

Cross to the north side of Nánjīng Lù and continue east, passing at no. 778 the 1928 Art Deco **Denis Apartments.** East of Shímén Yī Lù is the:

## 8 Former International Recreation Club (No. 722)

This handsome, sprawling colonial structure was designed by Palmer and Turner and built in 1929 as the International Recreation Club. In those days, the interiors included a dance hall with sprung floor, a theater, and a dining room. In 1941, it became the Jewish Club of Shànghăi. Unfortunately, the interiors are off limits these days as the building belongs to an air-conditioning manufacturing company.

Continue east on Nánjīng Lù past the skyscraper complex (the **Shànghăi Broadcasting & Television International News Exchange Centre** at no. 585) and cross the wide and very busy Chéngdū Bĕi Lù *very carefully*. On the south side of the street at no. 479 is:

## 9 Tóng Yì LīLòng (No. 479)

Here is an example of the classic lane (*lĭlòng*) housing that proliferated throughout Shànghăi for over a century. In this particular warren of lanes, bas-relief sculptures have been put up on the sides of houses by the local Party committee to boost residents' patriotism by reminding them of all the revolutionary activities that have gone on at the nearby People's Square. None of today's residents seem to pay much attention.

Continuing east on the south side of Nánjīng Lù, you'll pass **Gōngdélín** (no. 445), Shànghăi's most famous vegetarian restaurant (p. 114). In front of you is:

## 10 Tomorrow Square (Míntiān Guăngchăng)

This architecturally intriguing rocket tower, which does a 90-degree horizontal shift at the 38th floor, is home to the JW Marriott Hotel (the tallest hotel on the Bund side of the river), the first Mandara Spa in China, and a Ferrari dealership.

**11 Take a Break 💽**

If you need to freshen up or take a break, stop for a cup of tea on the 38th floor lobby lounge of the JW Marriott Hotel (Wànyí Jiǔdiàn), where you can choose from 40 different tea vintages while gazing on stunning panoramas of the city. The hotel also serves one of the best afternoon teas (Mon–Fri 2:30–5:30pm) if you're here in the afternoon. There's no better place for a bird's-eye appreciation of how far you've come and how much farther you have to go. Alternatively, you can jump straight to dessert and cappuccino at Kathleen's 5 (✆ 021/6327-0004) atop the upcoming Shànghǎi Art Museum, or kick back at the Moroccan-themed Barbarossa (p. 251), sitting pretty on a lake in the middle of People's Park, which is coming up.

Just east of Huángpí Běi Lù is:

## 12 Shànghǎi Art Museum (Shànghǎi Měishùguǎn, No. 325)

This five-story landmark has been beautifully restored to its colonial splendor (p. 182). There's a lovely restaurant (Kathleen's 5) inside, too. At this point, you're at the northwestern edge of Rénmín Gōngyuán and Rénmín Guǎngchǎng (People's Park and People's Square; see p. 176).

Enter via either the western or northwestern entrance:

## 13 People's Park (Rénmín Gōngyuán, No. 231)

This is the city's biggest downtown green, which, together with People's Square, covers what was the Shànghǎi Race Track in colonial times. Smack dab in the middle of this pleasant park is Shànghǎi's new Museum of Contemporary Art (p. 180), worth a quick tour if you are interested in the modern Chinese art scene. Or refresh yourself with a cup of coffee at Barbarossa in the middle of the lake. If you're here on weekend afternoons, you'll see a large crowd gathered around the lake in what has become a matchmaking marketplace. Older singles gather here, as do many parents of younger singles. The latter often have profiles of their offspring in hand or attached to nearby bulletin boards, in an attempt to find dates for their children, who are apparently too busy working to do it themselves. Such is life in modern China—perhaps not so different from life in any other modern city.

Exit the park via the northern (main) entrance. Cross to the north side of Nánjīng Lù. Straight ahead is the sleek **Grand Theatre,** built in 1933, which used to show first-run Hollywood movies before 1949 and, now refurbished, still screens the occasional American blockbuster. Head east, crossing Huánghé Lù (another restaurant street) to the:

## 14 Park Hotel (Guójì Fàndiàn, No. 170)

Designed by prolific Hungarian architect Ladislav Hudec (1893–1958), who also designed the Grand Theatre, this hotel was the tallest building outside North America when it was built in 1934. It also boasted the fastest elevators in Shànghǎi at the time. Young, fashionable Chinese people came here in droves to party the night away. Chinese-American Architect I. M. Pei reportedly said that it was the Park Hotel, which he first saw as a young boy in Shànghǎi, that inspired his interest in architecture. Don't miss its finely restored Art Deco interiors.

If colonial architecture excites you, right next door at no. 150 is the **former Foreign YMCA** building (1926–1933) with a gorgeous Beaux Arts facade; it is currently the Shànghǎi Sports Club. To its east is the:

## 15 Pacific Hotel (Jīnmén Dàjiǔdiàn, No. 108)

Built in 1926, serving first as the China United Assurance Company, then as the Overseas Chinese Hotel, this classic Italian-style hotel is a bit run-down but still has a stunning Art Deco lobby of coffered ceilings and carved columns. Just to the east, the building with the spaceship roof is the Radisson New World Hotel, and right next to it is the **New World City** Shopping Center (Nánjīng Dōng Lù 830), home to mainland China's first Madame Tussauds Museum (p. 180).

At this point, using the underpass on the south side of Nánjīng Lù, cross Xīzàng Zhōng Lù, one of Shànghǎi's main north-south thoroughfares and the beginning of the eastern section of Nánjīng Lù. As you emerge, on your right (south) past the sky-scraper Le Méridien Hotel is:

## 16 Moore Memorial Church (Mù'ēn Táng)

This Protestant church was established by American missionaries in 1887, and rebuilt in 1931 when it was designed by architect Ladislav Hudec. It was used as a middle school during the Cultural Revolution. In 1979, it was the first church to reopen in Shànghǎi (p. 173).

Return to the wide, vehicle-free:

## 17 Nánjīng Lù Pedestrian Mall (Nánjīng Lù Bùxíng Jiē)

From here east to Hénán Zhōng Lù (which is 2 blocks from the Bund and the river), strollers can enjoy a pedestrian-only mall, designed by Arle Jean Marie Carpentier and Associates (France), and opened in 1999. Here, new buildings dwarf the colonial-period landmarks of Nánjīng Lù, but there's still plenty of history along the way. *Caution:* Although this is a pedestrian mall, the cross streets (north-south) still permit vehicular traffic, so look both ways at controlled intersections.

At the northern end of Nánjīng Lù is:

## 18 The No. 1 Department Store (No. 800)

In the old days, this emporium was known as the **Sun,** one of Nánjīng Lù's "Big Four" department stores. The Sun's building was designed by Chinese architects, opened its doors in 1934, and was the first store in China to use an escalator. Later, renamed the No. 1 Department Store complex, it attracted more than 150,000 shoppers daily; and it may be doing more business than ever these days with the addition of the 22-story tower on its East Building, its first 11 floors devoted to retailing.

Those too tired to walk the rest of the street can take a **sightseeing trolley,** a three-car electric train that weaves its way up and down the length of the pedestrian mall; tickets, purchased onboard, cost ¥2 .

In the next block (across Guìzhōu Lù) on the north side is the:

## 19 Shànghǎi No. 1 Provisions Store (No. 700)

Formerly known as Sun Sun, another of Shànghǎi's "Big Four" department stores, this shop is still in its old building, where it opened in 1926. A Pizza Hut

*The Shanghainese were inordinately proud of Nanking Road, not only because of its shops overflowing with goods, but because there was truly nothing like it in the rest of China. It was so modern, and nothing enthralled the Shanghainese more than modernity. While the rest of the nation was still sunk in rusticity, here were young girls clacking about on Italian heels, photographic studios, department stores, special offers and seasonal sales, and publicity gimmicks which called for bands to play and even a dwarf got up in a top-hat to cry "Fantastic value! Fantastic value!" outside the shop.*

—Pan Ling, *In Search of Old Shànghǎi*, 1982

and McDonald's have attached themselves to the old store. Just to the east is a stunning block-long gray Art Deco building, the:

## 20 Shànghǎi Fashion Company (No. 650)

The third of the "Big Four," this was the former Sincere Department Store. A hotel now occupies part of the premises.

Across the street on the south side is the:

## 21 Huálián Commercial Building (No. 635)

The last of the "Big Four," this was the former **Wing On,** opened in 1918, a famous department store chain transplanted to Hong Kong after 1949.

At this point, the mall crosses a vast square at the busy intersection with Zhèjiāng Zhōng Lù and Húběi Lù. In the early colonial days, this intersection was the spot where electric trams heading west on Nánjīng Lù were rotated on a wooden plate so they could make the return journey eastward.

Continuing east on the south side is:

## 22 Century Square (Shìjì Guǎngchǎng)

This block-long square hosts open-air performances and exhibits. Stop for a cappuccino at the open-air cafe in the square, Bar Tazza D'Oro. If you're interested in a bit more shopping, there's a street of specialty shops at the next intersection running north of Nánjīng Lù along Fújiàn Zhōng Lù, where you can find stores selling traditional Chinese handicrafts such as chopsticks, tea, and carved-wood products. At this point, the walking tour is almost at an end, unless you want to engage in more shopping.

There are a number of ways to conclude this tour. You can head 3 blocks east past Fújiàn Zhōng Lù to Hénán Zhōng Lù, which marks the end of the pedestrian mall. From there you can hop on Metro Line 2 (Nánjīng Dōng Lù station) or catch a cab to your next destination. Or to see this through, visitors can wind up their stroll at the recently restored Art Deco **Peace Hotel** (**Hépíng Fàndiàn,** no. 20, p. 86), which is 3 more blocks east of Hénán Zhōng Lù. On the south side of Nánjīng Lù across from the Peace Hotel is the former **Palace Hotel,** now also restored as the Swatch Art Peace Hotel, no. 19. From here, you can catch a cab back to your hotel.

## 23  Winding Down ☕

The nicest place to end this stroll is the landmark Peace Hotel (Hépíng Fàndiàn, no. 20), at the intersection of Nánjīng Dōng Lù and the Bund (described in detail on p. 158). Check out the gorgeously restored Art Deco interiors, while you sip tea and refreshments in the lobby lounge. Or head upstairs to the terrace of the Cathy Room where you can admire some stunning views of the city skyline and the Bund.

## WALKING TOUR 3  THE OLD CHINESE CITY

| | |
|---|---|
| START: | **Shànghǎi Lǎo Jiē (Shànghǎi Old Street), Nánshì, Huángpǔ District (Metro: Yu Garden).** |
| FINISH: | **Dàjīng Lù, Nánshì, Huángpǔ District (Metro: Dàshìjiè or Yu Garden).** |
| TIME: | **2 to 4 hours.** |
| BEST TIMES: | **Weekday mornings or early Sunday morning (for the Fúyòu antiques market).** |
| WORST TIMES: | **Weekends are packed with tourists and shoppers. If you must tour on the weekend, go early.** |

The Old Chinese City (Nánshì), located just southwest of the Bund, was the first part of Shànghǎi to be settled. In the early days, Shànghǎi had a city wall (which followed the course of today's Rénmín Lù and Zhōnghuá Lù) that came down when the last dynasty fell, in 1911. During the colonial era (1842–1949) when Westerners had their own enclaves (concessions), this was the main Chinese district, where foreigners almost never ventured. Considerably more frequented by foreigners these days (though mostly around the Yù Yuán Old Town Bazaar area), Nánshì, with its narrow winding streets and old houses, is still one of the lesser-explored parts of town. Although this walk focuses mainly on the Old Town Bazaar (bounded by Rénmín Lù, Hénán Nán Lù, Fāngbāng Zhōng Lù, and Zhōnghuá Lù) with all its tourist attractions, hopefully you'll get from it a sense of traditional life around the old Chinese streets as well. Entire sections of the district are being torn down and replaced with new developments as quickly as this is being written, so hurry and get your walking shoes on.

---

There are many entry points into the maze of the Old Town Bazaar. To avoid congestion, begin your stroll at the intersection of Hénán Nán Lù and Fāngbāng Zhōng Lù on the southwest side of the Old Town Bazaar, where you'll pass through a traditional-style Chinese gate and enter:

## 1  Shànghǎi Lǎo Jiē (Shànghǎi Old Street)

This stretch of Fāngbāng Zhōng Lù was renovated in 1999 as an Old Town theme street. The traditional shop houses, selling antiques, collectibles, ethnic crafts, and tea, reflect the architectural and cultural evolution of Shànghǎi as you walk east, from the Míng Dynasty through the Qīng Dynasty into the Chinese Republican era.

Just inside the entrance and immediately to your left is the irresistible:

## 2  Fúyòu Antiques Market/Cáng Bǎo Lóu

This is still the best and liveliest antiques market for browsing in Shànghǎi (especially early Sun morning), where four floors of vendors sell everything

# Walking Tour 3: Nánshì (Shànghǎi's Old Chinese City)

南市
Nánshì

Shànghǎi

1 Shànghǎi Lǎo Jiē (Shànghǎi Old Street)
上海老街

2 Fúyòu Antiques Market/Cáng Bǎo Lóu
福佑市场 / 藏宝楼

3 Food Stalls and Lane Housing

4 Chénghuáng Miào (Temple of the Town God)
城隍庙

5 Curiosity Stores

6 Bridge of Nine Turnings (Jiǔqū Qiáo)
九曲桥

7 Húxīntíng (Mid-Lake Pavilion) Teahouse
湖心亭茶社

8 Yù Yuán (Yù Garden)
豫园

9 Small Commodities Street (Xiǎoshāngpǐn Jiè)
小商品街

10 Chénxiāng Gé
沉香阁

11 Dàjìng Lù Markets (Dàjìng Lù Shìchǎng)
大境路市场

12 Báiyún Guàn (White Cloud Daoist Temple)
白云观

13 Ancient City Wall (Gǔ Chéngqiáng)
古城墙

from coins and ceramics to jewelry and Russian cameras. Be prepared to stay awhile; there's a lot of junk to sift through, but also the occasional real find.

Continue east, entering or bypassing the shops as your interest warrants. In the second block after the Hòujiā Lù intersection, the two-story **Old Shànghǎi Teahouse** (Fāngbāng Zhōng Lù 385) can provide a refreshing cup of tea or juice if you're already fatigued from shopping. Otherwise, continue your way east past the Yu Fashion Center and Dragon Gate Mall to your right until you come to the **street Sì Pái Lóu** (right) with its :

## 3 Food Stalls & Lane Housing

Having been spared the bulldozer as of press time, this street allows a wonderful glimpse into the daily life of ordinary Chinese around the old city. Very basic food stalls sell everything from fresh vegetables and meat to local specialties like *chòu dòufu* (stinky tofu) and *shēngjiān bāo* (pan-fried dumplings). You'll also find little lanes branching off the street (such as *kāngjiā long*/Kāngjiā Lane about 50m/164 ft. down Sì Pái Lóu running east) that lead to the lane housing so common in Shànghǎi. The houses here are considerably older and more dilapidated and cramped than the lane houses in the foreign concessions. Wander around and you might still stumble upon the night-soil worker making his rounds in the morning or residents playing mah-jongg outdoors.

Head back to Fāngbāng Zhōng Lù and retrace your steps west (left) past Ānrén Jiē. On the north side of the street is the stone arch entrance of:

## 4 Chénghuáng Miào (Temple of the Town God)

This Daoist temple, rebuilt many times since the early–15th century and most recently in the 1990s, can be quickly toured from 8:30am to 4:30pm daily (admission ¥10; see p. 169).

Exit the temple and zigzag your way north by following the lane along the west side of the temple. Along the way you'll find a series of:

## 5 Curiosity Stores

Here, you'll find novelty stores such as the Pear Syrup Shop (selling old China's answer to cough drops) and the Five Flavor Bean Shop (selling a famous Shànghǎi snack, *wǔxiāng dòu* [five-flavor lima beans]) right next to a not-so-novel Starbucks. By now, you should be in the main square with the teahouse floating on the artificial lake to your north. To get there, follow the:

## 6 Bridge of Nine Turnings (Jiǔ Qū Qiáo)

This zigzag bridge is supposed to be propitious, as demons were believed to be afraid of corners. By contrast, camera-wielding tourists appear addicted to them.

The bridge leads to the fine:

## 7 Húxīngtíng (Mid-Lake Pavilion) Teahouse (Yùyuán Lù 257)

More than 200 years old, this is Shànghǎi's most famous place to drink tea (open 8:30am–10pm). Step inside, take a look at the teas for sale on the first floor, and head upstairs for a cup and a Shànghǎi snack.

8 Take a Break 🍴

**For a more substantial repast, lunch on a variety of Shànghǎi dumplings and noodle dishes at the Nánxiáng Mántou Diàn (p. 115) that lines the west shore of the lake.**

The north side of the lake is the location of the main entrance to Shànghǎi's most complete classical garden:

## 9 Yù Yuán (Yù Garden)

Completed in 1577, this pleasant private garden (Ānrén Lù 218) is a maze of ponds, bridges, pavilions, and small gardens, but it's impossible to get lost for long (p. 160). The garden is open from 8:30am to 5:30pm and is usually quite crowded (admission ¥40). Exit at the southern Inner Garden (Nèi Yuán) and find your way back to the Húxīntíng Teahouse by walking west a block on Yùyuán Lù. If you haven't had your fill of shopping, the whole northwest part of the bazaar complex is chock-full of large and small stores selling everything from glittering gems to Chinese medicinal herbs.

Those seeking more curios can follow the lane outside the Nánxiáng Mántou Diàn as it winds north. Take a left onto:

## 10 Small Commodities Street (Xiǎoshāngpīn Jiē)

Along this street (Yùyuán Lǎo Lù), you'll find shops specializing in everything from musical instruments and chopsticks to scissors and bamboo crafts.

At the northern end of the street, take a left onto Fúyòu Lù (west), passing the Shànghǎi Old Restaurant, then take another left (south) down Jiùjiàochǎng Lù. West of the Tóng Hán Chuán Táng Chinese Medicine Store, take a right (west) onto Chénxiānggé Lù, where you'll find the temple:

## 11 Chénxiāng Gé (Chénxiānggé Lù 29)

While Yù Yuán was built to honor Pān Yǔnduān's father, this small Buddhist temple was built for his mother (p. 170).

Continue west along Chénxiānggé Lù, take a left (south) onto Hòujiā Lù, then a right (west) onto Zǐhuá Lù, at the end of which is Hénán Nán Lù, marking the western boundary of the Old Town Bazaar. Cross Hénán Nán Lù, then jog slightly north and turn left (west) onto Dàjìng Lù. This area used to be full of old houses, many of which have been bulldozed to make way for the brand-new apartment complexes you see around you. All down the street you can still find various:

## 12 Dàjìng Lù Markets

There was a delightful open food market at Dàjìng Lù 150–160 that was in the process of being dismantled at press time, but there are still plenty of makeshift markets and smaller stalls selling everything from fresh fish and meats to spices, tea, and tofu. This is another wonderful street to catch a glimpse of daily life in the old Chinese city as housewives and grandmothers make their daily shopping rounds.

Farther west on the north side of the street is:

## 13 Báiyún Guàn (White Cloud Daoist Temple, Dàjìng Lù 239)

Peek inside this Daoist temple (p. 169), identifiable by its red walls, for a look at the hundreds of statues of Daoist deities and possibly even a Daoist service.

West of this temple on the same side of the street is the:

## 14 Ancient City Wall (Gǔchéngqiáng Dàjìng Gé, Dàjìnggé Lù 269)

Here is preserved the only remaining 50m (164 ft.) of Shànghǎi's old city wall, originally built in 1553 when it measured 8.1m (27 ft.) high and 4.8km (3 miles) around. There's a small exhibit on life in the old Chinese city for those who can't find enough signs of it in today's streets.

Although this is the end of the walk, options abound for those who have energy to spare. About 20 minutes by foot to the south is Wén Miào (Temple of Confucius), the Xiǎotáoyuán Qīngzhēn Sì (Peach Orchard Mosque), and more back streets and alleys for exploring. If more shopping is in order, Huáihǎi Zhōng Lù, the favorite modern shopping street of today's Shanghainese people, is about a 30-minute stroll to the west, while the Dōngtái Lù Antiques Market is an even closer 10-minute walk to the southwest. If food is all you can think about at this point, cross Rénmín Lù, then head north on Yúnnán Nán Lù.

## 15 Winding Down 🍺

Yúnnán Lù Měishí Jiē (Yúnnán Lù Food St.), only a quick 2 blocks north of the old city wall, is packed with a host of bright and lively Chinese restaurants, though most places don't carry English menus. For Western fare, a 10-minute taxi ride west will land you at the supermodern and chic Xīntiāndì, a pedestrian mall and a contrasting bookend to a day begun in the old Chinese city.

## WALKING TOUR 4 FRENCH CONCESSION

| | |
|---|---|
| START: | **Xīntiāndì, Lúwān District (Metro: Huangpi Rd. ★).** |
| FINISH: | **Héngshān Lù, Xúhuì District (Metro: Hengshan Rd.).** |
| TIME: | **4 to 6 hours.** |
| BEST TIMES: | **Weekday mornings and midafternoons.** |
| WORST TIMES: | **On weekends (especially Sun) and evenings, many of these streets are quite crowded with local shoppers and visitors. Lunchtime (11:30am–2pm) also brings out big crowds.** |

Shànghǎi's French Concession, consisting of a corridor running from the lower Bund between today's Yán'ān Lù and the Chinese Old Town west along Huáihǎi Lù, contains many of the city's most picturesque colonial mansions, parks, hotels, and town houses. The French arrived in 1846 and leased land just south of the British Concession's holdings. They established a series of fine residential neighborhoods west across today's Lúwān District, branching off Huáihǎi Lù, the main avenue known in colonial times as Avenue Joffre. The concession's northern border, today's Yán'ān Lù, was originally a creek named Yángjìngbāng, which was filled to become the street then known as Avenue Edouard VII. The streets in the long, sprawling settlement were lined with plane trees; the buildings, with their mansard roofs and shutters, resembled those of French towns of the time; and these neighborhoods, most now dating from the first 3 decades of the 1900s, remain much intact, although the modern construction boom has laid waste to considerable clusters of the French legacy.

# Walking Tour 4: French Concession

1 Xīntiāndì
(New Heaven and Earth)
新天地

2 Fùxīng Park
(Fùxīng Gōngyuán)
复兴公园

3 Former St. Nicholas Russian
Orthodox Church

4 Sun Yat-sen's Former Residence
(Sūn Zhōngshān Gùjū)
孙中山故居

5 Zhōu Ēnlái's Former Residence
(Zhōu Gōng Guǎn)
周公馆

"Take a Break" 

6 Ruìjīn Hotel (Ruìjīn Bīnguǎn)
瑞金宾馆

7 Màomíng Nán Lù
茂名南路

8 Okura Garden Hotel
(Huāyuán Fàndiàn)
花园饭店

9 Jǐnjiāng Hotel
(Jǐn Jiāng Fàndiàn)
锦江饭店

10 Lyceum Theatre 兰心大戏院

11 Former Russian Orthodox Cathedral
of the Holy Mother of God

12 Shànghǎi Conservatory of Music
(Shànghǎi Yīnyuè Xuéyuàn)
上海音乐学院

13 Shànghǎi Museum of Arts and Crafts
(Shànghǎi Gōngyì Měishù Bówùguǎn)
上海工艺美术博物馆

14 Tàiyuán Villa (Tàiyuán Biéshù)
太原别墅

15 Héngshān Lù 衡山路

Still, especially in recent years, a concerted effort has been made to preserve and spruce up many charming blocks of the original French residences, open historic houses, and convert some of the surviving mansions and estates to fine restaurants and retail shops—all making for a delightful, if spread out, stroll through colonial Shànghǎi. Refusing to join the International Settlement formed in 1863 by the British and Americans, the French had their own electric power, bus system, and legal system within their 10-sq.-km (4-sq.-mile) quarter. It was a neighborhood that attracted not only the French, but international adventurers, Chinese gangsters, White Russian refugees, Communist revolutionaries, and pimps and prostitutes as well. By the 1930s, the French were vastly outnumbered here, but their sense of style has endured.

From exit no. 1 of the Huangpi Rd. (S) Metro station, head west, past the Shui On Center (no. 333). Turn left (south) at Mǎdāng Lù for 2 short blocks to:

## 1 Xīntiāndì (New Heaven and Earth)

Beginning at Tàicàng Lù, this 2-square-block pedestrian mall of cafes and boutiques is one of the hottest venues in Shànghǎi, with its restored late-colonial architecture known as *shíkùmén* (row houses with courtyards and stone frame gates), though it must be said that many of the buildings are new constructions done in the traditional style. It's all quite faux but very upscale and worth a stroll. In the evenings, you'll often see Chinese tour groups traipsing through. The **Site of the First National Congress of the Communist Party** (Huángpí Nán Lù 374) anchors its southeast corner in an original *shíkùmén* building (p. 185).

Head west on Xìngyè Lù, crossing the massive Chéngdū Běi Lù/Chóngqìng Nán Lù elevated overpass. Descend, and proceed west on Nánchāng Lù as it snakes around. At the next intersection, take a left (south) down Yándāng Lù to the entrance to:

## 2 Fùxīng Park

Since the French established it as their park in 1909, it has been known locally as **French Park,** and it is still one of Shànghǎi's loveliest urban green spots, famous for its rose gardens. Looking diagonally southeast from the southeastern entrance to the park, you can spy the former residence (southeastern corner of Fùxīng Zhōng Lù and Chóngqìng Nán Lù) of American journalist **Agnes Smedley.** At the statues of Karl Marx and Friedrich Engel (a favorite point for Shànghǎi's ballroom dancers to practice), bear west past the club **Muse at Park 97,** and exit the park on Gāolán Lù (the former Rue Corneille).

Cross Sīnán Lù and continue 1 more block on Gāolán Lù to a decidedly strange sight, the:

## 3 Former St. Nicholas Russian Orthodox Church (Gāolán Lù 16)

Built in 1933, the high-domed church is testimony to the bygone presence of White Russians in the French quarter. After 1949, it served for a time as a warehouse for washing machines. In recent years, several restaurants have tried to make a go of it here, but none with much long-term success. The church's icons, stained glass, and religious murals inside are lovely, but of late, the place has fallen into some disrepair.

After a gawk, retrace your steps east along this pretty lane, back to the tree-lined Sīnán Lù (the old Rue Masenet), and take it 1 block south to Xiāngshān Lù (Rue de Moliere), passing along the way the lovely cafe cum antique shop **Antique Garden Shanghai.** Step in for a cup of tea if you need refreshment, or browse the interesting curios here, a number of them collected from the former mansions around the area. Across Sīnán Lù at the Xiāngshān Lù intersection, you'll find:

## 4 Sun Yat-sen's Former Residence (Sūn Zhōngshān Gùjū, Xiāngshān Lù 7)

The founder of the Chinese Republic, Sun lived here with his famous wife, Soong Ching-ling, from 1918 to 1924, the year before his death. You can tour the house from 9am to 4:30pm. This is a typical small mansion of the French concession (p. 186).

Continue south down Sīnán Lù, crossing busy Fùxīng Lù. On your left will be the **Sinan Mansion** compound (no. 53) consisting of 51 villas largely built in the 1920s and 1930s, which were recently restored to become a high-end residential and commercial area home to boutique hotels, luxury stores, and restaurants. Also on the same side of the street is:

## 5 Zhōu Ēnlái's Former Residence (Zhōu Gōng Guǎn, Sīnán Lù 73)

Zhōu eventually became second in power to Chairman Máo, but as head of the Shànghǎi branch of the Communist Party in the 1940s, he lived modestly in this French Concession house in 1946, whenever he was in town on Party business (p. 186).

Return to Fùxīng Zhōng Lù (1 block north) and take it west to Ruìjīn Èr Lù (the former Rte. Pere Robert), the next major street. Turn left (south) for a block or so to the:

## 6 Ruìjīn Hotel (Ruìjīn Bīnguǎn, Ruìjīn Èr Lù 118)

This beautiful estate on the west side of the street, now the grounds for a hotel and restaurant complex, was the **Morriss Estate** in colonial times. The owner of the villas that still stand in these spacious gardens built his fortune by running the *North China Daily News*, then the main English-language newspaper in Shànghǎi; he also bred greyhounds that he would race at the 50,000-seat Canidrome just to the west (today's Cultural Square). The last Morriss descendent to live here died in the gatekeeper's house a few years after the Communists took over in 1949. The wide green lawns and ornate villas with stained-glass windows are exquisite relics of the privileged life led by wealthy foreigners in old Shànghǎi.

Exit the estate by the west gate onto:

## 7 Màomíng Nán Lù

Known in colonial days as Route Cardinal Mercier, today's Màomíng Lù is a pretty and quaint, tree-lined street home to cafes, bars, and a slew of fashion shops.

8 Take a Break ☕

**At this point, if you need a refresher, you can head south (left) on Màomíng Lù to Blue Frog (Màomíng Nán Lù 207-6), a cafe-pub-restaurant that serves smoothies, stiffer libations, and American comfort food. If you prefer an old Chinese-Shànghǎi setting, head north on Màomíng Nán Lù to the 1931 Bar and Restaurant (Màomíng Nán Lù 112).** *Qípáo*-**clad waitresses will serve you teas, coffees, juices, wines, and classic Shànghǎi dishes and snacks while Nat King Cole croons in Portuguese in the background. It's all very dreamy and nostalgic.**

Head north up Màomíng Lù all the way to Huáihǎi Zhōng Lù, formerly Avenue Joffre, the main street of the old French Concession and stocked then with the latest fashions from Paris. Cross Huáihǎi Lù. In front on the left is the:

## 9 Okura Garden Hotel (Huāyuán Fàndiàn, Màomíng Nán Lù 58)

The towering Okura Garden Hotel, a Japanese-managed five-star property, opened in 1989 on the site of the 1926 **Cercle Sportif Française,** once the most luxurious private club in the French quarter, with its grand ballroom, swimming pool, lounges, and wicker sofas. For a look at its original Art Deco interiors now brilliantly restored, take a right inside the hotel lobby past the business center to the east wing. This was the original entrance to the Cercle Sportif's ballroom, complete with marble stairways and colonnades topped by nude female figures. The Grand Ballroom still bears its beautiful stained-glass ceiling lights. This club served as Máo Zédōng's private quarters whenever he visited Shànghǎi, which perhaps explains the eight-room underground concrete bunker that connects to the Jǐn Jiāng Hotel across the street (the entrance near the fountain is usually locked, though).

Outside, cross Màomíng Lù to the landmark:

## 10 Jīn Jiāng Hotel (Jīn Jiāng Fàndiàn, Màomíng Nán Lù 59)

The massive old hotel complex with its Art Deco buildings is most famous for being the site where Richard Nixon and Zhōu Ēnlái signed the Shànghǎi Communiqué in 1972, which opened China to the West for the first time since World War II. Originally built as exclusive apartments, the buildings became part of the Jǐn Jiāng Hotel in 1951. Since then, the various structures have been modernized, gaining in luxury but losing in character. No longer as lively as it was several years ago, the Jǐn Jiāng Shopping Lane (just inside the gate, parallel to Màomíng Lù) still has several restaurants and shops worth a browse, including the hip **Shànghǎi Tang** clothing and crafts store from Hong Kong.

Reemerging on Màomíng Lù and walking north (right) to the corner, you can see across Chánglè Lù (formerly Rue Bourgeat) the old:

## 11 Lyceum Theatre

The theater was built in 1931 by the British Consul for the Amateur Dramatic Society. Margot Fonteyn danced here as a girl. Today, it serves as a theater primarily for large pop concerts. You can check out its restored lobby inside.

Head west on Chánglè Lù for 2 blocks (passing a row of shops that sell and tailor traditional *qípáo* dresses), then turn left (south) on Xiāngyáng Běi Lù (the former Rue L.
Lorton). At the next intersection with Xīnlè Lù, you'll find in the southwest corner:

## 12 Former Russian Orthodox Cathedral of the Holy Mother of God (Xīnlè Lù 55)

Built in 1931, this building with the gorgeous peacock-blue domes was then
the most active church among Russians. At one point, the church housed a
stock exchange with an electronic trading board. It is currently partially occupied by a restaurant, the Grape, popular with expatriates for its inexpensive and
tasty Shànghǎi fare.

Continue south on Xiāngyáng Lù, passing on the east side of the street **Xiāngyáng
Gōngyuán,** formerly a private garden in French Concession days famous for its cherry
trees. Cross Huáihǎi Zhōng Lù to the south. Head west on Huáihǎi Lù, then left (southwest) down the slanting street of Fēnyáng Lù (the old Rte. Pichon). About halfway
down the block on the right (west), you'll pass the:

## 13 Shànghǎi Conservatory of Music (Shànghǎi Yīnyuè Xuéyuàn, Fēnyáng Lù 20)

Established in 1927, the Shànghǎi Music Conservatory moved to the current
premises in the 1950s. The three remaining colonial-era villas on today's campus, one of which was the former Belgian Consulate, date to the 1920s.

Continue south on Fēnyáng Lù past Fùxīng Lù (or Rte. Lafayette, as it was once
known) until you come to the intersection with Tàiyuán Lù, where you'll find (on the
eastern side of Fēnyáng Lù) hidden behind a tall wall the:

## 14 Shànghǎi Museum of Arts and Crafts (Shànghǎi Gōngyì Měishù Bówùguǎn, Fēnyáng Lù 79)

This marvelous 1905 French Renaissance–style marble-and-stone mansion
(open 8:30am–4:30pm) served as the private estate of the director of the
French Municipal Council, a French general, and finally the first mayor of
Communist Shànghǎi, Chén Yì, before housing the open workshops of some of
China's most skilled artisans. This survivor of colonial Shànghǎi packs a triple
punch: as a place to watch traditional arts and crafts being fashioned, as a
museum of those works, and as an architectural masterpiece, resplendent with
its unaltered interiors, sculptures, and marble fountains in its garden (p. 183).

At this point, you can take a quick detour south on Tàiyuán Lù past Yǒngjiā Lù to the:

## 15 Tàiyuán Villa (Tàiyuán Biéshù, Tàiyuán Lù 160)

This lovely 1920s colonial mansion hosted American Gen. George Marshall in
1946 when he was attempting to mediate a truce between Chiang Kai-shek and
Máo Zédōng (p. 96).

Head back (north) up Tàiyuán Lù, take a left (southwest) on Fēnyáng Lù until it ends
at a four-way intersection of Fēnyáng Lù, Táojiāng Lù, Dōngpíng Lù, and south-run-
ning Yuèyáng Lù. The **Pǔxījīn Monument** located on the tiny island in the middle was

dedicated to Russian poet Alexander Pushkin on his 200th birthday. From here, you can head west for your ultimate destination:

## 16 Héngshān Lù

Formerly Avenue Petain, a big, tree-lined avenue with orange-tile sidewalks, wrought-iron railings, and ivy-covered mansions, this is one of Shànghǎi's trendier streets. End your walk here with a bit of shopping; or have a look at the ivy-covered **International Community Church (Guójì Lǐbài Táng;** Héngshān Lù 53) established in 1925 and the former **Shànghǎi American School** (built in 1923) across the street. Or do a spot of people-watching at any of the cafes dotting the side streets. To get to Héngshān Lù, head west on Dōngpíng Lù with its row of quaint restaurants and shops. Don't miss the English-style villa with yellow walls at Dōngpíng Lù 9 where Chiang Kai-shek stayed with his wife Soong Mei-ling. Next door (west) at House no. 11 is another 1920s Soong family mansion (currently occupied by Sasha's restaurant).

## 17 Winding Down ☕

After this long jaunt through the old French quarter, there's no better reward than to enjoy some good food in one of the many splendid colonial mansions around Héngshān Lù. If you fancy Continental dishes presented in a 1920s Soong family mansion, try Sasha's (Dōngpíng Lù 9, House no. 11 at Héngshān Lù). More Continental and Asian fare is served next door in the serene Lapis Lazuli (which also has lunch specials). For Irish ale, live Irish music, and Irish stew, served in an old courtyard house, try O'Malley's (Táojiāng Lù 42, west 1 block off Héngshān Lù). If just taking a load off in a charming cottage adorned with antiques and bric-a-brac sounds like your cup of tea (or vodka-laced coffee), check out the Cottage (Táojiāng Lù 25a at Héngshān Lù), as undemanding a spot as any to wind down.

# SHOPPING

ven before economic reforms in China kicked into high gear in the 1990s, Shànghǎi was a shopper's city. All across the country, the Chinese dreamed of making one visit to the great port, not to sightsee, but to shop. Anything made and sold in Shànghǎi, it seems, had to be the best; non-Shànghǎi goods were by definition inferior—and this reputation for the best goods and great shopping persists today. Shoppers now are able and willing to indulge in everything from uniquely Chinese products to international brand-name items and luxury goods, at venues ranging from modern department stores to open-air markets and sidewalk stalls. Even if you have no interest in doing your part for the Chinese economic miracle, it's still worth entering the fray (preferably with all your wits, commercial and otherwise, sharpened) to witness, if not join in, Shànghǎi's favorite pastime.

## THE SHOPPING SCENE

Shànghǎi has long been an oasis of international shopping, so it is no surprise that Western-style malls have been replacing traditional shop fronts, Chinese department stores, and alley markets across Shànghǎi. Some of the best buys, however, can be found in the tens of thousands of privately run shops that dot the city, from the unique one-offs to the fly-by-night outfits. Colorful open-air markets and street-side vendors also offer more traditional arts and crafts, collectibles, and clothing at low prices. If you're looking for souvenirs or Chinese treasures, check out the cost and selection at hotel shops, modern shopping malls, or the Friendship Store first; then see what's available in the streets and at markets. Most stores are open daily from about 10am to 10pm (especially in the summer). Weekends (especially Sun) are the most hectic time to shop.

### Shànghǎi's Best Buys

Shànghǎi is no Hong Kong, but it has some of the best **antiques** shopping in mainland China. A red wax seal must be attached to any item created between 1795 and 1949 that is taken out of China; older items cannot be exported. Many hotel shops and modern department stores will ship purchases to your home, and the Friendship Store has an efficient shipping department. **Furniture,** old or new, in traditional Chinese styles can be purchased or custom-ordered at several antiques stores. Prices are high, but still lower than you'd pay at home; shipping, however, can add considerably to the bill.

Shànghǎi is also known for its selection and low prices in **silk** (both off the bolt and in finished garments). The Shanghainese people are connoisseurs of fashion and style, so shops selling **fashionable clothing** in cotton, wool, silk, and just about any imaginable material are a dime a dozen, and prices are low. **Traditional clothing** such as *qípáo* (mandarin collar dresses) and *mián ǎo* (padded jackets sometimes referred to as Máo jackets or Zhōngshān jackets) are once again fashionable purchases.

Jewelry can be a bargain, particularly **jade, gold, silver,** and **freshwater pearls,** but bargaining and a critical eye are required. **Electronics, cameras,** and other high-tech goods are not particularly good buys, but if you need anything replaced, you'll find a wide selection from which to choose.

Among **arts and crafts,** there are also especially good buys in **ceramics,** hand-stitched **embroideries, teapots, painted fans,** and **chopsticks.** These are often sold in markets and on the sidewalks by itinerant vendors. Collectibles include **Máo buttons, posters of Old Shànghǎi** (covering everything from cigarette advertisements to talcum powder), old Chinese **coins, wood carvings,** and **screens**—all priced lowest at markets and stands. Other popular crafts made in Shànghǎi are **handbags, carpets, lacquerware, painted snuff bottles,** and **peasant paintings.** Prices vary considerably. The best rule is to find something you truly like, then consider how much it is worth to you.

Designer-label **sportswear** and **stuffed toys** are abundant in department stores and street markets alike. Another popular gift is a **chop** (also called a seal), which is a small, stone, custom-engraved stamp with your name (in English, Chinese, or both), used with an ink pad to print your "signature" on paper. Chops can be created overnight, the same day, or sometimes even while you wait. Prices depend on the stone you select and the skill of the engraver.

## The Art of Bargaining

It helps to know the going prices for items in which you're interested. The Friendship Store is worth scoping out with prices in mind because it marks the high-end price for most items. Prices in hotel shops are usually your ceiling—you should be able to beat that price elsewhere. The street markets usually have the lowest prices. There, for example, you can buy porcelain chopstick rests for ¥10, painted fans for ¥15, silk shirts at around ¥100, quilts at ¥150, and ecru tablecloths at ¥200.

### Buyer Beware

A local saying goes, "Everything is fake, only the fake things are real." This is true of goods sold at many antiques markets, and especially the open-air markets that line the entrances to major tourist sites where, in general, you'll be charged extravagant prices for mass-produced kitsch of shoddy quality. Jade is particularly difficult to evaluate and prone to being fake, so buy only what you really like and don't pay much.

Haggling is not done at government-run stores, most hotel stalls, and modern shops, but it is expected on the street and in small private stores. A good rule of thumb is to offer no more than a quarter of the quoted price and not to accept the first counteroffer. Try to reach a compromise (no more than half the quoted price). Walking away with a firm but polite "No" often brings about a more favorable price. Smiling through the entire exchange (whatever the outcome) helps as well, as does negotiating alone with the vendor who will never give you the best price if he/she stands to lose face in front of other prying eyes. Remember that locals are demon shoppers who scrutinize each potential purchase and exercise mountains of patience before making a buy.

## Shànghǎi's Top Shopping Areas

Shànghǎi's top street to shop has always been **Nanjing Road/Nánjīng Lù,** enhanced recently by the creation of the **Nánjīng Lù Pedestrian Mall** on Nánjīng Dōng Lù downtown (described in chapter 8, "Shànghǎi Strolls"), where the most modern and the most traditional modes of retailing commingle.

Even more popular among locals, however, is **Huáihǎi Zhōng Lù,** the wide avenue south of Nánjīng Lù and parallel to it. The Huáihǎi shopping area tends to run far west across the city, from the Huángpí Nán Lù Metro station to the Chángshú Lù station. The modern shopping malls here have better prices than you'll find on Nánjīng Lù, and there are plenty of boutiques featuring fashions and silks. Some of the most interesting shopping for fashion and accessories is concentrated in the **Shaǎnxli Lù/Màomíng Lù/Chánglè Lù/Xīnlè Lù** area, just off Huáihǎi Lù. In the southern part of the concession, **Tàikàng Lù,** home to a burgeoning number of art galleries and trendy clubs, has many fashionable boutiques selling everything from designer handbags to pricey silks.

Another popular shopping street is **Héngshān Lù,** which continues at the western end of Huáihǎi Lù and runs south to the **Xújiāhuì** intersection and subway stop, where one of the city's largest collections of shopping centers is located.

Shànghǎi's **Old Town Bazaar** (see chapter 8, "Shànghǎi Strolls") is a fine place to shop for local arts and crafts and for antiques. In Pǔdōng, the shopping is concentrated mostly east of the riverfront and south of the Oriental Pearl TV Tower in the malls anchored by the massive **Nextage** department store on Zhāngyáng Lù and the **Super Brand Mall** (Zhèngdà Guǎngchǎng) in Lùjiāzuǐ, with the new **IFC Mall** (Guójīn Zhōngxīn Shāngcháng) being the latest magnet for all luxury goods.

# MARKETS & BAZAARS

Some of Shànghǎi's most interesting shopping experiences are provided by its colorful street markets and alley bazaars. Curios, crafts, collectibles, antiques, jewelry, and coins are all here for those who are willing to bargain hard, but perhaps the most common item you'll find in the markets these days is designer-label clothing, much of it knockoffs (copies) with upscale labels sewn in, although some items are factory seconds or overruns (sometimes smuggled out of legitimate brand-name factories). Many of the markets also sell fresh produce, seafood, spices, and other consumables to residents, along with snacks and drinks. At all such markets, cash is the only means of exchange, and pickpockets are plentiful, so keep all your valuables in a concealed pouch or money belt. If you're purchasing goods from an outdoor antiques

## WHAT TO KNOW ABOUT knockoffs

Leading up to and during the World Expo in 2010, Shànghǎi authorities made a concerted effort to crack down on pirated and knockoff goods (everything from North Face jackets, Louis Vuitton handbags, Rolex watches, and so on, to pirated DVDs), though knock-off Western-branded merchandise can still be found in several different locales, including Qīpǔ Lù Market in Hóngkǒu and A.P. Plaza in the Science and Technology Museum subway station in Pǔdōng. And of course, it can also be found from the hard-to-avoid vendors loitering around tourist-friendly areas, who will unerringly seek you out and thrust their crumpled laminated photos of fake goods at you, asking "Rolex? Rolex?" This guide doesn't recommend that you go anywhere with them, even if they can be very persuasive.

Know if you do, however, that the Customs services of many nations frown on the importation of knockoffs on trademarked goods. The U.S. Customs Service allows U.S. residents to return with one trademark-protected item of each type; that is, one counterfeit watch, one knockoff purse, one camera with a questionable trademark, and so on. For instance, you may not bring back a dozen "Polo" shirts as gifts for friends. Even if the brand name is legitimate, you are not a licensed importer. Copyrighted products like CD-ROMs and books must have been manufactured under the copyright owner's authorization; otherwise, tourists may not import even one of these items—they are pirated. The U.S. Customs Service booklet *Know Before You Go* and the U.S. Customs website (www.cbp.gov) provide further guidelines.

market, be aware that not all older (pre-1949) items sold at such markets will have the red-wax seal attached. A stern Customs inspector, finding an old item without a seal, might confiscate it. As well, many "antiques" these days are nothing but modern fakes aged and dirtied up. Caveat emptor!

### A.P. PLAZA (YÀDÀ SHÈNGHUÌ LǙYÓU GÒUWÙ GUĂNGCHĂNG) ★

For those who don't have the patience to rifle through the mess of shops at Qīpǔ Market, but still want their Western-branded knockoffs, this underground plaza in the Science and Technology Museum subway station (Metro Line 2) in Pǔdōng offers a more organized alternative. Individual shops here sell clothing, electronics, bags, toys, antiques, shoes, and accessories, though the brand-name knockoffs are usually hidden. The plaza is open daily 10am to 8pm.

### DŌNGTÁI LÙ ANTIQUES MARKET (DŌNGTÁI LÙ GǓWÁN SHÌCHĂNG) ★

This largest of Shànghǎi's antiques markets has hundreds of stalls and many permanent shops along a short lane, located on Dōngtái Lù and Liúhé Lù, 1 block west of Xīzàng Nán Lù, Lúwān (about 3 blocks south of Huáihǎi Lù). Dealers specialize in antiques, curios, porcelain, furniture, jewelry, baskets, bamboo and wood carvings, birds, flowers, goldfish, and nostalgic bric-a-brac from colonial and revolutionary days (especially Máo memorabilia). When it rains, most stalls aren't open, but the stores are. The market is open daily 9am to 5pm.

**FÚYÒU MARKET** If you like rummaging through lots of junk for the chance to find the rare real nugget, this is still the best place to do it in Shànghǎi. This favorite for weekend antique and curio hunting, located in the Cángbǎo Lóu (building) at Fāngbāng Zhōng Lù 457 and Hénán Nán Lù (the western entrance to Shànghǎi Old St. in the Old Town Bazaar, Nánshì) is also called a "ghost market" because the traders set out their wares before sunrise (when only ghosts can see what's for sale). Come as early as possible on Saturday or Sunday morning, preferably the latter, when vendors come in from the surrounding countryside. The goods are various and few are polished up; many of the items are from the attic or the farm, though increasingly also from some factory backroom that churns out modern pieces that are then scuffed up with mud to look old. Porcelains, old jade pendants, used furniture, Qīng Dynasty coins, Chairman Máo buttons, old Russian cameras, Buddhist statues, snuff bottles, and carved wooden screens are just a few of the treasures here, none with price tags. Three floors of the market building are open daily from 9am to 5pm; the weekend market (on the third and fourth floors) runs from 5am to 6pm, but tapers off by noon.

**QĪPǓ LÙ WHOLESALE CLOTHING MARKET (QĪPǓ FÚZHUĀNG SHÌCHǍNG)** For years, this gargantuan clothing market bounded by Qīpǔ Lù, Hénán Běi Lù, Tiāntóng Lù, and Zhèjiāng Lù in Hóngkǒu district has been where locals shop for low-cost, locally made daily clothing and accessories, but is now home also to some of the vendors of brand-name "fakes" who have been displaced by the closing of Xiāngyáng Market. Because of its size (three complexes spanning as many blocks), you'll need some patience and time to make your way through much that will probably not be to your taste, but finds can definitely be found. More likely, the vendors of the goods you're looking for will find you the minute you step

---

 **Vendors Behaving Badly**

When visiting the Fúyòu Market, be very careful when navigating your way through the makeshift vendors on the third and especially fourth floors; many are itinerant peddlers here for the weekend who merely display their wares on the ground wherever they can find space. Shoppers with large bags or heavy packs should be especially vigilant, as a careless swing of an arm or even a tiny push from the crowd can cause bodies to topple and wares to go flying. This has happened before and will happen again (whether by accident or design). If you are the hapless soul who ends up damaging something (even if you were pushed by someone else), you will be held responsible. This is open season for vendors who, smelling blood, will claim that you've broken their precious Táng Dynasty vase (when it has just come from the factory backroom), and cite a ridiculously marked-up charge that you must pay. Fortunately, the Fúyòu Market now has a supervising manager familiar with the quality and price of the goods on sale to monitor and mediate precisely such incidents. Should you ever find yourself in such an unlucky situation, don't attempt to bargain your way out; immediately consult the supervisor (*jiāndū*) whose office is in the small alley just east of the building.

## THE pearls OF CHINA

China's oyster beds remain among the world's most fertile grounds for pearls, of both the saltwater and freshwater variety. Seawater pearls are usually more expensive than the freshwater gems, but in both cases the qualities to look for are roundness, luster, and size. The bigger, rounder, and shinier the pearl, the better (and the more expensive). Here are a few ways to detect fakes, even if most shoppers don't bother:

o Nick the surface of the pearl with a sharp blade (the color should be uniform within and without).

o Rub the pearl along your teeth (you should hear a grating sound).

o Scrape the pearl on glass (real pearls leave a mark).

o Pass the pearl through a flame (fakes turn black, real pearls don't).

Try to pick a string of pearls that are of the same size, shape, and color. Here's a rough pricing guide, based on what's charged in Shànghǎi:

¥60 to ¥80 for a string of small rice-shaped pearls.

¥80 to ¥100 for a string of larger pearls of mixed or low luster.

¥100 to ¥200 for a string of larger pearls of different colors.

A string of very large, perfectly round pearls of the same color sells for considerably more, ¥10,000 to ¥20,000 and higher.

out of your taxi. As always, exercise caution and stick to the public stalls and shops. The market is open daily 10am to 5pm.

**SOUTH BUND FABRIC MARKET (NÁN WÀITĀN QĪNG FÁNG MIÁN-LIÀO SHÌCHǍNG)** ★ This popular fabric market, originally known as the Dǒngjiādù Fabric Market, moved from its original Dǒngjiādù location in 2006, hence the name change, though some taxi drivers and hotel concierges may still refer to it by its old name. Now relocated to nearby Lùjiābāng Lù 399 (intersection with Náncāng Jiē; ⓒ **021/6377-5858**) in the southeastern corner of the old Chinese city, this former outdoor market, a favorite with expatriates, has moved indoors. Hundreds of stalls still sell bales of fabric at ridiculously low prices (though prices have increased slightly since the move), from traditional Chinese silk and Thai silk to cotton, linen, wool, and cashmere, though the heavier fabrics are only carried during the colder months. Many shops have their own in-house tailors who can stitch you a suit, or anything else you want, at rates that are less than half what you'd pay at retail outlets like Silk King. Come with a pattern. Turnaround is usually a week or more, but can be expedited for an extra fee. The market is open daily 8:30am to 6pm.

# SHOPPING A TO Z

## Antiques & Furniture

The markets and bazaars (listed above) are a primary source of antiques, collectibles, and Chinese furniture and furnishings, as are some hotel shops; but there are also several private antiques stores worth checking out. Most of the warehouses are situated in west Shànghǎi's Chángníng District, near the Hóngqiáo Airport (no Metro). If you plan to make a day of shopping, ask your hotel concierge to haggle with the taxi driver over a price for the trip. A half-day of shopping should cost no more than ¥250.

**Annly's Antique Warehouse (Ān Lì)**  Annly Chan provides custom-made sofas, chairs, draperies, and cushions; picture framing; and pricey antique furniture. The warehouse is open daily 9am to 6pm. Zhōngchūn Lù 7611, no. 68 (by Hùsōng Lù), Mínháng Qū. ℂ **021/6406-0242.** www.annlyschina.com. No Metro.

**Chine Antiques (Chúntiān Gé)**  In business for the last 17 years, and noted for its high-end (and high-priced) antiques, mainly wooden pieces from the Qīng Dynasty, Chine will ship purchases overseas. The shop in the Dōngtái Market has pictures of what you can find in their warehouse showroom. The store is open daily 9am to 5pm. Liúhé Lù 38 (at Dōngtái Lù), Lúwān. ℂ **021/6387-4100.** Metro: Laoximen.

**Fúyòu Antique Market**  This is still the most fun place to scavenge for every imaginable antique and collectible, from Buddhist statuary to Qīng Dynasty coins (see above). The market is open Monday through Friday 9am to 5pm; Saturday and Sunday 5am to 5pm. Fāngbāng Lù 457 (at Hénán Lù), Nánshì. Metro: Yu Garden.

**Henry Antique Warehouse (Hēnglì Gǔdiǎn Jiājù)**  The English-speaking staff at this huge space shows off antique Chinese furniture and furnishings, with a carved Chinese bed costing around ¥13,000. Overseas shipping is provided. The warehouse is open daily 9am to 6pm. Hóngzhōng Lù 361 (near Héchuān Zhì Èr Lù). ℂ **021/6401-0831.** No Metro.

**Hu & Hu**  Sisters-in-law Lin and Marybelle Hu have some 20-plus years of experience collecting, valuating, and restoring antiques. Their showroom, full of antiques collected from the Chinese countryside, is a testament to their expert and discerning eye. Prices are high, but so is the quality of restoration. Staff is friendly and knowledgeable. The showroom is open daily 9am to 6pm. Cáobǎo Lù 1885, No. 8 (west of Hóngxīn Lù), Chángníng. ℂ **021/3431-1212.** www.hu-hu.com. Metro: Xingzhong Rd.

**Shànghǎi Antique and Curio Store (Shànghǎi Wénwù Shāngdiàn)**  The owners hope to make downtown Guǎngdōng Lù, which runs west off the south end of the Bund, into something of an antiques row for shoppers. One of the oldest and largest antiques stores, it has under its umbrella everything from calligraphy, old jades, and porcelain, to antique furniture, wood carvings, embroidery, and tapestries. Prices are even reasonable. The store is open daily 9am to 5pm. Guǎngdōng Lù 240, Huángpǔ. ℂ **021/6321-4697, ext. 301.** Metro: Nanjing Rd. (E).

## Books

The **Foreign Language Bookstore** (see below) offers the widest range of English-language material, but hotel kiosks and shops also have decent English-language guides to Shànghǎi attractions and books about China. The **Confucius Temple Book Market (Gǔshū Shìchǎng),** held every Sunday from 8am to 4pm at Wén-miào Lù 215 (east of Zhōnghuá Lù), traffics in secondhand and vintage books, including some foreign-language volumes.

**Chaterhouse Booktrader**  This chain, with several stores around town, has an excellent collection of English-language material, including literary fiction, the latest bestsellers, travel books, cookbooks, and international magazines. The stores are open daily 10am to 9pm. Nánjīng Xī Lù 1376 (at Shànghǎi Centre), 104. ☎ **021/6279-7633.** Metro: Jing'an Temple. Also at Huáihǎi Zhōng Lù 93, Shànghǎi Times Square, Basement 1K. ☎ **021/6391-8237.** Metro: Huangpi Rd. (S).

**Old China Hand Reading Room (Hànyuán Shūwū)**  Shànghǎi's most charming coffeehouse, opened in 1996 by photographer Deke Erh, is also a bookstore, with hundreds of old and new, obscure and popular books and magazines on its shelves. Relax at a Qīng Dynasty antique table by the window as you peruse your possible purchases over green tea or cappuccino. This is the best place to purchase the series of books on colonial architecture in China put out by Deke Erh and Tess Johnston. The reading room is open 10am to midnight. Shàoxing Lù 27 (btw. Ruìjīn Èr Lù and Shǎnxī Nán Lù), Lúwān. ☎ **021/6473-2526.** Metro: Shaanxi Rd. (S).

**Shànghǎi Book Mall (Shànghǎi Shū Chéng)**  Shànghǎi's state-of-the-art megamall for book lovers, this new store has eight floors of books, music, and DVDs. About 10% of its collection comprises English-language books. The mall is open daily 9am to 8pm. Fúzhōu Lù 465 (east of Húběi Lù), Huángpǔ. ☎ **021/6352-2222.** Metro: Nanjing Rd. (E).

**Shànghǎi Foreign Language Bookstore (Wàiwén Shūdiàn)**  The city's largest selection of English-language books and magazines (along with some maps, tapes, and CDs) can be found on the first and fourth floors of this big government-run store. They take credit cards and ship books overseas. The bookstore is open daily 9:30am to 6pm. Fúzhōu Lù 390 (east of Fújiàn Lù), Huángpǔ. ☎ **021/6322-3200.** Metro: Nanjing Rd. (E).

**Shànghǎi Museum Bookshop**  The gift shop on the museum's first floor carries a good selection of books in English on art, history, and culture, including coffee-table volumes. The bookshop is open daily 9am to 5pm (8pm on Sat). Rénmín Dà Dào 201 (People's Square), Huángpǔ District. ☎ **021/6372-3500.** Metro: People's Square.

# Cameras & Film

These days, one can purchase all the standard big brand digital cameras and accessories in Shànghǎi, especially in the big malls like Grand Gateway Plaza (p. 238) in Xújiāhuì; prices are comparable to those in the West, perhaps slightly higher depending on the brand. Analog cameras and film are considerably more difficult to find these days. Some of the same department stores may still have a few or check in the specialty camera markets (see below). Those looking for ancient Russian swing-lens cameras can sometimes find them in the Fúyòu Antique Market (p. 231).

**Huánlóng Dàshà**  This camera market is an excellent place to pick up used cameras (vintage, SLRs, and digital) and accessories. Prices vary, so look around. Booth 3051 on the third floor specializes in the home-grown Shànghǎi Seagull cameras. The market is open daily 10am to 8pm. Méiyuán Lù 360 (across from Shànghǎi Railway Station), Zhábēi District. ☎ **021/6354-9376.** Metro: Shànghǎi Railway Station (exit 4).

**Xīngguāng Photographic Equipment City**  You can find all the latest big brand cameras (SLRs and digital) at this huge camera market. Accessories and photography books are on the third and fourth floors. The market is open daily 10am to 7pm. Lǔbān Lù 300 (near Xiétǔ Lù), Lúwān. ☎ **021/6301-8248.** Metro: Luban Rd.

# Carpets

Check over carpets carefully, with an eye to faded colors. Colors should be bright and the threads fine. A 1.8m×2.4m (6 ft.×8 ft.) silk carpet, tightly woven (300–400 stitches per in.), can cost ¥50,000 or more.

**Bokhara Carpets**  This store has an excellent choice of new and old carpets from Iran, Pakistan, Afghanistan, India, and Uzbekistan. They do not accept credit cards. The shop is open daily 10am to 6:30pm. Xiānxiá Lù 679 (off Yán'ān Xī Lù, near Shuīchéng Lù), Chángníng. ☎ 021/6290-1745. No Metro.

**Torana House**  You'll find high-quality, handmade carpets and rugs direct from their workshop in Lhasa, Tibet. The shop is open daily 10:30am to 7pm. Ānfú Lù 164 (west of Wūlǔmùqí Lù), Lúwān. ☎ 021/5404-4886. www.toranahouse.com. Metro: Changshu Rd.

# Clothing

A number of shops along Chánglè Lù and Màomíng Lù sell ready-made *qípáos* (mandarin-collar dresses with high slits), Táng jackets, and other traditional Chinese-style clothing, and can also tailor the same.

**Huā Jiā Fúshì**  One of several stores on this strip of Màomíng Lù selling traditional Chinese clothing such as *qípáo*, this one has been the haunt of several Chinese celebrities, so you know you're at least getting star-quality goods. The shop is open daily 10am to 10pm. Màomíng Nán Lù 88 (south of Huáihǎi Zhōng Lù), Lúwān. ☎ 021/6467-2845. Metro: Shaanxi Rd. (S).

**Shànghǎi Tang (Shànghǎi Tān)**  This oh-so-hip store from Hong Kong fashion maven David Tang has spawned several branches worldwide since it first opened in Shànghǎi in 2003. Besides his signature and pricey traditional Chinese shirts and *qípáo*, you can also pick up elegant scarves, photo frames, bags, and candles. The stores are open daily 10am to 10pm. Màomíng Nán Lù 59, Shop E, Jǐnjiāng Hotel Promenade, Lúwān Qū. ☎ 021/5466-3006. www.shanghaitang.com. Metro: Shaanxi Rd. (S). Also at Xīntiāndì, Tàicāng Lù 181, 15 North Block. ☎ 021/6384-1601. Metro: Huangpi Rd. (S).

**Uniqlo**  The popular Japanese casual clothing chain (with stores in New York, London, and Paris) has opened a three-story flagship store (its biggest in the world) in Shànghǎi, where you can pick up wardrobe staples like coats, fashionable T-shirts, and jeans at very reasonable prices. The store is open daily 10am to 10pm. Nánjīng Xī Lù 969 (near Màomíng Běi Lù), Jìng Ān. ☎ 021/5250-9688. www.uniqlo.cn. Metro: West Nanjing Rd.

# Computers

**Apple**  The second Apple store in China after Beijing, this one commands its own building-in-the-round right outside the hip IFC mall in Pǔdōng. All the usual Apple gizmos and accessories are here, as are the crowds. The store is open daily 10am to 10pm. Shìjì Dàdào 8, LG2-27, IFC, Pǔdōng. ☎ 021/6084-6800. www.apple.com.cn/retail/pudong. Metro: Lujiazui.

**Cybermart (Sàibó Shùmǎ Guǎngchǎng)**  This huge mall is a cybergeek's dream come true, with stores selling everything from laptops and printers to mobile phones and MD and DVD players. International brands such as Apple, IBM, Sony, and NEC also have outlets here. Repair services are also available. The mall is open daily 10am to 8pm. Huáihǎi Zhōng Lù 282, Hong Kong Plaza, North Block (by Huángpí Nán Lù), Lúwān. ☎ 021/6390-8008. www.cybermart.com.cn. Metro: Huangpi Rd. (S).

# Crafts, Ceramics & Gifts

**Liúlí Gōngfáng**   With almost 10 outlets around town, this chain started by former Taiwanese actress Yáng Huìshān features unique and unusual pieces of crystal and glassware, from Buddhist statues to ritual vessels and decorative tableware. International glass art techniques have been adapted to create gorgeous Chinese-themed pieces you're unlikely to come across elsewhere. The shop is open daily 10am to 9pm. Huáihǎi Zhōng Lù 381 (above Huángpí Nán Lù subway station), Room 103, Central Plaza Shopping Center. ℂ 021/6391-6057. www.liuli.com. Metro: Huangpi Rd. (S).

**Madame Máo's Dowry (Máo Tài Shèjì)**   This wonderful shop near the French Concession sells antique furniture, silk clothing, unusual housewares, ceramics, and art, with an emphasis on Cultural Revolution posters and propaganda art. The shop is open Monday to Saturday 10am to 7pm; Sunday noon to 6pm. Fùmín Lù 207 (north of Chánglè Lù), Jìng Ān. ℂ 021/5403-3551. www.madamemaosdowry.com. Metro: Changshu Rd.

**Shànghǎi Arts & Crafts Museum (Shànghǎi Gōngyì Měishùguǎn)**   What you see made in the open workshops of this French Concession mansion is for sale in the shops here, from embroideries and eggshell porcelain to snuff bottles and kites. The museum is open daily 8:30am to 4:30pm. Fēnyáng Lù 79 (south of Fùxīng Zhōng Lù), Xújiāhuì. ℂ 021/6437-0509. Metro: Changshu Rd.

**Shànghǎi Jǐngdé Zhèn Porcelain Artware (Shànghǎi Jǐngdé Zhèn Yìshù Cíqì Shāngdiàn)**   An excellent selection of some of China's most prized ceramic creations, produced by factories and artisans in nearby Jǐngdé Zhèn, can be found here. Vases, plates, cups, and artware are expensive here, but the quality is high and the reputation good. The store is open daily 10am to 10pm. Nánjīng Xī Lù 1185 (at Shǎnxī Běi Lù), Jìng Ān. ℂ 021/6253-3178. Metro: Jing'an Temple.

**Simply Life (Yìjū Shēnghuó)**   Tasteful gifts from China and throughout Asia are the hallmark of the Simply Life stores. The vast foreigner-pleasing selection includes household decorations, painted bone china, tableware, crafts, linens, and silks. Alas, prices are simply sky-high. The stores are open daily 10am to 10pm. Xīntiāndì North Block, Mǎdāng Lù 159, Lúwān. ℂ 021/6387-5100. www.simplylife-sh.com. Metro: Huangpi Rd. (S). Also at Dōngpíng Lù 9, Xúhuì. ℂ 021/3406-0509. Metro: Changshu Rd.

# Department Stores

Shànghǎi has a large number of new, Western-style department stores that have almost completely replaced the traditional (but shoddy) Chinese versions. Most of them are joint ventures with overseas retailing chains.

**Friendship Store (Yǒuyì Shāngdiàn)**   Friendship stores once catered exclusively to foreigners, but now compete freely (though not always successfully) with department stores and shopping plazas. For some visitors, this is the ultimate one-stop shop, containing a generous sampling of nearly everything worth hauling home: arts and crafts, jewelry, silk, books, souvenirs, antiques. Prices are relatively high (no bargaining allowed), but are generally still lower than in high-end hotel shops, and quality is decent. You can start here to get an overview of what's available in Shànghǎi at a fair price, shop the streets and malls, then return to make any last-minute purchases. There is another branch in the western part of town. Both stores are open daily 10am to 10pm. Chángshòu Lù 1188, Jìng Ān. ℂ 021/6252-5252. Metro: Chángshòu Rd. Also at Friendship Shopping Centre (Hóng Qiáo Yǒuyì Shāngchéng), Zūnyì Nán Lù 6, Chángníng. ℂ 021/6270-0000. No Metro.

**Isetan (Yīshìdān)** This Japanese department store puts high prices on its exceptional goods and fashions. It also offers its own bakery and an Esprit boutique in the heart of Huáihǎi Lù's most upscale shopping area. The store is open daily 10am to 9pm. There's also a branch at the Westgate Shopping Mall. Huáihǎi Zhōng Lù 527 (at Chéngdū Lù), Lúwān. ☏ 021/5306-1111. Metro: Huangpi Rd. (S). Also at Nánjīng Xī Lù 1038. ☏ 021/6272-1111. Metro: Nanjing Rd. (W).

**Nextage Department Store (Shànghǎi Dìyī Bābǎibàn Xīnshìjì Shāngshà)** One of the largest department stores in the world, this megastore is 10 stories tall and a square block wide. It's chock-full of everything department stores ever carry (and some things they don't, such as automobiles). The Japanese supermarket Yaohan is also here. The store is open daily 10am to 10pm. Directly across the street (south) is another big shopping mall, **Times Square** (**Shídài Guǎngchǎng;** ☏ **021/5836-8888**), as if another were needed. Zhāngyáng Lù 501 (at Pǔdōng Nán Lù), Pǔdōng. ☏ 021/5830-1111. Metro: Dongfang Rd.

**Parkson (Bǎishèng Gòuwù Zhōngxīn)** At one of the busiest junctures in town, this Malaysian-based French Concession department store is yet another upscale emporium of Western fashions and cosmetics, with a McDonald's and a Gino's Café next door and an excellent Park 'n Shop supermarket carrying foreign goods in the basement. Prices are lower than on Nánjīng Lù. The store is open daily 10am to 10pm. Huáihǎi Zhōng Lù 918 (at Shǎnxī Nán Lù), Lúwān. ☏ 021/6415-6384. Metro: Shaanxi Rd. (S).

**Shànghǎi No. 1 Department Store (Shànghǎi Shì Dìyī Bǎihuò Shāngdiàn)** Shànghǎi's most famous department store, opened in 1934, has been thoroughly updated with the incorporation of a 22-story East Tower, the first 11 floors of which are devoted to retailing. All the usual suspects are here: clothing, shoes, children's wear, gifts, books, watches, toys, jewelry, cosmetics, housewares, sporting equipment, and electronic goods. The store has renown and volume, but not always the best selections or prices. It's open daily 10am to 10pm. Nánjīng Dōng Lù 800–830 (at Xīzàng Zhōng Lù), Huángpǔ. ☏ 021/6322-3344. Metro: People's Square.

## Drugstores

**Shànghǎi Number One Dispensary (Shànghǎi Dìyī Yīyào Shāngdiàn)** East meets West at this apothecary on the pedestrian mall that carries a considerable number of foreign medicines. Branches can be found all over town. They're open daily 9am to 10pm. Nánjīng Dōng Lù 616 (at Zhéjiāng Zhōng Lù), Huángpǔ. ☏ 021/6322-4567. Metro: Nanjing Rd. (E).

**Watson's (Qūchénshì)** Watson's is a large Western-style drugstore, with just about anything you might need, including a fairly wide range of imported beauty and health aids, from cosmetics to toothpaste. There are many outlets around town. They're open daily 10am to 10pm. Huáihǎi Zhōng Lù 787-789 (west of Ruìjīn Èr Lù), Lúwān. ☏ 021/6431-8650. www.watsons.com.cn. Metro: Huangpi Rd. (S).

## Embroideries

**Annabel Lee** Quality silk embroidery on a wide range of accessories is the name of the game here. Choose from a selection of handsome and pricey shoes, bags, wallets, cushion covers, table runners, and various pen/tissue/eyeglass/cellphone holders. The shop is open daily 10am to 10pm. Zhōngshan Dōng Yī Lù 8, No. 1 (the Bund by Guǎngdōng Lù), Huángpǔ. ☏ 021/6445-8218. www.annabel-lee.com. Metro: Nanjing Rd. (E).

**Brocade Country (Jǐngxiù Fáng)**  The Miao people, primarily found in Guizhou and Yunnan provinces, are known to sew their stories and history into their costumes because they have no written language. This wonderful little shop sells all kinds of Miao-minority embroideries, some of which are antique collectibles, and others more recent creations by the part Miao and English-speaking owner. The shop is open daily 10:30am to 7pm. Jùlù Lù 616, Jìng Ān. ✆ **021/6279-2677.** Metro: Shaanxi Rd. (S).

**Zhang's Textiles**  Here, you'll find a superb collection of framed embroidery (from Qīng Dynasty royal costumes) and dynastic-era robes and skirts for purchase. These are genuine antique fabrics. Zhang's also carries jade bracelets, silk pillows, and silk pillow boxes. Items are predictably pricey. The shop is open daily 10am to 9pm. Nánjīng Xī Lù 1376, Shànghǎi Centre 202A, Jìng Ān. ✆ **021/6279-8587.** www.zhangstextiles.com. Metro: Jing'an Temple.

## Jewelry

**Amylin's Pearls (Àimīnshì Zhūbǎo)**  High-quality (and fairly high-priced) pearls from China and Asia are sold by a knowledgeable and English-speaking staff (with outlets in Běijīng as well). The shop is open daily 10am to 8pm. Nánjīng Xī Lù 580, 3rd floor, Jìng Ān. ✆ **021/5228-2372.** www.amy-pearl.com. Metro: Nanjing Rd. (W).

**Angel Pearls**  This is one of Shànghǎi's best shops for pearls (freshwater pearls, South Sea pearls, Japanese cultured pearls). It also carries silk carpets and embroideries. The shop is open Monday to Friday 9am to 5:30pm; Saturday and Sunday 10am to 5:30pm. Xīnzhá Lù 1051, 1D (at Tàixīng Lù), Jìng Ān. ✆ **021/6215-5031.** Metro: Nanjing Rd. (W).

**Hóngqiáo Pearl Market (Hóngqiáo Zhēnzhū Chéng)**  Popular with expats, this complex in the western part of town has three floors of shops that sell everything from clothing and golf clubs to jewelry and shoes. Head for the second floor where the pearl shops are, bargain hard (pay no more than half the asking price), and you can end up with some very nice finds. The market is open daily 10am to 10pm. Hóngméi Lù 3721 (by Yán'ān Xī Lù), Chángníng. ✆ **021/6465-0000 or 6262-6588.** Metro: Longxi Rd.

**Lǎo Fèng Xiáng Jewelers (Lǎo Fèng Xiáng Yínlóu)**  Located on the north side of the Nánjīng Lù Pedestrian Mall, this jewelry store has long specialized (since the Qīng Dynasty) in jade, pearls, and fine silver and gold ornaments. It's open daily 9:30am to 10pm. Nánjīng Dōng Lù 432 (at Shǎnxī Nán Lù), Huángpǔ. ✆ **021/6322-0033.** Metro: Nanjing Rd. (E).

**Pearl Village (Zhēnzhū Cūn)**  Located a few blocks west of the Temple of the City God in the Yù Yuán Bazaar, Pearl Village has more than 50 vendors representing pearl dealers, pearl farms, and pearl factories from throughout China. Freshwater, seawater, inlaid, and black pearls are featured, often at reasonable wholesale prices. The village is open daily 9am to 5:30pm. Fúyòu Lù 288, Yàyī Jīndiàn, 3rd floor, Nánshì. ✆ **021/6355-3418.** Metro: Nanjing Rd. (E).

**Swatch Art Boutique**  Swiss-based watchmaker Swatch has brought its signature plastic watches, along with some of their other brands (Tiffany, Breguet, Blancpain, and Omega) to their own hotel (Swatch Art Peace Hotel) boutiques here in Shànghǎi. There's even a special Shànghǎi watch exclusive to the store, which features the words "No Smoking" and "Opium Commission" in reference to the fact that the hotel hosted the first meeting of the International Opium Commission in 1909. The store is open daily 10am to 10pm. Nánjīng Dōng Lù 23, Bund 19, Ground floor, Swatch Art Peace Hotel, Huángpǔ. ✆ **021/6329-9936.** Metro: Nanjing Rd. (E).

# Modern Art

The Chinese contemporary art scene has been thriving in Shànghǎi in the last few years, with galleries and showrooms cropping up all over town. Though contemporary Chinese artists are increasingly gaining more international recognition, they are still relatively unknown and their works often sell below international prices, making them potential investments for those so inclined—and many tourists are increasingly inclined. The **St. Regis Hotel** (p. 104) has taken to offering "art tours" for their guests who are interested in visiting local galleries. Otherwise, **Tiānzǐfáng** on Tàikàng Lù in the southern part of the French Concession (Lúwān District), **Mògānshān Lù 50** just south of the Sūzhōu Creek in the northern part of town (Pǔtuó District), and the **Shànghǎi Sculpture Space** (p. 190) at Huáihǎi Xī Lù 570 are home to a series of industrial warehouses that have been converted to galleries and artists' studios, and are a must-visit if you like modern art and photography. Various former warehouses and factories along Sūzhōu Creek are also being converted into galleries such as **Creek Art** at Guāngfù Lù 423. The area around the Bund (**Swatch Art Peace Hotel**) and **Yuánmíngyuán Lù** (fronted by the new Rockbund Art Museum) should also yield a slew of new galleries and studios. Check the local English-language magazines for listings.

**Deke Erh Centre (Ěr Dōng Qiáng Yìshù Zhōngxīn)**　This gallery of photographer, traveler, and cultural impresario Deke Erh, famous for, among other things, his photographs of Shànghǎi's colonial architecture published in a series of *Old China Hand* books, features Tibetan-themed oils as well as occasional photo exhibits and musical recitals. The gallery is open daily 9:30am to 5:30pm. Tàikàng Lù 210, Building 2, Lúwān. ✆ **021/6415-0675.** www.han-yuan.com. Metro: Dǎpǔqiáo.

**Shànghǎi Gallery of Art (Wàitān Sānhào Hùshēn Huàláng)**　Occupying 1,000 sq. m (10,764 sq. ft.) of floor space on the third floor of the ritzy Three on the Bund development, this gallery hosts high-profile rotating exhibits by both local and expatriate Chinese artists. It's open daily 11am to 11pm. Zhōngshān Dōng Yī Lù 3, Three on the Bund, 3rd floor, Húangpǔ. ✆ **021/6323-3355.** www.threeonthebund.com. Metro: Nanjing Rd. (E).

**ShanghART Gallery & H-space (Xiānggénà Huàláng)**　One of the earlier and more interesting galleries to show the works of contemporary Chinese artists, this much expanded gallery is often recommended as the first stop for modern connoisseurs. It's open daily 10am to 6pm; Building 18 (H-Space) is open Tuesday to Sunday 1 to 6pm. There's also a new ShanghART at 796 Huáihǎi Lù that's open daily 10am to 7pm. Mògānshān Lù 50, Building 16, Pǔtuó. ✆ **021/6359-3923.** www.shanghart gallery.com. No Metro. Also at Huáihǎi Zhōng Lù 796. ✆ **021/3395-0808.** www.796huaihailu.com. Metro: Húangpí Rd. (S).

# Shoes

Both fashionable and casual shoes can be found easily around town, although men's shoes in larger sizes (42 and up) are a considerably rarer find. For women, many small shops along Shǎanxī Lù, Chánglè Lù, and Xīnlè Lù can yield some inexpensive and fun finds if you can spare the time to browse.

**Mary Ching**　Taking advantage of her British-Chinese heritage, Shànghǎi-based designer Alison Yeung has created an aesthetic to match, coming up with some highly original and funky women's shoes (stiletto pumps on a platform base, for example), slippers, and handbags. The shop is open Wednesday to Sunday 11am to 7pm; Monday and Tuesday by appointment. Wŭkāng Lù 376, Boutique 106, Ferguson Lane (by Tài'ān Lù), Xúhuì). ✆ 021/6090-4599. www.marychingshanghai.com. No Metro.

**Suzhou Cobblers (Zhōngguó Lányìnhuā Bù Guǎn)**   This store sells some lovely all-silk, 100% hand-sewn, leather-soled Chinese slippers created by Shànghǎi designer Huang Mengqi (Denise). Recently, Denise has also branched out to making hats and bags. The store is open daily 10am to 6:30pm. Fúzhōu Lù 17, Rm. 101 (just off the Bund), Huángpǔ. ✆ 021/6321-7087. www.suzhou-cobblers.com. Metro: Nanjing Rd. (E).

# Shopping Malls & Plazas

Shànghǎi has plenty of mammoth shopping plazas (consisting of scores of independent brand-name and designer-label outlets selling international merchandise under one roof), particularly along Huáihǎi Zhōng Lù and at Xújiāhuì. Several other locations around town are also being converted to high-end lifestyle shopping and entertainment complexes, such as **1933** (**1933 Lǎo Chǎng Fáng;** www.1933-shanghai. com) in Hóngkǒu, on the grounds of a former abattoir, a stunning building well worth seeing.

**City Mall (Jiǔbǎi Chéngshì Guǎngchǎng)**   This gargantuan, rolling edifice of gleaming white marble (suspiciously resembling the ugly white tiles of many a Chinese building) right next to the Jìng Ān Temple was designed by Paul Andreu. He also designed Shànghǎi's Pǔdōng International Airport, Oriental Art Center, and the collapsed terminal at Charles de Gaulle airport. As expected, brand-name shops such as Montblanc, Burberry, and Jean Paul Gaultier share space with an eight-story department store, a basement supermarket and food court, and dining and beauty outlets on the ninth floor. The mall is open daily 10am to 10pm. Nánjīng Xī Lù 1618 (next to Jìng Ān Sì), Jìng'ān. ✆ 021/3217-4838. Metro: Jing'an Temple.

**Cool Docks (Lǎo Mǎ Tóu)**   About 2km (1¼ miles) south of the Bund near the Shíliùpǔ Wharf, this complex of shops and restaurants in restored old buildings and warehouses is supposed to be Shànghǎi's second Xīntiāndì (p. 116), but has yet to fully take off. For now, if you're looking to get away from the crowds, this is a "cool" place to dine, shop, or get a tattoo (there's a Shànghǎi Tattoo shop here). The complex is open daily 10am to 10pm. Zhōngshān Nán Lù 430–505 (by Máojiāyuán Lù), Huángpǔ. Metro: Xiāonánmén.

**Grand Gateway Plaza (Gǎnghuì Guǎngchǎng)**   The biggest and flashiest of the malls in the Xújiāhuì circle has a good mix of retail (clothing, books, accessories, electronic items), dining and entertainment outlets, a theater (occasionally showing English-language movies) on the fifth floor, and a plethora of food court restaurants. Prices here are slightly lower than on Nánjīng Lù, but still not the best in town. The plaza is open 10am to 10pm. Hóngqiáo Lù 1 (at Huáshān Lù), Xúhuì. ✆ 021/6404-0111. Metro: Xújiāhuì.

**High Street Loft (Shāng Jiē)**   Filippo Gabbiani, the designer of Bund 18, has put his design imprint on this cluster of former factories in the French Concession, converting them into one of the hippest fashion, dining, and entertainment complexes in town. Many of the clothing stores feature the works of up-and-coming local designers. The complex is open daily 10am to 10pm. Jiāshàn Lù 1 (south of Jiànguó Xī Lù), Xúhuì. ✆ 021/5466-6675. Metro: Jiashan Rd.

**IFC Mall (Guójīn Zhōngxīn Shāngcháng)**  As part of the Shànghǎi International Finance Centre designed by Cesar Pelli, this brand-new, glittering, six-story shopping complex is chock-full of luxury stores (25 to be precise) fronted by the likes of Louis Vuitton and Armani. Apple's flagship Shànghǎi store is here, as well as a multiplex cinema and some high-end restaurants. The complex is open daily 10am to 10pm. Shìjì Dàdào 8, Pǔdōng. (☏ **021/2020-7000.** Metro: Lujiazui.

**Plaza 66 (Hénglóng Guǎngchǎng)**  The glamorous Plaza 66 (there are 66 floors to the building, six of them dedicated to shops and restaurants) probably has the largest collection of luxury-brand shops under one roof in Shànghǎi. Louis Vuitton, Prada, Versace, Christian Dior, and more—they're all here. Max out the credit card, or simply gawk and have fun trying to guess the pecking order of the luxury stores. The plaza is open daily 10am to 10pm. Nánjīng Xī Lù 1266 (at Shaǎnxī Běi Lù), Jing Ān. (☏ **021/6279-0910.** Metro: Nanjing Rd. (W).

**Raffles City (Láifùshì Guǎngchǎng)**  This ultramodern Singapore joint venture, aided by a prime location across from People's Square, is one of the biggest draws for hip mall rats. There's a cineplex showing Chinese and occasional Hollywood films, an IMAX theater, a fitness center, and retail shops ranging from local outfits to international names like Nike, Guess, and Swatch; however, the many dining establishments (Starbucks, Häagen-Dazs, a popular bakery called Bread Talk, and an excellent food court called Megabite) are the main draw. The mall is open daily 10am to 10pm. Xīzàng Zhōng Lù 268, Huángpǔ. (☏ **021/6340-3600.** Metro: Rénmín Guǎngchǎng (People's Square).

**Shànghǎi Centre (Shànghǎi Shāngchéng)**  With outlets like Starbucks and Tony Roma's dotting the landscape, this self-contained hub makes you feel like you've never left home. Also here: a deluxe hotel (Portman Ritz-Carlton Hotel), a medical and dental clinic, a grand theater, ATMs, a supermarket with a wide selection of Western groceries, and offices for half a dozen international airlines—all in the same complex. The shops are among the most upscale in Shànghǎi, with such outlets as Salvatore Ferragamo, Miu Miu, and Stefano Ricci. Hours vary for shops and offices, but many are open daily 10am to 6pm. Nánjīng Xī Lù 1376, Jing Ān. (☏ **021/6279-8600.** www.shanghaicentre.com. Metro: Jing'an Temple.

**Super Brand Mall (Zhèngdà Guǎngchǎng)**  The largest mall in Pǔdōng, this gargantuan 10-story edifice has finally started to attract the crowds. The anchor is a four-story department store with all the usual super goods. There's also a well-stocked Liánhuā supermarket and a Bank of China ATM in the basement, and scores of clothing, jewelry, and accessories stores, as well as dining establishments competing for your attention. The mall is open daily 10am to 10pm. Lùjiāzuǐ Lù 168, Pǔdōng. (☏ **021/6887-7888.** Metro: Lujiazui.

**Tiānzǐfáng**  This charming little complex started out as a small artists' colony, but has since expanded into the neighboring lanes as traditional *shíkùmén* houses have been converted into a veritable maze of open-air cafes, artists' studios, and small shops and boutiques selling everything from the latest fashions to home furnishings and Tibetan collectibles. It's become a de rigueur stop for many visitors, resulting in big crowds and high prices. The complex is open daily 10am to 10pm. Tàikàng Lù 210–274, Lúwān. Metro: Dǎpǔqiáo.

**Three on the Bund (Wàitān Sān Hào)**    About as classy and pricey as you can get in Shànghǎi shopping, this ritzy development on the Bund has a Giorgio Armani flagship store (✆ **021/6339-1133;** daily 11am–10pm), and other not-too-shabby mouthfuls such as Ann Demeulemeester, Bottega Veneta, Vivienne Tam, Yves Saint Laurent, and more. Even if you are going to pick up that "Emporio Armani" knockoff watch at a roadside stall for less than ¥200, it may be fun to come and admire the real thing through the looking glass. The complex is open daily 10am to 10pm. Zhōngshān Dōng Yī Lù 3 (entrance on Guǎngdōng Lù), Huángpǔ. ✆ 021/6323-3355. Metro: Nanjing Rd. (E).

## Silk, Fabrics & Tailors

The **South Bund Fabric Market** (p. 230) is the best place to shop for a variety of inexpensive fabrics, though you'd have to bargain hard; tailors here also generally do yeoman's work in churning out suits, dresses, and other garments.

**Chinese Printed Blue Nankeen Exhibition Hall (Zhōngguó Lányìnhuā Bù Guǎn)**    In business for more than 20 years, this exhibition hall/shop started by Madam Kubo Mase revives the folk art of indigo batik dyeing. Bales of this *nankeen* (as indigo batik is known in China) cloth, so fashionable in ethnic restaurants and on fashion runways these days, are sold here, along with ready-made *nankeen* shirts, tablecloths, and craft souvenirs. The hall is open daily 9am to 5pm. Chánglè Lù 637, House 24 (by Chángshú Lù), Xúhuì. ✆ 021/5403-7947. Metro: Changshu Rd.

**Dave's Custom Tailoring**    Dave's specializes in men's fashion, with custom-made Savile Row three-piece suits starting from ¥3,500. Turnaround is normally 10 to 14 days, but can be shorter for a hefty fee. The shop is open daily 10:30am to 7pm. Wǔyuán Lù, Lane 288, no. 6 (between Wǔlǔmùqí Lù and Wǔkāng Lù), Xúhuì. ✆ 021/5404-0001. Metro: Changshu Rd.

**Silk King (Zhēnsī Dà Wáng)**    Silk and wool yardage and a good selection of shirts, blouses, skirts, dresses, ties, sheets, and other finished silk goods have made Silk King one of the top silk retailers in Shànghǎi, and a favorite stop for visiting heads of state and other VIPs. Silk or wool suits can be custom-tailored in as few as 24 hours. Silk starts around ¥100 per meter (3¼ ft.), while more delicate cashmere is almost 10 times that. The shops are open daily 9:30am to 10pm. There are several Silk King branches. Tiānpíng Lù 139, Xújiāhuì (headquarters). ✆ 021/6282-1533. Metro: Xújiāhuì. Also at: Nánjīng Dōng Lù 66. ✆ 021/6321-2193. Metro: Nanjing Rd. (E). Nánjīng Xī Lù 819. ✆ 021/6215-3114. Metro: Nanjing Rd. (W). Huáihǎi Zhōng Lù 550. ✆ 021/5383-0561. Metro: Huangpi Rd. (S).

**Woo Scarf & Shawl**    The neighborhood roadside stall may claim to sell "100% Pashmina" scarves, but this store *guarantees* that its shawls and scarves are 100% pashmina and of the highest quality cashmere and silk. The colors and designs are indeed quite gorgeous, the selection is wide, and the quality is tops, which the owners are hoping will justify the sky-high prices. The store is open daily 9am to 9pm. Tàikāng Lù 210, Yard 7, Room 12 (in Tiānzǐfáng), Xújiāhuì. ✆ 021/6445-7516. www.shanghaiwoo.com. Metro: Dǎpǔqiáo.

## Supermarkets

Shànghǎi's hotels might have a small shop with some Western snacks and bottled water, or a deli stand, but for a broad range of familiar groceries, try one of the large-scale supermarkets listed here. There is also a well-stocked Park 'n Shop in the basement of Parkson's (see "Department Stores," earlier in this chapter).

**Carrefour (Jiālèfú)**   This French commodities giant offers an extensive range of imported Western groceries, along with fresh fruits, vegetables, sporting goods, clothing, shoes, music, electronic items, books, bicycles, and film developing. It's open daily 8am to 10pm. Shuīchéng Nán Lù 268, Gǔběi Xīnqū, Chángníng. ☎ **021/6270-6829.** Metro: Shuīchéng Rd.

**City Supermarket (Chéngshì Chāoshì)**   This small but comprehensive supermarket in the Shànghǎi Centre is among the best places in town to pick up those Western foodstuffs you've been missing. It's pricey, but there's a nice selection, with a fine deli in the back. It's open daily 8am to 10pm. Nánjīng Xī Lù 1376 (at Shànghǎi Centre), Jing Ān. ☎ **021/6279-8018.** Metro: Jing'an Temple.

# Tea

**The Bund Tea Company (Shànghǎi Cháyuán Yǒuxiàn Gōngsī)**   Newly ensconced in a restored 1908 building just behind the Bund, this tea room and tea shop hearkens back to the early–20th century when this building was occupied by a British tea trading company. You can participate in tastings and purchase the various black, green, and flower teas on sale here. The shop is open daily 9am to 5pm. Diānchí Lù 100 (west of Yuánmíngyuán Lù), Lúwān. ☎ **021/6329-0989.** www.bundtea.com. Metro: Nanjing Rd. (E).

**Huángshān Tea Company (Huángshān Cháyè Diàn)**   There's a wide assortment of classic Yíxīng teapots (made in the adjacent province) and loose Chinese teas sold by weight here. The shops are open daily 10am to 10pm. Huáihǎi Zhōng Lù 605 (west of Chéngdū Běi Lù), Lúwān. ☎ **021/5306-2258.** Metro: Huangpi Rd. (S). Also at Huáihǎi Zhōng Lù 868 (east of Màomíng Lù), Lúwān. ☎ **021/5403-5412.**

# SHÀNGHĂI AFTER DARK

I n the first half of the 20th century, Shànghăi was the most notorious city in Asia, with a nightlife that rivaled that of Paris. Dubbed the "Whore of Asia," old Shànghăi presented countless opportunities for debauchery in its gambling dens, opium joints, rowdy nightclubs, and glamorous theaters. After the Communist Party came to power in 1949, Shànghăi was cleaned up overnight; drugs and prostitution were ended by decree, and entertainment was reduced to a few politically acceptable plays and dances. Well into the 1990s, visitors retired to their hotels after dark unless they were part of a group tour going to see the Shànghăi acrobats. In the last few years, however, the possibilities for an evening on the town have multiplied exponentially, and while Shànghăi is not in the same league as Hong Kong or Paris quite yet, it is fast becoming again a city that never sleeps.

Culture mavens can now find in Shànghăi large-scale performances of acrobatics, musicals, opera, dance, theater, and classical and contemporary music. New state-of-the-art theaters and auditoriums have attracted in recent years the likes of Yo-Yo Ma, Luciano Pavarotti, Diana Krall, the Kirov Ballet, and touring companies of *Les Misérables* and *Cats,* among others. Large-scale pop and rock concerts are happening with increasing frequency, many of them of the more benign Mando-pop or Canto-pop variety, but artists like the Rolling Stones, Christina Aguilera, and Celine Dion have all performed here in the last few years.

Nightclubs and bars are also booming, with joints opening and closing faster than night can turn into day. Barflies now have a choice of everything from glamorous Art Deco lounges to the seediest watering hole; live rock and jazz can be heard into the wee hours (although 2am is the official closing hour); and the dance club scene now employs DJs, foreign and local, to keep the younger set raving. With a return to the rollicking times has come the return of drugs and sexual exploitation, a phenomenon that

## BUYING tickets

Check the entertainment listings in the free English-language papers for tourists and expatriates, such as the bi-weekly *City Weekend* (www.cityweekend.com.cn), or the monthlies *Time Out Shànghǎi, Shanghai Talk*, or *that's Shanghai* (www.shanghai.urbanatomy.com). Tickets for all arts performances can be purchased at their individual venues, or at the Shànghǎi Cultural Information and Booking Centre, Fèngxián Lù 272 (© **021/6217-2426** or 021/6217-3055; www.culture.sh.cn; daily 9am–7pm), northeast of the Shànghǎi Centre, behind the Westgate Mall, as well as online at the above Web address. Tickets for the Grand Theatre can be purchased directly at the box office (Rénmín Dà Dào 200; © **021/ 6372-8701**), and movie tickets can be bought at the cinemas. If you don't want to do it yourself, your hotel concierge should be able to secure tickets for a fee.

periodically receives some government attention, but largely continues unchecked. Having converted some of its newly won wealth into so many venues for culture and entertainment, Shànghǎi, it seems, is not about to go gentle into that good night.

# THE PERFORMING ARTS

## Acrobatics

Chinese acrobats are justifiably world-famous, their international reputation cemented in no small part by the Shànghǎi Acrobatic Troupe, formed in 1951. While the troupe, one of the world's best, frequently tours internationally, it also performs at home, and an acrobatic show has become one of the most popular evening entertainment for tourists. These days, the juggling, contortionists, unicycling, chair-stacking, and plate-spinning have entered the age of modern staging; performances are beginning to resemble the high-tech shows of a Las Vegas–style variety act. You can catch a performance at the following stages.

**Shànghǎi Centre Theatre (Shànghǎi Shāngchéng Jùyuàn)**   A favorite with foreign tour groups, this luxurious, modern, 1,000-seat auditorium at Shànghǎi Centre is equipped for a variety of performances, but its specialty is the Shànghǎi Acrobatic Troupe. Almost nightly, the troupe gives a 90-minute variety show featuring both standard and inventive acts, from plate-spinning and tightrope-walking to clowns and magic. Shows are held most nights at 7:30pm with some seasonal variation. Nánjīng Lù (E) 1376, 4th floor, Jing Ān. © **021/6279-8663** or 021/6279-7132. Tickets ¥100–¥280. Metro: Jing'an Temple.

**Shànghǎi Circus World (Shànghǎi Mǎxìchéng)**   The home of the Shànghǎi Acrobatic Troupe, this glittering arena in the northern suburbs houses a 1,672-seat circus theater with computer-controlled lighting, state-of-the-art acoustics, and a motorized revolving stage, all the more to impress the already impressed crowd. On most nights, it's home to the stunning multimedia extravaganza "ERA—Intersection of Time," which is worth traipsing out here for if you like your acrobatics with flashing lights and pyrotechnics. Performances are at 7:30pm. Gònghé Xīn Lù 2266, Zhábběi. © **021/5665-6622,** ext. 2027. Tickets ¥80–¥580. Metro: Shànghǎi Circus World.

# Shànghǎi After Dark

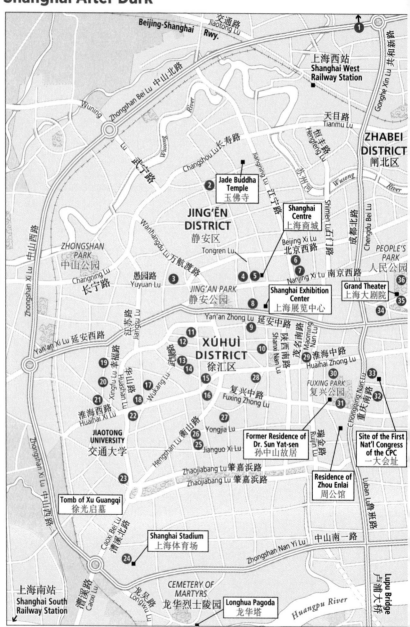

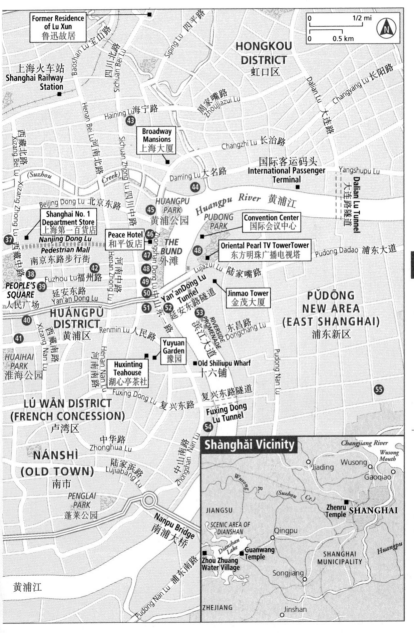

Former Residence
of Lu Xun
鲁迅故居

上海火车站
Shanghai Railway
Station

HONGKOU
DISTRICT
虹口区

Broadway
Mansions
上海大厦

43

Haining Lu 海宁路

Baoshan Lu 宝山路
Sichuan Bei Lu 四川北路
Siping Lu 四平路
Zhoujiazui Lu 周家嘴路
Dalian Lu 大连路
Changyang Lu 长阳路

Changzhi Lu 长治路

国际客运码头
International Passenger
Terminal

Yangshupu Lu

Daming Lu 大名路

44

Dalian Lu Tunnel
大连路隧道

Henan Bei Lu 河南北路
Xizang Bei Lu 西藏北路
(Suzhou Creek)

Beijing Dong Lu 北京东路

45

HUANGPU
PARK
黄浦公园

Huangpu River 黄浦江

PUDONG
PARK

Convention Center
国际会议中心

Shanghai No. 1
Department Store
上海第一百货店
Nanjing Dong Lu
Pedestrian Mall
南京东路步行街

37

Peace Hotel
和平饭店

46

THE
BUND
外滩

48

Oriental Pearl TV TowerTower
东方明珠广播电视塔

Pudong Dadao 浦东大道

Sichuan Zhong Lu 四川中路
Henan Zhong Lu 河南中路

47
48
49
50

38
39

Fuzhou Lu 福州路

42

Zhongshan Dong Lu 中山东一路

Lujiazui Lu 陆家嘴路

10

SHÀNGHĂI AFTER DARK    The Performing Arts

PEOPLE'S
SQUARE
人民广场

Yan'an Dong Lu

Yan'anDong Lu
Tunnel
延安东路隧道

Jinmao Tower
金茂大厦

PŬDŌNG
NEW AREA
(EAST SHANGHAI)
浦东新区

51
52
53

RIVERSIDE
PROMENADE
滨江大道

Dongchang Lu 东昌路

40

HUÁNGPŬ
DISTRICT
黄浦区

Renmin Lu 人民路

Dongchang Lu 东昌路

Pudong Nan Lu 浦东南路

41

HUAIHAI
PARK
淮海公园

Xizang Nan Lu 西藏南路
Henan Nan Lu 河南南路

Yuyuan
Garden
豫园

Old Shiliupu Wharf
十六铺

55

LÚ WĀN DISTRICT
(FRENCH CONCESSION)
卢湾区

Huxinting
Teahouse
湖心亭茶社

Fuxing Dong Lu 复兴东路

Fuxing Dong
Lu Tunnel

NÁNSHÌ
(OLD TOWN)
南市

中华路
Zhonghua Lu

陆家浜路
Lujiabang Lu

54

PENGLAI
PARK
蓬莱公园

中山南路
Zhongshan Lu

Nanpu Bridge
南浦大桥

黄浦江

Pudong Nan Lu 浦东南路

Shànghăi Vicinity

Changjiang River

Wusong
Mouth

Jiading

Wusong

Gaoqiao

JIANGSU

Wusong R. (Suzhou Cr.)

Zhenru
Temple

SHANGHAI

SCENIC AREA OF
DIANSHAN

Qingpu

Dianshan Lake

Guanwang
Temple

SHANGHAI
MUNICIPALITY

Huangpu

Zhou Zhuang
Water Village

Songjiang

ZHEJIANG

Jinshan

# Key for Shànghǎi After Dark

**THE PERFORMING ARTS**
Hèlǔtīng Concert Hall **28**
(Hèlǔtīng Yīnyuè Tīng)

Majestic Theater **6**
(Měiqí Dàxìyuàn)

Shànghǎi Centre Theatre **5**
(Shànghǎi Shāngchéng Jùyuàn)

Shànghǎi Circus World **1**
(Shànghǎi Mǎxìchéng)

Shànghǎi Concert Hall **40**
(Shànghǎi Yīnyuè Tīng)

Shànghǎi Dramatic Arts Centre **12**
(Shànghǎi Huàjù Yìshù Zhōngxīn)

Shànghǎi Grand Stage **24**
(Shànghǎi Dà Wǔtái)

Shànghǎi Grand Theatre **35**
(Dà Jùyuàn)

Shànghǎi Oriental Art Center **55**
(Shànghǎi Dōngfāng Yìshù Zhōngxīn)

Yìfū Theatre (Yìfū Wǔtái) **39**

**JAZZ CLUBS**
JZ Club (Juéshì) **14**

Cotton Club **15**
(Miánhuā Jùlèbù)

House of Blues and Jazz **48**
(Bùlǔsī Juéshì Zhī Wū

Peace Hotel Old Jazz Bar **46**

**DANCE CLUBS & DISCOS**
Babyface **41**
Guandii (Guāndǐ) **31**
LOgO **20**
M1NT **42**
MAO **27**
Muse **2**
Muse at Park 97 **30**
Paramount **3**
The Shelter **13**

**LOUNGES & BARS**
Atanu 1907 Bar **52**
Bar Rouge **47**
Barbarossa (Bābālùshā) **36**
Constellation **10**
Cotton's (Miánhuā Jiǔbā) **25**
Dada **19**
Eddy's Bar **22**
el Coctel **13**
Ferg and Sons **17**
Frangipani **34**
Glamour Bar (Mèilì Jiǔbā) **49**
Gosney & Kallman's Chinatown **43**
Jade on 36 Bar **53**
Kevin's **11**
Lost Heaven Bar (Huāmǎ Tiāntáng Jiǔbā) **51**
Malone's (Mǎlóng Měishì Jiǔlóu) **4**
Manifesto **9**
Mural (Mó Yàn) **26**
O'Malley's Irish Pub (Ōumǎlì ) **16**
Salon de Ning **45**
Shànghǎi Studio **18**
Sky Dome Bar **37**
The Long Bar at the Puli **8**
The Roof @ Waterhouse **54**
The Vault **50**
Vue Bar **44**
Xīntiāndì "Heavenly" Bars **33**

**CINEMAS**
Cathay Theatre **29**
(Guótài Diànyǐngyuàn)

Paradise Warner Cinema City **23**
(Yǒnghuá Diànyǐngchéng)

Peace Cinema **38**
(Hépíng Yǐngdū)

Shànghǎi Film Art Center **21**
(Shànghǎi Yǐngchéng)

Studio City **7**
(Huányì Diànyǐngchéng)

UME International Cineplex **32**
(Xīntiāndì Guójì Yǐngchéng)

The Performing Arts

SHÀNGHǍI AFTER DARK

# Opera

Shànghǎi has its own troupe that performs Běijīng opera (*Jīng Xì*) regularly at the Yìfu Theatre. Běijīng opera is derived from 8 centuries of touring song and dance troupes, but became institutionalized in its present form in the 1700s under the Qīng Dynasty. The stylized singing, costumes, acrobatics, music, and choreography of Chinese opera often strike uninitiated foreigners as rather screechy and incomprehensible. It helps to know the plot (usually a historical drama with a tragic outcome), which most Chinese do. Songs are performed on a five-note scale (not the eight-note scale familiar in the West), and gongs, cymbals, and string and wind instruments accompany the action on the stage. Faces are painted with colors symbolizing qualities such as valor or villainy, and masks and costumes announce the performer's role in society, from emperor to peasant. Most Běijīng opera these days consists of abridgements, lasting 2 hours or less (as opposed to 5 hr. or more in the old days). With martial arts choreography, spirited acrobatics, and brilliant costumes, these performances can be a delight even to the unaccustomed, untrained eye. Regional operas, including the Kūnjù form, are also performed in Shànghǎi. Kūnjù, which originated near Shànghǎi in the old city of Kūnshān, is the oldest form of opera in China, and Shànghǎi has China's leading troupe. This opera tradition uses traditional stories and characters, as does Běijīng opera, but it is known for being more melodic. Regular venues for opera include:

**Majestic Theater (Měiqí Dàxìyuàn)** Opera in Chinese is occasionally performed by local and touring groups in one of Shànghǎi's oldest and most ornate theaters. The theater is worth attending just for the traditional atmosphere. Jiāngníng Lù 66 (at Běijīng Xī Lù), Jìng Ān. ℂ **021/6217-4409.** Metro: Nanjing Rd. (E).

**Yifu Theatre (Yìfū Wǔtái)** This is the premier venue for Shànghǎi's opera companies. The Shànghǎi Peking Opera House Troupe, featuring some of China's greatest opera stars, performs here regularly, as do the Shànghǎi Kūnjù Opera Troupe and other visiting companies. Performances most nights are at 7:15pm, with occasional matinees on weekends at 1:30pm. Fúzhōu Lù 701, Huángpǔ. ℂ **021/6351-4668** or 021/6322-5294. Tickets ¥80–¥380. Metro: Nanjing Rd. (E).

# Other Performance Venues

Shànghǎi is the site of major national and international music, drama, and dance performances nearly every day of the year. The most frequent venues are listed here. In addition, local and international dramatic productions are often mounted at the **Shànghǎi Dramatic Arts Centre,** Ānfú Lù 288, Xúhuì (ℂ **021/6433-5133**), and at the **Shànghǎi Theatre Academy,** Huáshān Lù 630, Jìng Ān (ℂ **021/6248-2920,** ext. 3040), where experimental plays are sometimes presented.

**Hèlùtīng Concert Hall (Hèlùtīng Yīnyuè Tīng)** On the grounds of the Shànghǎi Conservatory of Music, this concert hall plays host mostly to a variety of classical music performances and chamber concerts. Fēnyáng Lù 20, Xúhuì. ℂ **021/6431-1792.** Tickets start from ¥20, depending on performance. Metro: Jing'an Temple.

**Shànghǎi Concert Hall (Shànghǎi Yīnyuè Tīng)** Recently renovated (and literally hoisted whole and moved), this classical concert hall used to be the former home of the Shànghǎi Symphony Orchestra, which still continues to perform here occasionally, despite its move to more permanent quarters in Pǔdōng. Yán'ān Dōng Lù 523 (south of People's Square), Huángpǔ. ℂ **021/6386-2836** or 021/5386-6666. Metro: People's Square.

**Shànghǎi Grand Stage (Shànghǎi Dà Wǔtái)**　　This stage, located inside the Shànghǎi Sports Stadium, is mostly used for large rock and pop concerts, including the Rolling Stones and Celine Dion. Cáoxī Běi Lù 1111 (inside Shànghǎi Stadium), Xúhuì. ✆ **021/6438-5200** or 021/6426-5678. Metro: Shanghai Stadium.

**Shànghǎi Grand Theatre (Shànghǎi Dà Jùyuàn)**　　This stunning space-age complex with three theaters (the largest seating 1,800) is the city's premier venue for international performers and concerts, ranging from Yo-Yo Ma to the touring company of *Cats* and *The Lion King*. Prices usually start at ¥80, and can top ¥1,600 for the best seats to popular world-class performers and groups. Rénmín Dà Dào 300, People's Square, Huángpǔ. ✆ **021/6372-8701** or 021/6386-8686. Metro: People's Square.

**Shànghǎi Oriental Art Center (Shànghǎi Dōngfāng Yìshù Zhōngxīn)**　　This modern, butterfly-shaped, Paul Andreu–designed complex (he also designed the Pǔdōng Airport) is Pǔdōng's answer to the Shànghǎi Grand Theatre. The 1,953-seat symphony hall is now a permanent home for the Shànghǎi Symphony Orchestra, and the center also has two smaller theaters. Dīngxiāng Lù 425 (by Jǐndài Lù), Pǔdōng. ✆ **021/3842-4800.** www.shoac.com.cn. Metro: Science and Technology Museum.

# JAZZ CLUBS

Shànghǎi's pre-revolutionary (before 1949) jazz legacy has been revived for the 21st century: Not only are the old standards being played once again, but more modern and improvisational sounds can also be heard around town, and there's a greater influx of international jazz artists to these shores than ever before. Hotel lounges and bars are the most obvious venues for jazz performances, though what you get here is mostly easy-listening jazz. Once a year, the jazz scene perks up with the Shànghǎi Jazz Festival in mid-October, which draws headline artists and groups from America, Europe, Japan, and Australia. During the rest of the year, live jazz can be heard at the following places.

**Cotton Club (Miánhuā Jùlèbù)**　　Live jazz nightly is the hallmark of this local institution, Shànghǎi's longest running venue and still the best one for live jazz and blues. The bands are skilled, the tunes are tight, and the informal, darkly atmospheric club often attracts standing-room-only crowds on weekends. The club is open Tuesday to Sunday 7:30pm to 2am. Live music plays on weeknights 9:30pm to midnight, Friday and Saturday 10:15pm to 1:30am. Fùxīng Xī Lù 8 (at Huáihǎi Zhōng Lù), Xúhuì. © **021/6437-7110.** No cover. Metro: Changshu Rd.

**House of Blues and Jazz (Bùlǔsī Juéshì Zhī Wū)** Relocated from the French Concession to just off the Bund across from the Captain hostel, this is thankfully still an excellent spot to sing the blues. The space is larger here, with two floors, but the vibe is still fairly intimate, relaxed, and unpretentious, with the music (international bands are the norm) usually taking center stage. The house is open Tuesday to Sunday, 7pm to 2am; a band plays 9:30pm to 1am. Fúzhōu Lù 60 (east of Sìchuān Lù), Huángpǔ. © **021/6323-2779.** No cover. One-drink minimum. Metro: Nanjing Rd. (E).

**JZ Club** Established by two musicians as a kind of informal jazz "living room," this is one of Shànghǎi's more popular venues for live jazz as it boasts a talented house band, good acoustics, and an intimate environment. The crowd is obviously here for the music, which features top foreign and local artists, and tends toward more improvisational jams. The club is open nightly from 8pm to 2am; a band plays 10pm to 1am. Fùxīng Xī Lù 46 (btw. Yǒngfú Lù and Wūlǔmùqí Lù), Xúhuì. © **021/6431-0269.** www.jzclub. cn. Cover Fri–Sat ¥30; no cover other days. Metro: Changshu Rd.

**Peace Hotel Old Jazz Bar** Relocated to the Huátíng Hotel and Towers in Xújiāhuì for the last 2 years while the Peace Hotel was closed for renovation, the famous Peace Hotel Jazz Band should, by the time you read this, be back in its place of origin. The band has been an institution, with nearly continuous performances since the 1930s. Expect a lot of nostalgic old standards. Performances run nightly from 7:30 to 9:30pm. Nánjīng Dōng Lù 20, Fairmont Peace Hotel (Hépíng Bīngguǎn), Huángpǔ. © **021/6138-6886.** Tickets ¥150; reservations highly recommended. Metro: Nanjing Rd. (E).

# DANCE CLUBS & DISCOS

Shànghǎi has some of the most sophisticated and elaborate dance clubs and discos in China. The bar scene is lively, too, but clubs and discos are for those who want to party on the dance floor as well as at the bar—or at least for those who want to observe Shànghǎi nightlife at a pitch it hasn't reached since the 1930s. Shànghǎi's dance club scene relies heavily on DJs, whether foreign superstars brought in on a short engagement or increasingly sophisticated locals. Here's a list of the top venues, which like all trends are subject to overnight revisions.

**Babyface** Originally the playground for Shanghainese nouveau riches, Babyface is as popular, crowded, and ultrapretentious as ever. A DJ spins pop music, but the sleek, sophisticated crowd is usually more interested in sizing up all who walk through the door. The club is open nightly from 9pm to 3am (5am on Fri–Sat). Huáihǎi Zhōng Lù 138, Shànghǎi Sq., Unit 101 (east of Sōngshān Lù at Pǔ'ān Lù), Lúwān. © **021/6375-6667**. www.babyface.com.cn. No cover. Metro: Huangpi Rd. (S).

**Guandii** A Táiwān import, this very popular club located in the southern part of Fùxīng attracts a Taiwanese, Hong Kong, and hip local crowd. Music ranges from house to hip-hop. The club is open nightly from 8:30pm to 3am (5am Fri–Sat). Gāo'ān Lù 2 (inside Fùxīng Gōngyuán), Lúwān. © **021/3308-0726.** No cover. Metro: Huangpi Rd. (S) or Shanxi Rd. (S).

**LOgO**   The first of the underground music clubs on Xìngfú Lù, LOgO has largely remained close to its alternative underground music roots. The artsy, young crowd comes for the music (house, electronic, techno, and the like), DJs, and the cheap drinks. The club is open nightly 8:30pm to late. Xìngfú Lù 13 (near Fǎhuázhèn Lù), Chángníng. ☎ 021/6281-5646. www.logoshanghai.net. No cover, except for special performances. Metro: Jiaotong University.

**MAO**   Weekend theme parties, a cover charge for men (women usually get in free), minimum-charge tables, and complaints of overpriced drinks don't seem to deter the sweaty crowds who dance and drink into the wee hours of the morning at this place. The club is open Wednesday and Thursday midnight to 6am, Friday and Saturday 11pm to 7am. Yuèyáng Lù 46 (by Yǒngjiā Lù), Xúhuì. ☎ 0/1580-039-1942. Cover ¥100 Fri-Sat for men, includes 1 drink; no cover for women. Metro: Hengshan Rd.

**M1NT**   Lodged on the 24th floor of a downtown high-rise, this upscale members club (nonmembers welcome) boasts brilliant floor-to-ceiling window views of the whole city, a much ballyhooed shark tank, and some of Shànghǎi's hottest parties. Frequented by a superchic clientele not dissuaded by the overpriced drinks, there's also a restaurant and lounge bar on the premises, though certain areas like the VIP terrace are reserved for members only. Voted Best Club in 2009, this is a place where appearance (and money) counts. The club is open Monday to Saturday 9pm to late; the lounge daily 6pm to late. Fúzhōu Lù 318, 24th floor (by Shāndōng Lù), Huángpǔ. ☎ **021/6391-2811.** www.m1nt.com.cn. Cover ¥100 Fri-Sat; no cover for members. Metro: Nanjing Rd. (E).

**Muse**   A bit off the trodden path in the northwestern part of town, Muse really heats up on weekends when young expats and oh-so-hip locals make this one of their de rigueur dance stops. House and hip-hop are played in different rooms separated by soundproof glass screens—dancers are preferred, but voyeurs are certainly welcome. The club is open Sunday to Wednesday 8pm to 2am; Thursday to Saturday 8pm to 4am. Yúyáo Lù 68, the New Factories (west of Xīkāng Lù), Jìng Ān. ☎ 021/5213-5228. www.museshanghai.cn. No cover, except for special events and guest DJs. Metro: Changping Rd.

**Muse at Park 97**   This third outlet of the Muse chain has taken over one of the original longstanding clubs in Shànghǎi in the lovely Fùxīng Park. Thankfully, the lively partying continues, and the drinks are even reasonably priced. The club is open nightly 8pm to 2am (4am on Fri–Sat). Gāolán Lù 2, Lan Kwai Fong at Park 97, Fùxīng Gōngyuán, Lúwān. ☎ **021/5383-2328.** No cover. Metro: Huangpi Rd. (S).

**Paramount**   The outer trappings are cool—a nightclub in a refurbished 1930s Art Deco theater complete with flashing strobe lights and a large dance floor. Oh, and the place is purportedly haunted. You can decide for yourself if those apparitions you see are ghostly spirits or just the frenzied gyrating bodies of young locals at your standard Shànghǎi nightclub. The club is open nightly 8pm to 2am (4am on Fri–Sat). Yùyuán Lù 218 (west of Wūlǔmùqí Lù), Jìng Ān. ☎ **021/6249-8866.** Cover ¥250. Metro: Jing'an Temple.

**The Shelter**   Tired of all the same slick trance and techno? Mix it up at this former bomb shelter (hence the name), a popular spot for alternative indie music in town. Great DJs (who sometimes spin soul, too), a large dance floor with rooms in the back, and reasonably priced drinks make this a popular hangout for the young and the restless expat set. The club is open Wednesday to Sunday 9pm to 2am. Yǒngfú Lù 5 (north of Fùxīng Xī Lù), Xúhuì. No phone. Cover ¥10-¥80. Metro: Shanghai Library.

# THE LOUNGE & BAR SCENE

The big hotels often have elegant lounges on their top floors and some of Shànghǎi's best bars in their lobbies. Independent spots outside the hotels run the gamut from upscale to down-and-dirty, but those listed here are frequented by plenty of English-speaking foreigners (residents and tourists alike) in addition to hip, well-to-do Shanghainese. In recent years, Shànghǎi's lively nightlife seems to have cleaved along the lines of the Bund crowd (favoring the many bars that have sprouted there), and those who wouldn't be caught dead anywhere near there, the latter including a growing underground scene. Expect drink prices, especially for imports, to be the same as, if not more than, what you'd pay in the bars of a large city in the West. Tipping is not necessary, although it does make the bartenders happy.

Gay-friendly nightspots (subject to change, as the scene shifts but never disappears) include the mainstay **Eddy's Bar,** Huáihǎi Zhōng Lù 1877, by Tiānpíng Lù (☎ 021/6282-0521; nightly 8pm–2am, Fri–Sun to 3am); **Kevin's,** Chánglè Lù 946, no. 4, at Wūlǔmùqí Běi Lù (☎ 021/6248-8985; nightly 9pm–2am); **Frangipani,** Dàgǔ Lù 399, by Shímén Yī Lù (☎ 021/5375-0084); and the part bar, part art studio **Shànghǎi Studio,** Huáihǎi Zhōng Lù 1950, no. 4, by Xìngguó Lù (☎ 021/6283-1043; www.shanghai-studio.com; nightly 9pm–late).

**Atanu 1907 Bar**   Soak in some Shànghǎi history as you imbibe your cocktails at this cool little bar located right on the Bund promenade. Drinking quarters are lodged on the second floor of what used to be Shànghǎi's old Signal Tower (1907), which was used to control river traffic during colonial times. There are displays of old photos of the Bund on the first floor, and at press time, the bar was restricting access to the third-floor patio. It's open daily 9am to 2am. Zhōngshān Dōng Èr Lù 1 (at Yán'ān Dōng Lù), Huángpǔ. ☎ 021/6350-7649. Metro: Nanjing Rd. (E).

**Bar Rouge**   Perched atop Bund 18, Bar Rouge, with its glamorous vibe, great views, grand terrace, and creative cocktails, is *the* bar of choice for Shànghǎi's beautiful jet set used to glamming it up. Late at night, international DJs ratchet it up a notch. Even if you forget your Gauloises, someone there should be able to bum you one. It's open daily 6pm to 1:30am (Fri–Sat to 4:30am). Zhōngshān Dōng Yī Lù 18, 7th floor (at Bund 18), Huángpǔ. ☎ 021/6339-1199. www.bar-rouge-shanghai.com. Metro: Nanjing Rd. (E).

**Barbarossa**   Built on the lake in the middle of People's Park, this Moroccan-themed fantasia features four floors of drinking, dining, dancing, and, most popularly, Sheesha pipes for smoking. With panoramic views of the park and surrounding skyscrapers, both indoor and outdoor seating on chairs and cushions, and those exotic fragrances wafting from the pipes, this is a popular stop on any evening, even if it's not your final destination. It's open daily 11am to 2am (Fri–Sat 3am). Nánjīng Xī Lù 231 (inside People's Park), Huángpǔ. ☎ 021/6318-0220. Metro: People's Square.

**Constellation**   A favorite of connoisseurs in the know, this longstanding sophisticated Japanese-style bar features some of the most impeccably mixed cocktails in town. The original location on Xīnlè Lù is still preferred. It's open daily 7pm to 2am. Xīnlè Lù 86 (by Xiāngyáng Běi Lù), Xúhuī. ☎ 021/5404-0970. Metro: Shaanxi Rd. (S). Also at Yǒngjiā Lù 33 (by Màomíng Nán Lù), Lúwān. ☎ 021/5465-5993. Metro: Shaanxi Rd. (S). Huáihǎi Zhōng Lù 1276 (near Huátíng Lù). ☎ 021/5404-7211. Metro: Changshu Rd.

**Cotton's**   This place is popular with many expats for its friendly vibe and quintessential Shànghǎi setting in a romantic French Concession mansion. There are big fireplaces, color-themed rooms, and a delightful garden bar for the warmer months. It's open daily 11am to 2am (Fri–Sat 4am). Āntíng Lù 132 (by Jiànguó Xī Lù), Xúhuì. *℃* **021/6433-7995.** www.cottons-shanghai.com. Metro: Hengshan Rd.

**Dada** Far from the din of the luxury Bund bars, this is your regular unpretentious neighborhood dive bar that's a favorite of the young keepin'-it-real crowd. Both locals and expats love the cheap drinks, friendly management, varied dance sets, and indie movie nights (Tues at 9pm). The bar is open nightly 9pm to late. Xingfú Lù 115 (by Fǎhuázhèn Lù), Chángníng. *℃* **1500-018-2212.** Metro: Jiaotong University.

**el Cóctel** Opened by the owner of the tapas restaurant el Willy (p. 120), this second-floor bar, like your regular neighborhood bar in Barcelona or Paris, is a cozy place for cool sophisticates to unwind and socialize. Prices are on the high end, but the bartenders are skilled and they don't skimp. The martinis are mean, and *The Godfather* (scotch and amaretto) will have your loyalty. The bar is open Monday to Saturday 5pm to late. Yǒngfú Lù 47, Unit 202 (by Wǔkāng Lù), Xúhuì. *℃* **021/6433-7995.** www.elwilly.com.cn. Metro: Shanghai Library.

**Ferg and Sons** Next to the bistro Franck (p. 120), this intimate bar by the same owner features an eclectic decor (antique foosball table, anyone?), an outdoor terrace, a tapas bar, and a small but good-quality wine and beer selection. It's far from the usual tourist crowds, but popular with expats looking to unwind after a long week. For quieter conversation with your Prosecco, pop into Franck next door if they're still open. It's open Thursday to Sunday 6pm to late. Wǔkāng Lù 376, Ferguson Lane (near Tài'ān Lù), Xúhuì. *℃* **021/6433-1213.** Metro: Shanghai Library.

**Glamour Bar** The glamorous bar in M on the Bund has romantic views of the Bund through its picture windows and a full range of creative cocktails and champagnes to complement its tasteful Art Deco surroundings. Try the Kumquat Mojito if you fancy some zing. There is live music as well to keep the well-heeled set happy. It's open nightly 5pm to 2am. Guǎngdōng Lù 20, 6th floor (off the Bund), Huángpǔ. *℃* **021/6350-9988.** www.m-theglamourbar.com. Metro: Nanjing Rd. (E).

**Gosney & Kallman's Chinatown** *Willkommen, bienvenue, welcome.* Burlesque returns to Shànghǎi, this time in a former 1930s Buddhist temple. The three-story cavernous Chinatown, as the joint is commonly referred to, plays host nightly to 1920s-style cabaret acts with international musicians, vaudevillians, and showgirls in revealing costumes. It's open Wednesday to Saturday 8pm to 2am. Zhápǔ Lù 471 (by Hǎiníng Lù), Hóngkǒu. *℃* **021/6258-2078.** www.chinatownshanghai.com. Metro: Hailun Rd.

**Jade on 36 Bar** Perched on the 36th floor of the Shangri-La Hotel Tower, this bar is part of the hotel's signature restaurant and has probably the best views of the Bund and Pǔxī, especially at night. Drinks (try their Apple Mojito, or the Jelly Freeze—of vodka and Chambord) don't come cheap, but neither does real glamour and some highly creative mixology. International DJs funk it up most nights. Don't leave without checking out the space-age toilets. It's open nightly 5:30pm to 1am (Fri–Sat to 2am). Fùchéng Lù 33 (36th floor, Pǔdōng Shangri-La Hotel), Pǔdōng. *℃* **021/6882-3636.** Metro: Lujiazui.

**The Long Bar at the PuLi** Nestled within a grove of bamboo next to an infinity pool, this 32m-long (105-ft.) bar inside the PuLi Hotel and Spa is a great place to relax away from the hustle and bustle of the city. It's definitely quiet enough for cocktails and conversation. The bar boasts one of the largest whiskey selections in

The Lounge & Bar Scene

SHÀNGHǍI AFTER DARK

town, and its signature Pulitini cocktail featuring Kahlúa, vodka, and espresso is buzz-worthy as well. The bar is open daily 5:30pm to 1am (Fri–Sat to 2am). Chángdé Lù 1, PuLi Hotel and Spa (corner of Yán'ān Xī Lù), Jìng Ān. ℂ **021/3203-9999.** Metro: Jing'an Temple.

**Lost Heaven Bar (Huāmǎ Tiāntáng Jiǔbā)** This two-story bar and lounge is atop the Yunnan/Tibet/Burma-themed Lost Heaven on the Bund restaurant. It has a lovely rooftop terrace, Yunnan dance performances, and a wide selection of the usual cocktails, along with drinks and snacks featuring Yunnan ingredients. The bar is open daily 6pm to 2am. Yán'ān Dōng Lù 17 (east of Sichuān Nán Lù), Huángpǔ. ℂ **021/6330-0967.** Metro: Nanjing Rd. (E).

**Malone's (Mǎlóng Měishì Jiǔlóu)** Once the earliest and still most popular sports bar in town, Malone's is an informal American-style pub and restaurant with a dartboard, pool tables, and a slew of TV monitors beaming Western sports events. It still gets crowded here despite the fact that the young waitstaff is a little inexperienced. It's open daily 11am to 2am. Tóngrén Lù 255 (northwest of Shànghǎi Centre), Jìng Ān. ℂ **021/6247-2400.** Metro: Jing'an Temple.

**Manifesto** Designed to be your regular neighborhood bar where you'll feel free to kick up your heels and down a few Brazilian cocktails, the classy Manifesto's deep, soft cushion banquettes encourage doffing the shoes and stretching out. Exposed ceiling pipes, floor-to-ceiling windows, and a well-stocked bar lend this place a cool, trendy vibe. It consistently earns high marks from loyal patrons for its creative cocktails. Best of all, you can order tapas and sinful chocolate desserts from its sister restaurant next door, Mesa. The bar is open daily 4pm to 2am. Jùlù Lù 748 (east of Fùmín Lù), Jìng Ān. ℂ **021/6289-9108.** Metro: Changshu Rd.

**Mural (Mó Yàn)** Complete with faux stalactites and stalagmites, this funky, cave-like underground bar has, yes, wall murals with Buddhist iconography to go with its opium beds, but it all adds to the cool quotient, as does the bar's various all-you-can-drink deals. Live bands and DJs trade off. The bar is open daily 6:30pm to 2am. Yǒngjiā Lù 697 (east of Héngshān Lù), Xúhuì. ℂ **021/6433-5023.** www.muralbar.com. Metro: Hengshan Rd.

**O'Malley's Irish Pub (Ōumǎlì Cāntīng)** This very comfortable pub in a colonial villa is extremely popular with Shànghǎi's foreign residents (especially with its outdoor garden). Kilkenny and Guinness are on tap, and it's easy to quaff one too many here. The bartenders are tops. It's open Monday to Saturday 11:30am to 2am; Sunday 10am to 1am. Táojiāng Lù 42 (1 block west of Héngshān Lù), Jìng Ān. ℂ **021/6474-4533.** Metro: Changshu Rd.

**The Roof @ Waterhouse** Adjacent to the Cool Docks and the Shíliùpǔ Wharf, this lovely terrace bar on the roof of the Waterhouse boutique hotel puts you far enough from the madding crowds of the main Bund, but still gives you gorgeous rooftop views of Pǔdōng, the South Bund, and traffic along the Huángpǔ River. Just open at press time, I'm predicting (and hoping) that this bar will be the cool place to be as the South Bund develops in the coming years. It's open nightly from 5pm to 1am. Máojiāyuán Lù 1-3 (at Cool Docks, Zhōngshān Nán Lù 479), Huángpǔ. ℂ **021/6080-2988.** Metro: Xiaonanmen.

**Salon de Ning** The cocktails are tasty (and predictably pricey), but it's the ambience that's the big draw at this bar in the basement of the Peninsula Hotel. Four semiprivate rooms face the stage, each decorated in its own highly eclectic style: the Indian room, the Upside Down room, the Old Movies room, and the Submarine

# heavenly BARS

Shànghǎi's trendiest upscale pedestrian mall, Xīntiāndì (New Heaven and Earth), located just a short stroll south of Huangpi Road (S) Metro station downtown, is famous for its upscale restaurants and international shops. But this impressive development comes truly alive only after dark when Shànghǎi's hip and wealthy spill out of its pretty bars and lounges. For now, the top nightspots here include:

**Brown Sugar** A lively jazz venue with bar, restaurant, international and domestic artists, and high table minimums. Performances start around 9pm. Open daily 6pm to 2am. North Block, House 15. © 021/5382-8998. www.brownsugarlive.com.

**Club G Plus** A massive dance floor and a host of international DJs playing trance and techno help pack in the party people. Open daily 5pm to 1am. South Block, No. 6, fifth floor. © 021/5386-8088. www.clubgplus.com.

**Dr Bar** The quietest place in Xīntiāndì for a chat and drink over candlelight. Open daily 5pm to 2am. North Block, House 15. © 021/6311-0358.

**KABB** This American bar and cafe with candlelight in the evenings is the place for laid-back music and musings. Open daily 7pm to 2am. North Block, House 5. © 021/3307-0798.

**Luxe** Hip-hop beats attract a mostly local crowd. Open daily 8:30pm to 4am. South Block, fifth floor. © 021/6336-0000.

**Paulaner Bräuhaus** This is the second branch of the popular and festive Bavarian *bierhaus* with home-brewed beer, hearty food, and a hoppin' live band. Open daily 11am to 2am. North Block, House 19–20. © 021/6320-3935.

**Rendezvous** The staples here are the Filipino band, which the local patrons seem to like well enough. Open daily 10am to 2am. North Block, House 22. © 021/6336-5383.

**TMSK** Here's a bar made entirely from colored glass, owned by a Taiwanese actress and glass entrepreneur. Even the wine and martini glasses are works of glass art. Open daily 1:30pm to midnight (Fri–Sat to 2am). North Block, House 11. © 021/6326-2223.

room. Pick your poison, or try them all, and if/when claustrophobia strikes, you can always bar-hop upstairs to **Sir Elly's Terrace** on the 14th floor, with its outdoor terrace and breathtaking views of the city. Salon de Ning is open Tuesday to Saturday 8pm to 1am. Sir Elly's Terrace is open daily 6pm to late. Zhōngshān Dōng Yī Lù 32 (Basement, the Peninsula Shànghǎi), Huángpǔ. © 021/2327-6731. Metro: Nanjing Rd. (E).

**Sky Dome Bar** It may be a bit of an out-of-this-world experience, sipping pricey drinks in a good ol' flying saucer lodged 47 floors atop the Radisson New World Hotel. The views of People's Square and People's Park are tremendous, and the drink list is varied and creative. It's open daily 5pm to 1am. Nánjīng Dōng Lù 88, Radisson New World Shànghǎi, 47th floor, Huángpǔ. © 021/6359-9999. Metro: People's Square.

**The Vault** One of sophisticated Shànghǎi's favorite bars, the stylish Vault stirs up some of the fanciest concoctions in town, with the apple martinis justifiably receiving raves. Or try the passion and peach margarita between dance sets. It is easy and highly recommended to move back and forth between here and the attached Laris restaurant. Thursday Martini Night seems to be everybody's favorite. The bar is open daily 6pm to midnight (Thurs–Sat to 2am). Zhōngshān Dōng Yī Lù 3, Three on the Bund, 6th floor, Huángpǔ. ✆ **021/6321-9922.** Metro: Nanjing Rd. (E).

**Vue Bar**  Its name gives it away. Here at this sophisticated and fun bar sitting atop the Hyatt on the Bund hotel, you'll get one of the most spectacular night *vues* in all of Shànghǎi, with both Pǔdōng and the Bund at your feet. If that's not enough reason to bring you out to Hóngkǒu at night, then perhaps the open-air Jacuzzi that's part of the bar might tempt you to get wet. The bar is open daily 5pm to 1am (Fri–Sat to 2am). Huángpǔ Lù 199 (33rd floor, Hyatt on the Bund), Hóngkǒu. ✆ **021/6393-1234,** ext. 6348. www.shanghai.bund.hyatt.com. No Metro.

# CINEMA

Although Shànghǎi is no longer the center of Chinese filmmaking today, there is still a large and eager movie-going audience here. China limits the release of new Hollywood films to just 20 a year. In the past, most of these movies were dubbed in Chinese, but recently, some have been shown in Shànghǎi in their original language with Chinese subtitles. In the last 2 decades, Chinese directors have made some of the best films in the world, but some of these still can't be officially shown in China. Of course, the pirated versions of these politically sensitive films and of hundreds of Hollywood movies are usually circulating on Shànghǎi streets within hours of (and even sometimes before) the film's world premiere, wherever it might be. Given this sad state of cinematic affairs in Shànghǎi, there isn't too much here for the non-Chinese-speaking visitors eager for a night at the pictures. The only exception is when the **Shànghǎi International Film Festival** comes to town every June. Originated in 1993, when Oliver Stone chaired the jury, the festival attracts more than 250,000 viewers to the screenings.

In the long interval between festivals, cinephiles can also get their fix at regular screenings sponsored by the **Canadian Consulate** (✆ **021/6279-8400**), **German Consulate** (✆ **021/6391-2068,** ext. 602), and **Cine-Club de l'Alliance Française** (✆ **021/6357-5388**). The following are the best venues for flicks in Shànghǎi, which still has a long road to travel to regain its reputation as China's Hollywood. Tickets range from ¥30 to ¥120 depending on the theater and the movie shown. For up-to-date listings, consult the English-language monthlies, such as *that's Shanghai* (www.shanghai.urbanatomy.com).

**Cathay Theatre (Guótài Diànyīngyuàn)**  Chinese and Hollywood movies are screened in this 1930s Art Deco theater. Huáihǎi Zhōng Lù 870 (at Màomíng Nán Lù), Lúwān. ✆ **021/5403-2980** or 021/5404-0415. Metro: Shanxi Rd. (S).

**Paradise Warner Cinema City (Yǒnghuá Diànyīngchéng)**  Warner Bros. helped with the design of this 11-theater multiplex in the sparkling Grand Gateway mall, so you can expect state-of-the-art screening and sound systems, all the better to amp up the latest Hollywood fare and Chinese blockbusters. Hóngqiáo Lù 1, Gateway Mall, 6th floor, Xúhuì. ✆ **021/6407-6622,** ext. 8002. Metro: Xújiāhuì.

**Peace Cinema (Hépíng Yīngdū)**  This big multiplex located in the Raffles City mall has wide screens (including an IMAX screen), DTS and Dolby sound systems, and all the up-to-date conveniences. Hollywood and foreign films are often shown here, sometimes dubbed and sometimes in the original language. Xīzàng Zhōng Lù 290 (by Hànkǒu Lù), Huángpǔ. ✆ **021/6361-2898** or 021/6322-5252. Metro: People's Square.

**Shànghǎi Film Art Center (Shànghǎi Yīngchéng)**　The leading venue during the Shànghǎi International Film Festival, this modern cinema complex with five spacious theaters features Hollywood releases on the big screen. Xīnhuá Lù 160 (next to Crowne Plaza Hotel), Chángníng. ✆ **021/6280-4088.** www.filmcenter.com.cn. Metro: Jiaotong University.

**Studio City (Huányì Diànyīngchéng)**　One of Shànghǎi's top multiplex theaters with six cinemas, it features Dolby surround-sound system, seats with built-in cup holders, and popcorn from the concession in the lobby. Nánjīng Xī Lù 1038, 10th floor, Westgate Mall, Jing Ān. ✆ **021/6218-2173,** ext. 244. Metro: Nanjing Rd. (W).

**UME International Cineplex**　The latest, greatest multiplex in the Xīntiāndì complex, it's fully modern and screens Hollywood movies in their original language, just like you never left home. The English schedule follows Chinese when you call. Xìngyè Lù, Lane 123, no. 6, 4th floor, Huángpǔ. ✆ **021/6373-3333,** ext. 807. www.ume.com.cn. Metro: Huangpi Rd. (S).

# SŪZHŌU, HÁNGZHŌU & OTHER SIDE TRIPS FROM SHÀNGHĂI

he over-quoted Chinese saying, "In heaven there is paradise, on earth there are Sūzhōu and Hángzhōu" *(shàng yǒu tiāntáng, xià yǒu sūháng),* promises more than today's reality can deliver, but it nevertheless calls deserved attention to two famous destinations within an easy day trip of Shànghǎi: Sūzhōu, to the northwest, with its famous gardens and canals; and Hángzhōu, to the southwest, renowned for beautiful West Lake and the surrounding tea plantations. Sandwiched in between are a host of water villages of the Yángzī River delta, with their arched bridges, narrow canals, and Chinese garden estates all spruced up for mass tourism. It's worth visiting at least one of these pastoral towns, though picking one can be difficult. The most famous, and perhaps most complete water village, Zhōu Zhuāng, has unfortunately become a nightmarish tourist trap, and has been replaced in my recommendations by the villages of Nánxún and Tónglǐ, which are not only less commercial, but boast unique features not found elsewhere.

Many travelers to these destinations book a group tour with an English-speaking guide to smooth the way. The main drawback to such an arrangement is that you will have but a short time to explore the sites, the duration dictated by the tour company's schedule rather than your interest (or lack of it) at any point. Alternatives are to hire a driver and car yourself, with the assistance of your hotel concierge, or to use public transportation (trains and buses), which is more grueling, but is also the cheapest and most fun way to experience this beautiful corner of China.

# SŪZHŌU, CITY OF GARDENS

81km (50 miles) NW of Shànghǎi

Sūzhōu's interlocking canals—which once earned it the moniker of "Venice of the East"—its unparalleled collection of classic gardens, and its embroidery and silk factories are the chief surviving elements of a cultural center that dominated China's artistic scene for long periods during the Míng (1368–1644) and Qīng (1644–1911) dynasties. Rapid modernization in the last decade has robbed the city of much of its mystique, but enough beauty remains, especially in quiet corners of its celebrated gardens, to merit at least a day of your time.

## Essentials

**GETTING THERE**   Sūzhōu can easily be visited on your own. There are frequent **trains** (approx. 40 min.; ¥26–¥31 from the Shànghǎi Railway Station), with the most popular trains for day-trippers being the D196, which leaves Shànghǎi at 7:56am and arrives at 8:32am; and the D232, which departs at 8:26am and arrives at 9:02am. There are many return trains to Shànghǎi in the afternoon, including no. D5435 (departs 5:54pm, arrives 6:38pm). There is also an express direct train from Sūzhōu to Běijīng, D386, departing at 9:38pm and arriving at 7:09am. At press time, there were plans for new China Railway High Speed (CRH) trains to depart from Shànghǎi's Hóngqiáo Railway Station (Hóngqiáo Huǒchē Zhàn) that will reduce travel time to Sūzhōu to less than 30 minutes. For the most up-to-date information on Sūzhōu train schedules in English, check the website travelchinaguide.com (www.travelchinaguide.com). The **Sūzhōu Railway Station (Sūzhōu Zhàn)** (✆ 0512/6753-2831) is in the northern part of town on Chēzhàn Lù just west of the Rénmín Lù intersection.

If you miss your train back, Sūzhōu is also well connected by **bus** to Shànghǎi. From Sūzhōu's **North Bus Station (Qìchē Běi Zhàn)** (✆ 0512/6577-6577), just to the east of the railway station, buses depart for Shànghǎi (90 min.; ¥33) every 20 minutes from 6:30am to 7:40pm. There is also a direct **airport bus** (at least one every hour between 10:40am and 7:40pm; ¥82) from Shànghǎi's Pǔdōng Airport (PVG) to Sūzhōu, but no direct return bus to PVG. You'll have to first take a bus from Sūzhōu's China Eastern Airlines office at Gānjiāng Xī Lù 115 to Shànghǎi's Hóngqiáo Airport (SHA) (11 buses between 6:20am and 2:50pm; ¥50) and then take Airport Bus 1 to Pǔdōng Airport. Buses depart hourly between 10am and 4pm and at 5:30pm and 7pm from Hóngqiáo Airport to Sūzhōu.

If you don't wish to visit on your own, check with your hotel tour desk to book a bus tour of Sūzhōu. The **Jǐn Jiāng Optional Tours Center,** Chánglè Lù 191 (✆ 021/5466-7936), offers a convenient 1-day group bus tour to Sūzhōu and the village of Zhōuzhuāng with an English-speaking guide and lunch, departing daily between 8am and 9am and returning in the late afternoon. At press time, the price

苏州
**Sūzhōu**

0      1/2 mi
0    0.5 km

**North Bus Terminal**
汽车北站

**Suzhou Railway Station**
苏州火车站

Chezhan Lu 车站路

西汇路
Xihui Lu

Donghui Lu 东汇路

**Humble Administrator's Garden** (Zhuō Zhèng Yuán)
拙政园

**Suzhou Museum**
苏州博物馆

Qimen Lu 齐门路

**Forest of Lions Garden** (Shī Zi Lín Yuán)
狮子林园

**Beisi Ta**
北寺塔

东北街
Dongbei Jie

Loujiang R.

**The Zoo**
动物园

Shantang Jie 山塘街

Xi Bei Lu

**Xiyuan Garden**
西园

**Lingering Garden** (Liú Yuán)
留园

白塔西路
Báita Xilu

白塔东路
Báita Donglu

**EAST GARDEN**
东园

留园路
Liuyuan Lu

**To Tiger Hill** (Hǔ Qiū Shān)
虎丘山

Tongjing Bei Lu

金门路
Jinmen Lu

**Temple of Mystery**
玄妙观

观前街
Guanqian Jie

Lindun Lu

临顿路

Pingjiang Lu 平江路

Jingde Lu 景德路

Ganjiang Lu 干将路

Changxu Lu 阊胥路

Yuanmiao Lu 园妙路

**GRAND PARK**
大公园

**Twin Pagodas**
双塔

**Yiyuan Garden** (Joyous Garden)
怡园

Ganjiang Lu

Renmin Lu 人民路

Wuzhou Lu 五州路

十梓街
Shizi Jie

凤凰街
Fenghuang Jie

Daoqian Jie 道前街

**Blue Wave Pavilion**
沧浪亭

Panmu Lu 盘门路

Shiquan Jie 十全街

**CITS**

**Master of the Nets Garden** (Wǎng Shī Yuán)
网师园

**South Bus Terminal**
汽车南站

**Steamer Wharf**
轮船码头

Nanmen Lu

**Panmen Gate** (Pán Gate)
盘门

**Ruiguang Pagoda**
瑞光塔

**CHINA**
Beijing ★
Suzhou ●
Shanghai

Xujiang River

Outer Moat
外城河

🚌 Bus Station
🔺 Pagoda
🚉 Rail Station

**ACCOMMODATIONS** ■

Pan Pacific Sūzhōu **9**
(Sūzhōu Wúgōng Fàn Tàipíngyáng Jiǔdiàn)
苏州吴宫泛太平洋酒店

Scholars Inn **5**
(Shūxiāng Méndì Shāngwù Jiǔdiàn)
书香门第商务酒店

Shangri-La Hotel Sūzhōu **3**
(Sūzhōu Xiānggélǐlā Fàndiàn)
苏州香格里拉饭店

Sofitel Sūzhōu **7**
(Sūzhōu Xuánmiào Suōfēitè Dàjiǔdiàn)
苏州玄妙索菲特大酒店

Sūzhōu Marriott Hotel **2**
(Sūzhōu Wànháo Jiǔdiàn)
苏州万豪酒店

**DINING** ◆

Sōng Hè Lóu **6**
(Pine and Crane Restaurant)
松鹤楼

The Bookworm (Lǎo Shū Chóng) **8**
老书虫

**ATTRACTIONS** ●

Gūsū Yuán (Gūsū Garden) 姑苏园 **10**

Shāntáng Jiē (Shāntáng Street) 山塘街 **1**

Sūzhōu Silk Museum **4**
(Sūzhōu Sīchóu Bówùguǎn)
苏州丝绸博物馆

was ¥650 for adults, ¥300 for children ages 2 to 7, and free for children up to age 2. The same tour operator can also arrange a private tour with a guide, air-conditioned car, lunch, and door-to-door service (¥2,000 for one person, ¥1,200 each for two people, ¥1,000 each for three or four people).

China International Travel Service (CITS), at Dàjǐng Xiàng 18, off Guānqián Jiē (© 0512/6511-7505), can provide an English-speaking guide and vehicle for the day at around ¥500 (lunch and entrance tickets not included), but it's just as easy, and a whole lot cheaper, to see the town on your own.

## Exploring Sūzhōu

Central Sūzhōu, where most of the tourist attractions are, is surrounded by remnants of a moat and canals linked to the Grand Canal in the west, and is a protected historical district, 3×5km (2×3 miles) across, in which little tampering and no skyscrapers are allowed. More than 170 bridges arch over the 32km (20 miles) of slim waterways within the town. The poetic private gardens number about 70, with a dozen of the finest open to public view. No other Chinese city contains such a concentration of canals and gardens. **Taxis** are the most convenient way to get around, with trips about town averaging between ¥10 and¥20. In 2011, Sūzhōu will also open two **subway** lines: a north-south line running from the new high-speed railway station in the north through the old town, and an east-west line connecting the old town with the Sūzhōu Industrial Park in the west.

### CLASSIC GARDENS

Sūzhōu's magnificent, formerly private gardens are small, exquisite jewels of landscaping art, often choked with visitors, making a slow, meditative tour difficult. Built primarily in the Míng and Qīng dynasties by retired scholars, generals, merchants, and government officials, these gardens, designed on different principles than those of the West, aimed to create the illusion of the universe in a limited setting by borrowing from nature and integrating such elements as water, plants, rocks, and buildings. Poetry and calligraphy were added as the final touches. Listed below are some classic gardens worth visiting.

**FOREST OF LIONS GARDEN (SHĪZI LÍN YUÁN) ★★** Built in 1342 by a Buddhist monk to honor his teacher and reportedly last owned (privately) by relatives of renowned American architect I. M. Pei, this large garden consists of four small lakes, a multitude of buildings, and big chunks of tortured rockeries that are supposed to resemble lions. Many of these oddly shaped rocks come from nearby Tài Hú (Lake Tài), where they've been submerged for a very long time to achieve the desired shapes and effects. During the Sòng Dynasty (A.D. 960–1126), rock appreciation reached such extremes that the expense in hauling stones from Tài Hú to the capital is said to have bankrupted the empire. Containing the largest rocks and most elaborate rockeries of any garden in Sūzhōu, Shīzi Lín can be a bit ponderous, but then again, you won't see anything like this anywhere else. The garden is located at Yuánlín Lù 23 (© **0512/6727-2428**). It's open daily from 7:30am to 5:30pm; admission is ¥30.

**HUMBLE ADMINISTRATOR'S GARDEN (ZHUŌ ZHÈNG) ★★** Usually translated as "Humble Administrator's Garden," but also translatable tongue-in-cheek as "Garden of the Stupid Officials," this largest of Sūzhōu's gardens, which dates from 1513, makes complex use of the element of water. Linked by zigzag bridges, the maze of connected pools and islands seems endless. The creation of multiple vistas and the dividing of spaces into distinct segments are the garden artist's means of expanding the compressed spaces of the estate. As visitors stroll through the garden, new spaces and vistas open up at every turn. The garden is located at Dōng Běi Jiē 178 (✆ 0512/6751-0286). It's open daily from 7:30am to 5pm; admission is ¥70 from May to September, ¥50 from October to April.

**LINGERING GARDEN (LIÚ YUÁN)** ★★ This garden in the northwest part of town is the setting for the finest Tài Hú rock in China, a 6m-high (20-ft.), 5-ton contorted castle of stone called Crown of Clouds Peak (Jùyún Fēng). Composed of four sections connected by a 700m-long (2,297-ft.) corridor, Liú Yuán is also notable for its viewing pavilions, particularly its **Mandarin Duck Hall,** which is divided into two sides: an ornate southern chamber for men, and a plain northern chamber for women. Lingering Garden is located at Liúyuán Lù 80 (✆ 0512/6533-7940). It's open daily from 7:30am to 5:30pm; admission is ¥40.

**MASTER OF THE NETS GARDEN (WĂNG SHĪ YUÁN)** ★★★ Considered to be the most perfect, and also smallest, of Sūzhōu's gardens, the Master of the Nets Garden is a masterpiece of landscape compression. Hidden at the end of a blind alley, its tiny grounds have been cleverly expanded by the placement of walls, screens, and pavilion halls, producing a maze that seems endless. The eastern sector of the garden consists of the residence of the former owner and his family. At the center of the garden is a small pond encircled by verandas, pavilions, and covered corridors, and traversed by two arched stone bridges. Strategically placed windows afford different views of bamboo, rockeries, water, and inner courtyards, all helping to create an illusion of the universe in a garden. In the northwest of the garden, don't miss the lavish **Diànchūn Yí (Hall for Keeping the Spring),** the former owner's study furnished with lanterns and hanging scrolls. This was the model for Míng Xuān, the Astor Chinese Garden Court and Ming Furniture Room in the Metropolitan Museum of Art in New York City. Master of the Nets Garden is located at Kuotao Xiàng 11, off Shíquán Jiē (✆ 0512/6529-3190). It's open daily from 7:30am to 5:30pm; admission is ¥30. In the summer, daily performances of traditional music and dance are staged in the garden (7:30pm; ¥100).

**TIGER HILL (HŬ QIŪ SHĀN)** ★ This multipurpose theme park can be garishly tacky in parts, but it's also home to some local historic sights, chief among them the remarkable leaning **Yúnyán Tǎ (Cloud Rock Pagoda)** at the top of the hill. Now safely shored up by modern engineering (although it still leans), this seven-story octagonal pagoda dating from A.D. 961 is thought to be sitting on top of the legendary grave of Hé Lǔ, king of Wú during the Spring and Autumn period (770–464 B.C.), and also Sūzhōu's founder. Hé Lǔ was reportedly buried with his arsenal of 3,000 swords, his tomb guarded by a white tiger, which was said to have appeared 3 days after the king's death (hence the name of the hill).

Partway up Tiger Hill is a natural ledge of rocks, the **Ten Thousand People Rock (Wànrén Shí),** where according to legend a rebel delivered an oratory so fiery that the rocks lined up to listen. Another version claims they represent Hé Lǔ's followers who were buried along with him, as was the custom at that time. A deep stone cleavage, the **Pool of Swords (Jiàn Chí),** runs along one side of it, reputedly the remnants of a pit dug by order of the First Emperor (Qín Shǐ Huáng) 2,000 years ago in a search for the 3,000 swords. Tiger Hill is located 3km (2 miles) northwest of the city at Hŭqiū Shān 8 (© **0512/6532-3488**). It's open daily from 7:30am to 6pm; admission is ¥60.

## WATER GATES & CANALS

Your best chance of catching what remains of Sūzhōu's once-famous canal life is in the southern part of town in the scenic area just south of the Pan Pacific Sūzhōu Hotel known as **Gūsū Yuán (Gūsū Garden).** Here, you'll find in the southwestern corner **Pán Mén (Pán Gate),** built in A.D. 1351, and the only major piece of the Sūzhōu city wall to survive. **Pán Mén** once operated as a water gate and fortress when the Grand Canal was the most important route linking Sūzhōu to the rest of China. To the south is a large arched bridge, **Wúmén Qiáo,** a fine place to view the ever-changing canal traffic. Near the main garden entrance in the east is **Ruìguāng Tă,** a seven-story, 37m-high (121-ft.) pagoda built in A.D. 1119, which affords some excellent views of the old city from its top floors. The rest of the grounds are not very interesting. Gūsū Yuán is located at Dōng Dà Jiē 1. It's open daily from 8am to 5pm; admission is ¥25.

In the northwest part of town near Liú Yuán, **Shāntáng Jiē (Shāntáng St.),** chock-full of Sūzhōu's old houses, narrow alleyways, arched bridges, and canals, is being slowly developed for tourists and pedestrians, with entrance to seven mansions and community halls of note being included in the ¥45 entrance fee (open daily 8am–9pm; © **0512/6723-6980**). You can also take the de rigueur canal boat ride here (¥25 per person).

## MUSEUMS

Sūzhōu is synonymous not only with gardens and canals, but also with silk. Its silk fabrics have been among the most prized in China for centuries, and the art of silk embroidery is still practiced at the highest levels. The **Sūzhōu Silk Museum (Sūzhōu Sīchóu Bówùguăn),** Rénmín Lù 2001 (© **0512/6753-6538**), just south of the railway station, takes visitors through the history of silk in China, with an interesting section on sericulture complete with silkworms, cocoons, and mulberry leaves. Weavers demonstrate on traditional looms. The museum is open daily from 9am to 5pm; admission is ¥15.

Opened in October 2006, the I. M. Pei–designed **Sūzhōu Museum (Sūzhōu Bówùguăn)** just west of the Humble Administrator's Garden at Dōngbĕi Jiē 204 (© **0512/6757-5666;** www.szmuseum.com), and reportedly the last design of his career, combines characteristics of a typical Sūzhōu garden with modern geometric designs, and is worth a visit both for the building and its well-laid-out collection of locally discovered cultural relics, including an exquisite Pearl Pillar of the Buddhist Shrine from the Northern Sòng Dynasty. The museum is open Tuesday to Sunday, 9am to 5pm (last admission 4pm); free admission.

# Where to Stay & Dine

If you plan to spend the night in Sūzhōu, a traditional favorite for its quintessential Chinese garden setting is the former Sheraton Hotel and Towers, now the **Pan Pacific Sūzhōu (Sūzhōu Wúgōng Zhī Tàipíngyáng Jiŭdiàn),** Xīn Shì Lù 259, near Pán Mén in southwest Sūzhōu (© **800/325-3535** or 0512/6510-3388; fax 0512/6510-0888; www.panpacific.com/suzhou). With 481 rooms and prices starting as low as around ¥800 to ¥1,000 in the low season for a standard room, this five-star

# A quick GETAWAY

For visitors eager to glimpse a Yángzǐ River delta water village, but who are unable to spare an entire day, the ancient water town of **Qībǎo** (information ✆ 021/6461-5308) located in Mínháng District a scant 18km (11 miles) southwest of downtown Shànghǎi, makes for an acceptable if not terribly exciting alternative.

Like many water towns in the area, Qībǎo was built in the Northern Sòng Dynasty (960–1127), but only came into its own in the Míng (1368–1644) and Qīng (1644–1911) dynasties. Local lore has it that Qībǎo (literally, "seven treasures") was once home to seven treasures including, among other exotica, a Míng Dynasty bronze bell and a Lotus sutra, both the only artifacts remaining today. Opened as a tourist attraction in 2002, the "old town" (many of the structures are newly built to look old) spans about 2 sq. km (¾ sq. mile) and has the usual narrow alleyways, arched bridges, and canals. Unfortunately, it's also surrounded by a new town and many ugly, modern concrete structures.

There are no must-sees here, but structures of note include the Catholic Church (Tiānzhǔ Jiàotáng) in the southern part, with its whitewashed interiors; the completely rebuilt Qībǎo Temple (Qībǎo Jiào Sì); the Opera House, where

shadow plays are occasionally still performed; a cotton spinning workshop (Miánzhì Fáng); and a distillery workshop (Lǎojiǔ Fáng), where you can sample some of the freshly distilled wine for which the town is famous. You can also take the de rigueur canal boat ride. There is the usual gauntlet of shops proffering all the same souvenirs you've likely seen elsewhere, but of more interest may be the many local snacks, the most famous of which is *qībǎo fāngzhèng gāo*, a steamed pastry made of glutinous rice with sweet bean paste, best eaten when it's just a few minutes out of the steamer.

Both a blessing and a curse, Qībǎo's proximity to downtown Shànghǎi means that it can be easily reached, but it is also overrun with tourists, making a relaxed leisurely visit (the ideal way to see a water town) all but impossible. To get here, take Metro Line 9 to Qībǎo Station; from there, follow directions to the old town, just a short walk from the station. A taxi from downtown Shànghǎi will cost around ¥90. There is no admission fee to wander the old town, but if you wish to visit any of the designated sights, you can either pay separate admission fees (¥5–¥10) at each place or purchase a ¥45 ticket that will gain you entry into eight sights.

hotel receives rave reviews for its Chinese-style buildings, which blend seamlessly into the environment. Another excellent choice is the luxury **Shangri-La Hotel Sūzhōu (Sūzhōu Xiānggélǐlā Fàndiàn)** (Tǎyuán Lù 168; ✆ 0512/6808-0168; fax 0512/6808-1168; www.shangri-la.com), but located less conveniently in the Sūzhōu Hi-Tech Industrial Development Zone about 20 minutes west of the old town. Delightfully luxurious rooms (¥1,880, 30% discount) offer high ceilings and panoramic views of the city. Between the Sūzhōu Industrial Park and the old city is the new **Sūzhōu Marriott Hotel (Sūzhōu Wànháo Jǐndiàn)** at Gānjiāng Xī Lù 1296 (✆ 0512/8225-8888; fax 0512/8225-8899; www.marriott.com), a modern high-rise with all the familiar luxury rooms and amenities. Standard rooms start at around ¥1,000.

If you want to be in the heart of the old town, the best location belongs to the **Sofitel Sūzhōu (Sūzhōu Xúanmiào Suŏfēitè Dàjiŭdiàn)** (Gānjiāng Dōng Lù 818; ℂ **0512/6801-9888;** fax 0512/6801-1218; www.sofitel.com/asia), with plush standards (with free Internet access) starting at ¥1,488 (up to 50% discount), but its proximity to the nearby shopping and pedestrian streets can be a bit noisy for some guests. For those on a budget, the lovely 37-unit **Scholars Inn (Shūxiāng Méndì Shāngwù Jiŭdiàn)** in the center of town at Jīngdé Lù 277 (ℂ **0512/6521-7388;** fax 0512/6521-7326; www.soocor.com) offers simple but clean standard rooms with air-conditioning, phone, TV, showers, and broadband Internet for ¥520, with discounts up to 50%.

Although hotel restaurants serve the most reliable fare and accept credit cards, Sūzhōu has a number of good restaurants that deserve to be tried, many of which are located on Tàijiān Nòng (Tàijiān Lane), also known as Gourmet Street, around the Guànqián Jiē area. One of the most famous local restaurants on this street is the more than 200-year-old **Sōng Hè Lóu (Pine and Crane Restaurant)** at Tàijiān Nòng 72 (ℂ **0512/6727-2285;** 8am–9pm), which serves Sūzhōu specialties such as *Sōngshŭ Guìyú* (squirrel-shaped Mandarin fish), *Gūsū Lŭyā* (Gūsū marinated duck), *Huángmèn Hémàn* (braised river eel) and the exquisitely shredded *Luóbòsī Sū Bĭng* (pan-fried turnip cake). Dinner for two ranges from ¥140 to ¥250. The **Bookworm (Lăo Shū Chóng)** at Shíquán Jiē, Gŭnxiūfáng 77 (ℂ **0512/6526-4720;** www.suzhoubookworm.com), is a lovely bookstore-restaurant-cafe offering coffees, smoothies, salads, sandwiches, pastas, and desserts guaranteed to cure any homesickness.

# HÁNGZHŌU & WEST LAKE

185km (115 miles) SW of Shànghăi

Seven centuries ago, Marco Polo pronounced Hángzhōu "the finest, most splendid city in the world . . . where so many pleasures may be found that one fancies oneself to be in Paradise." Hángzhōu's claim to paradise has always been centered on its famous **West Lake (Xī Hú),** surrounded on three sides by verdant hills. The islets and temples, pavilions and gardens, causeways and arched bridges of this small lake (about 5km/3 miles across and 14km/8¾ miles around) have constituted the supreme example of lakeside beauty in China ever since the Táng Dynasty, when Hángzhōu came into its own with the completion of the Grand Canal (Dà Yùnhé) in A.D. 609. Hángzhōu reached its zenith during the Southern Sòng Dynasty (A.D. 1127–1279), when it served as China's capital.

In 2003, much to the horror of purists, Xī Hú was enlarged in the western section with an additional causeway along its new western shoreline. New sights, shops, and restaurants were added to the eastern and southern shores. But the news is not all bad. Away from the commercial eastern edges of the lake, and especially in the surrounding hills and countryside, it's still possible to find pockets of peace and quiet. In the last few years, the Hángzhōu government has also been positioning the city as a resort destination worthy of a visit in its own right. While this has meant more hotels being built and inevitably more traffic jams, there are also a few more worthwhile attractions for visitors, including a National Wetland Park. An overnight visit will allow you to appreciate more fully Hángzhōu's fabled beauty.

# Essentials

Like Sūzhōu, Hángzhōu is perfectly tourist-friendly and is possible to see on your own. There have been on-again, off-again plans for the building of a magnetic levitation train from Shànghăi to Hángzhōu, which, if ever completed (at press time, plans were on again, with the line to be built between 2010 and 2014), will reduce the train traveling time from 1½ hours to around 40 minutes. In the meantime, however, you can book a taxi for the day through your Shànghăi hotel (Hángzhōu is a 2–3 hr. ride via the Hú Háng Expwy.) or better yet, and faster, venture there completely on your own by **train** (1½ hr.).

The majority of Hángzhōu-bound trains leave throughout the day from the **Shànghăi South Railway Station (Shànghăi Nán Zhàn)** (© 021/6317-9090) in the southern part of town (reachable by Metro Lines 1 and 3). There are a few Hángzhōu-bound trains that leave from Shànghăi Railway Station, but the times are less convenient and the journey takes longer than from South Station. The D5685, D3105, D5551, and D5689 bullet trains all depart the South Station between 7am and 8am and arrive in Hángzhōu around 90 minutes later. If you plan to stay overnight, the D5557 leaves Shànghăi at 6:35pm and arrives at 8:04pm while the D5681 departs at 7:03pm and arrives at 8:21pm. Return train D5680 leaves Hángzhōu at 6:24pm and arrives at South Station at 7:42pm, and the D5672 leaves at 8:50pm and arrives at 10:12pm. Soft-seat train tickets range from ¥54 to ¥75, plus a typical ¥20 service charge if purchased from hotel tour desks. A daily express direct train D310 also leaves Hángzhōu at 8:15pm and arrives in Běijīng at 7:44am.

For the most up-to-date information on Hángzhōu train schedules, check the website **travelchinaguide.com** (www.travelchinaguide.com). The **Hángzhōu Railway Station (Hángzhōu Huǒchē Zhàn)** (© 0571/5672-0222 or 0571/8782-9983) is in the eastern part of town. The no. 7 or no. K7 bus connects the station to downtown and the Shangri-La Hotel for ¥2, while a taxi should cost around ¥12 to West Lake.

There are also **buses** traveling between Shànghăi and Hángzhōu, but they are a lot less convenient than trains. A direct bus (¥100) to Hángzhōu leaves from Shànghăi Pǔdōng International Airport (© 021/6834-5743 or 021/6834-6467) and runs between 9:30am and 7pm.

Hángzhōu also has an **airport** (© 0571/8666-1234 or 0571/8666-2999; www. hzairport.com; airport code HGH) with a newly built international terminal (Terminal A) about a 30-minute drive from downtown, with international connections to Amsterdam, Hong Kong, Macau, Seoul, Singapore, Bangkok, Osaka, Tokyo, Taipei, and to Běijīng and other major Chinese cities, but not Shànghăi. A taxi into town costs around ¥130 while an air-conditioned airport bus (© 0571/8666-2539; ¥20) runs to the railway station, the Merchant Marco Hotel (nearest stop to the Shangri-La Hotel), and the Wǔlínmén CAAC ticket office in town.

If you want to see Hángzhōu on a group tour, the **Jǐn Jiāng Optional Tours Center,** Chánglè Lù 191 (© 021/5466-7936), in Shànghăi offers a convenient, if expensive, 1-day group bus tour with an English-speaking guide and lunch, departing Shànghăi around 8am every Tuesday, Thursday, and Saturday, and returning in the late afternoon. The price is ¥850 for adults. The same tour operator can also arrange a private 1- or 2-day tour (on any day) with a guide, air-conditioned car, lunch, and door-to-door service for significantly more. The top Hángzhōu hotels recommended in this guide can also organize half- or full-day city tours.

# Hángzhōu

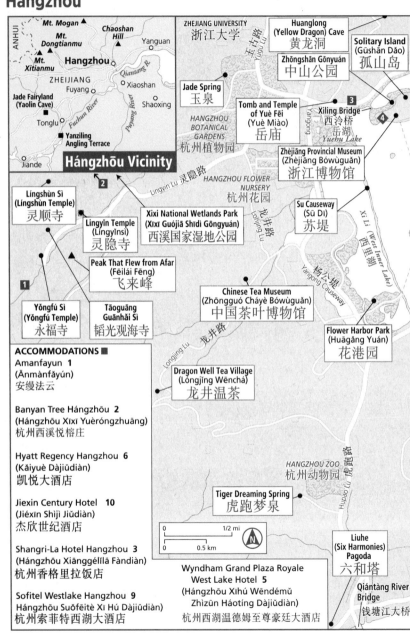

ANHUI

Mt. Mogan ▲
Chaoshan Hill
Mt. Dongtianmu ▲
Yanguan
▲ Mt. Xitianmu
**Hangzhou**
ZHEIJANG
Qiantang R.
Fuyang
× Xiaoshan
Jade Fairyland (Yaolin Cave) ■
Fuchun River
Shaoxing
Tonglu
Poyang River
■ Yanziling Angling Terrace
Jiande

**Hángzhōu Vicinity**
▲2

ZHEJIANG UNIVERSITY
浙江大学

Huanglong (Yellow Dragon) Cave
黄龙洞

Solitary Island (Gūshān Dǎo)
孤山岛

Zhōngshān Gōngyuán
中山公园

Jade Spring
玉泉

Tomb and Temple of Yuè Fēi (Yuè Miào)
岳庙

Xiling Bridge
西泠桥

▲3

▲4

Yangong

Yuehu Lake

HANGZHOU BOTANICAL GARDENS
杭州植物园

Zhèjiāng Provincial Museum (Zhèjiāng Bówùguǎn)
浙江博物馆

Lingyin Lu 灵隐路

HANGZHOU FLOWER NURSERY
杭州花园

Su Causeway (Sū Dī)
苏堤

Língshùn Sì (Língshùn Temple)
灵顺寺

Lingyin Temple (Língyǐnsì)
灵隐寺

Xixi National Wetlands Park (Xīxī Guójiā Shīdì Gōngyuán)
西溪国家湿地公园

龙井路 Lóngjǐng Lu

Xi Li (West Inner Lake)
西里湖

Yangong Causeway 杨公堤

▲
Peak That Flew from Afar (Fēilái Fēng)
飞来峰

Chinese Tea Museum (Zhōngguó Cháyè Bówùguǎn)
中国茶叶博物馆

▲1

Yǒngfú Sì (Yǒngfú Temple)
永福寺

Tāoguāng Guānhǎi Sì
韬光观海寺

Flower Harbor Park (Huāgǎng Yuán)
花港园

Lóngjǐng Lu 龙井路

Dragon Well Tea Village (Lǒngjǐng Wēnchá)
龙井温茶

**ACCOMMODATIONS** ■

Amanfayun **1**
(Ānmànfǎyún)
安缦法云

Banyan Tree Hángzhōu **2**
(Hángzhōu Xīxī Yuèróngzhuāng)
杭州西溪悦榕庄

Hyatt Regency Hangzhou **6**
(Kǎiyuè Dàjiǔdiàn)
凯悦大酒店

Jiexin Century Hotel **10**
(Jiéxīn Shìjì Jiǔdiàn)
杰欣世纪酒店

Shangri-La Hotel Hangzhou **3**
(Hángzhōu Xiānggélǐlā Fàndiàn)
杭州香格里拉饭店

Sofitel Westlake Hangzhou **9**
(Hángzhōu Suǒfēitè Xī Hú Dàjiǔdiàn)
杭州索菲特西湖大酒店

Tiger Dreaming Spring
虎跑梦泉

HANGZHOU ZOO
杭州动物园

Hǔpáo Lu 虎跑路

0          1/2 mi
0      0.5 km
N

Liuhe (Six Harmonies) Pagoda
六和塔

Wyndham Grand Plaza Royale West Lake Hotel **5**
(Hángzhōu Xīhú Wēndémù Zhìzūn Háotíng Dàjiǔdiàn)
杭州西湖温德姆至尊豪廷大酒店

Qiántàng River Bridge
钱塘江大桥

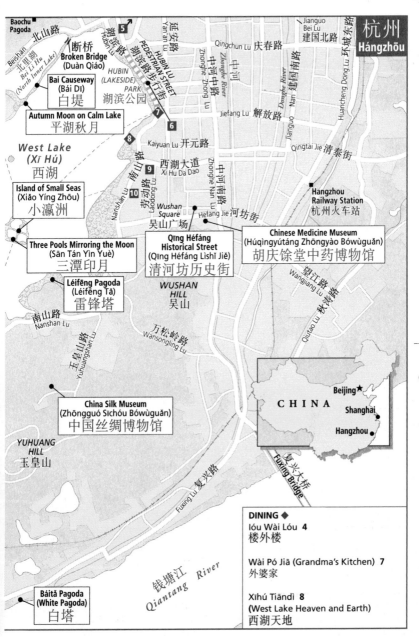

Baochu
Pagoda

北山路
Beishan

断桥
**Broken Bridge**
(Duàn Qiáo)

北里湖
*Bei Li Hu*
*(North Inner Hu)*

**Bai Causeway**
(Bái Dī)
白堤

HUBIN
(LAKESIDE)
PARK
湖滨公园

延安路
Yan'an Lu

HUBIN LU
PEDESTRIAN
STREET
湖滨路步行街

**Autumn Moon on Calm Lake**
平湖秋月

Qingchun Lu 庆春路

Jianguo
Bei Lu
建国北路

杭州
**Hángzhōu**

Huancheng Dong Lu 环城东路

*West Lake*
*(Xī Hú)*
西湖

Kaiyuan Lu 开元路

Zhonghe Zhong Lu

Zhonghe River

Donghe River

中河

Jiefang Lu 解放路

Jianguo
Nan Lu
建国南路

Qingtai Jie 清泰街

**Island of Small Seas**
(Xiǎo Yíng Zhōu)
小瀛洲

西湖大道
Xī Hu Da Dao

劳动路
Laodong Lu

南山路
Nanshan Lu

中河南路
Zhonghe Nan Lu

**Hangzhou
Railway Station**
杭州火车站

**Three Pools Mirroring the Moon**
(Sān Tán Yìn Yuè)
三潭印月

Wushan
Square
吴山广场

Hefang Jie 河坊街

**Qīng Héfáng
Historical Street**
(Qīng Héfáng Lìshǐ Jiē)
清河坊历史街

**Chinese Medicine Museum**
(Húqìngyútáng Zhōngyào Bówùguǎn)
胡庆馀堂中药博物馆

望江路
Wangjiang Lu

**Léifēng Pagoda**
(Léifēng Tǎ)
雷锋塔

*WUSHAN
HILL*
吴山

万松岭路
Wansongling Lu

玉皇山路
Yuhuangshan Lu

秋涛路
Qiutao Lu

**China Silk Museum**
(Zhōngguó Sīchóu Bówùguǎn)
中国丝绸博物馆

*YUHUANG
HILL*
玉皇山

*CHINA*

Beijing ★

Shanghai

Hangzhou

复兴路
Fuxing Lu

Fuxing
Bridge
复兴大桥

钱塘江
*Qiantang River*

**Báitǎ Pagoda**
(White Pagoda)
白塔

**DINING ◆**
Ióu Wài Lóu **4**
楼外楼

Wài Pó Jiā (Grandma's Kitchen) **7**
外婆家

Xǐhú Tiāndì **8**
**(West Lake Heaven and Earth)**
西湖天地

# Getting Around

The city surrounds the shores of West Lake, with modern Hángzhōu spread to the north and east. The lake is best explored on foot and by boat, while sights farther afield will require a taxi or bus. **Taxis** cost ¥10 for 3km (1¾ miles), then ¥2 per kilometer until 10km (6¼ miles) and ¥3 per kilometer after that. There is a ¥1 gas surcharge on all trips. Air-conditioned **buses** cost ¥2, while tour buses with a Y prefix (*yóukè*) cost ¥3 to ¥5. Bus no. K7 runs from the railway station to Língyǐn Sì via the northern shore of the lake (Běishān Lù) and the Shangri-La Hotel, while bus no. 27 runs along Běishān Lù to Lóngjǐng Cūn (Dragon Well Village), and bus no. Y1 makes a loop of the lake starting from Língyǐn Sì. **Bicycles** are available for rental at public leasing points around the city, but it's a bit of a hassle as you have to first purchase a stored value card at Lóngxiáng Qiáo 20 (© **0571/8533-1122**), with proof of ID and a ¥300 deposit. **Water taxis** (© **0571/8802-4368;** ¥3) also ply a small section of the Grand Canal in the northern part of town from Wǔlíng Mén (Wǔlíng Gate/Westlake Cultural Square) north to Gǒngchén Qiáo and Canal Cultural Square around Xiǎohé Lù, stopping at Xìnyìfáng along the way. Hángzhōu has a tourist information hot line (© **0571/96123**).

## Exploring Hángzhōu

### XĪ HÚ (WEST LAKE)

Strolling the shores and causeways of West Lake and visiting the tiny islands by tour boat should not be missed. A **Lakeshore Promenade** ★—a combination walkway and roadway—encircles the lake, with the busiest parts along the eastern edge of the lake. The once-busy thoroughfare Húbīn Lù has now become a rather pleasant, tree-lined pedestrian walkway home to such outlets as Starbucks and Häagen-Dazs, while the area immediately to the south around Nánshān Lù and Xīhú Dà Dào is now known as Xī Hú Tiāndì (West Lake Heaven and Earth), a miniature version of Shànghǎi's Xīntiāndì (p. 116), right down to the *shíkùmén* (stone-frame) style housing and with some of the exact same restaurants. Following are the top attractions around the lake.

**SOLITARY ISLAND (GŪSHĀN DǍO)** ★   Situated just off the lake's northwest shore, this big island is accessible via the Xīlíng Bridge in the west and the Bái Causeway (Bái Dī) in the northeast. A roadway sweeps across the island, which is home to a number of minor sights, including the park **Zhōngshān Gōnyuán** (daily sunrise–sunset; free admission), which was once part of the old Southern Song imperial palace built in 1252, though nothing remains of it. A climb to the top of the hill affords views of the lake to the south. Also here is Hángzhōu's famous restaurant, Lóu Wài Lóu, and the large **Zhèjiāng Provincial Museum (Zhèjiāng Shěng Bówùguǎn)** (© **0571/8798-0281**), which contains the oldest grains of cultivated rice in the world (developed 7,000 years ago in a nearby Hémǔdù village). The museum is open Monday from noon to 4pm and Tuesday through Sunday from 9am to 4pm; free admission.

**BÁI CAUSEWAY (BÁI DĪ)** ★★   Solitary Island is connected in the east to downtown Hángzhōu by **Bái Dī,** a man-made causeway providing some of the finest strolls around West Lake. Named after famous Táng Dynasty poet Bái Jūyì, who served as prefectural governor here in A.D. 822 to 824, the causeway runs east for half a mile, rejoining the north shore road (Běishān Lù) at **Duàn Qiáo (Broken Bridge),** so named because when winter snows first melt, the bridge appears from a distance to be broken.

**CRUISING WEST LAKE** ★★ All along the lakeshore, but particularly on Húbīn Lù and near Gūshān Dǎo (northwest corner of the lake), there are boats for hire, from 3m (9¾-ft.), heavy wooden rowboats (where you take the oars) to small junks propelled by the owner's single oar to full-fledged ferries—flat-bottomed launches seating 20 under an awning. To tour the lake in a small junk costs ¥80 for an hour. Larger passenger ferries sell tickets for ¥35 (80-min. cruise with no stops), and ¥45, which includes entrance to the Island of Small Seas (below). Ticket booths are across the street from the Shangri-La Hotel and along the east side of the lake.

**ISLAND OF SMALL SEAS (XIǍO YÍNG ZHŌU)** ★★ Make sure your boat docks on this island at the center of West Lake. The **Island of Small Seas** was formed during a silt-dredging operation in 1607. As a Chinese saying goes, this is "an island within a lake, a lake within an island." Its form is that of a wheel with four spokes, its bridges and dikes creating four enclosed lotus-laden ponds. The main route into the hub of this wheel is the **Bridge of Nine-Turnings,** built in 1727. Occupying the center is the magnificent **Flower and Bird Pavilion,** an exceedingly graceful structure that is notable for its intricate wooden railings, lattices, and moon gates, though it only dates from 1959. It's open daily from 8am to 5pm; admission is ¥20 (included if you take a large passenger ferry to the island).

**THREE POOLS MIRRORING THE MOON (SĀN TÁN YÌN YUÈ)** ★★ Located just off the southern shore of the Island of Small Seas are three little water pagodas, each about 2m (6½ ft.) tall, that have "floated" like buoys on the surface of West Lake since 1621. Each pagoda has five openings. On evenings when the full moon shines on the lake, candles are placed inside. The effect is of four moons shimmering on the waters. Even by daylight, the three floating pagodas are quite striking.

**SŪ CAUSEWAY (SŪ DĪ)** ★ The best view from land of the Three Pools Mirroring the Moon is from the Sū Causeway (Sū Dī), the original great dike that connects the north and south shores along the western side of the lake. (A third causeway added in 2003, the Yánggōng Dī running parallel to Sū Dī in the west, is primarily for vehicles and is not as scenic.) Running nearly 3km (1¾ miles), Sū Dī, named for Hángzhōu's poet-governor Sū Dōngpō (A.D. 1036–1101), is lined with weeping willows, peach trees, and shady nooks, and crosses six arched tone bridges.

Sū Dī begins in the north across from the **Tomb and Temple of Yuè Fēi** (Yuè Miào; ℭ **0571/8797-9133;** daily 7:30am–6:30pm; admission ¥25), a 12th-century general famous in Chinese history for his unwavering patriotism. He was nevertheless accused of treason and executed, though his reputation was later restored. Near the southern tip of Sū Dī is **Huāgǎng Yuán (Flower Harbor Park)** (daily 8am–6pm; free admission), where there's a peony garden and ponds full of fat carp and goldfish.

**LÉIFĒNG PAGODA (LÉIFĒNG TǍ)** ★ Completely rebuilt in 2003 on the south bank of West Lake, this modern steel-and-copper pagoda affords some of the best panoramic views of the lake. Beneath the modern construction are the brick foundations of the original Buddhist Léifēng Pagoda built in A.D. 977 by Qiān Chū, the king of the Wúyuè Kingdom. The bricks you see were part of an underground vault used to store precious Buddhist relics, including a rare woodcut sutra, which was found among the ruins. The pagoda and surrounding gardens (© 0571/8798-2111, ext. 123) are open daily from 7:30am to 9pm (to 5:30pm Dec–Mar); admission is ¥40.

## OTHER ATTRACTIONS

*Largest Buddhist Temple in S.E.*

**LÍNGYĪN TEMPLE (LÍNGYĪN SÌ)** ★   Located in the lush hills just west of West Lake, Língyīn Sì (Temple of the Soul's Retreat) has been rebuilt a dozen times since its creation in A.D. 326. Don't expect to find much peace here, though, as the surrounding area seems to have been turned into one large amusement park. Entrance to the whole complex (7am–5:30pm) costs ¥35, while entrance to the temple itself is a separate ¥30.

The main attraction on the way to the temple is a limestone cliff, called **Fēilái Fēng (Peak That Flew from Afar),** so named because it resembles a holy mountain in India seemingly transported to China. The peak, nearly 150m high (492 ft.), contains four caves and about 380 Buddhist rock carvings. The most famous carving is of a Laughing Buddha from the year A.D. 1000. Scholars have deemed these stone carvings the most important of their kind in southern China.

The present temple buildings go back decades rather than centuries. The main Dàxióng Bǎodiàn (Great Hall) contains a gigantic statue of Buddha carved in 1956 from 24 sections of camphor and gilded with nearly 3,000 grams (106 oz.) of gold—the largest sitting Buddha in China, and not a bad modern re-creation.

If you want to get away from the crowds, farther west along the pathway past Língyīn Sì is a quieter pretty temple, **Yǒngfú Sì (Temple of Goodness),** set amidst groves of bamboo and willow. A climb to the Dàxióng Bǎodiàn (Grand Hall) at the top allows wonderful views of the surrounding hills and even glimpses of West Lake on a clear day. More exalted views are available at two other temples even higher up, **Tāoguāng Guānhǎi Sì,** and the 1,600-year-old **Língshùn Sì,** often known as Cáishén Miào (Temple of Wealth) which sits atop **Běigāo Fēng (North Peak Mountain).** It's a fairly strenuous climb to the top, or you can take the cable car from behind Língyīn Sì, the preferred transportation of the crowds who ascend the mountain to pray for wealth and good fortune. For a relaxing end to the visit, follow the Língyī Sì thoroughfare west past Yǒngfú Sì (you've now left the Língyīn Sì scenic area) into **Fǎyún Cūn (Fǎyún Village),** formerly home to villagers who worked the surrounding tea fields, and now part of the Amanfayun hotel complex, complete with restored original village dwellings. A tea house here offers tea for sampling and for sale.

### DRAGON WELL TEA VILLAGE (LÓNGJǏNG WĒNCHÁ)   West of West Lake is the village of **Lóngjǐng (Dragon Well),** the source of Hángzhōu's famous **Lóngjǐng tea,** grown only on these hillsides and revered throughout China as a supreme vintage for its fine fragrance and smoothness. The best tea here is still picked and processed by hand. A popular stop near the village is the **Zhōngguó Cháyè Bówùguǎn (Chinese Tea Museum)** (© 0571/8796-4221), open daily from 8:30am to 4:30pm. Here, you can comb through the extensive displays of Chinese teas, pots, cups, and ceremonial tea implements. Admission is free.

Dragon Well Village itself, a few miles beyond the museum, is where much of the tea is grown and processed. Independent travelers are sometimes accosted by local

*Mr. Hu mansion —*

farmers who will invite them into their homes, ply them with tea, and sell them a few pounds at inflated prices. This can actually be a good opportunity to buy this relatively expensive vintage at the source if you know how to bargain. The highest grade Xī Hú Lóngjǐng tea retails in Hángzhōu's stores for around ¥68 to ¥88 per 50 grams (2 oz.), so aim for a price well below that. It also helps if you are or are with a tea connoisseur, as vendors may sometimes try to pass off last year's vintage as the most recent. Caveat emptor!

**CHINA SILK MUSEUM (ZHŌNGGUÓSĪCHÓU BÓWÙGUǍN)** Though Sūzhōu may be better known as a silk capital, Hángzhōu, too, produced its share of this much-sought-after commodity. This large, modern museum south of West Lake boasts a surprisingly comprehensive exhibit on the history and art of silk weaving and embroidery. Displays range from mulberry bushes and silkworms to traditional looms and exquisite pieces of damask brocades, all well annotated in English. There are demonstrations of traditional weaving techniques as well. The museum is located at Yùhuáng Shān Lù 73–1 (✆ **0571/8706-2129**) and is open daily from 8:30am to 4:30pm; free admission.

**CHINESE MEDICINE MUSEUM (QĪNG HÉFÁNG/HÚQÌNGYÚTÁNG ZHŌNGYÀO BÓWÙGUǍN)** Located east of West Lake in downtown Hángzhōu, **Qīng Héfáng Lìshǐ Jiē (Qīng Héfáng Historical Street)** has been the commercial center of Hángzhōu since the late 6th century. Restored in 2001 with Míng and Qīng dynasty–style buildings, this pedestrian mall has your usual quota of teahouses, restaurants, specialty stores, and also a few small museums. The most interesting of the lot is the **Húqìngyútáng Chinese Medicine Museum** on Dàjǐng Xiàng (✆ **0571/8701-5379**). Established in 1874 by a rich merchant, Hú Xuěyán, the original apothecary, housed in a traditional courtyard mansion, has a striking dispensary hall with Chinese lanterns, and finely carved wooden pillars and brackets. Cubicle drawers along the walls contain an assortment of herbs, leaves, barks, seeds, and roots, much of which is on display in the many rooms that follow. There's also a large collection of stuffed animals whose parts are valued for their particular curative properties, such as leopard bone or the oil of the fur seal; this last section is best avoided by animal lovers or PETA advocates. There are English explanations throughout. The museum is open daily from 9am to 5pm; admission is ¥10.

**SIX HARMONIES PAGODA (LIÙ HÉ TǍ)** Situated on Yuèlún Hill above the Qiántáng River about a 15-minute ride south of town, this seven-story (13-story from the outside), octagonal, wood and brick tower was originally built in A.D. 970 to ward off evil spirits thought to be responsible for the heavy tides. Destroyed in 1127, today's structure was rebuilt and added to in the Southern Sòng, Míng, and Qīng dynasties. What's best today are the views of the river, the Qiántáng Bridge, and the surrounding city from the top of the pagoda. Nearby is an exhibit of China's many pagodas. The park is open daily from 6:30am to 5:30pm; admission is ¥30 including entrance to the pagoda.

**XIXI NATIONAL WETLANDS PARK (XĪXĪ GUÓJIĀ SHĪD GŌNGYUÁN)** Located about 5km (3 miles) northwest of West Lake, this first national wetland park in the country covers an area of 12 sq. km (4½ sq. miles), and encompasses an ecological preserve, pretty natural landscapes with different seasonal plants and flowers (willow, persimmon, bulrush, plum blossoms, and lotus, for starters), and a tourist village area complete with shops and restaurants inside traditional buildings. It's worth a visit if you're into birding or wildlife, or if you find yourself with an extra day in town. Crisscrossed by causeways and winding waterways, it's best to tour both on foot and by boat. The boat trip (¥60) begins at Zhōujiācūn Mătóu (Zhōujiācūn Dock), which is just inside the main entrance off Tiānmùshān Lù, and makes three stops at the Plum and Bamboo Cottage (Méizhú Shānzhuāng), Deep Pool Mouth (Shēntán Kŏu), and Autumn Snow Hut (Qiūxuĕ Ān). You may alight at any of the stops, wander to your heart's content, and then catch the next boat to the next stop. After 4pm, boats make a loop without stopping. The park (© **0571/8810-6698**) is open daily from 8:30am to 5:30pm (5pm Nov–Mar); admission is ¥80.

# Where to Stay & Dine

If you're spending the night, and don't mind splurging, a number of luxury resorts have opened in Hángzhōu in the last few years. The loveliest is **Amanfayun (Ānmànfăyún)**, Făyún Nòng 22, Xīhújiēdào, in the redeveloped Táng dynasty village Făyún Cūn in the hills just west of Língyĭn Temple (© **0571/8732-9999**; fax 0571/8732-9900; www.amanresorts.com). Aspiring to the simplicity of village life (Făyún Cūn's villagers used to tend the neighboring tea fields), the hotel has 42 rooms, suites, and villas scattered among the original, but now refurbished (and unmarked) village houses. There's under-floor heating, free Wi-Fi, daybeds, but no bathtubs (except in the Aman spa), and TVs are available only on request. Lighting is on the dim side, but service is discreet and first-rate, making for a private pampering retreat. Rooms start from ¥3,944. To the west, nestled within the XīXī National Wetland Park is the **Banyan Tree Hángzhōu (Hángzhōu Xīxī Yuèróngzhuāng)**, Zĭjīngăng Lù 21 (© **0571/8586-0000**; fax 0571/8586-2222; www.banyantree. com). Highlights here include the resort's tranquil, traditional Chinese-garden setting with arched bridges and flowing streams, its 72 rooms and villas (all newly built), fully furnished with all the expected luxury amenities (including bathtubs), and the award-winning Banyan Tree Spa. Rooms start from around ¥2,500 to ¥2,700.

Closer to West Lake, the most atmospheric hotel is still the five-star, 382-unit **Shangri-La Hotel Hángzhōu (Hángzhōu Xiānggélĭlā Fàndiàn)**, Bĕishān Lù 78, on the north shore of West Lake (© **800/942-5050** or 0571/8797-7951; fax 0571/8799-6637; www.shangri-la.com). Standard rooms, spacious and comfortable, cost ¥1,650 to ¥2,250, depending on whether they have garden or lake views. Expect around 35% discounts off the rack rate. Another top choice is the classy **Hyatt Regency Hángzhōu (Kăiyuè Dàjiŭdiàn)**, Hébīn Lù 28, on the northeastern shore of West Lake (© **0571/8779-1234**; fax 0571/8779-1818; www.hangzhou. regency.hyatt.com). Rooms are plush and modern, with standard doubles ranging from ¥1,600 to ¥2,050 (30%–50% discount). Request a nonsmoking room if so desired.

A little farther south on the eastern shore of the lake is the slightly faded, 200-unit **Sofitel Westlake Hángzhōu (Hángzhōu Suŏfēitè Xīhú Dàjiŭdiàn)**, Xīhú Dà Dào 333 (© **800/221-4542** or 0571/8707-5858; fax 0571/8707-8383; www.sofitel. com). Standard rooms start at ¥1,200, while lake-view rooms cost ¥1,736 before the average 40% discounts. The trade-off at the new 283-unit **Wyndham Grand Plaza Royale West Lake Hotel (Hángzhōu Xīhú Wēndémŭ Zhìdūn Háotíng**

**Dàjiǔdiàn),** at Fēngqǐ Lù 555 (✆ **0571/8761-6888;** www.wyndham.com), is that it's still a short walk northeast of the lake, but the facilities are still new, and the staff very helpful. Fully appointed rooms start from around ¥1,100. For a cheaper alternative, the 60-unit **Jiéxīn Century Hotel (Jiéxīn Shìjì Jiǔdiàn),** also known as the Yìyuàn Bīnguǎn, Nánshān Lù 220 (✆ **0571/8707-0100;** fax 0571/8708-7010), on the eastern edges of the lake, is affiliated with the China Academy of Fine Arts and offers clean doubles from ¥680 (discounted to around ¥300 in low season).

For dining, the Hángzhōu institution **Lóu Wài Lóu,** Gūshān Lù 30 (✆ **0571/8796-9023**), on Solitary Hill Island, between the Xīlíng Seal Engraving Society and the Zhèjiāng Library, is a tourist favorite. Hours are daily from 11:30am to 2pm and from 5 to 8pm; local specialties, such as Beggar's Chicken (*jiàohuà jī*), the excellent local *dōngpō* pork, and Lóngjǐng shrimp can all be tried here. Or avoid the whole tourist trap (and prices) and head to where locals go for their Hángzhōu food fix: the perennially crowded **Wài Pó Jiā (Grandma's Kitchen),** with branches all over the city, including at Húbīn Lù 3, second floor (✆ **0571/8510-1939;** www.waipojia.com; daily 10:30am–2pm and 4:40–9pm). There's a picture menu with all kinds of delicious local dishes you will not find at home; dinner for two ranges from ¥100 to ¥200. The international restaurants at **Xī Hú Tiāndì (West Lake Heaven and Earth),** on the southeastern shore of the lake, should provide plenty of comfort food. Or dine in style at Amanfayun's the **Restaurant** (Fǎyún Nòng 22, Xīhújiēdào; ✆ **0571/8732-9999**), which serves tasty international fare with a varied wine list.

# NÁNXÚN

90km (56 miles) W of Shànghǎi, 66km (41 miles) S of Sūzhōu, 100km (62 miles) NE of Hángzhōu

Of all the many water villages in the upper reaches of the Yángzǐ River, the Sòng Dynasty town of Nánxún is, for now, my favorite. Besides having it all—a charming mix of traditional houses that back right onto flowing streams, ancient stone arched bridges, narrow cobblestone lanes, friendly residents, and some of the most interesting mansions and estates to be found in any Yángzǐ water village (for their highly unusual mix of Chinese and Western architectural styles)—Nánxún is, at press time, still comparatively free of the usual tourist glitter. Located at the southern edge of Tài Hú (Lake Tài) on the boundary between Jiāngsū and Zhèjiāng provinces (it's officially in the latter), it can be visited as a long day trip from Shànghǎi or combined with a longer trip to Sūzhōu or Hángzhōu.

## Essentials

The easiest way to reach Nánxún (a 2–2½-hour ride from Shànghǎi) is by car, whether rented as part of an organized private tour, or separately arranged by your hotel concierge. Travel agencies can, of course, arrange private tours with the **Jǐn Jiāng Optional Tours Center** (Chánglè Lù 191; ✆ **021/6415-1188**) charging around ¥2,500 for one person, ¥1,500 each for two. A cheaper alternative is the daily Nánxún tour bus (2½ hr.; ¥150 round-trip, including the ¥100 admission ticket), which leaves the Shànghǎi Sightseeing Bus Center (Gate 25 of the Shanghai Stadium/ Shànghǎi Tǐyùguǎn) at 9am and returns at 5pm. Departure times may change, so call ahead (✆ **021/6426-5555**) to confirm.

Entry into the old town is free, but tickets to all the major sights cost ¥100. The ticket office (© **0572/391-5115** or 0572/301-6999; www.chinananxun.com) is open daily 8am to 5pm.

## Exploring Nánxún

Though a village existed here as early as A.D. 746, Nánxún was officially established around 1252 during the Southern Sòng Dynasty; the town reached its prominence only later in the Míng and Qīng dynasties. Today's town is made of a new (1980) urban section to the west and the old town located in the east. Life in the old section, still a haven of relative peace and quiet, is largely clustered around the Gŭ Yùnhé canal in the north, and the small north-south tributary that flows from it. The main streets are Dōng Dàjiē in the north, and the north-south Nánxī Jiē and Nándōng Jiē.

Since the tourist entrance is in the south, start your visit around Jiāyè Táng and Xiăo Lián Zhuāng and slowly meander your way north. Along the way, there are several docks from which you can take a **gondola** ride (¥13–¥30 per person for a one-way 30-min. ride).

Many of Nánxún's traditional houses and garden estates are from the late Míng (1368–1644) through the Qīng (1644–1911) dynasties, when the town was a thriving center of trade, first in silk, then later in rice and salt. In fact, the town was so awash in wealth in the 19th century that it had its own list of the 100 richest residents, known as *sì xiàng bā gǔniú qīshíèr zhī huángjīnggǒu,* literally "4 elephants, 8 bulls, and 72 golden retrievers."

The richest animal of them all was a Qīng Dynasty merchant named Liú Yŏng (1826–99) who built his fortune from cotton, silk, salt, and real estate. His legacy is on view in Nánxún's most famous garden, the lovely **Xiăo Lián Zhuāng (Little Lotus Villa),** which was built in 1885 as his private garden. The centerpiece here is an immense lotus pond that's especially beautiful in the summer. Anchoring the southeastern end of the pond is a Western-style, two-story red-brick house that was used as a retreat for the women of the house. To the southeast are two striking stone memorial archways *(páifáng)* built to honor Liú Yŏng's many charitable works as well as the chastity of the Liú womenfolk. Also here is the family ancestral hall.

In 1920, Liú Chénggān, Liú Yŏng's grandson, built the two-story courtyard-style **Jiāyè Táng Cángshū Lóu (Jiāyè Táng Library)** in the lot just west of Xiăo Lián Zhuāng, where he reportedly spent a fortune accumulating up to 600,000 volumes of ancient books, among them rare finds such as the official histories of the Sòng and Yuán dynasties, as well as block-printed books that were banned by the Qīng government. In the 1930s, the family was forced to sell much of its collection, and after 1949, what was left (of the books and the building) was given over to the Zhèjiāng Library. The rest of the compound is taken up by a sprawling garden with ponds, pavilions, and large clusters of rocks dredged up from Tài Hú (Lake Tài).

East of Xiăo Lián Zhuāng is one of Nánxún's true treasures, the magnificent **Zhāng Shímíng Jiùzhái.** Built in 1905 by businessman Zhāng Shímíng (the grandson of one of the original four richest men in town), this unusual 4,000-sq.-m (43,056-sq.-ft.) estate features a front section done in a quintessentially Chinese style with beautifully carved stone frames, lattice windows and doors, and traditional Qīng Dynasty furniture. The buildings in the back, though, are distinctly Western in

# Nánxún Water Village

南浔
Nánxún

Bǎijiān Lóu
(One Hundred Rooms)
百间楼

Zhāng Jìngjiāng
Gùjū
张静江故居

Baijian Lou River
百间楼河

Baoshan Jie
宝善街

西大街
Xi Da Jie

Dong Da Jie
东大街

Hóngjì Qiáo
洪济桥

Tōngjīn Qiáo
通津桥

Xiatang Dong Jie
下塘东街

Dock

南东街
Nandong Jie

南西街
Nanxi Jie

Ying Garden
颖园

Bianmin Lu
便民路

Tai'an Lu
泰安路

NANXUN
NEW TOWN
南浔新镇

NANXUN
OLD TOWN
南浔古镇

Guanghui Bridge
广惠桥

Dock

Nanxun Historical Museum
南浔史官

Liúshì Tīhào
刘氏梯号

Jiaye Lu
嘉业路

Shiyuan Lu
适园路

Zhāng Shímíng Jiùzhái
张石铭旧宅

Xin Kai River
新开河

Dock

Xiǎo Lián Zhuāng
(Little Lotus Villa)
小莲庄

Jiāyè Táng Cángshū Lóu
(Jiāyè Táng Library)
嘉业堂藏书楼

Ticket Office
售票处

Renrui Lu 人瑞路

N

style (Zhāng did a great deal of business with the French): a rear courtyard, seemingly lifted right out of a New Orleans plantation, down to its abandoned, slightly decrepit air, sports a red-and-gray-brick facade with French windows, wrought-iron banisters, and Roman columns. Inside is an enormous ballroom with wainscoting, chandeliers, and a French mosaic floor. You can almost hear the music and see the waltzing dancers, except, of course, this was during the time when female footbinding was still the norm, so there wouldn't have been many debutante balls. Don't miss the absolutely gorgeous blue-and-white flower-patterned, stained-glass windows on the second floor, which served as the women's quarters.

A little way up across the main canal from here is another residence worth seeing: **Liúshì Tīhào.** Built by Liú Ānshēng, third son of Liú Yǒng, this splendid **Hóng Fángzi (Red House),** designed in a similar Chinese-front/Western-back style, has a massive red-brick rear facade with a second-floor balcony propped up by Greek columns, and deep-set arched French windows concealing dusty, but still beautiful panes of stained glass. The building would look right at home in the West were it not for the unmistakably Chinese-style black-tile roof.

Working your way north, cross the stone arched bridge **Tōngjīn Qiáo** (rebuilt in 1798) onto Dōng Dàjiē. Depending on the time of day, you should be able to get a pretty picture of the **Hóngjì Qiáo** (bridge) to the east. Dōng Dàjiē was one of the two busiest thoroughfares in Nánxún's heyday. At the eastern end of the street is **Zhāng Jìngjiāng Gùjū,** the former residence of Zhāng Jìngjiāng, a supporter of Sun Yat-sen during the 1911 Republican revolution. Built in 1898, his house is much more traditionally Chinese, with none of the Western flourishes found in the earlier mansions.

The real highlight in this northern section of town, however, is **Bǎijiān Lóu (One Hundred Rooms),** so named for the 100 or so houses that wind along both sides of the Bǎijiānlóu Hé (One Hundred Rooms River). These more than 400-year-old row houses with white walls and black-tiled roofs, attached to each other by a high white wall with a stepped crenellated roof, were reportedly built by Míng Dynasty official Dǒng Fèn for the servants of his female family members, though some find it hard to believe that such beautiful houses would be wasted on the help. Then again, it was a rich town. The front of each house typically has a covered walkway; lined up together, these walkways make for one long corridor running along each side of the canal. Bǎijiān Lóu offers one of the best photo opportunities in town—if you don't mind the modern-day wires, TV antennae, and hanging laundry, that is.

## Where to Dine

There are a number of informal restaurants and teahouses along Nánxī Jiē, Nándōng Jiē, and Dōng Dàjiē where you can take a break. The restaurants will serve inexpensive *jiācháng cài* (home-style Chinese cooking), with rice, noodles, and a variety of stir-fries such as *yúxiāng ròusī* (garlic pork) or *jiācháng dòufu* (home-style tofu). Local snacks include gelatinous candy like *júhóng gāo* and *gǔsǎo bǐng*, which some Westerners have likened to eating flavored chalk. Most of these restaurants are open from 11am to 2pm for lunch and from 5 to 7 or 8pm for dinner, though some are open all day and can easily fry up some meat and vegetables or make a bowl of noodles as long as staff is around and willing.

# TÓNGLĬ

18km (11 miles) SE of Sūzhōu, 80km (50 miles) W of Shànghǎi

Surrounded by five lakes and crisscrossed by a skein of canals, the Sòng Dynasty town of Tónglĭ is more built up and commercialized than Nánxún, but it's still a pleasant enough water village, with several impressive residences and gardens, and China's first sex museum. It's not as if this picturesque town a half-hour east of Sūzhōu needs any more publicity, having been a magnet for television and film crews since 1983. Try to visit on a weekday when you won't be overrun by the masses, though you just may find yourself in the midst of a film set.

## Essentials

**VISITOR INFORMATION**     Entrance to Tónglĭ's old town is free, but there is a ¥80 fee to visit all the major sights listed below except for the sex museum. Visiting hours are daily 7:30am to 5:30pm. There are introductory captions in English at the

# Tónglǐ Water Village

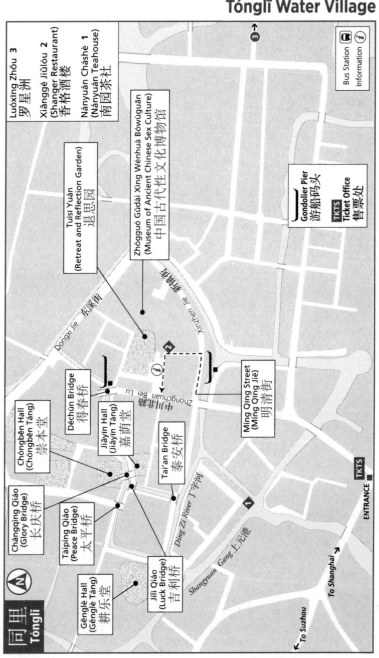

同里 Tónglǐ

Luóxīng Zhōu **3**
罗星洲

Xiānggé Jiǔlóu **2**
(Shanger Restaurant)
香格酒楼

Nányuán Cháshè **1**
(Nányuán Teahouse)
南园茶社

Tuìsī Yuán
(Retreat and Reflection Garden)
退思园

Zhōngguó Gǔdài Xìng Wénhuà Bówùguǎn
(Museum of Ancient Chinese Sex Culture)
中国古代性文化博物馆

Déchūn Bridge
得春桥

Chóngběn Hall (Chóngběn Táng)
崇本堂

Jiāyìn Hall (Jiāyìn Táng)
嘉荫堂

Tài'ān Bridge
泰安桥

Míng Qīng Street (Míng Qīng Jiē)
明清街

Chángqìng Qiáo (Glory Bridge)
长庆桥

Tàipíng Qiáo (Peace Bridge)
太平桥

Gēnglè Hall (Gēnglè Táng)
耕乐堂

Jílì Qiáo (Luck Bridge)
吉利桥

Dōngxī Jiē 东溪街

Zhōngchuān Běi Lù

Xīnzhèn Jiē

驳岸街

Ding Zé River 丁字河

Shàngyuán Gǎng 上元港

Gondolier Pier
游船码头

TKTS Ticket Office
售票处

Bus Station
Information

ENTRANCE   TKTS

To Shanghai

To Suzhou

N

sights, but if you want greater detail, the **Tónglǐ Tourist Information Center** (© 0512/6333-1145) southwest of Tuìsī Yuán can sometimes offer English-speaking guides for a fee, though they prefer that you call ahead to book.

**GETTING THERE**    Only a half-hour away from Sūzhōu, Tónglǐ can just as easily be visited from there, especially if you decide to overnight in Sūzhōu. Your hotel tour desk in Shànghǎi or Sūzhōu can organize a day trip out here, as can any of the major travel agencies, but it's equally easy to do the trip on your own. From Shànghǎi, there are Tónglǐ buses (2 hr., ¥130 round-trip, includes ¥80 entrance fee) that leave the Shànghǎi Sightseeing Bus Center (Gate 25 of the Shànghǎi Stadium/Shànghǎi Tǐyùguǎn) daily at 8:30am. Departure times may change, so call ahead (© 021/6426-5555) to confirm. From Tónglǐ, buses return to Shànghǎi around 4pm. Tónglǐ's public bus station (qìchēzhàn) is in the south in the new part of town on Sōngběi Gōnglù. From here, buses run to Sūzhōu (40–50 min.; ¥8) every hour between 7am and 5pm.

## Exploring Tónglǐ

Buffeted in the south by new, ugly concrete buildings, Tónglǐ's picturesque old town, located north of the Shàngyuán Canal (Shàngyuán Gǎng), is actually made up of seven islets connected to each other by more than 40 arched stone bridges and fed by a network of some 15 canals. The town dates to the Sòng Dynasty (960–1279), though many of its surviving mansions are of later Míng and Qīng origin. As recently as 2 years ago, residents were still blithely going about their lives along the canals (it was not uncommon to see children bathing and women washing clothes in the streams), but all that messy living has now been largely cleaned up for tourists. The most common sight in the canals these days is a flotilla of tourist gondolas (and, of course, the inevitable trash that still results from hordes of visitors). You, too, can soak up the watery atmosphere by renting a **gondola** (¥70 per boat for 30 min.) from various piers scattered along the canals.

Waterways aside, the rest of the old town is easily traversed on foot. The busiest street is **Míngqīng Jiē,** a winding lane flanked with Míng and Qīng dynasty–style wooden houses that have mostly been converted to shops and restaurants. The north end of this street leads to the old town's main attraction, **Tuìsī Yuán (Retreat and Reflection Garden).** Built in 1886 by a dismissed court official, this World Heritage garden is laid out from west to east in three sections, with the family's residences in the west, meeting and entertaining rooms in the center, and a small, but cleverly designed landscaped garden in the east. The use of winding walkways with different shaped windows, jutting pavilions, and a reflecting pond make the garden appear larger than it is.

East of the garden is the former Lìzé Girls' School and the current home of the **Zhōghuá Xìng Wénhuà Bówùguǎn (Chinese Sex Museum)** (© 0512/6332-2973; www.chinasexmuseum.com). Relocated here from its two previous sites in Shànghǎi (see the "China's sex Museum" box), the museum showcases the private collection of more than 1,200 sex artifacts amassed through the years by Professor Liú Dálín of Shànghǎi University. Displays are divided into sections covering themes from sex and evolution to the sexual oppression of women, and sex in literature and the arts. The wide array of sexual relics includes ancient tomb paintings, statuary,

# CHINA'S SEX MUSEUM

When it first opened in 1999 on the eighth floor of the Old Sincere Building on Nánjīng Lù in Shànghǎi, China's first official sex museum was welcomed by some as an indication of an increasingly progressive attitude in a puritanical empire where the sale of pornography is still ostensibly punishable by death. The creation of Professor Liú Dálín of Shànghǎi University, this pioneering **Chinese Sex Museum (Zhōghuá Xìng Wénhuà Bówùguǎn)** displayed most of his private collection of over 1,200 sex artifacts, many of them proof that China's putative Puritanism is really no more than a 60-year-old yoke. Unfortunately, exorbitant rents in 2004 forced the museum to move to the town of Tónglǐ 80km (50 miles) away. The museum's eviction received some press attention and Tónglǐ, not surprisingly, has also received more visitors.

and erotic devices, including a pottery penis with a woman's head dated 2000 B.C. There are also exhibits devoted to foot-binding, furniture designed to enhance love-making, and "trunk bottoms" (explicit china figures placed at the bottom of dowry trunks by parents to instruct prospective brides). The museum is open daily from 8:30am to 5pm; admission is ¥20.

West of Tuìsī Yuán are three of the town's better-preserved traditional residences. The westernmost, **Gēnglè Hall (Gēnglè Táng),** which belonged to the Míng Dynasty nobleman Zhū Xiáng, is also the largest of the residences, with three major courtyards encompassing 41 rooms and a sprawling yard in the back. **Jiāyīn Hall (Jiāyīn Táng),** built in 1922 as the residence of famous local scholar Liǔ Yàzǐ, has high white walls and doorways fronted by upturned eaves—a style more reminiscent of the Southern Ānhuī Huīzhōu architecture. Here, the garden is in the center of the residence. The highlight at the 1912 **Chóngběn Hall (Chóngběn Táng),** with its four courtyards and three doorways, is the refined brick, stone, and wood carvings of scenes from Chinese literary classics, as well as of various propitious symbols such as cranes and vases (the Chinese word for vase, *píng*, is also a homonym for peace). Each row of buildings here is stepped increasingly higher than the previous, symbolizing the owner's wish that each subsequent generation in his family would attain greater success than the last.

The last two residences are connected by three bridges, **Tàipíng Qiáo (Peace Bridge), Jílì Qiáo (Luck Bridge),** and **Chángqìng Qiáo (Glory Bridge).** It was the custom in the old days to carry a bride in her sedan chair over all three bridges. Today, that custom has been resurrected for tourists who can don the proper red Chinese wedding finery and be carried in an old-fashioned sedan chair accompanied by a wailing *lúshēng* (wind musical instrument) and beating drums.

Also included in the price of the entrance ticket is **Luóxīng Zhōu (Luóxīng Islet),** located in the middle of Tónglǐ Hú (Tónglǐ Lake). Although there's been a temple here since the Yuán Dynasty (1206–1368), today's buildings are a strictly new (1996) mishmash of Buddhist, Daoist, and Confucian influences. The boat ride over makes for a pleasant enough trip if you've exhausted the rest of the town's attractions.

# Where to Dine

As the official restaurant catering to foreign tour groups, **Xiānggé Jiǔlóu (Shanger Restaurant)** on Míngqīng Jiē (Míngqīng St.; © **0512/6333-6988;** daily 8:30am– 8pm) has a handy English menu and serves local specialties and generic foreigner-friendly Chinese food. There are also many nondescript small restaurants along the same **Míngqīng Jiē** that serve basic *jiācháng cài* (Chinese home-style cooking) at reasonable prices, with a meal for two averaging ¥30 to ¥50. The **Nányuán Cháshè (Nányuán Teahouse)** at the intersection of Dōngkāng Lù and Nánkāng Lù in the southern part of the old town is a restored Qīng Dynasty building where you can sip tea and nosh on local snacks as you look out over the canals from the second floor. Local specialties include the Tónglǐ version of braised pig's trotters, *zhuàngyuán tí; xiǎo xūnyú* (small smoked fish); and *mín bǐng* (a sweet glutinous rice pastry). Also look for the roasted chestnuts on sale in the streets.

# FAST FACTS

## FAST FACTS: SHÀNGHǍI

**Area Codes**   China's country code is 86, and Shànghǎi's area code is 021. In mainland China, all area codes begin with a zero, which is dropped when calling China from abroad. The entire area code can be dropped when making local calls.

**Business Hours**   Offices are open Monday through Friday from 9am to 6pm, although some still close at the lunch hour (about noon–1:30pm); a few maintain limited Saturday hours. Bank opening hours are Monday to Friday 9am to 5pm. Sights, shops, restaurants, and transportation systems offer the same service 7 days a week. Department stores are typically open from 10am to 10pm. Restaurants outside of hotels are generally open from 11:30am to 2pm and 5 to 9:30pm, while those catering to foreign visitors usually stay open later. The official closing time for bars is 2am, though some stay open later on weekends.

**Cellphones (Mobile Phones)**   See "Staying Connected" p. 66.

**Doctors & Dentists**   Shànghǎi has the most advanced medical treatment and facilities in China. The higher-end hotels usually have in-house or on-call doctors, but almost all hotels can refer foreign guests to dentists and doctors versed in Western medicine. The following medical clinics and hospitals specialize in treating foreigners and provide international-standard services: With multiple branches around town, **Parkway Health Medical Center** (formerly World Link Medical Center), Nánjīng Xī Lù 1376, Shànghǎi Centre, Ste. 203 (24-hr. hot line ☏ **021/6445-5999;** www.parkwayhealth.cn), offers family medical care, 24-hour emergency services, a 24-hour hot line, Western dental care, OB-GYN services, and inpatient care (Dànshuǐ Lù 170, second and third floors; ☏ **021/6385-9889**). Walk-in hours at the main clinic at Nánjīng Lù 1376 are Monday through Friday 9am to 7pm, Saturday and Sunday 9am to 5pm. Call for times at other clinics. **Huá Shān Hospital,** Wūlǔmùqí Zhōng Lù 12, Jìng Ān District, has a Foreigners Clinic on the eighth floor of Building 1, and a 24-hour hot line (☏ **021/6248-3986**). A representative office of **International SOS** (Hóngqiáo Lù 3, 2 Grand Gateway, Unit 2907–2910; ☏ **021/5298-9538**) provides medical evacuation and repatriation throughout China on a 24-hour basis.

Dental care to foreign visitors and expatriates is provided by **Parkway Health Dental Centers** Monday to Saturday from 8:30am to 6:30pm (see above), and by **DDS Dental Care,** Huáihǎi Zhōng Lù 1325 (at Bǎoqìng Lù), Evergo Plaza, B1-05 (☏ **021/5465-2678;** www.ddsdentalcare.com). DDS Dental Care has multilingual Western-trained dentists and its own lab.

**Drinking Laws**   There are no liquor laws in Shànghǎi worth worrying about (in other words, no legal drinking age). Bars keep irregular closing hours, some not shutting down until well after the official 2am closing time. Supermarkets, hotel shops, and international restaurants sell imported and domestic beer, wine, and spirits. Inexpensive domestic beer and liquor can be bought anytime at the 24-hour neighborhood convenience stores.

**Driving Rules**  See "Getting There & Around," p. 35.

**Drugstores**  In general, bring any and all of your own prescription medicines, and your favorite over-the-counter pain and cold remedies. A limited selection of Western amenities like cough drops, toothpaste, shampoo, and beauty aids are available in international hotel kiosks, and most reliably at **Watson's Drug Store,** which has branches throughout town, including at Huáihǎi Zhōng Lù 787–789 (✆ **021/6474-4775;** 9:30am–10pm). If necessary, prescriptions can be filled at the **Parkway Health Medical Center,** Nánjīng Xī Lù 1376, Shànghǎi Centre, Ste. 203 (✆ **021/6279-7688**). Chinese medicines (as well as some Western remedies) are dispensed at the **Shànghǎi No. 1 Pharmacy,** Nánjīng Dōng Lù 616 (✆ **021/6322-4567,** ext. 0; 9am–10pm).

**Electricity**  The electricity used throughout China is 220 volts, alternating current (AC), 50 cycles. Except for laptop computers and most mobile-phone chargers, other North American electrical devices will require the use of a transformer. Outlets come in a variety of configurations, the most common being the flat two-pin (but not the three-pin or the two-pin where one is wider than the other), and also the round two-pin, the slanted two-prong, and slanted three-prong types. Most hotels have a variety of outlets and can supply a range of adapters. Transformers and adapters can be purchased in department stores.

**Embassies & Consulates**  The consulates of many countries are located in the French Concession and Jìng Ān districts several miles west of downtown. Visa and passport sections are open only at certain times of the day, so call in advance. The consulates are open from Monday to Friday only, and are often closed for lunch (noon–1pm). The Consulate General of **Australia** is in CITIC Square at Nánjīng Xī Lù 1168, 22nd floor (✆ **021/2215-5200;** fax 021/2215-5252; www.shanghai.china.embassy.gov.au). The **British** Consulate General is in the Shànghǎi Centre, Nánjīng Xī Lù 1376, Ste. 301 (✆ **021/3279-2000;** fax 021/6279-7651; www.uk.cn). The **Canadian** Consulate General is in the Shànghǎi Centre at Nánjīng Xī Lù 1376, West Tower, Ste. 604 and 668 (visa section, ✆ **021/3279-2800;** fax 021/3279-2801; www.shanghai.gc.ca). The **New Zealand** Consulate General is at Chánglè Lù 989, the Centre, Room 1605–1607A (✆ **021/5407-5858;** fax 021/5407-5068; www.nzembassy.com). The Consulate General of the **United States** is at Huáihǎi Zhōng Lù 1469 (✆ **021/6433-6880;** fax 021/6433-4122; http://shanghai.usembassy-china.org.cn), although the American Citizens Services Unit is at Nánjīng Xī Lù 1038, Westgate Mall, eighth floor (✆ **021/3217-4650,** ext. 2102, 2103, 2114).

**Emergencies**  The emergency phone numbers in Shànghǎi are ✆ **110** for police (English operators available), ✆ **119** for fire, and ✆ **120** for ambulance, though no English is spoken at the last two.

**Etiquette & Customs**  **Appropriate attire:** The Shanghainese have a long-held reputation of being fashion-conscious and are, on the whole, a comparatively well-dressed bunch. For the worldly Shanghainese who've seen it all, foreigners tend to get a pass when it comes to attire anyway, so wear whatever you find comfortable. Chances are, you'll be out-dressed (or under-dressed in some cases) by the trendy fashion plates. When in doubt, err on the side of modesty even if some of the younger locals don't. Business attire is similar to that in the West.

**Gestures:** The handshake is now commonplace, as is the exchange of business cards (*míng piàn*), so bring some along if you have them. Cards and gifts should be presented and received with both hands. Speaking a few words of Mandarin will go a long way in pleasing your host; you'll be told you speak very well, to which the proper reply should be a self-effacing denial, even if you are fluent. When invited to someone's house, never go empty-handed; always bring a small gift, even if it's just some fruit picked up at the last minute at the corner store.

**Avoiding offense:** Causing someone to lose face is the surest way to offend, and should be avoided as much as possible. This means not losing your temper and yelling at someone in public, not calling public attention to their mistakes, and not publicly contradicting them, no matter how great the grievance. Instead, take up the matter privately or complain to a superior, when appropriate.

**Eating & drinking:** If possible, master the use of chopsticks before you go. Chinese food is eaten family-style with everyone serving themselves from several main dishes. As the guest, you'll be served first; accept graciously. Then reciprocate the gesture by serving your host in return. Use the communal serving spoon(s) or chopsticks provided. Eat with your chopsticks, but don't leave them sticking out of the bowl. Never criticize the food in front of your host. Your cup of tea will be constantly topped up. A Cantonese custom that has started to catch on in Shànghǎi is to acknowledge the pour by tapping your fingers lightly on the table. Feel free to top up other people's cups of tea every now and then, though it's likely that after the first time, your host will remove the teapot from your reach. If you're invited to eat at someone's home, always bring a small gift (fruit is always a fail-safe gift) and take off your shoes at the entrance even if your host/hostess demurs. They're merely being polite. If you're invited to a banquet, expect a great deal of drinking. Toasts are usually made with *báijiǔ* (potent Chinese spirits), often to the tunes of *"gān bēi"* (literally dry glass, the equivalent of "bottoms up"). If you can't keep up, don't drain your glass (for it will be filled up again quickly, sparking another round of drinking), but do return the toast, if necessary with beer, mineral water, or tea.

**Holidays**   See "When to Go," p. 29, and "Shànghǎi Calendar of Events," p. 70.

**Hospitals**   See "Doctors & Dentists" above.

**Hot Lines**   The 24-hour **Shànghǎi Call Center** (© **021/962-288**) should be able to handle most tourist queries in both English and Chinese.

**Insurance**   Check your existing insurance policies and credit card coverage before you buy travel insurance. You may already be covered for lost luggage, cancelled tickets, or medical expenses. The cost of travel insurance varies widely, depending on the cost and length of your trip, your age and health, and the type of trip you're taking, but expect to pay between 5% and 8% of the vacation itself. You can get estimates from various providers through **InsureMyTrip.com**. Enter your trip cost and dates, your age, and other information, for prices from more than a dozen companies.

**Note:** Many tour operators, including those catering to China, include insurance in the cost of the trip or can arrange insurance policies through a partnering provider, a convenient and often cost-effective way for the traveler to obtain insurance. Make sure the tour company is a reputable one; however, some experts suggest you avoid buying insurance from the tour company you're traveling with, saying it's better to buy from a "third party" insurer than to put all your money in one place.

**Medical insurance:** Check with your individual health plan to see if it provides coverage for travel to China. In any event, consider purchasing travel insurance that includes an air ambulance or scheduled airline repatriation, but be clear as to the terms and conditions of repatriation. With several advanced clinics staffed by foreign doctors in Shànghǎi, travelers can expect a fairly high quality of health care, though avoid, if possible, regular Chinese hospitals. In the latter, you'll have to pay your (more than likely substantial) bill upfront and in cash, and then only submit your claim after you've returned home. Be sure you have adequate proof of payment.

If you require additional medical insurance, try **MEDEX Assistance** (☎ **410/453-6300;** www.medexassist.com) or **Travel Assistance International** (☎ **800/821-2828;** www.travelassistance.com; for general information on services, call the company's Worldwide Assistance Services, Inc., at ☎ **800/777-8710**).

**Internet Access** See "Staying Connected," p. 66.

**Language** Mandarin is the official language throughout China. However, while many Shanghainese speak Mandarin, you're just as likely to hear locals conversing everywhere (shops, businesses, restaurants) in Shanghainese, which is as different from Mandarin as Cantonese is from English. Written Chinese, however, follows one standard script. Outside of international hotels, restaurants, and shops, English is still seldom spoken, though compulsory English classes from primary grade one was implemented in local schools in 2003. Many younger urbanites should recognize at least a smattering of English words and phrases. See chapter 13, "The Chinese Language," p. 289.

**Legal Aid** If you end up on the wrong side of the "still evolving" law in China, call your consulate immediately.

**Lost & Found** Be sure to tell all of your credit card companies the minute you discover your wallet has been lost or stolen, and file a report at the nearest police precinct. Contact the PSB (see "Police," below) for this. Your credit card company or insurer may require a police report number or record of the loss. Most credit card companies have an emergency toll-free number to call if your card is lost or stolen; they may be able to wire you a cash advance immediately or deliver an emergency credit card in a day or two. In China, the emergency toll-free numbers for lost or stolen credit cards are as follows: Visa (☎ **010/800-440-2911** or 021/6374-4418); American Express, which will also replace lost or stolen traveler's checks (☎ **021/6279-8082** or 010/800-610-0277); and MasterCard (☎ **010/800-110-7309**). Diners Club members should call Hong Kong at ☎ **852/2860-1800** or call the U.S. collect at ☎ **001/416/369-6313.** If you need emergency cash, you can have money wired to you at many post offices and a few Agricultural Bank of China branches throughout China via Western Union (☎ **800/325-6000;** www.westernunion. com). The loss of your passport should be immediately reported to your consulate. For other personal items, contact the site where you think you lost it, then report the loss to your hotel staff or the police, but don't expect much sympathy, let alone results.

**Mail** Sending mail from China is remarkably reliable. Most hotels sell postage stamps and will mail your letters and parcels, the latter at a hefty fee, so take your parcels to the post office yourself, if possible. Overseas letters and postcards require 5 to 10 days for delivery. Current costs are as follows: overseas airmail: **postcard** ¥4.20, **letters under 10g** ¥5.40, **letters under 20g** ¥6.50. Domestic letters are ¥1.20. EMS (**express parcels** under 500g/18 oz.): to the U.S. and Canada ¥180 to ¥240; to Europe and the U.K. ¥220 to ¥280; to Australia and New Zealand ¥160 to ¥210. **Normal parcels** up to 1kg (2.2 lb.): to the U.S. and Canada by air ¥102, by sea ¥20 to ¥84; to Europe and the U.K. by air ¥142, by sea ¥22 to ¥108; to Australia and New Zealand by air ¥135, by sea ¥15 to ¥89. Customs declaration forms in Chinese and French are available at post offices. When sending parcels, bring your package to the post office unsealed, as packages are often subject to inspection. Large post offices will sell packaging material.

The main Post Office (*yóuzhèng jú*) (7am–10pm daily) is located at Běi Sūzhōu Lù 276 (☎ **021/6325-2070**), at the intersection of Sìchuān Běi Lù, in downtown Shànghǎi just north of Sūzhōu Creek; international parcels are sent from a desk in the same building, but that entrance is actually around the corner at Tiāntóng Lù 395. Other post offices where employees can speak some English are located at Shànghǎi Centre, Nánjīng Xī Lù 1376, lower level (☎ **021/6279-8044**), and at Huáihǎi Lù 1337.

International parcel and courier services in Shànghǎi include **FedEx,** Shílóng Lù 411, no. 28 (☏ **021/5411-8333**); **DHL-Sinotrans,** Jìniàn Lù 303 (☏ **021/6536-2900**); and **UPS,** Lùjiāzuǐ Dōng Lù 166, China Insurance Building, 23rd floor (☏ **021/3896-5599**). Pickup and delivery can usually be arranged by your hotel.

**Measurements**   China uses the metric system.

**Newspapers & Magazines**   See "Staying Connected," p. 66.

**Passports**   Allow plenty of time before your trip to apply for a passport; processing normally takes 3 weeks, but can take longer during busy periods (especially spring). And keep in mind that if you need a passport in a hurry, you'll pay a higher processing fee.

**For Residents of Australia:** You can pick up an application from your local post office or any branch of Passports Australia, but you must schedule an interview at the passport office to present your application materials. Call the **Australian Passport Information Service** at ☏ **131-232,** or visit the government website at www.passports.gov.au.

**For Residents of Canada:** Passport applications are available at travel agencies throughout Canada or from the central **Passport Office,** Department of Foreign Affairs and International Trade, Ottawa, ON K1A 0G3 (☏ **800/567-6868;** www.ppt.gc.ca).

**For Residents of Ireland:** You can apply for a 10-year passport at the **Passport Office,** Setanta Centre, Molesworth Street, Dublin 2 (☏ **01/671-1633;** www.irlgov.ie/iveagh). Children under age 3 must apply for a €15 3-year passport; children ages 3 to 17 must apply for a €25 5-year passport. You can also apply at 1A South Mall, Cork (☏ **021/272-525**), or at most main post offices.

**For Residents of New Zealand:** You can pick up a passport application at any New Zealand Passports Office or download it from their website. Contact the **Passports Office** at ☏ **0800/225-050** in New Zealand or 04/474-8100, or log on to www.passports.govt.nz.

**For Residents of the United Kingdom:** To pick up an application for a standard 10-year passport (5-year passport for children under 16), visit your nearest passport office, major post office, or travel agency, or contact the **United Kingdom Passport Service** at ☏ **0300/222-0000** or search its website at www.ips.gov.uk.

**For Residents of the United States:** Whether you're applying in person or by mail, you can download passport applications from the U.S. State Department website at **http://travel.state.gov.** To find your regional passport office, either check the U.S. State Department website or call the **National Passport Information Center** toll-free number (☏ **877/487-2778**) for automated information.

**Police**   Known as the **PSB** (**Public Security Bureau,** *gōng'ān jú*), the Shànghǎi police force has its headquarters at Fúzhōu Lù 185 (☏ **021/6231-0110** or 021/6854-1199). Known as *jīngchá,* the police are no more keen to get involved in your business than you are to contact them. Ideally, any interaction with them should be limited to visa extensions. These are handled at the Foreign Affairs Section at Mínshēng Lù 1500 in Pǔdōng (☏ **021/2895-1900,** ext. 2; Metro: Shànghǎi Kèjìguǎn/Science and Technology Museum, exit 3). The emergency telephone number for the police is ☏ **110.**

**Smoking**   China has more smokers than any other nation, an estimated 350 million, accounting for one of every three cigarettes consumed worldwide. About 70% of the men smoke. Recent antismoking campaigns have led to laws banning smoking on all forms of public transport (including taxis) and in waiting rooms and terminals, a ban, which has, surprisingly, been largely observed (except on long-distance buses). Top hotels provide nonsmoking rooms and floors, and a few restaurants have begun to set aside nonsmoking tables and sections. Still, expect to encounter more smoking in public places in China than in most Western countries.

**Taxes**   Most four- and five-star hotels levy a 10% to 15% tax on rooms (including a city tax), while a few restaurants and bars have taken to placing a similar service charge on bills. In the case of the latter, you can almost be assured that the service will not justify the charge. There is no sales tax. Airport departure taxes are now included in the price of your airline ticket.

**Telephones**   See "Staying Connected," p. 66.

**Time**   Shànghǎi (and all of China) is on Běijīng time, which is 8 hours ahead of Greenwich Mean Time (GMT + 8), 13 hours ahead of New York, 14 hours ahead of Chicago, and 16 hours ahead of Los Angeles. There's no daylight saving time, so subtract 1 hour in the summer. For the current time in Shànghǎi, dial ✆ **117.**

**Tipping**   There is officially *no* tipping in China, but the reality is that it has become quite commonplace in Shànghǎi's hospitality industry, especially where bellhops (four- and five-star hotels), tour guides, and tour bus drivers are concerned. Though you may feel pressured to do so, only tip if you feel truly inclined to or for exceptional service. Restaurant waitstaff and taxi drivers usually do not expect tips, and will return any change due you.

**Toilets**   For hygienic restrooms, rely on the big hotels, restaurants catering to foreigners, new malls, and fast-food outlets, in that order. There are, of course, hundreds of public restrooms in the streets, parks, cafes, department stores, and tourist sites of Shànghǎi, but most of these consist primarily of squat toilets (a trough in the ground), are not always clean, and do not provide tissues or soap as a rule. Some public restrooms charge a small fee (¥.50) and will give you a rough sheet of what passes for toilet paper. Look for wc or ᴛᴏɪʟᴇᴛ signs at intersections pointing the way to all public facilities.

**Visas**   For details about visa requirements, see "Visas," p. 32.

**Visitor Information**   China's travel industry, though ostensibly controlled by a central authority, is generally quite mired in misinformation and obfuscation, so that it is often difficult for visitors to get truly reliable and accurate information either inside or outside the country. The all-controlling China National Tourism Administration has branches in foreign countries known as **China National Tourist Offices (CNTO);** their purpose is supposedly to provide tourist information and services. Traditionally, however, CNTO has usually funneled visitors to the agency handling all travel within China, **China International Travel Service** (**CITS** or *guójì lǚxíngshè*). There are more tour operators inside China now, but don't expect the information CNTO provides to always be accurate or up-to-date. For a list of CNTO office addresses, see below.

   **Shànghǎi online:** The best way to receive fairly up-to-date information on Shànghǎi before departure is to use the Internet, though it's best to surf a variety of websites so you can compare information. Treat with some skepticism "official sources" of information, including the official city website (www.shanghai.gov.cn), which is not always up-to-date either. Also beware of unofficial Chinese-run sites, especially those that also sell travel services—they are a dime a dozen on the Web and there is no guarantee of reliability.

   Shànghǎi's English-language newspaper, *Shanghai Daily* (www.shanghaidaily.com), offers both Shànghǎi and China news, albeit of the highly filtered and uncontroversial variety.

   Of the online editions of the English-language magazines, the best of the lot are the long-running bi-weekly *City Weekend* (www.cityweekend.com.cn) which offers news and features, along with its restaurant, bar, and arts reviews and listings; the 2010-launched *Time Out Shanghai* (www.timeoutcn.com/tosh); and the monthly *that's Shanghai* (www.shanghai.urbananatomy.com), with longer feature articles and listings for just about everything the visitor or even expat can want to look up. "Smart Shanghai" (www.smart shanghai.com) is an urban webzine on local nightlife, dining, and culture, while "Shanghaiist" (www.shanghaiist.com) is one of the best blogs on the latest happenings in Shànghǎi. Other Shànghǎi blogs include www.sinosplice.com and www.wangjianshuo.com.

*The Oriental-List* offers an ad- and spam-free discussion of issues relating to travel in China, and is a good place to ask questions that may not be addressed in this book. To subscribe, send a blank e-mail to: subscribe-oriental-list@list.datasinica.com.

**In Shànghǎi:** The best source of visitor information is the 24-hour **Shànghǎi Call Center** (✆ 021/962-288). Staffed by very helpful English- and Chinese-speaking university graduates, it's the first of its kind to offer such a service in the country, providing information on culture, entertainment, medical services, the economy, tourism, dining, transportation, entry-exit issues, and other related topics on Shànghǎi.

Otherwise, Shànghǎi has an official **Tourism Hot Line** (✆ 021/6439-8947 or 021/962020) with the occasional English speaker who can be helpful. You can also try the 24-hour **Tourist Information Line** maintained by Spring Travel Service (✆ 021/6252-0000). Hotel staff and concierges can be a font of information as well, though even the most friendly and knowledgeable guest-relations officers at the top hotels can sometimes still be in the dark about any options off the beaten path. Also, beware of those who would try to sell you expensive tours.

There are about a dozen **Tourist Information Service Centers (Lǚyóu Zīxún Fúwù Zhōngxīn)** around Shànghǎi. They appear to exist mainly to sell various city tours and to book hotels but, depending on who is sitting behind the desk, they may be able to offer some guidance. You can also pick up city maps, postcards, brochures, and information on local sights, shopping, and restaurants here. The main office is at Zhōngshān Xī Lù 2525, Room 410, Chángníng District (✆ 021/6439-9806), with smaller branch offices at Nánjīng Xī Lù 1699, Jìng Ān District (✆ 021/6248-3259); Nánjīng Dōng Lù 561, Huángpǔ District (✆ 021/5353-1117); Chéngdū Nán Lù 127, Lúwān District (✆ 021/6372-8330); and Lùjiāzuǐ Xī Lù 168, Zhèngdà Guǎngchǎng first floor, Pǔdōng (✆ 021/6887-7888).

The best sources for **current information** about Shànghǎi events, shopping, restaurants, and nightlife are the free English-language newspapers and magazines (listed above) distributed to hotels, shops, and cafes around town.

Contact these **China National Tourist Offices** (www.cnto.org):

o In the **United States:** 350 Fifth Ave., Ste. 6413, New York, NY 10118 (✆ **212/760-8218;** fax 212/760-8809; ny@cnta.gov.cn); 600 W. Broadway, Ste. 320, Glendale, CA 91204 (✆ **818/545-7505;** fax 818/545-7506; la@cnta.gov.cn).

o In the **U.K.:** 71 Warwick Rd., London SW5 9HB (✆ **020/7373-0888;** fax 020/7370-9989; london@cnta.gov.cn).

o In **Australia:** 44 Market St., Level 19, Sydney NSW 2000 (✆ **02/9299-4057;** fax 02/9290-1958; sydney@cnta.gov.cn).

o In **Canada:** 480 University Ave., Ste. 806, Toronto, ON M5G 1V2 (✆ **416/599-6636;** fax 416/599-6382; www.tourismchina-ca.com).

**Water** Tap water throughout China is not safe for drinking (or for brushing teeth). Use only bottled water, widely available almost everywhere (supermarkets, convenience stores, neighborhood shops, vendors' stalls), and also provided in most hotel rooms.

**Weather** The *China Daily* newspaper, CCTV 9 (China Central Television's English-language channel), and some hotel bulletin boards furnish the next day's forecast. You can also dial Shànghǎi's weather number, ✆ **121.**

**Wi-Fi** See "Staying Connected," p. 66.

# AIRLINE & HOTEL WEBSITES

## MAJOR AIRLINES

**Air Canada**
www.aircanada.com

**Air China**
www.airchina.com

**Air New Zealand**
www.airnewzealand.com

**American Airlines**
www.aa.com

**British Airways**
www.british-airways.com

**Cathay Pacific**
www.cathaypacific.com

**China Airlines**
www.china-airlines.com

**China Eastern**
www.flychinaeastern.com

**China Southern**
www.flychinasouthern.com

**Continental Airlines**
www.continental.com

**Delta Air Lines**
www.delta.com

**Dragonair**
www.dragonair.com

**Hainan Airlines**
http://global.hnair.com

**Qantas Airways**
www.qantas.com

**Shandong Airlines**
www.shandongair.com.cn

**Shanghai Airlines**
www.shanghai-air.com

**Singapore Airlines**
www.singaporeair.com

**United Airlines**
www.united.com

**Virgin Atlantic Airways**
www.virgin-atlantic.com

## BUDGET AIRLINE

**Spring Airlines**
www.china-sss.com
(operates within China only)

## MAJOR HOTEL & MOTEL CHAINS

**Four Seasons**
www.fourseasons.com

**Hilton Hotels**
www.hilton.com

**Holiday Inn**
www.holidayinn.com

**Hyatt**
www.hyatt.com

**InterContinental Hotels & Resorts**
www.ichotelsgroup.com

**Marriott**
www.marriott.com

**Radisson Hotels & Resorts**
www.radisson.com

**Ramada Worldwide**
www.ramada.com

**Renaissance**
www.renaissance.com

**The Ritz-Carlton**
www.ritzcarlton.com

**Shangri-La Hotels**
www.Shangri-La.com

**Sheraton Hotels & Resorts**
www.starwoodhotels.com/sheraton

**Westin Hotels & Resorts**
www.starwoodhotels.com/westin

# THE CHINESE LANGUAGE

Chinese is not as difficult a language to learn as it may first appear to be—at least not once you've decided what kind of Chinese to learn. There are six major languages called Chinese and there are, in addition, a host of dialects. The Chinese you are likely to hear spoken in your local Chinatown, or used by your friends of Chinese descent, is more than likely to be Cantonese, which is the version of Chinese used in Hong Kong and in much of southern China. But the official national language of China is **Mandarin** (PŭtōNihau—"common speech"), sometimes called Modern Standard Chinese, and viewed in mainland China as the language of administration, of the classics, and of the educated. While throughout much of mainland China, people speak their own local flavor of Chinese for everyday communication, they've all been educated in Mandarin.

Chinese grammar is considerably more straightforward than that of English or other European languages, even Spanish or Italian. There are no genders, so there is no need to remember long lists of endings for adjectives and to make them agree, with variations according to case. There are no equivalents for the definite and indefinite articles ("the," "a," "an"), so there is no need to make those agree either. Singular and plural nouns are the same. Best of all, verbs cannot be declined. The verb "to be" is *shì*. The same sound also covers "am," "are," "is," "was," "will be," and so on, since there are also no tenses. Instead of past, present, and future, Chinese is more concerned with whether an action is continuing or has been completed, and with the order in which events take place. To make matters of time clear, Chinese depends on simple expressions such as "yesterday," "before," "originally," "next year," and the like. "Tomorrow I go

New York," is clear enough, as is "Yesterday I go New York." It's a little more complicated than these brief notes can suggest, but not much.

There are a few sounds in Mandarin that are not used in English (see the rough pronunciation guide below), but the main difficulty for foreigners lies in tones. Most sounds in Mandarin begin with a consonant and end in a vowel (or -n, or -ng), which leaves the language with very few distinct noises compared to English. Originally, one sound equaled one idea and one word. Even now, each of these monosyllables is represented by a single character, but often words have been made by putting two characters together, sometimes both with the same meaning, thus reinforcing one another. The solution to this phonetic poverty is to multiply the available sounds by making them tonal—speaking them at different pitches, thereby giving them different meanings. *Mā* spoken on a high level tone (first tone) offers a set of possible meanings different from those of *má* spoken with a rising tone (second tone), *mǎ* with a dipping then rising tone (third tone), or *mà* with an abruptly falling tone (fourth tone). There's also a different meaning for the neutral, toneless *ma*.

In the average sentence, context is your friend (there are not many occasions in which the third-tone *mǎ* or "horse" might be mistaken for the fourth-tone *mà* or "grasshopper," for instance), but without tone, there is essentially no meaning. The novice had best sing his or her Mandarin very clearly, as Chinese children do—a chanted sing-song can be heard emerging from the windows of primary schools across China. With experience, the student learns to give particular emphasis to the tones on words essential to a sentence's meaning, and to treat the others more lightly. Sadly, most books using modern Romanized Chinese, called *Hànyǔ pīnyīn* ("Hàn language spell-the-sounds"), do not mark the tones, nor do these appear on **pīnyīn** signs in China. But in this book, the author has added tones to every Mandarin expression, so you can have a go at saying them for yourself. Where tones do not appear, that's usually because the name of a person or place is already familiar to many readers in an older form of Romanized Chinese such as Wade-Giles or Post Office (in which Běijīng was written misleadingly as Peking), or because it is better known in Cantonese: Sun Yat-sen, or Canton, for instance.

Cantonese has *eight* tones plus the neutral, but its grammatical structure is largely the same, as is that of all versions of Chinese. Even Chinese people who can barely understand each other's speech can at least write to each other, since written forms are similar. However many different meanings for each tone of *ma* there may be, for each meaning there's a different character. This makes the written form a far more successful communication medium than the spoken one, which leads to misunderstandings even between native speakers, who can often be seen sketching characters on their palms during conversation to confirm which one is meant.

But knowledge of the language is not needed to get around China, and it's almost a plus that Chinese take it for granted that outlandish foreigners (meaning you and me, unless of Chinese descent) can speak not a word (poor things) and must use whatever other limited means we have to communicate—this book and a phrase book, for instance. For help with navigation to sights, simply point to the characters in this book's map keys. When leaving your hotel, take one of its cards with you, and show it to the taxi driver when you want to return. Below is a limited list of useful words and phrases, which is best supplemented with a proper phrase book.

# A GUIDE TO PĪNYĪN PRONUNCIATION

Letters in *pīnyīn* mostly have the values any English speaker would expect, with the following exceptions:

**c** *ts* as in bi*ts*

**q** *ch* as in *ch*in, but much harder and more forward, made with tongue and teeth

**r** has no true equivalent in English, but the *r* of *r*eed is close, although the tip of the tongue should be near the top of the mouth, and the teeth together

**x** also has no true equivalent, but is nearest to the *sh* of *sh*eep, although the tongue should be parallel to the roof of the mouth and the teeth together

**zh** is a soft j, like the *dge* in ju*dge*

The vowels are pronounced roughly as follows:

**a** as in f*a*ther

**e** as in *e*rr (*leng* is pronounced as English "lung")

**i** is pronounced *ee* after most consonants, but after c, ch, r, s, sh, z, and zh is a buzz at the front of the mouth behind closed teeth

**o** as in s*o*ng

**u** as in t*oo*

**ü** is the purer, lips-pursed u of French t*u* and German *ü*. Confusingly, **u** after j, x, q, and y is always ü, but in these cases the accent over "ü" does not appear.

**ai** sounds like *eye*

**ao** as in *ou*ch

**ei** as in h*ay*

**ia** as in *ya*k

**ian** sounds like *yen*

**iang** sounds like *yang*

**iu** sounds like *you*

**ou** as in t*oe*

**ua** as in g*ua*va

**ui** sounds like *way*

**uo** sounds like *or,* but is more abrupt

Note that when two or more third-tone "ˇ" sounds follow one another, they should all, except the last, be pronounced as second-tone "ˊ."

# MANDARIN BARE ESSENTIALS

## GREETINGS & INTRODUCTIONS

| English | Pīnyīn | Chinese |
|---|---|---|
| Hello | Nǐ hǎo | 你好 |
| How are you? | Nǐ hǎo ma? | 你好吗? |
| Fine. And you? | Wǒ hěn hǎo. Nǐ ne? | 我很好。你呢? |
| I'm not too well/Things aren't going well | Bù hǎo | 不好 |

| English | Pīnyīn | Chinese |
|---|---|---|
| What is your name? (very polite) | Nín guì xìng? | 您贵姓? |
| My (family) name is | Wǒ xìng | 我姓…… |
| I'm known as (family, then given name) | Wǒ jiào | 我叫…… |
| I'm from [America] | Wǒ shì cóng [Měiguó] lái de | 我是从美国来的 |
| I'm [American] | Wǒ shì [Měiguó] rén | 我是美国人 |
| [Australian] | [Àodàlìyà] | 澳大利亚人 |
| [British] | [Yīngguó] | 英国人 |
| [Canadian] | [Jiānádà] | 加拿大人 |
| [Irish] | [Àiěrlán] | 爱尔兰人 |
| [a New Zealander] | [Xīnxīlán] | 新西兰人 |
| Excuse me/I'm sorry | Duìbùqī | 对不起 |
| I don't understand | Wǒ tīng bù dǒng | 我听不懂 |
| Thank you | Xièxie nī | 谢谢你 |
| Correct (yes) | Duì | 对 |
| Not correct | Bú duì | 不对 |
| No, I don't want | Wǒ bú yào | 我不要 |
| Not acceptable | Bù xíng | 不行 |

## BASIC QUESTIONS & PROBLEMS

| English | Pīnyīn | Chinese |
|---|---|---|
| Excuse me/I'd like to ask | Qīng wènyíxià | 请问一下 |
| Where is . . . ? | . . . zài nǎr? | ……在哪儿? |
| How much is . . . ? | . . . duōshǎo qián? | ……多少钱? |
| . . . this one? | Zhèi/Zhè ge . . . | 这个…… |
| . . . that one? | Nèi/Nà ge . . . | 那个…… |
| Do you have . . . ? | Nī yǒu méi yǒu . . . | 你有没有……? |
| What time does/is . . . ? | . . . jī diǎn? | ……几点? |
| What time is it now? | Xiànzài jī diǎn? | 现在几点? |
| When is . . . ? | . . . shénme shíhou? | ……什么时候? |
| Why? | Wèishénme? | 为什么? |
| Who? | Shéi? | 谁? |
| Is that okay? | Xíng bù xíng? | 行不行? |
| I'm feeling ill | Wǒ shēng bìng le | 我生病了 |

## TRAVEL

| English | Pīnyīn | Chinese |
|---|---|---|
| luxury (bus, hotel rooms) | háohuá | 豪华 |
| high speed (buses, expressways) | gāosù | 高速 |
| air-conditioned | kōngtiáo | 空调 |
| When is the last bus? | mòbānchē jīdiǎn kāi? | 末班车几点开? |

## NUMBERS

Note that more complicated forms of numbers are often used on official documents and receipts to prevent fraud—see how easily the number one can be changed to two, three, or even 10. Familiar Arabic numerals appear on bank notes, most signs, taxi meters, and other places. Be particularly careful with *four* and *ten*, which sound very alike in many regions—hold up fingers to make sure. Note, too, that *yī,* meaning "one," tends to change its tone all the time, depending on what it precedes. Don't worry about this—once you've started talking about money, almost any kind of squeak for "one" will do. Finally note that "two" alters when being used with expressions of quantity.

| English | Pīnyīn | Chinese |
|---------|--------|---------|
| zero | líng | 零 |
| one | yī | 一 |
| two | èr | 二 |
| two (of them) | liǎng ge | 两个 |
| three | sān | 三 |
| four | sì | 四 |
| five | wǔ | 五 |
| six | liù | 六 |
| seven | qī | 七 |
| eight | bā | 八 |
| nine | jiǔ | 九 |
| 10 | shí | 十 |
| 11 | shí yī | 十一 |
| 12 | shí èr | 十二 |
| 21 | èr shí yī | 二十一 |
| 22 | èr shí èr | 二十二 |
| 51 | wǔ shí yī | 五十一 |
| 100 | yì bǎi | 一百 |
| 101 | yì bǎi líng yī | 一百零一 |
| 110 | yì bǎi yī (shí) | 一百一（十） |
| 111 | yì bǎi yī shí yī | 一百一十一 |
| 1,000 | yì qiān | 一千 |
| 1,500 | yì qiān wǔ (bǎi) | 一千五百 |
| 5,678 | wǔ qiān liù bǎi qī shí bā | 五千六百七十八 |
| 10,000 | yí wàn | 一万 |

## MONEY

The word *yuán* (¥) is rarely spoken, nor is *jiǎo,* the written form for one-tenth of a *yuán,* equivalent to 10 *fēn* (there are 100 *fēn* in a *yuán*). Instead, the Chinese speak of "pieces of money," *kuài qián,* usually abbreviated just to *kuài,* and they speak of *máo* for one-tenth of a *kuài. Fēn* have been overtaken by inflation and are almost useless. Often all zeros after the last whole number are simply omitted, along with *kuài qián*, which is taken as read, especially in direct reply to the question *duōshǎo qián*—"How much?"

| English | Pīnyīn | Chinese |
|---|---|---|
| ¥1 | yí kuài qián | 一块钱 |
| ¥2 | liǎng kuài qián | 两块钱 |
| ¥.30 | sān máo qián | 三毛钱 |
| ¥5.05 | wǔ kuài líng wǔ fēn | 五块零五分 |
| ¥5.50 | wǔ kuài wǔ | 五块五 |
| ¥550 | wǔ bǎi wǔ shí kuài | 五百五十块 |
| ¥5,500 | wǔ qiān wǔ bǎi kuài | 五千五百块 |
| small change | língqián | 零钱 |

## BANKING & SHOPPING

| English | Pīnyīn | Chinese |
|---|---|---|
| I want to change money (foreign exchange) | Wǒ xiǎng huàn qián | 我想换钱 |
| credit card | xìnyòng kǎ | 信用卡 |
| traveler's check | lǚxíng zhīpiào | 旅行支票 |
| department store | bǎihuò shāngdiàn | 百货商店 |
| *or* | gòuwù zhōngxīn | 或购物中心 |
| convenience store | xiǎomàibù | 小卖部 |
| market | shìchǎng | 市场 |
| May I have a look? | Wǒ Kànyíxià, hǎo ma? | 我看一下，好吗？ |
| I want to buy | Wǒ xiǎng mǎi | 我想买…… |
| How many do you want? | Nǐ yào jǐ ge? | 你要几个？ |
| two of them | liǎng ge | 两个 |
| three of them | sān ge | 三个 |
| 1 kilo (2¼ lb.) | yì gōngjīn | 一公斤 |
| half a kilo | yì jīn | 一斤 |
| *or* | bàn gōngjīn | 半公斤 |
| 1 meter (3¼ ft.) | yì mǐ | 一米 |
| Too expensive! | Tài guì le! | 太贵了！ |
| Do you have change? | Yǒu língqián ma? | 有零钱吗？ |

## TIME

| English | Pīnyīn | Chinese |
|---|---|---|
| morning | shàngwǔ | 上午 |
| afternoon | xiàwǔ | 下午 |
| evening | wǎnshang | 晚上 |
| 8:20am | shàngwǔ bā diǎn èr shí fēn | 上午八点二十分 |

| English | Pīnyīn | Chinese |
|---|---|---|
| 9:30am | shàngwǔ jiǔ diǎn bàn | 上午九点半 |
| noon | zhōngwǔ | 中午 |
| 4:15pm | xiàwǔ sì diǎn yí kè | 下午四点一刻 |
| midnight | wǔ yè | 午夜 |
| 1 hour | yí ge xiǎoshí | 一个小时 |
| 8 hours | bā ge xiǎoshí | 八个小时 |
| today | jīntiān | 今天 |
| yesterday | zuótiān | 昨天 |
| tomorrow | míngtiān | 明天 |
| Monday | Xīngqī yī | 星期一 |
| Tuesday | Xīngqī èr | 星期二 |
| Wednesday | Xīngqī sān | 星期三 |
| Thursday | Xīngqī sì | 星期四 |
| Friday | Xīngqī wǔ | 星期五 |
| Saturday | Xīngqī liù | 星期六 |
| Sunday | Xīngqī tiān | 星期天 |

## TRANSPORT

| English | Pīnyīn | Chinese |
|---|---|---|
| I want to go to . . . | Wǒ xiǎng qù . . . | 我想去 . . . . . . |
| plane | fēijī | 飞机 |
| train | huǒchē | 火车 |
| bus | gōnggòng qìchē | 公共汽车 |
| long-distance bus | chángtú qìchē | 长途汽车 |
| taxi | chūzū chē | 出租车 |
| airport | fēijīchǎng | 飞机场 |
| stop or station (bus or train) | zhàn | 站 |
| (plane/train/bus) ticket | piào | 票 |

## NAVIGATION

| English | Pīnyīn | Chinese |
|---|---|---|
| North | Běi | 北 |
| South | Nán | 南 |
| East | Dōng | 东 |
| West | Xī | 西 |
| Turn left | zuǒ guǎi | 左拐 |
| Turn right | yòu guǎi | 右拐 |
| Go straight on | yìzhí zǒu | 一直走 |
| Crossroads | shízì lùkǒu | 十字路口 |
| 10 kilometers | shí gōnglǐ | 十公里 |
| I'm lost | Wǒ mi lùle | 我迷路了 |

## HOTEL

| English | Pīnyīn | Chinese |
|---|---|---|
| How many days? | Zhù jǐ tiān? | 住几天? |
| standard room (twin or double with private bathroom) | biāozhǔn jiān | 标准间 |
| passport | hùzhào | 护照 |
| deposit | yājīn | 押金 |
| I want to check out | Wǒ tuì fáng | 我退房 |

## RESTAURANT

| English | Pīnyīn | Chinese |
|---|---|---|
| How many people? | Jǐ wèi? | 几位 |
| waiter/waitress | fúwùyuán | 服务员 |
| menu | càidān | 菜单 |
| I'm vegetarian | Wǒ shì chī sù de | 我是吃素的 |
| Don't add MSG | qīng bù fàng wèijīng | 请别放味精 |
| Do you have . . . ? | Yǒu méi yǒu . . . ? | 有没有……？ |
| Please bring a portion of . . . | Qǐng lái yí fèn . . . | 请来一份…… |
| I'm full | Wǒ chībǎo le | 我吃饱了 |
| beer | píjiǔ | 啤酒 |
| coffee | kāfēi | 咖啡 |
| mineral water | kuàngquán shuǐ | 矿泉水 |
| tea | cháshuǐ | 茶水 |
| Bill, please | jiézhàng | 结帐 |

## POPULAR DISHES & SNACKS

| English | Pīnyīn | Chinese |
|---|---|---|
| bābǎo zhōu | rice porridge with nuts and berries | 八宝粥 |
| bāozi | stuffed steamed buns | 包子 |
| bīngqílín | ice cream | 冰淇淋 |
| chǎofàn | fried rice | 炒饭 |
| chǎomiàn | fried noodles | 炒面 |
| diǎnxin | dim sum (snacks) | 点心 |
| dòujiāng | soy bean milk | 豆浆 |
| gānbiān sìjìdòu | sautéed string beans | 干煸四季豆 |
| gōngbào jīdīng | spicy diced chicken with cashews | 宫爆鸡丁 |
| guōtiē | fried dumplings/pot stickers | 锅贴 |
| huíguō ròu | twice-cooked pork | 回锅肉 |
| húntun | wonton (dumpling soup) | 馄饨 |
| huǒguō | hot pot | 火锅 |

| English | Pīnyīn | Chinese |
|---------|--------|---------|
| jiācháng dòufu | homestyle tofu | 家常豆腐 |
| jiǎozi | dumplings/Chinese ravioli | 饺子 |
| jīngjiàng ròusī | shredded pork in soy sauce | 京酱肉丝 |
| júhuā chá | chrysanthemum tea | 菊花茶 |
| lā miàn | hand-pulled noodles | 拉面 |
| lóngjǐng chá | Lóngjǐng Tea (from Hángzhōu) | 龙井茶 |
| mápó dòufu | spicy tofu with chopped meat | 麻婆豆腐 |
| miàntiáo | noodles | 面条 |
| mǐfàn | rice | 米饭 |
| mòlihuā chá | jasmine tea | 茉莉花茶 |
| mù xū ròu | sliced pork with fungus (mushu pork) | 木须肉 |
| niúròu miàn | beef noodles | 牛肉面 |
| ròu chuàn | kabobs | 肉串 |
| sānxiān | "three flavors" (usually prawn, mushroom, pork) | 三鲜 |
| shuǐjiǎo | boiled dumplings | 水饺 |
| suānlà báicài | hot-and-sour cabbage | 酸辣白菜 |
| suānlà tāng | hot-and-sour soup | 酸辣汤 |
| sù shíjǐn | mixed vegetables | 素什锦 |
| xiàn bǐng | pork- or vegetable-stuffed fried pancake | 馅饼 |
| xīhóngshì chǎo jīdàn | tomatoes with eggs | 西红柿炒鸡蛋 |
| yángròu chuan | barbecued lamb skewers with ground cumin and chili powder | 羊肉串 |
| yóutiáo | fried salty doughnut | 油条 |
| yúxiāng qiézi | eggplant in garlic sauce | 鱼香茄子 |
| yúxiāng ròusī | shredded pork in garlic sauce | 鱼香肉丝 |
| zhēngjiǎo | steamed dumplings | 蒸饺 |
| zhōu | rice porridge | 粥 |

## SPECIALTY DISHES (FROM SHÀNGHǍI & ELSEWHERE) RECOMMENDED IN RESTAURANT REVIEWS

| English | Pīnyīn | Chinese |
|---------|--------|---------|
| báopí yángròu juǎn | minced lamb wrapped in pancakes | 薄皮羊肉卷 |
| càixīn xièhuángyóu | vegetarian crab (carrot, mushroom, bamboo) | 菜心蟹黄油 |
| chénpí sùyā | orange peel vegetarian duck | 陈皮素鸭 |

| English | Pīnyīn | Chinese |
|---|---|---|
| cōngyóu bǐng | scallion pancakes | 葱油饼 |
| dàjiùjià | rice-flour pastry stir-fried with ham, mushrooms, and vegetables | 大救架 |
| dāndān miàn | noodles in spicy peanut sauce | 担担面 |
| dàzhá xiè | hairy crab | 大闸蟹 |
| dōngpō ròu | braised fatty pork in small clay pot | 东坡肉 |
| dòushā sūbǐng | crispy pastry with mashed bean filling | 豆沙酥饼 |
| duòjiāo yútóu | fish head steamed with red chili | 剁椒鱼头 |
| fūqī fèipiàn | beef and tongue doused in chili oil and peanuts | 夫妻肺片 |
| gānbiān tǔdòu bā | fried potato pancake | 干煸土豆粑 |
| gānguōjī guōzi | spicy chicken with peppers | 干锅鸡锅子 |
| Hángzhōu jiàohuà jī | "beggar's chicken"—baked in clay | 杭州叫化鸡 |
| huíguōròu jiābǐng | twice-cooked lamb wrapped in pancakes | 回锅肉夹饼 |
| huǒyán niúròu | beef with red and green peppers | 火焰牛肉 |
| jiāobái | wild rice stems | 茭白 |
| kǎofū | braised wheat gluten | 烤麸 |
| kǎo quányáng | roast lamb | 烤全羊 |
| kǎo yángròu | barbecued lamb skewers | 烤羊肉 |
| kòu sān sī | julienne strips of tofu skin, ham and bamboo | 扣三丝 |
| lǎohǔ cài | Xīnjiāng salad | 老虎菜 |
| làzi jīdīng | spicy chicken nuggets | 辣子鸡丁 |
| liǎngmiàn huáng | pan-fried noodles | 两面黄 |
| luóbòsī sūbǐng | pan-fried turnip cake | 萝卜丝酥饼 |
| mìzhī chāshāo fàn | barbecue pork rice | 蜜汁叉烧饭 |
| mìzhī huǒfāng | pork and taro in candied sauce | 蜜汁火舫 |
| Nánxiáng xiǎolóng bāo | Nánxiáng crabmeat and pork dumplings | 南翔小龙包 |
| pídàn dòufu | tofu with "thousand year" eggs | 皮蛋豆腐 |
| qícài dōngsǔn | winter shoots with local greens | 荠菜冬笋 |
| qīngzhēng dòuní | creamy mashed beans | 青蒸豆泥 |
| rìběn jièmo chǎo niúliǔlì | wasabi stir-fried beef | 日本芥末炒牛柳粒 |

| English | Pīnyīn | Chinese |
|---|---|---|
| sānsī méimao sū | pork, bamboo, and mushroom-stuffed crisp | 三丝眉毛酥 |
| shèngguā chǎo zhūjǐngròu | crispy-skinned pork | 胜瓜炒猪颈肉 |
| shīzi tóu | lion's head meatballs | 狮子头 |
| shuǐzhǔ yú | fish slices and vegetables in spicy broth | 水煮鱼 |
| shuǐjīng xiārén | stir-fried shrimp | 水晶虾仁 |
| sōngshǔ lúyú | sweet-and-sour fried perch | 松鼠鲈鱼 |
| suān dòujiǎo ròuní | diced sour beans with minced pork | 酸豆角肉泥 |
| suān jiāngdòu làròu | sour long beans with chilies and bacon | 酸豇豆腊肉 |
| sùjī | vegetarian chicken | 素鸡 |
| sùyā | vegetarian duck | 素鸭 |
| xiǎolóng bāo | pork-stuffed steamed bread dumplings | 小笼包 |
| xiāngwèi hóngshǔ bō | fragrant sweet potato in monk's pot | 香味红薯钵 |
| Xīnjiāng píjiǔ | Xīnjiāng black beer | 新疆啤酒 |
| xiānggū miànjīn miàn | noodle soup with gluten and mushrooms | 香菇面筋面 |
| xiānxiā yúntūn miàn | shrimp wonton noodles in soup | 鲜虾云吞面 |
| xiāròu xiǎohúntūn | soup wontons with shrimp filling | 虾肉小馄饨 |
| xiāngwèi hóngshǔ bō | fragrant sweet potato in monk's pot | 香味红薯钵 |
| xièfěn huì zhēnjūn | braised mushroom with crabmeat | 蟹粉烩珍菌 |
| xièfěn shēngjiān | crabmeat and pork buns steamed in oil | 蟹粉生煎 |
| xièfěn xiǎolóng | pork and powdered crabmeat dumplings | 蟹粉小笼 |
| XO jiàng chǎo sìjìdòu | stir-fried string beans in XO sauce | XO酱炒四季豆 |
| zhūyóu lāofàn | rice with lard and soya sauce | 猪油捞饭 |

## SIGNS

Here's a list of common signs and notices to help you identify what you are looking for, from restaurants to condiments, and to help you choose the right door at the public toilets. These are the simplified characters in everyday use in China, but note that it's increasingly fashionable for larger businesses and for those with a long history to use more complicated traditional characters, so not all may match what's below. Also, very old restaurants and temples across China tend to write their signs from right to left.

| English | Pīnyīn | Chinese |
|---|---|---|
| hotel | bīnguǎn | 宾馆 |
| | dàjiǔdiàn | 大酒店 |
| | jiǔdiàn | 酒店 |
| | fàndiàn | 饭店 |
| restaurant | fànguǎn | 饭馆 |
| | jiǔdiàn | 酒店 |
| | jiǔjiā | 酒家 |
| vinegar | cù | 醋 |
| soya sauce | Jiàngyóu | 酱油 |
| bar | jiǔbā | 酒吧 |
| Internet bar | wǎngbā | 网吧 |
| cafe | kāfēiguǎn | 咖啡馆 |
| teahouse | cháguǎn | 茶馆 |
| department store | bǎihuò shāngdiàn | 百货商店 |
| shopping mall | gòuwù zhōngxīn | 购物中心 |
| market | shìchǎng | 市场 |
| bookstore | shūdiàn | 书店 |
| police (Public Security Bureau) | gōng'ānjú | 公安局 |
| Bank of China | Zhōngguó Yínháng | 中国银行 |
| public telephone | gōngyòng diànhuà | 公用电话 |
| public toilet | gōngyòng cèsuǒ | 公用厕所 |
| male | nán | 男 |
| female | nǚ | 女 |
| entrance | rùkǒu | 入口 |
| exit | chūkǒu | 出口 |
| bus stop/station | qìchē zhàn | 汽车站 |
| long-distance bus station | chángtú qìchē zhàn | 长途汽车站 |
| luxury | háohuá | 豪华 |
| using highway | gāosù | 高速公路 |
| railway station | huǒchē zhàn | 火车站 |
| hard seat | yìng zuò | 硬座 |
| soft seat | ruǎn zuò | 软座 |
| hard sleeper | yìng wò | 硬卧 |
| soft sleeper | ruǎn wò | 软卧 |
| direct (through) train | zhídá | 直达 |
| express train | tèkuài | 特快 |
| Metro/subway station | dìtiě zhàn | 地铁站 |
| airport | fēijīchǎng | 飞机场 |
| dock/wharf | mǎtóu | 码头 |
| passenger terminal (bus, boat, and so on) | kèyùn zhàn | 客运站 |

| English | Pīnyīn | Chinese |
|---|---|---|
| up/get on | shàng | 上 |
| down/get off | xià | 下 |
| ticket hall | shòupiào tīng | 售票厅 |
| ticket office | shòupiào chù | 售票处 |
| left-luggage office | xíngli jìcún chù | 行李寄存处 |
| temple | sì | 寺 |
| | miào | 庙 |
| museum | bówùguǎn | 博物馆 |
| memorial hall | jìniànguǎn | 纪念馆 |
| park | gōngyuán | 公园 |
| hospital | yīyuàn | 医院 |
| clinic | zhěnsuǒ | 诊所 |
| pharmacy | yàofáng/yàodiàn | 药房/药店 |
| travel agency | lǚxíngshè | 旅行社 |

# Index

## General Index

### A
Abercrombie and Kent, 65
Academic Travel Abroad, 65
Accessibility, 58
Accommodations, 81–105. *See also* Accommodations Index
    airport hotels, 102
    best, 5–6, 85–86
    business motels, 90
    Chángníng/Hóngqiáo Development Zone (West Shànghǎi), 101
    Downtown Shànghǎi (Huángpǔ), 84, 86–91
    Hángzhōu, 272
    Jìng Ān (Northwest Shànghǎi), 97–101
    location of, 84
    Lúwān (French Concession), 92–94
    price categories, 85
    Pǔdōng (East of River), 103–105
    rankings of, 81–82
    saving on, 83
    Sūzhōu, 262–264
    types of, 81
Acrobatics, 243
Acting and Singing Stage (Gǔ Xìtái), 163
Adventure Center, 65
Aeroflot, 35
Aimǐnshì Zhūbǎo (Amylin's Pearls), 236
Air Canada, 35
Air China, 35
Air France, 35
Air New Zealand, 35
Airport Bus, 37
Airport hotels, 102
Air travel, 35–40
All Nippon Airways, 35
All Saints Church (Zhūshèng Táng), 173
American Airlines, 35
American Express, traveler's checks, 54–55
Ampire Building, 203
Amylin's Pearls (Aimǐnshì Zhūbǎo), 236
Anantara Spa, 196
Ancient Chinese Bronze Gallery, 164
Ancient Chinese Sculpture Gallery, 164
Ancient City Wall (Gǔchéngqiáng DàJīng Gé), 218

Angel Pearls, 236
Ān Lì (Annly's Antique Warehouse), 231
Annabel Lee, 235
Annly's Antique Warehouse (Ān Lì), 231
Antique Garden Shanghai, 221
Antiques and furniture, 230–231
A.P. Plaza (Yàdà Shènghuì Lǚyóu Gòuwù Guǎngchǎng), 228
Apple, 233
Aquariums, 191–192
Architecture, 21–22
Area codes, 281
Art, 22–23
Art galleries, 237
Asiana Airlines, 35
Asiatic Petroleum Building (McBain Building), 206
Associated Mission Building, 203
Astor House Hotel, 202
Atanu 1907 Bar, 251
ATMs (automated-teller machines), 53
Austrian Airlines, 35

### B
Babyface, 249
Bái Causeway (Bái Dī; Hángzhōu), 268–269
Bǎijiān Lóu (One Hundred Rooms; Nánxún), 276
Bǎishèng Gòuwù Zhōngxīn (Parkson), 235
Báiyán Guàn (White Cloud Daoist Temple), 169, 217
Bangkok Bank, 206
Bank of China, 203
Bank of Communications Building, 205
Bank of Taiwan Building, 204
Banyan Tree Spa, 196
Bǎolíng Qiú (bowling), 195
Barbarossa, 251
Bargaining, 226–227
Bar Rouge, 251
Bars, wine 124
Bars and lounges, 251–255
Běigāo Fēng (North Peak Mountain), 270
Běijīng/Northern cuisine, 108
Big Bus Tours, 194
Biking, 45
    tours, 194
Bīnjiāng Dà Dào (Riverside Promenade), 175
Boat travel and cruises, 39, 41
Bodhi Bikes, 45, 194
Bóduōlù Táng (St. Peter's Church), 173
Bokhara Carpets, 233
Books, recommended, 24–25
Bookstores, 231–232
Bowling (Bǎolíng Qiú), 195
Bridge of Nine Turnings (Hángzhōu), 269

Bridge of Nine Turnings (Jiǔ Qū Qiáo), 216
British Airways, 35
British Consulate, Former, 202
Broadway Mansions (Shànghǎi Mansions), 201–202
Brocade Country (Jǐngxiù Fáng), 236
Broken Bridge (Duàn Qiáo; Hángzhōu), 269
Brown Sugar, 254
Bùlǔsī Juéshì Zhī Wū (House of Blues and Jazz), 249
The Bund (Wàitān), 46–47, 158–160
    walking tour, 200–207
Bund 18 (formerly Chartered Bank of India, Australia, and China), 204
Bund History Museum, 159–160
Bund Promenade, 158, 200
Bund Sightseeing Avenue (Wàitān Guānjǐng Dàdào), 202
Bund Sightseeing Tunnel (Wàitān Guànguāng Suìdào), 46, 160
The Bund Tea Company (Shànghǎi Cháyuán Yǒuxiàn Gōngsī), 241
Buses, 45
    airport, 37
Business, 19–21
Business hours, 281

### C
Calendar of events, 30–32
Calligraphy Gallery, 164
Cameras and accessories, 232
Cángbǎo Lóu (Treasury Hall), 162
Cantonese cuisine, 108
Captain Hostel, 67
Carpets, 233
Carrefour (Jiālèfú), 241
Car travel, 38, 44
Cathay Theatre (Guótài Diànyǐngyuàn), 255
Cellphones, 66
Centers for Disease Control and Prevention, 55
Century Park (Shìjì Gōngyuán), 177
Century Square (Shìjì Guǎngchǎng), 213
Ceramics Gallery, 164
Chángníng District/Hóngqiáo Development Zone (West Shànghǎi), 71, 84
    accommodations, 101
    restaurants, 130–132
Chángqīng Qiáo (Glory Bridge; Tónglǐ), 279
Chaterhouse Booktrader, 231–232
Chénghuáng Miào (Temple of the Town God), 169–170, 216

## Accommodations